MANAGEMENT SKILLS

ASSESSMENT AND DEVELOPMENT

RICKY W. GRIFFIN
Texas A&M University

DAVID D. VAN FLEET
Arizona State University

SOUTH-WESTERN
CENGAGE Learning®

Australia • Brazil • Japan • Korea • Mexico • Singapore • Spain • United Kingdom • United States

Management Skills: Assessment and Development
Ricky W. Griffin and David D. Van Fleet

Senior Vice President, LRS/Acquisitions & Solutions Planning: Jack W. Calhoun

Editorial Director, Business & Economics: Erin Joyner

Executive Editor: Scott Person

Sr. Developmental Editor: Julia Chase

Marketing Manager: Jonathan Monahan

Sr. Content Project Manager: Colleen A. Farmer

Media Editor: Rob Ellington

Manufacturing Planner: Ron Montgomery

Marketing Communications Manager: Libby Shipp

Production Service: Integra Software Services Pvt. Ltd.

Sr. Art Director: Stacy Shirley

Cover and Internal Designer: Red Hangar Design, Ltd.

Cover Image: © Jon Feingerish Photograph, Inc/Getty Images

Rights Acquisitions Specialist (Text and Photo): John Hill

Photo Credits for Brief TOC:
Chapter 1: © Istockphoto.com/Jacob Wackerhausen; Chapter 2: © Yuri Arcurs/Shutterstock.com; Chapter 3: Stephen Coburn/Shutterstock.com; Chapter 4: © iStockphoto.com/Robert Churchill; Chapter 5: © iStockphoto.com/Jacob Wackerhausen; Chapter 6: © SelectStock; Chapter 7: Dmitriy Shironosov; Chapter 8: © iStockphoto.com/Steve Cole; Chapter 9: © Christian Delbert/Shutterstock.com, erwinova/Shutterstock.com; Chapter 10: © iStockphoto.com/kali9

© 2014 South-Western, Cengage Learning

ALL RIGHTS RESERVED. No part of this work covered by the copyright herein may be reproduced, transmitted, stored, or used in any form or by any means graphic, electronic, or mechanical, including but not limited to photocopying, recording, scanning, digitizing, taping, Web distribution, information networks, or information storage and retrieval systems, except as permitted under Section 107 or 108 of the 1976 United States Copyright Act, or applicable copyright law of another jurisdiction, without the prior written permission of the publisher.

For permission to use material from this text or product, submit all requests online at **www.cengage.com/permissions**
Further permissions questions can be emailed to
permissionrequest@cengage.com

Library of Congress Control Number: 2012944414

International Edition:

ISBN-13: 978-1-133-58295-3

ISBN-10: 1-133-58295-8

Cengage Learning International Offices

Asia
www.cengageasia.com
tel: (65) 6410 1200

Australia/New Zealand
www.cengage.com.au
tel: (61) 3 9685 4111

Brazil
www.cengage.com.br
tel: (55) 11 3665 9900

India
www.cengage.co.in
tel: (91) 11 4364 1111

Latin America
www.cengage.com.mx
tel: (52) 55 1500 6000

UK/Europe/Middle East/Africa
www.cengage.co.uk
tel: (44) 0 1264 332 424

Represented in Canada by Nelson Education, Ltd.
www.nelson.com
tel: (416) 752 9100/(800) 668 0671

Cengage Learning is a leading provider of customized learning solutions with office locations around the globe, including Singapore, the United Kingdom, Australia, Mexico, Brazil, and Japan. Locate your local office at: **www.cengage.com/global**

For product information and free companion resources: **www.cengage.com/international**

Visit your local office: **www.cengage.com/global**

Visit our corporate website: **www.cengage.com**

Printed in the United States of America
1 2 3 4 5 6 7 16 15 14 13 12

AVAILABILITY OF RESOURCES MAY DIFFER BY REGION. Check with your local Cengage Learning representative for details.

DEDICATION

For Griffin Grace Hilgemeier, the newest star in her Granddad's universe (RWG)
For Ella, a valued and loved collaborator (DDVF)

BRIEF CONTENTS

CHAPTER 1 Basic Management Skills 2

CHAPTER 2 Learning and Developing Management Skills 26

CHAPTER 3 Time-Management Skills 50

CHAPTER 4 Interpersonal Skills 98

CHAPTER 5 Conceptual Skills 144

CHAPTER 6 Diagnostic Skills 188

CHAPTER 7 Communication Skills 234

CHAPTER 8 Decision-Making Skills 272

CHAPTER 9 Technical Skills 320

CHAPTER 10 Transitioning from Managing to Leading 362

CONTENTS

1 BASIC MANAGEMENT SKILLS 2

©ISTOCKPHOTO.COM/ JACOB WACKERHAUSEN

Basic Management Skills 4

How do I Rate as a Manager? 4

Self-Described Profile 6

What Is Management? 8

The Core Management Skills 9

- Time-Management Skills 9
- Interpersonal Skills 10
- Conceptual Skills 11
- Diagnostic Skills 11
- Communication Skills 11
- Decision-Making Skills 11
- Technical Skills 12

The Organizational Compass 12

- Levels of Management 13
  - *Top Managers 13* • *Middle Managers 13* • *First-Line Managers 14*
- Areas of Management 14
  - *Marketing Managers 14* • *Financial Managers 14* • *Operations Managers 14* • *Human Resource Managers 14* • *Administrative Managers 14* • *Other Kinds of Managers 14*

The Functional Perspective on Management 15

- Planning and Decision Making: Determining Courses of Action 15
- Organizing: Coordinating Activities and Resources 15
- Leading: Motivating and Managing People 16
- Controlling: Monitoring and Evaluating Activities 16

The Role Perspective on Management 16

- Interpersonal Roles 16
- Informational Roles 17
- Decisional Roles 17

Summary and a Look Ahead 18

Determining Why Individuals Become Entrepreneurs 18

Job Skills 19

The Nature of Managerial Work 19

What Do You Think? 20

Success Leads to … 21

Kodak's Fuzzy Picture 22

Group Extensions 23

Individual Extensions 23

How do I Rate as a Manager? 24

Self-Described Profile 24

The Nature of Managerial Work 24

2 LEARNING AND DEVELOPING MANAGEMENT SKILLS 26

© YURI ARCURS/SHUTTERSTOCK.COM

What's Your Learning Style? 28
Assessing Your Mental Abilities 29
The Nature of Managerial Work 30
The Model of Skill Development 31
The Science and the Art of Management 32
- The Science of Management 32
- The Art of Management 32

The Role of Education 33
The Role of Experience 34
Personal Skills 35
- Self-Awareness 35
- Understanding Our Own Personality 35
  - *The "Big Five" Personality Traits* 35 • *The Myers-Briggs Framework* 37 • *Other Personality Traits at Work* 37
- Emotional Intelligence 38
- Generalizability/Discrimination 39
- Understanding Personal Values, Ethics, and Priorities 39

The Scope of Management 41
- Managing in Profit-Seeking Organizations 41
- Managing in Not-for-Profit Organizations 42

Summary and a Look Ahead 42
What Do You Bring to the Table? 43
Inner Circle 43
What Are Your Learning Goals? 43
What about Me, What about You? 44
Body Shop and Education 44
Learning at Kyocera 46
Group Extensions 47
Individual Extensions 47
What Is Your Learning Style? 47
Assessing Your Mental Abilities 48

3 TIME-MANAGEMENT SKILLS 50

Behavior Activity Profile 52
Are You a Good Planner? 53
Stress Management 54
Time-Management Assessment 55
Understanding Prioritization 57
- Setting Priorities 57
- Misjudging Priorities 58

Effective Delegation 58
- Reasons for Delegation 58
- Parts of the Delegation Process 58
- Problems in Delegation 59
- Decentralization and Centralization 60

Scheduling Meetings and Controlling Intrusions 61
- Scheduling and Managing Meetings 61
- Controlling Intrusions 61

Managing Stress 62
- Causes of Stress 64
- Consequences of Stress 65
- Limiting Stress 66

STEPHEN COBURN/SHUTTERSTOCK.COM

Summary and a Look Ahead 68
Time-Management Skills in Action—1 68
Time-Management Skills in Action—2 69
Controlling Your Own Work 69
Balancing Urgent and Important Tasks 70
Demands that Cause Stress 73
Staircasing Your Goals 74
Effectiveness of Communication Exchanges 75
How Is Time Being Spent? 76
Personal Goal Sheet 77

Prioritizing Tasks 78
Stressful Jobs 79
Identifying Stressors 79
Running Team Meetings 80
Using Time More Efficiently 80
What to do Now 80
Time Flexibility 88
United Parcel Service 89
Group Extensions 91
Individual Extensions 91
Time-Management Skills Assessment 92
Time-Management Skills 92
Summary of Your Scores 93
Interpretation of Your Scores 93
Behavior Activity Profile: A "Type A Measure" 94
Are You a Good Planner? 95
Stress Management 95
Time-Management Assessment 96

4 INTERPERSONAL SKILLS 98

© ISTOCKPHOTO.COM/ ROBERT CHURCHILL

Assessing Your Needs 100
Job Involvement 100
Team Effectiveness Inventory 101
Using Teams 102
The Interpersonal Nature of Organizations 104
Interpersonal Dynamics 105
Outcomes of Interpersonal Behaviors 105
Understanding Individual Differences 106
The Psychological Contract 106
The Person-Job Fit 107
The Nature of Individual Differences 107
Motivating Employees 108
Content Perspectives on Motivation 108
The Needs Hierarchy Approach 108 • The Two-Factor Theory 109
Process Perspectives on Motivation 110
Expectancy Theory 110 • Equity Theory 112 • Goal-Setting Theory 114
Working with Diversity, Teams, and Conflict 114
Understanding Diversity 114
Reasons for Increased Diversity 115 • Dimensions of Diversity 115 • Working With Diversity 117
Managing Teams 118
Types of Teams 118 • Benefits and Costs of Teams 119
Managing Conflict 120
The Nature of Conflict 121 • Causes of Conflict 121 • Managing Conflict in Organizations 122
Managing Workplace Behaviors 124
Performance Behaviors 124
Dysfunctional Behaviors 124
Organizational Citizenship 125
Summary and a Look Ahead 125
Interpersonal Skills in Action—1 126
Interpersonal Skills in Action—2 126
Managing During a Period of Change 127
Selecting Modes of Communication 127
Skills Related to Motivation and Satisfying Needs in a Career 128
Surviving in a Period of Change 128
Understanding the Perceptual Process 129
Understanding Decision Makers (1) 130
Understanding Decision Makers (2) 131
Identifying Personality Traits for Different Jobs 132
Assessing Entrepreneurial Personality Traits 132
Assessing Your Personality Type 133
Nordstrom Cares 134
Campbell's Continues Canning 135
Group Extensions 137
Individual Extensions 137
Interpersonal Skills Assessment 137
Interpersonal Skills 138

Summary of Your Scores 140
Interpretation of Your Scores 140
Assessing Your Needs 140
Job Involvement 141
Team Effectiveness 141
Using Teams 141

5 CONCEPTUAL SKILLS 144

Goal-Setting Questionnaire 146
How Creative Are You? 147
Innovative Attitudes Scale 150
Personal Risk Taking 152
Strategic Thinking 154
The Components of a Strategy 155
Types of Strategic Alternatives 156
Strategy Formulation and Implementation 156
Using SWOT Analysis to Formulate Strategy 157
Evaluating an Organization's Strengths 157 • Evaluating an Organization's Weaknesses 158 • Evaluating an Organization's Opportunities and Threats 158
Managing Creativity 158
The Creative Individual 159
Background Experiences and Creativity 159 • Personal Traits and Creativity 159 • Cognitive Abilities and Creativity 159
The Creative Process 159
Preparation 159 • Incubation15 160 • Insight 160 • Verification 160
Enhancing Creativity in Organizations 160
Managing Innovation 161
The Innovation Process 161
Innovation Development 161 • Innovation Application 161 • Application Launch 161 • Application Growth 162 • Innovation Maturity 162 • Innovation Decline 162
Forms of Innovation 162
Radical Versus Incremental Innovations 162 • Technical Versus Managerial Innovations 162 • Product Versus Process Innovations 163
The Failure to Innovate 164
Lack of Resources 164 • Failure to Recognize Opportunities 164 • Resistance to Change 164
Promoting Innovation in Organizations 164
The Reward System 164 • Organization Culture 165 • Intrapreneurship in Larger Organizations 165
Managing Change 165
Forces for Change 166
External Forces 166 • Internal Forces 166
Planned Versus Reactive Change 166

© ISTOCKPHOTO.COM/ JACOB WACKERHAUSEN

The Lewin Change Model 167
A Comprehensive Approach to Change 167
Understanding Resistance to Change 168
Uncertainty 168 • Threatened Self-Interests 168 • Different Perceptions 168 • Feelings of Loss 168
Overcoming Resistance to Change 168
Participation 168 • Education and Communication 169 • Facilitation 169 • Force-Field Analysis 169
Managing Risk 169
Summary and a Look Ahead 171
Conceptual Skills in Action—1 171
Conceptual Skills in Action—2 172
Management Functions in Different Organizations 172
Choosing a New Business Startup 172
Using Conceptual Skills to Understand the Behavior of Others 173
Job Values as Perceived by Students and Employers 174
Learning from Other Organizations 175
To Cheat or Not? 175
Factors Affecting Organizational Design 176
Can You Predict? 176
The Relationship Between Quality and Financial Performance 177
Determining Why Teams Are Successful 178
Creativity at Kellogg 178
Creativity at Merck 179
Group Extensions 181
Individual Extensions 182
Conceptual Skills Assessment 182

Conceptual Skills 183
Summary of Your Scores 184
Interpretation of Your Scores 184
Goal-Setting Questionnaire 184
How Creative Are You? 184
Innovative Attitude Scale 184
Personal Risk Taking 184

6 DIAGNOSTIC SKILLS 188

© SELECTSTOCK

How Is Your Organization Managed? 190
Organizational Climate Questionnaire 191
Assessing Your Feedback Style 193
Organizational Structure Preferences 195
Understanding Cause and Effect 197
Understanding Control 198
The Purpose of Control 199
Adaptation 199 • Limiting the Accumulation of Error 199 • Coping with Organizational Complexity 200 • Minimizing Costs 200
Areas of Control 200
Levels of Control 200
Responsibilities for Control 201
Designing Control Systems 201
Steps in the Control Process 201
Establish Standards 201 • Measure Performance 203 • Compare Performance Against Standards 203 • Determine Need for Corrective Action 203
Operations Control 204
Preliminary Control 204 • Screening Control 204 • Postaction Control 205
Characteristics of Effective Control 205
Integration with Planning 205 • Flexibility 205 • Accuracy 205 • Timeliness 206 • Objectivity 206
Managing Control 206
Resistance to Control 206
Overcontrol 206 • Inappropriate Focus 207 • Rewards for Inefficiency 207 • Too Much Accountability 207
Overcoming Resistance to Control 207
Encourage Employee Participation 207 • Develop Verification Procedures 207
Rewarding Employees 208
Reinforcement Perspectives on Motivation 208
Kinds of Reinforcement in Organizations 208 • Providing Reinforcement in Organizations 209 • Implications of the Reinforcement Perspectives 210
Popular Motivational Strategies 210
Empowerment and Participation 210 • Techniques and Issues in Empowerment 211 • Alternative Forms of Work Arrangements 211
Using Reward Systems to Motivate Performance 212
Merit Reward Systems 212 • Incentive Reward Systems 213 • Common Team and Group Reward Systems 214 • Other Types of Team and Group Rewards 214 • New Approaches to Performance-Based Rewards 215
Summary and a Look Ahead 215
Diagnostic Skills in Action—1 216
Diagnostic Skills in Action—2 216
Relating Needs to Reality 217
Issues of Centralization and Decentralization 217
Determining Why Individuals Become Entrepreneurs 218
Negotiating a Franchise Agreement 218
Ethics in Decision Making 219
Using Different Methods of Power 220
Using Different Types of Power 220
Quality Relative to Price and Expectations 221
Diagnosing Causes of Problems 222
Weighing Organization Change Alternatives 222
Dealing with Equity and Justice Issues 223
Diagnosis at DuPont 224
International Training 225
Group Extensions 226
Individual Extensions 227
Diagnostic Skills Assessment 227
Diagnostic Skills 228
Summary of Your Scores 229
Interpretation of Your Scores 229
How Is Your Organization Managed? 229

Organizational Climate Questionnaire 229
Assessing Your Feedback Style 230
Organizational Structure Preferences 230
Mechanistic 230
Organic 231

7 COMMUNICATION SKILLS 234

A Communication Skills Survey 236
Becoming Aware of Your Communication Style 237
Feedback Skills Questionnaire 239
Gender Differences in Communication 240
The Meaning of Communication 242
The Role of Communication in Management 243
The Communication Process 243
Forms of Communication in Organizations 244
Interpersonal Communication 244
Oral Communication 245 • Written Communication 245 • Choosing the Right Form 245
Communication in Networks and Work Teams 246
Organizational Communication 247
Vertical Communication 247 • Horizontal Communication 248
Electronic Communication 248
Information Systems 248 • Personal Electronic Technology 249
Informal Communication in Organizations 249
The Grapevine 250
Management by Wandering Around 251
Nonverbal Communication 251
Managing Organizational Communication 252
Barriers to Communication 252
Individual Barriers 252 • Organizational Barriers 253
Improving Communication Effectiveness 254
Individual Skills 254 • Organizational Skills 254
Summary and a Look Ahead 255
Communication Skills in Action—1 255
Communication Skills in Action—2 256
Alone or Together? 256

DMITRIY SHIRONOSOV

"Best/Worst" Presentations 257
Can You Communicate Accurately? 258
Communicating a Change in Strategy 258
Ethical Issues 259
Communicating Human Resource Information 259
Communication in International Business 260
Announcing Unpopular Decisions 260
Slide Presentation 261
Communicating Across Time Zones 262
Japan and America—Alike But Different 262
Workplace Violence 263
Group Extensions 265
Individual Extensions 265
Communication Skills Assessment 266
Communication Skills 266
Summary of Your Scores 268
Interpretation of Your Scores 268
A Communication Skills Survey 268
Becoming Aware of Your Communication Style 268
Feedback Skills Questionnaire 269
Gender Differences in Communication 269

8 DECISION-MAKING SKILLS 272

© ISTOCKPHOTO.COM/STEVE COLE

Decision-Making Styles 274
Internal-External Control Sampler 274
Problem-Solving Style Questionnaire 275
Your Decision-Making Style 278
The Decision-Making Context 281
Kinds of Decisions 282
Conditions for Making Decisions 282
Rational Decision Making 284
Recognizing and Defining the Decision Situation 285
Identifying Alternatives 285
Evaluating Alternatives 285
Selecting an Alternative 286
Implementing the Chosen Alternative 287
Following Up and Evaluating the Results 288
Behavioral Processes and Decision Making 288
The Administrative Model 288
Coalitions and Decision Making 289
Intuition 289
Escalation of Commitment 290
Risk Propensity and Decision Making 291
Ethics and Decision Making 291
Participative and Group Decision Making 291
Employee Participation and Involvement 291
Group and Team Decision Making 292
Forms of Group and Team Decision Making 292 • Advantages of Group and Team Decision Making 293 • Disadvantages of Group and Team Decision Making 293 • Managing Group and Team Decision-Making Processes 294
How Much Participation Should Be Allowed? 294
Making Decisions For Contingencies and During Crisis 296
Summary and a Look Ahead 298
Decision-Making Skills in Action—1 298
Decision-Making Skills in Action—2 299
Making Career Choices 299
Choosing Team Members 300
Decision Making and Communication 302
Examining One Component of an Organization's Control System 303
Cost Reduction Decisions 304
Evaluating Training 305
Individual vs. Nominal Group Decision Making 306
Journaling and Affinity Diagrams in Decision-Making 306
Designing a New Organization 307
Decision Making and Communicating in a Small Business 308
Decisions, Decisions, Decisions 309
Lufthansa 310
Group Extensions 312
Individual Extensions 312
Decision-Making Skills Assessment 313
Decision-Making Skills 313
Summary of Your Scores 314
Interpretation of Your Scores 314
Decision-Making Styles 314
Internal-External Control Sampler 315
Problem-Solving Style Questionnaire 315
Your Decision-Making Style 316

9 TECHNICAL SKILLS 320

PBS (Power Bases Score) Questionnaire 322
Defining Quality and Productivity 323
Understanding Control 324
Are You Technically Oriented? 325
Technology, Product and Service, Industry, and Business Knowledge 328
Accounting and Financial Management Techniques 329
Budgets 329
Financial Statements 332
Ratio Analysis 332
Forecasting Techniques 332
Sales and Revenue Forecasting 332
Technological Forecasting 333
Other Types of Forecasting 333
Forecasting Techniques 333
Time-Series Analysis 334 • *Causal Modeling* 334 • *Qualitative Forecasting Techniques* 335
Other Planning Techniques 336
Linear Programming 336
Breakeven Analysis 338
Simulations 339
PERT 340
Decision-Making Tools 341
Payoff Matrices 341
Decision Trees 342
Other Techniques 343
Inventory Models 343 • *Queuing Models* 343 • *Distribution Models* 344 • *Game Theory* 344 • *Artificial Intelligence* 344
Summary and a Look Ahead 344
Technical Skills in Action—1 345
Technical Skills in Action—2 345
Applying Technical Skills to Budgeting 346
Using Your Technical Skills on the Internet 346
Getting Organized 347
Using the Internet to Obtain Data 348

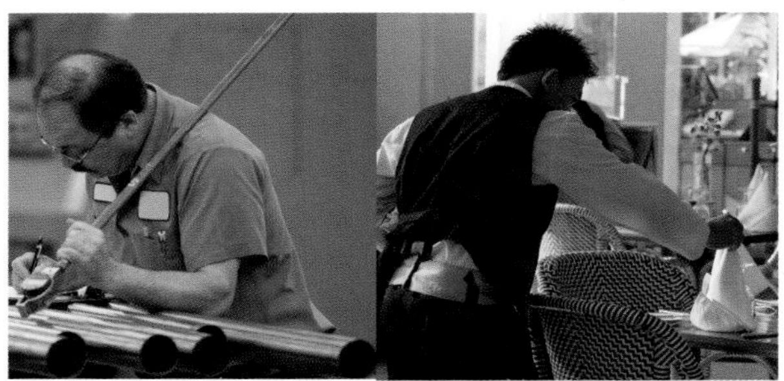
© CHRISTIAN DELBERT/SHUTTERSTOCK.COM, ERWINOVA/SHUTTERSTOCK.COM

Identifying Technical Skills Related to Quality and Productivity 349
Span of Management 349
Using SWOT to Evaluate Work-Life Strengths and Weaknesses 350
Identifying Technical Skills Needed in Different Organizations 351
Impact of Organizational Strategy on Structure 352
Your Problems 353
Perrier Keeps Flowing 353
Restaurant Operations 354
Group Extension 356
Individual Extension 356
Technical Skills Assessment 357
Technical Skills 357
Summary of Your Scores 358
Interpretation of Your Scores 359
PBS (Power Bases Score) Questionnaire 359
Defining Quality and Productivity 359
Understanding Control 359
Are You Technically Oriented? 359

10 TRANSITIONING FROM MANAGING TO LEADING 362

© ISTOCKPHOTO.COM/KALI9

How Charismatic Are You? 364
Managerial Leader Behavior Questionnaire 365
Differences Between Managing and Leading 367
Understanding The Basics of Leadership 368
Power and Leadership 368
Legitimate Power 368 • Reward Power 368 • Coercive Power 369 • Referent Power 369 • Expert Power 369 • Using Power 369
Leadership Traits 370
Leadership Behaviors 370
Michigan Studies 370 • Ohio State Studies 370 • Leadership Grid 371
Understanding Situational Approaches to Leadership 372
LPC Theory 372
Favorableness of the Situation 373 • Favorableness and Leader Style 373 • Flexibility of Leader Style 374
Path–Goal Theory 374
Leader Behavior 374 • Situational Factors 374
The Leader–Member Exchange Approach 375
Understanding Related Perspectives on Leadership 376
Substitutes for Leadership 376
Charismatic Leadership 377
Transformational Leadership 378
Cross-Cultural Leadership 378
Ethical Leadership 378
Summary and a Look Ahead 379
Leadership Skills in Action—1 379
Leadership Skills in Action—2 380
Draw Leadership 380
Analyze Leadership Style 380
Managers and Leaders 381
Who Are the Leaders? 381
The Struggles of Leadership 382
Paper or Not—Xerox Has It Covered 383
Group Extensions 385
Individual Extensions 386
How Charismatic Are You? 386
Managerial Leader Behavior Questionnaire 387

APPENDIX A 391

APPENDIX B 401

GLOSSARY 415

INDEX 421

ABOUT THE AUTHORS

Ricky W. Griffin serves as Distinguished Professor and Blocker Chair in Business at Texas A&M. A Fellow in both the Academy of Management and the Southern Management Association, he received his Ph.D. in organizational behavior from the University of Houston. He has served as editor of the *Journal of Management* and as an officer in the Southwest Regional Division of the Academy of Management, the Southern Management Association, and the Research Methods Division and the Organizational Behavior Division of the Academy of Management. Griffin spent three years on the faculty at the University of Missouri (Columbia) before moving to Texas A&M University in 1981. His research interests include workplace violence, employee health and well-being in the workplace, and workplace culture. A well-respected author, recognized for his organizational behavior and management research, Griffin has written many successful textbooks, including: *Management, Fundamentals of Management, Organizational Behavior, Human Resource Management, Introduction to Business,* and *International Business.*

David D. Van Fleet is a Professor of Management in the Morrison School of Agribusiness and Resource Management at Arizona State University. A Fellow in both the Academy of Management and the Southern Management Association, he received his Ph.D. in economics and management from the University of Tennessee—Knoxville. He has served as editor of the *Journal of Management* and the *Journal of Behavioral and Applied Management,* as well as an officer in the Southwest Regional Division of the Academy of Management, the Southern Management Association, and the Management History Division of the Academy of Management. Van Fleet taught at the University of Tennessee, the University of Akron, and Texas A&M University before moving to Arizona State in 1989. His research interests include: workplace violence, management history, and leadership. A well-respected author, Van Fleet has written many successful books, including: *The Violence Volcano, Workplace Survival, Contemporary Management, Behavior in Organizations,* and *Organizational Behavior: A Managerial Viewpoint.*

PREFACE

Business schools have been teaching management courses for decades. Our vision in planning and creating this book was to take an entirely new perspective to better enable you to learn about management. Our focus is on basic management skills, and our approach is derived from an active learning perspective. Specifically, while we believe you can learn definitions, models, frameworks, and theories by reading about them, in order for you to actually enhance your managerial capabilities you must be an active participant in the learning process.

STYLE AND APPROACH

To achieve our goals, we approached the creation of this book with a specific set of characteristics in mind. In particular, we wanted our book to have:

Research- and/or theory-based content Every concept and premise in the book is based on valid research- and/or theories. We don't subscribe to the "fad-of-the-month" club based on popular press anecdotes of what worked for one manager in one organization in one particular situation. Instead, we derive our material from serious and systematic theories and/or research by leading experts in the field.

Realistic, applied practitioner focus At the same time, we don't rely solely on ideas from research and/or theory and then assume that you will know how to apply that knowledge. Instead, we present myriad examples that illustrate how managers in a wide variety of organizations and realistic settings have succeeded or failed by doing things consistently or inconsistently with sound theory and research.

Active learning model We also believe that you will learn most effectively if you are an active participant in the learning process. As a result, while our book presents basic content in a traditional manner, that content is surrounded by a wide array of action-based exercises, cases, and other activities.

Integrated assessment framework Assessment is traditionally approached in a single manner—exams, cases, projects, and so forth that are evaluated by the instructor. While that form of assessment will likely be a part of your course, there is also an integrated assessment framework incorporated in this book. Specifically, you have the opportunity to assess your current level of proficiency on each of the core management skills and then re-assess after you have studied and practiced using the skills. Hence, you will get a direct reading on how much you improve. You can complete these assessments in the text as well as online on the CourseMate site.

Readability and engagement Some textbooks are dry and boring. We have made every effort to present this material in a friendly, easy-to-read style with numerous examples to make the book more interesting and accessible.

LOGICAL ORGANIZATION

At its most basic level this book is about the basic core skills both current and future managers need. Our goal is to help you learn about and develop these core skills so you are prepared to either begin a managerial career or perform more effectively in your current management position. If you have already started your career, the book will help you to prepare for future higher-level managerial positions. This book focuses on the following core skills: time-management skills, interpersonal skills, conceptual skills, diagnostic skills, communication skills, decision-making skills, and technical skills.

The first chapter discusses the nature of the manager's job and relates management skills to the functions and roles that comprise the manager's job. Chapter 2 examines how you can most effectively learn and develop the core managerial skills. Chapters 3–9 focus on each of the core skills individually. Chapter 10 discusses the processes associated with synthesizing all of these skills and how they can be applied to make the transition from managerial positions to positions of leadership. Appendix A includes a comprehensive assessment instrument created to help you understand your current strengths and weaknesses on each of the core skills covered in this book (you will be directed to that Appendix early in Chapter 1). Finally, there is an appendix (Appendix B) to help you with your career and job-hunting skills.

PEDAGOGICAL FEATURES

This book employs several pedagogical features to facilitate learning and applying the knowledge and skills. Those features include:

Introduction and Assessment Each chapter begins with a brief introduction. The introduction is followed by a diagnostic assessment questionnaire designed to evaluate your current proficiency in using the skill taught in the chapter. The initial assessment questionnaire, found in Appendix A, is quite long because it covers all of the core skills. The individual chapter assessment questionnaires are all considerably shorter because they cover only one skill. The assessments conclude with normative interpretation data to help you see how your skills proficiency compares to that of other managers.

Learning About the Skill A discussion of the skill follows each assessment and includes details of how it relates to other areas of managerial work and why it is important.

Visualizing the Skill Next, we help you to visualize the skills by examining scenes from films provided with the book. In addition, the Instructor's Manual suggests scenes from numerous popular movies that also illustrate the skills in action. These movies are generally available at public and/or university libraries as well as from online sources and movie rental firms.

Practicing and Using the Skills Additional sections present exercises and cases to assist you in putting your skills into practice and providing opportunities for additional reflection and refinement. Following these sections are other exercises that will further extend your skill proficiency in both individual and group contexts.

Reassessments Chapters 3–9 focus in detail on the core management skills and have a post-learning assessment to help you evaluate your improvement in using the skills covered in those chapters.

Interpretations Finally, each chapter concludes with additional interpretation data.

Additional Features In addition to creating strong and effective content, we also worked closely with our editors to insure that the book would be designed and presented in an accessible and inviting format. Effective use of color, photographs, and other innovative design elements will help engage you in the learning process. An array of web-based support materials will also enhance your learning experience.

Support Materials

Our text offers a full suite of instructor and student support materials.

- ***Instructor's Resource CD***. Instructors can find everything they need to create a dynamic, interactive learning environment with all of the key instructor ancillaries (Instructor's Manual, Test Bank, ExamView®, and PowerPoint® slides.) This powerful CD-ROM provides the ultimate timesaving tool for customizing lectures and presentations. The indispensable Instructor's Manual contains chapter overviews and outlines, lecture enhancements, suggestions for administering exercises, interpretations for the assessments, suggested answers for the chapter case questions, and more. The Test Bank offers multiple-choice, true/false, and essay questions. Each question is tagged with useful metadata. ExamView® contains all of the questions in the printed Test Bank. Instructors can easily add, edit, or select specific questions, instructions, and answers (randomly or numerically) on the screen. Bring lectures to life with the dynamic PowerPoint® Lecture Presentation slides. Slides are organized by chapter and can be easily modified.

- ***DVD.*** Students can watch text concepts come to life with this video collection. These clips have corresponding Visualizing the Skill exercises in 8 chapters and 1 appendix. These clips are from contemporary, popular movies like *In Good Company*, *Failure to Launch*, *Friday Night Lights*, *Casino*, and *Charlie Wilson's War*. The accompanying DVD guide (available on the Instructor's Companion Web site) offers detailed descriptions of the segments, including chapter learning goals and a synopsis. The DVD is fantastic for in-class use, and these same videos can be accessed for outside-of-class use through CengageNOW, CourseMate, and WebTutor.
- ***Text Companion Web Site.*** Access important teaching resources on this companion Web site. Instructors can download electronic versions of the instructor supplements at the password-protected section of the site, including the Instructor's Manual, Test Bank, and PowerPoint® presentations.
- To access these additional course materials and companion resources, please visit www.cengagebrain.com. At the CengageBrain.com home page, search for the ISBN of your title (from the back cover of your book) using the search box at the top of the page. This will take you to the product page where free companion resources can be found.
- ***MANAGEMENT CourseMate.*** Engaging, trackable, and affordable, the new MANAGEMENT CourseMate Web site offers a dynamic way to bring course concepts to life with interactive learning, study, and exam preparation tools that support this printed edition of the text. Watch student comprehension soar with all-new flash cards and engaging games, interactive self assessments, streaming videos, and more in this textbook-specific Web site. A complete e-book provides you with the choice of an entire online learning experience. MANAGEMENT CourseMate goes beyond the book to deliver what you need!
- ***CengageNOW.*** This robust, online course management system gives you more control in less time and delivers better student outcomes—NOW. CengageNOW for Griffin/VanFleet, *Management Skills*, includes teaching and learning resources organized around lecturing, creating assignments, grading, quizzing, and tracking student progress and performance. Flexible assignments options include Self Assessments, Experiential Exercises, Role-Play Exercises, Case analysis questions, and more. Video Quizzes feature segments covered in the chapters' Visualize the Skill section. These clips are from contemporary, popular movies including *In Good Company*, *Failure to Launch*, *Friday Night Lights*, *Casino*, and *Charlie Wilson's War*. Students can test their understanding of the skills by watching a short clip and answering the corresponding multiple choice questions. These features enhance the text's unique approach to not only explaining but also showing management skills in action. Automatic grading and a gradebook option provide more control while saving you valuable time. A Personalized Study diagnostic tool empowers students to master concepts, prepare for exams, and become more involved in class.

WebTutor™ for Blackboard® or WebCT®. Jumpstart your course with this interactive, Web-based, teaching and learning resource that is designed specifically for Griffin/VanFleet, *Management Skills*. Easily blend, add, edit, reorganize, or delete content, including media assets, quizzing, Web links, discussion topics, interactive games and exercises, and more. These tools supplement the classroom experience and ensure that students leave with the resources they need to succeed in management today.

We hope you find this book to be a valuable resource as you develop a solid grounding in management. The practice of management is both challenging and exhilarating. We have tried to create a book that will prepare you for your first management position and for subsequent promotions to higher-level positions. Please feel free to provide us with comments and feedback at rgriffin@tamu.edu and ddvf@asu.edu.

Ricky W. Griffin
David D. Van Fleet

ACKNOWLEDGEMENTS

We each began our teaching careers more years ago than we would like to admit! Since our first classes we have taught literally thousands of students. While many of these have been traditional full-time students, many others have been non-traditional students, part-time students, practicing managers, and senior executives. One of the greatest joys of teaching is what we ourselves have learned from our students. Hence, our first acknowledgement must go to the thousands of students we have had the privilege to know and to learn from.

We would also like to acknowledge a strong team of professionals at Cengage Learning. Scott Person and Julia Chase are top-notch professionals who have guided and directed this project from its beginnings. Jonathan Monahan has played a key role in developing marketing plans for the book. Other key contributors include Erin Joyner, Colleen Farmer, Rob Ellington, Tamara Grega, Scott Rosen, and Christie Barros. We would also like to thank our wonderful supplements preparers: Carol Heeter, Cheryl Meheden, Charlie Cook, Susan Leshnower, and Damaris Herlihy. Special thanks to Karen Baker for providing outstanding research assistance.

Several reviewers also helped us refine our thinking and sharpen our approach. We offer our thanks to the following key professionals:

Kathryn Archard
University of Massachusetts Boston

Genie Black
Arkansas Technical University

Scott Bryant
Montana State University

Jonathan Bundy
University of Georgia

Frank Carothers
Somerset Community College

Duane Collette
Skagit Valley College

Christine Day
Eastern Michigan University

Daniel Degravel
California State University: Northridge

Ivan Filby
Greenville College

Monica C. Gavino
Saint Xavier University

David Glew
University of North Carolina Wilmington

Dr. Alan Goldman
Arizona State University

Kimberly Goudy
Central Ohio Technical College

Douglas A. Greiner
University of Toledo

George Griffin
Spring Arbor University

Joanne Hix
Dallas Baptist University

John Humphreys
Texas A&M University

Gerri Hura
Buffalo State College

Jonatan Jelen
The City College of New York

Toni Knechtges
Eastern Michigan University

Barbara Limbach
Chadron State College

Jerry Luckett
Dakota Wesleyan University

Karen Markel
Oakland University

Erin Makarius
Canisius College

Donald W. McCormick
California State University: Northridge

Heather S. McMillan
Southeast Missouri State University

Cheryl Meheden
University of Lethbridge

Tracy K. Miller
University of Dayton

Morgan Milner
Eastern Michigan University

Elouise Mintz
Saint Louis University

Peter Morgan
British Columbia Institute of Technology

David W. Murphy
Madisonville Community College

David Nemi
Niagara County Community College

Buddy Jo Tanck
Miami County Campus of Fort Scott Community College

Elaine Tweedy
The University of Scranton

Paula Weber
St. Cloud State University

Carolyn Wiethoff
Indiana University

John Yudelson
California State University: Channel Islands

Maria Vitale
Chaffey College

Paula Weber
St. Cloud State University

Robert Zahrowski
Oregon Institute of Technology - OIT (Portland campus)

Finally, we would be remiss if we did not acknowledge the myriad contributions that our families make to our work. Glenda, Dustin, Ashley, and Matt enrich Ricky's life in more ways than can be imagined; they also help keep his hat size in check and remind him to stop and smell the roses. Ella, Dirk, and Marijke constantly help David to understand and appreciate the world of work and provide opportunities for getting away from it all as needed.

Chapter 1

Assessing Your Skills

How Do I Rate as a Manager?
Self-Described Profile

Learning About the Skills

What Is Management?
The Core Management Skills
Time-Management Skills
Interpersonal Skills
Conceptual Skills
Diagnostic Skills
Communication Skills
Decision-Making Skills
Technical Skills
The Organizational Compass
Levels of Management
Top Managers
Middle Managers
First-Line Managers
Areas of Management
Marketing Managers
Financial Managers
Operations Managers
Human Resource Managers
Administrative Managers
Other Kinds of Managers
The Functional Perspective on Management
Planning and Decision Making: Determining Courses of Action
Organizing: Coordinating Activities and Resources
Leading: Motivating and Managing People
Controlling: Monitoring and Evaluating Activities
The Role Perspective on Management
Interpersonal Roles
Informational Roles
Decisional Roles
Summary and a Look Ahead

Practicing Your Skills

Determining Why Individuals Become Entrepreneurs
Job Skills
The Nature of Managerial Work
What Do You Think?

Using Your Skills

Success Leads to ....
Kodak's Fuzzy Picture

Extending Your Skills

Group Extensions
Individual Extensions

Interpretations

How Do I Rate as a Manager?
Self-Described Profile
The Nature of Managerial Work

Basic Management Skills

©ISTOCKPHOTO.COM/JACOB WACKERHAUSEN

This chapter sets the stage for moving toward mastery of the core management skills (or competencies) by helping you to better understand the nature of management—its meaning, its basic functions, and how the functions and roles of managers fit together to help create, guide, and direct an organization. First, management is defined, and the core skills necessary for managers to perform effectively are introduced. Next, the concept of the organizational compass through which managers can better assess both the skills they need for their current position and the skills they will need for their future positions are introduced. Then, the basic functions and roles of managers are introduced and discussed.

ASSESSING YOUR SKILLS

BASIC MANAGEMENT SKILLS

To achieve maximum benefit from this book, you should have a reasonably accurate initial assessment of your skills before reading and working through it. This assessment in Appendix A will serve as a baseline measure of your skills. Because management involves a wide variety of skills, a comprehensive and detailed assessment instrument is needed. So, *go to Appendix A and complete this comprehensive assessment now.*

Throughout the book there are opportunities to reassess your skills in certain areas. Comparing these assessments with this initial, more comprehensive one will help you to understand how you are progressing or possibly identify areas that you need to revisit. Each chapter begins with several brief self-assessments to help you understand the skills necessary to be a successful manager. This chapter begins with two of these self-assessments.

HOW DO I RATE AS A MANAGER?

The following self-assessment will help you determine your current understanding of and approach to the practice of management. This assessment outlines four important functions of management: planning, organizing, leading, and controlling. You should respond in *one* of three ways:

1. Respond based on your own managerial experience, if you have any.
2. Respond about effective (or ineffective) managers you have observed in your work experience.
3. Respond in terms of how you think an ideal manager should behave.

Instructions:
Recall a situation in which you were a member of a group or team that had a specific task or project to complete. This may have been at work, in a class, or in a church, club, or civic organization. Now assess your behavior in each of the functions. For each question, rate yourself according to the following scale:

Rating Scale
5 Definitely true of me
4 Probably true of me
3 Neither true or not true; undecided
2 Probably not true of me
1 Definitely not true of me

I. Planning

_____ 1. I prepare an agenda for meetings.

_____ 2. I try to anticipate what will happen in the future as a result of my current actions and decisions.

_____ 3. I establish clear goals for myself and others.

_____ 4. I carefully analyze the pros and cons involved in situations before reaching decisions.

_____ 5. I am quite willing to try new things, to experiment.

_____ 6. I have a clear vision for accomplishing the task at hand.
_____ 7. I put plans in writing so that others can know exactly what they are.
_____ 8. I try to remain flexible so that I can adapt to changing conditions.
_____ 9. I try to anticipate barriers to goal accomplishment and how to overcome them.
_____ 10. I discuss plans and involve others in arriving at those plans.

_____ **Section I Total**

II. Organizing

_____ 1. I try to follow the plan while working on the task.
_____ 2. I try to develop an understanding of the different steps or parts needed to accomplish the task at hand.
_____ 3. I evaluate different ways of working on the task before deciding on which course of action to follow.
_____ 4. I have a clear sense of the priorities necessary to accomplish the task.
_____ 5. I arrange for others to be informed about the degree of progress in accomplishing the task.
_____ 6. I am open to alternative, even novel ways of working on the task.
_____ 7. I adapt the sequence of activities involved if circumstances change.
_____ 8. I have a clear sense of how the steps involved in accomplishing the task should be structured.
_____ 9. I lead or follow where appropriate to see to it that progress is made toward accomplishing the task.
_____ 10. I coordinate with others to assure steady progress on the task.

_____ **Section II Total**

III. Leading

_____ 1. I set an example for others to follow.
_____ 2. I am effective at motivating others.
_____ 3. I try to keep a balance between getting the work done and keeping a spirit of teamwork.
_____ 4. I try to handle conflict in non-threatening, constructive ways.
_____ 5. I provide guidance and training to help others in the group better perform their roles.
_____ 6. I am open to suggestions from others.
_____ 7. I keep everyone informed about the group's activities and progress.
_____ 8. I show a genuine interest in the work of others.
_____ 9. I am considerate when providing constructive suggestions to others.
_____ 10. I understand the needs of others and encourage others to take initiative in meeting those needs.

_____ **Section III Total**

IV. Controlling

_____ 1. I regularly assess the quantity and quality of progress on the task at hand.
_____ 2. I try to assure that the information I have is timely, accurate, complete, and relevant.
_____ 3. I routinely share information with others to help them accomplish their tasks.

_____ 4. I compare progress with plans and take corrective action as warranted.

_____ 5. I manage my time and help others to manage theirs.

_____ 6. I have good sources of information or methods for obtaining information.

_____ 7. I use technology (computers, tablets, smartphones, etc.) to monitor progress and communicate with others.

_____ 8. I anticipate possible negative reactions and take action to minimize them.

_____ 9. I recognize that "fixing problems before they occur" is better than "fixing problems after they occur."

_____ 10. I try to balance my attention on the many and different steps required to accomplish the task at hand.

_____ **Section IV Total**

Source: Adapted from Van Fleet, D. D., Van Fleet, E. W., & Seperich, G. J. 2013. *Principles of Management for Agribusiness.* Clifton Park, NY: Delmar/Cengage Learning; Griffin, R. W. 2011. *Management.* Mason, OH: South-Western Cengage Learning; and Van Fleet, D. D. 1991. *Behavior in Organizations.* Boston: Houghton Mifflin, in collaboration with G. Moorhead and R. W. Griffin.

See Interpretations at the end of the chapter.

SELF-DESCRIBED PROFILE

This assessment offers a self-described profile of your basic management skills. The items on the list are recommended by the American Assembly of Collegiate Schools of Business (AACSB) as skills and personal characteristics that should be nurtured in college and university business students.

Instructions:
Rate yourself on the following ten personal characteristics, using this scale:

S = *Strong – I am very confident about this one.*
G = *Good – I still have room to grow.*
W = *Weak – I really need work on this one.*
? = *Unsure – I just don't know.*

_____ 1. *Critical thinking:* The ability to carefully assess assumptions and aspects of your own thinking in order to arrive at viable alternative courses of action.

_____ 2. *Stamina and resistance to stress:* The ability to perform your tasks working long hours and under stressful conditions.

_____ 3. *Multicultural skills:* The ability to act free of racial, ethnic, gender, and other prejudices or biases.

_____ 4. *Tolerance for uncertainty:* The ability to perform your tasks even under uncertain and ambiguous conditions.

_____ 5. *Interpersonal skills:* The ability to interact effectively with others.

_____ 6. *Inner work goals:* The ability to personally set and work toward high-performance goals.

_____ 7. *Change management skills:* The ability to be flexible and adapt to changes.

_____ 8. *Self-confidence:* The ability to consistently act effectively and decisively.

_____ 9. *Teamwork skills:* The ability to work cooperatively as part of a group.

_____ 10. *Self-objectivity:* The ability to evaluate personal strengths and weaknesses and to understand one's motives and skills relative to required tasks.

ASSESS

_____ 11. *Negotiation skills:* The ability to discuss differences with others and reach jointly acceptable results.

_____ 12. *Introspection:* The ability to learn from your own experience, awareness, and self-study.

_____ 13. *Communication skills:* The ability to use appropriate media to transmit information and achieve understanding.

_____ 14. *Entrepreneurism:* The ability to address problems and take advantage of opportunities for constructive change.

_____ 15. *Leadership skills:* The ability to influence and motivate others to accomplish a common task or achieve objectives.

Scoring:

Give yourself one point for each **Strong** *answer, and 1/2 point for each* **Good** *answer. No points are awarded for* **Weak** *answers or* **Unsure** *answers.*

Total score: _________

Source: Recommendations to AACSB International from the Globalization of Management Education Task Force (Tampa, FL: AACSB International – The Association to Advance Collegiate Schools of Business, 2011); Management Education at Risk (St. Louis, MO: AACSB International – The Association to Advance Collegiate Schools of Business, April 2002); Outcome Measurement Project, Phase I and Phase II Reports (St. Louis, MO: American Assembly of Collegiate Schools of Business, 1986 & 1987).

See Interpretations at the end of the chapter.

GO ONLINE to the Griffin/Van Fleet Assessment Library for online versions of these and other assessments.

LEARNING ABOUT THE SKILLS

What Is Management?

The Core Management Skills

- *Time-Management Skills*
- *Interpersonal Skills*
- *Conceptual Skills*
- *Diagnostic Skills*
- *Communication Skills*
- *Decision-Making Skills*
- *Technical Skills*

The Organizational Compass

- *Levels of Management*
  - *Top Managers*
  - *Middle Managers*
  - *First-Line Managers*
- *Areas of Management*
  - *Marketing Managers*
  - *Financial Managers*
  - *Operations Managers*
  - *Human Resource Managers*
  - *Administrative Managers*
  - *Other Kinds of Managers*

The Functional Perspective on Management

- *Planning and Decision Making: Determining Courses of Action*
- *Organizing: Coordinating Activities and Resources*
- *Leading: Motivating and Managing People*
- *Controlling: Monitoring and Evaluating Activities*

The Role Perspective on Management

- *Interpersonal Roles*
- *Informational Roles*
- *Decisional Roles*

Summary and a Look Ahead

WHAT IS MANAGEMENT?

management a set of activities (including planning and decision making, organizing, leading, and controlling) directed at an organization's resources (human, financial, physical, and information) with the aim of achieving organizational goals in an efficient and effective manner

Management is generally defined as a set of activities (including planning and decision making, organizing, leading, and controlling) directed at an organization's resources (human, financial, physical, and information) with the aim of achieving organizational goals in an efficient and

AFOTOSHOP/SHUTTERSTOCK.COM

AP PHOTOS/KEVIN P. CASEY

AP PHOTO/TED S. WARREN

Starbucks uses a variety of resources, including coffee beans, employees, and financial information. Other firms use different combinations of resources.

effective manner. The last phrase in our definition is especially important because it highlights the basic purpose of management—to ensure that an organization's goals are achieved in an efficient and effective manner. By efficient, we mean using resources wisely and in a cost-effective way. For example, a firm such as Honda, which produces high-quality products at relatively low costs, is efficient. By effective, we mean making the right decisions and successfully implementing them. Honda also makes cars with the styling and quality to inspire consumer interest and confidence. Alternatively, a firm might efficiently produce heavy and bulky laptop computers with few options and limited capabilities but still not succeed, because laptop users today want small, lightweight machines with different capabilities. A firm that produces products that no one wants is not effective. In general, organizations that are successful over the long run are both efficient and effective.[1]

All organizations use four basic kinds of resources from their environment: human, financial, physical, and information. *Human resources* include managerial talent and labor. *Financial resources* are the capital used by the organization to finance initial, ongoing, and long-term operations. *Physical resources* include raw materials, office and production facilities, and equipment. *Information resources* are usable data needed to make effective decisions.

Managers are responsible for combining and coordinating these various resources to achieve the organization's goals. A manager at Chevron, for example, uses the talents of executives and drilling platform workers, profits earmarked for reinvestment, existing refineries and office facilities, and sales forecasts to make decisions regarding the amount of petroleum to be refined and distributed during the next quarter. Similarly, the mayor (manager) of Chicago might use police officers, a government grant (perhaps supplemented with surplus tax revenues), existing police stations, and detailed crime statistics to launch a major crime prevention program in the city.

> "Business is simple. Management's job is to take care of employees. The employees' job is to take care of the customers. Happy customers take care of the shareholders. It's a virtuous circle."
>
> JOHN MACKEY
> Founder and CEO of Whole Foods[2]

FORBES, FEBRUARY 14, 2005, P. 110.

How do these and other managers combine and coordinate the various kinds of resources in ways that are effective and efficient? They do so by relying on a set of core management skills to carry out basic managerial functions.

MATTHEW MAHON/REDUX

THE CORE MANAGEMENT SKILLS

Decades of theory, research, and practice have identified numerous skills that managers need to exhibit in various circumstances. There is, however, no universal agreement on the specific skill set managers need. It is also the case that skills differ in their importance and frequency across different settings. To complicate things further, in some cases the differences among the skills are apparent and, in other cases, there is overlap across the skills. Nevertheless, theory and research provide relative agreement on the importance of seven core management skills. The skills framework used in this book, based on these seven core skills, was developed from this body of theory and research. The framework was then refined and validated through detailed interviews with hundreds of managers. These managers reflect a cross section of industry, organization size and level, and functional area. As shown in *Figure 1.1*, the core skills around which this book is organized are time-management, interpersonal, conceptual, diagnostic, communication, decision-making, and technical skills.[3]

Time-Management Skills

All managers need effective time-management skills. Time-management skills refer to the manager's

efficient using resources wisely and in a cost-effective way. For example, a firm such as Honda, which produces high-quality products at relatively low costs, is efficient

effective making the right decisions and successfully implementing them

time-management skills the manager's ability to prioritize work, to work efficiently, and to delegate appropriately

LEARN

FIGURE 1.1 THE CORE MANAGEMENT SKILLS

Managers need proficiency in using seven core skills: technical, interpersonal, conceptual, diagnostic, communication, decision-making, and time-management skills. Effectively blending these skills in behavior and action with the effective execution of basic managerial functions and roles will enhance the likelihood of personal, team, unit, and organizational success.

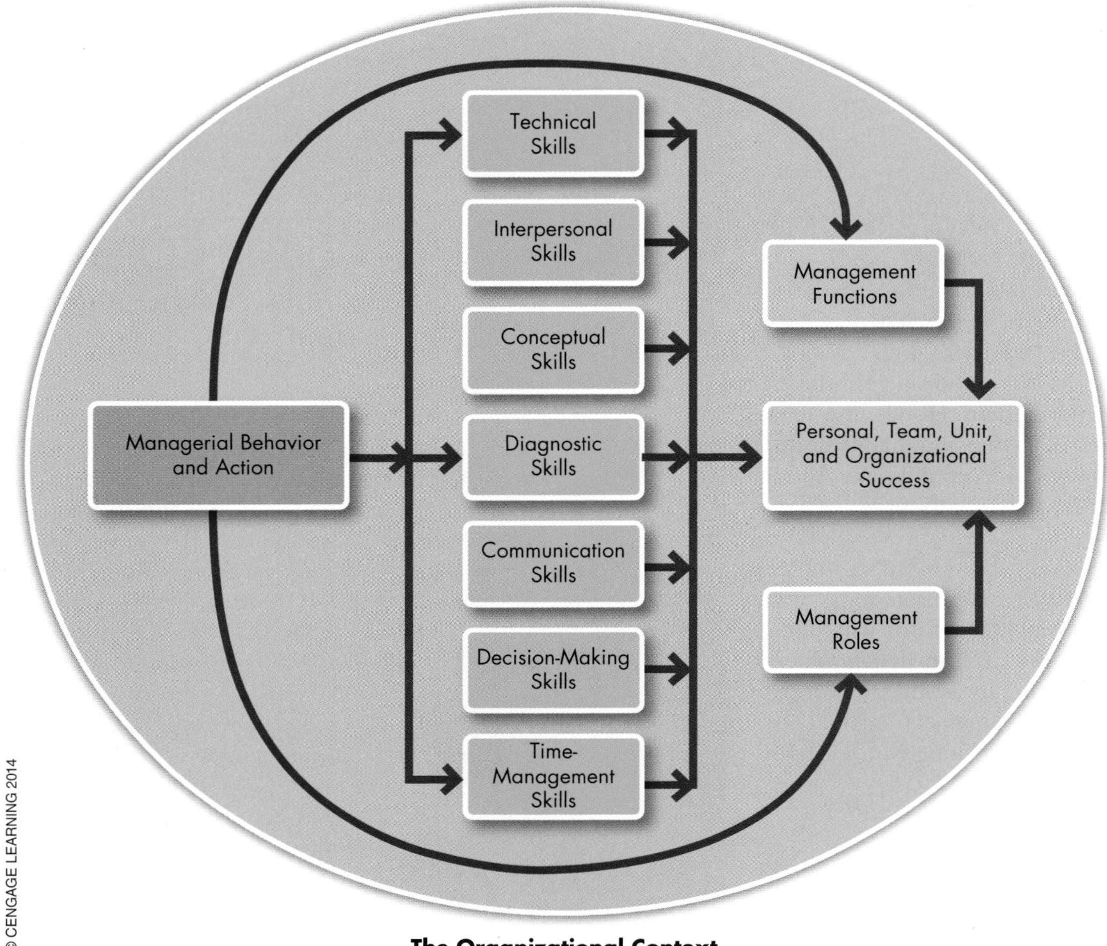

ability to prioritize effectively, work efficiently, and delegate appropriately. Managers face many different pressures and challenges. It is easy for a manager to get bogged down doing work that can easily be postponed or delegated to others.[4] When this happens, unfortunately, more pressing and higher-priority work may be neglected.[5] Similarly, poor time-management skills can result in inefficiency and stress. Key elements of time-management skills include understanding how to prioritize, delegate effectively, schedule meetings, control intrusions, and manage stress. Jeff Bezos, CEO of Amazon.com, schedules all of his meetings on three days a week but insists on keeping the other two days clear so he can pursue his own ideas and maintain the flexibility to interact with his employees informally.[6] Chapter 3 will help you assess and develop your time-management skills.

interpersonal skills the manager's abilities to understand and relate to both individuals and groups, as well as to motivate others to perform at their highest levels

Interpersonal Skills

Managers spend considerable time interacting with people both inside and outside the organization. A manager needs **interpersonal skills**—the abilities to understand and relate to both individuals and groups, as well as to motivate others to perform at their highest levels. As a manager climbs the organizational ladder, he or she must be able to get along with subordinates, peers, and those at higher levels of the organization. Because of the many roles managers must fulfill, a manager must be able to work with suppliers, customers, investors, and others outside of the organization. Although some managers have succeeded with poor interpersonal skills, a manager who has good interpersonal skills will likely be more successful. Basic elements of interpersonal skills include being able to recognize individual differences, understand diversity, work with teams, manage conflict, motivate others, and manage workplace behaviors. Sheryl Sandberg joined Facebook in 2008 as chief operating officer following successful stints at the World Bank, the Treasury Department, and Google. Sandberg is renowned for her interpersonal skills and sharp intellect, balancing CEO Mark Zuckerberg's introversion. These skills have helped to cultivate strong relationships with key advertisers and bring continued growth and stability to Facebook. Interpersonal skills are the focus of Chapter 4.

Conceptual Skills

Conceptual skills depend on the manager's ability to think in the abstract. Managers need to understand the overall workings of the organization and its environment, to grasp how all the parts of the organization fit together, and to view the organization in a holistic manner. This allows them to think strategically, to see the "big picture," and to make broad-based decisions that serve the overall organization. Strategic thinking, managing innovation and creativity, and managing change are key components of conceptual skills. Dave Gilboa and Neil Blumenthal recently founded Warby Parker, a business that sells prescription eyewear through the mail. The entrepreneurs realized that most consumers disliked the experience of going to an optical shop to try on glasses and then were irritated at the price of those glasses. So, Warby Parker offers lower-priced glasses with hip designs and a money-back guarantee. Astute marketing then allowed them to get a quick start with their niche business, selling more than 50,000 pairs of glasses and generating profits after only a single year of operation.[7] Chapter 5 will help you assess and start developing your conceptual skills.

Diagnostic Skills

Successful managers also possess diagnostic skills, or the ability to visualize the most appropriate response to a situation. A physician diagnoses a patient's illness by analyzing symptoms and determining their probable cause. Similarly, a manager can diagnose and analyze a problem in the organization by studying its symptoms and then developing a solution.[8] Core elements of diagnostic skills include understanding cause-and-effect relationships, managing control, and linking rewards to desired employee behaviors. When the original owners of Starbucks failed to make a success of the business, Howard Schultz took over. He reoriented the business away from mail order and moved it into retail coffee outlets. His diagnostic skills enabled him to understand both why the current business model was not working and how to construct a better one. Diagnostic skills are the focus of Chapter 6.

LEARN

Communication Skills

Communication skills refer to the manager's abilities both to effectively convey ideas and information to others and to effectively receive ideas and information from others. These skills enable a manager to transmit ideas to subordinates so they know what is expected, to coordinate work with peers and colleagues so that they work well together properly, and to keep higher-level managers informed about what is going on. In addition, communication skills help the manager listen to what others say and to understand the real meaning behind letters, reports, and other written communication. Understanding the meaning of communication, being competent in different forms of communication, having awareness of informal communication, and being able to manage communication all contribute to communication skills. Communication skills are the subject of Chapter 7.

Decision-Making Skills

Effective managers also have good decision-making skills. Decision-making skills refer to the manager's ability to correctly recognize and define problems and opportunities and to then select an appropriate course of action to solve problems and capitalize on opportunities. No manager makes the right decision *all*

conceptual skills the manager's ability to think in the abstract

diagnostic skills the manager's ability to visualize the most appropriate response to a situation

communication skills the manager's abilities both to effectively convey ideas and information to others and to effectively receive ideas and information from others

decision-making skills the manager's ability to correctly recognize and define problems and opportunities and to then select an appropriate course of action to solve problems and capitalize on opportunities

the time. However, effective managers make good decisions *most* of the time. When they do make a bad decision, they usually recognize their mistake quickly and then make good decisions to recover with as little cost or damage to their organization as possible. Decision-making skills include understanding both rational and behavioral perspectives on decision making, the role of participation in making decisions, and making decisions for contingencies and during crisis. Chapter 8 is devoted to decision-making skills.

> "...set realistic goals, achieve them, and recalibrate your goals so that you're constantly moving forward, as opposed to setting dreamer-type goals that you're going to get frustrated by."
>
> MEREDITH WHITNEY
> Founder, Meredith Whitney Advisory Group[9]

QUOTED IN FORTUNE, JULY 6, 2009, P. 47.

Technical Skills

Technical skills are necessary to perform or understand tasks that require specialized knowledge. Technical skills are especially important for first-line managers. These managers spend much of their time training subordinates and answering questions about work-related problems. They must know how to perform the tasks assigned to those they supervise if they are to be effective managers. Technical skills should include knowledge about technology, products, services, finance, accounting, forecasting, planning, decision making, and the business itself. Brian Dunn, director and CEO of Best Buy, began his career in 1985 as a store associate when Best Buy consisted of only 12 stores. He continued to work his way up into various positions including store manager, district manager, regional manager, regional VP, senior VP, executive VP, and president of Retail (North America). Hence, he literally learned the technical aspects of retailing from the ground up. We discuss technical skills in Chapter 9.

THE ORGANIZATIONAL COMPASS

One key ingredient to managerial success is to understand and appreciate how you contribute to your organization's efficiency and effectiveness. This will enable you to maximize your contributions to your organization and, ultimately, enhance your own personal career success. From a skills perspective managers must be able to answer two key questions: (1) What skills do I need to perform my *current job* effectively? (2) What skills do I need to perform my *next job* effectively? Clearly, you need to already understand and be developing the skills needed for your current job. At the same time, though, you must understand and be developing the skills you need for your next job. The organizational compass, illustrated in *Figure 1.2*, can help serve as a roadmap for this assessment. Managers must understand where their current position fit in terms of level and area, as well as the location—again by both level and area—of your most likely future jobs.

technical skills the manager's abilities to perform or understand relatively concrete tasks that require specialized knowledge

FIGURE 1.2 THE ORGANIZATIONAL COMPASS

Managers must understand their current level and functional area within their organization. This will enable them to assess the skills they need to perform their current job more effectively. To the extent possible, they should also understand where their next job is likely to be in terms of level and area in order to be better prepared when they assume that position.

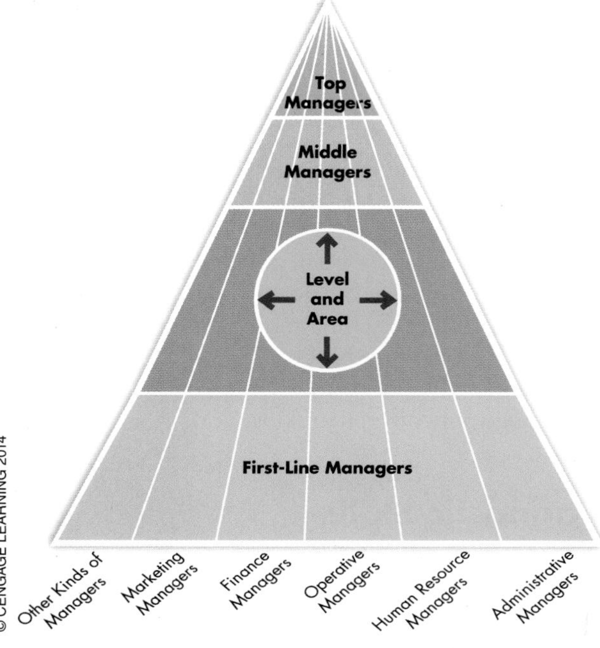

© CENGAGE LEARNING 2014

REB IMAGES

JACOBS STOCK PHOTOGRAPHY

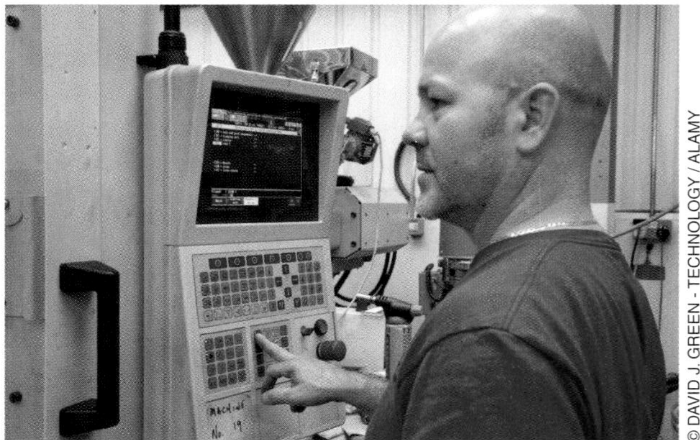
© DAVID J. GREEN - TECHNOLOGY / ALAMY

Most organizations are populated by managers across a variety of hierarchical levels. Experts generally classify these levels as top managers, middle managers, and first-line (or supervisory) managers.

Levels of Management

Managers can be classified according to their level in the organization. Although large organizations typically have a number of levels of management, the most common view considers three basic levels: top, middle, and first-line managers.

LEARN

Top Managers Top managers make up the relatively small group of executives who manage the overall organization. Titles found in this group include president, vice president, and chief executive officer (CEO). Top managers create the organization's goals, overall strategy, and operating policies. They also officially represent the organization to the external environment by meeting with government officials, executives of other organizations, and so forth.

Howard Schultz, CEO of Starbucks, is a top manager, as is Troy Alstead, the firm's executive vice president. The job of a top manager is likely to be complex and varied. Top managers make decisions about such activities as acquiring other companies, investing in research and development, entering or leaving various markets, and building new plants and office facilities. They often work long hours and spend much of their time in meetings or on the telephone. In most cases, top managers are also very well paid. In fact, the elite top managers of very large firms sometimes make several million dollars a year in salary, bonuses, and stock.[10]

Middle Managers Middle management is probably the largest group of managers in most organizations. Common middle-management titles include plant manager, operations manager, and division head. Middle managers are responsible primarily for implementing the policies and plans developed by top managers and for supervising and coordinating the activities of lower-level managers.[11] Plant managers, for example, handle inventory management, quality control, equipment failures, and minor union problems. They also coordinate the work of supervisors within the plant. Jason Hernandez, a regional manager at Starbucks responsible for the firm's operations in three eastern states, is a middle manager.

In recent years, many organizations have thinned the ranks of middle managers to lower costs and eliminate excess bureaucracy. Still, middle managers are necessary to bridge the upper and lower levels of the organization and to implement the strategies developed at the top. Although many organizations have found that they can indeed survive with fewer middle managers, those who remain play an even more important role in determining how successful the organization will be.

levels of management top, middle, and first-line managers

LEARN

First-Line Managers First-line managers supervise and coordinate the activities of operating employees. Common titles for first-line managers are supervisor, coordinator, and office manager. Positions like these are often the first held by employees who enter management from the ranks of operating personnel. Wayne Maxwell and Jenny Wagner, managers of Starbucks coffee shops in Texas, are first-line managers. They oversee the day-to-day operations of their respective stores, hire operating employees to staff them, and handle other routine administrative duties required of them by the parent corporation. In contrast to top and middle managers, first-line managers typically spend a large proportion of their time supervising the work of subordinates.

Areas of Management

Regardless of their level, managers may work in various areas within an organization. In any given firm areas of management may include marketing, finance, operations, human resources, administration, and other areas.

Marketing Managers Marketing managers work in areas related to the organization's marketing function—getting consumers and clients to buy the organization's products or services (be they iPads, Ford automobiles, *Time* magazines, Associated Press news reports, flights on Southwest Airlines, or cups of latte at Starbucks). These areas include new-product development, promotion, and distribution. Given the importance of marketing for virtually all organizations, developing good managers in this area can be critical.

Financial Managers Financial managers deal primarily with an organization's financial resources. They are responsible for such activities as accounting, cash management, and investments. In some businesses, such as banking and insurance, financial managers are found in especially large numbers, because financial management is really the core function at those businesses.

Operations Managers Operations managers are concerned with creating and managing the systems that create an organization's products and services. Typical responsibilities of operations managers include production control, inventory control, quality control, plant layout, and site selection. Operations managers are needed in both manufacturing and service businesses.

areas of management marketing, financial, operations, human resource, administrative, and other areas

Human Resource Managers Human resource managers are responsible for hiring and developing employees. They are typically involved in human resource planning, recruiting and selecting employees, training and development, designing compensation and benefit systems, formulating performance appraisal systems, and discharging low-performing and problem employees.

Administrative Managers Administrative, or general, managers are not associated with any particular management specialty. Probably the best example of an administrative management position is that of a hospital or clinic administrator. Administrative managers tend to be generalists; they have some basic familiarity with all functional areas of management rather than specialized training in any one area.[12]

Other Kinds of Managers Many organizations have specialized management positions in addition to those already described. Public relations managers, for example, deal with the public and media for firms like Philip Morris Companies and the Dow Chemical Company to protect and enhance the image of the organization. Research and development (R&D) managers coordinate the activities of scientists and engineers working on scientific projects in organizations such as Monsanto Company, NASA, and Merck & Company. Internal consultants are used in organizations such as Prudential Insurance to provide specialized expert advice to operating managers. Specialized managers in organizations like Eli Lilly and Rockwell International coordinate international operations. In some cases, organizations create temporary management positions to handle specialized activities with a limited duration. For instance, during the merger of Continental and United Airlines in 2011–2012, a team of senior managers was created to oversee the integration of the two firms. When the merger was completed, these positions were eliminated. The number, nature, and importance of these specialized managers vary tremendously from one organization to another. As contemporary organizations continue to grow in complexity and size, the number and importance of such managers are also likely to increase.

> "I spend more time on the people-development priorities that I do any other single thing as CEO."
>
> MIKE DUKE
> Walmart CEO[13]

QUOTED IN USA TODAY, SEPTEMBER 19, 2011, P. 3B.

THE FUNCTIONAL PERSPECTIVE ON MANAGEMENT

We noted earlier that management involves the four basic functions of planning and decision making, organizing, leading, and controlling. Consider, for example, Sergey Brin and Larry Page, founders and top managers at Google. As they run their organization, Brin and Page must first create goals and plans that articulate what they want the company to become. Then they rely on effective organization to help make those goals and plans reality. Brin and Page also pay close attention to the people who work for the company. They must also monitor how well the company is performing. Each of these activities represents one of the four basic managerial functions illustrated in *Figure 1.3*—setting goals is part of planning, setting up the organization is part of organizing, managing people is part of leading, and monitoring performance is part of controlling.

The functions of management are not necessarily executed in a tidy, step-by-step fashion, however. Managers do not plan on Monday, make decisions on Tuesday, organize on Wednesday, lead on Thursday, and control on Friday. At any given time, a manager is likely to be engaged in several different activities simultaneously. From one setting to another, managerial work is as different as it is similar. The similarities that pervade most settings are the phases in the management process. Important differences include the emphasis, sequencing, and implications of each phase.[14]

FIGURE 1.3 THE FUNCTIONAL PERSPECTIVE ON MANAGEMENT

The functional perspective on management suggests that most managerial activities involve planning and decision making, organizing, leading, and controlling. A clear understanding of these functions and how they relate to the core management skills can promote more effective performance. As suggested by the interconnections, most managers engage in more than one activity at a time and often move back and forth between the activities in unpredictable ways.

© CENGAGE LEARNING 2014

Planning and Decision Making: Determining Courses of Action

In its simplest form **planning** means setting an organization's goals and deciding how best to achieve them. **Decision making**, a part of the planning process, involves selecting a course of action from a set of alternatives. Planning and decision making help maintain managerial effectiveness by providing both general and specific direction for future activities. In other words, the organization's goals and plans clearly help managers know how to allocate their time and resources. Planning and decision making require an understanding of the role and importance of organizational goals, strategy and strategic planning, tactical planning, and operational planning. While all of the core management skills affect planning, conceptual and diagnostic skills are often the most important, and decision-making skills are at the heart of effective decision making as a basic management function.

Organizing: Coordinating Activities and Resources

Once a manager has set goals and developed a workable plan, the next management function is to organize people and the other resources necessary to carry out the plan. **Organizing** involves determining how to group activities and resources. Organizing requires an understanding of job design, departmentalization, authority relationships, span of control, and line-and-staff roles. It also requires an understanding of how managers fit these elements and concepts together to form an overall organization design. Further, organizing requires an understanding of how to manage organizational change and

planning setting an organization's goals and deciding how best to achieve them

decision making selecting a course of action from a set of alternatives

organizing determining how to group and coordinate activities and resources

HELDER ALMEIDA/SHUTTERSTOCK.COM

innovation, and processes associated with managing the organization's workforce. Technical, conceptual, and diagnostic skills also often play important roles in organizing.

Leading: Motivating and Managing People

The third basic managerial function is leading. Some people consider leading to be both the most important and the most challenging of all managerial activities. **Leading** is the set of processes used to get members of the organization to work together to further the interests of the organization. To effectively engage in the leading function, managers must possess an understanding of individual and interpersonal processes. They also must have an appreciation for employee motivation, interpersonal relations and communication, the dynamics of managing work groups and teams, and leadership itself. Interpersonal and communication skills may be especially important in carrying out the leading function.

Controlling: Monitoring and Evaluating Activities

leading the set of processes used to get members of the organization to work together to further the interests of the organization

controlling monitoring the organization's progress toward its goals

interpersonal roles figurehead, leader, and liaison roles

The final phase of the management process is **controlling**, or monitoring the organization's progress toward its goals. As the organization moves toward its goals, managers must monitor progress to ensure that it is performing in such a way as to arrive at its "destination" at the appointed time. A good analogy is that of a space mission to Mars. NASA does not simply shoot a rocket in the general direction of the planet and then look again in four months to see whether the rocket hit its mark. NASA monitors the spacecraft almost continuously and makes the necessary course corrections to keep it on track. Controlling helps ensure the effectiveness and efficiency needed for successful management. To engage effectively in the control function, managers need to understand the basic elements of the control process, including the increasing importance of strategic control; the management of operations, quality, and productivity; and the management of information and information technology. Technical, diagnostic, decision-making, and time-management skills all play important roles in control.

THE ROLE PERSPECTIVE ON MANAGEMENT

As you develop and refine your core management skills, you also need to understand the various roles that managers play. Mintzberg offers a number of interesting insights into the nature of managerial roles.[15] He closely observed the day-to-day activities of a group of CEOs by literally following them around and taking notes on what they did. From his observations, Mintzberg concluded that managers play ten different roles, as summarized in *Table 1.1*, and that these roles fall into three basic categories: interpersonal, informational, and decisional roles.

Interpersonal Roles

There are three **interpersonal roles** inherent in the manager's job. First, the manager is often expected to serve as a *figurehead*—taking visitors to dinner, attending ribbon-cutting ceremonies, and the like. These activities are typically more ceremonial and symbolic than substantive. The manager is also expected to serve as a *leader*—hiring, training, and motivating employees. A manager who formally or informally shows subordinates how to do things and how to perform under pressure is leading. Finally, managers can have a *liaison* role. This role often involves serving as a coordinator or link among people, groups, or organizations.

For example, companies in the computer industry may use liaisons to keep other companies informed about their plans. This enables Microsoft, for example,

TABLE 1.1 TEN BASIC MANAGERIAL ROLES

Category	Role	Sample Activities
Interpersonal	Figurehead	Attending ribbon-cutting ceremony for new plant
	Leader	Encouraging employees to improve productivity
	Liaison	Coordinating activities of two project groups
Informational	Monitor	Scanning industry reports to stay abreast of developments
	Disseminator	Sending memos outlining new organizational initiatives
	Spokesperson	Making a speech to discuss growth plans
Decisional	Entrepreneur	Developing new ideas for innovation
	Disturbance handler	Resolving conflict between two subordinates
	Resource allocator	Reviewing and revising budget requests
	Negotiator	Reaching agreement with a key supplier or labor union

© CENGAGE LEARNING 2014

LEARN

to create software for interfacing with new Hewlett-Packard printers while those printers are being developed. At the same time, managers at Hewlett-Packard can incorporate new Microsoft features into the printers they introduce. There are numerous linkages between these roles and the core management skills. For instance, interpersonal skills help play the role of figurehead, and interpersonal skills can help fulfill both the leader and liaison roles.

Informational Roles

The three informational roles flow naturally from the interpersonal roles just discussed. The process of carrying out the interpersonal roles places the manager at a strategic point to gather and disseminate information. The first informational role is that of *monitor*, one who actively seeks information that may be of value. The manager questions subordinates, is receptive to unsolicited information, and attempts to be as well informed as possible. The manager is also a *disseminator* of information, transmitting relevant information back to others in the workplace. When the roles of monitor and disseminator are viewed together, the manager emerges as a vital link in the organization's chain of communication. The third informational role focuses on external communication. The *spokesperson* formally relays information to people outside the unit or outside the organization.

SEAN LOCKE/JUPITERIMAGES

©ISTOCKPHOTO.COM/KUTAY TANIR

For example, a plant manager at Union Carbide may transmit information to top-level managers so that they will be better informed about the plant's activities. The manager may also represent the organization before a chamber of commerce or consumer group. Although the roles of spokesperson and figurehead are similar, there is one basic difference between them. When a manager acts as a figurehead, the manager's presence as a symbol of the organization is what is of interest. In the spokesperson role, however, the manager carries information and communicates it to others in a formal sense. Communication, diagnostic, and time-management skills all come into play as managers fulfill the informational roles.

Decisional Roles

The manager's informational roles typically lead to the decisional roles. The information

informational roles monitor, disseminator, and spokesperson roles

decisional roles entrepreneur, disturbance handler, resource allocator, and negotiator roles

acquired by the manager as a result of performing the informational roles has a major bearing on important decisions that he or she makes. Mintzberg identified four decisional roles. First, the manager has the role of *entrepreneur*, the voluntary initiator of change. A manager at 3M Company developed the idea for the Post-it note pad but had to "sell" it to other skeptical managers inside the company. A second decisional role is initiated not by the manager but by some other individual or group. The manager responds to his or her role as *disturbance handler* by handling such problems as strikes, copyright infringements, or problems in public relations or corporate image.

The third decisional role is that of *resource allocator*. As resource allocator, the manager decides how resources are distributed and with whom he or she will work most closely. For example, a manager typically allocates the funds in the unit's operating budget among the unit's members and projects. A fourth decisional role is that of *negotiator*. In this role the manager enters into negotiations with other groups or organizations as a representative of the company. For example, managers may negotiate a union contract, an agreement with a consultant, or a long-term relationship with a supplier. Negotiations may also be internal to the organization. The manager may, for instance, mediate a dispute between two subordinates or negotiate with another department for additional support.

Again, there are numerous clear connections between the core management skills and the decisional roles. Decision-making skills are obviously the most important. However, technical, interpersonal, communication, and diagnostic skills will also be important in most situations.

SUMMARY AND A LOOK AHEAD

You now understand the basic meanings of the core management skills around which this book is organized. Further, in terms of organizational level and area, you see the importance of understanding where your current position is and recognize the value of understanding where your next position most likely will be. You also appreciate the nature of the basic management functions—planning, organizing, leading, and controlling—and see how these functions relate to the core management skills. Finally, you know the general roles that managers must play and can begin to recognize how the core management skills relate to these roles.

So, now it's time to start developing your own personal skills. On the next several pages you will find several basic exercises and cases that will enable you to begin putting your skills into practice. Following these exercises and cases, additional activities will enable you to further extend your mastery of the core management skills into both group and individual settings. The chapter concludes with some interpretation data to help you better understand how you measure up on various skills.

PRACTICING YOUR SKILLS

DETERMINING WHY INDIVIDUALS BECOME ENTREPRENEURS

This exercise provides an opportunity to analyze your own personal background to determine whether you are likely to choose an entrepreneurial career as a way to use your management skills.

Scholars of entrepreneurship are concerned with understanding why some individuals choose to start a new business whereas others do not. Investigators have surveyed thousands of entrepreneurs and non-entrepreneurs in an attempt to discover factors that can distinguish between the two groups. Hundreds of studies have been conducted and some consensus has emerged. For example, entrepreneurship is more likely when an individual:

- is the parent, child, spouse, or sibling of an entrepreneur
- is an immigrant to the United States or the child of an immigrant

- is a parent
- is a member of the Jewish or Protestant faith
- holds a professional degree in a field such as medicine, law, or engineering
- has recently experienced a life-changing event, such as getting married, having a child, moving to a new city, or losing a job

Your Assignment

1. Choose one of the categories above and explain why this factor might make an individual more likely to become a business owner.
2. From the categories listed above, choose one that is true of yourself (don't choose the same category that you chose in Question 1). In your opinion, does that factor make it more likely that you will become an entrepreneur? Why or why not?
3. If none of the categories above applies to you, tell whether that fact makes it less likely that you will become an entrepreneur, and explain why.

PRACTICE

JOB SKILLS

This exercise allows you to consider how different jobs require the use of different management skills. Some jobs, for example, depend heavily on specific technical skills while others require the use of more abstract thinking as in conceptual skills. Time-management skills are more likely to be necessary in highly structured and fast-paced jobs, whereas communications and interpersonal skills are crucial in situations where people interact on the job.

Your Assignment

1. Identify ten jobs that are markedly different from one another. List them and note three skills that would be necessary to perform effectively in each of those jobs.
2. Your instructor will now organize the class into teams to discuss the lists of the team members.
   (a) Each team's task is to develop a consensus list of two jobs that are the most interesting or unique.
   (b) Next, the teams will agree upon three skills for each of those two jobs.
   (c) Then each team will narrow the list to only one job, from the two they selected.
3. Next, your instructor will reassemble the class and the teams will share their results (oral "reports," writing on charts or whiteboards, or using shared computer technology).
   (a) Add or delete skills if the discussion warrants.
   (b) Note how much agreement or disagreement there is among students regarding the requisite skills.

THE NATURE OF MANAGERIAL WORK

This exercise is designed to help you understand the complicated nature of managerial work. You will compare your rankings of how a typical high-level manager spends her or his time with the results of research by Mintzberg (Mintzberg, H. *The Nature of Managerial Work*. New York: Harper and Row, 1973).

Your Assignment

Read the following descriptions of the thirteen management tasks. Order the tasks by percentage of time that you think a typical high-level manager spends on each in a typical week. A ranking should be from 1 (most time) to 13 (least time).

Task	Ranking
Non-managerial work: Work involved in specialized tasks of the organization	_____
Scheduling: Brief communications to formally schedule the day, such as calls and meetings	_____
Ceremony: Conducting, or participating in, organizational ceremonial events, such as banquets and greeting new employees	_____
External board work: Working on the boards of directors of other corporations	_____
Status requests and solicitations: Non-work-related requests for the manager's time that are made by individuals both internal and external to the organization—chiefly related to her or his high-status position	_____
Action requests: Work-related requests for the manager's time—for information and advice, for influencing pressures, or to initiate a project	_____
Manager requests: Manager requests of a subordinate—for information or to delegate a task	_____
Observational tour: Tour of the organization to see a specific item of interest or to generally observe	_____
Receiving information: Taking in information—such as by phone calls, unscheduled meetings, briefings, and so forth	_____
Giving information: Supplying information to others inside and outside of the organization	_____
Review: Discussing a wide range of issues with immediate subordinates	_____
Strategy: Attending formal meetings in which major organizational decisions are made	_____
Negotiation: Talking with other companies to reach mutually satisfactory agreements	_____

Source: From DAFT. Management, 9E. © 2010 South-Western, a part of Cengage Learning, Inc. Reproduced by permission. www.cengage.com/permissions.

See Interpretations at the end of the chapter.

WHAT DO YOU THINK?

This exercise gives you an opportunity to think about the management skills that may be involved in jobs that you or your classmates may seek upon graduation. Combining your assumptions with those of your classmates should give you a more detailed and accurate assessment of the skills that you will need.

Your Assignment

1. Your instructor will organize the class into small groups.
2. One person in each group will be designated as "The Interviewer." Everyone else in the group will play the role of "New College Graduate" looking for their first managerial job.
3. The Interviewer will talk with each New College Graduate privately outside the classroom or in a corner away from the others in the group. The Interviewer will ask each New College Graduate what he or she thinks are the most important skills for a manager to have.

4. The group should reconvene and combine the lists compiled by The Interviewer.
5. The group lists should be shared with the whole class (oral "reports," writing on charts or whiteboards, or using shared computer technology). The class should discuss the variety of managerial skills identified.

USING YOUR SKILLS

USE

SUCCESS LEADS TO …

AmeriHost Properties was a small but fast-growing Illinois firm that specialized in buying run-down, distressed motel and hotel properties, refurbishing them, and then operating them profitably. While perhaps not the most glamorous of businesses, AmeriHost developed a solid reputation in its industry for being a well-managed and tightly controlled enterprise.

The firm was started in 1984 as America Pop Inc., selling popcorn and sodas from kiosks in Chicago subways. The new business never earned a profit. Thus, in 1986 the founders sold the kiosk operation, changed the corporation's name to AmeriHost, and began investing in hotels. Losses were incurred initially as it hired new managers, invested in the development of new property designs, and opened hotels under its own brand, AmeriHost Inn. By 1990, however, AmeriHost earned its first profits and was poised for future growth and expansion.

AmeriHost's strategy was a simple one: Focus on small but growing communities in the Midwest and buy failed motels or build new ones. Provide limited services at each property—no grand lobby, no restaurant, no laundry facilities, etc. These new hotels were operated as part of a national or regional franchise system, including Days Inn and Holiday Inn.

In evaluating a potential property or building site, AmeriHost relied on a 20-page checklist of criteria. For instance, one important factor was the existence of one or more so-called "demand generators"—things like universities, new businesses, or major highways which provide on-going potential customers.

AmeriHost also practiced tight control throughout its operations. For example, it used the same contractors and suppliers to refurbish or build its properties. And it used only one of three basic designs, again to hold down costs. These tactics allowed the company to build fifteen hotels without going over budget.

Then at the end of the 1990s, the franchise rights were sold to Cendant Corporation. Cendant continued to build and develop AmeriHost Inns, but it handed out AmeriHost franchises to other, existing properties. Then in 2006 the Cendant Hotel Group became part of a Cendant spin-off hospitality company called Wyndham Worldwide. It also announced that all AmeriHost Inns would be rebranded as Baymont Inns and that the name, AmeriHost Inn, would be dropped from the brands. Management success in this instance led to takeovers. Wyndham, however, is regarded as a highly respected hotel operating group.

Case Questions

Go Online

1. What skills seem to have been used by managers at AmeriHost?
2. What additional skills might have prevented the takeovers?
3. Do you think that your skills would be compatible with managing a hotel? Why or why not?
4. If your skills are not compatible but you would like them to be, how would you go about changing your skills?

Case References

Maha Atal, "Best corporate citizens: Hotels," *Fortune*, October 2, 2009. http://money.cnn.com/2009/10/02/news/companies/good_citizen_hotels.fortune/index.htm; Telis Demos and Jia Lynn Yang, "On the radar: What to watch in the weeks ahead," *Fortune*, August 2, 2006. http://money.cnn.com/magazines/fortune/fortune_archive/2006/08/07/8382595/index.htm; "AmeriHost Finds Niche in Restoring Distressed Motels," *The Wall Street Journal*, June 6, 1991, p. B2.

KODAK'S FUZZY PICTURE

Economic conditions and global competition impact even huge, market-dominant firms. One such firm, Eastman Kodak, the Rochester, New York-based photography company, underwent at least four restructurings beginning in the 1980s in its efforts to respond to increased global competition. More than 20,000 people left the company through early retirements, resignations, or dismissals. Despite these efforts, however, Kodak's profits declined from more than $1 billion in 1980 to a little more than $300 million in 1985. Profits began to recover after that, though, reaching more than $500 million by 1989.

Kodak is organized around three major market sectors at the corporate level: the Consumer Digital Imaging Group; the Film, Photofinishing and Entertainment Group; and the Graphic Communications Group. Two former units were divested earlier. The chemical sector, Eastman Chemical, was spun off in 1994; and the health group Kodak had acquired in 1988, Sterling-Winthrop, in 2007.

For several years now, within these sectors Kodak has been moving toward high involvement management approaches, especially the use of teams and process organization. That teamwork, which has been achieving outstanding results, takes the form of employee involvement and self-direction linked with a continuous improvement philosophy. Process organization results when flow charts are used to reengineer departments into customer streams or business units.

USE

Kodak has been developing new products in an effort to maintain its strong historical position. It developed a series of inkjet printers that some felt would earn it a substantial share of that market. It made new forays into the commercial printing business and health imaging. However, its transition from film to digital hasn't really clicked yet. Amid rumors of bankruptcy in 2011, Kodak still derived much of its revenue from traditional film.

Case Questions

Go Online

1. What skills can you suggest are being used by management at Kodak? Why do you think those skills are being used?
2. What skills do you feel managers at Kodak need to compete effectively in the several market sectors in which they engage?
3. Do you think your skills would be compatible with working at Kodak? Why or why not?
4. If your skills are not compatible but you would like them to be, how would you go about changing your skills?

Case References

Mina Kimes, "Ouch! 15 worst-performing stocks," *Fortune*, April 15, 2010, http://money.cnn.com/galleries/2010/fortune/1004/gallery.fortune500_worst_performing_stocks.fortune/index.html; Jon Fortt, "Kodak inkjets target the heart of HP's profit," *Fortune*, February 5, 2007. http://tech.fortune.cnn.com/2007/02/05/kodak-inkjets-target-the-heart-of-hps-profit/; "Teamwork Is Key to KAD Site Management's Success," Plant Engineering, September 17, 1992, p. 72; Thomas A. Stewart, "The Search for the Organization of Tomorrow," *Fortune*, May 18, 1992, pp. 92–98; "Integrative Learning Speeds Teamwork," *Management Review*, December 1, 1991, p. 43.

EXTENDING YOUR SKILLS

Your instructor may use one or more of these **Group Extensions** to provide you with yet another opportunity to develop your skills. On the other hand, you may continue your development on your own by doing one or more of the **Individual Extensions**.

GROUP EXTENSIONS

- A good icebreaking exercise for the first day of class is to have students form into small groups, select two or three different kinds of organizations and management positions, and have students discuss the skills they feel are needed in those positions.
- Have students brainstorm examples of the most important information that should be included in an employee skills inventory.
- Ask students to identify common skills that are likely to be reflected in all organizations.
- Have student groups research and collect information about a large diversified firm. Then have the groups classify the skills of managers at different levels within that firm.
- Break students up into small groups. Have them select an organization and a management position. Then have them identify the skills needed by a person in that position.
- Have student groups locate copies of job advertisements that specify skills and share them with the class.
- Have groups of students identify differences and similarities between the skills needed by an executive and those needed by a front-line supervisor.
- Have students examine their own personal choices regarding management in terms of the skills they currently have.
- Have students construct a hypothetical job advertisement specifying the skills needed for a job they have or would like to have in the future.
- Have small groups of students discuss what they would consider to be a "perfect" job. Ask them to identify the similarities and differences in skills among the various jobs suggested.

EXTEND

INDIVIDUAL EXTENSIONS

- Think of an organization with which you have some familiarity. Describe the skills of the personnel in that organization.
- Think about different managerial positions. Do the skills needed for some positions differ from the skills needed for other positions? Why or why not?
- Do all top executives use the same skills regardless of the size or type of organization in which they work? Why or why not?
- Go to the library and see how many different managerial skills you can identify in the literature. Can you find ones not mentioned in this text? Share your results with the class.
- Watch a television program that is set in an organization. Identify as many management skills as you can.
- Can you think of skill dimensions that are not discussed in the text? Indicate their linkage to those that are discussed.

INTERPRETATIONS

HOW DO I RATE AS A MANAGER?

Your *Total Score* for each section provides you with a general evaluation of your performance on that function. If your Total Score on a section is 40–50, you are doing quite well. A score of 30–40 suggests the need for some improvement. A score of less than 30 suggests a strong need for improvement.

At the end of the course, if you have participated in any group activities in which you incorporated any of these areas, take this assessment again to see if you have improved your score.

SELF-DESCRIBED PROFILE

This assessment offers a self-described profile of your basic management skills. While a perfect score is 15, few people are likely to rate themselves that highly. However, this should be a good starting point for deciding where and how to expand the development of your own managerial skills and personal characteristics.

Growing and developing these and other management skills will require hard work, but the importance of doing so cannot be overstated. Managerial success may well rest on managers appreciating the importance of these skills and their willingness to strive continually to strengthen them throughout their work careers.

After you have completed the profile for yourself, ask someone who knows you to assess you on this instrument. You can be sure that your score as self-described will differ from your score as described by someone else.

THE NATURE OF MANAGERIAL WORK

Below are the results of Mintzberg's research. Two tasks tied for requiring the most time, receiving information and review.

Rank	Task
7	Non-managerial work
6	Scheduling
3	Ceremony
5	External board work
8	Status requests and solicitations
3	Action requests
5	Manager requests
8	Observational tour
1	Receiving information
4	Giving information
1	Review
2	Strategy
4	Negotiation

Source: Mintzberg, H. *The Nature of Managerial Work*. New York: Harper and Row, 1973

ENDNOTES

[1] Fred Luthans, "Successful vs. Effective Real Managers," *Academy of Management Executive*, May 1988, pp. 127–132. See also "The Best Performers," *Business Week*, Spring 2011 Special Issue, pp. 46–72. Spring 2012 Special Issue, pp. 52–70.

[2] *Forbes*, February 14, 2005, p. 110.

[3] See Robert L. Katz, "The Skills of an Effective Administrator," *Harvard Business Review*, September–October 1974, pp. 90–102, for a classic discussion of several of these skills. For a recent perspective, see J. Brian Atwater, Vijay R. Kannan, and Alan A. Stephens, "Cultivating Systemic Thinking in the Next Generation of Business Leaders," *Academy of Management Learning & Education*, 2008, Vol. 7, No. 1, pp. 9–25. See also Peterson, T.O., & Van Fleet, D.D. "The Ongoing Legacy of R. L. Katz: An Updated Typology of Management Skills," *Management Decision* incorporating the *Journal of Management History*, (2004), Vol. 42, No. 10, 1297–1308.

[4] See "The Real Reasons You're Working so Hard … And What You Can Do About It," *BusinessWeek*, October 3, 2005, pp. 60–68; "I'm Late, I'm Late, I'm Late," *USA Today*, November 26, 2002, pp. 1B, 2B.

[5] For a thorough discussion of the importance of time-management skills, see David Barry, Catherine Durnell Cramton, and Stephen J. Carroll, "Navigating the Garbage Can: How Agendas Help Managers Cope with Job Realities," *Academy of Management Executive*, May 1997, pp. 26–42.

[6] "Taming the Out-of-Control In-Box," *Wall Street Journal*, February 4, 2000, pp. B1, B4.

[7] "A Startup's New Prescription for Eyewear," *BusinessWeek*, July 4–10, 2011, pp. 49–51.

[8] See Mark Gottfredson, Steve Schaubert, and Hernan Saenz, "The New Leader's Guide to Diagnosing the Business," *Harvard Business Review*, February 2008, pp. 63–72 for an interesting application.

[9] Quoted in *Fortune*, July 6, 2009, p. 47.

[10] See "Executive Pay," *BusinessWeek*, April 15, 2002, pp. 80–100. See also Jim Collins, "The Ten Greatest CEO's of All Times," *Fortune*, July 21, 2003, pp. 54–68.

[11] Rosemary Stewart, "Middle Managers: Their Jobs and Behaviors," in Jay W. Lorsch (ed.), *Handbook of Organizational Behavior* (Englewood Cliffs, N.J.: Prentice-Hall, 1987), pp. 385–391. See also Bill Woolridge, Torsten Schmid, and Steven W. Floyd, "The Middle Management Perspective on Strategy Process: Contributions, Synthesis, and Future Research," *Journal of Management*, 2008, Vol. 34, No. 6, pp. 1190–1221 and Anneloes Raes, Mrielle Heijltjes, Ursula Glunk, and Robert Row, "The Interface of the Top Management Team and Middle Managers: A Process Model," *Academy of Management Review*, January 2011, pp. 102–126.

[12] John P. Kotter, "What Effective General Managers Really Do," *Harvard Business Review*, March–April 1999, pp. 145–155. See also Peter Drucker, "What Makes an Effective Executive," *Harvard Business Review*, June 2004, pp. 58–68.

[13] Quoted in *USA Today*, September 19, 2011, p. 3B.

[14] Sumantsa Ghospal and Christopher A. Bartlett, "Changing the Role of Top Management: Beyond Structure to Process," *Harvard Business Review*, January–February 1995, pp. 86–96.

[15] Henry Mintzberg, *The Nature of Managerial Work* (Englewood Cliffs, N.J.: 1973).

CHAPTER 2

ASSESSING YOUR SKILLS

What's Your Learning Style?
Assessing Your Mental Abilities

LEARNING ABOUT THE SKILLS

The Nature of Managerial Work
A Model of Skill Development
The Science and Art of Management
The Science of Management
The Art of Management
The Role of Education
The Role of Experience
Personal Skills
Self-Awareness
Understanding Our Own Personality
The "Big Five" Personality Traits
The Myers-Briggs Framework
Other Personality Traits at Work
Emotional Intelligence
Generalizability/Discrimination
Understanding Our Personal Values, Ethics, and Priorities
The Scope of Management
Managing in Profit-Seeking Organizations
Managing in Not-for-Profit Organizations
Summary and a Look Ahead

PRACTICING YOUR SKILLS

What Do You Bring to the Table?
Inner Circle
What Are Your Learning Goals?
What About Me, What About You?

USING YOUR SKILLS

Body Shop and Education
Learning at Kyocera

EXTENDING YOUR LEARNING SKILLS

Group Extensions
Individual Extensions

INTERPRETATIONS

What Is Your Learning Style?
Assessing Your Mental Abilities

Learning and Developing Management Skills

© YURI ARCURS/SHUTTERSTOCK.COM

Chapter 1 introduced you to the core management skills and related those skills to the basic management functions and roles. It also noted the importance of understanding both your current and future level in the development of management skills as well as the area of the organization in which you work. Chapter 2 considers how managers learn, develop, and refine those skills. It provides additional perspectives about the nature of managerial work, and then introduces and describes a model of skill development. This chapter discusses management as science and as art, and describes the roles of education and experience. Chapter 2 also examines personal skills and how they contribute to the development of management skills. Finally, it summarizes the broad scope across which management skills are relevant.

ASSESS

ASSESSING YOUR SKILLS

WHAT'S YOUR LEARNING STYLE?

Learning style refers to the ways you prefer to approach new information. Each of us learns and processes information in our own special style, although we share some learning patterns, preferences, and approaches. Knowing your own style also can help you to realize that other people may approach the same situation differently than you do.

Instructions:
Complete the following questionnaire to assess your preferred learning style. First, read the words in the left-hand column. Circle one of the three responses to the right that best characterizes you. Answer honestly with the description that applies to you right now. Count the number of circled items and write your total at the bottom of each column. The questions you prefer provide insight into how you learn.

1. When I try to **concentrate...**	I am distracted by clutter or movement, and I notice things around me other people don't notice.	I am distracted by sounds, and I attempt to control the amount and type of noise around me.	I am distracted by commotion, and I tend to retreat inside myself.
2. When I **visualize...**	I see vivid, detailed pictures in my thoughts.	I think in voices and sounds.	I see images in my thoughts that involve movement.
3. When I **talk with others...**	I find it difficult to listen for very long.	I enjoy listening, or I get impatient to talk myself.	I gesture and communicate with my hands.
4. When I **contact people...**	I prefer face-to-face meetings.	I prefer speaking by telephone for serious conversations.	I prefer to interact while walking or participating in some activity.
5. When I **see an acquaintance...**	I forget names but remember faces, and I tend to replay where we first met.	I know people's names and I can usually quote what we discussed.	I remember what we did together and I may almost "feel" our time together.
6. When I **relax...**	I watch TV, see a play, visit an exhibit, or go to a movie.	I listen to the radio, play music, read, or talk with a friend.	I play sports, make crafts, or build something with my hands.
7. When I **read...**	I like descriptive examples and I may pause to imagine the scene.	I enjoy the narrative most and I can almost "hear" the characters talk.	I prefer action-oriented stories, but I do not often read for pleasure.
8. When I **spell...**	I envision the word in my mind or imagine what the word looks like when written.	I sound out the word, sometimes aloud, and tend to recall rules about letter order.	I get a feel for the word by writing it out or pretending to type it.
9. When I **do something new...**	I seek out demonstrations, pictures, or diagrams.	I want verbal and written instructions, and to talk it over with someone else.	I jump right in to try it, and keep trying different approaches.
10. When I **assemble an object...**	I look at the picture first and then I may read the directions.	I read the directions, or I talk aloud as I work.	I usually ignore the directions and figure it out as I go along.
11. When I **interpret someone's mood...**	I examine facial expressions.	I listen to tone of voice.	I focus on body language.
12. When I **teach other people...**	I show them.	I tell them, I write it out, or I ask them questions.	I demonstrate how it is done and then ask them to try.
Total	Visual: ____________	Auditory: ____________	Tactile/Kinesthetic: __________

Scoring:
The column with the highest total represents your primary processing style. The column with the second-most choices is your secondary style.
Your primary learning style: _____
Your secondary learning style: _____

Source: © Marcia Conner, What's Your Learning Style? 1993–2012, All rights reserved. http://marciaconner.com

See Interpretations at the end of the chapter.

ASSESSING YOUR MENTAL ABILITIES

Mental abilities are important to both learning and job performance, especially in this information age. The following assessment surveys your judgments about your personal mental abilities.

Instructions:
Judge how accurately each of the following statements describe you. In some cases, it may be difficult to make a decision, but force a choice. Record your answers next to each statement, using the following scale:

Rating Scale
5 = *Very descriptive of me*
4 = *Fairly descriptive of me*
3 = *Somewhat descriptive of me*
2 = *Not very descriptive of me*
1 = *Not descriptive of me at all*

_____ 1. I am at ease learning visually. I can readily take in and hold visual images of instructions in my mind.
_____ 2. I can produce remotely associated, clever, or uncommon responses to statements or situations.
_____ 3. I can formulate and test hypotheses directed at finding relationships among elements of a problem.
_____ 4. I can remember and recall bits of unrelated material.
_____ 5. I can recall perfectly for immediate reproduction a series of items after only one presentation.
_____ 6. I can rapidly manipulate numbers in arithmetic operations.
_____ 7. I can quickly find figures, make comparisons, and carry out other simple tasks involving visual perception.
_____ 8. I can reason from stated premises to their necessary conclusions.
_____ 9. I can perceive spatial patterns or maintain orientation with respect to objects in space. I can manipulate or transform the image of spatial patterns into other visual arrangements.
_____ 10. I have a large knowledge of words and their meanings, and can apply this knowledge in understanding discourse.

Source: Adapted from M. D. Dunnette, "Aptitudes, Abilities, and Skills," in M. D. Dunnette (ed.). *Handbook of Industrial and organizational Psychology*, Rand McNally, pp. 481–483. ©1976 by Rand McNally. Reprinted by permission of the author.

See Interpretations at the end of the chapter.

GO ONLINE to the Griffin/Van Fleet Assessment Library for online versions of these and other assessments.

LEARN

LEARNING ABOUT THE SKILLS

The Nature of Managerial Work
A Model of Skill Development
The Science and Art of Management
The Science of Management
The Art of Management
The Role of Education
The Role of Experience
Personal Skills
Self-Awareness
Understanding Our Own Personality
The "Big Five" Personality Traits
The Myers-Briggs Framework
Other Personality Traits at Work
Emotional Intelligence
Generalizability/Discrimination
Understanding Our Personal Values, Ethics, and Priorities
The Scope of Management
Managing in Profit-Seeking Organizations
Managing in Not-for-Profit Organizations
Summary and a Look Ahead

© YURI ARCURS/SHUTTERSTOCK.COM

People don't simply walk into their first job and start managing. This chapter looks at the complex and life-long processes that go into the development of management capabilities. We first discuss the nature of managerial work. Then we examine the science and the art of management, and discuss the role of education and experience. In addition, we introduce a number of personal skills that can help you develop your management skills. Finally, we discuss a variety of settings in which management skills may be important.

THE NATURE OF MANAGERIAL WORK

Managerial work does not follow an orderly, systematic progression through the workweek. The manager's job is fraught with uncertainty, change, interruption, and fragmented activities. Mintzberg's early study of managerial roles, introduced in Chapter 1, found that in a typical day CEOs were likely to spend 59 percent of their time in scheduled meetings, 22 percent doing "desk work," 10 percent in unscheduled meetings, 6 percent on the telephone, and the remaining 3 percent on tours of company facilities. (These proportions, of course, are different for managers at lower levels.) Moreover, the nature of managerial work continues to change in complex and often unpredictable ways.[1] For instance, Mintzberg's work was done before the advent of email, smartphones, social networking, and other communication technologies that most managers use today. If his study were replicated today, the range and diversity of activities would no doubt be far greater.

In addition, managers perform a wide variety of tasks. In the course of a single day, for example, a manager might have to make a decision about the design of a new product, settle a complaint between two subordinates, hire a new assistant, write a report for his boss, coordinate a joint venture with an overseas colleague, form a task force to investigate a problem, search for information on the Internet, and deal with a labor grievance. Moreover, the pace of the manager's job can be relentless. She may feel bombarded by email, telephone calls, and people waiting to see her. Decisions may have to be made quickly and plans formulated with little time for reflection.[2] But, in many ways, these same characteristics of managerial work also contribute to its richness and meaningfulness. Making critical decisions under intense pressure, and making them well, can be a major source of intrinsic satisfaction. And managers usually are well paid for the pressures they bear.

THE MODEL OF SKILL DEVELOPMENT

Our primary goal in this book is to help you develop the skills needed for a successful managerial career. *Figure 2.1* illustrates the basic model we will use to achieve this goal and represents the fundamental model of skill development around which this book is organized.

Our model suggests three essential antecedents to skill development. Education—early childhood, high

FIGURE 2.1 THE MODEL OF SKILL DEVELOPMENT

The model of skill development proposes that a combination of education, experience, and personal skills lead to our ability to assess our strengths and weaknesses. This self-assessment, combined with skills knowledge and visualization allow us to practice, apply, and extend our skills. Practicing the science and art of management then allow us to further enhance our education, experience, and personal skills.

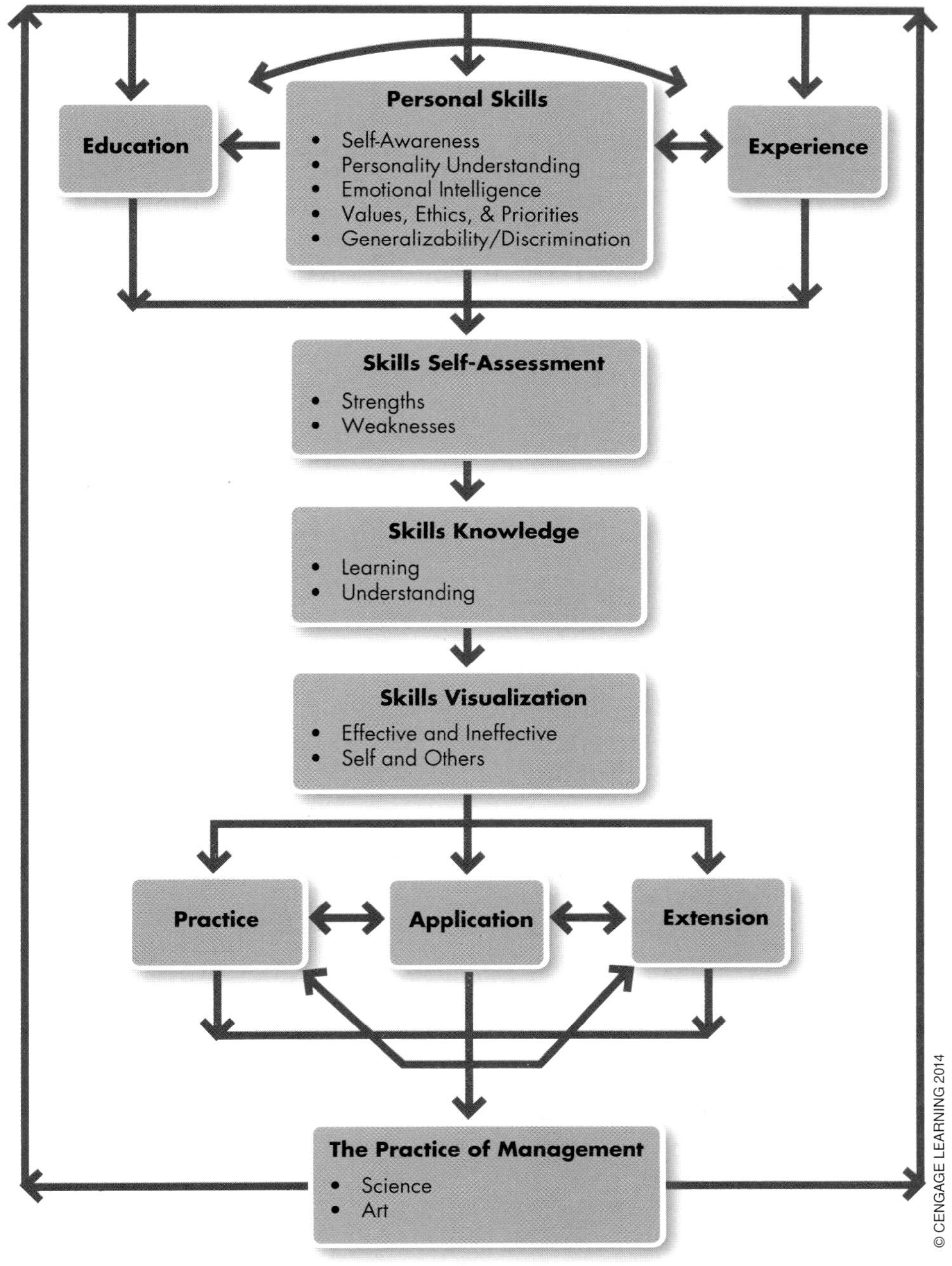

© CENGAGE LEARNING 2014

school, college, graduate study, and/or continuing education—can all play important roles. A wide array of experiences can also come into play. These experiences can include summer jobs while in school, internships, entry-level professional jobs, jobs from an earlier (different) career, and jobs to which you are promoted. In addition, experiences can also come from other domains, such as leadership positions in other organizations, volunteer work, and so forth. The third antecedent condition is a set of personal skills. These are centered around and drawn from self-awareness, personality understanding, emotional intelligence; values, ethics, and priorities; motivation, self-control, and the ability to generalize and discriminate across settings. Each of these three antecedents is discussed later in this chapter.

Secondly, antecedent conditions are fed into skills knowledge. It is important to learn about and understand each of the skills. This is acquired through reading and studying text-based commentary, discussion, theory analysis, research, and practice.

The next step in our skill development model is visualization—"seeing" the skill being enacted in various situations. It is instructive to observe various skills being used both effectively and ineffectively. It also is useful to visualize skills being used both by others and by ourselves. Visualization helps us interpret our self-assessments and understand how to translate knowledge into action. Visualization occurs by watching the behaviors of others, interpreting the impact of those behaviors, and applying our observations to our own situations.

Properly equipped with self-assessment, knowledge, and visualization, the manager (or would-be manager) is now ready to practice, apply, and extend her or his skills. Practice and application refer to the actual use of the skill to workplace situations, decisions, problems, and opportunities. Extension means using the skill in different contexts. For instance, if we are proficient in using a skill at an individual level we might extend it to a group setting. Alternatively, having mastered a skill in the workplace we might become even more proficient by using the same skill in a different context.

Of course, managers also have jobs to do—they can't spend all of their time focusing solely on developing their skills! As they practice, apply, and extend their skills they also go about their normal managerial work, behaviors, and activities keeping in mind that managerial work has elements of both art and science. That is, they engage in the practice—the work, if you will—of management.

Finally, consistent with the premises of life-long learning, skill development never really "ends." As skills get refined, developed, and mastered, they become a part of our experience base and our educational knowledge and may affect our personal skills. Hence, the process begins anew as we reassess our skills, as we climb the organizational hierarchy, or move to different challenges in a different context.

education early childhood, high school, college, graduate study, and/or continuing education that contribute to managerial effectiveness

experiences summer jobs while in school, internships, entry-level professional jobs, jobs from an earlier (different) career, and jobs to which a person is promoted that contribute to managerial effectiveness

personal skills centered around and drawn from self-awareness, emotional intelligence, values, ethics, priorities, motivation, and self-control

THE SCIENCE AND THE ART OF MANAGEMENT

The practice of management may involve elements of science and of art. Effective management is a blend of both science and art. Successful executives recognize the importance of combining both the science and the art of management as they practice their craft.[3]

The Science of Management

Many management issues can be approached in a rational, logical, objective, and systematic way. For decades researchers assumed that there was likely to be "one best way" to manage, lead, make decisions, and run organizations. Hence, much of the early literature about management—academic articles, books, and popular press—all sought to prescribe for managers how they should do their jobs.

Good managers often gather data, facts, and objective information. They can use quantitative models and decision-making techniques to arrive at "correct" decisions. They need to take this scientific approach to solving problems, especially when they are dealing with relatively routine and straightforward issues. When Starbucks considers building a new store or entering a new market, for example, its managers look closely at a wide variety of objective details as they formulate their plans. Variables such as traffic patterns, income levels, adjacent retail outlets, and dozens of other objective variables can be used to select sites. Technical, diagnostic, and decision-making skills are especially important when practicing the science of management.

The Art of Management

Even though managers may try to be scientific, they must frequently make decisions and solve problems on the basis of intuition, experience, instinct, and personal insights. A good manager relies heavily on his or her conceptual, communication, interpersonal, and time-management skills to decide among multiple courses of action that look equally attractive. Even "objective facts" may prove to be wrong. When Starbucks was planning its first store in New York City, market research clearly showed that New Yorkers preferred drip coffee to more exotic espresso-style coffees. After installing more drip coffee makers and fewer espresso makers than in their other stores, managers had to backtrack when New Yorkers lined up clamoring for espresso. Starbucks now introduces a standard menu and layout in all its stores, regardless of presumed market differences, and then makes necessary adjustments later. Thus, managers must blend an element of intuition and personal insight with hard data and objective facts.[4]

> *"Business is really an art form. At its best, it's the artistry of how people create things together."*
>
> PETER SENGE
>
> A leading business expert[6]

BIZ ED, MAY/JUNE 2010, P. 23.

How does one acquire the skills necessary to blend the science and art of management and to become a successful manager? Although there are as many variations as there are managers, the most common path involves a combination of education and experience.[5]

THE ROLE OF EDUCATION

Many of you are reading this book because you are enrolled in a management course at a college or university. Thus, you are beginning to learn about and develop your management skills in an educational setting. When you complete this book and the course, you will have a basic understanding of and ability to use your management skills in more advanced courses. A college degree has become a requirement for career advancement in business, and virtually all CEOs in the United States have college degrees. MBA degrees are also common among successful executives today. *Table 2.1* lists the top-ranked MBA programs in the United States. Also listed are the most popular online MBA programs. More and more foreign universities, especially in Europe and Asia, are beginning to offer academic programs in management, as well.

Even after obtaining a degree, most prospective managers have not seen the end of their management education. Many middle and top managers periodically return to campus to participate in executive or management development programs ranging in duration from a few days to several weeks. First-line managers also take advantage of extension and continuing education programs offered by institutions of higher education. A recent innovation in extended management education is the executive MBA program (EMBA) offered by many top business schools, in which middle and top managers with several years of experience complete an accelerated program of study on weekends.[7] Top EMBA programs are also listed in *Table 2.1*.

LEARN

TABLE 2.1 REPRESENTATIVE TRADITIONAL MBA, ONLINE MBA, AND EMBA PROGRAMS (UNITED STATES)

Top-Ranked Full-Time MBA Programs	Popular Online MBA Programs	Top-Ranked EMBA Programs
1. Univ. of Chicago	1. Indiana Univ.	1. Univ. of Chicago
2. Harvard Univ.	2. Univ. of Maryland	2. Columbia Univ.
3. Univ. of Pennsylvania	3. Walden Univ.	3. Northwestern Univ.
4. Northwestern Univ.	4. Arizona State Univ.	4. UCLA
5. Stanford Univ.	5. Babson College	5. Univ. of Michigan
6. Duke Univ.	6. Drexel Univ.	6. SMU
7. Univ. of Michigan	7. Northeastern Univ.	7. USC
8. Univ. of California	8. Syracuse Univ.	8. Wharton
9. Columbia Univ.	9. Univ. of Texas-Dallas	9. Duke Univ.
10. MIT	10. George Washington Univ.	10. Univ. of North Carolina

© CENGAGE LEARNING 2014

Sources and Notes: These are representative rankings compiled from multiple sources, including *Business Week*, *U.S. News and World Report*, and *Financial Times*, in January 2012. Rankings vary from year to year and depend on criteria used. There are no reliable rankings of online MBA programs. Those listed all have relative large enrollments.

LEARN

© LISA F. YOUNG/SHUTTERSTOCK.COM

Education is an important ingredient to managerial success. Some people continue their education after working for several years.

Finally, many large companies have in-house training programs for furthering managers' education. Some firms have created what are essentially corporate universities to provide the specialized education they feel is required for their managers to remain successful.[8] McDonald's and Shell Oil are among the leaders in this area. There is also a distinct trend toward online educational development for managers.[9] The primary advantage of a management skills education is that a person can follow a well-developed program of study, becoming familiar with current research and thinking on management. In some cases, students can devote full-time energy and attention to learning. On the negative side, management education is often too general to meet the needs of a wide variety of students, or to provide the specific job-related knowledge needed by managers. Further, many aspects of the manager's job can be discussed in a book but cannot really be appreciated and understood until they are experienced.

THE ROLE OF EXPERIENCE

This book provides a solid foundation for enhancing your management skills. However, even if you were to memorize every word in every management book ever written, you could not step into a top-management position and be effective. Why? Management skills also must be learned through experience. Most managers advanced to their present positions from other jobs. Only by experiencing the day-to-day pressures a manager faces and by meeting a variety of managerial challenges can an individual develop insights into the real nature and character of managerial work. This book provides the opportunity for you to "see" both more effective and less effective management skills portrayed in cases and in films allowing you the opportunity to practice and, thus, gain experience through the exercises.

Because practice is essential, most large companies and many smaller ones as well, have developed management training programs for their prospective managers. People are hired from college campuses, from other organizations, or from the ranks of the organization's first-line managers and operating employees. These people are systematically assigned to a variety of jobs. Over time, the individual is exposed to most, if not all, of the major aspects of the organization. In this way the manager learns by experience. The training programs at some companies such as Procter & Gamble, General Mills, and Shell Oil, are so good that other companies try to hire people who have graduated from them.[10] Even without formal training programs, managers can achieve success as they learn from varied experiences. For example, Herb Kelleher was a practicing attorney before he took over at Southwest Airlines. Of course, natural ability, drive, and self-motivation also play roles in acquiring experience and developing management skills.

Most effective managers learn their skills through a combination of education and experience. Some type of college degree, even if it is not in business administration, usually provides a foundation for a management career. The individual then gets his or her first job and subsequently progresses through a variety of management situations. During the manager's rise in the organization, occasional education "updates," such as management development programs, may supplement on-the-job experience. Increasingly, managers also may need to acquire international expertise as part of their professional development. As with general managerial skills, international expertise can be acquired through a combination of education and experience.[11]

> *"Growth is a new skill to learn for us. We've been good at restructuring businesses over the last decade. Growth takes practice."*
>
> LEWIS BOOTH
> Ford Motor chief financial officer[12]

BUSINESS WEEK, JUNE 13, 2011, P. 23.

PERSONAL SKILLS

In our model of skill development (*Figure 2.1*), personal skills play a key role in the development of management skills. Personal skills are the individual strengths and weaknesses we bring with us to the workplace. As with management skills, personal skills can also be developed and refined as we grow, mature, and gain new knowledge and experience. The development of management skills can play a reciprocal role in further developing our personal skills.

Self-Awareness

One key personal skill is self-awareness. Self-awareness is the extent to which we are aware of how we are seen by others. Self-awareness may refer to appearance, behaviors, words and expressions, decisions, or other factors that cause others to form impressions of us.

A person with *high self-awareness*, then, has a relatively accurate understanding of how she is seen by others. She may come to know, for instance, that others see her as a well-spoken, strong-willed manager who is quick to make decisions and who is a good role model for others. She develops this awareness by recognizing how others respond to her and the level of confidence they seem to have in her over time and across different settings. Further, this high level of self-awareness will enable her to function more effectively in the future. For instance, if she knows that others see her as an excellent public speaker she will gain confidence in her abilities when she is called upon to speak to a group of investors or potential new employees.

But other people have *low self-awareness*. These individuals are much less conscious of how others see them. Suppose a different manager, for example, also sees herself as a good public speaker while others (unfortunately) see her as a poor speaker. She may eagerly volunteer for speaking opportunities but then not understand why she is not selected or why others do not exhibit enthusiasm for listening to her. Eventually she will become frustrated and may even come to feel that people just dislike her or are discriminating against her. People have low self-awareness because they fail to pay attention to how others respond to them, they overestimate their own skills, or they attempt to provide a rationale for situations in which they do not recognize a shortcoming on their parts (for example, explaining away low performance to a lack of sleep or too much stress).

It is important to recognize that no one is perfect, and no one sees him or herself exactly as they are seen by others. Different people may also see the same individual differently. But by paying attention to cues we get from others, candidly diagnosing our successes and failures, and developing a real understanding of our own personal strengths and weaknesses we can have a higher degree of self-awareness. Developing a clear understanding of our own personality can also contribute to heightened self-awareness. A heightened self-awareness enables us to function in a positive and constructive fashion.

LEARN

Understanding Our Own Personality

Personality is the relatively stable set of psychological attributes that distinguish one person from another. A longstanding debate among psychologists—often expressed as "nature versus nurture"—is the extent to which personality attributes are inherited from our parents (the "nature" argument) or shaped by our environment (the "nurture" argument). In reality, both biological and environmental factors play important roles in determining our personalities. Managers should strive to understand basic personality attributes and how they can affect people's behavior in organizational situations, not to mention their perceptions of and attitudes toward the organization. Developing a sophisticated understanding of personality is a key element in knowing ourselves and can result in greater self-awareness. In addition, knowing more about personality will also enable us to better understand others.

The "Big Five" Personality Traits Psychologists have identified literally thousands of personality traits that differentiate one person from another. But in recent years, researchers have identified five fundamental traits that are especially relevant to organizations.[13] These traits, illustrated in *Figure 2.2*, are now commonly called the "big five" personality traits.

Agreeableness refers to a person's ability to get along with others. Agreeableness causes some people to be gentle, cooperative, forgiving, understanding, and good-natured in their dealings with others. But it results in others being irritable, short-tempered, uncooperative, and generally antagonistic toward other people. Researchers have not yet fully investigated the effects of agreeableness, but it seems likely that highly

self-awareness the extent to which we are aware of how we are seen by others

personality the relatively stable set of psychological attributes that distinguish one person from another

"big five" personality traits five fundamental personality traits that are especially relevant to organizations: agreeableness, conscientiousness, neuroticism, extraversion, and openness

agreeableness a person's ability to get along with others

LEARN

FIGURE 2.2 THE "BIG FIVE" MODEL OF PERSONALITY

The "Big Five" personality model represents the most commonly accepted framework for understanding personality traits in organizational settings. In general, experts agree that personality traits toward the left end of each continuum, as illustrated in this figure, are more positive in organizational settings, whereas traits closer to the right are less positive.

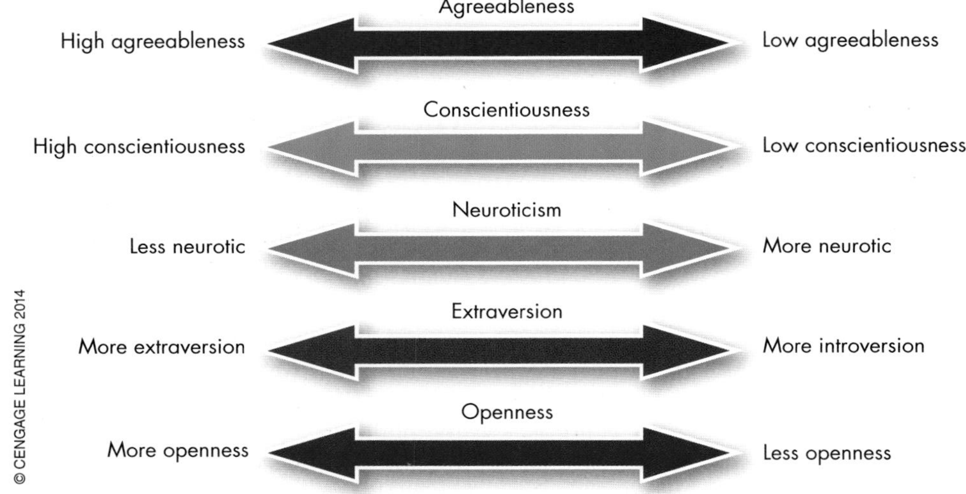

agreeable people are better at developing good working relationships with coworkers, subordinates, and higher-level managers, whereas less agreeable people are not likely to have particularly good working relationships. The same pattern might extend to relationships with customers, suppliers, and other key organizational constituents. Understanding your own level of agreeableness will help you more effectively work with others and perhaps better see the role of your own personality in interpersonal relationships that may be more or less positive.

Conscientiousness refers to the number of goals on which a person focuses. People who focus on relatively few goals at one time are likely to be organized, systematic, careful, thorough, responsible, and self-disciplined; they tend to focus on a small number of goals at one time. Others, however, tend to pursue a wider array of goals, and, as a result, are more disorganized, careless, and irresponsible, as well as less thorough and self-disciplined. Research has found that more conscientious people tend to be higher performers than less conscientious people in a variety of different jobs. This pattern seems logical, because conscientious people take their jobs seriously and approach their jobs in a highly responsible fashion. Having a realistic view of your own conscientiousness will contribute to how well you manage time and provide guidance as you decide whether or not to take on additional responsibilities.

The third of the "big five" personality dimensions is **neuroticism**. People who are neurotic tend to experience unpleasant emotions such as anger, anxiety, depression, and feelings of vulnerability more often than people who are less neurotic. People who are less neurotic are poised, calm, resilient, and secure. People who are neurotic are more excitable, insecure, reactive, and subject to extreme mood swings. People with less neuroticism might be expected to better handle job stress, pressure, and tension. Their stability might also lead them to be seen as being more reliable than their less-stable counterparts. Understanding our own neuroses is difficult, but by doing so we will be better equipped to deal with the stresses and pressure of both work and non-work situations.

Extraversion reflects a person's comfort level with relationships. Extroverts are sociable, talkative, assertive, and open to establishing new relationships. Introverts are much less sociable, talkative, and assertive, and more reluctant to begin new relationships. Research suggests that extroverts tend to be higher overall job performers than introverts, and that they are more likely to be attracted to jobs based on personal relationships, such as sales and marketing positions. Understanding our own level of extraversion can be an important factor in assessing why we may like or dislike certain kinds of work and serve as a guide as we consider career options. For instance, if a person knows he is an extrovert he

conscientiousness the number of goals on which a person focuses, including effective time management and meeting work obligations

neuroticism the extent to which a person commonly experiences unpleasant emotions such as anger, anxiety, depression, and feelings of vulnerability versus poise, calmness, resilience, and security

extraversion a person's comfort level with relationships

might work harder to move into a position that involves a great deal of personal interaction, while an introvert might avoid such a position.

Finally, **openness** reflects a person's rigidity of beliefs and range of interests. People with high levels of openness are willing to listen to new ideas and to change their own ideas, beliefs, and attitudes in response to new information. They also tend to have broad interests and to be curious, imaginative, and creative. On the other hand, people with low levels of openness tend to be less receptive to new ideas and less willing to change their minds. Further, they tend to have fewer and narrower interests and to be less curious and creative. People with more openness might be expected to be better performers due to their flexibility and the likelihood that they will be better accepted by others in the organization. Openness may also encompass a person's willingness to accept change. People with high levels of openness may be more receptive to change, whereas people with little openness may resist change. It is helpful to understand our own level of openness, especially if we tend to have a lower level of openness. This awareness, for example, might enable us to avoid reaching hasty decisions or rejecting ideas too quickly just because they don't fall in line with our current views and attitudes.

The "big five" framework continues to attract the attention of both researchers and managers. The potential value of this framework is that it encompasses an integrated set of traits that appear to be valid predictors of certain behaviors in certain situations. Thus, managers who can understand the framework, rationally assess how their own personality maps onto these traits, and assess these traits in their employees are in a good position to understand how and why they behave as they do. On the other hand, managers must be careful to not overestimate their ability to assess the "big five" traits in either themselves or others. Even assessment using the most rigorous and valid measures is likely to be somewhat imprecise. Another limitation of the "big five" framework is that it is primarily based on research conducted in the United States. Thus, its generalizability to other cultures presents unanswered questions. Even within the United States a variety of other factors and traits are also likely to affect behavior in organizations.

> *"I've changed from a person known for making snap decisions to someone who's viewed as thoughtful and analytical."*
>
> LAUREN ZALAZNICK
> NBC television executive[14]

QUOTED IN FORTUNE, JULY 6, 2009, P. 49.

The Myers-Briggs Framework Another interesting approach to understanding personalities in organizations is the Myers-Briggs framework. This framework, based on the classical work of Carl Jung, differentiates people in terms of four general dimensions: sensing/intuiting; judging/perceiving; extraversion/introversion; and thinking/feeling. Higher and lower positions in each of the dimensions are used to classify people into one of sixteen different personality categories.

The Myers-Briggs Type Indicator (MBTI) is a popular questionnaire some organizations use to assess personality types. Indeed, it is among the most popular selection instruments used today, with as many as 2 million people taking it each year. Research suggests that the MBTI is a useful method for determining communication styles and interaction preferences. In terms of personality attributes however, questions exist about both the validity and the stability of the MBTI.

Other Personality Traits at Work Besides these complex models of personality, several other specific personality traits are also likely to influence behavior in organizations. Among the most important are locus of control, self-efficacy, authoritarianism, Machiavellianism, self-esteem, and risk propensity.

Locus of control is the extent to which people believe that their behavior has a real effect on what happens to them.[15] Some people, for example, believe that if they work hard they will succeed. They may also believe that people who fail do so because they lack ability or motivation. People who believe that individuals are in control of their lives are

© ISTOCKPHOTO.COM/TRIGGERPHOTO

openness a person's rigidity of beliefs and range of interests

locus of control the extent to which people believe that their behavior has a real effect on what happens to them

LEARN

said to have an internal locus of control. Other people think that fate, chance, luck, or other people's behavior determines what happens to them. For example, an employee who fails to get a promotion may attribute that failure to a politically motivated boss or just bad luck, rather than to her or his own lack of skills or poor performance record. People who think that forces beyond their control dictate what happens to them are said to have an external locus of control.

Self-efficacy is a related but subtly different personality characteristic. A person's self-efficacy is that person's belief about his or her capabilities to perform a task. People with high self-efficacy believe that they can perform well on a specific task, but people with low self-efficacy tend to doubt their ability to perform a specific task. Self-assessments of ability contribute to self-efficacy, but so does the individual's personality. Some people simply have more self-confidence than others. This belief in their ability to perform a task effectively results in their being more self-assured and better able to focus their attention on performance.[16]

Another important personality characteristic is authoritarianism, the extent to which a person believes that power and status differences are appropriate within hierarchical social systems such as organizations.[17] For example, a person who is highly authoritarian may accept directives or orders from someone with more authority purely because the other person is "the boss." On the other hand, a person who is not highly authoritarian, although she may still carry out reasonable directives from the boss, is more likely to question things, express disagreement with the boss, and even refuse to carry out orders if they are for some reason objectionable.

A highly authoritarian manager may be relatively autocratic and demanding, and highly authoritarian subordinates are more likely to accept this behavior from their leader. On the other hand, a less authoritarian manager may allow subordinates a bigger role in making decisions, and less authoritarian subordinates respond positively to this behavior. Dennis Kozlowski, the indicted former CEO of Tyco International, was an authoritarian manager to the point of being Machiavellian. He came to believe that his position of power in the company gave him the right to do just about anything he wanted with company resources.[18]

self-efficacy a person's belief about his or her capabilities to perform a task

authoritarianism the extent to which a person believes that power and status differences are appropriate within hierarchical social systems such as organizations

Machiavellianism behavior directed at gaining power and controlling the behavior of others

self-esteem the extent to which a person believes that he or she is a worthwhile and deserving individual

risk propensity the degree to which a person is willing to take chances and make risky decisions

emotional intelligence (EQ) the extent to which people are self-aware, can manage their emotions, can motivate themselves, can express empathy for others, and possess social skills

Machiavellianism is another important personality trait. This concept is named after Niccolo Machiavelli, a sixteenth-century author. In his book *The Prince*, Machiavelli explained how the nobility could more easily gain and use power. The term "Machiavellianism" is now used to describe behavior directed at gaining power and controlling the behavior of others. Research suggests that the degree of Machiavellianism varies from person to person. Machiavellian individuals tend to be rational and non-emotional, may be willing to lie to attain their personal goals, put little emphasis on loyalty and friendship, and enjoy manipulating others' behavior. Less Machiavellian individuals are more emotional, less willing to lie to succeed, value loyalty and friendship highly, and get little personal pleasure from manipulating others.

Self-esteem is the extent to which a person believes that he or she is a worthwhile and deserving individual. A person with high self-esteem is more likely to seek higher-status jobs, be more confident in her ability to achieve higher levels of performance, and derive greater intrinsic satisfaction from her accomplishments. In contrast, a person with less self-esteem may be more content to remain in a lower-level job, be less confident of his ability, and focus more on extrinsic rewards. Among the major personality dimensions, self-esteem is the one that has been most widely studied in other countries. Although more research is clearly needed, the published evidence suggests that self-esteem as a personality trait does indeed exist in a variety of countries and that its role in organizations is reasonably important across different cultures.

Risk propensity is the degree to which a person is willing to take chances and make risky decisions. A manager with a high risk propensity, for example, might experiment with new ideas and gamble on new products. He might also lead the organization in new and different directions. This manager might be a catalyst for innovation, or on the other hand, might jeopardize the continued well-being of the organization if the risky decisions prove to be bad ones. A manager with low risk propensity might lead an organization to stagnation and excessive conservatism, or he might help the organization successfully weather turbulent and unpredictable times by maintaining stability and calm. Thus, the potential consequences of a manager's risk propensity depend heavily on the organization's environment.

Emotional Intelligence

The concept of emotional intelligence provides interesting insights into personality. Emotional intelligence, or EQ, refers to the extent to which people are self-aware, in control of their emotions, self-motivated, empathetic, and sociable.[19] These various dimensions can be described as follows:

Self-awareness This is the basis for the other components. It refers to a person's capacity for being aware of how he or she is feeling. In general, more self-awareness allows a person to more effectively guide his or her own lives and behaviors.

Managing Emotions This refers to a person's ability to balance anxiety, fear, and anger so as not to overly interfere with getting things accomplished.

Motivating Oneself This dimension refers to a person's ability to remain optimistic and to continue striving in the face of setbacks, barriers, and failure.

Empathy Empathy refers to a person's ability to understand how others are feeling even without being explicitly told.

Social Skill This refers to a person's ability to get along with others and to establish positive relationships.

Preliminary research suggests that people with high EQs may perform better than others, especially in jobs that require a high degree of interpersonal interaction and that involve influencing or directing the work of others. Moreover, EQ appears to be something that isn't biologically based but which can be developed.[20]

Generalizability/Discrimination

Another personal skill is the ability to generalize across and discriminate between different situations. For example, suppose a project manager who works for a large organization volunteers for a Habitat for Humanity building project. During the course of the project, he observes numerous instances of how people working together can get things done effectively. He also notes situations where people disagree over how to do something but then resolve their disagreement in an amicable way. He sees that some people look to other people as informal leaders. He also has sufficient self-awareness to understand his own strengths and weaknesses and how others on the Habitat project see him. As it turns out, he has just been assigned to lead a new project team at work charged with managing the construction of a new shopping mall. It may be possible for him to take some of the things he learned at the Habitat project and effectively apply them to the new work project. If he can do this, he has demonstrated the ability to generalize from one setting to another.

On the other hand, suppose a different manager has just left her job working as a sales representative for a large pharmaceutical company and started a new job selling commercial real estate. While her selling skills may be transferrable, she also needs to understand the differences in advocating products to physicians and hospitals as opposed to promoting real estate to big box retailers. To the extent that this is apparent to her, she is demonstrating an ability to discriminate. The personal skills of generalizability and discrimination refer to your understanding of similarities and differences across various settings, and how behaviors in one setting may or may not be effective in another setting. The better you are at generalizing and discriminating correctly, the more effective you are likely to be.

Understanding Personal Values, Ethics, and Priorities

Finally, it is important that you clearly understand your personal values, ethics, and priorities. For instance, some people might be uncomfortable working for a defense contractor building a guided missile system, a logging company that cuts down trees, a tobacco company that markets cigarettes in developing countries, or an advertising agency that is prone to hyperbole in its promotional campaigns. Others might have no issues with these employers and think that as long as they function within the law they are attractive employers. Similarly, some people might not enjoy working for an insurance company and having to make decisions about whether or not to reimburse policyholders for an expensive surgery. Some people might get satisfaction from working with a social service agency helping disadvantaged people, while others would see the work as depressing.

The ethical climate of the organization is also important. *Figure 2.3* presents a way to assess the key areas where ethics come into play and offers a framework for evaluating the degree to which ethics might affect us. As shown, these issues generally relate to how the organization treats its employees, how employees treat the organization, and how employees and the organization treat other economic agents.

How an organization treats its employees encompasses areas such as hiring and firing, wages and working conditions, and employee privacy and respect. For example, both ethical and legal guidelines suggest that hiring and firing decisions should be based solely on an individual's ability to perform the job. A manager who discriminates against African Americans in hiring is exhibiting both unethical and illegal behavior. But consider the case of a manager who does not discriminate in general, but who hires a family friend when other applicants might be just as qualified. Although these hiring decisions may not be illegal, they may be objectionable on ethical grounds. Wages and working conditions, although regulated, also are areas for

LEARN

FIGURE 2.3 THE ORGANIZATIONAL CONTEXT OF ETHICS

The organizational context of ethics generally involves three basic areas: how the organization treats its employees, how employees treat the organization, and how both employees and the organization treat other economic agents. Understanding these areas can help managers better match their own personal values, ethics, and priorities to those of their employer.

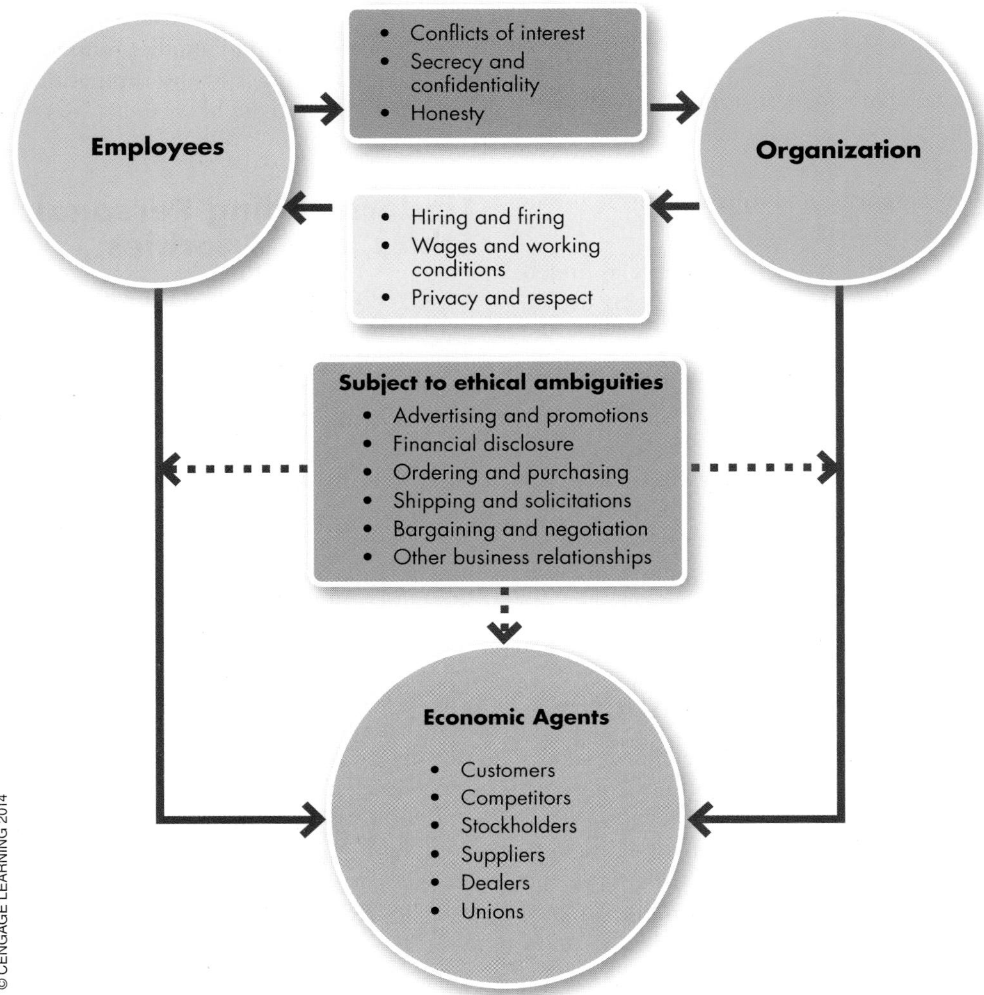

© CENGAGE LEARNING 2014

potential controversy. For example, a manager paying an employee less than he deserves, simply because the manager knows the employee cannot afford to quit or risk losing his job by complaining, might be considered unethical. Finally, most would agree that an organization is obligated to protect the privacy of its employees.

Numerous ethical issues stem from how employees treat the organization, especially regarding conflicts of interest, secrecy and confidentiality, and honesty. A conflict of interest occurs when a decision potentially benefits the individual to the possible detriment of the organization. To guard against such practices, most companies have policies that forbid their buyers from accepting gifts from suppliers. Divulging company secrets is also clearly unethical. Employees who work for businesses in highly competitive industries—electronics, software, and fashion apparel, for example—might be tempted to sell information about company plans to competitors. Another area of concern is honesty in general. Common problems in this area include activities such as using a business telephone to make personal long-distance calls, stealing supplies, and padding expense accounts. Recently, behaviors such as personal Internet use at work have become more pervasive.

Ethics also come into play in the relationship between the firm and its employees with other economic agents. As listed previously in *Figure 2.3*, the primary agents of interest include customers, competitors, stockholders, suppliers, dealers, and unions. The behaviors between the organization and these agents subject to ethical ambiguity include advertising and promotions, financial disclosures, ordering and purchasing, shipping and solicitations, bargaining and negotiation, and other business relationships.

Personal priorities also must be recognized. One person, for instance, might want a job that involves very little travel and allows him to be home every evening and weekend. Someone else, though, might find a job with a lot of travel to be exciting and be indifferent to working evenings and weekends. Some people put a high premium on pay and may be willing to work longer hours and to move frequently to advance in the organization and increase their salaries. But other people value a balanced life with ample time for personal interests, socializing, and family activities. These individuals may be less interested in jobs that require them to move. And of course, priorities change over the course of our lives and careers. For instance, people may be more willing to work longer hours and to move in the early stages of their careers, but prefer greater balance and stability later. We need to understand our own personal priorities and match those with our jobs as best we can.

THE SCOPE OF MANAGEMENT

Management takes place in a wide variety of settings. Any group of two or more persons working together to achieve a goal and that has human, material, financial, or informational resources at its disposal requires the practice of management.

Managing in Profit-Seeking Organizations

Most of what we know about management comes from large profit-seeking organizations because their long survival has depended on efficiency and effectiveness. Examples of large businesses include industrial firms such as ExxonMobil, Toyota, BMW, Xerox, Unilever, and Levi Strauss; commercial banks such as Citicorp, Fuji Bank, and Wells Fargo; insurance companies such as Prudential, State Farm, and Metropolitan Life; retailers such as Sears, Safeway, and Target; transportation companies such as United Airlines and Consolidated Freightways; utilities such as Pacific Gas & Electric, and Consolidated Edison of New York; communication companies such as CBS and the New York Times Company; and service organizations such as Kelly Services, KinderCare Learning Centers, and Century 21 real estate.

STAN HONDA/AFP/GETTY IMAGES/NEWSCOM

Although many people associate management primarily with large businesses, effective management is also essential for small businesses, which play an important role in the country's economy. In fact, most of this nation's businesses are small. In some respects, effective management is more important in a small business than in a large one. A large firm such as ExxonMobil or Monsanto can recover relatively easily from losing several thousand dollars on an incorrect decision; even losses of millions of dollars would not threaten their long-term survival. But a small business may ill afford even a much smaller loss. Of course, some small businesses become big ones. Dell Computer, for example, was started by one person—Michael Dell—in 1984. By 2011 it had become one of the largest businesses in the United States, with annual sales of more than $60 billion.

In recent years, the importance of international management has increased dramatically. The list of US firms doing business in other countries is staggering. ExxonMobil, for example, derives almost 75 percent of its revenues from foreign markets, and Coca-Cola derives more than 80 percent of its sales from foreign markets. Other major US exporters include General Motors, General Electric, Boeing, and Caterpillar. Some numbers, however, like Ford's are deceptive. For example, the automaker has large subsidiaries based in many European countries whose sales are not included as foreign revenue. Moreover, a number of major firms that do business in the United States have their headquarters in other countries. Firms in this category include the Royal Dutch/Shell Group (the Netherlands), Fiat S.p.A. (Italy), Nestlé S.A. (Switzerland), and Massey Ferguson

(Canada). International management is not confined to profit-seeking organizations, however. Several international sports federations, such as Little League Baseball, branches of the federal government, and the Roman Catholic Church are established in most countries as well. In some respects, the military was one of the first multinational organizations.

Managing in Not-for-Profit Organizations

Intangible goals such as education, social services, public protection, and recreation are often the primary aim of not-for-profit organizations. Examples include United Way of America, the US Postal Service, Girl Scouts of the USA, the International Olympic Committee, art galleries, museums, and the Public Broadcasting System (PBS). Although these and similar organizations may not have to be profitable to attract investors, they must still employ sound management practices if they are to survive and work toward their goals.[21] They must handle money in an efficient and effective way. If the United Way were to begin to spend large portions of its contributions on administration, contributors would lose confidence in the organization and make their charitable donations elsewhere.

The management of government organizations and agencies often is regarded as a separate specialty: public administration. Government organizations include the Federal Trade Commission (FTC), the Environmental Protection Agency (EPA), the National Science Foundation, all branches of the military, state highway departments, and federal and state prison systems. Tax dollars support government organizations, so politicians and citizens' groups are acutely sensitive to the need for efficiency and effectiveness.

Public and private schools, colleges, and universities all stand to benefit from the efficient use of resources. Taxpayer "revolts" in states such as California and Massachusetts have drastically cut back the tax money available for education, forcing administrators to make tough decisions about allocating remaining resources.

Managing healthcare facilities such as clinics, hospitals, and HMOs (health maintenance organizations) is now considered a separate field of management. Here, as in other organizations, scarce resources dictate an efficient and effective approach. In recent years many universities have established healthcare administration programs to train managers as specialists in this field.

Good management is also required in nontraditional settings. Management is practiced in religious organizations, terrorist groups, fraternities and sororities, organized crime, street gangs, neighborhood associations, and individual households. In short, management and managers have a profound influence on all of us. It is critical, then, that those managers work to develop their skills so they can lead their organizations as efficiently and as effectively as possible.

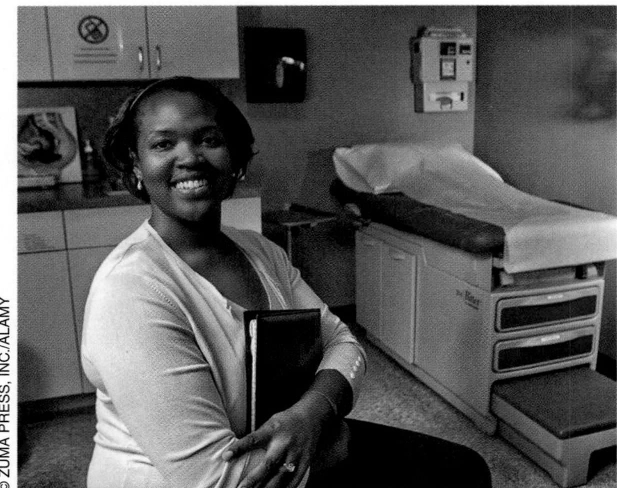

© ZUMA PRESS, INC./ALAMY

DeAnna Warren manages Genesis Community Health, a not-for-profit clinic in Florida. Even though Genesis does not seek to earn profits, Ms. Warren must still practice effective management in order for the clinic to survive.

SUMMARY AND A LOOK AHEAD

Now you understand the nature of managerial work and the model of skill development we will use throughout this book. You recognize the differences between the science and the art of management and you appreciate the importance of both education and experience in developing your skills. You also have a better appreciation of the importance of personal skills, including self-awareness and an understanding of the role and importance of personality, emotional intelligence, generalizability and discrimination, and personal values, ethics, and priorities. You also recognize the breadth of managerial opportunities across a variety of both profit-seeking and not-for-profit organizations. The next several pages provide a number of exercises and cases that will provide additional insights to help you as you continue to develop and refine your managerial skills.

PRACTICING YOUR SKILLS

WHAT DO YOU BRING TO THE TABLE?

This exercise provides an opportunity to see how your background and experience contribute to the learning goals of not just yourself but also others in your class.

Your Assignment

1. Think about three to five things about you that shape your learning and your potential contributions to the class. These might be your work experience, your education, languages that you know, contacts you have, other courses you have taken, or organizations in which you are a member.
2. Assemble in small groups to share your thoughts with other group members. Then each group should discuss its members' lists, focusing on how relevant or useful the various items may or may not be.
3. Each group should present to the whole class a brief summary of the most relevant things that the group identified for further discussion.

INNER CIRCLE

This exercise provides an opportunity to explore various learning goals with others in your class. It should give you a new appreciation for the skills that managers need for resolving differences of opinion and forging a consensus of employees with different needs.

Your Assignment

1. Form groups of about 12 students, and divide each group into two teams of six members.
2. For each group, have one of the six-member teams get together and discuss "What we hope to learn in this course." The other six-member team from each group will watch and listen to the first team's discussion.
3. Then have all the six-member teams reverse positions and repeat the exercise. This time around, the discussion teams can build upon what happened the first time.
4. The two teams from each group will then meet as a whole to discuss their findings and attempt to resolve any differences that have been noted.
5. All the groups should report their findings to the class to give students an idea of how similar or dissimilar their goals were.

WHAT ARE YOUR LEARNING GOALS?

This exercise will give you an opportunity to see how your learning goals compare with those of your classmates. It will also let you see the feasibility of trying to satisfy all individuals. It should help you appreciate the dilemma of a manager (instructor, in this case) in trying to address a wide variety of student goals and the skills needed to resolve the disappointments experienced by the students.

Your Assignment

1. Prepare a list of five things you want to learn from this course. These can be very specific (such as learning how to properly format business letters) or very general (such as learning how to work with others).
2. In small groups, share your list with the other members. Then discuss each item and arrive at a group list of five "things I want from this course" to be shared with the whole class.
3. The whole class should then discuss the feasibility of achieving those learning goals through this course. Why are some more or less feasible than others?

WHAT ABOUT ME, WHAT ABOUT YOU?

This exercise will give you an opportunity to explore, with others, what you believe are the various goals of yourself and individuals who supposedly share similar goals.

Your Assignment

Form small groups to answer the following questions. Each group should arrive at a short answer to each question and then share the group answer with the whole class for discussion.

1. Will students study the assigned textbook material on a timely basis or postpone studying until exam time?
2. How committed do you think other class members are to learning versus just getting a grade or completing a curriculum requirement?
3. How cooperative and engaged will class members be in group exercises?
4. How honest will class members be when doing self-assessments and group exercises?
5. How honest will students be when taking tests in this course?

USE

USING YOUR SKILLS

BODY SHOP AND EDUCATION

The first Body Shop opened in 1976 in Brighton, England. By 1992, there were more than 800 stores—more than 200 in the United Kingdom and Channel islands, more than 100 in the United States, nearly 100 in Canada, and others scattered within 40 other countries. That same year the stock value of the organization was approximately $1 billion. Not bad for a retail chain that did not believe in advertising and emphasized that it is more important to have an interesting conversation that imparts information to a customer than for the customer to walk out of a shop having bought something. The management style of founder Anita Roddick was described as loosely structured, collaborative, imaginative, and improvisatory. She strongly believed in nurturing entrepreneurs and renegades to bring about effective groups in her organization.

Educating consumers and practicing environmental and social responsibility is pushed in Body Shop stores. Leaflets and cards offer health and beauty tips and product content information. Brochures and pamphlets about recycling and Amnesty International are scattered throughout the stores. Well-educated customers not only buy Body Shop products but also convince their friends to do likewise. Thus, by word of mouth, the business expands without spending money on advertising or marketing. Of course, getting lots of free publicity by supporting social causes doesn't hurt.

Employees are also educated. They are deluged with information about the business from newsletters, videos, brochures, posters, training programs, and so on. The message is not about the selling or profit aspects of the business, however, but rather about the nature and use of the products. Thus, the employee is given the knowledge to educate the customer. This keeps the employees learning, interested, and excited about the products, which in turn makes for better customer relations (which ultimately results in sales but without having created stress in the first place). Or the message is about a social issue, such as saving the rain forest or banning ozone-depleting chemicals, again to educate the employee so that she or he can better educate the customer.

As a result, employees understand why it's important to have good merchandise displays, clean shops, treat customers respectfully, and so on. They don't need rules about these things; they have learned the importance and so they do them. They work together as a team to get them done. The corporate culture bonds employees and customers together. The common bond is a belief that businesses should do more than make money, create jobs, and sell products—businesses should also help solve major social problems.

That common bond enables groups of Body Shop employees to function as energetic teams of educators about its products and about important social issues. The corporate staff and franchisees are strongly encouraged to work on community projects of their choice in their local areas. Groups of Body Shop personnel have worked on projects that included cooking and serving meals in soup kitchens, working in battered-women and -children's shelters, and assisting in literacy programs. Employees are allowed as much as a half day of paid company time every four weeks to participate in these activities, but groups frequently spend their own time and energies on these social projects as well.

Imitators eventually eroded the markets of the Body Shop. In an effort to improve the company, in 2002, Body Shop founders Anita and Gordon Roddick gave up their roles as co-chairmen. Improved efficiencies and a spruced-up image enabled the company to return to strong performance by the mid-2000s, and in 2006 L'Oréal purchased it. In 2007 Anita Roddick died of an acute brain hemorrhage, a complication of Hepatitis C that was contracted through a blood transfusion several years previously. In her final years she promoted the work of the Hepatitis C Trust in the United Kingdom and campaigned courageously to educate others about this "silent disease."

Case Questions

Go Online

1. Why was education emphasized at Body Shop?
2. How did employees learn about products? About the importance of customers? About keeping the store clean and neat?
3. What might you learn from this company about the way employees can learn?
4. Do you think that learning in this way is efficient? Effective? Why or why not?
5. Do you think that your skills would be compatible with working at Body Shop? Why or why not? If not compatible, but you would like them to be, how would you go about changing your skills?

Case References

Beth Carney, "Toning up the Body Shop," *Business Week*, May 18, 2005 http://www.businessweek.com/bwdaily/dnflash/may2005/nf20050518_6631_db016.htm; Carlye Adler, "The disenfranchised owning a Body Shop store seemed like the perfect business, with great products and earth-friendly management. So why are some franchisees now suing the company?" *Fortune*, September 17, 2001 http://money.cnn.com/magazines/fortune/fortune_archive/2001/09/17/310263/index.htm;

Various "Fact Sheets" provided in the press packet by The Body Shop Communications Office, Cedar Knolls, New Jersey, November 1992; Rahul Jacob, "What Selling Will Be Like in the '90s," *Fortune*, January 13, 1992, pp. 63–64; Tom Peters, Liberation Management (New York: Alfred A. Knopf, 1992), pp. 594–596.

USE

LEARNING AT KYOCERA

Kyocera Corporation was started by a maverick, Kazuo Inamori. An ordained Buddhist priest who earned a Ph.D. in Chemical Engineering, Inamori first went to work for a big Japanese manufacturer. But he soon found that he did not enjoy working within that firm's traditional Japanese bureaucratic system. Thus, he left his first employer and started Kyocera. Kyocera is not nearly as well known outside of Japan as firms like Sony, Honda, and Nissan, but within Japan, Kyocera has a reputation for being among that country's highest quality manufacturers. A recent survey of Japanese executives ranked Kyocera as the firm they admired most.

Kyocera specializes in electronics. The firm sees its competitive advantage as making the highest possible quality products. The thing Inamori had resisted most in his first job was having to bow to authority. He felt that individual managers should be free to learn and pursue entrepreneurial opportunities without being constrained by a rigid bureaucracy. Thus, when he founded Kyocera one of his highest priorities was to avoid rigid channels of authority and to instead promote opportunities for learning, creativity, and innovation.

His concept of Kyocera was derived from the notion of amoebas. He views the organization as simply being a collection of individual people without permanent job assignments or a departmental affiliation. Instead, each person is assigned to a project group that grows, changes, and dissolves as dictated by its particular job assignment. Thus, each group is like an amoeba and, to survive, the amoeba must learn.

Each group, or amoeba, starts with the assignment of an executive or supervisor to a project. That person then scans the roster of available employees and recruits those who are best suited to the needs of the project. As the group takes shape, it takes on more and more control, and the supervisor becomes more and more a team member as opposed to the group's boss. Ultimately, the group itself recruits new members as they are needed. Likewise, individual group members transition out of the group when their services are no longer needed. Each group also makes its own decisions about supplies, materials, and purchases, and schedules its own work assignments.

At any given time, several dozen amoebas are at work, their memberships ranging from as few as two to as many as several hundred members. This evolutionary and constantly changing structure might be difficult for many people to understand, but Kyocera makes the highest quality products in its industry. And Inamori credits his amoebas for being the critical ingredient in the firm's success, which includes the development of the Finecam SL300R and the highly successful Smart Phone.

Case Questions

Go Online

1. How do employees learn at Kyocera? Is this efficient? Effective?
2. Why do you think the amoebas are so successful at Kyocera?
3. Would this concept work in all organizations? Why or why not?
4. What unique personal skills would be necessary for an individual to be comfortable working for Kyocera?
5. Do you think your skills would be compatible with working at Kyocera? Why or why not? If not compatible but you would like them to be, how would you go about changing your skills?

Case References

William Pesek, "He's not Steve Jobs, but this tycoon might fix it," *Business Week*, January 20, 2010 http://www.businessweek.com/globalbiz/content/jan2010/gb20100120_195894.htm; Peter Lewis, "A camera to outsmart your smart-aleck kid," *Fortune*, January 12, 2004 http://money.cnn.com/magazines/fortune/fortune_archive/2004/01/12/357943/index.htm; Peter H. Lewis, "Smart Phone Invasion: Kyocera's Smartphone combines a wireless phone with a Palm computer," *Fortune*, May 28, 2001 http://money.cnn.com/magazines/fortune/fortune_archive/2001/05/28/303878/index.htm; Gene Bylinsky, "The Hottest High-Tech Company in Japan," *Fortune*, January 1, 1990, pp. 82–88.

EXTENDING YOUR LEARNING SKILLS

Your instructor may use one or more of these Group Extensions to provide you with yet another opportunity to develop your learning skills. On the other hand, you may continue your development on your own by doing one or more of the Individual Extensions.

GROUP EXTENSIONS

- Have groups of students share their preferred learning strategies and discuss the pros and cons of each.
- Have groups of students identify various techniques used in teaching/learning. They should share which they feel is best and which is worst with the class.

INDIVIDUAL EXTENSIONS

- Identify something that you want to learn that can be "broken" into parts. Try to learn one part in your usual, preferred way and then try to learn another part in a very different way. Does it help to try different approaches?
- Do research on what seems to be the best method for learning skills and share your results with the class.

INTERPRETATIONS

WHAT IS YOUR LEARNING STYLE?

Now that you know which learning style you rely on, you can boost your learning potential when working to learn more. For instance, the following suggestions can help you get more from reading a book.

If your primary learning style is *visual*, draw pictures in the margins, look at the graphics, and read the text that explains the graphics. Envision the topic or play a movie in your thoughts of how you will act out the subject matter.

If your primary learning style is *auditory*, listen to the words you read. Try to develop an internal conversation between you and the text. Don't be embarrassed to read aloud or talk through the information.

If your primary learning style is *tactile/kinesthetic*, use a pencil or highlighter pen to mark passages that are meaningful to you. Take notes, transferring the information you learn to the margins of the book, into your journal, or onto a computer. Doodle whatever comes to mind as you read. Hold the book in your hands instead of placing it on a table. Walk around as you read. Feel the words and ideas. Get busy—both mentally and physically.

More information on each style, along with suggestions on how to maximize your learning potential, is available in the book by Marcia Conner, *Learn More Now* (Hoboken, NJ; John Wiley & Sons, 2004).

ASSESSING YOUR MENTAL ABILITIES

For each of the ten behavior categories, the higher your score, the more descriptive that mental ability is of you.

1. visualization
2. clever and uncommon responses
3. formulate hypotheses
4. remember unrelated material
5. remembering items
6. manipulate numbers, arithmetic
7. fast in comparison
8. reason from stated premises
9. spatial patterns
10. vocabulary

Think about how each of these mental abilities might relate to different managerial skills and functions.

ENDNOTES

[1] Michael A. Hitt, "Transformation of Management for the New Millennium," *Organizational Dynamics*, Winter 2000, pp. 7–17.

[2] James H. Davis, F. David Schoorman, and Lex Donaldson, "Toward a Stewardship Theory of Management," *Academy of Management Review*, January 1997, pp. 20–47.

[3] Gary Hamel and C. K. Prahalad, "Competing for the Future," *Harvard Business Review*, July–August 1994, pp. 122–128.

[4] James Waldroop and Timothy Butler, "The Executive as Coach," *Harvard Business Review*, November–December 1996, pp. 111–117.

[5] Steven J. Armstrong and Anis Mahmud, "Experiential Learning and the Acquisition of Managerial Tacit Knowledge," *Academy of Management Learning & Education*, 2008, Vol. 7, No. 2, pp. 189–208.

[6] *Biz Ed*, May/June 2010, p. 23.

[7] "The Executive MBA Your Way," *BusinessWeek*, October 18, 1999, pp. 88–92.

[8] "Despite Cutbacks, Firms Invest in Developing Leaders," *Wall Street Journal*, February 9, 2009, p. B4.

[9] "Turning B-School into E-School," *BusinessWeek*, October 18, 1999, p. 94.

[10] See "Reunion at P&G University," *Wall Street Journal*, June 7, 2000, pp. B1, B4, for a discussion of Procter & Gamble's training programs.

[11] For an interesting discussion of these issues, see Rakesh Khurana, "The Curse of the Superstar CEO," *Harvard Business Review*, September 2002, pp. 60–70.

[12] *BusinessWeek*, June 13, 2011, p. 23.

[13] R.W. Griffin and G. Moorhead, *Organizational Behavior*, 11th Ed. (Mason, OH: Cengage, 2013) Chapter 3.

[14] Quoted in *Fortune*, July 6, 2009, p. 49.

[15] J. B. Rotter, "Generalized Expectancies for Internal vs. External Control of Reinforcement," *Psychological Monographs*, vol. 80, 1966, pp. 1–28; Bert De Brabander and Christopher Boone, "Sex Differences in Perceived Locus of Control," *Journal of Social Psychology*, vol. 130, 1990, pp. 271–276.

[16] Jeffrey Vancouver, Kristen More, and Ryan Yoder, "Self-Efficacy and Resource Allocation: Support for a Nonmonotic, Discontinuous Model," *Journal of Applied Psychology*, 2008, Vol. 93, No. 1, pp. 35–47.

[17] T. W. Adorno, E. Frenkel-Brunswick, D. J. Levinson, and R. N. Sanford, *The Authoritarian Personality* (New York: Harper & Row, 1950).

[18] "The Rise and Fall of Dennis Kozlowski," *Business Week*, December 23, 2002, p. 64–77.

[19] Daniel Goleman, *Emotional Intelligence: Why it Can Matter More Than IQ* (New York: Bantam Books, 1995).

[20] Daniel Goleman, "Leadership That Gets Results," *Harvard Business Review*, March-April 2000, pp. 78–90.

[21] James L. Perry and Hal G. Rainey, "The Public-Private Distinction in Organization Theory: A Critique and Research Strategy," *Academy of Management Review*, April 1988, pp. 182–201. See also Ran Lachman, "Public and Private Sector Differences: CEOs' Perceptions of Their Role Environments," *Academy of Management Journal*, September 1985, pp. 671–680.

CHAPTER 3

ASSESSING YOUR TIME-MANAGEMENT SKILLS

Behavior Activity Profile
Are You a Good Planner?
Stress Management
Time-Management Assessment

LEARNING ABOUT TIME-MANAGEMENT SKILLS

Understanding Prioritization
Setting Priorities
Misjudging Priorities
Effective Delegation
Reasons for Delegation
Parts of the Delegation Process
Problems in Delegation
Decentralization and Centralization
Scheduling Meetings and Controlling Intrusions
Scheduling and Managing Meetings
Controlling Intrusions
Managing Stress
Causes of Stress
Consequences of Stress
Limiting Stress
Summary and a Look Ahead

VISUALIZING TIME-MANAGEMENT SKILLS

Time-Management Skills in Action—1
Time-Management Skills in Action—2

PRACTICING YOUR TIME-MANAGEMENT SKILLS

Controlling Your Own Work
Balancing Urgent and Important Tasks
Demands that Cause Stress
Staircasing Your Goals
Effectiveness of Communication Exchanges
How Is Time Being Spent?
Personal Goal Sheet
Prioritizing Tasks
Stressful Jobs
Identifying Stressors
Running Team Meetings
Using Time More Efficiently
What to Do Now

USING YOUR TIME-MANAGEMENT SKILLS

Time Flexibility
United Parcel Service

EXTENDING YOUR TIME-MANAGEMENT SKILLS

Group Extensions
Individual Extensions

YOUR TIME-MANAGEMENT SKILLS NOW

Time-Management Skills Assessment

INTERPRETATIONS

Behavior Activity Profile: A "Type A" Measure
Are You a Good Planner?
Stress Management
Time-Management Assessment

Time-Management Skills

STEPHEN COBURN/SHUTTERSTOCK.COM

Chapter 2 described how management skills are learned and developed and discussed the differences between the science and the art of management. Understanding these differences will help you appreciate the importance of both education and experience in developing your management skills. Chapter 2 also discussed the importance of personal skills and the breadth of managerial opportunities across a variety of organizations. In Chapter 3 we begin our examination of specific management skills with one that is truly universal—time management. Using time effectively and efficiently is important in virtually every aspect of life. We begin our discussion with an examination of establishing priorities. We then describe the delegation process. Next, we discuss basic issues in scheduling meetings and controlling intrusions. Finally, we examine the causes and consequences of stress and how it can be managed. The chapter concludes with several cases and exercises to help you further develop and master your time-management skills.

ASSESS

ASSESSING YOUR TIME-MANAGEMENT SKILLS

BEHAVIOR ACTIVITY PROFILE

This self-assessment allows you to better understand the traits that may cause stress as you attempt to manage your time.

Instructions:

Each of us displays certain kinds of behaviors and thought patterns as personal characteristics. For each of the 21 descriptions below, circle the number that you feel best describes where you are between each pair. The best answer for each set of descriptions is the response that most nearly describes the way you feel, behave, or think. Respond in terms that reflect your regular or typical behavior, thoughts, or characteristics.

Descriptions

1.	I'm always on time for appointments.	7 6 5 4 3 2 1	I'm never quite on time.
2.	When someone is talking to me, chances are I'll anticipate what he or she is going to say by nodding, interrupting, or finishing sentences.	7 6 5 4 3 2 1	I listen quietly without showing impatience.
3.	I frequently try to do several things at once.	7 6 5 4 3 2 1	I tend to do things one at a time.
4.	When it comes to waiting in line (at banks, theaters, etc.), I really get impatient and frustrated.	7 6 5 4 3 2 1	It simply doesn't bother me.
5.	I always feel rushed.	7 6 5 4 3 2 1	I never feel rushed.
6.	When it comes to my temper, I find it hard to control at times.	7 6 5 4 3 2 1	I just don't seem to have one.
7.	I tend to do most things like eating, walking, and talking rapidly.	7 6 5 4 3 2 1	Slowly
TOTAL SCORE 1-7 = _____ = S [See interpretation of "S" at the end of the chapter].			
8.	Quite honestly, the things I enjoy most are job-related activities.	7 6 5 4 3 2 1	Leisure-time activities
9.	At the end of a typical workday, I usually feel like I needed to get more done than I did.	7 6 5 4 3 2 1	I accomplished everything I needed to.
10.	Someone who knows me very well would say that I would rather work than play.	7 6 5 4 3 2 1	I would rather play than work.
11.	When it comes to getting ahead at work, nothing is more important.	7 6 5 4 3 2 1	Many things are more Important.
12.	My primary source of satisfaction comes from my job.	7 6 5 4 3 2 1	I regularly find satisfaction in non-job pursuits, such as hobbies, friends, and family.
13.	Most of my friends and social acquaintances are people I know from work.	7 6 5 4 3 2 1	Not connected with my work.
14.	I'd rather stay at work than take a vacation.	7 6 5 4 3 2 1	Nothing at work is important enough to interfere with my vacation.
TOTAL SCORE 8–14 = _____ = J [See interpretation of "J" at the end of the chapter].			

15.	People who know me well would describe me as hard-driving and competitive.	7 6 5 4 3 2 1	Relaxed and easy-going.
16.	In general, my behavior is governed by a desire for recognition and achievement.	7 6 5 4 3 2 1	What I want to do—not by trying to satisfy others.
17.	In trying to complete a project or solve a problem, I tend to wear myself out before I'll give up on it.	7 6 5 4 3 2 1	I tend to take a break or quit if I'm feeling fatigued.
18.	When I play a game (tennis, cards, etc.), my enjoyment comes from winning.	7 6 5 4 3 2 1	The social interaction.
19.	I like to associate with people who are dedicated to getting ahead.	7 6 5 4 3 2 1	Easy-going and take life as it comes.
20.	I'm not happy unless I'm always doing something.	7 6 5 4 3 2 1	Frequently, "doing nothing" can be quite enjoyable.
21.	What I enjoy doing most are competitive activities.	7 6 5 4 3 2 1	Noncompetitive pursuits.
TOTAL SCORE 15–21 = _____ = H [See interpretation of "H" at the end of the chapter].			

Source: From John M. Ivancevich and Michael T. Matteson, *Organizational Behavior and Management*, 3rd ed., pp. 274–276. ©1990, 1993 by Richard D. Irwin, Inc. Reproduced by permission of The McGraw-Hill Companies.

See Interpretations at the end of the chapter.

ARE YOU A GOOD PLANNER?

Do you set goals and identify ways to accomplish them? This brief assessment will help you understand how your work habits fit with making plans and setting goals.

Instructions:

Answer the following questions as they apply to your work or study habits. Indicate whether each is Mostly True or Mostly False for you.

	Mostly True	Mostly False
1. I have clear, specific goals in several areas of my life.	_____	_____
2. I have a definite outcome in life I want to achieve.	_____	_____
3. I prefer general to specific goals.	_____	_____
4. I work better without specific deadlines.	_____	_____
5. I set aside time each day or week to plan my work.	_____	_____
6. I am clear about the measures that indicate when I have achieved a goal.	_____	_____
7. I work better when I set more challenging goals for myself.	_____	_____
8. I help other people clarify and define their goals.	_____	_____

Source: Adapted from Richard L. Daft, *Management*, 10th ed., Mason, OH: South-Western Cengage Learning, 2012, p. 177. Used by permission.

See Interpretations at the end of the chapter.

ASSESS

STRESS MANAGEMENT

This survey is designed to help you discover your level of competency in stress management so you can tailor your learning to your specific needs. When you have completed the survey, a scoring key will help you identify the skill areas that are most important for you to master.

Instructions:

Respond to the following statements by writing a number from the rating scale in the column below. Your answers should reflect your attitudes and behavior as they are now, not as you would like them to be. Be honest.

Rating Scale:
6 – *Strongly agree*
5 – *Agree*
4 – *Slightly agree*
3 – *Slightly disagree*
2 – *Disagree*
1 – *Strongly disagree*

When faced with stressful or time-pressured situations:

_____ 1. I use effective time-management methods such as keeping track of my time, making to-do lists, prioritizing, and so on.

_____ 2. I maintain a program of regular exercise for fitness.

_____ 3. I maintain an open, trusting, relationship with someone with whom I can share my frustrations.

_____ 4. I know and practice several temporary relaxation techniques such as deep breathing, muscle relaxation, and so on.

_____ 5. I frequently affirm my priorities so that less important things don't drive out more important things.

_____ 6. I maintain balance in my life by pursuing a variety of interests outside of work.

_____ 7. I have a close relationship with someone who serves as my mentor or advisor.

_____ 8. I effectively use others to accomplish work assignments.

_____ 9. I encourage others to recommend solutions, not just questions, when they come to me with problems or issues.

_____ 10. I strive to redefine problems as opportunities for improvement.

When I delegate tasks to others at work or in other groups:

_____ 11. I make sure that they have the necessary resources and authority to accomplish the tasks.

_____ 12. I specify clearly the level of performance I expect and the degree of initiative the other person should assume.

_____ 13. I continually pass along new information and resources to them to assists in their work.

_____ 14. I make sure that the other person understands completely the results I expect when I delegate tasks.

_____ 15. I always follow up and maintain accountability for delegated tasks.

Scoring:

Add your numerical answers for all 15 items, and write the total here:

TOTAL _____

See Interpretations at the end of the chapter.

TIME-MANAGEMENT ASSESSMENT

While anyone can complete the first section of the instrument, the second section applies primarily to individuals currently serving in some kind of managerial or organizational leadership position.

Instructions:

In responding to the statements below, enter the number that indicates the frequency with which you do each activity. Assess your behavior as it is, not as you would like it to be. How useful this instrument will be to you depends on your ability to accurately assess your own behavior. A scoring key and an interpretation of your scores will be provided.

Rating Scale
0 – Never
1 – Seldom
2 – Sometimes
3 – Usually
4 – Always

SECTION I

_____ 1. I read selectively, skimming the material until I find what is important and highlighting it.

_____ 2. I make a list of tasks to accomplish each day (a to-do list).

_____ 3. I keep everything in a place at work where it can be located.

_____ 4. I prioritize the tasks I have to do during the day according to their importance and urgency.

_____ 5. I concentrate on only one important task at a time, but I do multiple trivial tasks at once (like signing letters while talking on the phone).

_____ 6. I make a list of short five- or ten-minute tasks to do.

_____ 7. Where possible, I divide large projects into smaller, separate stages.

_____ 8. I identify which 20 percent of my tasks will produce 80 percent of the results.

_____ 9. I do the most important tasks at my best time during the day.

_____ 10. I have some time during each day when I can work uninterrupted.

_____ 11. I don't procrastinate. I do it today when it needs to be done.

_____ 12. I keep track of my use of time, with tools such as a time log.

_____ 13. I set deadlines for myself.

_____ 14. I do something productive whenever I am waiting.

_____ 15. I do redundant "busy work" at one set time during the day.

_____ 16. I finish at least one thing every day.

_____ 17. I schedule some time during the day for personal time alone (for planning, meditation, prayer, exercise).

_____ 18. I allow myself to worry about things only at one particular time of the day, not all the time.

_____ 19. I have clearly defined long-term objectives I am working toward.

_____ 20. I continually try to find little ways to improve my efficient use of time.

SECTION II

_____ 1. I hold routine meetings at the end of the day.

_____ 2. I hold all short meetings standing up.

_____ 3. I set a time limit at the outset of each meeting.

_____ 4. I cancel meetings that are scheduled but are not absolutely necessary.

_____ 5. I have a written agenda for every meeting.

_____ 6. I stick to the agenda and reach closure on each item.

_____ 7. Someone is assigned to take minutes and to watch the time in every meeting.

_____ 8. I start all meetings on time.

_____ 9. I have minutes prepared after the meeting and see that follow-up occurs promptly.

_____ 10. When subordinates come to me with a problem, I require that they suggest solutions.

_____ 11. I meet visitors to my office outside of the office or in the doorway.

_____ 12. I go to subordinates' offices when feasible so that I can control when I leave.

_____ 13. I leave at least one-fourth of my day free from meetings and appointments.

_____ 14. I have someone who can answer my calls and greet visitors for me at least some of the time.

_____ 15. I have one place where I can work uninterrupted.

_____ 16. I do something definite with every piece of paper I handle.

_____ 17. I keep my workplace clear of all materials except those I am working on.

_____ 18. I delegate tasks to others.

_____ 19. I specify the amount of personal initiative I want others to take when I assign them tasks.

_____ 20. I am willing to let others get the credit for tasks they accomplish.

Scoring:

Add the numerical answers that you gave for the 20 items in Section 1 and the 20 items in Section II, and write them here:

Section I total_____ Section II total_____

See Interpretations at the end of the chapter.

GO ONLINE to the Griffin/Van Fleet Assessment Library for online versions of these and other assessments.

LEARNING ABOUT TIME-MANAGEMENT SKILLS

Understanding Prioritization
- *Setting Priorities*
- *Misjudging Priorities*

Effective Delegation
- *Reasons for Delegation*
- *Parts of the Delegation Process*
- *Problems in Delegation*
- *Decentralization and Centralization*

Scheduling Meetings and Controlling Intrusions
- *Scheduling and Managing Meetings*
- *Controlling Intrusions*

Managing Stress
- *Causes of Stress*
- *Consequences of Stress*
- *Limiting Stress*

Summary and a Look Ahead

LEARN

Time-management skills refer to the manager's ability to prioritize work, to work efficiently, and to delegate work appropriately. As the pace of managerial work increases and demand on the manager's time grows, it is more important than ever to manage your time effectively. Effective time management allows you to get work done on time, facilitates the work of others, and forestalls problems. But ineffective time management can cause you to miss deadlines, adversely affect the work of others, and create problems throughout the organizations. It can also result in unmanageable stress for both yourself and others. This chapter will help you improve your time- management skills as we discuss prioritization, effective delegation, scheduling and managing meetings, controlling access and intrusion, and managing stress.

UNDERSTANDING PRIORITIZATION

One of the most important ingredients in managing time effectively is the ability to prioritize activities. Prioritization refers to the ability to understand the relative importance of different goals and activities. Suppose that you have two tasks that need to be done. One is to create the executive summary for a major report that is due to your boss tomorrow, and the other is to respond to a marketing survey for a trade association that is in two weeks. It is clear that the first task has a higher priority than the second. Why? It's an important internal document, it's due quickly, and you are accountable to your boss to get it done. You can do it now, and complete the survey tomorrow. If you spend your day completing the survey and don't finish the executive summary, you may face serious repercussions.

Setting Priorities

At virtually any point in time, managers have multiple activities that require their attention and a variety of tasks on which they can be working. The decisions about which activities and tasks to handle and in what order require the ability to prioritize. (In addition, other skills, especially diagnostic and conceptual skills, help managers understand the relative priorities of different activities and tasks). Priorities generally should be based on the following elements:

- Time: When is the activity or task due to be completed? All else equal, activities and tasks with shorter deadlines should be tackled first.
- Responsibility: Who is responsible for the activity or task? Does the manager have to handle it personally, or can she legitimately delegate or assign it to someone else?
- Accountability: To whom is the manager accountable for completing the activity or task? All else equal, accountability to someone at a higher level in the organization should likely take precedence.
- Significance: How important is the activity or task? What are the consequences if it is late?
- Impact on others: Does timely completion of the activity or task impact others? For instance, if a manager is charged with the early work on a report that is not due for six months, but others will be completing the latter parts of it, the manager must know the schedule for their work as well as his own.

Some people find it helpful to maintain a "to-do" list. This list helps them keep track of what they need to do and when it has to be done. The manager can then

time-management skills the manager's ability to prioritize work, to work efficiently, and to delegate appropriately

prioritization the ability to understand the relative importance of different goals and activities

prioritize the activities and tasks using the criteria listed above. Some people feel that they can maintain such a list "in their heads." However, most time-management experts advocate putting the list in writing—either on paper or electronic media—to prevent overlooking inadvertently. Managers must continually update the list as new activities and tasks come up and others are completed. Managers also have individual differences in how they complete their lists. Some people, for example, prefer to start their day by tackling a couple of the easy and quick activities and tasks. This allows them to mark those items off and have a sense of accomplishment as they move on to tougher items. Others prefer to deal with the most challenging things first. The key is to understand what works best for you.

Misjudging Priorities

Even managers with strong time-management skills may occasionally misjudge priorities and subsequently recognize their errors. When this happens, they need to do several things. First, the manager should move the activity or task to the top of the "list" and tackle it immediately. This may allow her or him to meet the deadline by postponing other activities. It also may be possible to marshal additional resources to help. For instance, the manager might be able to call in a "favor" from a colleague and get additional support, or perhaps hire temporary staff.

However, if it becomes apparent that a deadline will be missed, the manager should immediately notify all affected parties of what is going to happen. This notification should include (1) a clear statement that the deadline will be missed, (2) a sincere apology (with an explanation, if appropriate), and (3) an unambiguous statement of when the activity or task will be completed.

EFFECTIVE DELEGATION

Another important element in effective time management is effective delegation. Delegation is the establishment of a pattern of authority between a superior and one or more subordinates. Specifically, **delegation** is the process by which managers assign a portion of their total workload to others.[1]

Reasons for Delegation

delegation the process by which managers assign a portion of their total workload to others

The primary reason for delegation is to enable the manager to get more work done. Subordinates help ease the manager's burden by doing major portions of the organization's work. In some instances, a subordinate may have more expertise in addressing a particular problem than the manager does. For example, the subordinate may have had special training in developing information systems or may be more familiar with a particular product line or geographic area. Delegation also helps develop subordinates. By participating in decision making and problem solving, subordinates learn about overall operations and improve their managerial skills.

Parts of the Delegation Process

In theory, as shown in *Figure 3.1*, the delegation process involves three steps. First, the manager assigns responsibility or gives the subordinate a job to do. The assignment of responsibility might range from telling a subordinate to prepare a report to placing the person in charge of a task force. Along with the assignment, the individual is given the authority to do the job. The manager may give the subordinate the power to obtain needed information from confidential files or to direct a group of other workers. Finally, the manager establishes the subordinate's accountability—that is, the subordinate accepts an obligation to carry out the task assigned by the manager. For instance, the CEO of AutoZone will sign off for the company on financial performance only when the individual manager responsible for each unit has certified his or her own results as being accurate. The firm believes that this high level of accountability will help it avoid the kind of accounting scandal that has hit many businesses in recent times.[2]

MICHAL KOWALSKI /SHUTTERSTOCK.COM

Effective delegation is a key element in time management. This senior manager (left) is delegating a project and explaining its timetable to a member of his team.

FIGURE 3.1 THE DELEGATION PROCESS

Delegation is generally a three-stage process. First, the manager assigns responsibility for a task, decision, activity, or project. Second, the manager grants the authority necessary to meet the responsibility. Finally, accountability is created so that the individual(s) responsible for the task, decision, activity, or project has an obligation to the manager.

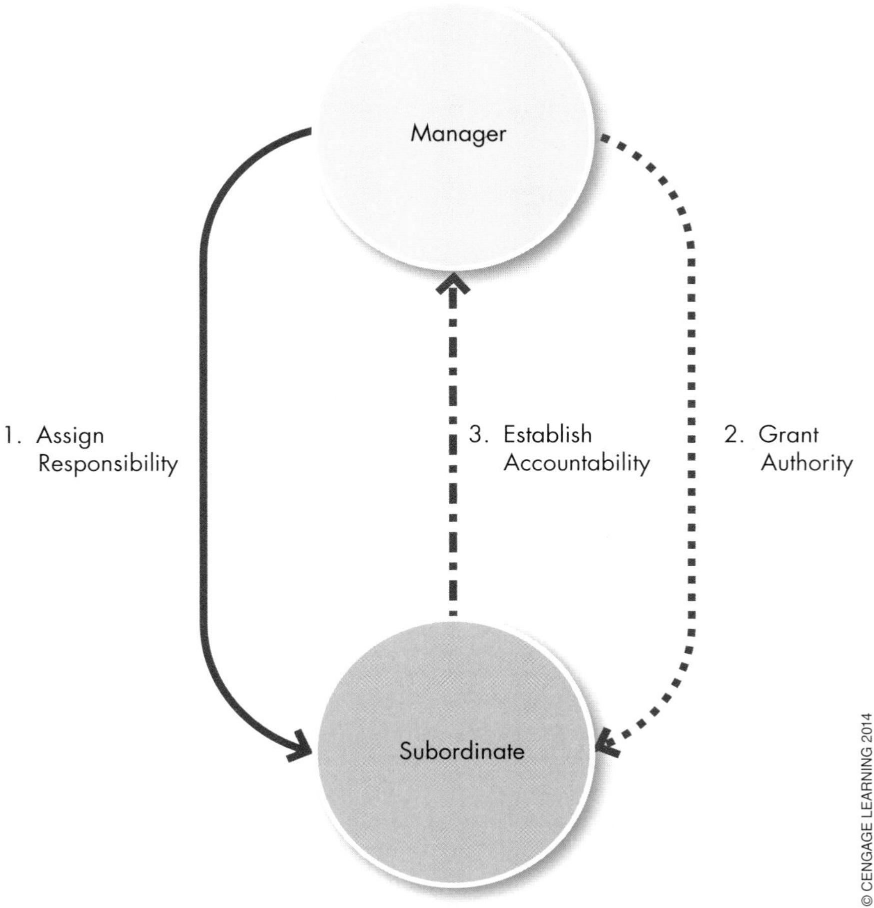

© CENGAGE LEARNING 2014

These three steps do not occur mechanically, however. Indeed, when a manager and a subordinate have developed a good working relationship, the major parts of the process may be implied rather than stated. The manager may simply mention that a particular job must be done. A perceptive subordinate may realize that the manager is actually assigning the job to her. From past experience with the boss, she also may know, without being told, that she has the necessary authority to do the job and that she is accountable to the boss for finishing the job as "agreed."

Problems in Delegation

Unfortunately, problems often arise in the delegation process. For example, a manager may be reluctant to delegate. Some managers are so disorganized that they are unable to plan work in advance and, as a result, cannot delegate appropriately. Other managers may worry that subordinates will do too well and pose a threat to their own advancement. Some managers may not trust the subordinate to do the job well. Finally, some subordinates are reluctant to accept delegation. They may be afraid that failure will result in a reprimand from their superior. They also may perceive that there are no rewards for accepting additional responsibility. Or, they may simply prefer to avoid risk and therefore want their boss to take all responsibility.

Norm Brodsky, a small-business owner who built six successful companies, learned firsthand what happens when the CEO cannot effectively delegate. It took Brodsky seven years to build a messenger service

LEARN

into a $120 million operation—and just 14 months to go from $120 million into bankruptcy. "Where did I go wrong?" he asks rhetorically and then provides his own answer: "The company needed management, stability, and structure, and I kept it from getting them. I was so desperate to sustain the head rush of start-up chaos that I made all the final decisions and didn't let the managers do their jobs. In the end I paid a steep price."[3]

QUOTED IN BLOOMBERG BUSINESSWEEK, JANUARY 16, 2012, P. 49.

There are no quick fixes for these problems. The basic issue is communication. Subordinates must understand their own responsibility, authority, and accountability, and the manager must come to recognize the value of effective delegation. With the passage of time, subordinates should develop to the point at which they can make substantial contributions to the organization. At the same time, managers should recognize that a subordinate's satisfactory performance is not a threat to their own careers, but an accomplishment by both the subordinate who did the job and the manager who trained the subordinate and was astute enough to entrust the subordinate with the project. Ultimate responsibility for the outcome, however, continues to reside with the manager.

> "The only way to get great execution with great ideas is to have guys in our leadership who can really take things to the next level—not wait to hear from me on what the instruction is but to take things to the next level."
>
> STEVE BALLMER
> Microsoft CEO[4]

Decentralization and Centralization

Just as authority can be delegated from one individual to another, organizations also develop patterns of authority across a wide variety of positions and departments. **Decentralization** is the process of systematically delegating power and authority throughout the organization to middle and lower-level managers. It is important to remember that decentralization is actually one end of a continuum anchored at the other end by **centralization**, the process of systematically retaining power and authority in the hands of higher-level managers. A decentralized organization is one in which decision-making power and authority are delegated as far down the chain of command as possible. Conversely, in a centralized organization, decision-making power and authority are retained at the higher levels of management. No organization is ever completely decentralized or completely centralized; some firms position themselves toward one end of the continuum, and some lean the other way.

decentralization the process of systematically delegating power and authority throughout the organization to middle and lower-level managers

centralization the process of systematically retaining power and authority in the hands of higher-level managers

KIMIHIRO HOSHINO/AFP/GETTY IMAGES/NEWSCOM

What factors determine an organization's position on the decentralization–centralization continuum? One common determinant is the organization's external environment. Usually, the greater the complexity and uncertainty of the environment, the greater the tendency to decentralize. Another crucial factor is the history of the organization. Firms have a tendency to do what they have done in the past, so there is likely to be some relationship between what an organization did in its early history and what it chooses to do today in terms of centralization or decentralization. The nature of the decisions to be made also is considered. The costlier and riskier the decisions, the more pressure there is to centralize. Organizations also consider the abilities of lower-level managers. If lower-level managers do not have the ability to make high-quality decisions, there is likely to be a high level of centralization. If lower-level managers are well qualified, top management can take advantage of their talents by decentralizing. In fact, if top management does not decentralize power and authority, talented lower-level managers may leave the organization.[5]

A manager has no clear-cut guidelines for determining whether to centralize or decentralize. Many successful organizations, such as General Electric and Johnson & Johnson, are quite decentralized. Equally successful firms, such as McDonald's and Walmart, have remained centralized. IBM has recently undergone a transformation from using a highly centralized approach to a much more decentralized approach to managing its operations. A great deal of decision-making authority was passed from the hands of a select group of top executives down to six product and marketing groups. The reason for the move was to speed the company's ability to make decisions, introduce new products, and respond to customers. In contrast, Royal Dutch Shell, which has long operated in a highly decentralized manner, has recently gone through several major changes all intended to make the firm more centralized. New CEO Peter Voser went so far as to note that, "fewer people will make strategic decisions."[6] Yahoo! Inc. also has initiated a change toward increased centralization.[7]

> "When you have command and control by the top 10 people, you can only do one or two things at a time. The future is about collaboration and teamwork and making decisions with a process that offers scale, speed, and flexibility."
>
> JOHN CHAMBERS
> Cisco CEO[8]

BUSINESS WEEK, MARCH 23/30, 2009, P. 33.

While meetings should start on time, some people think it's best to wait if others are late. But doing this both rewards those who come late (because they don't miss anything) and punishes those who are on time (because they waste time sitting and waiting on the latecomers). To the extent possible, the meeting organizer should follow the agenda, covering everything that was announced for the meeting but not introducing other topics unless absolutely necessary. The agenda should indicate both a start and an end time, and the meeting organizer should end the meeting as scheduled. Finally, any follow-up actions that individuals at the meeting are to undertake should be carefully noted.

SCHEDULING MEETINGS AND CONTROLLING INTRUSIONS

Scheduling and managing meetings and controlling information and intrusions are also important components of effective time management.

Scheduling and Managing Meetings

Meetings are a normal and frequent part of the day-to-day functioning in any organization. Effectively scheduled and run meetings can be an excellent way to make decisions, discuss issues, resolve conflicts, develop strategies, and communicate information. At the same time, poorly scheduled and run meetings can be an enormous waste of time and a source of irritation. *Table 3.1* summarizes a number of suggestions for effectively scheduling and managing meetings.

Scheduled meetings should be announced with sufficient lead time so that everyone who needs to attend is available to do so. It should also be scheduled in a room conducive to the group that is to meet—it should be convenient for everyone and large and comfortable enough. Some managers suggest that attendees stand for brief meetings. It is useful to send a reminder to everyone shortly before the meeting. Further, most experts suggest sending an agenda ahead of time so that people will know what is to be discussed. Today electronic scheduling techniques make it easier than ever to schedule meetings.

Controlling Intrusions

Another useful practice that can improve time management is to control unexpected intrusions. Most managers like to be available to others in the organization and often talk about having an "open-door" policy, suggesting that people feel free to just drop in. But this practice can lead to a lot of informal conversation that, if allowed to get out of hand, can result in the manager not having enough time to get her or his work done. So, even if a manager wants to have an open-door

YURI ARCURS/SHUTTERSTOCK.COM

Business meetings can be a highly effective way to get things done. At the same time, though, poorly conducted meetings can waste a lot of time.

LEARN

TABLE 3.1 GUIDELINES FOR EFFECTIVE MEETINGS

Hold creative meetings early in the day and routine meetings at the end of the day.
Have attendees stand for short meetings.
Have a time limit.
Schedule meetings regularly, cancel them when not needed.
Have an agenda and take minutes.
Distribute minutes promptly after the meeting and follow up.
If the meeting is to deal with a problem:
Present the problem
• make your presentation of the problem brief
• share all necessary information
• avoid suggesting causes or solutions
• call upon mutual interests
Diagnose the problem
• encourage alternatives
• evaluate alternatives
Generate solutions
• focus on the present
• encourage novelty
Evaluate the solutions
• list advantages/disadvantages, costs/benefits
• find the time to do it right
• choose a solution

© CENGAGE LEARNING 2014

PURESTOCK/AGEFOTOSTOCK

Having people stop by to visit informally can be a good way to communicate. But too many intrusions can waste time and reduce efficiency.

policy it may still be necessary to occasionally close the door to concentrate on a project for a short period of time. Similarly, using a receptionist to screen potential visitors can also be an effective way to control intrusions. For instance, visitors can be asked to schedule an appointment so that meetings can be handled in a systematic fashion rather than an ad hoc basis. Another increasingly common practice for controlling intrusions is for the manager to spend time working away from the office—at home, in a conference room, etc.

Regulating the flow of information is also a useful method for controlling intrusions. Regulating information flow means that people communicating with each other take steps to ensure that overload does not occur. For the sender, this could mean not passing too much information through the system at one time. For the receiver, it might mean calling attention to the fact that he is being asked to do too many things at once. Many managers limit the influx of information by periodically weeding out the list of journals and routine reports they receive, or they use their assistant to screen phone calls and visitors. Some executives get so much email that they have it routed to an assistant. That person reviews the email, discards those that are not useful (such as "spam"), responds to those that are routine, and passes on to the manager only those that require her or his personal attention.

stress an individual's response to a strong stimulus

MANAGING STRESS

Another important consideration for time management in organizations is stress. As illustrated in *Figure 3.2*, stress and time management affect each other in a cyclical and mutually reinforcing manner. For example, if poor time management results in the manager falling behind on important projects, her or his stress will likely increase. Too much stress can lead to the manager not being able to manage his or her time effectively, causing further delays.

Stress is an individual's response to a strong stimulus.[9] This stimulus is called a *stressor*. Stress generally follows a cycle referred to as the General Adaptation Syndrome, or GAS,[10] shown in *Figure 3.3*. According to this view, when an individual first encounters a stressor, the GAS is initiated, and the Stage 1 alarm is activated. He may feel panic, wonder how to cope, and feel helpless. For example, suppose a manager is told to prepare a detailed evaluation of a plan by his firm to buy one of its competitors. His first reaction may be, "How will I ever get this done by tomorrow?"

If the stressor is too intense, the individual may feel unable to cope and never really try to respond to its demands. In most cases, however, after a short period of alarm, the individual gathers some strength and starts to resist the negative effects of the stressor. For example, the manager with the evaluation to write may calm down, call home to say he is working late, roll up his sleeves, order out for coffee, and get to work. Thus, at Stage 2 of the GAS, the person is resisting the effects of the stressor.

In many cases, the resistance phase may end the GAS. If the manager is able to complete the evaluation earlier than expected, he may drop it in his briefcase, smile to himself, and head home tired but satisfied.

FIGURE 3.2 THE TIME-MANAGEMENT STRESS CYCLE

Stress and time management are interrelated. For instance, poor time management can cause a person to get behind on his or her obligations, with a commensurate increase in stress. Additional stress, further, can result in further inefficient time management, only leading to more stress. On the other hand, effective time management and help limit stress, and effective stress management can help someone work more efficiently.

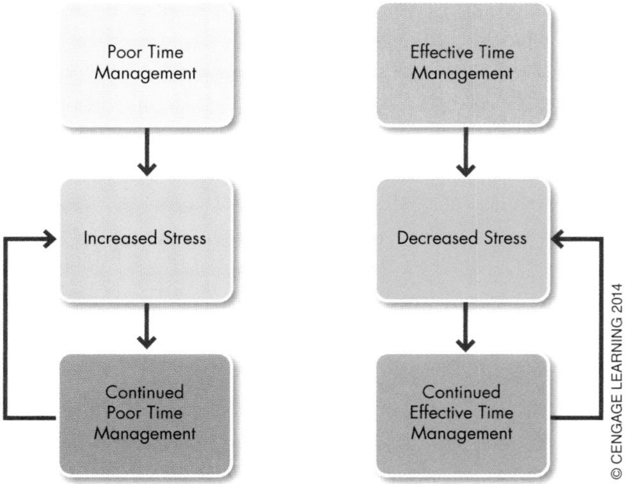

© CENGAGE LEARNING 2014

FIGURE 3.3 THE GENERAL ADAPTATION SYNDROME

The General Adaptation Syndrome represents the normal process by which we react to stressful events. At Stage 1 (alarm), we feel panic, and our level of resistance to stress drops. Stage 2 (resistance) represents our efforts to confront and control the stressful circumstance. If we fail, we may eventually reach Stage 3 (exhaustion) and just give up or quit.

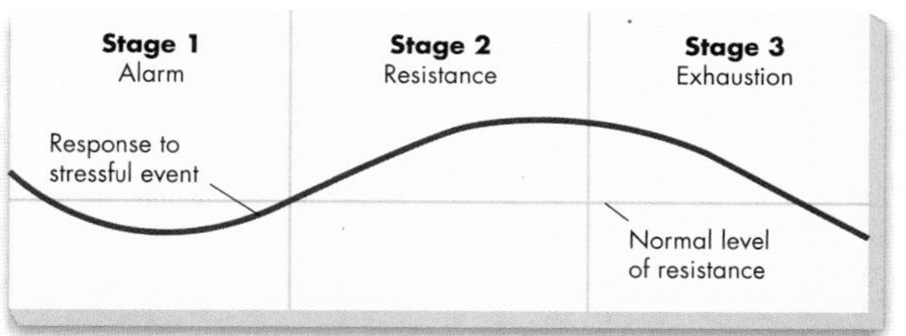

© CENGAGE LEARNING 2014

On the other hand, prolonged exposure to a stressor without resolution may bring on Stage 3 of the GAS—exhaustion. At this stage, the individual literally gives up and can no longer resist the stressor. The manager, for example, might fall asleep at his desk at 3:00 A.M. and never finish the evaluation.

Stress is not always bad. In the absence of stress, we may experience lethargy and stagnation. An optimal level of stress, on the other hand, can result in motivation and excitement. Too much stress, however, can have negative consequences. It is also important to understand that stress can be caused by "good" as well as "bad" things. Excessive pressure, unreasonable demands on our time, and bad news can all cause stress. But receiving a bonus and then having to decide what to do with the money also can be stressful. So, too, can receiving a promotion, gaining recognition, and similar good things.

One important line of thinking about stress focuses on Type A and Type B personalities.[11] Type A individuals are extremely competitive, very devoted to work, and have a strong sense of urgency. They are likely to be aggressive, impatient, and very work oriented. They have a lot of drive and want to accomplish as much as possible as quickly as possible. Type B individuals are less competitive, less devoted to work, and have a weaker sense of urgency. Such individuals are less likely to experience conflict with other people and more likely to have a balanced, relaxed

General Adaptation Syndrome Three-stage process of alarm, resistance, and exhaustion

Type A individuals who are extremely competitive, very devoted to work, and have a strong sense of time urgency

Type B individuals who are less competitive, less devoted to work, and have a weaker sense of time urgency

LEARN

approach to life. They are able to work at a constant pace without urgency. Type B people are not necessarily more or less successful than are Type A people, but they are less likely to experience stress. Moreover, Type A people may react more negatively when they fall behind schedule or encounter delays in getting things accomplished.

"...your people will be very influenced by how you carry yourself under stress."

LLOYD BLANKFEIN
Chairman and CEO
Goldman Sachs[12]

FORTUNE, JULY 6, 2010, P. 44.

Causes of Stress

Work-related stressors fall into one of four categories—task, physical, role, and interpersonal demands. These are illustrated in *Figure 3.4*. *Task demands* are associated with the task itself. Some occupations are inherently more stressful than others. Situations that can make some jobs more stressful are having to make fast decisions, decisions with less than complete information, or decisions that have relatively serious consequences. The jobs of surgeon, airline pilot, and stockbroker are relatively more stressful than the jobs of general practitioner, baggage handler, and office receptionist. Although a general practitioner makes important decisions, he is also likely to have time to make a considered diagnosis and fully explore a number of different treatments. During surgery, though, the surgeon must make decisions quickly while realizing that the wrong one may endanger her patient's life.

Physical demands are stressors associated with the job setting. Working outdoors in extremely hot or cold temperatures, or even in an improperly heated or cooled office, can lead to stress. Likewise, jobs that have rotating work shifts make it difficult for people to have stable sleep patterns. A poorly designed office that makes it difficult for people to have privacy or promotes too little social interaction can result in stress, as can poor lighting and inadequate work surfaces. Even more severe are jobs that pose threats to one's health. Examples include coal mining, poultry processing, and toxic waste handling. Similarly, some jobs carry risks associated with higher incident rates of violence such as armed robberies. Examples include law enforcement officers, taxi drivers, and convenience store clerks.

Role demands can also cause stress. A role is a set of expected behaviors associated with a position in a group or organization. Stress can result from either role conflict or role ambiguity that people can experience in groups. For example, an employee who is feeling pressure from her boss to work longer hours or to travel more, while also being asked by her family for more time at home, will almost certainly experience stress

FIGURE 3.4 CAUSES OF WORK STRESS

There are several causes of work stress in organizations. Four general sets of organizational stressors are task demands, physical demands, role demands, and interpersonal demands.

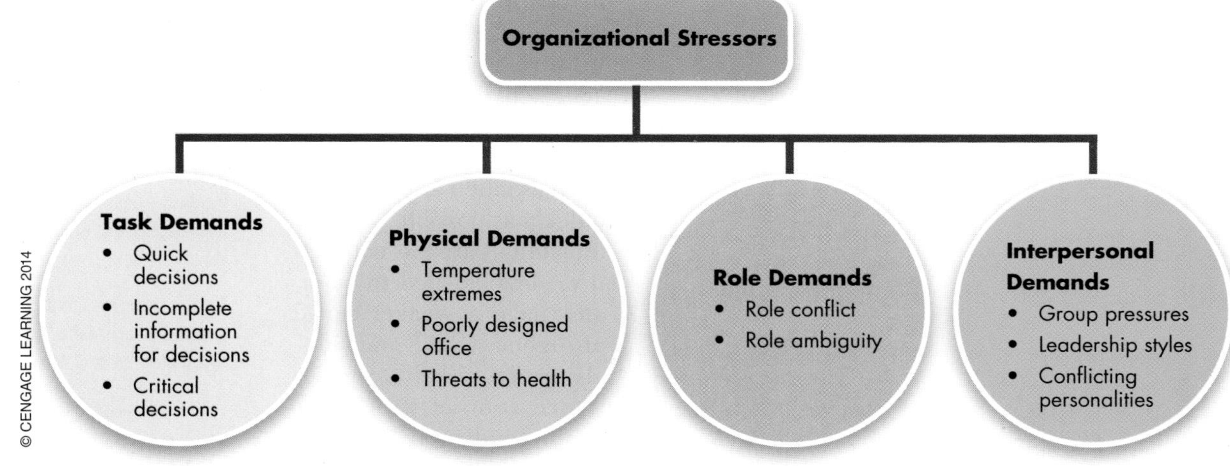

© CENGAGE LEARNING 2014

as a result of role conflict.[13] Similarly, a new employee experiencing role ambiguity because of poor orientation and training practices by the organization will also suffer from stress. Excessive meetings are also a potential source of stress.[14] While job cuts and layoffs during the 2008–2009 recession focused on the stress experienced by those losing their jobs (and appropriately so), many of the managers imposing the layoffs experienced stress as well.[15]

Interpersonal demands are stressors associated with relationships that confront people in organizations. For example, group pressures regarding restriction of output and norm conformity can lead to stress. Leadership styles may also cause stress. An employee who feels a strong need to participate in decision making may feel stress if his boss refuses to allow participation. And individuals with conflicting personalities may experience stress if required to work too closely together. For example, a person with an internal locus of control might be frustrated when working with someone who prefers to wait and just let things happen.[17]

> *"Some of [the people I laid off] I'd worked with for a very long time. I saw such pain in their faces, but felt I couldn't show my emotions to them....As soon as I could, I'd close the door, draw the blinds, and have a good sob."*
>
> ALICIA SANERA
> HR Executive[16]

USA TODAY, APRIL 23, 2009, P. 5D.

Consequences of Stress

As noted earlier, the results of stress may be positive or negative. The negative consequences may be behavioral, psychological, or medical. Behavioral stress may lead to detrimental or harmful actions, such as smoking, alcohol or drug abuse, and overeating. Other stress-induced behaviors are accident proneness, violence toward self or others, and appetite disorders. Substance abuse is also a potential consequence.[18]

GREG PEASE/GETTY IMAGES

Psychological consequences of stress interfere with an individual's mental health and well-being. These outcomes include sleep disturbances, depression, family problems, and sexual dysfunction. Managers are especially prone to sleep disturbances when they experience stress at work.[19] Medical consequences of stress affect an individual's physiological well-being. Heart disease and stroke have been linked to stress, as have headaches, backaches, ulcers, and skin conditions such as acne and hives.

Individual stress also has direct consequences for businesses. For an operating employee, stress may translate into poor-quality work and lower productivity. For a manager, it may mean faulty decision making and disruptions in working relationships.[20] Withdrawal behaviors can also result from stress. People who are having difficulties with stress in their jobs are more likely to call in sick or to leave the organization. More subtle forms of withdrawal may also occur. A manager may start missing deadlines or taking longer lunch breaks. Employees also may withdraw by developing feelings of indifference. The irritation displayed by people under great stress can make them difficult to get along with. Job satisfaction, morale, and commitment can all suffer as a result of excessive levels of stress. So, too, can motivation to perform.

Another consequence of stress is **burnout**—a feeling of exhaustion that may develop when someone experiences too much stress for an extended period. Burnout results in constant fatigue, frustration, and helplessness. Increased rigidity follows, as do a loss of self-confidence and

burnout a feeling of exhaustion that may develop when someone experiences too much stress for an extended period of time

LEARN

psychological withdrawal. The individual dreads going to work, often puts in longer hours but gets less accomplished than before, and exhibits mental and physical exhaustion. Because of the damaging effects of burnout, some firms are taking steps to help employees avoid it. For example, British Airways provides all of its employees with training designed to help them recognize the symptoms of burnout and develop strategies for avoiding it.

LEARN

Limiting Stress

Given the potential consequences of stress, it follows that both people and organizations should be concerned about how to limit its more damaging effects. Numerous ideas and approaches have been developed to help manage stress. As summarized in *Table* 3.2, some are strategies for individuals while others are strategies for organizations.[21]

POLARIC/SHUTTERSTOCK.COM

One way people manage stress is through exercise. People who exercise regularly feel less tension and stress, are more self-confident, and feel more optimistic. Their better physical condition also makes them less susceptible to many common illnesses. People who do not exercise regularly, tend to feel more stress and are more likely to be depressed. They are also more likely to have heart attacks. And, because of their physical condition, they are more likely to become ill.

Another method people use to manage stress is relaxation. Relaxation allows individuals to adapt to, and therefore better deal with, their stress. Relaxation comes in many forms, such as taking regular vacations and engaging in non-work activities on the weekends. A recent study found that people's attitudes toward a variety of workplace characteristics improved significantly following a weekend when they were able to fully disengage from their work.[22] People can also learn to relax while on the job. For example, some experts recommend that people take regular rest breaks during their normal workday.

ANDRESR/SHUTTERSTOCK.COM

As noted earlier, people also can use time management to control stress. The idea behind time management is that many daily pressures can be reduced or eliminated if individuals do a better job of managing time. Finally, people can manage stress through support groups. A support group can be as simple as a group of family members or friends. Going out after work with a couple of coworkers to a basketball game or a movie, for example, can help relieve stress built up during the day. Family and friends can help people cope with stress on an ongoing basis and during times of crisis. For example, an employee who has just learned that she did not get the promotion she has been working toward for months may find it helpful to have a good friend to lean on, talk to, or vent their frustrations with. People also may seek more formal support groups. Community centers or churches, for example, may sponsor support groups for people who have recently gone through a divorce, the death of a loved one, or some other difficult situation.

Organizations are also beginning to realize that they should be involved in helping employees cope with stress. One argument for this is that, because the business is at least partially responsible for stress, it should also help relieve it. Another is that stress-related insurance claims by employees can cost the organization considerable sums of money. Still another is that workers experiencing lower levels of detrimental stress will be able to function more effectively. AT&T has initiated a series of seminars and workshops to help its employees cope with the stress they face in their jobs. The firm was prompted to develop these seminars for all three of the reasons noted above.

A wellness stress program is a special part of the organization specifically created to help deal with stress. Organizations have adopted stress-management programs, health promotion programs, and other kinds of programs for this purpose. The AT&T seminar program noted earlier is similar to this idea, but true wellness programs are ongoing activities that have a number of different components. They commonly include exercise-related activities as well as classroom instruction programs dealing with smoking cessation, weight reduction, and general stress management.

Some companies develop their own wellness programs or use existing programs. Johns Manville, for example, has a gym at its corporate headquarters. Other firms negotiate discounted health club membership rates with local establishments. For the instructional part of the program, the organization can again either sponsor its own training or jointly sponsor seminars with a local YMCA, civic

TABLE 3.2 METHODS AND TECHNIQUES FOR MANAGING STRESS

Plan Goals
Keep long-term goals in mind even when doing small tasks and unpleasant activities.
Review and revise your longer-term goals periodically—don't worry if they change.
Review your shorter-term goals frequently and identify activities to do each day to accomplish those goals.
Prioritize
Priority refers to importance in accomplishing longer-term goals—just because something is due "tomorrow" doesn't mean that it is a priority item.
Use a daily "to do" list of specific items to complete each day.
Arrange tasks in priority order [A = highest priority, that is the most likely to move you toward achieving your goals; B = intermediate priority; C = lowest priority]
Try to do A goals, not Bs or Cs.
Use a "C drawer" for storage of those items which you do not immediately throw away.
Use the "80–20" rule or Pareto's Law as a reminder to keep focused on those things which are highest priority (80% of your goal accomplishment will come from 20% of your activities—the A items)
Do not skip items on the daily "to do" list just because they are difficult or unpleasant.
Use your workplace area for work, not storage; put the most important thing in the center of the work area.
Analyze
Examine old habits for possible elimination or streamlining.
Keep a diary or time log to help you identify your major problems and opportunities.
Identify the portion of the day when you are most creative or productive and try to schedule routine meetings and administrative duties at other times.
Use Techniques
Give up waiting time—consider it a gift of time to relax, plan, or do something that you would otherwise not have had time to do.
Carry blank 3 × 5 cards or a small notebook to jot down ideas and notes.
Concentrate on only one thing at a time.
Set deadlines for yourself and others.
Delegate where feasible and practicable, given the time demands on others.
Screen visitors, mail, and phone calls, when possible.
Write replies directly on original memos or letters (keep a copy for yourself or keep the original and send the copy).
Be considerate of others' time as you want them to be considerate of yours. Generate as little paperwork as possible, and throw away as much as possible.
Do something with each piece of paper you handle—route to someone else, request other information before completion is possible, etc. (This is sometimes referred to as "handling each piece of paper only once.")
Have a Time-Management Philosophy
Take time to relax and do non-work activities, especially at night and on weekends.
Remember the importance of interpersonal networks—don't cut off your friends.
Always keep in mind that it is time quality, not quantity, that matters.

© CENGAGE LEARNING 2014

LEARN

organization, or church. Organization-based fitness programs facilitate employee exercise, a very positive consideration, but such programs are also quite costly. Still, more and more companies develop fitness programs for employees. Similarly, some companies offer their employees periodic sabbaticals—extended breaks from work that presumably allow people to revitalize and reenergize themselves. Intel and McDonald's are among the firms offering the benefit.[23]

SUMMARY AND A LOOK AHEAD

After reading and studying this chapter, you should have a better understanding of time management. For example, you should have a clearer perspective on how to set priorities and what to do if you misjudge them. You should understand effective delegation, another central part of effective time management, and you should be better equipped to schedule and run meetings and to control intrusions into your schedule. Finally, you should better understand how time management relates to stress, know the causes and consequences of stress, and how to limit stress.

The remainder of this chapter provides opportunities for you to continue to develop and refine your time-management skills. For instance, you will be directed to resources where you can visualize both effective and less effective time management. Subsequent sections provide several different opportunities for you to practice and explore time-management skills from different perspectives. The chapter concludes with some additional assessment and interpretation data.

VISUALIZE

VISUALIZING TIME-MANAGEMENT SKILLS

TIME-MANAGEMENT SKILLS IN ACTION—1

Your Assignment

Consider the two BizFlix film clips for this chapter.

Dr. Seuss' *How the Grinch Stole Christmas* (2000) is a loose adaptation of the story, but recognizable nonetheless. Whoville, a magical, mythical land, features the Whos who love Christmas and the Grinch (Jim Carrey) who hates it. The Grinch is a nasty creature who plots to steal Christmas away from the Whos whom he equally detests. A small child, Cindy Lou Who (Taylor Momsen), tries to befriend the Grinch and bring him back to the Yuletide celebrations, an effort that backfires on all involved.

Played (2006) is about the London underworld and its criminal underground. One of those criminals, Ray Burns (Mick Rossi), does prison time for a crime he did not commit. After serving eight years, he is released and focuses his attention on getting even with his enemies. This fast-moving film peers deeply into London's criminal world, which includes some crooked London police, especially Detective Brice (Vinnie Jones). The film's unusual ending reviews all major parts of the plot.

Note how time-management skills are shown in these two scenes.

1. In the first clip, you see both positive and negative time management from the Grinch. He keeps a schedule book to organize his time but then wastes time procrastinating over the decision to accept the invitation from Cindy Lou Who. Does the Grinch's behavior remind you of time-management skills you or others have used?
2. In the second clip, the importance of time management to planning, even planning a criminal endeavor, is clear as Ray says, "OK, what we got, guys? Nathan. One, two, three, four moves, okay?" Each move must be carefully timed to accomplish the caper successfully. Can you suggest how these characters could have handled time management differently in planning the caper?

TIME-MANAGEMENT SKILLS IN ACTION—2

This exercise gives you an opportunity to think about time-management skills that may be involved in the management positions you will have in the future.

Your Assignment

1. Think about time-management skills and try to identify a scene that illustrates a positive or effective use of such skills in a movie, a TV show, or perhaps a video on YouTube.
2. Now do the same for a scene that illustrates a negative or ineffective use of such skills.

Share your results with the class and discuss how each clip shows the positive and negative use of time-management skills. You should also suggest how the negative situation could have been changed for the better.

PRACTICING YOUR TIME-MANAGEMENT SKILLS

PRACTICE

CONTROLLING YOUR OWN WORK

Time-management skills play a major role in the control function of managers. They can use those skills to more effectively control their own work. This exercise helps demonstrate the relationship between time-management skills and control.

Assume you are a middle manager in a small manufacturing plant. Today is Monday, your first day back from a one-week vacation. The first thing you discover is that your assistant will not be in the office today because he is out of town for his aunt's funeral. He did, however, leave you the following note:

Dear Boss:

Sorry I could not be here today. Here are some things you need to know before I return tomorrow:

(a) *Ms. Jantzen [your boss] wants to see you today at 4:00.*

(b) *The shop steward wants to see you ASAP about a labor problem.*

(c) *George Littman [big customer] has a complaint about a recent shipment.*

(d) *Jolene Fajinski [major supplier] wants to discuss a change in the delivery schedule.*

(e) *Mr. Prescott from the Chamber of Commerce wants you to attend a breakfast meeting on Wednesday and discuss our expansion plans.*

(f) *The legal office wants to discuss our upcoming OSHA inspection.*

(g) *HR wants to know when you can interview someone for the new supervisor's position.*

(h) *Jack Williams, the machinist you fired last month, has been hanging around the parking lot.*

Your Assignment

1. Explain the difference between importance and timeliness.
2. Try to prioritize the work into three categories: very timely, moderately timely, and less timely.

3. Explain what additional information you need before you can prioritize the individual tasks effectively.
4. Consider how your approach would differ if your secretary had come in today.

BALANCING URGENT AND IMPORTANT TASKS

This exercise allows you to assess your current time-management skills and to improve them by prioritizing your tasks and other activities.

Effective managers must be prepared to switch between basic activities in the management process. They also must be able to fulfill a number of different roles in their organizations and employ many different managerial skills as they do so. In addition, managers' schedules are busy and full of complex, unpredictable, and brief tasks, requiring managers to "switch gears" frequently throughout a workday.

Stephen Covey, management consultant and author of *The 7 Habits of Highly Effective People* and other best-selling books, has developed a way of prioritizing tasks. He uses the terms *urgent* and *important* to characterize tasks. **Urgent tasks** are those that must be done right away, such as tasks that have an approaching deadline. **Important tasks** are those that are critical; that is, tasks that have a big impact on key areas of one's life. Covey claims that most people spend too much time on tasks that are urgent when they should instead give high priority to tasks that are important. He asserts that workers who concentrate on urgent tasks meet their deadlines but may neglect critical areas such as long-term planning. These workers may also neglect critical areas of their personal lives. To help managers make better use of their time, Covey developed a 2 × 2 matrix to illustrate how tasks fall into one of four quadrants: (1) both urgent and important, (2) not urgent but important, (3) not important but urgent, or (4) neither urgent nor important.

Covey claims that those who spend most of their time in Quadrant 1 may be meeting their deadlines but are not making good long-term use of time. Over time, people who stay in Quadrant 1 most of the time will become consumed by problems. If you spend a large proportion of time in Quadrant 1, you are likely to experience stress, which may lead you to escape by engaging in Quadrant 4 activities. Minimize time spent in Quadrant 1. Instead, spend some time in Quadrant 2 to get ahead of your problems through better planning and preparation.

Folks who send much of their time in Quadrant 2 tend to be effective in their personal and professional lives. They are proactive, focused on opportunities rather than problems. They often make profound and positive changes in the people and organizations around them. It is virtually impossible to spend too much time in this quadrant. If you spend a high proportion of your time here, you are in control, balanced, disciplined, experience few crises, and remain focused on your long-term vision.

A person who spends a lot of time in Quadrant 3 feels and is busy; but, looking back, this person has accomplished little. You may enjoy pleasing others and being needed, but you also need to spend time on your own long-term goals. Too much time spent in Quadrant 3 can leave you feeling frustrated or even victimized as you try to meet the expectations of others. Other results of Quadrant 3 activities can include feeling out of touch with your own feelings or goals, feeling worthless, and experiencing shallow relationships. Engage in some Quadrant 3 activities, but be sure to balance that time with activities in Quadrant 2.

Quadrant 4 is perhaps the most dangerous quadrant. People who spend too much time in Quadrant 4 are irresponsible, neglecting themselves and others. If Quadrant 4 activities account for a very large proportion of your time, you likely have broken relationships, are dependent on others for basic support, and have difficulty completing courses or holding a job. If you spend a moderately large amount of time spent in Quadrant 4, you need to improve your time-management skills. Minimize Quadrant 4 activities and spend the time in Quadrant 2, if possible. If you do engage in some trivial activities, make sure that you truly enjoy them and limit the time spent.

Effective managers can balance the demands of their urgent tasks with an understanding of the need to spend an appropriate amount of time on those tasks that are important.

Your Assignment

1. On a separate sheet of paper, draw a 2 × 2 cell matrix (below) that reflects Covey's ideas about time management:

	URGENT	NOT URGENT
IMPORTANT	Quadrant 1 **"The Quadrant of Necessity"**	Quadrant 2 **"The Quadrant of "Leadership"**
NOT IMPORTANT	Quadrant 3 **"The Quadrant of Deception"**	Quadrant 4 **"The Quadrant of Waste"**

2. What portion of your time do you spend in each quadrant? In each cell of the matrix, list some of your activities over the last day or several days.
   (a) In Quadrant 1 (Necessity) list items such as emergencies, work crises, problems, tasks with near deadlines, and last-minute tasks.
   (b) In Quadrant 2 (Leadership) list activities that were aimed at accomplishing long-term goals or preventing problems. For example, exercise prevents future health problems, while time spent on building important family relationships or friendships accomplishes a key long-term goal. Other examples include planning, preparation, getting a start on tasks with far-off deadlines, recreation and stress relief, and exploring new opportunities and ideas.
   (c) In Quadrant 3 (Deception) lists tasks that had urgent deadlines but in fact did not help you to accomplish important goals, such as time spent on other people's problems, routine meetings and reports, and interruptions. Parties, social activities, and anything you feel "pressured" to do may also fit in Quadrant 3.
   (d) Quadrant 4 (Waste) is also called The Quadrant of Default because people tend to default to Quadrant 4 activities to avoid activities in other quadrants: watching television, surfing the Web, instant messaging, chatting aimlessly, reading junk mail, and so on. Anything done to excess can be put in Quadrant 4.
3. What is one thing that you can do today to make better use of your time? Try it and see if your time-management skills improve.

PRACTICE

Daily Time Log

1. HOW are you spending your time? Don't rely on memory—systematically find out by using a DAILY TIME LOG. Complete the log for at least one day—preferably a week.

Daily Time Log				
			Check here if	
Time	Activity	Comments*	Job	Non-Job
8:01 - 8:15				
8:16 - 8:30				
8:31 - 8:45				
8:46 - 9:00				
9:01 - 9:15				
9:16 - 9:30				
9:31 - 9:45				
9:46 - 10:00				
10:01 - 10:15				
10:16 - 10:30				
10:31 - 10:45				
10:46 - 11:00				
11:01 - 11:15				
11:16 - 11:30				
11:31 - 11:45				
11:46 - 12:00				
12:01 - 12:15				
12:16 - 12:30				
12:31 - 12:45				
12:46 - 1:00				
1:01 - 1:15				
1:16 - 1:30				
1:31 - 1:45				
1:46 - 2:00				
2:01 - 2:15				
2:16 - 2:30				
2:31 - 2:45				
2:46 - 3:00				
3:01 - 3:15				
3:16 - 3:30				
3:31 - 3:45				
3:46 - 4:00				
4:01 - 4:15				
4:16 - 4:30				
4:31 - 4:45				
4:46 - 5:00				
5:01 - 5:15				
5:16 - 5:30				
5:31 - 5:45				
5:46 - 6:00				

PRACTICE

*For example: Who initiated the activity—superior, subordinate, peer, family member, client? Was the activity important or urgent? Was it "delegated in" to you? Did you "delegate out" to someone else?

2. After completing several daily time logs (we recommend a week of them), use the following Activity Summary to organize and summarize your findings.

Activity Summary								
	Person or Group Involved							
Activity	Sub	Sup	Peer	Civic	Family	Importance	Urgency	Delegate?
Desk Work:								
Letters								
Memos								
Reports								
Periodicals								
Books								
Other								
Phone Calls:								
Initiated								
Received								
Tours								
Co. Meetings:								
Scheduled								
Unscheduled								
Travel:								
Inside Co.								
Outside Co.								
Civic								
Family								
Other								

3. Once you complete the exercises "Desired Behavior" and "Personal Goal Sheet," try to estimate the degree or extent to which each activity contributes to your particular goals. Mark any activities that are not making substantial contributions ("time wasters") and try to eliminate them. This should help ensure that all of your activities contribute to your goals.

DEMANDS THAT CAUSE STRESS

Stress is very common both in organizations and in non-work settings, such as school or family life. We attribute much of our stress to "just the nature of the job." However, you can reduce a significant amount of stress by managing your time more effectively. Thus, you need to learn time-management skills.

This exercise will help you analyze your work or personal life for the purpose of identifying and removing causes of stress.

PRACTICE

Your Assignment

1. Working alone, assess the *task demands* associated with your management class. In this category, include items such as the extent to which you are fully informed and can, therefore, make informed decisions about your job duties and responsibilities. Also consider the time pressure and the possible consequences of your actions.
2. Assess the *physical demands* associated with your management class. In this category, include items such as the location of facilities available in the classroom. Also include lighting, heating, ventilation, seating, amount of space, flexibility of the space, and so on.
3. Assess the *role demands* associated with your management class. In this category, consider the role that you play as a student. Do you understand what is expected of you in this role? Are you comfortable in this role? Does your role as a student conflict with any of the other important roles that you play?
4. Assess the *interpersonal demands* associated with your management class. In this category, consider your relationship with the instructor and with your classmates. Any personality conflicts or pressure to conform to group norms would tend to increase stress.
5. In small groups, discuss your answers and try to recognize patterns of similarities and differences. Then discuss changes that could be made to reduce stress. Be sure to consider changes that could be made by your institution or department, by your instructor, and by the students.
6. Discuss your group conclusions with the class and with your instructor.

PRACTICE

STAIRCASING YOUR GOALS

To decide how to spend your time now, you must first determine what you really want to accomplish—your long-term goals. One way to do this is to use a means-end staircase.

Your Assignment

Use a diagram like the one below to chart your major goals from long-term (3–5 years) to medium-term (1–3 years) to short-term (from now to one year).

(A) Beginning on the right, identify your highest priority LONG-term goal (1).

(B) Working backwards, identify several MEDIUM-term goals (1, 1 and 1, 2 and 1, 3 etc.) that will be the means to achieving your one LONG-term goal.

(C) Working backwards again, on the left, identify several SHORT-term goals (1, 1, 1 and 1, 1, 2 plus 1, 2, 1 and 1, 2, 2 plus 1, 3, 1 and 1, 3, 2, etc.) that will be the submeans for achieving MEDIUM-term goals 1, 1 and 1, 2 and 1, 3.

(D) Now repeat this for your second priority LONG-term goal (2).

(E) You should repeat this for all of your high priority long-term goals (there should not be very many of them if they really are high priority).

To use a means-end staircase, after building it starting on the right, you implement it starting on the left. Doing what it takes to accomplish your short-term goals automatically helps you to accomplish your medium-term goals. In like manner, accomplishing your medium-term goals helps you to accomplish your long-term goals.

Things change, though. So you should repeat this exercise every year or so to adjust your means and ends to respond to such changes.

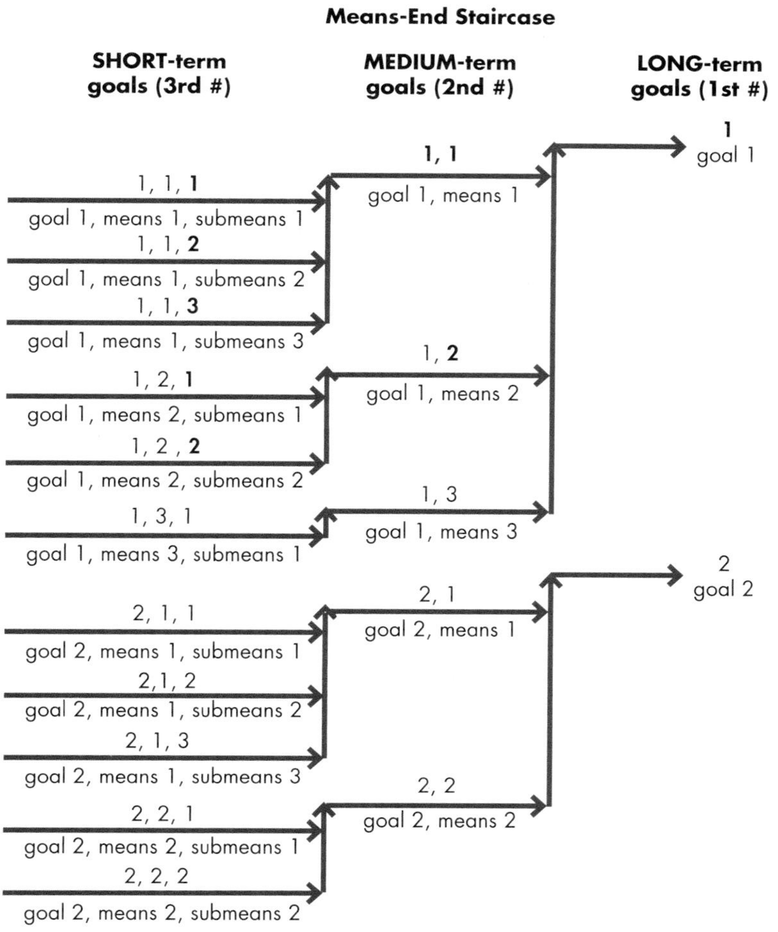

PRACTICE

EFFECTIVENESS OF COMMUNICATION EXCHANGES

This exercise helps you develop your time-management skills as they relate to communication.

Communication is a vital part not only of management but also of our daily lives. We benefit when communication takes place in effective ways, but ineffective communication can be a major source of wasted time and energy.

Your Assignment

1. Reflect back on your communication for one day. Write down with whom you talked, when, for how long, and about what subjects:
   - … in face-to-face and telephone conversations
   - … in mail or email messages that you received or sent
   - … in text messages that you received or sent
2. Evaluate each communication exchange as being more valuable or less valuable.
3. Estimate how much time you spent on less-valuable communication.

4. Decide how you could have either avoided those less-valuable communication exchanges or made them more valuable.
5. Consider how much control we really have over our communication.

HOW IS TIME BEING SPENT?

This exercise allows you to analyze a daily time log to determine how time-management skills could be improved.

Your Assignment

The following is from a one-day time log of a busy executive.

1. How much of the time was (1) personal, (2) family, (3) school, and (4) work?
2. In the personal category, how much was time was spent on leisure/relaxation and how much on personal growth (education/development)?
3. In the work category, how much time was spent on various subcategories such as (A) alone, one-on-one, or group; and (B) with subordinates, peers, superiors, and so on?
4. Finally, what suggestions could you make to this executive for improving his/her time-management skills?

Time Log, Jim Atcheson, Tuesday, October 14	
5:00 a.m.	Awoke; took care of bathroom affairs; got dressed
5:30	Picked up newspaper; fixed breakfast
6:00	Read paper; ate breakfast; relaxed
6:30	Got family "up and at 'em"
6:45	Got breakfast for children; helped children find school supplies
7:00	Helped get children ready for school
7:15	Left for office; picked up coffee on the way; called assistant
8:00	Arrived at work; stopped by several offices to greet peers and touch base
8:30	Arrived at own office; went "to do" list
8:45	Worked through email; returned phone call from late yesterday
9:00	Assistant arrived with mail; sorted mail; continued going through email
9:15	Scanned several articles for ideas to help with current issues and read one more closely
9:30	Transferred notes from last evening to report template
10:00	Delegated report to assistant for completion
10:05	Scanned reports from various units in the organization; noted several issues for follow-up
10:40	Restroom break; picked up coffee from vending machine to take back to office
10:50	Stopped in hall by colleague to discuss problem
11:00	Subordinate waiting in office with concern
11:15	Began writing emails and memos to peers and subordinates about issues noted in the unit reports

PRACTICE

STRESSFUL JOBS

Time-management and other skills are closely linked to stress and stressful jobs. As one example, the failure to manage time effectively leads to missed deadlines and work backup, and the lack of technical and other skills can interfere with the successful performance of a job. Both of these, in turn, create additional stress. The more stressful the job, the more you need to manage your time effectively and avoid more stress. But the ability to manage time can depend heavily on an employee's skills or lack of skills for performing the job effectively and in a timely manner. This exercise should give you an opportunity to identify the similar or different skills needed in high- and low-stress jobs.

Your Assignment

1. Individuals: Identify the ten *most* stressful and the ten *least* stressful jobs you can think of (they must be real jobs). Put them in order of their stress levels, and indicate why you classified each of them as you did.
2. Small groups: Your instructor will now organize the class into teams. Each team should discuss the lists of each team member and develop a group list of the five jobs that are considered most stressful and the five considered the least stressful.
3. Entire class: Share the team lists with the whole class (oral "reports," writing on charts or whiteboards, or using shared computer technology). Then discuss the skills necessary in these ten jobs, noting similarities and differences in skills that are needed in the most stressful and the least stressful jobs.

PRACTICE

IDENTIFYING STRESSORS

This exercise will help you relate time-management skills to stress reduction. Poor time-management skills prevent you from prioritizing work, delegating appropriately, and working more efficiently, which can result in additional stress.

Your Assignment

1. List several major events or expectations that cause stress for you. Stressors might involve school (difficult classes, too many exams), work (demanding schedule, tight deadlines, financial pressures), or personal circumstances (friends, romance, family). Be as specific as possible. Try to identify at least 10 different stressors.
2. Using the list developed in item 1 above, evaluate the extent to which poor time-management skills on your part play a role in how each stressor affects you. For example, do exams cause stress because you delay studying?
3. For each stressor related to time in item 2 above, develop a strategy for using time more efficiently in that situation.
4. Note interrelationships among different kinds of stressors and time. For example, financial pressures may motivate you to work, but work may interfere with school. Can you manage any of these interrelationships more effectively with regard to time?
5. How do you manage the stress in your life? Is it possible to manage stress in a more time-effective manner?

RUNNING TEAM MEETINGS

This exercise helps you develop your time-management skills as they relate to running team meetings.

Although teams and team meetings are becoming more and more common, some managers worry that meetings waste too much time. Listed below are some of the many suggestions that experts have made for running a meeting more efficiently:

- Have an agenda and distribute it in time for members to prepare.
- Meet only when there is a reason.
- Set clear starting and ending times, and put a clock in front of everyone
- Take away all the chairs and make people stand.
- Lock the door at starting time to "punish" latecomers or embarrass them in some manner.
- Give everyone a role in the meeting.
- Use visual aids.
- Have a recording secretary to document what transpires.
- Have a one-day-a-week meeting "holiday"—a day on which no one can schedule a meeting.

PRACTICE

Your Assignment

1. Evaluate the likely effectiveness of each of the above suggestions.
2. Rank the suggestions in order in terms of their likely value.
3. Identify at least three other suggestions that you think might improve the efficiency of a team meeting.

USING TIME MORE EFFICIENTLY

Using time-management skills wisely can change how a person works. Almost every task you perform can, theoretically, be performed more efficiently.

Your Assignment

1. The next time you work on a particular task such as studying for a test, writing a paper, or working on a project, take note of your work habits. Consider videotaping yourself while you work and reviewing the tape later. Take special note of the things that do not seem to contribute to task performance: going to the refrigerator, watching TV, daydreaming, making or answering an unnecessary phone call, text messaging, etc. Then estimate how much of your so-called "total work time" was actually spent on other activities.
2. Assess the extent to which each non-work activity was wasted effort or failed to contribute in some way to task performance.
3. Describe how you might have completed the work if you had not performed any of the non-work activities.
4. Assuming that you want to change your work habits to use your time more efficiently, describe a change approach that you might use.

WHAT TO DO NOW

Time management involves prioritizing. This exercise can help you sharpen your skills by giving you an opportunity to set priorities and discuss them with others.

Your Assignment

1. Use the following form for your notes as you work through the various items in this assignment.

NOTES

Urgency Code: 1 = Urgent 2 = Deadline Approaching 3 = No Rush

Priority Code: 1 = Do Now 2 = Do Soon 3 = Do Whenever 4 = Don't Bother

Item	Urgency	Priority	Action Taken
A			
B			
C			
D			
E			
F			
G			
H			
I			
J			
K			
L			
M			
N			
O			
P			
Q			
R			

2. Assume it is Wednesday, May 5; you, Brooke Salerno, are the XYZ Corporation manager whose desk currently holds the following letters, phone messages, emails, etc.—some of which have been around for a while.

A • LETTER

April 30, 2010

Brooke Salerno
XYZ Corporation
29 North Central Avenue
Main City, USA

Dear Ms. Salerno:

Our winter meeting was a big success thanks to people like you. Having solid practical and interesting presentations is important and yours was one of the best ever.

Now it's time to look ahead. Will you be available to participate again next year? Details about dates and locations will be sent shortly.

Thanks again for your help and we look forward to a productive, continuing relationship.

PRACTICE

Yours,

David

David Smith
Program Chair
Major Managers Association

B • LETTER

April 30, 2010

Ms Brooke Salerno
XYZ Corporation
29 North Central Avenue
Main City, USA

Dear Ms. Salerno:

Estimado y fino amigo:

The Executive Committee of SMC has asked me to inquire if you will be disposed to serve on the Board of Directors of the Commission. We generally hold three meetings each year for about one and one-half or two hours in the Governor's Conference Room and we try to make these meetings brief and to the point.

If you would like to join the board, please let me know and I will process the paper work.

Abrazos.

Sincerely yours,
Tony

Antonio Certosimo
Executive Director
State Mexico Commission
The Office of the Governor

C • EMAIL

From: Global Business Solutions
Sent: May 3, 2010 4:00 AM
To: Brooke Salerno
Subject: Weekly Report

To help you maximize your firm's prospects for profits in a key market, you might be interested in the following research report:

Doing Business in China: A Risky but Rich Market. This report outlines the pros and cons of entering this greatly expanding market. It covers all aspects—economic, political, cultural, demographic—in sufficient detail that will benefit you immediately.
Click here to order: www.globalbussolutions.com/research

D • EMAIL

From: Susan Hunt
Sent: May 3, 2010 8:34 AM
To: Brooke Salerno
Subject: Accident Claim

Brooke,

As you know, Ralph Lawler, a file clerk in the African Group, was injured when he slipped and fell in the file room. He received normal benefits but now claims that he did not get his full entitlements. I understand that he has hired legal counsel and plans to bring action against the company and several individuals. What should we do?

Susan

Susan Hunt
Human Resources Department

E • LETTER

May 3, 2010

Ms. Brooke Salerno
XYZ Corporation
29 North Central Avenue
Main City, USA

Dear Ms. Salerno:

Organizations doing business in the global marketplace are seldom able to effectively deal with the social and political issues they encounter. As a result, confrontation and even litigation can result.
Based on research currently underway, here are some facts about global businesses:

1. Global businesses increasingly are becoming aware of the need for top executives to be personally involved in their companies' external relations.
2. External relations and public affairs executives are rarely involved in planning processes or in top-management decision-making in socially or politically sensitive areas.
3. Operating managers, especially those overseas, have neither the time nor the formal training nor proper incentives to become involved in issue analysis and external affairs in any meaningful or systematic way.
4. Corporate plans frequently are formulated based on economic data and do not take into account social, political, and cultural issues.
5. Companies often lack the communication systems needed to share information among subsidiaries, regional headquarters, and home offices.

These and other findings will be detailed exclusively to sponsoring companies in a special report, *Managing in the Global Economy*, to be followed by workshops for executives offered in the United States and Asia.

The special report will be available to sponsoring organizations in six months. The US workshop will be held about a month later. The Asian workshop will be held shortly after that. The special report and the workshops will be practical, using everyday business language. Sponsoring organizations will get the special report before it is available to others, and the first workshops will be exclusively for executives from sponsoring organizations.

Your organization still has time to participate as a sponsor. The cost of the special report and participation in the workshops is only $15,000.

I hope that you will want to participate in the program.

Best Wishes,

Frank

Francisco Fernandez
Director, Public Policy Development
Global Business Solutions Corporation
29 Portside Street
Boston, MA

F • EMAIL

From: Mary Cochran
Sent: May 3, 2010 8:45 AM
To: Brooke Salerno
Subject: Don't Forget

Brooke,

DON'T FORGET!!! The final meeting of the Association of Managers and Administrators will be on Friday, May 14, at the Doubletree Inn in the Ironwood Room. Cocktails at 7:30 p.m. with dinner at 8:00. We plan on London Broil, Lover's Salad, Crème de Cocoa Sundae, and wine with dinner.

Next year's officers will be installed and afterwards there will be dancing and listening in the lounge. The group "One Foot in the Grave" is scheduled to entertain.

Reservations must be made no later than noon on Monday, May 10.

Hope to see you there.

Mary

G • EMAIL

From: Mary Cochran
Sent: May 3, 2010 8:45 AM
To: Department List
Subject: Coffee

If you want to participate in the coffee fund, contact Joan.

H • EMAIL

From: Susan Hunt
Sent: May 3, 2010 1:20 PM
To: Brooke Salerno
Subject: Vacation Schedules

Brooke, You need to approve the vacation schedule.

June 1 through July 27

Period	Employee
June 4–8	Cherri Miller
June 11–21	Michael Dupree
June 18–22	Susan Hunt
June 25–29	Patrick Hurley
July 9–13	Loretta Pence
July 16–20	Juan Lopez
July 23–27	Helen Marie Feeney-Schmidt

Susan Hunt
Human Resources Department

I • EMAIL

From: W. J. Kelley
Sent: May 4, 2010 8:34 AM
To: Brooke Salerno
Subject: John Greenberg

Brooke,

I have heard through the grapevine and "unimpeachable" sources that John Greenberg has been looking around and has had a firm job offer on which he is going to give a firm answer next week. I don't think anyone else knows this yet. I just happened to find out about it. I know that you and Mr. Thomas feel that he is one of the most valuable people in the Group and thought I would let you know about this for whatever action you want to take.

W.J.

William J. Kelley
Human Resources Department

J • EMAIL

From: Howard Fritz
Sent: May 4, 2010 9:20 AM
To: Brooke Salerno
Subject: Budget

Brooke, We are getting awfully late in preparing our new budget figures and several group reports are not yet in. Can you do something to speed up action?
Howie
Howard Q. Fritz
Accounting Department

K • EMAIL

From: Ted Lawrence
Sent: May 4, 2010 2:30 PM
To: Brooke Salerno
Subject: State Employment Related to Tourism and Travel

Per your request see attached

Theodore J. Lawrence
Marketing Department

Attachment

State Employment Related to Tourism and Travel

County	Lodging Industry Jobs	Food Industry Jobs	All Other Industry Jobs	Totals
A	36	78	27	141
B	227	391	353	971
C	2,135	2,911	3,006	8,052
D	155	567	307	1,029
E	24	59	380	463
F	5,357	8,500	12,884	26,741
G	441	586	626	1,653
H	370	430	437	1,237
I	2,291	4,142	6,304	12,737
J	84	156	142	382
K	95	215	721	1,031
L	179	625	401	1,205
M	537	899	1,365	2,801
TOTAL				

Source: Based on the Tourism and Travel Industry Statistics for the State Office of Tourism.

PRACTICE

PRACTICE

L • EMAIL

From: Ted Lawrence
Sent: May 4, 2010 3:35 AM
To: Brooke Salerno
Subject: Business Development

Brooke, listed below are customers George and I visited on Wednesday, April 28.
Miller Industries
Wilson Products
Sun Valley Properties

As you may recall, these customers were initially visited by George and me in February.

We were accompanied by Mary Blythe, Manager of the FCIA office in Los Angeles on our recent visits. She made a special trip here, at our request, to further explain the FCIA program that was of interest to these customers.
Ted

Theodore J. Lawrence
Marketing Department

M • PHONE CALL

This phone call took place on May 5. *Brooke's part of the conversation is shown in italics.*

"Hello, Brooke. This is Jerry Murphy. How is everything up your way?"

"Outstanding. How are you, Jerry, and your family? It is difficult to believe that Megan will graduate from high school this year. We received her invitation to graduation yesterday."

"We hope you can make it, but the reason I'm calling is I would like for you to help me with a project. If you can, that is. Yesterday, George Grills, chief auditor for the State Bank, asked if I would be one of the reviewers for the new services that will be offered by banks in the next decade. George mentioned the importance of telecommunications, satellite transmissions, and highly sophisticated automated systems. Plus more advanced fund transfer systems, bill-paying services, check-verification services, and direct data input by customers. What do you see on the horizon as further expansion of international operations? George needs my reaction by May 31. Can you help me with the international view?"

"Surely. I'll get someone to help me and I'll call you on Monday, May 24."

"Thanks, Brooke. I really appreciate your help."

"No problem. Talk to you soon."

"Bye."

"Bye."

N • LETTER

May 3, 2010

Ms. Brooke Salerno
XYZ Corporation

29 North Central Avenue
Main City, USA

Dear Ms. Salerno:

I was fortunate to have been in the audience for your presentation at the Winter Major Managers Association. It was superb! Congratulations on a job well done.

GER is planning programs in London, New York, Montreal, and San Francisco during 2011. We would very much like for you to be involved. We cordially invite you to join one of our panels on the impact of international operations on organizations.

Please let us know if you will be able to participate as soon as possible.

Sincerely yours,

Alex

Alexander Holmes
Executive Director
Global Executives Roundtable

O • COPY OF ARTICLE

The article is from a highly respected business journal and details changes in international operations resulting from developments in wireless technology.

Note attached to article says, "Thought you would find this interesting. Ted"

P • LETTER

May 3, 2010

Ms. Brooke Salerno
XYZ Corporation
29 North Central Avenue
Main City, USA

Dear Ms. Salerno:

Congratulations!

You have been named as a recipient of our "Doing Business Internationally" award for 2010.

The award is scheduled to be presented at our annual dinner, which will be Friday, May 14, at the Mountain View Resort at 8:00 p.m.

We would like to have an 8" × 10" glossy photograph of you for PR purposes. Please send it to Margaret Stephens so that she can get things going.

I look forward to seeing you, and, again, congratulations.

Yours,

Alice

Alice Woodward, Chair
Department of International Business
Local Small College

Q • STICKY NOTE ON COMPUTER MONITOR

[no date] check on car maintenance

USING YOUR TIME-MANAGEMENT SKILLS

TIME FLEXIBILITY

Several years ago, the customer service unit of Stride Rite Corporation's Sperry Topsider division increased its hours of availability from 40 to nearly 70, with only about a 3 percent increase in costs. Xerox's administrative center in Dallas saw absences fall by one-third, teamwork improve, and morale rise with little change in costs. Carter Hawley Hale Stores, GTE, IBM, and Chicago's Harris Bank all have had similar experiences. The common link in these situations was a move to be more flexible with regard to employees' working schedules.

Once a relatively rare phenomenon in corporate America, time flexibility has become more commonplace. Workers frequently rank it at the top of desired job characteristics along with pay and security. In its report, "The National Study of the Changing Workforce," the Families and Work Institute stated that about one-third of those surveyed who do not have the option of taking time off for childbirth or parenting would be willing to trade pay or other benefits for that choice. Another survey of 80 Fortune 500 companies found that only about 25 percent of employees actually used flextime, and slightly less than 2 percent worked part-time arrangements. Harris Bank, on the other hand, found that 64 percent of its requests for flexible work schedules were for a compressed workweek, 24 percent were for flextime, 7 percent for flexplace (telecommuting), and 5 percent for part-time arrangements.

At Xerox, the Dallas administrative center had many single parents and dual-career couples with child-care and family problems. The flexible arrangements were widely popular; and even though managers were very uncomfortable with their use, those managers stuck with it and it proved so successful that it was being tried elsewhere in the organization. Stride Rite found that, even though employees were stretched thinner at certain times, they were able to complete clerical tasks much faster at other times to compensate. At GTE's telephone-operations division, employees requested more flexibility. When GTE gave it to them, they responded so well that they essentially have 100 percent responsibility for scheduling, and GTE planned to expand the effort to other facilities as well.

With compressed workweeks, individuals can work longer hours but with fewer days. Two income and dual career couples can arrange schedules so that one or the other is available for parenting for longer blocks of time. Flextime permits individuals to arrive at and leave from work at different times. It enables fitting work schedules better to traffic flows and parenting duties such as taking children to soccer games or gymnastics classes. Flexplace, or telecommuting, permits individuals to work from their homes or other locations rather than travel to a central office. This approach provides maximum opportunity for individuals to work at their own pace and fit multiple time demands into their schedules. Part-time arrangements usually involve job sharing, in which two individuals each working half of the time perform a job normally held by one person. Almost all of these approaches make family responsibilities easier to manage along with job responsibilities.

Catalyst, a national organization that researches women's career issues, conducted a survey in an effort to determine the effects of workplace flexibility on organizations. It surveyed human-resource personnel from 50 organizations that had people working in flexible arrangements of one kind or another. Catalyst found that flexible work arrangements can be successful in a wide range of jobs and areas. These flexible arrangements were even used in line jobs, supervisory positions, and jobs that have a large amount of contact with customers.

Most of the people using these arrangements, it turned out, were women with preschool-age children. Given that women make up a large proportion of the workforce, flexible work arrangements represent a potentially powerful fringe benefit an organization can offer.

While flexible work arrangements can lead to improved productivity, morale, and retention rates, they may make little difference unless the organization's culture also is flexible. The managerial mindset of "face-time" must change. "Face-time" refers to the strongly held and deeply ingrained view that if people are present at work for 40 hours a week, then they must be accomplishing their work no matter how little output they produce. But if an employee is not clocked in, no work is being accomplished. Managers must give up the notion of face-time in order for flexible policies to have an impact. Further, communication is critical. Coworkers, subordinates, superiors, and customers all must clearly understand how the arrangement works including responsibilities and day-to-day schedules of availability for those using the system.

Case Questions

Go Online

1. What different types of flexible work arrangements exist? What are the advantages and disadvantages to each one?
2. What time-management skills are necessary for each of these different flexible work arrangements?
3. Would the time-management skills identified in item 2 also serve other organizational arrangements? If so, what? If not, why not?
4. What are the assumptions underlying face-time? If you owned a company, would you be willing to allow your employees some flexible time instead of face-time? Why or why not?
5. What would be a way to acquire the time-management skills needed for such flexible work arrangements?
6. How do you feel about allowing flextime for some categories of employees (for example, parents of children under age 6, or employees with some job titles or classifications) but not all employees?

Case References

Amy Dunkin, "Working dads want flextime, too," *BusinessWeek*, June 13, 2007 http://www.businessweek.com/careers/workingparents/blog/archives/2007/06/working_dads_wa.html; Anne Fisher, "Forget the raise, give me flexible hours," *Fortune*, August 22, 2007 http://money.cnn.com/2006/07/27/news/economy/annie.0726.fortune/index.htm; Anne Fisher, "7 ways to make your office greener," *Fortune*, December 5, 2007 http://money.cnn.com/2007/12/04/news/economy/environment.fortune/index.htm; Sue Shellenbarger, "More Companies Experiment with Workers' Schedules," *Wall Street Journal*, January 13, 1994, pp. B1, B6; Catherine Romano, "What's Your Flexibility Factor?" *Management Review*, January 1994, p. 9.

UNITED PARCEL SERVICE

Two teenagers, Jim Casey and Claude Ryan, began the American Messenger company in 1907 in Seattle. In 1913 they changed the name to Merchants Parcel Company to reflect the business that had developed. By 1918 it was handling all deliveries for three of Seattle's largest department stores. It began to expand operations and changed its name to United Parcel Service (UPS). By 1930 it had expanded from the West Coast to New York City. During the 1950s, UPS expanded its services to include door-to-door parcel pickup and delivery and the air express business. By the 1980s, it had become the largest delivery service in the US. UPS now operates in more than 200 countries worldwide.

The time-saving methods of Frank Gilbreth, the time-and-motion study pioneer, intrigued Jim Casey, and he adopted many of them. Casey ran the organization for more than 50 years. As a result of his influence, an emphasis on efficiency and time management dominates the firm. For example, delivery truck seats were beveled to enable drivers to get out of their trucks more easily and thus make pickups and deliveries more quickly. Later, technology became a major factor in efficiency. UPS maintains computerized, daily records of each driver's performance and has supervisors ride along with the "least-best" (the worst) drivers to help them improve as one part of its emphasis on efficiency. UPS uses computers to monitor every aspect of performance in the firm.

By the early 1990s, UPS had more than 60,000 drivers and handled more than one million accounts in the United States alone. To conduct this vast business, it used more than 70,000 handheld pen computers. These were linked through more than 300 local area networks into its global communications network, which had nearly 3 terabytes of data storage space (a terabyte is one trillion bytes of information). This gigantic information system enabled it to trace the progress of more than 12 million packages each day.

UPS developed its own version of the bar code to handle even more information than usual. It is called a *dense code* because, in about the same space, it packs about twice as much information. Scanners can read a package's origin, destination, contents, and price and send that information to the central computer system. Even in emergencies, UPS has carefully developed time-management plans. It uses "contingency workers" to keep things going.

This use of technology has enabled UPS to expand into Europe, providing door-to-door service throughout the European Union. Through an advanced data link in airplane cockpits, it is also able to compete in the airfreight business. UPS's technology is designed so that it is easy to connect to its computer information system. This has enabled it to put package-shipping centers in supermarkets for customer convenience.

USE

Rising fuel costs are a constant concern to trucking companies, and UPS is no exception. In the face of almost uncontrollable fuel costs, UPS has used creative ideas to boost demand, such as lending money to small businesses to use for shipping. Then, in 2004, UPS announced that it would save fuel (and also reduce the odds of truck accidents) by minimizing left turns. When trucks sit at intersections waiting to make left turns, they use fuel but don't move toward their goals. UPS developed software that routes the day's packages with a minimum of left turns. Given the size of the UPS fleet of trucks, the fuel savings are considerable.

Go Online

Case Questions

1. What time-management tools can you note at UPS?
2. What time-management skills are necessary for each of these different tools?
3. What strengths and weaknesses can you suggest about UPS's time-management approaches? How might the weaknesses be reduced?
4. How would you go about acquiring the time-management skills needed by UPS?

Case References

Brent Adams, "UPS delivers through weather challenges," *BusinessWeek*, January 30, 2009 http://louisville.bizjournals.com/louisville/stories/2009/02/02/story3.html?b=1233550800^1770768; Matthew Boyle, "UPS: Making Loans to Small Biz," *BusinessWeek*, September 4, 2008 http://www.businessweek.com/magazine/content/08_37/b4099064499029.htm; Greg Nieman, (2007). *Big Brown: The Untold Story of UPS*, Hoboken, NJ: John Wiley & Sons; "UPS Ups Rates," *The Traffic World*, January 11, 1993, pp. 15–21; Frank Hammel, "A Little 'Wrap' Music," *Supermarket Business*, November 1, 1992, pp. 73–79; "Langley Data Link Systems Provides ATC Communications," *Aviation Week & Space Technology*, January 6, 1992, pp. 52–53; Dennis Livingston, "United Parcel Service Gets A Special Delivery," *Systems Integration*, November 1, 1991, pp. 54–61.

EXTENDING YOUR TIME-MANAGEMENT SKILLS

Your instructor may use one or more of these Group Extensions to provide you with yet another opportunity to develop your time-management skills. On the other hand, you may continue your development on your own by doing one or more of the Individual Extensions.

These Group Extensions are repeated exactly for each of the seven specific skills. Doing the exact Extension for different skills will help you to sharpen both the skills and the subtle differences between them.

GROUP EXTENSIONS

- Form small groups of students. Have each group select an organization and a management position. Then have them identify the time-management skills needed by a person in that position.
- Form small groups of students. Have each group identify a problem or opportunity facing a business or other organization. Then have them identify the time-management skills needed by managers in dealing with that problem or opportunity.
- Form small groups of students. Assign each group one or more corporations to analyze. Have them identify the members who serve on its board of directors and research their backgrounds. Then have students describe the time-management skills those directors need to have.
- Form small groups of students. Have each group select a job they see regularly (e.g., retail clerk, fast-food worker, staff person at school). Ask them to describe the time-management skills those workers need to have on the job.
- Form small groups of students. Have students sketch the time-management skills they would need if they were going to start a specific type of new business.
- Form small groups of students. Have each group identify situations they have recently faced that called for them to use time-management skills.

INDIVIDUAL EXTENSIONS

- Go to the library and research a company. Characterize its level of effectiveness and identify the time-management skills its top executives need to have. Share your results with the class.
- Select a highly visible manager and analyze his or her time-management skills.
- Interview a manager from a local organization. Learn about what time-management skills he or she needs to perform effectively.
- Think of someone you know who is a manager. Describe that person's management position in terms of the type of organization, level in the organization, and the area of management in which he or she practices. What time-management skills does that person need to be effective?
- Plan a hypothetical change in your school focusing on the use of time-management skills.

- You may wish to complete some of the exercises in the "Toolkit" provided at http://www.mindtools.com/.
- You also may use computer-based "to do" lists such as those provided at rememberthe-milk.com, todoist.com, tadalist.com, or toodledo.com.

YOUR TIME-MANAGEMENT SKILLS NOW

TIME-MANAGEMENT SKILLS ASSESSMENT

Now that you have completed Chapter 3, it is time once again to assess your time-management skills. To do so, complete the following instrument. Think about your current situation, job, or organization in which you are a member. You should respond in terms of your current situation and not by how you think you should respond or how a manager should respond. If a statement doesn't pertain to your current situation, respond in terms of what you think would be accurate for you in that situation.

Use this scale in your responses.

1	2	3	4	5
Not true at all	Somewhat Untrue	Sometimes true Sometimes not	Somewhat true	Completely true

Total your scores and record them in the table at the end of instrument.

Given that many experts suggest the use of 360° feedback in performance appraisals, you may find it useful to obtain the views of others about your managerial skills. You may get a form from your instructor that is designed for others to complete and then record their scores in the table as well. Look for areas where there are major differences between your views and those of others and spend more time on developing those skills.

TIME-MANAGEMENT SKILLS

[Note: The numbers correspond to those on the baseline assessment in Appendix A.]

____ 301. I almost always complete my tasks on time.
____ 302. I am able to "unwind" after a trying day at work.
____ 303. I am not stressed about deadlines and commitments.
____ 304. I analyze new tasks or assignments to establish their priorities.
____ 305. I deal with higher priority problems and tasks first.
____ 306. I deal with issues one at a time.
____ 307. I don't over-schedule; I leave time for "the unexpected" and relaxation.
____ 308. I exercise to relieve tension.
____ 309. I generally am punctual.
____ 310. I generally can prioritize tasks without too much trouble.

____ 311. I generally manage my time well.
____ 312. I get others to help when necessary.
____ 313. I handle interruptions quickly so that they don't delay my work.
____ 314. I handle paperwork quickly and effectively.
____ 315. I have "confidants" with whom I can release frustrations.
____ 316. I keep a "to do" list.
____ 317. I keep a well-organized and orderly workspace.
____ 318. I keep information and documents in an orderly manner.
____ 319. I know how much time I spend on the various tasks I do.
____ 320. I make good use of time.
____ 321. I meet goals.
____ 322. I minimize distractions that could keep me from working on critical tasks.
____ 323. I organize and schedule my tasks.
____ 324. I organize my activities.
____ 325. I organize my time effectively.
____ 326. I pay attention to details.
____ 327. I practice relaxation techniques (e.g., reciting a mantra, slowing breathing).
____ 328. I prioritize my activities.
____ 329. I respond promptly to written requests.
____ 330. I return phone calls quickly.
____ 331. I seldom have to ask for extensions.
____ 332. I set and meet deadlines.
____ 333. I set aside time for planning and scheduling.
____ 334. I set daily goals and prepare daily "to do" lists.
____ 335. I set specific deadlines on projects.
____ 336. I take time to meet with others.
____ 337. I try to never leave things to the last minute.
____ 338. I use goal setting to establish priorities for my tasks and activities.
____ 339. I use plans to manage my tasks.
____ 340. I work in a tidy and organized way.

Summary of Your Scores

Skill (max. possible score)	**Your Score Now**	**Scores from Others**	**Your Score From Chapter 1**
Time Management (200)			

Interpretation of Your Scores

Compare your score with the one you reported at the beginning of Chapter 1. If there is no or only a modest improvement in your score, you should examine the same set of items from the Managerial Skills Assessment from Chapter 1 and compare each of them with these to see where change has and has not occurred. You should then spend more time on developing the particular skills where change either decreased or stayed the same.

INTERPRETATIONS

BEHAVIOR ACTIVITY PROFILE: A "TYPE A MEASURE"

(1) Transfer your scores from the self-assessment activity to the following table:

Impatience	Job Involvement	Hard Driving and Competitive	Total Score
(S)	(J)	(H)	(A) = S + J + H

(2) The Behavior Activity Profile attempts to assess the three Type A coronary-prone behavior patterns, as well as provide a total score. The three a priori types of Type A coronary-prone behavior patterns are shown below. Compare your scores with these.

Items	Behavior Pattern	Characteristics
1–7	(S) Impatience	Anxious to interrupt Fails to listen attentively Frustrated by waiting (e.g., in line, for others to complete a job)
8–14	(J) Job involvement	Focal point of attention is the job Lives for the job Relishes being on the job Immersed in job activities
15–21	(H) Hard-driving, competitive	Hard-working, highly competitive Competitive in most aspects of life, sports, work, etc. Racing against the clock
1–21	(A) Total score	Total of S+J+H represents your global Type A behavior

Score ranges for total score are:

Score	Behavior Type
122 and above	Hard-core Type A
99–121	Moderate Type A
90– 98	Low Type A
80– 89	Type X
70– 79	Low Type B
50– 69	Moderate Type B
40 and below	Moderate Type B

(3) Now you can compare your score to a sample of more than 1,200 respondents.

Percentile Score (Percent of individuals scoring lower)	Raw Score	
	Males	Females
99%	140	132
95%	135	126
90%	130	120
85%	124	112
80%	118	106
75%	113	101
70%	108	95
65%	102	90
60%	97	85
55%	92	80
50%	87	74
45%	81	69
40%	75	63
35%	70	58
30%	63	53
25%	58	48
20%	51	42
15%	45	36
10%	38	31
5%	29	26
1%	21	21

ARE YOU A GOOD PLANNER?

Give yourself one point for each item you marked as Mostly True except items 3 and 4. For items 3 and 4, give yourself one point for each one you marked Mostly False. A score of 5 or higher suggests a positive level of goal-setting behavior and planning. If you scored 4 or less, you might want to evaluate and begin to change your behavior. An important part of a manager's job is setting goals and planning.

These questions indicate the extent to which you have already adopted the disciplined use of goals in your life and work. But if you scored low, don't despair. Goal setting can be learned. Research indicates that setting clear, specific, and challenging goals in key areas will produce better performance.

STRESS MANAGEMENT

This self-assessment is designed to help you discover your level of competency in stress management so you can tailor your learning to your specific needs. The first ten items deal with your direct handling of stressful or time-pressured situations and the last five deal with your use of delegation in handling stress.

The higher your scores, the better you are at dealing with stress.

TIME-MANAGEMENT ASSESSMENT

Time management is important to everyone, but especially managers. So the first section of the instrument is for anyone, while the second section applies primarily to individuals currently serving in some kind of managerial position.

The higher the score in each section, the better you are at time management.

ENDNOTES

[1] Carrie R. Leana, "Predictors and Consequences of Delegation," *Academy of Management Journal*, December 1986, pp. 754–774.

[2] Jerry Useem, "In Corporate America It's Cleanup Time," *Fortune*, September 16, 2002, pp. 62–70.

[3] Norm Brodsky, "Necessary Losses," *Inc.*, December 1997, pp. 116–119.

[4] Quoted in *Bloomberg Businessweek*, January 16, 2012, p. 49.

[5] "Toppling the Pyramids," *Canadian Business*, May 1993, pp. 61–65.

[6] "New Shell CEO Begins Shake-Up," *Wall Street Journal*, May 28, 2009, p. B4.

[7] "Yahoo CEO to Install Top-Down Management," *Wall Street Journal*, February 23, 2009, p. B1.

[8] *BusinessWeek*, March 23/30, 2009, p. 33.

[9] Frank Landy, James Campbell Quick, and Stanislav Kasl, "Work, Stress, and Well-Being," *International Journal of Stress Management*, 1994, vol. 1, no. 1, pp. 33–73.

[10] Hans Selye, *The Stress of Life* (New York: McGraw-Hill, 1976).

[11] M. Friedman and R. H. Rosenman, *Type A Behavior and Your Heart* (New York: Knopf, 1974).

[12] *Fortune*, July 6, 2010, p. 44.

[13] Richard S. DeFrank, Robert Konopaske, and John M. Ivancevich, "Executive Travel Stress: Perils of the Road Warrior," *Academy of Management Executive*, 2000, vol. 14, no. 2, pp. 58–67.

[14] Steven Rogelberg, Desmond Leach, Peter Warr, and Jennifer Burnfield, "'Not Another Meeting!' Are Meeting Time Demands Related to Employee Well Being?" *Journal of Applied Psychology*, 2006, vol. 91, no. 1, pp. 86–96.

[15] "Those Doing Layoffs Can Feel the Pain," *USA Today*, April 23, 2009, p. 5D.

[16] *USA Today*, April 23, 2009, p. 5D.

[17] Remus Ilies, Michael Johnson, Timothy Judge, and Jessica Keeney, "A Within-Individual Study of Interpersonal Conflict as a Work Stressor: Dispositional and Situational Moderators," *Journal of Organizational Behavior*, January 2011, pp. 44–64.

[18] Michael R. Frone, "Are Work Stressors Related to Employee Substance Abuse? The Importance of Temporal Context in Assessments of Alcohol and Illicit Drug Use," *Journal of Applied Psychology*, 2008, Vol. 93, No. 1, pp. 199–216.

[19] "Breaking Point," *Newsweek*, March 6, 1995, pp. 56–62; see also "Rising Job Stress Could Affect Bottom Line," *USA Today*, July 28, 2003, p. 1B.

[20] Christopher M. Barnes and John R. Hollenbeck, "Sleep Deprivation and Decision-Making Teams: Burning the Midnight Oil or Playing with Fire?" *Academy of Management Review*, Vol. 34, No. 1, January 2009, pp. 56–66.

[21] John M. Kelly, "Get a Grip on Stress," *HRMagazine*, February 1997, pp. 51–58; see also Marilyn Macik-Frey, James Campbell Quick, and Debra Nelson, "Advances in Occupational Health: From a Stressful Beginning to a Positive Future," *Journal of Management*, 2007, Vol. 33, No. 6, pp. 809–840.

[22] Charlotte Fritz, Sabine Sonnentag, Paul Spector, and Jennifer McInroe, "The Weekend Matters: Relationships Between Stress Recovery and Affective Experiences," *Journal of Organizational Behavior*, November 2010, pp. 1137–1162.

[23] "Nice Work if You Can Get It," *BusinessWeek*, January 9, 2006, pp. 56–57; see also "Wellness," *Time*, February 23, 2009, pp. 78–79.

CHAPTER 4

ASSESSING YOUR INTERPERSONAL SKILLS

Assessing Your Needs
Job Involvement
Team Effectiveness Inventory
Using Teams

LEARNING ABOUT INTERPERSONAL SKILLS

The Interpersonal Nature of Organizations
- *Interpersonal Dynamics*
- *Outcomes of Interpersonal Behaviors*

Understanding Individual Differences
- *The Psychological Contract*
- *The Person-Job Fit*
- *The Nature of Individual Differences*

Motivating Employees
- *Content Perspectives on Motivation*
  - *The Needs Hierarchy Approach*
  - *The Two-Factor Theory*
- *Process Perspectives on Motivation*
  - *Expectancy Theory*
  - *Equity Theory*
  - *Goal Setting Theory*

Working with Diversity, Teams, and Conflict
- *Understanding Diversity*
  - *Reasons for Increased Diversity*
  - *Dimensions of Diversity*
  - *Working with Diversity*
- *Managing Teams*
  - *Types of Teams*
  - *Benefits and Costs of Teams*
- *Managing Conflict*
  - *The Nature of Conflict*
  - *Causes of Conflict*
  - *Managing Conflict in Organizations*

Managing Workplace Behaviors
- *Performance Behavior*
- *Dysfunctional Behavior*
- *Organizational Citizenship*

Summary and a Look Ahead

VISUALIZING INTERPERSONAL SKILLS

Interpersonal Skills in Action—1
Interpersonal Skills in Action—2

PRACTICING YOUR INTERPERSONAL SKILLS

Managing During a Period of Change
Selecting Modes of Communication
Skills Related to Motivation and Satisfying Needs in a Career
Surviving in a Period of Change
Understanding the Perceptual Process
Understanding Decision Makers (1)
Understanding Decision Makers (2)
Identifying Personality Traits for Different Jobs
Assessing Entrepreneurial Personality Traits
Assessing Your Personality Type

USING YOUR INTERPERSONAL SKILLS

Nordstrom Cares
Campbell's Continues Canning

EXTENDING YOUR INTERPERSONAL SKILLS

Group Extensions
Individual Extensions

YOUR INTERPERSONAL SKILLS NOW

Interpersonal Skills Assessment
- *Interpersonal Skills*
- *Summary of your Scores*
- *Interpretation of Your Scores*

INTERPRETATIONS

Assessing Your Needs
Job Involvement
Team Effectiveness
Using Teams

Interpersonal Skills

© ISTOCKPHOTO.COM/ROBERT CHURCHILL

The previous chapter described time-management skills and how you can more effectively learn and develop those skills. In managing your time, you must understand how what you do impacts those around you. For instance, while you may have a week to write a memo, others may need to take action following the submission of your memo. There is a ripple effect if you are late or early in submitting the memo. Dealing with those around you involves interpersonal skills, which is the subject of this chapter. We begin the chapter by examining the nature of individual differences and what motivates the behavior of individuals in organizations. We then discuss diversity, teams, and conflict management. Following the text section are several cases and exercises to help you further develop and master your interpersonal skills.

ASSESSING YOUR INTERPERSONAL SKILLS

ASSESS

ASSESSING YOUR NEEDS

Needs are one factor that influences motivation. The following assessment surveys your judgments about some of the personal needs that might be partially shaping your motivation.

Instructions:
Judge how descriptively accurate each of the following ten statements is about you. You may find it difficult to make a decision in some cases, but you should force yourself to make a choice. Record your answers next to each statement according to the following scale:

Rating Scale
5 – Very descriptive of me
4 – Fairly descriptive of me
3 – Somewhat descriptive of me
2 – Not very descriptive of me
1 – Not descriptive of me at all

_____ 1. I aspire to accomplish difficult tasks and maintain high standards and am willing to work toward distant goals.

_____ 2. I enjoy being with friends and people in general and accept people readily.

_____ 3. I am easily annoyed and am sometimes willing to hurt people to get my way.

_____ 4. I try to break away from restraints or restrictions of any kind.

_____ 5. I want to be the center of attention and enjoy having an audience.

_____ 6. I speak freely and tend to act on the spur of the moment.

_____ 7. I assist others whenever possible, giving sympathy and comfort to those in need.

_____ 8. I believe in the saying that "there is a place for everything and everything should be in its place." I dislike clutter.

_____ 9. I express my opinions forcefully, enjoy the role of leader, and try to control my environment as much as I can.

_____ 10. I want to understand many areas of knowledge and value synthesizing ideas and generalization.

See Interpretations at the end of the chapter.

JOB INVOLVEMENT

When employees are given a greater voice in how things are done, they become more involved and committed to the organization. When employees enjoy their job, they become more involved in the work. This self-assessment examines your level of involvement starting with your job.

Instructions:
Think of the job that you currently have. If you are not now working, think of the job you most recently held. Then beside each of the following 20 items, respond according to whether you (1) Strongly Disagree, (2) Disagree, (3) Agree, (4) Strongly Agree.

ASSESS

_____ 1. I'll stay overtime to finish a job, even if I'm not paid for it.
_____ 2. You can measure a person pretty well by how good a job is done.
_____ 3. The major satisfaction in my life comes from my job.
_____ 4. For me, mornings at work really fly by.
_____ 5. I usually show up for work a little early to get things ready.
_____ 6. The most important things that happen to me involve work.
_____ 7. Sometimes I lie awake at night thinking ahead to the next day's work.
_____ 8. I'm really a perfectionist about my work.
_____ 9. I feel depressed when I fail at something connected with my job.
_____ 10. I have other activities more important than my work.
_____ 11. I live, eat, and breathe my job.
_____ 12. I would probably keep working even if I didn't need the money.
_____ 13. Quite often I feel like staying home from work instead of coming in.
_____ 14. To me, my work is only a small part of who I am.
_____ 15. I am very much involved personally in my work.
_____ 16. I avoid taking on extra duties and responsibilities in my work.
_____ 17. I used to be more ambitious about my work than I am now.
_____ 18. Most things in life are more important than work.
_____ 19. I used to care more about my work, but now other things are more important to me.
_____ 20. Sometimes I'd like to kick myself for the mistakes made in my work.

Source: Thomas M. Lodahl and Mathilde Kejner, "The Definition and Measurement of Job Involvement," *Journal of Applied Psychology*, February 1965, Vol. 49, Issue 1, pp. 24–33. ©1965 by the American Psychological Association. Reprinted by permission.

See Interpretations at the end of the chapter.

TEAM EFFECTIVENESS INVENTORY

All organizations must have highly performing teams to be successful. Many different factors contribute to a team's effectiveness. This self-assessment measures some of the most critical team characteristics that contribute to effectiveness.

Instructions:

Think of a group or team in which you are currently or have been a member. Please respond on the basis of your degree of agreement or disagreement with each statement. Use the following scale: Strongly Disagree (SD), Disagree (D), Undecided/Neutral (U), Agree (A), Strongly Agree (SA).

Statements	SD	D	U	A	SA
Task Performance:					
1. We plan ahead for problems that might arise.	1	2	3	4	5
2. We are an effective problem-solving team.	1	2	3	4	5
3. We achieve high performance goals	1	2	3	4	5
Influence:					
4. Team members are willing to listen to and understand each other.	1	2	3	4	5
5. Members are active in influencing the future of the team.					
6. Members are willing to disagree and make suggestions to each other.	1	2	3	4	5

(continued)

ASSESS

Statements	SD	D	U	A	SA
Satisfaction:					
7. I enjoy working with my team members.	1	2	3	4	5
8. I am able to make good use of my skills and abilities on this team.	1	2	3	4	5
9. Considering everything, it is a pleasure to be a member of this team.	1	2	3	4	5
Member Relations:					
10. I trust the members of my team.	1	2	3	4	5
11. There is no free riding by members.	1	2	3	4	5
12. We are a cooperative and cohesive group.	1	2	3	4	5
Creativity:					
13. Divergent ideas are encouraged.	1	2	3	4	5
14. Our norms encourage change.	1	2	3	4	5
15. The creative talents of members are drawn on to improve the quality and quantity of the team's outputs.	1	2	3	4	5

Scoring:

Add the point values for each of the scales:

_____ *Task Performance*
_____ *Influence*
_____ *Satisfaction*
_____ *Member Relations*
_____ *Creativity*
_____ *TOTAL POINTS*

Source: Reprinted by permission from Hellriegel, Slocum and Woodman, Organizational Behavior, 6th edition, pp. 344–345. © 1992 South-Western, a part of Cengage Learning, Inc. www.cengage.com/permissions.

See Interpretations at the end of the chapter.

USING TEAMS

The use of groups and teams is increasingly common in organizations throughout the world. The following assessment surveys your beliefs and understanding about the effective use of teams in work organizations.

Instructions:

You will agree with some of the statements and disagree with others. In some cases you may find making a decision difficult, but you should force yourself to make a choice. Record your answers next to each statement using the following scale:

4 – *Strongly Agree*
3 – *Somewhat Agree*
2 – *Somewhat Disagree*
1 – *Strongly Disagree*

_____ 1. All teams are alike.
_____ 2. It is not necessary for a team to have much structure for effective functioning.
_____ 3. All organizations can use teams.
_____ 4. A team must have complete authority over all aspects of its task in order to be effective.
_____ 5. Creativity is not important to effective team functioning.
_____ 6. Teams develop any skills that they need as they go along so training is necessary.

_____ 7. Managers determine the means to the end while the team itself determines the end.

_____ 8. An advantage of teams is that managers can focus on other issues once the team gets going.

_____ 9. The most effective teams are formed by just getting people together, giving them a general idea of what to do, and then letting them do it.

_____ 10. Individual accountability assures team effectiveness.

Source: Adapted from John Mathieu, M. Travis Maynard, Tammy Rapp, & Lucy Gilson. 2008. "Team Effectiveness 1997–2007: A Review of Recent Advancements and a Glimpse Into the Future". *Journal of Management*, 34(3): 410–476; J. Richard Hackman, ed., *Groups That Work (and Those That Don't)*. San Francisco, Jossey-Bass Publishers, 1990, pp. 493–504; and Van Fleet, D. D. 1991. *Behavior in Organizations*. Boston: Houghton Mifflin, in collaboration with G. Moorhead and R. W. Griffin.

See Interpretations at the end of the chapter.

GO ONLINE to the Griffin/Van Fleet Assessment Library for online versions of these and other assessments.

LEARN

LEARNING ABOUT INTERPERSONAL SKILLS

The Interpersonal Nature of Organizations
Interpersonal Dynamics
Outcomes of Interpersonal Behaviors
Understanding Individual Differences
The Psychological Contract
The Person-Job Fit
The Nature of Individual Differences
Motivating Employees
Content Perspectives on Motivation
The Needs Hierarchy Approach
The Two-Factor Theory
Process Perspectives on Motivation
Expectancy Theory
Equity Theory
Goal Setting Theory
Working with Diversity, Teams, and Conflict
Understanding Diversity
Reasons for Increased Diversity
Dimensions of Diversity
Working with Diversity
Managing Teams
Types of Teams
Benefits and Costs of Teams
Managing Conflict
The Nature of Conflict
Causes of Conflict
Managing Conflict in Organizations
Managing Workplace Behaviors
Performance Behavior
Dysfunctional Behavior
Organizational Citizenship
Summary and a Look Ahead

Interpersonal skills refer to the manager's ability to communicate with, understand, and relate to both individuals and groups. Managers interact with many different people, including subordinates, peers, those at higher levels of the organization, and colleagues from other organizations. Because of the multitude of roles managers must fulfill, a manager must also be able to work with suppliers, customers, investors, and others outside of the organization. Although some managers have succeeded with poor interpersonal skills, a manager who has good interpersonal skills is likely to be more successful. This chapter first provides context for the interpersonal nature of organizations. We then look at a variety of factors that affect interpersonal relations, including individual differences, employee motivation, diversity, teams, conflict, and various forms of workplace behavior.

interpersonal skills the manager's ability to communicate with, understand, and relate to both individuals and groups

THE INTERPERSONAL NATURE OF ORGANIZATIONS

A great deal of what all managers do involves interacting with other people, both directly and indirectly and both inside and outside of the organization. The schedule that follows is a typical composite day for the president of a Houston-based company, part of a larger corporation headquartered in California. He kept a log of his activities for several different days so that you could better appreciate the nature of managerial work.

6:00–6:30 A.M. Read and respond to email from home; scan major news stories.
7:45–8:15 A.M. Arrive at work; review hardcopy mail sorted by assistant.
8:15–8:30 A.M. Scan the online version of *The Wall Street Journal*; read and respond to email.
8:30–9:00 A.M. Meet with labor officials and plant manager to resolve minor labor disputes.
9:00–9:30 A.M. Review internal report; read and respond to new email.
9:30–10:00 A.M. Meet with two marketing executives to review advertising campaign; instruct them to fax approvals to advertising agency.
10:00–11:30 A.M. Meet with company executive committee to discuss strategy, budgetary issues, and competition (this committee meets weekly).
11:30–12:00 noon. Send several emails; read and respond to new email.
12:00–1:15 P.M. Lunch with the financial vice president and two executives from another subsidiary of the parent corporation. Primary topic of discussion is the Houston Rockets basketball team. Place three calls from cell phone en route to lunch and receive one call en route back to office.
1:15–1:45 P.M. Meet with human resource director and assistant about a recent OSHA inspection; establish a task force to investigate the problems identified and to suggest solutions.

1:45–2:00 P.M. Read and respond to new email.
2:00–2:30 P.M. Conference call with four other company presidents.
2:30–3:00 P.M. Meet with financial vice president about a confidential issue that came up at lunch (unscheduled).
3:00–3:30 P.M. Work alone in office; read and respond to new email; send several emails.
3:30–4:15 P.M. Meet with a group of sales representatives and the company purchasing agent.
4:15–5:30 P.M. Work alone in office.
5:30–7:00 P.M. Play racquetball at nearby athletic club with marketing vice president.
9:00–9:30 P.M. Read and respond to email from home; send email to assistant about an emergency meeting to be scheduled for the next day.

How did this manager spend his time? He spent most of it working, communicating, and interacting with other people. And this compressed daily schedule does not include several other brief telephone calls, brief conversations with his assistant, and brief conversations with other managers. Clearly, interpersonal relations, communication, and group processes are a pervasive part of all organizations and a vital part of all managerial activities.[1] So, just imagine the differences in effectiveness if this manager has strong interpersonal skills (which he does) as compared to someone else with poor interpersonal skills.

Interpersonal Dynamics

The nature of interpersonal relations in an organization is as varied as the individual members themselves. At one extreme, interpersonal relations can be personal and positive. This occurs when the two parties know each other, have mutual respect and affection, and enjoy interacting. Two managers who have known each other for years, play golf together on weekends, and are close personal friends will likely interact at work in a positive fashion. At the other extreme, interpersonal dynamics can be personal but negative. This is most likely when the parties dislike each other, do not have mutual respect, and do not enjoy interacting. Suppose a manager has fought openly for years to block the promotion of another manager within the organization. Over the objections of the first manager, however, the other manager eventually gets promoted to the same rank. When the two of them must interact, it will most likely be in a negative manner.

"When the company was younger and smaller, [Microsoft CEO Steve Ballmer] could, quite honestly, overwhelm most of the issues he faced with his energy and smarts. Now he's learned to manage through people. … I think he will come off looking like a really unique and special leader."

JAMES CASH, Former Microsoft director[3]

QUOTED IN BLOOMBERG BUSINESSWEEK, JANUARY 16, 2012, P. 49.

Most interactions fall between these extremes, as members of the organization interact in a professional way and focus primarily on goal accomplishment. These interactions deal with the job at hand, are relatively formal and structured, and are task directed. In another example, two managers may respect each other's work and recognize the professional competence that each brings to the job. However, they may also have few common interests and little to talk about besides the job they are doing. These different types of interactions may occur between individuals, between groups, or between individuals and groups, and they can change over time. Two managers may decide to bury the hatchet and adopt a detached, professional manner. In doing so they could find more common ground than they anticipated, and their interactions could help their relationship evolve into one that is more positive on a professional as well as personal level.

Outcomes of Interpersonal Behaviors

A variety of things can happen as a result of interpersonal behaviors. Numerous perspectives on motivation suggest that most people have social needs. For many people, interpersonal relations in organizations can be a primary source for satisfying this need. For a person with a strong need for affiliation, high-quality interpersonal relations can be an important positive element in the workplace. However, when this same person is confronted with poor-quality working relationships, the effect can be just as great in the other direction.

Interpersonal relations also serve as a solid basis for social support. Suppose that an employee receives a poor performance evaluation or is denied a promotion.

LEARN

Others in the organization can lend support because they share a common frame of reference—an understanding of the causes and consequences of what happened. Good interpersonal relations throughout an organization can also be a source of synergy. People who support one another and who work well together can accomplish much more than people who do not support one another and who do not work well together. Another outcome is conflict—people may leave an interpersonal exchange feeling angry or hostile. A common thread is woven through all of these outcomes—interactions between people in the organization.[2] A manager with strong interpersonal skills is well-positioned to understand, manage, capitalize on, and help improve interactions among others.

UNDERSTANDING INDIVIDUAL DIFFERENCES

An effective place to start understanding the role and impact of interpersonal skills in the workplace is the basic nature of the relationship between individuals and organizations. It is also helpful to gain an appreciation of the nature of individual differences.

The Psychological Contract

Most people have a basic understanding of a contract. Whenever we buy a car or sell a house, for example, both buyer and seller sign a contract that specifies the terms of the agreement. A psychological contract is similar in some ways to a standard legal contract but is less formal and well defined. In particular, a **psychological contract** is the overall set of expectations held by an individual with respect to what he or she will contribute to the organization and what the organization will provide in return.[4] Thus a psychological contract is not written on paper, nor are all of its terms explicitly negotiated.

The essential nature of a psychological contract is illustrated in *Figure 4.1*. The individual makes a variety of **contributions** to the organization—effort, skills, ability, time, loyalty, and so forth. These contributions presumably satisfy various needs and requirements of the organization. In other words, because the organization may have hired the person because of her skills, it is reasonable for the organization to expect that she will subsequently display those skills in the performance of her job.

psychological contract the overall set of expectations held by an individual with respect to what he or she will contribute to the organization and what the organization will provide in return

contributions *(psychological contract)* what an individual offers to the organization—effort, skills, ability, time, loyalty, and so forth

inducements *(psychological contract)* what an organization provides to the individual—pay, career opportunities, job security, status, and so forth

FIGURE 4.1 THE PSYCHOLOGICAL CONTRACT

Psychological contracts are the basic assumptions that individuals have about their relationships with their organization. Such contracts are defined in terms of contributions by the individual relative to inducements from the organization. Individuals can have psychological contracts with the organization itself, and/or with their leader and team members.

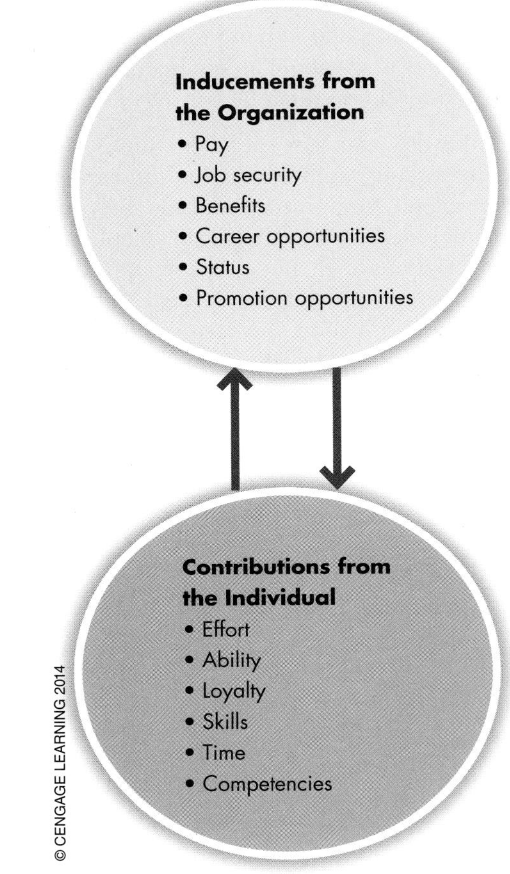

In return for these contributions, the organization provides **inducements** to the individual. Some inducements, like pay and career opportunities, are tangible rewards. Others, like job security and status, are more intangible. Just as the contributions available from the individual must satisfy the needs of the organization, the inducements offered by the organization must serve the needs of the individual. Thus, if a person accepts employment with an organization because he thinks he will earn an attractive salary and have an opportunity to advance, he will subsequently expect that those rewards will actually be forthcoming.

If both the individual and the organization perceive that the psychological contract is fair and equitable, they will be satisfied with the relationship and will likely continue it. On the other hand, if either party sees an imbalance or inequity in the contract, it may initiate a change. For example, the individual may request a pay raise or promotion, decrease her contributed effort, or look for a better job elsewhere. The organization can also initiate change by requesting that the individual improve his skills through training, transfer the person to another job, or terminate the person's employment altogether.[5]

A basic challenge faced by the manager, then, is to fully understand psychological contracts. The manager must ensure that the organization is getting value from its employees. At the same time, the manager must be sure that the organization is providing employees with appropriate inducements. If the organization is underpaying its employees for their contributions, for example, they may perform poorly or leave for better jobs elsewhere. On the other hand, if they are being overpaid relative to their contributions, the organization is incurring unnecessary costs.[6] Effective interpersonal skills can help managers understand psychological contracts and enable her or him to more effectively explain and implement such contracts.

DREAMPICTURES

Person-job fit is an important consideration in organizations. Not everyone, for example, would be willing or able to perform high-floor window cleaning work like this man.

LEARN

The Person-Job Fit

One specific aspect of using interpersonal skills to manage psychological contracts is managing the person-job fit. **Person-job fit** is the extent to which the contributions made by the individual match the inducements offered by the organization. In theory, each employee has a specific set of needs that he wants fulfilled and a set of job-related behaviors and abilities to contribute. If the organization can take complete advantage of those behaviors and abilities, and entirely fulfill his needs, it will have achieved a perfect person-job fit.

Of course, such a precise level of person-job fit is seldom achieved. There are several reasons for this. For one, organizational selection procedures are imperfect. Organizations can make approximations of employee skill levels when making hiring decisions and can improve those skills through training. But even simple performance capabilities are difficult to measure in objective and valid ways.

Another reason for imprecise person-job fits is that both people and organizations change. An individual who finds a new job stimulating and exciting may find the same job boring and monotonous after a few years of performing it. On the other hand, when the organization adopts new technology, it has changed the skills it needs from its employees. Some employees may find it too challenging to adapt to this change.

Another reason for imprecision in the person-job fit is that each individual is unique. Measuring skills and performance is difficult enough. Assessing needs, attitudes, and personality is far more complex. Each of these individual differences serves to make matching individuals with jobs a difficult and complex process.[7]

The Nature of Individual Differences

Individual differences are personal attributes that vary from one person to another. Individual differences may be physical, psychological, or emotional. In Chapter 2 we discussed the importance of understanding our own personality and identified a

person-job fit the extent to which the contributions made by the individual match the inducements offered by the organization

individual differences personal attributes that vary from one person to another

number of fundamental personality traits. These personality traits define us in unique ways and are the basic framework that makes each of us different.

The individual differences that characterize any specific person serve to make them unique from everyone else. Are specific differences that characterize a given individual good or bad? Do they contribute to or detract from performance? It depends on the circumstances. One person may be very dissatisfied, withdrawn, and negative in one job setting, but very satisfied, outgoing, and positive in another. Working conditions, coworkers, and leadership all contribute to and determine performance.

LEARN

When an organization attempts to assess or account for individual differences among its employees, it must also consider the situation in which behavior occurs. Individuals who are satisfied or productive workers in one context may prove to be dissatisfied or unproductive workers in another context. Consider individual differences and contributions in relation to inducements and contexts is a major challenge for organizations as they attempt to establish effective psychological contracts with their employees and achieve optimal fits between people and jobs.

MOTIVATING EMPLOYEES

One of the basic functions of management is to motivate employees. The process of motivating people relies heavily on the manager's interpersonal skills. **Motivation** is the set of forces that cause people to behave in certain ways.[8] On any given day, an employee may choose to work as hard as possible at a job, work just hard enough to avoid a reprimand, or do as little as possible. The goal for the manager is to maximize the likelihood of the first behavior and minimize the likelihood of the last. This goal becomes all the more important when we understand how important motivation is in the workplace. Individual performance is generally determined by three things: motivation (the desire to do the job), ability (the capability to do the job), and the work environment (the resources needed to do the job). If an employee lacks ability, the manager can provide training or replace the worker. If there is a resource problem, the manager can correct it. But, if motivation is the problem, the task for the manager is more challenging.[9] Individual behavior is a complex phenomenon, and the manager may have difficulty determining the precise nature of the problem and how to solve it. Motivation and its intangible characteristics are important because they significantly determine performance.[10]

motivation the set of forces that cause people to behave in certain ways

content perspectives (*on motivation*) theories and concepts that address the question of what factors in the workplace motivate people

Maslow's hierarchy of needs content perspective that suggests there are five levels of needs arranged in a hierarchy of importance

Content Perspectives on Motivation

Content perspectives on motivation deal with needs and need deficiencies. **Content perspectives** address the question: What factors in the workplace motivate people? Labor leaders often argue that workers can be motivated by more pay, shorter working hours, and improved working conditions. Some experts suggest that motivation can be enhanced by providing employees with more autonomy and greater responsibility.[11] Both of these views represent content views of motivation. The former asserts that motivation is a function of pay, working hours, and working conditions; the latter suggests that autonomy and responsibility are the causes of motivation. Two widely known content perspectives on motivation are the needs hierarchy and the two-factor theory.

The Needs Hierarchy Approach The needs hierarchy approach assumes that people have different needs that can be arranged in a hierarchy of importance. The best known is Maslow's hierarchy of needs.[12] **Maslow's hierarchy of needs** suggests there are five levels of needs.

At the bottom of the hierarchy are *physiological needs*—things like food, sex, and air, which represent basic issues of survival and biological function. In organizations, these needs are generally satisfied by adequate wages and the work environment itself, which provides restrooms, adequate lighting, comfortable temperatures, and ventilation.

Next are the *security needs* for a secure physical and emotional environment. Examples include the need for housing and clothing, and the need to be free from worry about money and job security. These needs can be satisfied in the workplace by job continuity (no layoffs), a grievance system (to protect against arbitrary supervisory actions), and an adequate insurance and retirement benefit package (for security against illness and provision of income in later life). Even today, however, depressed industries and economic decline can put people out of work and restore the primacy of security needs.

Belongingness needs relate to social processes. They include the need for love and affection and the need to be accepted by one's peers. These needs are satisfied for most people by family and community relationships outside of work and by friendships on the job. A manager can help satisfy these needs by allowing social interaction and by making employees feel like part of a team or work group.

Esteem needs comprise two different sets of needs: the need for a positive self-image and self-respect, and the need for recognition and respect from others. A manager can help address these needs by providing a variety of extrinsic symbols of accomplishment, such as job titles, nice offices, and similar rewards as appropriate. At a more intrinsic level, the manager can provide challenging job assignments and opportunities for the employee to feel a sense of accomplishment.

At the top of the hierarchy are the *self-actualization needs*. These involve realizing one's potential for continued growth and individual development. The self-actualization needs are perhaps the most difficult for a manager to address. In fact, it can be argued that these needs must be met entirely from within the individual. But a manager can help by promoting a culture wherein self-actualization is possible. For instance, a manager could give employees a chance to participate in making decisions about their work and the opportunity to learn new things.

Maslow suggests that an individual is motivated first and foremost to satisfy physiological needs. As long as they remain unsatisfied, the individual is motivated to fulfill only those needs. When satisfaction of physiological needs is achieved, they cease to act as primary motivational factors, and the individual moves "up" the hierarchy and becomes concerned with security needs. This process continues until the individual reaches the self-actualization level. Maslow's concept of the need hierarchy has a certain intuitive logic and is known by many managers. But research has revealed certain shortcomings and defects in the theory. Some research has found that five levels of need are not always present and that the order of the levels is not always the same, as postulated by Maslow.[14] In addition, people from different cultures are likely to have different need categories and hierarchies.

"I wanted to do something with my life where I felt I was contributing. Somehow, selling more tacos and margaritas than the week before wasn't."

CATHEY GARDNER,
Former restaurant manager, on her decision to become a nurse[13]

USA TODAY, AUGUST 16, 2004, P. 2B.

The Two-Factor Theory Another popular content perspective is the two-factor theory of motivation.[15] Frederick Herzberg developed his theory by asking employees to recall occasions when they had been satisfied and motivated, and occasions when they had been dissatisfied and unmotivated. Surprisingly, he found that different sets of factors were associated with satisfaction and with dissatisfaction—that is, a person might identify "low pay" as causing dissatisfaction but would not necessarily mention "high pay" as a cause of satisfaction. Instead, different factors—such as recognition or accomplishment—were cited as causing satisfaction and motivation.

This finding led Herzberg to conclude that the traditional view of job satisfaction was incomplete. That view assumed that satisfaction and dissatisfaction are at opposite ends of a single continuum. People might be satisfied, dissatisfied, or somewhere in between. But Herzberg's interviews had identified two different dimensions: one ranging from satisfaction to no satisfaction, and the other ranging from dissatisfaction to no dissatisfaction. This perspective, along with several examples of factors that affect each continuum, is shown in *Figure 4.2*. Note that the factors influencing the satisfaction continuum—called motivation factors—are related specifically to the work content. The factors presumed to cause dissatisfaction—called hygiene factors—are related to the work environment.

© GERARDO ANTONIO SANCHEZ TORRES

Based on these findings, Herzberg argued that there are two stages in the process of motivating employees. First, managers must ensure that the hygiene factors are not deficient. Pay and security must be appropriate, working conditions must be safe, technical supervision must be acceptable, and so on. By providing hygiene factors at an appropriate

two-factor theory of motivation
content perspective based on two different dimensions, one ranging from satisfaction to no satisfaction and the other ranging from dissatisfaction to no dissatisfaction

LEARN

FIGURE 4.2 THE TWO-FACTOR THEORY OF MOTIVATION

The two-factor theory suggests that job satisfaction has two dimensions. A manager who tries to motivate an employee using only hygiene factors, such as pay and good working conditions, will likely not succeed. To motivate employees and produce a high level of satisfaction, managers must also offer factors such as responsibility and the opportunity for advancement (motivation factors).

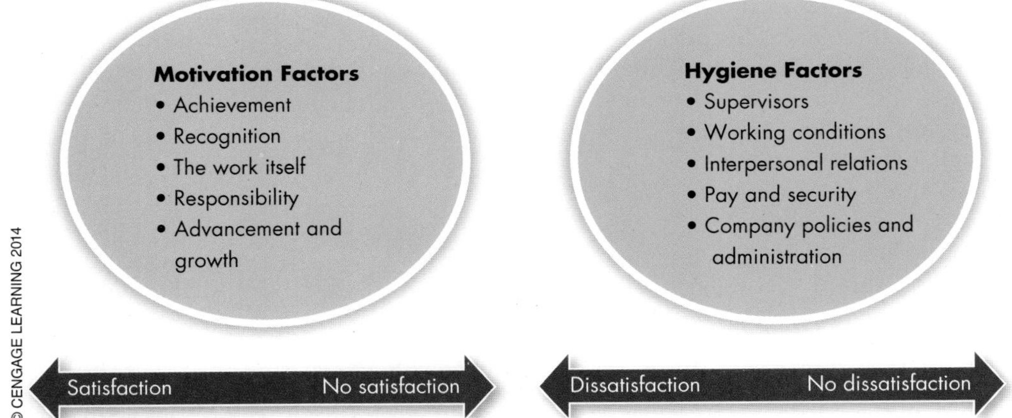

level, managers do not stimulate motivation but merely ensure that employees are "not dissatisfied." Employees whom managers attempt to "satisfy" through hygiene factors alone will usually do just enough to get by. Thus, managers should proceed to stage two—giving employees the opportunity to experience motivation factors such as achievement and recognition. The result is predicted to be a high level of satisfaction and motivation. Herzberg also went a step further than most other theorists and described exactly how to use the two-factor theory in the workplace. Specifically, he recommended job enrichment, an approach to job design intended to provide higher levels of the motivation factors.

Although widely known by many managers, Herzberg's two-factor theory is not without its critics. One criticism is that the findings in Herzberg's initial interviews are subject to different interpretations. Another charge is that his sample was not representative of the general population, and that subsequent research often failed to uphold the theory.[16] Herzberg's theory is not held in high esteem by researchers in the field. The theory has had a major impact on managers, however, and it has played a key role in increasing their awareness of motivation and its importance in the workplace.

process perspectives (*on motivation*) theories and concepts that focus on why people choose certain behavioral options to satisfy their needs and how they evaluate their satisfaction after they have attained these goals

expectancy theory process perspective that suggests that motivation depends on two things—how much we want something and how likely we think we are to get it

Process Perspectives on Motivation

Process perspectives are concerned with how motivation occurs. Rather than attempting to identify motivational stimuli, process perspectives focus on why people choose certain behavioral options to satisfy their needs and how they evaluate their satisfaction after they have attained these goals. Three useful process perspectives on motivation are the expectancy, equity, and goal-setting theories.

Expectancy Theory Expectancy theory suggests that motivation depends on two things—how much we want something and how likely we think we are to get it.[17] Assume that you are fresh out of college and looking for a job. You have learned that General Motors is seeking a new vice president with a starting salary of $1,500,000 per year. Even though you might want the job, you will not apply because you realize that you have little chance of getting it. You also know of a job scraping chewing gum from underneath theater seats for minimum wage. Even though you could probably get this job, you do not apply because you do not want it. Then you learn about an attractive job that matches your credentials and offers a salary that is comparable to those offered to your classmates. You will probably apply for this job because you want it and you think you have a reasonable chance of getting it.

Expectancy theory rests on four basic assumptions:

1. Behavior is determined by a combination of forces in the individual and in the environment.

FIGURE 4.3 THE EXPECTANCY MODEL OF MOTIVATION

The expectancy model of motivation is a complex but relatively accurate portrayal of how motivation occurs. According to this model, a manager must understand what employees want (such as pay, promotions, or status) in order to motivate them. For example, offering a reward that no one wants will not motivate behavior.

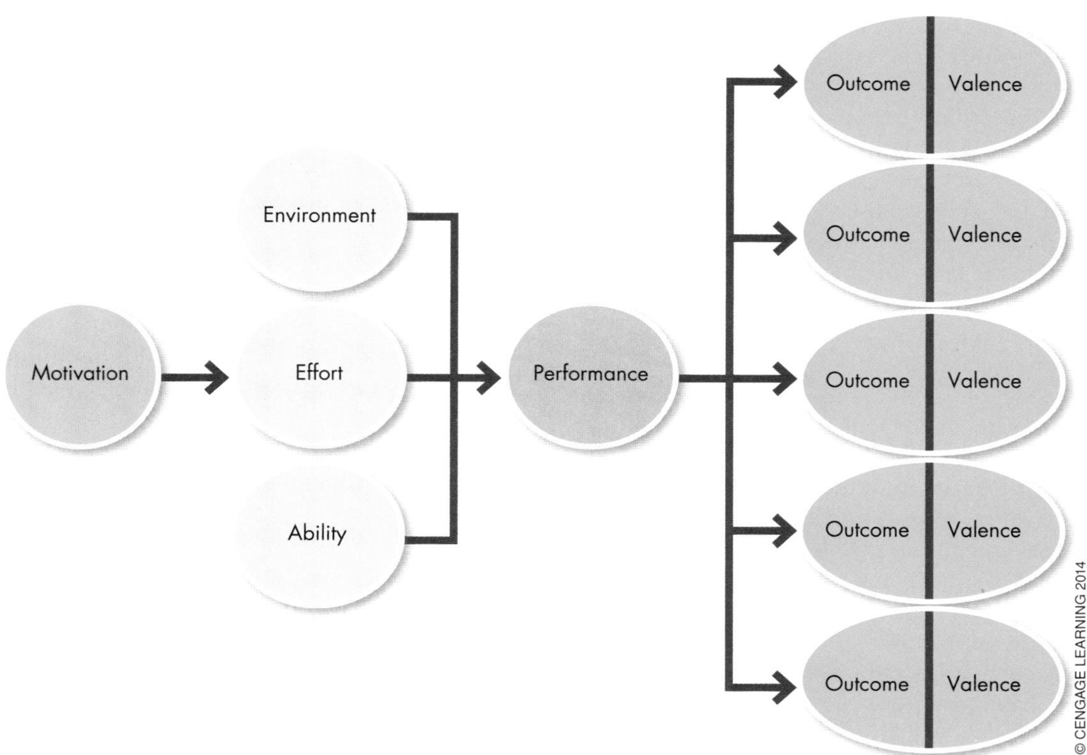

LEARN

2. People make decisions about their own behavior in organizations.
3. Different people have different types of needs, desires, and goals.
4. People make choices from among alternative plans of behavior, based on their perceptions of the extent to which a given behavior will lead to desired outcomes.

Figure 4.3 summarizes the basic expectancy model. The model suggests that motivation leads to effort and that effort, combined with employee ability and environmental factors, results in performance. Performance, in turn, leads to various outcomes, each of which has an associated value, called its valence. The most important parts of the expectancy model cannot be shown in the figure, however. These are the individual's expectation that effort will lead to high performance, that performance will lead to outcomes, and that each outcome will have some kind of value.

- *Effort-to-Performance Expectancy* The effort-to-performance expectancy is the individual's perception of the probability that effort will lead to high performance. When the individual believes that effort will lead directly to high performance, expectancy will be quite strong (close to 1.00). When the individual believes that effort and performance are unrelated, the effort-to-performance expectancy is very weak (close to 0). The belief that effort is somewhat but not strongly related to performance carries with it a moderate expectancy (somewhere between 0 and 1.00).
- *Performance-to-Outcome Expectancy* The performance-to-outcome expectancy is the individual's perception that performance will lead to a specific outcome. For example, if the individual believes that high performance will result in a pay raise, the performance-to-outcome expectancy is high (approaching 1.00). The individual who believes that high performance may lead to a pay raise has a moderate expectancy (between 1.00 and 0).

effort-to-performance expectancy the individual's perception of the probability that effort will lead to high performance

performance-to-outcome expectancy the individual's perception that performance will lead to a specific outcome

The individual who believes that performance has no relationship to rewards has a low performance-to-outcome expectancy (close to 0).

- *Outcomes and Valences* Expectancy theory recognizes that an individual's behavior results in a variety of **outcomes**, or consequences, in an organizational setting. A high performer, for example, may get bigger pay raises, faster promotions, and more praise from the boss. On the other hand, she may also be subject to more stress and incur resentment from coworkers. Each of these outcomes also has an associated value, or **valence**—an index of how much an individual values a particular outcome. If the individual wants the outcome, its valence is positive; if the individual does not want the outcome, its valence is negative; and if the individual is indifferent to the outcome, its valence is zero. It is this part of expectancy theory that goes beyond the content perspectives on motivation. Different people have different needs, and they will try to satisfy these needs in different ways. For an employee who has a high need for achievement and a low need for affiliation, the pay raise and promotions cited above as outcomes of high performance might have positive valences, the praise and resentment zero valences, and the stress a negative valence. For a different employee, with a low need for achievement and a high need for affiliation, the pay raise, promotions, and praise might all have positive valences, whereas both resentment and stress could have negative valences.

© VARIO IMAGES GMBH & CO.KG/ALAMY

outcomes in expectancy theory, the perceived consequences of motivated behavior

valence in expectancy theory, an index of how much an individual values a particular outcome

For motivated behavior to occur, three conditions must be met. First, the effort-to-performance must be greater than zero (the individual must believe that if effort is expended, high performance will result). Second, the performance-to-outcome expectancy must also be greater than zero (the individual must believe that if high performance is achieved, certain outcomes will follow). And, third, the sum of the valences for the outcomes must be greater than zero. (One or more outcomes may have negative valences if they are more than offset by the positive valences of other outcomes. For example, the attractiveness of a pay raise, a promotion, and praise from the boss may outweigh the unattractiveness of more stress and resentment from coworkers.) Expectancy theory suggests that when these conditions are met, the individual is motivated to expend effort. Starbucks credits its unique stock ownership program with maintaining a dedicated and motivated workforce. Based on the fundamental concepts of expectancy theory, Starbucks employees earn stock as a function of their seniority and performance. Thus, their hard work helps them earn shares of ownership in the company.[18]

> *"When we're productive and we've done something good together (and we are recognized for it), we feel satisfied, not the other way around."*
>
> J. RICHARD HACKMAN, Leading organizational psychologist[19]

HARVARD BUSINESS REVIEW, MAY 2009, P. 101.

An extension of expectancy theory has also shed interesting light on the relationship between performance and satisfaction.[20] Many people would assume that employee satisfaction causes good performance. However, this causal relationship has not been supported by research. Expectancy theory suggests that there may indeed be a relationship between satisfaction and performance but that it goes in the opposite direction—that is, high performance may lead to high satisfaction. *Figure 4.4* summarizes this logic. Performance results in rewards for an individual. Some of these are extrinsic (such as pay and promotions); others are intrinsic (such as self-esteem and accomplishment). The individual evaluates the equity, or fairness, of the rewards relative to the effort expended and the level of performance attained. If the rewards are perceived to be equitable, the individual is satisfied.

Equity Theory After needs have stimulated the motivation process and the individual has chosen an action that is expected to satisfy those needs, the individual assesses the fairness, or equity, of the resultant

FIGURE 4.4 EXTENSION OF EXPECTANCY THEORY

An expanded version of expectancy theory suggests that if performance results in equitable rewards, people will be more satisfied. Thus, performance can lead to satisfaction. Managers must therefore be sure that any system of motivation includes rewards that are fair, or equitable, for all.

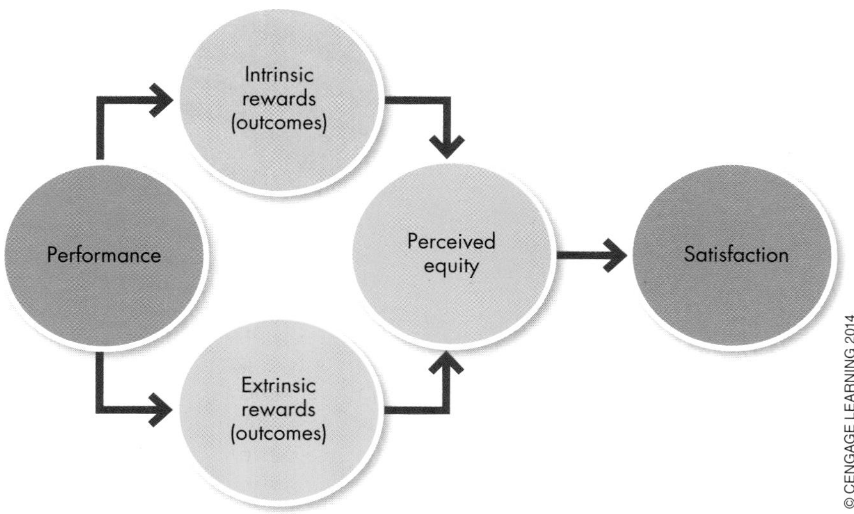

outcome. **Equity theory** contends that people are motivated to seek social equity in the rewards they receive for performance.[21] Equity is an individual's belief that the treatment he or she is receiving is fair relative to the treatment received by others. According to equity theory, outcomes from a job include pay, recognition, promotions, social relationships, and intrinsic rewards. To get these rewards, the individual makes inputs to the job, such as time, experience, effort, education, and loyalty. The theory suggests that people view their outcomes and inputs as a ratio, and then compare it to someone else's ratio. This other "person" may be someone in the work group or some sort of group average or composite. The process of comparison looks like this:

$$\frac{\text{Outcomes (self)}}{\text{Inputs (self)}} \text{ compared with } \frac{\text{Outcomes (other)}}{\text{Inputs (other)}}$$

Both the formulation of the ratios and comparisons between them are very subjective and based on individual perceptions. As a result of comparisons, three conditions may result: The individual may feel equitably rewarded, under-rewarded, or over-rewarded.

A feeling of equity will result when the two ratios are equal. This may occur even though the other person's outcomes are greater than the individual's own outcomes—if the other's inputs are also proportionately greater. Suppose that Mark has a high school education and earns $35,000. He may still feel equitably treated relative to Susan, who earns $45,000, because she has a college degree.

People who feel under-rewarded try to reduce the inequity. Such an individual might decrease her inputs by exerting less effort, increase her outcomes by asking for a raise, distort the original ratios by rationalizing, try to get the other person to change her or his outcomes or inputs, leave the situation, or change the object of comparison.

An individual may also feel over-rewarded relative to another person. This is not likely to be terribly disturbing to most people, but research suggests that some people who experience inequity under these conditions are somewhat motivated to reduce it. Under such a circumstance, the person might increase his inputs by exerting more effort, reduce his outcomes by producing fewer units (if paid on a per-unit basis), distort the original ratios by rationalizing, or try to reduce the inputs or increase the outcomes of the other person.

Managers today may need to pay even greater attention to equity theory and its implications. Many firms are moving toward performance-based reward systems as opposed to standard or across-the-board salary increases. Hence, they must ensure that the basis for rewarding some people more than others are clear and objective. Beyond legal issues such as discrimination, managers need to be sure that they are providing fair rewards and incentives to those

equity theory process theory that contends that people are motivated to seek social equity in the rewards they receive for performance

who do the best work.[22] Moreover, they must be sensitive to cultural differences that affect how people may perceive and react to equity and inequity.[23]

> "People have long memories. They'll remember whether they think they were dealt with equitably."
>
> WILLIAM CONATY, Former director of HR for General Electric[24]
>
> BUSINESSWEEK, JUNE 8, 2009, P. 48.

LEARN

Goal-Setting Theory

The goal-setting theory of motivation assumes that behavior is a result of conscious goals and intentions.[25] Therefore, by setting goals for people in the organization, a manager should be able to influence their behavior. Given this premise, the challenge is to develop a thorough understanding of the processes by which people set goals and then work to reach them. The basic premise of goal-setting theory is that managers should work with their subordinates and help them to develop meaningful, relevant, and effective goals. Two specific goal characteristics—goal difficulty and goal specificity—are predicted to shape performance.

- *Goal Difficulty* Goal difficulty is the extent to which a goal is challenging and requires effort. If people work to achieve goals, it is reasonable to assume that they will work harder to achieve more difficult goals. But a goal must not be so difficult that it is unattainable. If a new manager asks her sales force to increase sales by 300 percent, the group may become disillusioned. A more realistic but still difficult goal—perhaps a 30 percent increase—would be a better incentive. A substantial body of research supports the importance of goal difficulty. In one study, for example, managers at Weyerhaeuser set difficult goals for truck drivers hauling loads of timber from cutting sites to wood yards. Over a nine-month period, the drivers increased the quantity of wood they delivered by an amount that would have required $250,000 worth of new trucks at the previous per-truck average load.[26]
- *Goal Specificity* Goal specificity is the clarity and precision of the goal. A goal of "increasing productivity" is not very specific; a goal of "increasing productivity by 3 percent in the next six months" is quite specific. Some goals, such as those involving costs, output, profitability, and growth, are readily amenable to specificity. Other goals, however, such as improving employee job satisfaction, morale, company image and reputation, ethics, and socially responsible behavior, may be much harder to state in specific terms. Like difficulty, specificity has been shown to be consistently related to performance. The study of timber truck drivers mentioned above, for example, also examined goal specificity. The initial loads the truck drivers were carrying were found to be 60 percent of the maximum weight each truck could haul. The managers set a new goal for drivers of 94 percent, which the drivers were soon able to reach. Thus, the goal was both specific and difficult.

goal-setting theory process theory of motivation that assumes that behavior is a result of conscious goals and intentions

diversity exists in a community of people when its members differ from one another along one or more important dimensions

The content perspectives on motivation help managers understand the needs that may result in motivated behavior. The process perspectives, meanwhile, provide insight into the motivational process that direct behavior in specific directions. Interpersonal skills can enable managers to more effectively motivate employees through an appreciation of both needs and motivational process.

WORKING WITH DIVERSITY, TEAMS, AND CONFLICT

Individual differences represent one major lens through which we can understand others and hence have positive interpersonal relations with them. Motivation theory provides another lens that focuses on why people make behavioral choices. Other important perspectives are diversity, teams, and conflict.

Understanding Diversity

Diversity exists in a community of people when its members differ from one another along one or more important dimensions. Diversity is not an absolute phenomenon that specifies that a group or organization is or is not diverse. Instead, diversity can be conceptualized as a continuum. If everyone in the community is exactly like everyone else, there is no diversity whatsoever. If everyone is different along every imaginable dimension, total diversity exists. In reality these extremes are more hypothetical than real. Most settings are characterized by a level of diversity somewhere between these two extremes. Therefore, diversity should be thought of in terms of degree or level of diversity along relevant dimensions.

In general, there will usually be a reciprocal relationship between interpersonal skills and diversity. For instance, a manager with strong interpersonal skills is likely to help enhance the diversity of the organization's workforce. And at the same time, as an organization becomes more diverse, open-minded managers will come to understand a broader array of employee behavior and thus strengthen her or his interpersonal skills.

C. THATCHER

Diversity can take many forms. In this small group of medical professionals, for instance, several obvious dimensions are apparent. Other less apparent differences also exist.

Reasons for Increased Diversity There are several reasons that organizations are becoming more diverse. One reason organizations are becoming more diverse is because the composition of the labor force is becoming more diverse. A related factor contributing to diversity is the recognition that organizations can improve the overall quality of their workforce by hiring and promoting the most talented people available. By casting a broader net in recruiting and looking beyond traditional sources for new employees, organizations are finding more broadly qualified and better-qualified employees from many different segments of society. Thus, these organizations are finding that diversity can be a source of competitive advantage.[27]

Another reason for the increase in diversity is that both legislation and judicial decisions have forced organizations to hire more broadly. In earlier times, organizations in the United States were essentially free to discriminate against women, African Americans, and other minorities. Although not all organizations consciously or openly engaged in these practices, many firms nevertheless came to be dominated by white males. But starting with the passage of the Civil Rights Act in 1964, numerous laws have outlawed discrimination against these and most other groups. Today organizations must hire and promote people solely on the basis of their qualifications.

A final factor contributing to increased diversity is globalization. Organizations that have opened offices and related facilities in other countries have had to learn to deal with different customs, social norms, and mores. Strategic alliances and foreign ownership also contribute, as managers today are more likely to have job assignments in other countries or to work with foreign managers within their own countries. As employees and managers move from assignment to assignment across national boundaries, organizations and their subsidiaries within each country become more diverse.

Dimensions of Diversity Many different dimensions of diversity can characterize an organization. These include age, gender, and ethnicity. Recent trends along several dimensions are illustrated in *Figure 4.5*. One dimension is age. The average age of the US workforce is gradually increasing and will continue to do so for the next several years. For example, *Figure 4.5* presents age distributions in the United States in 2000 and projected age distributions through the year 2050. Over that span, the median age is expected to rise from 35.5 years to 39 years.

Several factors are contributing to this pattern. For one, the baby boom generation (a term used to describe the unusually large number of people who were born in the 20-year period after World War II) continues to age. Declining birthrates among the post-baby boom generations simultaneously account for smaller percentages of new entrants into the labor force. Another factor that contributes to the aging workforce is improved health and medical care. As a result of these improvements, people are able to remain productive and active for longer periods of time. Finally, and unfortunately, many people approaching traditional retirement ages do not have sufficient savings to pay for retirement and so must work longer. These reasons combine to result in more and more people working beyond the age at which they might have retired just a few years ago.

How does this trend affect organizations? Older workers tend to have more experience, to be more stable, and to make greater contributions to productivity than younger workers. On the other hand, despite the improvements in health and medical care, older workers are likely to require higher levels of insurance coverage and medical benefits. The declining labor pool of younger workers will continue to pose problems for organizations as they find fewer potential new entrants

FIGURE 4.5 THE AGING US WORKFORCE

The US population is gradually growing older. For example, in 2010 the median age in the United States was 36.9 years; by 2050, however, this figure will rise to 39 years. By that same year, more than one-third of the entire US population will be over age 50.

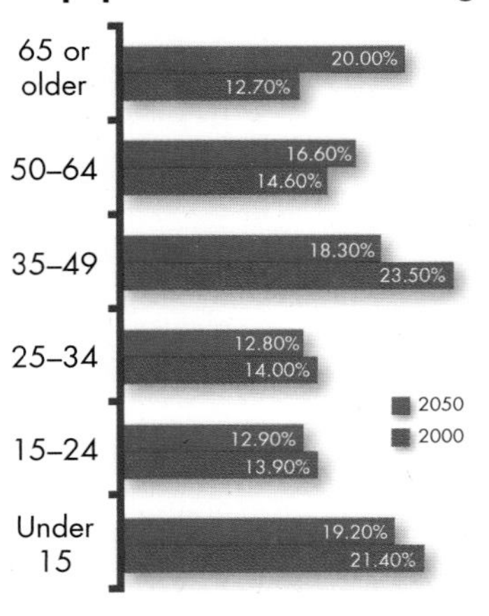

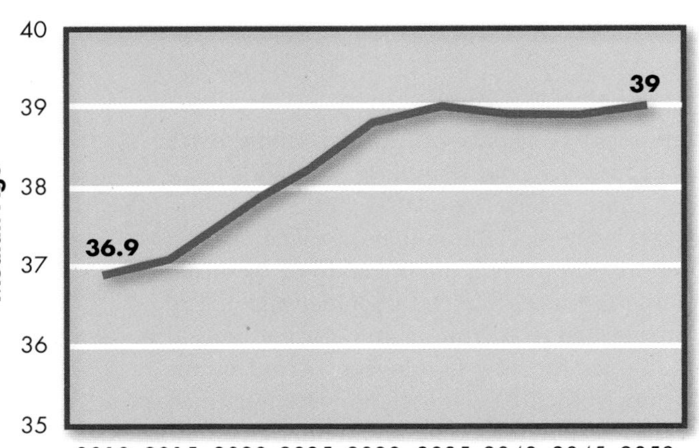

Source: U.S. Census Bureau

into the labor force.[28] Age disparities can be a challenge to interpersonal relations. With all else equal, a large age gap between a manager and subordinate (in either direction) can make common understanding more difficult and increase the likelihood of misunderstandings and conflict.

As more and more women have entered the workforce, organizations have subsequently experienced changes in the relative proportions of male and female employees. In the United States, for example, the workforce in 1964 was 66 percent male and 34 percent female. By 2010 the proportions were around 50.1 percent male and 49.9 percent female. During the next ten years, the gap between these percentages is expected to continue to shrink.

These trends aside, a major gender-related problem that many organizations face is the glass ceiling. The **glass ceiling** describes a barrier that keeps women from advancing to top management positions in many organizations.[29] This ceiling is difficult to break because its presence is subtle and not always apparent. Whereas women comprise more than 38 percent of all managers, there are very few female CEOs among the thousand largest businesses in the United States. Similarly, the average pay of women in organizations is lower than that of men. Although the pay gap is gradually shrinking, inequalities are still prominent.

glass ceiling describes a barrier that keeps women from advancing to top management positions in many organizations

ethnicity refers to the ethnic composition of a group or organization

Why does the glass ceiling still exist? One reason may be that obstacles to advancement for women, such as subtle discrimination, may still exist in some organizations.[30] Another is that many talented women choose to leave their job in a large organization and start their own business. Still another factor is that some women choose to suspend or slow their career progression to have children. But there are also many talented women continuing to work their way up the corporate ladder and getting closer and closer to a corporate "top spot."[31]

A third major dimension of diversity in organizations is ethnicity. **Ethnicity** refers to the ethnic composition of a group or organization. Within the United States, most organizations reflect varying degrees of ethnicity, comprising Caucasian, African Americans, Latinos, and Asians. As is the case with age and gender, the ethnic composition of the US population is becoming more diverse.[32] *Figure 4.6* shows ethnicity distribution trends in the United States projected from 2000 through 2025.

The biggest projected changes involve Caucasians and Latinos. In particular, the percentage of Caucasians in the United States is expected to drop from 72 percent to 53 percent by 2025. At the same time, the percentage of Latinos is expected to climb from 11.5 percent to 24.5 percent.[33] The percentage of African Americans, Asians, and others is also expected to climb, but at lower rates. As with women, members of the African American, Latino, and Asian groups generally are underrepresented in the executive ranks of most organizations. In addition, their pay is lower than might be expected. As is also the case for women,

FIGURE 4.6 TRENDS IN ETHNICITY IN THE UNITED STATES

Ethnic diversity in the United States is also increasing. For example, although 72 percent of the US population was white in 1999, this will drop to 53 percent by 2050. Latinos will reflect the largest percentage increase, moving from 11.5 percent in 2000 to 24.5 percent of the US population by 2050.

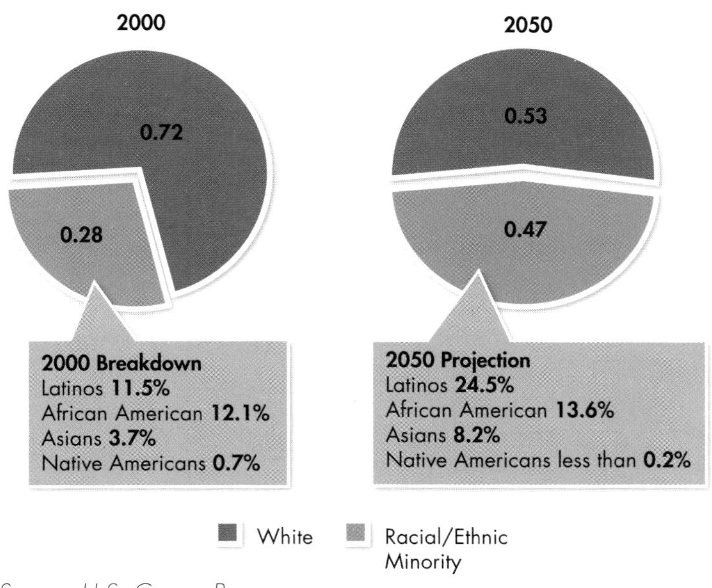

Source: U.S. Census Bureau

LEARN

the differences are gradually disappearing as organizations fully embrace equal employment opportunity and recognize the higher overall level of talent available to them.[34]

In addition to age, gender, and ethnicity, organizations are confronting other dimensions of diversity. Different religious beliefs, for example, constitute an important dimension of diversity.[35] Single parents, dual-career couples, gays and lesbians, people with special dietary preferences (such as vegetarians), and people with different political ideologies and viewpoints represent major dimensions of diversity in today's organizations.[36] Handicapped and physically challenged employees are increasingly important in many organizations, especially since the 1990 passage of the Americans with Disabilities Act.

In addition to these various diversity-related dimensions, organizations are being characterized by multicultural differences as well. Some organizations, especially international businesses, are actively seeking to enhance the multiculturalism of their workforce. Even organizations that are more passive in this regard may still become more multicultural because of changes in the external labor market. Immigration into the United States is at its highest rate since 1910. More than 5 million people from Asia, Mexico, Europe, and other parts of the world entered the United States between 1991 and 1995 alone.[37]

Working With Diversity Because of the tremendous potential that diversity holds for competitive advantage, as well as the possible consequences of associated conflict, much attention has been focused in recent years on how to better manage diversity. Interpersonal skills play a significant role in effectively managing diversity. Managers should keep four things in in mind when considering diversity.

First is to understand the nature and meaning of diversity. Some managers have taken the basic concepts of equal employment opportunity to an unnecessary extreme. They know that, by law, they cannot discriminate against people on the basis of sex, race, and so forth. In following this mandate, they come to believe that they must treat everyone the same. But this belief can cause problems when translated into workplace behaviors among people after they have been hired, because people are not the same. Although all people need to be treated fairly and equitably, managers must understand that differences among people do, in fact, exist. Thus any effort to treat everyone the same, without regard for their fundamental human differences, will lead only to problems. Managers must understand that cultural factors cause people to behave in different ways and that these differences should be accepted.

Related to understanding, the second diversity-related issue is empathy. People in an organization should try to understand the perspectives of others. For example, suppose a woman joins a group that has traditionally been comprised white men. Each man may be a little self-conscious about how to act toward the new member and may be interested in making her feel comfortable and welcome. They may be able to do this more effectively by empathizing with how she may feel. For example, she may feel disappointed or elated about her new assignment, she may be confident or nervous about her position in the group, or she may be experienced or inexperienced in working with male colleagues. By learning more about her feelings, the group members can further facilitate their ability to work together effectively.

LEARN

A third strategy for dealing with diversity is tolerance. Even though people learn to understand others, and even though they may try to empathize with others, the fact remains that they still may not accept or enjoy some aspect of their behavior. For example, one organization reported that it experienced considerable conflict among its US and Israeli employees. The Israeli employees always seemed to want to argue about every issue that arose. The US managers preferred to conduct business more harmoniously and became uncomfortable with the conflict. Finally, after considerable discussion, the US employees realized that many of the Israeli employees simply enjoyed debating or arguing and saw it as part of getting the work done. The firm's US employees still did not enjoy the arguing, but they were more willing to tolerate it as a fundamental cultural difference between themselves and their colleagues from Israel after they realized that it was not hostile in nature.[38]

The fourth and final approach to dealing with diversity is communication. While we address communication skills in Chapter 7, the willingness to communicate also is clearly related to interpersonal skills because problems often are magnified when people are afraid or unwilling to openly discuss issues that relate to diversity or multiculturalism. For example, suppose that a young employee has a habit of making jokes about the age of an older colleague. Perhaps the young colleague means no harm and is just engaging in what she sees as good-natured kidding, but the older employee may find the jokes offensive. If they do not communicate, the jokes will continue, and the resentment will grow. Eventually, what started as a minor problem may evolve into a much bigger one. For communication to work, it must work two ways. If a person wonders whether a certain behavior on her or his part is offensive to someone else, the curious individual should just ask. Similarly, if someone is offended by the behavior of another person, he or she should explain to the offending individual how the behavior is perceived and request that it stop. As long as such exchanges are friendly, low key, and nonthreatening, they will generally have a positive outcome. Of course, if the same message is presented in an overly combative manner or if a person continues to engage in offensive behavior after having been asked to stop, problems will only escalate. At this point, third parties within the organization may have to intervene. Most organizations today have one or more systems in place to address questions and problems that arise as a result of diversity.

team a small number of people with complementary skills who are committed to a common purpose, performance goals, and approach for which they hold themselves mutually accountable

work teams tend to be permanent and are the teams that do the daily work of an organization

problem-solving teams temporary teams established to attack specific problems in the workplace

Managing Teams

While organizations have used teams for decades, they have become much more prevalent in recent years. We will define a team as "a small number of people with complementary skills who are committed to a common purpose, performance goals, and approach for which they hold themselves mutually accountable."[39] Effective interpersonal skills in both managing a team and serving as a member of a team are very important. For example, managing a team requires the manager to interact effectively with each individual member of the team as well as the team itself. Similarly, being an effective team member requires that a person be capable of working productively with peers.

Types of Teams There are several different types of teams. Work teams tend to be permanent and are the teams that do the daily work of an organization.[40] The nurses, orderlies, and various technicians responsible for all patients on a floor or wing in a hospital comprise a work team. Rather than investigate a specific problem, evaluate alternatives, and recommend a solution or change, a work team does the actual daily work of the unit. The difference between a traditional work group of nurses and the patient care team is that the latter has the authority to decide how the work is done, in what order, and by whom. The entire team is responsible for all patient care. In general, work teams are teams that make or do things and that have appropriate levels of authority and autonomy.

Problem-solving teams are temporary teams established to attack specific problems in the workplace. Teams can use any number of methods to solve the problem. After solving the problem, the team usually is disbanded, allowing members to return to their normal work. One survey found that 91 percent of US companies utilize problem-solving teams regularly.[41] High-performing problem-solving teams are often

© PHOTOALTO/ALAMY

Teams are common in many work settings today. This team of contractors and architects is reviewing the plans for a new office complex at the work site.

cross-functional, meaning that team members come from many different functional areas. Crisis teams are problem-solving teams created only for the duration of an organizational crisis and are usually composed of people from many different areas. Problem-solving teams are teams that make recommendations for others to implement.

Management teams consist of managers from various areas and coordinate work teams. They are relatively permanent because their work does not end with the completion of a particular project or the resolution of a problem. Management teams must concentrate on the teams that have the most impact on overall corporate performance. The primary job of management teams is to coach and counsel other teams to be self-managing by making decisions within the team. The second most important task of management teams is to coordinate work between work teams that are interdependent in some manner. Digital Equipment Corporation abandoned its team matrix structure because the matrix of teams was not well organized and coordinated. Team members at all levels reported spending hours and hours in meetings trying to coordinate among teams, leaving too little time to get the real work done.[42] Top-management teams may have special types of problems. First, the work of the top-management team may not always be conducive to teamwork. Vice presidents or heads of divisions may be in charge of different sets of operations that are not related and do not need to be coordinated. Forcing that type of top-management group to be a team may be inappropriate. Second, top managers often have reached high levels in the organization because they have certain characteristics or abilities to get things done. For successful managers to alter their style, to pool resources, and to sacrifice their independence and individuality can be very difficult.[43]

Product development teams are combinations of work teams and problem-solving teams that create new designs for products or services that will satisfy customer needs. They are similar to problem-solving teams because when the product is fully developed and in production, the team may be disbanded. As global competition and electronic information storage, processing, and retrieving capabilities increase, companies in almost every industry are struggling to cut product development times. The primary organizational means of accomplishing this important task is the "blue-ribbon" cross-functional team. Boeing's team that developed the 787 commercial airplane and the platform teams of Chrysler are typical examples. The rush to market with new designs can lead to numerous problems for product development teams. The primary problems of poor communication and coordination of typical product development processes in organizations can be rectified by creating self-managing cross-functional product development teams.[44]

Virtual teams are teams that may never actually meet together in the same room—their activities take place on the computer via teleconferencing and other electronic information systems. Engineers in the United States can directly connect audibly and visually with counterparts all around the globe, sharing files via Internet, electronic mail, and other communication utilities. All participants can look at the same drawing, print, or specification, so decisions are made much faster. With electronic communication systems, team members can move in or out of a team or a team discussion as the issues warrant.

Benefits and Costs of Teams Why are so many organizations today using teams? With the popularity of teams increasing so rapidly around the world, it is possible that some organizations are starting to use teams simply because everyone else is doing it, which is obviously the wrong reason. But the fundamental reason for a company to create teams should be that teams make sense for that particular organization. The best reason to start teams in any organization is to recap the positive benefits that can result from a team-based environment: enhanced performance, employee benefits, reduced costs, and organizational enhancements.

management teams consist of managers from various areas and coordinate work teams

product development teams combinations of work teams and problem-solving teams that create new designs for products or services that will satisfy customer needs

virtual teams teams that may never actually meet together in the same room—their activities take place digitally via teleconferencing and other electronic information systems

Enhanced performance can come in many forms, including improved productivity, quality, and customer service. Working in teams enables workers to avoid wasted effort, reduce errors, and react better to customers, resulting in more output for each unit of employee input. Such enhancements result from pooling of individual efforts in new ways and from continuously striving to improve for the benefit of the team.[45] For example, a General Electric plant in North Carolina experienced a 20 percent increase in productivity after team implementation.[46] K Shoes reported a 19 percent increase in productivity and significant reductions in rejects in the manufacturing process after it started using teams.

Employees tend to benefit as much as organizations in a team environment. Much attention has been focused on the differences between the baby boom generation and the "post-boomers" in their attitudes toward work, its importance to their lives, and what they want from it. In general, younger workers tend to be less satisfied with their work and the organization, to have lower respect for authority and supervision, and to want more than a paycheck every week. Teams can provide the sense of self-control, human dignity, identification with work, and sense of self-worth and self-fulfillment for which current workers seem to strive. Rather than relying on the traditional, hierarchical, manager-based system, teams give employees the freedom to grow and to gain respect and dignity by managing themselves, making decisions about their work, and really making a difference in the world around them.[47] As a result, employees have a better work life, face less stress at work, and make less use of employee assistance programs.

As empowered teams reduce scrap, make fewer errors, file fewer worker compensation claims, and reduce absenteeism and turnover, organizations based on teams are showing significant cost reductions. Team members feel that they have a stake in the outcomes, want to make contributions because they are valued, and are committed to their team and do not want to let it down. Wilson Sporting Goods reported saving $10 million per year for five years thanks to its teams. Colgate-Palmolive reported that technician turnover was extremely low—more than 90 percent of technicians were retained after five years—once it changed to a team-based approach.

Other improvements in organizations that result from moving from a hierarchically based, directive culture to a team-based culture include increased innovation, creativity, and flexibility.[48] Teams can eliminate redundant layers of bureaucracy and flatten the hierarchy in large organizations. Employees feel closer and more in touch with top management. Employees who think their efforts are important are more likely to make significant contributions. In addition, the team environment constantly challenges teams to innovate and solve problems creatively. If the "same old way" does not work, empowered teams are free to throw it out and develop a new way. With increasing global competition, organizations must constantly adapt to keep abreast of changes. Teams provide the flexibility to react quickly. One of Motorola's earliest teams challenged a long-standing top-management policy regarding supplier inspections in order to reduce the cycle times and improve delivery of crucial parts.[49] After several attempts, management finally allowed the team to change the system and consequently reaped the expected benefits.

The costs of teams are usually tied to the difficulty of changing to a team-based organization. Managers have expressed frustration and confusion about their new roles as coaches and facilitators, especially if they developed their managerial skills under the old traditional hierarchical management philosophy. Some managers have felt as if they were working themselves out of a job as they turned over more and more of their old directing duties to a team.[50] Employees may also feel like losers during the change to a team culture. Some traditional staff groups, such as technical advisory staffs, may feel that their jobs are in jeopardy as teams do more and more of the technical work formerly done by technicians. New roles and pay scales may need to be developed for the technical staff in these situations. Often, technical people have been assigned to a team or a small group of teams and become members who fully participate in team activities.

Another cost associated with teams is the slowness of the process of full team development. It takes a long time for teams to go through the full development cycle and become mature, efficient, and effective. If top management is impatient with the slow progress, teams may be disbanded, returning the organization to its original hierarchical form with significant losses for employees, managers, and the organization. Probably the most dangerous cost, though, is premature abandonment of the change to a team-based organization. If top management gets impatient with the team change process and cuts it short, never allowing teams to develop fully and realize benefits, all the hard work of employees, middle managers, and supervisors is lost. As a result, employee confidence in management in general and in the decision makers in particular may suffer for a long time.[51] The losses in productivity and efficiency will be very difficult to recoup. Management must therefore be fully committed before initiating a change to a team-based organization.

Managing Conflict

When people work together in an organization, whether in teams or traditional dyads, things do not always go smoothly. Conflict is an inevitable element of interpersonal relationships in organizations. In this section, we look at how conflict affects overall performance. We also explore the causes of conflict between individuals, groups, and an organization and its environment. Interpersonal skills are essential to helping the manager understand conflict, as well as to manage and resolve it when it arises.

The Nature of Conflict A disagreement among two or more individuals, groups, or organizations results in conflict. This disagreement may be relatively superficial or very strong. It may be short-lived or exist for months or even years, and it may be work related or personal. Conflict may manifest itself in a variety of ways. People may compete with one another, glare at one another, shout, or withdraw. Groups may band together to protect popular members or oust unpopular members. Organizations may seek legal remedies.

Most people assume that conflict is something to be avoided because it connotes antagonism, hostility, unpleasantness, and dissension. Managers and management theorists have traditionally viewed conflict as a problem to be avoided.[52] In recent years, however, we have come to recognize that, although conflict can be a major problem, certain kinds of conflict may also be beneficial.[53] For example, when two members of a site selection committee disagree over the best location for a new plant, each may be forced to more thoroughly study and defend his or her preferred alternative. As a result of more systematic analysis and discussion, the committee may make a better decision and be better prepared to justify it to others than if everyone had agreed from the outset and accepted an alternative that was perhaps less well analyzed. As long as conflict is being handled in a cordial and constructive manner, it is probably serving a useful purpose in the organization. On the other hand, when working relationships are being disrupted and the conflict has reached destructive levels, it has likely become dysfunctional and needs to be addressed.[54]

Figure 4.7 depicts the general relationship between conflict and performance for a group or organization. If there is absolutely no conflict in the group or organization, its members may become complacent and apathetic. As a result, group or organizational performance and innovation may begin to suffer. A moderate level of conflict among group or organizational members, on the other hand, can spark motivation, creativity, innovation, and initiative, and raise performance. Too much conflict, though, can produce such undesirable results as hostility and lack of cooperation, which lowers performance. The key for managers is to find and maintain the optimal amount of conflict that fosters performance. Of course, what constitutes optimal conflict varies with both the situation and the people involved.[55]

FIGURE 4.7 THE NATURE OF ORGANIZATIONAL CONFLICT

Either too much or too little conflict can be dysfunctional for an organization. In either case, performance may be low. However, an optimal level of conflict that sparks motivation, creativity, innovation, and initiative can result in higher levels of performance.

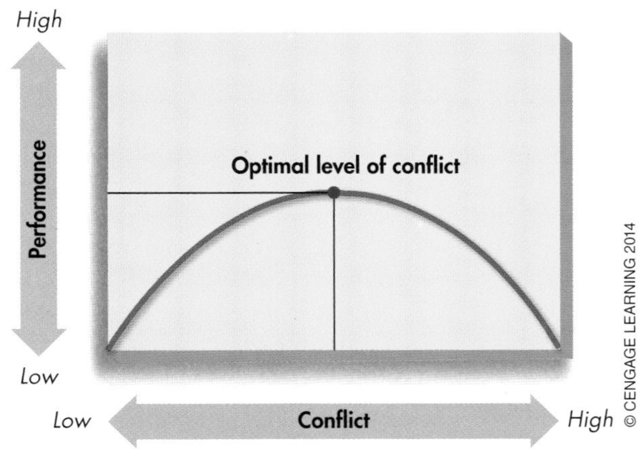

Causes of Conflict Conflict between two or more individuals is almost certain to occur in any organization, given the great variety in perceptions, goals, attitudes, and so forth among its members. William Gates, founder and CEO of Microsoft, and Kazuhiko Nishi, a former business associate from Japan, once ended a lucrative long-term business relationship because of interpersonal conflict. Nishi accused Gates of becoming too political, while Gates charged that Nishi became too unpredictable and erratic in his behavior.[56]

A frequent source of interpersonal conflict in organizations is what many people commonly refer to as a "personality clash"—when two people distrust each other's motives, dislike each other, or for some other reason simply cannot get along.[57] Conflict may also arise between people who have different beliefs or perceptions about some aspect of their work or their organization. For example, one manager might want the organization to require that all employees use Microsoft Office software, to promote standardization. Another manager might believe that a variety of software packages should be allowed, in order to recognize individuality. Similarly, a male manager may disagree with his female colleague over whether the organization is guilty of discriminating against women in promotion decisions. Conflict can also result from excess competitiveness among individuals. Two people vying for the same job, for example, may resort to political behavior in an

conflict the result of a disagreement among two or more individuals, groups, or organizations

LEARN

effort to gain an advantage. If either competitor sees the other's behavior as inappropriate, accusations are likely to result. Even after the "winner" of the job is determined, such conflict may continue to undermine interpersonal relationships, especially if the reasons given in selecting one candidate are ambiguous or open to alternative explanations. A former CEO of Delta Air Lines resigned because he disagreed with other key executives over how best to reduce the carrier's costs. After he began looking for a replacement for one of his rivals without the approval of the firm's board of directors, the resultant conflict and controversy left him no choice but to leave.[58] Similar problems once plagued Boeing as its top executives publicly disagreed over routine matters and sometimes went to great lengths to make each other look bad.[59]

Conflict between two or more organizational groups is also quite common. For example, the members of a firm's marketing group may disagree with the production group over product quality and delivery schedules. Two sales groups may disagree over how to meet sales goals, and two groups of managers may have different ideas about how best to allocate organizational resources. Many intergroup conflicts arise more from organizational causes than from interpersonal causes. For instance, increased interdependence makes coordination more difficult and increases the potential for conflict. For example, in sequential interdependence work is passed from one unit to another. Intergroup conflict may arise if the first group turns out too much work (the second group will fall behind), too little work (the second group will not meet its own goals), or poor-quality work. At one J. C. Penney department store, conflict arose between stockroom employees and sales associates. The sales associates claimed that the stockroom employees were slow in delivering merchandise to the sales floor so that it could be priced and shelved. The stockroom employees, in turn, claimed that the sales associates were not giving them enough lead time to get the merchandise delivered and failed to understand that they had additional duties besides carrying merchandise to the sales floor.

Just like people, different departments often have different goals. Further, these goals may often be incompatible. A marketing goal of maximizing sales, achieved partially by offering many products in a wide variety of sizes, shapes, colors, and models, probably conflicts with a production goal of minimizing costs, achieved partially by long production runs of a few items. Reebok recently confronted this very situation. One group of managers wanted to introduce a new sportswear line as quickly as possible, but other managers wanted to expand more deliberately and cautiously. Because the two groups were not able to reconcile their differences effectively, conflict between the two factions led to quality problems and delivery delays that plagued the firm for months.

Competition for scarce resources can also lead to intergroup conflict. Most organizations—especially universities, hospitals, government agencies, and businesses in depressed industries—have limited resources. In one New England town, for example, the public works department and the library battled over funds from a federal construction grant. The Buick, Pontiac, and Chevrolet divisions of General Motors frequently fought over the right to manufacture various new products developed by the company. This in-fighting was identified as one of many factors that led to GM's bankruptcy in 2009. As part of the solution, the Pontiac brand was eventually discontinued.

Managing Conflict in Organizations How do managers cope with all this potential conflict? Fortunately, as *Table 4.1* shows, there are ways to stimulate conflict for constructive ends, to control conflict before it gets out of hand, and to resolve it if it does. Below we look at ways of managing conflict.[60]

Some organizations may stimulate conflict by placing individual employees or groups in competitive situations. In these situations, a manager's interpersonal skills will be especially important because it is the orgnization itself that is creating the potential for conflict. Managers can establish sales contests, incentive plans, bonuses, or other competitive stimuli to spark competition. As long as the ground rules are equitable and all participants perceive the contest as fair, the conflict created by the competition is likely to be constructive because each participant will work hard to win (thereby enhancing some aspect of organizational performance).

Another useful method for stimulating conflict is to bring in one or more outsiders who will shake things up

TABLE 4.1 METHODS FOR MANAGING CONFLICT

Stimulating Conflict
Increase competition among individuals and teams.
Hire outsiders to shake things up.
Change established procedures.
Controlling Conflict
Expand resource base.
Enhance coordination of interdependence.
Set superordinate goals.
Match personalities and work habits of employees.
Resolving and Eliminating Conflict
Avoid conflict.
Convince conflicting parties to compromise.
Bring conflicting parties together to confront and negotiate conflict.

© CENGAGE LEARNING 2014

and present a new perspective on organizational practices. Outsiders may be new employees, current employees assigned to an existing work group, or consultants or advisors hired on a temporary basis. Of course, this action can also provoke resentment from insiders who feel they were qualified for the position. The Beecham Group, a British company, hired an executive from the United States for its CEO position, expressly to change how the company did business. His arrival brought new ways of doing things and an enthusiasm for competitiveness. Unfortunately, some valued employees also chose to leave Beecham because they resented some of the changes that were made.

Changing established procedures, especially procedures that have outlived their usefulness, can also stimulate conflict. Such actions cause people to reassess how they perform their job and whether they perform it correctly. For example, one university president announced that all vacant staff positions could be filled only after written justification had received his approval. Conflict arose between the president and the department heads, who felt they were doing more paperwork than was necessary. Most requests were approved, but because department heads now had to think through their staffing needs, a few unnecessary positions were appropriately eliminated.

One method of controlling conflict is to expand the resource base. Suppose a top manager receives two budget requests for $100,000 each. If she has only $180,000 to distribute, the stage is set for conflict because each group will believe their proposal is worth funding and will be unhappy if it is not fully funded. If both proposals are indeed worthwhile, it may be possible for the manager to come up with the extra $20,000 from some other source and thereby avoid difficulty.

As noted earlier, interdependence can result in conflict. If managers use an appropriate technique for enhancing coordination, they can reduce the probability that conflict will arise. Techniques for coordination include making use of the managerial hierarchy, relying on rules and procedures, enlisting liaison people, forming task forces, and integrating departments. At the J. C. Penney store mentioned earlier, the conflict was addressed by providing salespeople with clearer forms on which to specify the merchandise they needed and in what sequence. If one coordination technique does not have the desired effect, a manager might shift to another one.

Competing goals can also be a source of conflict among individuals and groups. Managers can sometimes focus employee attention on higher-level, or superordinate, goals as a way of eliminating lower-level conflict. When labor unions like the United Auto Workers make wage concessions to ensure survival of the automobile industry, they are responding to a superordinate goal. Their immediate goal may be higher wages for members, but they realize that, without the automobile industry, their members would not even have jobs.

Finally, managers should try to match the personalities and work habits of employees to avoid conflict between individuals. For instance, two valuable subordinates, one a chain smoker and the other a vehement antismoker, probably should not be required to work together in an enclosed space. If conflict does arise between incompatible individuals, a manager might seek an equitable transfer for one or both of them to other units.

Despite everyone's best intentions, conflict sometimes flares up. If it is disrupting the workplace, creating too much hostility and tension, or otherwise harming the organization, attempts must be made to resolve it.[61] Some managers who have weak interpersonal skills and are uncomfortable dealing with conflict choose to avoid the conflict and hope it will go away. Avoidance may sometimes be effective in the short run for some kinds of interpersonal disagreements, but it does little to resolve long-run or chronic conflicts. Even more unadvisable, though, is "smoothing"—minimizing the conflict and telling everyone that things will "get better" with time. Often the conflict only worsens as people continue to brood over it.

Compromise is striking a middle-range position between two extremes. This approach can work if it is used with care, but in most compromise situations, someone wins and someone loses. Budget problems are one of the few areas amenable to compromise because of their objective nature. Assume, for example, that additional resources are not available to the manager mentioned earlier. She has $180,000 to divide, and each of two groups claims to need $100,000. If the manager believes that both projects warrant funding, she can allocate $90,000 to each. The fact that the two groups have at least been treated equally may minimize the potential conflict.

The confrontational approach to conflict resolution—also called *interpersonal problem solving*—consists of bringing the parties together to confront the conflict. The parties discuss the nature of their conflict and attempt to reach an agreement or a solution. Confrontation requires a reasonable degree of maturity on the part of the participants, and the manager must structure the situation carefully. If handled well, this approach can be an effective means of resolving conflict. In recent years, many organizations have experimented with a technique called *alternative dispute resolution*, using a team of employees to arbitrate conflict in this way.[62] Interpersonal skills clearly play an important role in using the confrontational approach.

© ISTOCKPHOTO.COM/TROELS GRAUGAARD

Businesses sometimes conduct seminars to help their employees better understand the nature of conflict. The instructor leading a seminar for these managers has just used humor to make an important point.

Regardless of the approach, organizations and their managers should realize that conflict must be addressed if it is to serve constructive purposes and be prevented from bringing about destructive consequences. Conflict is inevitable in organizations, but its effects can be constrained with proper attention. For example, Union Carbide sent 200 of its managers to a three-day workshop on conflict management. The managers engaged in a variety of exercises and discussions to learn with whom they were most likely to come in conflict and how they should try to resolve it. As a result, managers at the firm later reported that hostility and resentment in the organization had been greatly diminished and that people in the firm reported more pleasant working relationships.[63]

performance behaviors the total set of work-related behaviors that the organization expects the individual to display

dysfunctional behaviors behaviors detract from, rather than contribute to, organizational performance

absenteeism the rate at which employees do not show up for work

MANAGING WORKPLACE BEHAVIORS

One of the more significant outcomes that managers attempt to achieve through effective use of interpersonal skills includes various forms of workplace behaviors by their subordinates. Workplace behavior is a pattern of action by the members of an organization that directly or indirectly influences the organization's effectiveness. One way to talk about workplace behavior is to describe its impact on performance and productivity, absenteeism and turnover, and organizational citizenship. Unfortunately, employees can exhibit dysfunctional behaviors as well.

Performance Behaviors

Performance behaviors are the total set of work-related behaviors that the organization expects the individual to display. You might think of these as the "terms" of the psychological contract discussed earlier in this chapter. For some jobs, performance behaviors can be narrowly defined and easily measured. For example, an assembly line worker who sits by a moving conveyor and attaches parts to a product as it passes by has relatively few performance behaviors. He or she is expected to remain at the workstation and correctly attach the parts. Performance can often be assessed quantitatively by counting the percentage of parts correctly attached.

For many other jobs, however, performance behaviors are more diverse and much more difficult to assess. For example, consider the case of a research-and-development scientist at Merck. The scientist works in a lab trying to find new scientific breakthroughs that have commercial potential. The scientist must apply knowledge learned in graduate school and experience gained from previous research. Intuition and creativity are also important. The desired breakthrough may take months or even years to accomplish. Organizations rely on a number of different methods to evaluate performance. The key is to match the evaluation mechanism with the job being performed.

Dysfunctional Behaviors

Some work-related behaviors are dysfunctional in nature. Dysfunctional behaviors are those that detract from, rather than contribute to, organizational performance. Two of the more common ones are absenteeism and turnover.

Absenteeism occurs when an employee does not show up for work. Some absenteeism has a legitimate cause, such as illness, jury duty, or death or illness in the family. At other times, the employee may report a feigned legitimate cause that's actually just an excuse to stay home. When an employee is absent, legitimately or not, her or his work does not get done at all or a substitute must be hired to do it. In either case, the quantity or quality of actual output is likely to suffer. Some absenteeism is expected, but organizations strive to minimize feigned absenteeism and reduce legitimate absences as much as possible.

Turnover occurs when people quit their jobs. An organization usually incurs costs in replacing workers who have quit, and if turnover involves especially productive people, it is even more costly. Turnover seems to result from a number of factors, including aspects of the job, the organization, the individual, the labor market, and family influences. In general, a poor person-job fit is also a likely cause of turnover. People may also be prone to leave an organization if its inflexibility makes it difficult to manage family and other personal matters and may be more likely to stay if an organization provides sufficient flexibility to make it easier to balance work and non-work considerations.[64] One Chick-fil-A operator in Texas has cut the turnover rate in his stores by offering flexible work schedules, college scholarships, and such perks as free bowling trips.[65]

Other forms of dysfunctional behavior may be even more costly for an organization. Theft and sabotage, for example, result in direct financial costs for an organization. Sexual and racial harassment also cost an organization, both indirectly (by lowering morale, producing fear, and driving off valuable employees) and directly (through financial liability if the organization responds inappropriately). Workplace violence is also a growing concern in many organizations. Violence by disgruntled or former workers results in dozens of deaths and injuries each year.[66]

Organizational Citizenship

Managers strive to minimize dysfunctional behaviors while trying to promote organizational citizenship. Organizational citizenship refers to the behavior of individuals who make a positive overall contribution to the organization.[67] Consider, for example, an employee who does work that is acceptable in terms of both quantity and quality. However, she refuses to work overtime, won't help newcomers learn the ropes, and is generally unwilling to make any contribution beyond the strict performance of her job. This person may be seen as a good performer, but she is not likely to be seen as a good organizational citizen.

Another employee may exhibit a comparable level of performance. In addition, however, he always works late when the boss asks him to, he takes time to help newcomers learn their way around, and he is perceived as being helpful and committed to the organization's success. He is likely to be seen as a better organizational citizen.

A complex mosaic of individual, social, and organizational variables determine organizational citizenship behaviors. For example, the personality, attitudes, and needs of the individual must be consistent with citizenship behaviors. In addition, the social context, or work group, in which the individual works must facilitate and promote such behaviors. And the organization itself, especially its culture, must be capable of promoting, recognizing, and rewarding these types of behaviors if they are to be maintained. The study of organizational citizenship is still in its infancy, but preliminary research suggests that it may play a powerful role in organizational effectiveness.

SUMMARY AND A LOOK AHEAD

After reading and studying this chapter you should now have a better understanding of interpersonal skills. You should be better equipped to recognize different forms of interpersonal dynamics in organizations and the various outcomes that result from those dynamics. You should also have a stronger appreciation of individual differences, including psychological contracts and person-job fit. In addition, you should have developed a clear understanding of how both content and process perspectives impact employee motivation. The role and impact of diversity, teams, and conflict and how they are affected by interpersonal skills should also be apparent. Finally, you should see a clear distinction across performance and dysfunctional behaviors and organizational citizenship.

The remainder of this chapter provides opportunities for you to continue to develop and refine your own interpersonal skills. For instance, you will be directed to resources where you can visualize both effective and less effective interpersonal skills. Subsequent sections provide several different opportunities for you to practice and explore interpersonal skills from different perspectives. The chapter concludes with some additional assessment and interpretation data.

turnover the rate at which people quit their jobs

organizational citizenship the behavior of individuals who make a positive overall contribution to the organization

LEARN

VISUALIZING INTERPERSONAL SKILLS

VISUALIZE

INTERPERSONAL SKILLS IN ACTION—1

Your Assignment

Consider the two BizFlix film clips for this chapter.

Lost in Translation (2003) deals with culture shock. Jet lag conspires with culture shock to force the meeting of Charlotte (Scarlett Johansson) and Bob Harris (Bill Murray). Neither can sleep after their Tokyo arrival. They meet in their luxury hotel's bar, forging an enduring relationship as they experience Tokyo's wonders, strangeness, and complexity. Based on director Sophia Coppola's Academy-Award-winning screenplay, this film was shot entirely on location in Japan. It offers extraordinary views of various parts of Japanese culture that are not available to you without a visit.

Friday Night Lights (2004) is based on H.G. Bissinger's book about Odessa, Texas and how the high school football team provides spirit for the whole city. The passion in Odessa for Friday night, high school football and the Permian High Panthers comes through clearly in this cinematic treatment. Coach Gary Gaines (Billy Bob Thornton) leads them to the 1988 semifinals where they must compete against a team of much larger players. Fast-moving pace in the football sequences and a slower pace in the serious, introspective sequences give this film many fine moments.

Note how interpersonal skills are shown in these two clips.

1. The first clip is an edited composite taken from different parts of the film. It shows selected aspects of Tokyo and Kyoto, Japan. Charlotte has her first experience with the complex, busy Tokyo train system. She later takes the train to Kyoto, Japan's original capital city for more than ten centuries. What interpersonal skills does she need to be able to handle living, if only for a short time, in a foreign culture?
2. The second clip starts with a panning shot of the Winchell's house. Coach Gaines says to Mike Winchell (Lucas Black), "Can you get the job done, Mike?" Coach Gaines not only seeks to motivate Mike to play his best at the upcoming game but also to motivate him to think about a life beyond high school in Odessa. Do you feel that Coach Gaines is effectively using his interpersonal skills? Why or why not?

INTERPERSONAL SKILLS IN ACTION—2

This exercise gives you an opportunity to think about interpersonal skills that may be involved in management positions for you in the future.

Your Assignment

1. Think about interpersonal skills and try to identify a scene that illustrates a positive or effective use of such skills in a movie, a TV show, or perhaps a video on YouTube.
2. Now do the same for a scene that illustrates a negative or ineffective use of those same skills.

Share your results with the class and discuss how the positive and negative use of interpersonal skills is shown in each clip. You should also see if you can suggest how the negative situation could have been changed for the better.

PRACTICING YOUR INTERPERSONAL SKILLS

MANAGING DURING A PERIOD OF CHANGE

This exercise will help you understand how to apply your interpersonal skills during a period of change.

Assume that you are the manager of a retail store in a local shopping mall. Your staff consists of seven full-time and ten part-time employees. The full-timers have worked together as a team for three years. The part-timers are all local college students, but a couple of them have worked here more than a year. Your boss, the Regional Manager, has just informed you that the national chain that owns your store is planning to open a second store in the same mall and that you must plan and implement the following changes:

- You will serve as manager of both stores until the sales volume of the new store warrants its own full-time manager.
- You will designate one of the full-time employees in your present store as the assistant manager to cover the hours you will be out of the store.
- To have experienced workers in the new store, you will select three of your current full-time workers to move there, with one of them appointed to be the assistant manager.
- You are permitted to hire three new full-time employees to replace those transferred from your present store and three new full-time employees to work at the new store.
- You may decide for yourself how to deploy your part-timers, but you will need a total of ten in the present store and eight in the new store.

You realize that many of your employees will be unhappy with these changes as they all know each other and work well together. However, the new store will be in a new expansion of the mall and will be a very nice place to work.

Your Assignment

1. Determine the likely reasons for the workers to resist this change.
2. Determine how you will make decisions about promotions and transfers (make whatever assumptions that you think are warranted).
3. Outline how you will inform your employees about what is going to happen.
4. An alternative strategy that could be adopted is keeping the existing staff intact and hiring new employees for the new store. Outline a persuasion strategy for convincing your boss that this is what should be done.

SELECTING MODES OF COMMUNICATION

This exercise applies interpersonal skills in selecting modes of communication to convey various kinds of news. This exercise also is relevant to Communication Skills that are covered in Chapter 7.

Assume that you are the regional branch manager for a large insurance company. This past week you have been so tied up in meetings that you have had little opportunity to communicate with any of your subordinates. You have now caught up on things and have a lot of information to convey:

- Three persons need to be told that they are getting a 10-percent pay raise.
- One person needs to be told that she has been placed on probation and will lose her job if her excessive absenteeism problem isn't corrected.

- One person deserves congratulations for receiving his master's degree.
- Everyone needs to be informed about the schedule for the next cycle of performance reviews.
- Two people need to be informed that their transfer requests have been approved, whereas a third was denied. In addition, one other person is being transferred even though she did not request a transfer and will be unhappy to receive one.

Your Assignment

1. Choose an interpersonal communication mode for each message you need to convey; for example, a telephone call during regular office hours, a cell phone call as you are driving home this evening, a formal written letter, a handwritten memo, a face-to-face meeting, or email.
2. What factors went into your selection of each mode?
3. What would be the least appropriate interpersonal communication mode for each message? Why?
4. What would be the likely consequences for each inappropriate choice?

SKILLS RELATED TO MOTIVATION AND SATISFYING NEEDS IN A CAREER

This exercise will give you an opportunity to see how management skills can be used to learn what motivating factors tend to be present in a career of your choice and whether your needs can be met by the career you choose.

Your Assignment

1. Prepare a list of approximately 15 things you need or want from an entry-level job that you will seek following graduation. These needs can be very specific (such as a new car) or very general (such as a feeling of accomplishment).
2. Use the Internet to research your entry-level job. (Hint: One good source is the *Occupational Outlook Handbook* on the Bureau of Labor Statistics website, at http://www.bls.gov/oco/hoe.htm.) Investigate any items related to the needs you specified in response to question one, such as compensation, benefits, working conditions, etc.
3. In what ways does your chosen entry-level job fulfill your needs? In what ways does it fail to do so? If it does satisfy your needs, will you be motivated? If it does not satisfy your needs, will you be unmotivated, or will you find another way to address any discrepancies (such as working a second job or developing a hobby)? Explain.

SURVIVING IN A PERIOD OF CHANGE

This exercise will help you to further understand how to apply interpersonal skills during a period of change.

Assume that you are the manager of a medium-size branch of a large corporation in the Southwestern United States. As one of the largest employers in this city, your company has been a leader in the effort to "Go Green." Not only have your employees been active in projects to save energy, but many of them have been recognized as leaders of the effort to "Save the Planet."

The CEO, who is located at the corporate headquarters in Minneapolis, has agreed to adopt several of the ideas that have been suggested by various "Go Green" committees and government agencies such as the local utility company. Today you and the other divisions received notice that the following actions would be implemented first:

- Thermostats, protected by locked boxes, will be set at 80° in the summer, 70° in winter.
- Microwaves, personal refrigerators, and fans will be banned in offices. If found, these items will have their electrical cords cut.
- Recycling barrels will be provided throughout the buildings for glass, cans, and paper.
- Computers will be turned off automatically at 7 P.M. daily and on weekends; however, anyone who needs to work later or earlier can restart their computers normally.

Your Assignment

You are responsible for communicating this information to all your employees, and you realize that most of them will be unhappy, even if they have previously supported environmental causes.

1. Rank in order the new actions according to how employees will react—for example, from "that's fine" to "that's overkill" to "that's insane."
2. Then think about any actions that you and the local managers may be able to take that will offset some of the resistance of employees. For example, can you change the dress code seasonally to make the office environment more comfortable? What changes can employees themselves make to minimize the negative effects of the changes?
3. What questions can you anticipate? What excuses can you expect for not complying?
4. To minimize the negative effect on morale, should you deliver this news in person at a meeting or in writing?
5. Outline your presentation, showing a balance of managerial behavior and empathy with employees.

PRACTICE

UNDERSTANDING THE PERCEPTUAL PROCESS

The Johari Window is a particularly good model for understanding the perceptual process in interpersonal relationships. Small groups are typically more trusting and work better together, as you will be able to see after this exercise has been completed.

This skill-builder focuses on interpersonal skills and will help you develop your self-awareness. The exercise encourages you to share data about yourself and then to assimilate and process feedback. It has two purposes: to encourage you to analyze yourself more accurately and to start you working on small-group cohesiveness.

Each individual has four sets of personality characteristics. One set, which includes such characteristics as working hard, is well known to the individual and to others. A second set is unknown to the individual but obvious to others. For example, in a working situation a peer group might observe that when you jump in to get the group moving off dead center, that behavior is appropriate. At other times, when you jump in before the group is really finished, you appear to interrupt. A third set of personality characteristics is known to the individual but not to others. These are situations that you have elected not to share, perhaps because of a lack of trust. Finally, there is a fourth set, which is not known to the individual or to others, such as why you are uncomfortable at office parties.

Your Assignment

1. Look at the Johari Window below. In Quadrant 1, list three things that you know about yourself and that you think others also know about you. In Quadrant 3, list three things that others do not know about you. Finally, in Quadrant 2, list three things that you did not know about yourself last semester that you learned from others.

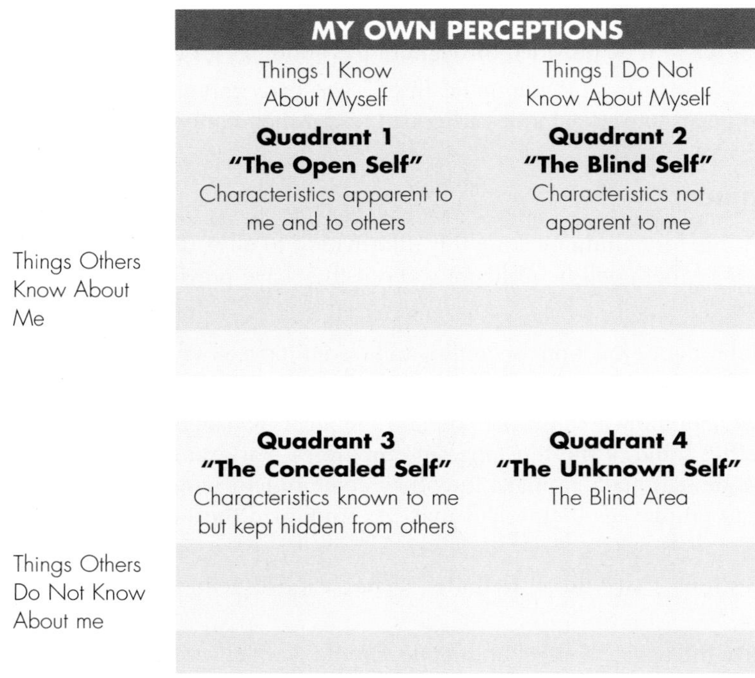

	MY OWN PERCEPTIONS	
	Things I Know About Myself	Things I Do Not Know About Myself
Things Others Know About Me	**Quadrant 1** **"The Open Self"** Characteristics apparent to me and to others	**Quadrant 2** **"The Blind Self"** Characteristics not apparent to me
Things Others Do Not Know About me	**Quadrant 3** **"The Concealed Self"** Characteristics known to me but kept hidden from others	**Quadrant 4** **"The Unknown Self"** The Blind Area

2. After completing the exercise, you will be asked to form small groups to share and discuss your perceptions.

Sources: Adapted from Joseph Luft, *Group Processes: An Introduction to Group Dynamics* (Palo Alto, CA: Mayfield, 1970), pp. 10–11; William C. Morris and Marshall Sashkin, *Organizational Behavior in Action* (St. Paul, MN: West, 1976), p. 56.

UNDERSTANDING DECISION MAKERS (1)

This exercise provides you with the opportunity to sharpen your interpersonal skills by attempting to gain a better understanding of high-level decision makers.

President Lyndon Baines Johnson introduced a great deal of social legislation, termed the "Great Society." That legislation dealt with civil rights, Medicare, Medicaid, environment protection, the "War on Poverty," public broadcasting, and aid to education. However, he also escalated the American involvement in the Vietnam War. He had many individuals providing advice on that latter issue. Among them were Clark M. Clifford (Defense Department), Dean Rusk (State Department), and McGeorge Bundy (National Security Adviser).

Your Assignment

Your instructor may ask you to do this in groups.

1. Construct a table like the following to record information that you find on the Internet and/or in the library about each of these three presidential advisors. Your last date should be in the 1970s.

Public History (general knowledge)		Private History (from public records)		
Date	Event	**Clifford**	**Rusk**	**Bundy**

2. Starting with the year each was born, try to identify significant events (schooling, military service, career, positions held, etc.) in their personal lives or important aspects of their personal lives (economic status of family when a child, relatives, etc.).
3. Then look up major events in the "world" that these individuals would have heard about, experienced, or lived through.
4. Now examine your table and draw inferences about the skills, personalities and biases each of these advisers might have had as a result of their "histories."

Source: Adapted with the permission of Free Press, a Division of Simon & Schuster, Inc., from THINKING IN TIME: The Users of History for Decision Makers by Richard E. Neustadt and Ernest R. May. Copyright © 1986 by Richard E. Neustadt and Ernest R. May. All rights reserved.

PRACTICE

UNDERSTANDING DECISION MAKERS (2)

This is an assignment that you should find very interesting. The objective is to identify significant events or important aspects of the lives of highly successful business executives that may have contributed to their behaviors and subsequent success. It is a repeat of the exercise "Understanding Decision Makers (1)" but using successful businesspeople rather than political figures.

Your Assignment

1. Construct a table like the following to record information that you find on the Internet and/or in the library about Steve Jobs, Bill Gates, and Meg Whitman. Your last date should be in the early 1990s.

Public History (general knowledge)		Private History (from public records)		
Date	**Event**	**Jobs**	**Gates**	**Whitman**

2. Starting with the year each was born, try to identify significant events (schooling, military service, career, positions held, etc.) in their personal lives, or important aspects of their personal lives (economic status of family when a child, relatives, etc.).
3. Then look up major events in the "world" that these individuals would have heard about, experienced, or lived through.
4. Now examine your table and draw inferences about the skills, personalities, and biases each of these individuals may have had as a result of their "histories."

Source: Adapted with the permission of Free Press, a Division of Simon & Schuster, Inc., from THINKING IN TIME: The Users of History for Decision Makers by Richard E. Neustadt and Ernest R. May. Copyright © 1986 by Richard E. Neustadt and Ernest R. May. All rights reserved.

IDENTIFYING PERSONALITY TRAITS FOR DIFFERENT JOBS

Implicit in the definition of interpersonal skills is the notion that a manager should try to understand important characteristics of others, including their personalities. This exercise gives you insights into the importance of personality in the workplace as well as some of the difficulties associated with assessing personality traits.

Assume that your job in a new firm will require you to hire three employees, whose duties have been described as follows:

Sales Representative: This position involves calling on existing customers to ensure that they continue to be happy with your firm's products. It also requires the sales representative to try to get those customers to buy more of your products, as well as to attract new customers. A sales representative should be aggressive but not pushy.

Office Manager: The Office Manager oversees the work of a staff of 20 secretaries, receptionists, and clerks. He or she hires them, trains them, evaluates their performance, and sets their pay. The manager also schedules working hours and disciplines or fires workers when necessary.

Warehouse Worker: Warehouse Workers unload trucks and carry shipments to shelves for storage. They also pull customers' orders from shelves and take products to packaging. The job requires workers to follow orders precisely and has little room for autonomy or interaction with others during work.

Your Assignment

1. Based on the above job descriptions, try to determine which personality traits are most relevant for each job.
2. For each job, identify a single personality trait that you think is especially important for a person to effectively perform that job. Then write five questions which, when answered by a job applicant, will help you assess or measure those traits in prospective employees. These questions should be of the type that can be answered on a five-point scale (for example, strongly agree, agree, neither agree or disagree, disagree, strongly disagree).
3. Exchange questions with a classmate. Then pretend you are a job applicant. Provide honest and truthful answers to each question. Next, discuss the traits that each of you identified for each position and how well you think the questions actually measure those traits.
4. Conclude by considering the following questions:
   (A) How easy is it to measure personality?
   (B) How important do you believe it is for organizations to consider personality in hiring decisions?
   (C) Do perception and attitudes affect how people answer personality questions?

ASSESSING ENTREPRENEURIAL PERSONALITY TRAITS

This exercise asks you to assess personality traits that some experts have associated with entrepreneurship. Do you agree with the experts?

Your Assignment

Check the appropriate column to indicate your level of agreement with the following 20 traits. There are no right or wrong choices.

Traits	Strongly Disagree	Disagree	Don't Know	Agree	Strongly Agree
1. I believe success depends on ability, not luck.					
2. I am consistent.					
3. I have little influence over things that happen to me.					
4. I have original ideas.					
5. I am stimulating.					
6. I am thorough.					
7. I often risk doing things differently.					
8. I can stand out in disagreement against a group.					
9. I prefer to work on one problem at a time.					
10. I enjoy detailed work.					
11. I prefer friends who do not "rock the boat."					
12. I will always think of something when stuck.					
13. I am methodical.					
14. I need the stimulation of frequent change.					
15. I like to vary my routines at a moment's notice.					
16. I never seek to bend or break the rules.					
17. I am predictable.					
18. When I make plans, I am sure I can achieve them.					
19. I prefer changes to occur gradually.					
20. I am more willing than other people to take risks.					

Source: Adapted from Ricky W. Griffin, *Fundamentals of Management* (Boston: Houghton Mifflin), p. 149. Reprinted by permission of the author, Margaret Hill.

ASSESSING YOUR PERSONALITY TYPE

This exercise shows how an understanding of personality can aid in developing effective interpersonal relationships within organizations. It introduces a widely used tool for personality assessment, the Myers-Briggs Type Indicator. According to Isabel Myers, each individual's personality type varies in four dimensions:

- Extroversion (E) versus Introversion (I). Extroverts get their energy from being around other people, whereas introverts are worn out by others and need solitude to recharge their energy.
- Sensing (S) versus Intuition (N). The sensing type prefers concrete things and physical experiences, whereas intuitive types prefer abstract concepts and imagination.
- Thinking (T) versus Feeling (F). Thinking individuals base their decisions more on logic and reason, whereas feeling individuals base their decisions more on feelings and emotions.
- Judging (J) versus Perceiving (P). People who are the judging type enjoy completion or being finished, whereas perceiving types enjoy the process and open-ended situations.

On the basis of their answers to a survey, individuals are classified into 16 personality types—all the possible combinations of the four dimensions above. The resulting personality type is then expressed as a 4-letter code, such as ESTP or INFJ. These 4-letter codes can then be used to describe an individual's preferred way of interacting with others.

Your Assignment

1. Use an online Myers-Briggs assessment form to assess your personality type. One place to find the form on line is http://www.humanmetrics.com/cgi-win/jtypes2.asp. Alternatively, your institution's Career Center may offer a Myers-Briggs assessment service.
2. When you have determined the 4-letter code for your personality type, see interpretations at http://www.dec.co.th/mbti_explanation.htm.

Source: Adapted from Ricky W. Griffin, *Fundamentals of Management* (Boston: Houghton Mifflin), pp. 285–286. Reprinted by permission of the author, Margaret Hill.

USING YOUR INTERPERSONAL SKILLS

USE

NORDSTROM CARES

In 1901, John W. Nordstrom came from Sweden and opened a retail store in Seattle, Washington. Later his three sons expanded the business and focused on shoe selling, making Nordstrom the largest shoe store chain in the United States by the late 1950s. Then in the 1960s it began to expand beyond shoes. It acquired Best Apparel of Seattle in 1963 and Nicholas Ungar, a Portland fashion outlet, in 1966. By 1975 Nordstrom had 11 stores in three Western states. By 1985 it had surpassed Saks Fifth Avenue to become the leading specialty fashion retailer in the United States.

Three grandsons of the founder ran the company until the late 1960s. They ran the company as a team, even rotating the title of president among themselves. Then a third generation of Nordstrom children and cousins took the company public in 1971 but held officer positions to maintain control. In 1991 they expanded this management by a team approach to include four non-family members. Then in 1995 the fourth generation of brothers and cousins served as co-presidents for a time. Finally, after having a non-Nordstrom CEO for a few years, the family reasserted its control in 2001.

By stressing outstanding customer service, Nordstrom had sales in excess of $2 billion from its 48 stores in 1988 and was giving rivals a strong run for their money. By 1990 it had expanded its retail empire to the East coast, grown to 59 stores, and was becoming a leader in the use of high technology to keep employees, buyers, and vendors in touch with one another. In 1993 Nordstrom announced plans to expand to the South with a store in Dallas.

Customer service is the sine qua non for employees at Nordstrom. New employees are told that customer service is the number one goal and are given Nordstrom's famous 75-word "handbook" that calls on employees to use "good judgment in all situations" and that there are "no additional rules." As a result, many loyal employees, called "Nordies," are clearly highly motivated. They have been known to write thank-you notes to customers, telephone them to let them know about the arrival of merchandise, and even warm up their cars for them on cold winter days. Two hundred of them even paid their own way to move across the country when stores opened up on the East coast. These employees spend a lot of time and energy assuring that high customer service is the hallmark of Nordstrom.

Not all employees share this enthusiasm, though. Nordstrom's pay practices were labeled as unfair by some labor unions and employees. Those employees claimed that they were not paid for overtime work or for many service-related activities that occurred after hours. Lawsuits by shareholders and employees coupled with adverse rulings by the National Labor Relations Board and the State of Washington during 1990 caused the firm to announce the first drop in annual profits in the history of the firm.

Profits returned by the mid-1990s, however, and they seemed headed for strong results by 2010 despite the negative impact of the poor economic conditions of the mid- to late-2000s. In addition, in 2010 *Fortune* magazine named Nordstrom one of the best big companies to work for and any employee unease seemed settled.

Case Questions

Go Online

1. What interpersonal skills seem to underlie the 75-word "handbook?"
2. How might interpersonal skills work for both employees and customers?
3. Which particular interpersonal skills seem to be particularly important for success at Nordstrom? Why?
4. Would your skills be compatible with working at Nordstrom? Why or why not?
5. If not compatible but you would like them to be, how would you go about assuring that you have the sort of skills for jobs in a successful retail firm like Nordstrom?

Case References

"Best big companies to work for," *Fortune*, April 15, 2010 http://money.cnn.com/galleries/2010/fortune/1004/gallery.fortune500_best_employers.fortune/18.html; Anne D'Innocenzio, "Retailers prepare for consumer comeback," *BusinessWeek*, May 16, 2010 http://www.businessweek.com/ap/financialnews/D9FO318G0.htm; Robert Spector and Patrick McCarthy, *The Nordstrom Way to Customer Service Excellence*, Hoboken, NJ: John Wiley & Sons, 2005; "News Briefs," *The Arizona Republic*, January 6, 1993, p. C1; Dori Jones Yang, "Nordstrom's Gang of Four," *BusinessWeek*, June 15, 1992, pp. 122–123; "Electronic Mail," *Chain Store Age Executive*, October 1, 1992, p. 72; "Technology Leaders," *Stores*, January 1, 1992, p. 112.

USE

CAMPBELL'S CONTINUES CANNING

The canned soup business of Joseph Campbell and Abram Anderson, like that of their two competitors, was struggling when Dr. John Thompson Dorrance joined the firm in the late 1800s. Dorrance invented condensed soup to enable easier transportation of the product. Campbell's condensed soup swept the nation, and by 1911 the brand was known coast to coast in the United States. In 1915 Campbell's acquired Franco-American. Forty years passed before its next acquisition (Swanson's in 1955), but then a period of rapid expansion and acquisition ensued, lasting all the way through the 1980s. As a result, Campbell's is the largest US maker of canned soups and a major producer of numerous other products including frozen dinners and related products, pickles, baked goods, vegetable juices, spaghetti sauces, canned beans, and pasta. Recently, however, Campbell's has been divesting itself of less profitable lines to become more competitive. Results during the early 1990s indicate that it was succeeding.

When David W. Johnson, a successful Gerber products executive, came to Campbell's in 1990, he brought about significant changes. He closed or sold 20 plants worldwide, cut unprofitable brands, and reduced the workforce by more than 20 percent. Johnson followed four basic precepts: (1) act fast—once a decision has been made, act on it quickly; (2) don't change the lineup—set a direction or focus and use existing personnel to achieve it; (3) make 'em sweat—motivate people to reach high standards through their pride in performance; and (4) manage by the numbers—empower and motivate people to be creative but keep a scoreboard (VERC: volume, earnings, return, cash) against which to measure performance.

Johnson also changed the corporate culture. Campbell's divisions had been so independent that the soup unit ran a promotion with Nabisco crackers while the Pepperidge

Farm unit made a competing product! Johnson reorganized Campbell's to eliminate such "protective turf" attitudes. He tied a large proportion of managerial bonuses to overall corporate performance as a further way to further reduce turf attitudes and behavior. He instituted succession planning to enable managers to know that they are constantly being evaluated for advancement and to provide them with feedback as to how well they are doing.

Elements of advanced management techniques and high-involvement management were introduced at many locations, and their success suggests that their use will be expanded throughout Campbell's. Training in communication skills and quality management were implemented. Quality circles and work teams were established. In Canadian operations, for instance, workers quickly began to handle plant scheduling, hiring, staffing, and even some capital projects. Costs were also trimmed. The workers essentially freed up the equivalent of a plant's worth of capacity which enabled the Canadian operation to expand its market, even possibly taking some business away from US factories.

The use of groups and strong motivational programs has made parts of Campbell's excellent places to work. For instance, its headquarters in Camden, New Jersey, has an on-site childcare center where much of the cost is covered by the company. Flextime, job sharing, and even adoption aid are offered by Campbell's to support diverse employee working situations. But other parts of the company have been different.

As Johnson moved from president to chairman, restructuring continued throughout the 1990s. He retired in 1999, but not for long! Dissatisfied with the company's stock performance, the founding Dorrance family (which still owned more than 50 percent of the company) and the board of directors pressured the new president to resign. They brought Johnson back on an interim basis in 2000, after which time Douglas R. Conant was brought on board as the new president and CEO. In 2009, despite severe economic challenges, Campbell's reported solid business performance.

Case Questions

Go Online

1. Johnson was a successful manager. What interpersonal skills did he demonstrate when he took over at Campbell's?
2. How do your skills match up with those of Johnson? Are you prepared to be a manager?
3. Johnson's restructuring and his four precepts created stress in the organization. Was that stress motivational? What criteria might be appropriate in making this judgment?
4. What is your reaction to improving a company's economic performance by getting rid of units/brands that don't meet standards? What might the impact be on people in the company? How would you use interpersonal skills to deal with those impacts?

EXTEND

Case References

2009 Annual Review at www.campbellsoupcompany.com/annualreview2009/letter.asp; Tina Grant (ed.) *International Directory of Company Histories*, Vol. 71. St. James Press, 2005; "Campbell Soup Posts 29% Increase in Net For Latest Quarter," *The Wall Street Journal*, September 11, 1992, p. A7; Bill Saporito, "Campbell Soup Gets Piping Hot," *Fortune*, September 9, 1991, pp. 142–148; Bruce Hager, Lisa Driscoll, Joseph Weber, and Gary McWilliams, "CEO Wanted. No Insiders, Please," *BusinessWeek*, August 12, 1991, pp. 44–45.

EXTENDING YOUR INTERPERSONAL SKILLS

Your instructor may use one or more of these **Group Extensions** to provide you with yet another opportunity to develop your time-management skills. On the other hand, you may continue your development on your own by doing one or more of the **Individual Extensions**.

These **Group Extensions** are repeated exactly for each of the seven specific skills. Doing the exact extension for different skills will help you to sharpen both the skills and the subtle differences between the several skills.

GROUP EXTENSIONS

- Form small groups of students. Have each group select an organization and a management position. Then have them identify the interpersonal skills needed by a person in that position.
- Form small groups of students. Have each group identify a problem or opportunity facing a business or other organization. Then have them identify the interpersonal skills needed by managers in dealing with that problem or opportunity.
- Form small groups of students. Assign each group one or more corporations to analyze. Have them identify the members who serve on its board of directors and research their backgrounds. Then have the students describe the interpersonal skills those directors need to have.
- Form small groups of students. Have each group select a job they see regularly (e.g., retail clerk, fast-food worker). Ask them to describe the interpersonal skills those workers need to have on that job.
- Form small groups of students. Have students sketch the interpersonal skills they would need if they were going to start a specific type of new business.
- Form small groups of students. Have each group identify situations they have recently faced that called a situation that called for them to use interpersonal skills.

INDIVIDUAL EXTENSIONS

- Go to the library and research a company. Characterize its level of effectiveness and identify the interpersonal skills its top executives need to have. Share your results with the class.
- Select a highly visible manager and analyze his or her interpersonal skills.
- Interview a manager from a local organization. Learn about what interpersonal skills he or she needs to perform effectively.
- Think of someone you know who is a manager. Describe that person's management position in terms of the type of organization, level in the organization, and the area of management in which he or she practices. What interpersonal skills does that person need to be effective?
- Plan a hypothetical change in your school focusing on the use of interpersonal skills.

YOUR INTERPERSONAL SKILLS NOW

INTERPERSONAL SKILLS ASSESSMENT

Now that you have completed Chapter 4, it is time once again to assess your interpersonal skills. To do so, complete the following instrument. Think about your current situation, job, or organization in which you are a member. You should respond in terms of your current situation and not by how you think you should respond or a manager should respond. If a statement doesn't currently pertain to your situation, respond in terms of what you think would currently be accurate for you in that situation.

Use this scale in your responses.

1	2	3	4	5
Not true at all	Somewhat untrue	Sometimes true Sometimes not	Somewhat true	Completely true

Total your scores and record them in the table at the end of instrument.

Given that many experts suggest the use of 360° feedback in performance appraisal, you may find it useful to obtain the views of others about your interpersonal skills. You may get a form from your instructor that is designed for others to complete and then record their scores in the table as well. Areas where there is a large discrepancy between your views and those of others should draw your attention and you should spend more time on developing those skills.

INTERPERSONAL SKILLS

[Note: The numbers correspond to those on the baseline assessment in Appendix A.]

____ 51. I admit and accept responsibility for my own mistakes.
____ 52. I always do my share in group activities.
____ 53. I am ambitious and competitive.
____ 54. I am assertive or forceful when the need arises.
____ 55. I am aware of potential conflicts in dealing with others.
____ 56. I am comfortable in leadership positions.
____ 57. I am generally an outgoing person.
____ 58. I am generally lively and enthusiastic.
____ 59. I am genuinely interested in what others are doing in terms of their careers.
____ 60. I am patient with others.
____ 61. I am pretty good at getting others to adopt my ideas.
____ 62. I am sensitive to other people's needs and feelings.
____ 63. I am very tough mentally and physically.
____ 64. I am willing to take an unpopular position if I feel it is right.
____ 65. I am willing to work long hours when necessary.
____ 66. I assure that those to whom I delegate have the authority and resources to do the work.
____ 67. I avoid compromising too quickly.
____ 68. I can act as a spokesperson for a group.
____ 69. I can be assertive when necessary.
____ 70. I can handle stress and pressure effectively.
____ 71. I care about my relationships with others.
____ 72. I consider the opinions and feelings of others when they are presenting their ideas.
____ 73. I cooperate with others.
____ 74. I delegate when appropriate.
____ 75. I develop and maintain good, cooperative working relationships with others.

____ 76. I feel that people are mostly trustworthy and ethical.
____ 77. I find that people generally live up to my expectations.
____ 78. I generally am aware of the strengths and weaknesses of those in my group.
____ 79. I generally display enthusiasm about meeting objectives and deadlines.
____ 80. I generally earn the attention and respect of others in a group.
____ 81. I genuinely care about the feelings of others.
____ 82. I get along well with coworkers/peers.
____ 83. I get along well with superiors.
____ 84. I give people the opportunity to show what they are capable of.
____ 85. I go out of my way to help people develop.
____ 86. I handle setbacks effectively.
____ 87. I have a wide range of contacts and friends.
____ 88. I have confidence in others.
____ 89. I help others learn when they are doing new tasks.
____ 90. I help resolve conflicting demands among group members.
____ 91. I inspire confidence.
____ 92. I keep others informed as to how things are going.
____ 93. I let others know when they are doing good work.
____ 94. I let others know when they are doing things wrong.
____ 95. I let people know if their performance is not up to what is desired.
____ 96. I listen to the views of others.
____ 97. I prefer to lead rather than follow.
____ 98. I provide advice to others when appropriate.
____ 99. I provide information to others on what they need to do to do well.
____ 100. I recognize and deal with problems between individuals and groups.
____ 101. I recognize and reward others for helping me.
____ 102. I rely on persuasion and expertise to motivate people.
____ 103. I seek additional responsibility to improve myself.
____ 104. I share credit for group work.
____ 105. I take time to get to know people.
____ 106. I tend to be a strong team player.
____ 107. I trust people to do the right thing.
____ 108. I try to always be courteous.
____ 109. I try to avoid being upset when I am criticized.
____ 110. I try to avoid getting irritable or moody when I am under stress.
____ 111. I try to avoid taking sides in arguments.
____ 112. I try to be a good role model.
____ 113. I try to be confident even in ambiguous and stressful situations.
____ 114. I try to be involved in group activities.
____ 115. I try to coach others to help them with their tasks.
____ 116. I try to convey my feelings so that others will know how I feel.
____ 117. I try to create an environment in which people will perform at their best.
____ 118. I try to deal with conflict by focusing on the real reasons underlying the conflict.
____ 119. I try to develop rapport with others.

____ 120. I try to empower people to help them perform better.
____ 121. I try to get everyone involved in group activities.
____ 122. I try to get people to work well together.
____ 123. I try to help others learn from their mistakes.
____ 124. I try to motivate others to do well.
____ 125. I try to provide support for others.
____ 126. I try to see to it that tasks are evenly distributed among group members.
____ 127. I try to set an example through my performance to encourage excellence by others.
____ 128. I try to set high standards of performance for group members.
____ 129. I try to suggest that everyone's work is important.
____ 130. I try to treat everyone fairly.

Summary of Your Scores

Skill (max. possible score)	Your Score Now	Scores from Others	Your Score From Chapter 1
Interpersonal (400)			

Interpretation of Your Scores

Compare your score with the one you reported at the beginning of Chapter 1. If there is no or only a modest improvement in your score, you should examine the same set of items from the **Managerial Skills Assessment** from Chapter 1 and compare each of them with these to see where change has and has not occurred. You should then spend more time on developing the particular skills where change either decreased or stayed the same.

INTERPRETATIONS

INTERPRET

ASSESSING YOUR NEEDS

A psychologist, H. A. Murray, developed a set of ten needs in 1938. They were later operationalized by J. W. Atkinson, another psychologist. Because they are visible through a person's behavior, they are known as Murray's Manifest Needs. They are:

1. Achievement
2. Affiliation
3. Aggression
4. Autonomy
5. Exhibition
6. Impulsivity
7. Nurturance
8. Order
9. Power
10. Understanding

To score your results, look at each question individually—the needs correspond one-to-one to the items on the assessment questionnaire.

Although little research has evaluated Murray's theory, the different needs have been investigated. People seem to have a different profile of needs underlying their motivations at different ages. The more any one or more of these needs are descriptive of you, the more you see that particular need as being active in your motivational makeup.

For more information, see H. A. Murray, *Exploration in Personality* (NY: Oxford University Press, 1938) and J. W. Atkinson, *An Introduction to Motivation* (Princeton, NJ: Van Nostrand, 1964).

JOB INVOLVEMENT

Your job involvement score on this self-assessment can range from 20 points to 80 points. An individual with a score less than 40 has low job involvement. These individuals feel indifferent toward work. They may be alienated from their organization. They see work only as an instrumentality to other pleasures.

On the other hand, those who score more than 40 are highly involved in their job. They find enjoyment in their work. They are high in achievement, desire, and drive. They enjoy going to work and willingly put in extra hours.

TEAM EFFECTIVENESS

Point values of 12 to 15 on any one of the five scales suggest that the team is effective on that dimension, whereas point values of 3 to 8 suggest ineffectiveness. Point values of 9 to 11 on any one scale suggest uncertainty and ambiguity on that dimension.

Total point values of 60 to 75 for all 15 items suggest a highly effective team, whereas a total score of 15 through 30 suggests a team that is probably ineffective.

USING TEAMS

All of the statements are false. If you have a very high score (30 or higher), you should examine the research evidence for yourself.

ENDNOTES

[1] John J. Gabarro, "The Development of Working Relationships," in Jay W. Lorsch (ed.), *Handbook of Organizational Behavior* (Englewood Cliffs, N.J.: Prentice-Hall, 1987), pp. 172–189; see also [[new reference to come]]

[2] C. Gopinath and Thomas E. Becker, "Communication, Procedural Justice, and Employee Attitudes: Relationships Under Conditions of Divestiture," *Journal of Management*, 2000, vol. 26, no. 1, pp. 63–83.

[3] Quoted in *Bloomberg Businessweek*, January 16, 2012, p. 49.

[4] Lynn McGarlane Shore and Lois Tetrick, "The Psychological Contract as an Explanatory Framework in the Employment Relationship," in C. L. Cooper and D. M. Rousseau (eds.), *Trends in Organizational Behavior* (London: Wiley, 1994); see also Jacqueline Coyle-Shapiro and Neil Conway, "Exchange Relationships: Examining Psychological Contracts and Perceived Organizational Support," *Journal of Applied Psychology*, 2005, vol. 90, no. 4, pp. 774–781.

[5] For an illustration see Zhen Xiong Chen, Anne Tsui, and Lifeng Zhong, "Reactions to Psychological Contract Breach: A Dual Perspective," *Journal of Organizational Behavior*, 2008, Vol. 29, pp. 527–548.

[6] Elizabeth Wolfe Morrison and Sandra L. Robinson, "When Employees Feel Betrayed: A Model of How Psychological Contract Violation Develops," *Academy of Management Review*, January 1997, pp. 226–256.

[7] Arne Kalleberg, "The Mismatched Worker: When People Don't Fit Their Jobs," *Academy of Management Perspectives*, 2008, Vol. 22, No. 1, pp. 24–40.

[8] Richard M. Steers, Gregory A. Bigley, and Lyman W. Porter, *Motivation and Leadership at Work*, 6th ed. (New York: McGraw-Hill, 1996); see also Maureen L. Ambrose and Carol T. Kulik, "Old Friends, New Faces: Motivation Research in the 1990s," *Journal of Management*, 1999, vol. 25, no. 3, pp. 231–292; and Edwin Locke and Gary Lartham, "What Should We Do About Motivation Theory? Six Recommendations for the Twenty-First Century," *Academy of Management Review*, 2004, vol. 29, no. 3, pp. 388–403.

[9] Nigel Nicholson, "How to Motivate Your Problem People," *Harvard Business Review*, January 2003, pp. 57–67; see also Hugo Kehr, "Integrating Implicit Motives, Explicit Motives, and Perceived Abilities: The Compensatory Model of Work Motivation and Volition," *Academy of Management Review*, 2004, vol. 29, no. 3, pp. 479–499; see also James M. Diefendorff and Megan M. Chandler, "Motivating Employees," in Sheldon Zedeck, (Ed.), *Handbook of Industrial and Organizational Psychology* (American Psychological Association: Washington, D.C., 2010).

[10] Jeffrey Pfeffer, *The Human Equation* (Cambridge, Mass.: Harvard Business School Press, 1998); see also Nitin Nohria, Boris Groysberg, and Linda-Eling Lee, "Employee Motivation—A Powerful New Model," *Harvard Business Review*, July–August 2008, pp. 78–89.

[11] For a recent discussion of these questions, see Eryn Brown, "So Rich So Young—But Are They Really Happy?" *Fortune*, September 18, 2000, pp. 99–110.

[12] Abraham H. Maslow, "A Theory of Human Motivation," *Psychological Review*, 1943, vol. 50, pp. 370–396; Abraham H. Maslow, *Motivation and Personality* (New York: Harper & Row, 1954). Maslow's most recent work is Abraham H. Maslow and Richard Lowry, *Toward a Psychology of Being* (New York: Wiley, 1999).

[13] *USA Today*, August 16, 2004, p. 2B.

[14] For a review, see Pinder, *Work Motivation in Organizational Behavior.*

[15] Frederick Herzberg, Bernard Mausner, and Barbara Snyderman, *The Motivation to Work* (New York: Wiley, 1959); Frederick Herzberg, "One More Time: How Do You Motivate Employees?" *Harvard Business Review*, January–February 1987, pp. 109–120 (reprinted in *Harvard Business Review*, January 2003, pp. 87–98).

[16] Robert J. House and Lawrence A. Wigdor, "Herzberg's Dual-Factor Theory of Job Satisfaction and Motivation: A Review of the Evidence and a Criticism," *Personnel Psychology*, Winter 1967, pp. 369–389; Victor H. Vroom, *Work and Motivation* (New York: Wiley, 1964); see also Pinder, *Work Motivation in Organizational Behavior.*

[17] Victor H. Vroom, *Work and Motivation* (New York: Wiley, 1964).

[18] "Starbucks' Secret Weapon," *Fortune*, September 29, 1997, p. 268.

[19] *Harvard Business Review*, May 2009, p. 101.

[20] Lyman W. Porter and Edward E. Lawler III, *Managerial Attitudes and Performance* (Homewood, Ill.: Dorsey, 1968).

[21] J. Stacy Adams, "Towards an Understanding of Inequity," *Journal of Abnormal and Social Psychology*, November 1963, pp. 422–436.

[22] "The Best vs. the Rest," *The Wall Street Journal*, January 30, 2006, pp. B1, B3.

[23] Mark C. Bolino and William H. Turnley, "Old Faces, New Places: Equity Theory in Cross-Cultural Contexts," *Journal of Organizational Behavior*, 2008, Vol. 29, pp. 29–50.

[24] *BusinessWeek*, June 8, 2009, p. 48.

[25] See Edwin A. Locke, "Toward a Theory of Task Performance and Incentives," Organizational *Behavior and Human Performance*, 1968, vol. 3, pp. 157–189.

[26] Gary P. Latham and J. J. Baldes, "The Practical Significance of Locke's Theory of Goal Setting," *Journal of Applied Psychology*, 1975, vol. 60, pp. 187–191.

[27] Gail Robinson and Kathleen Dechant, "Building a Business Case for Diversity," *Academy of Management Executive*, August 1997, pp. 21–31; see also Orlando C. Richard, "Racial Diversity, Business Strategy, and Firm Performance: A Resource-Based View," *Academy of Management Journal*, 2000, vol. 43, no. 2, pp. 164–177.

[28] "The Coming Job Bottleneck," *BusinessWeek*, March 24, 1997, pp. 184–185; Linda Thornburg, "The Age Wave Hits," *HR Magazine*, February 1995, pp. 40–46; "How to Manage an Aging Workforce," *The Economist*, February 18, 2006, p. 11.

[29] Gary Powell and D. Anthony Butterfield, "Investigating the 'Glass Ceiling' Phenomenon: An Empirical Study of Actual Promotions to Top Management," *Academy of Management Journal*, 1994, vol. 37, no. 1, pp. 68–86.

[30] Karen S. Lyness and Donna E. Thompson, "Above the Glass Ceiling? A Comparison of Matched Samples of Female and Male Executives," *Journal of Applied Psychology*, 1997, vol. 82, no. 3, pp. 359–375.

[31] "What Glass Ceiling?" *USA Today*, July 20, 1999, pp. 1B, 2B; see also Patricia Sellers, "The 50 Most Powerful Women in Business," *Fortune*, November 14, 2005, pp. 125–170.

[32] *Occupational Outlook Handbook* (Washington, D.C.: U.S. Bureau of Labor Statistics, 1990–1991).

[33] "Hispanic Nation," *BusinessWeek*, March 15, 2004, pp. 58–70.

[34] "The Power of Diversity: Who's Got the Clout?" *Fortune*, August 22, 2005, special issue.

[35] "In a Factory Schedule, Where Does Religion Fit In?" *The Wall Street Journal*, March 4, 1999, pp. B1, B12.

[36] Jane Easter Bahls, "Make Room for Diverse Beliefs," *HR Magazine*, August 1997, pp. 89–95; see also Cliff Edwards, "Coming Out in Corporate America," *BusinessWeek*, December 15, 2003, pp. 64–72.

[37] "Immigration Is on the Rise, Again," *USA Today*, February 28, 1997, p. 7A.

[38] "Firms Address Workers' Cultural Variety," *The Wall Street Journal*, February 10, 1989, p. B1.

[39] See Jon R. Katzenbach and Douglas K. Smith, *The Wisdom of Teams: Creating the High-Performance Organization* (Boston: Harvard Business School Press, 1993), p. 45.

[40] *Ibid.*

[41] *Ibid.*

[42] *Ibid.*

[43] Ellen Hart, "Top Teams," *Management Review*, February 1996, pp. 43–47.

[44] Dan Dimancescu and Kemp Dwenger, "Smoothing the Product Development Path," *Management Review*, January 1996, pp. 36–41; see also "The World's 50 Most Innovative Companies," *Fast Company*, March 2008, pp. 72–117.

[45] Ramon Rico, Miriam Sanchez-Manzanares, Francisco Gil, and Christina Gibson, "Team Implicit Knowledge Coordination Processes: A Team Knowledge-Based Approach," *Academy of Management Review*, 2008, Vol. 33, No. 1, pp. 163–184.

[46] Orsburn, Moran, Musselwhite, and Zenger, *Self-Directed Work Teams*, p. 15.

[47] Manz and Sims, *Business Without Bosses*, pp. 10–11.

[48] Deborah Ancona, Henrik Bresman, and Katrin Kaeufer, "The Competitive Advantage of X-Teams," *Sloan Management Review*, Spring 2002, pp. 33–42.

[49] Katzenbach and Smith, *The Wisdom of Teams*, pp. 184–189.

[50] Manz and Sims, *Business Without Bosses*, pp. 74–76.

[51] Jason Colquitt, Raymond Noe, and Christine Jackson, "Justice in Teams: Antecedents and Consequences of Procedural Justice Climate," *Personnel Psychology*, 2002, vol. 55, pp. 83–95.

[52] Suzy Wetlaufer, "Common Sense and Conflict," *Harvard Business Review*, January–February 2000, pp. 115–125.

[53] Kathleen M. Eisenhardt, Jean L. Kahwajy, and L. J. Bourgeois III, "How Management Teams Can Have a Good Fight," *Harvard Business Review*, July–August 1997, pp. 77–89.

[54] Thomas Bergmann and Roger Volkema, "Issues, Behavioral Responses and Consequences in Interpersonal Conflicts," *Journal of Organizational Behavior*, 1994, vol. 15, pp. 467–471; see also Carsten K.W. De Dreu, "The Virtue and Vice of Workplace Conflict: Food for (Pessimistic) Thought," *Journal of Organizational Behavior*, 2008, Vol. 29, pp. 5–18.

[55] Robin Pinkley and Gregory Northcraft, "Conflict Frames of Reference: Implications for Dispute Processes and Outcomes," *Academy of Management Journal*, 1994, vol. 37, no. 1, pp. 193–205.

[56] "How 2 Computer Nuts Transformed Industry Before Messy Breakup," *The Wall Street Journal*, August 27, 1996, pp. A1, A10.

[57] Bruce Barry and Greg L. Stewart, "Composition, Process, and Performance in Self-Managed Groups: The Role of Personality," *Journal of Applied Psychology*, 1997, vol. 82, no. 1, pp. 62–78.

[58] "Delta CEO Resigns After Clashes with Board," *USA Today*, May 13, 1997, p. B1.

[59] "Why Boeing's Culture Breeds Turmoil," *BusinessWeek*, March 21, 2005, pp. 34–36.

[60] Patrick Nugent, "Managing Conflict: Third-Party Interventions for Managers," *Academy of Management Executive*, 2002, vol. 16, no. 1, pp. 139–148.

[61] Kristin J. Behfar, Randall S. Peterson, Elizabeth A. Mannix, and William M.K. Trochim, "The Critical Role of Conflict Resolution in Teams: A Close Look at the Links Between Conflict, Conflict Management Strategies, and Team Outcomes," *Journal of Applied Psychology*, 2008, Vol. 93, No. 1, pp. 170–188.

[62] "Solving Conflicts in the Workplace Without Making Losers," *The Wall Street Journal*, May 27, 1997, p. B1.

[63] "Teaching Business How to Cope with Workplace Conflicts," *BusinessWeek*, February 18, 1990, pp. 136, 139.

[64] Peter Hom, Loriann Roberson, and Aimee Ellis, "Challenging Conventional Wisdom About Who Quits: Revelations From Corporate America," *Journal of Applied Psychology*, 2008, Vol. 93, No. 1, pp. 1–34.

[65] "Chick-fil-A Cuts Job Turnover Rates," *Houston Chronicle*, January 9, 2002, p. B3.

[66] See Anne O'Leary-Kelly, Ricky W. Griffin, and David J. Glew, "Organization-Motivated Aggression: A Research Framework," *Academy of Management Review*, January 1996, pp. 225–253; see also Ramona Paetzold, Anne O'Leary-Kelly, and Ricky W. Griffin, "Workplace Violence, Employer Liability, and Implications for Organizational Research," *Journal of Management Inquiry*, 2007, Vol. 16, No. 4, pp. 362–370.

[67] Dennis W. Organ, "Personality and Organizational Citizenship Behavior," *Journal of Management*, vol. 20, no. 2, 1994, pp. 465–478. For more recent information, see Jeffrey LePine, Amir Erez, and Diane Johnson, "The Nature and Dimensionality of Organizational Citizenship Behavior: A Critical Review and Meta-Analysis," *Journal of Applied Psychology*, Vol. 87, No. 1, 2002, pp. 52–65 and Mark Bolino and William Turnley, "Going the Extra Mile: Cultivating and Managing Employee Citizenship Behavior," *Academy of Management Executive*, 2003, Vol. 17, No. 3, pp. 60–70.

CHAPTER 5

ASSESSING YOUR CONCEPTUAL SKILLS

Goal-Setting Questionnaire
How Creative Are You?
Innovative Attitude Scale
Personal Risk Taking

LEARNING ABOUT CONCEPTUAL SKILLS

Strategic Thinking
- *The Components of a Strategy*
- *Types of Strategic Alternatives*
- *Strategy Formulation and Implementation*
- *Using SWOT Analysis to Formulate Strategy*

Managing Creativity
- *The Creative Individual*
- *The Creative Process*
- *Enhancing Creativity in Organizations*

Managing Innovation
- *The Innovation Process*
- *Forms of Innovation*
- *The Failure to Innovate*
- *Promoting Innovation in Organizations*

Managing Change
- *Forces for Change*
- *Planned Versus Reactive Change*
- *The Lewin Change Model*
- *A Comprehensive Approach to Change*
- *Understanding Resistance to Change*
- *Overcoming Resistance to Change*

Managing Risk
Summary and a Look Ahead

VISUALIZING CONCEPTUAL SKILLS

Conceptual Skills in Action—1
Conceptual Skills in Action—2

PRACTICING YOUR CONCEPTUAL SKILLS

Management Functions in Different Organizations
- *Choosing a New Business Startup*
- *Using Conceptual Skills to Understand the Behavior of Others*
- *Job Values as Perceived by Students and Employers*
- *Learning from Other Organizations*
- *To Cheat or Not?*
- *Factors Affecting Organizational Design*
- *Can You Predict?*
- *The Relationship Between Quality and Financial Performance*
- *Determining Why Teams Are Successful*

USING YOUR CONCEPTUAL SKILLS

Creativity at Kellogg
Creativity at Merck

EXTENDING YOUR CONCEPTUAL SKILLS

Group Extensions
Individual Extensions

YOUR CONCEPTUAL SKILLS NOW

Conceptual Skills Assessment
Conceptual Skills
- *Summary of Your Scores*
- *Interpretation of Your Scores*

INTERPRETATIONS

- *Goal-Setting Questionnaire*
- *How Creative Are You?*
- *Innovative Attitude Scale*
- *Personal Risk Taking*

Conceptual Skills

© ISTOCKPHOTO.COM/JACOB WACKERHAUSEN

A key skill for managers to have is the ability to understand complex, dynamic situations and effectively anticipate and respond to those situations. That understanding comes about through the development of conceptual skills. In this chapter we explain the nature of conceptual skills in thinking strategically about the organization and its environment. We also examine how conceptual skills include the abilities to manage creativity, innovation, change, and risk. Following the text section are several cases and exercises to help you further develop and master your conceptual skills.

ASSESS

ASSESSING YOUR CONCEPTUAL SKILLS

GOAL-SETTING QUESTIONNAIRE

This exercise will help you understand how to conceptualize the elements of goal setting and your own goal-setting tendencies.

Instructions:

Indicate your goal-setting behaviors and feelings by circling the appropriate number on the scale for each statement.

Statements	Strongly Agree	Slightly Agree	Not Sure	Slightly Disagree	Strongly Disagree
1. Rewards should be allocated based on goal achievement.	5	4	3	2	1
2. I set goals for all key results areas.	5	4	3	2	1
3. Goals should have clear deadlines.	5	4	3	2	1
4. I work hard to give others feedback on how they're doing.	5	4	3	2	1
5. I tend to set goals that I can't quite achieve to force me to try harder.	1	2	3	4	5
6. Sometimes when I think maybe I'm not doing so well, I don't want feedback from others.	1	2	3	4	5
7. My goals are always clearly stated.	1	2	3	4	5
8. My goals are stated in quantifiable terms.	5	4	3	2	1
9. Achieving goals is the way to promotion and success.	5	4	3	2	1
10. My boss (parent, etc.) will not get on my case if I don't achieve my goals.	1	2	3	4	5
11. My boss (parent, etc.) usually sets my goals.	1	2	3	4	5
12. I don't always know what the key result areas are.	1	2	3	4	5
13. I work better without specific deadlines.	1	2	3	4	5
14. Others allow me to take part in setting my goals.	5	4	3	2	1
15. The more challenging my goals, the better I work.	5	4	3	2	1
16. If I'm not on target to achieve my goals, my boss (parent, etc.) should get on my case.	5	4	3	2	1
17. When I'm working on my goals, my boss (parent, etc.) doesn't always give me the support I need.	1	2	3	4	5

18. Specific goals make me nervous, so I prefer general goals.	1	2	3	4	5
19. My goals state exactly what results I plan to achieve.	5	4	3	2	1
20. I challenge myself by setting goals that are just out of my reach.	1	2	3	4	5

Scoring:
Sum all of your responses on the questionnaire and place your total score here: _______. Scores can range from 20 to 100. The higher your score, the closer you are to having effective goal-setting behaviors.

Source: From Burton, Exercises in Management, 3E. © 1990 South-Western, a part of Cengage Learning, Inc. Reproduced by permission. www.cengage.com/permissions.

See Interpretations at the end of the chapter.

HOW CREATIVE ARE YOU?

The following exercise is designed to help you understand an important aspect of your conceptual skill—your creativity, a valuable characteristic to have in assessing and responding to your organizational environment. If managers do not hone their creativity, they are likely to be passive reactors to the environment rather than shapers of the future.

Instructions:
Using the following scale, in the spaces to the left of each statement, indicate the degree to which you agree or disagree with it. Mark your answers as accurately and frankly as possible. Try not to guess how a creative person might respond to each statement.

Rating Scale:
A – *Strongly Agree*
B – *Agree*
C – *In Between or Don't Know*
D – *Disagree*
E – *Strongly Disagree*

_____ 1. I always work with a great deal of certainty that I'm following the correct procedures for solving a particular problem.

_____ 2. It would be a waste of time for me to ask questions if I had no hope of obtaining answers.

_____ 3. I feel that a logical, step-by-step method is best for solving problems.

_____ 4. I occasionally voice my opinions in groups that seem to turn some people off.

_____ 5. I spend a great deal of time thinking about what others think of me.

_____ 6. I feel that I may have a special contribution to make to the world.

_____ 7. It is more important for me to do what I believe to be right than to try to win the approval of others.

_____ 8. People who seem uncertain about things lose my respect.

_____ 9. I am able to stick with difficult problems over extended periods of time.

_____ 10. On occasion I get overly enthusiastic about things.

_____ 11. I often get my best ideas when doing nothing in particular.

_____ 12. I rely on intuitive hunches and the feeling of "rightness" or "wrongness" when moving toward the solution of a problem.

_____ 13. When problem solving, I work faster when analyzing the problem and slower when synthesizing the information I've gathered.

_____ 14. I like hobbies that involve collecting things.

_____ 15. Daydreaming has provided the impetus for many of my more important projects.

_____ 16. If I had to choose, I would rather be a physician than an explorer.

_____ 17. I can get along more easily with people if they belong to the same social and business class as I.

_____ 18. I have a high degree of aesthetic sensitivity.

_____ 19. Intuitive hunches are unreliable guides in problem solving.

_____ 20. I am much more interested in coming up with new ideas than I am in trying to sell them to others.

_____ 21. I tend to avoid situations in which I might feel inferior.

_____ 22. When I evaluate information, its source is more important to me than its content.

_____ 23. I like people who follow the rule, "Business before pleasure."

_____ 24. Self-respect is much more important than the respect of others.

_____ 25. I feel that people who strive for perfection are unwise.

_____ 26. I like work in which I must influence others.

_____ 27. It is important for me to have a place for everything and to have everything in its place.

_____ 28. People who are willing to entertain "crackpot" ideas are impractical.

_____ 29. I enjoy fooling around with new ideas, even if there is no practical payoff.

_____ 30. When a certain approach to a problem doesn't work, I can quickly reorient my thinking.

_____ 31. I don't like to ask questions that show ignorance.

_____ 32. I am able to change my interests to pursue a job or career more easily than I can change a job to pursue my interests.

_____ 33. Inability to solve a problem is frequently due to asking the wrong questions.

_____ 34. I can frequently anticipate the solution to my problems.

_____ 35. It is a waste of time to analyze one's failures.

_____ 36. Only fuzzy thinkers resort to metaphors and analogies.

_____ 37. At times I have so enjoyed the ingenuity of a crook that I hoped he or she would go scot-free.

_____ 38. I frequently begin work on a problem that I can only dimly sense and not yet express.

_____ 39. I frequently forget things such as names of people, streets, highways, and small towns.

_____ 40. I feel that hard work is the basic factor in success.

_____ 41. To be regarded as a good team member is important to me.

_____ 42. I know how to keep my inner impulses in check.

_____ 43. I am a thoroughly dependable and responsible person.

_____ 44. I resent things being uncertain and unpredictable.

_____ 45. I prefer to work with others in a team effort rather than alone.

_____ 46. The trouble with many people is that they take things too seriously.

_____ 47. I am frequently haunted by my problems and cannot let go of them.

_____ 48. I can easily give up immediate gain or comfort to reach the goals I have set.

_____ 49. If I were a college professor, I would rather teach factual courses than those involving theory.

_____ 50. I'm attracted to the mystery of life.

Scoring:

To compute your score, circle the value corresponding to each of your responses in the table below, then add the values.

	A	B	C	D	E
	Strongly Agree	Agree	In Between or Don't Know	Disagree	Strongly Disagree
1.	−2	−1	0	+1	+2
2.	−2	−1	0	+1	+2
3.	−2	−1	0	+1	+2
4.	+2	+1	0	−1	−2
5.	−2	−1	0	+1	+2
6.	+2	+1	0	−1	−2
7.	+2	+1	0	−1	−2
8.	−2	−1	0	+1	+2
9.	+2	+1	0	−1	−2
10.	+2	+1	0	−1	−2
11.	+2	+1	0	−1	−2
12.	+2	+1	0	−1	−2
13.	−2	−1	0	+1	+2
14.	−2	−1	0	+1	+2
15.	+2	+1	0	−1	−2
16.	−2	−1	0	+1	+2
17.	−2	−1	0	+1	+2
18.	+2	+1	0	−1	−2
19.	−2	−1	0	+1	+2
20.	+2	+1	0	−1	−2
21.	−2	−1	0	+1	+2
22.	−2	−1	0	+1	+2
23.	−2	−1	0	+1	+2
24.	+2	+1	0	−1	−2
25.	−2	−1	0	+1	+2
26.	−2	−1	0	+1	+2
27.	−2	−1	0	+1	+2
28.	−2	−1	0	+1	+2
29.	+2	+1	0	−1	−2
30.	+2	+1	0	−1	−2
31.	−2	−1	0	+1	+2
32.	−2	−1	0	+1	+2

(continued)

ASSESS

	A	B	C	D	E
	Strongly Agree	Agree	In Between or Don't Know	Disagree	Strongly Disagree
33.	+2	+1	0	−1	−2
34.	+2	+1	0	−1	−2
35.	−2	−1	0	+1	+2
36.	−2	−1	0	+1	+2
37.	+2	+1	0	−1	−2
38.	+2	+1	0	−1	−2
39.	+2	+1	0	−1	−2
40.	+2	+1	0	−1	−2
41.	−2	−1	0	+1	+2
42.	−2	−1	0	+1	+2
43.	−2	−1	0	+1	+2
44.	−2	−1	0	+1	+2
45.	−2	−1	0	+1	+2
46.	+2	+1	0	−1	−2
47.	+2	+1	0	−1	−2
48.	+2	+1	0	−1	−2
49.	−2	−1	0	+1	+2
50.	+2	+1	0	−1	−2
Subtotals	______	______	______	______	______
TOTAL	______				

Source: From E. Raudsepp, *How Creative Are You?* ©1981. Reprinted by permission of Dominick Abel Literary Agency.

See Interpretations at the end of the chapter.

INNOVATIVE ATTITUDES SCALE

Change and innovation are important to organizations. This assessment surveys your readiness to accept and participate in innovation as part of your conceptual skill set.

Instructions:

Indicate the extent to which each of the following statements is true of either your actual *behavior or your* intentions *at work. That is, describe the way you are or the way you intend to be on the job. Use this scale for your responses:*

Rating Scale
5 – Almost always true
4 – Often true
3 – Not applicable
2 – Seldom true
1 – Almost never true

_____ 1. I feel very energetic when working with innovative colleagues.
_____ 2. I openly discuss with my boss on what I should do to get ahead.

_____ 3. I enjoy finding good solutions that nobody has looked at yet.
_____ 4. I try new ideas and approaches to problems.
_____ 5. I take things or situations apart to find out how they work.
_____ 6. I am always on the lookout for ways to improve efficiency or effectiveness in my tasks.
_____ 7. I welcome uncertainty and unusual circumstances related to my tasks.
_____ 8. I usually take control in unstructured situations.
_____ 9. I negotiate my salary openly with my supervisor.
_____ 10. I can be counted on to find a new use for existing methods or equipment.
_____ 11. Among my colleagues and coworkers, I will be the first or nearly the first to try out a new idea or method.
_____ 12. I take the opportunity to explain communications from other departments for my work group.
_____ 13. I demonstrate originality.
_____ 14. I will work on a problem that has caused others great difficulty.
_____ 15. I am drawn to ideas that no one else has thought of or implemented.
_____ 16. I provide critical input toward a new solution.
_____ 17. I provide written evaluations of proposed ideas.
_____ 18. I try to spend time each day developing new opportunities.
_____ 19. I develop contacts with experts outside my firm.
_____ 20. I use personal contacts to maneuver myself into choice work assignments.
_____ 21. I collect ideas and make connections from a wide range of areas.
_____ 22. I make time to pursue my own pet ideas or projects.
_____ 23. I set aside resources for the pursuit of a risky project.
_____ 24. I get a thrill from doing new, unusual things.
_____ 25. I tolerate people who depart from organizational routine.
_____ 26. I speak out in staff meetings.
_____ 27. I work in teams to try to solve complex problems.
_____ 28. I like to take ideas and fit them into my current situation or adapt them to my current activities.
_____ 29. If my coworkers are asked, they will say I have a good sense of humor.
_____ 30. I get excited when I think of new ideas or methods that can stimulate the organization of which I am a member.

Scoring:

Count the number of times you circled each of the 5 responses, and then use the following table to compute your score:

Answer Scale	# of Times Circled	×	# of Points	=	Totals
5 – Almost always true	_____	×	5	=	_____
4 – Often true	_____	×	4	=	_____
3 – Not applicable	_____	×	3	=	_____
2 – Seldom true	_____	×	2	=	_____
1 – Almost never true	_____	×	1	=	_____
TOTAL					_______

ASSESS

Source: Based on L. G. Gibson and R. A. Gibson, "Predictors of Entrepreneurial Innovation Attitude: Implications for Arts and Business Pedagogy." *United States Association for Small Business and Entrepreneurship Proceedings*, January 2011, 1007–1020; D. Killen and G. Williams, *Introduction to Type® and Innovation*. Mountain View, CA: CPP, Inc., 2009; J. E. Ettlie and R. D. O'Keefe, (1982). "Innovative Attitudes, Values, and Intentions in Organizations," *Journal of Management Studies*, 19, p. 176.

The higher the total score, the more willing and likely you are to be innovative. Your attitude toward innovation is more positive than that of people who score low. A score of 115 or greater is high, while a score of 85 or less is low. People who are not innovators have a tendency to maintain the status quo. Innovative people are entrepreneurs and individuals who like to create changes in their organizations.

See Interpretation at the end of the chapter.

PERSONAL RISK TAKING

Risk-taking involves incurring the potential for some danger or harm, but at the same time providing the potential to obtain some form of reward, recognition, or enjoyment.

Instructions:
For each of the following statements, indicate how you see yourself using the following scale:

Rating Scale
5 – Definitely true of me
4 – Probably true of me
3 – Neither true or not true of me; undecided
2 – Probably not true of me
1 – Definitely not true of me

_____ 1. I am generally willing to take risks.
_____ 2. I have invested time and/or money in chancy financial endeavors.
_____ 3. I frequently drive above the posted speed limit.
_____ 4. I have gone swimming in lakes or rivers with no lifeguards present.
_____ 5. I have cheated on examinations or quizzes.
_____ 6. I frequently arrive late for classes or meetings.
_____ 7. I am usually the first to get new technology devices.
_____ 8. I have knowingly written bad checks or made late payments on charge accounts or rent.
_____ 9. I participate in dangerous sports such as scuba diving, surfing, skiing, or sky diving.
_____ 10. I frequently drive on long trips when tired and/or sleepy.
_____ 11. I feel that rules are meant to be broken.
_____ 12. I have engaged in unprotected sex.
_____ 13. I use alcohol.
_____ 14. I smoke.
_____ 15. I have tried "recreational drugs."
_____ 16. I frequently accelerate on yellow traffic signals to "beat the red light."
_____ 17. I participate in sports activities at least once a month.
_____ 18. I don't want to be self-employed.
_____ 19. I have "stretched the truth" on resumes or application forms.
_____ 20. I tend to spend more than I can pay off at the end of the month.

_____ 21. I frequently gamble.

_____ 22. I have copied others' work for classes.

_____ 23. I don't mind asking people to lend me money.

_____ 24. I have driven after having had a few drinks.

_____ 25. I rarely have physical examinations to check up on my health.

Source: Adapted from Thomas Dohmen, Armin Falk, David Huffman, and Uwe Sunde, 2011, "Individual Risk Attitudes: Measurement, Determinants and Behavioral Consequences," *Journal of The European Economic Association*, Vol. 9, No. 3: pp. 522–550; C. W. Lejuez, Jennifer P. Read, Christopher W. Kahler, Jerry B. Richards, Susan E. Ramsey, Gregory L. Stuart, David R. Strong, and Richard A. Brown, 2002, "Evaluation of a Behavioral Measure of Risk Taking: The Balloon Analogue Risk Task (BART)," *Journal of Experimental Psychology*, Vol. 8, No. 2: pp. 75–84; and Mark P. Reilly, Mark K. Greenwald, and Chris-Ellyn Johanson, 2006, "The Stoplight Task: A Procedure for Assessing Risk Taking in Humans," *The Psychological Record*, Vol. 56: pp. 191–204.

See Interpretations at the end of the chapter.

GO ONLINE to the Griffin/Van Fleet Assessment Library for online versions of these and other assessments.

LEARNING ABOUT CONCEPTUAL SKILLS

Strategic Thinking
- *The Components of a Strategy*
- *Types of Strategic Alternatives*
- *Strategy Formulation and Implementation*
- *Using SWOT Analysis to Formulate Strategy*
  - *Evaluating an Organization's Strengths*
  - *Evaluating an Organization's Weaknesses*
  - *Evaluating an Organization's Opportunities and Threats*

Managing Creativity
- *The Creative Individual*
  - *Background Experiences and Creativity*
  - *Personal Traits and Creativity*
  - *Cognitive Abilities and Creativity*
- *The Creative Process*
  - *Preparation*
  - *Incubation*
  - *Insight*
  - *Verification*
- *Enhancing Creativity in Organizations*

Managing Innovation
- *The Innovation Process*
  - *Innovation Development*
  - *Innovation Application*
  - *Application Launch*
  - *Application Growth*
  - *Innovation Maturity*
  - *Innovation Decline*
- *Forms of Innovation*
  - *Radical Versus Incremental Innovations*
  - *Technical Versus Managerial Innovations*
  - *Product Versus Process Innovations*
- *The Failure to Innovate*
  - *Lack of Resources*
  - *Failure to Recognize Opportunities*
  - *Resistance to Change*
- *Promoting Innovation in Organizations*
  - *The Reward System*
  - *Organization Culture*
  - *Intrapreneurship in Larger Organizations*

Managing Change
- *Forces for Change*
  - *External Forces*
  - *Internal Forces*
- *Planned Versus Reactive Change*
- *The Lewin Change Model*
- *A Comprehensive Approach to Change*
- *Understanding Resistance to Change*
  - *Uncertainty*
  - *Threatened Self-Interests*
  - *Different Perceptions*
  - *Feelings of Loss*
- *Overcoming Resistance to Change*
  - *Participation*
  - *Education and Communication*
  - *Facilitation*
  - *Force-Field Analysis*

Managing Risk

Summary and a Look Ahead

As introduced in Chapter 1, conceptual skills refer to the manager's ability to think in the abstract. Managers need the mental capacity to understand the overall workings of the organization and its environment, to grasp how all the parts of the organization fit together, and to view the organization in a holistic manner. This allows them to think strategically, to see the "big picture," and to make broad-based decisions that serve the overall organization. This chapter will help you extend your conceptual skills though discussions of strategic thinking, creativity, innovation, change management, and risk management.

STRATEGIC THINKING

One cornerstone of a manager's conceptual skills is her or his ability to think strategically. In order to think strategically, in turn, managers need to understand the basic elements of strategy and strategic management. A **strategy** is a comprehensive plan for accomplishing an

strategy a comprehensive plan for accomplishing an organization's goals

LEARN

organization's goals. Strategic management, by extension, is a way of approaching business opportunities and challenges—it is a comprehensive and ongoing management process aimed at formulating and implementing effective strategies. Finally, effective strategies are those that promote a superior alignment between the organization and its environment and the achievement of strategic goals.[1] Strategic leadership, also closely related to strategic thinking, is a relatively new concept that explicitly relates leadership to the role of top management. We define strategic leadership as the capability to understand the complexities of both the organization and its environment and to lead change in the organization in order to achieve and maintain a superior alignment between the organization and its environment.

> "I wanted to create a new way of looking at retail. At the time a lot of stores were very minimalist, very clean. I wanted stores that would feel like a comfortable room in my apartment, cozy and colorful and different."
>
> TORY BURCH
> co-founder and creative director
> Tory Burch[4]

To be an effective strategic leader and thinker, a manager must have a thorough and complete understanding of the organization—its history, its culture, its strengths, and its weaknesses. In addition, the leader needs a firm grasp of the organization's environment. This understanding must encompass current conditions and circumstances as well as significant trends and issues on the horizon. The strategic leader and thinker also needs to recognize how the firm is currently aligned with its environment—where it relates effectively and where it relates less effectively with that environment. Finally, looking at environmental trends and issues, the strategic leader and thinker works to improve both the current and future alignment between the organization and its environment.[2]

Jeffrey Immelt (CEO of General Electric), Hector Ruiz (CEO of Advanced Micro Devices), Michael Dell (founder and CEO of Dell Computers), Anne Mulcahy (former CEO of Xerox) and A. G. Lafley (former CEO of Procter & Gamble) all have been recognized as strong strategic leaders. Reflecting on his dramatic turnaround at Procter & Gamble, for instance, Lafley commented, "I have made a lot of symbolic, very physical changes so people understand we are in the business of leading change." On the other hand, Raymond Gilmartin (CEO of Merck), Scott Livengood (CEO of Krispy Kreme), and Howard Pien (CEO of Chiron) have been cited as less-effective strategic leaders. Under Livengood's leadership, for instance, Krispy Kreme's stock plummeted by 80 percent, and the firm was investigated by the SEC; moreover, most critics believe that the chain tried to expand far too rapidly, with the result being major cutbacks and retrenchment.[3]

The Components of a Strategy

In general, a well-conceived strategy addresses three areas: distinctive competence, scope, and resource deployment. A distinctive competence is something the organization does exceptionally well. A distinctive competence of Abercrombie & Fitch is speed in moving inventory. It tracks consumer preferences daily with point-of-sale computers, electronically transmits orders to suppliers in Hong Kong, charters 747s to fly products to the United States, and has products in stores 48 hours later. Because other retailers take weeks or sometimes months to accomplish the same things, Abercrombie & Fitch uses this distinctive competence to remain competitive.[5]

The scope of a strategy specifies the range of markets in which an organization will compete. The Hershey Company has essentially restricted its scope to the confectionery business, with a few related activities in other food-processing areas. In contrast, its biggest competitor, Mars, has adopted a broader scope by competing in the pet food business and the electronics industry, among others. Some organizations, called conglomerates, compete in dozens or even hundreds of markets. Strategic thinking as a part of effective conceptual skills enables a manager to make the best decisions regarding scope.

strategic management a way of approaching business opportunities and challenges—a comprehensive and ongoing management process aimed at formulating and implementing effective strategies

effective strategies those that promote a superior alignment between the organization and its environment and the achievement of strategic goals

strategic leadership the capability to understand the complexities of both the organization and its environment and to lead change in the organization in order to achieve and maintain a superior alignment between the organization and its environment

distinctive competence something the organization does exceptionally well

scope (*as part of strategy*) specifies the range of markets in which an organization will compete

LEARN

LEARN

A strategy also should include an outline of the organization's projected resource deployment—how it will distribute its resources across the areas in which it competes. General Electric, for example, uses profits from its US operations to invest in new businesses in Europe and Asia. Alternatively, the firm might have chosen to invest in different industries in its domestic market or to invest more heavily in Latin America. The choices it makes as to where and how much to invest reflects issues of resource deployment. And again, conceptual skills help enable a manager to make the best decisions about resource deployment.

© IAN DAGNALL/ALAMY

Types of Strategic Alternatives

Most businesses today develop strategies at two distinct levels. These levels provide a rich combination of strategic alternatives for organizations. The two general levels are business-level strategies and corporate-level strategies. Business-level strategy is the set of strategic alternatives from which an organization chooses as it conducts business in a particular industry or market. Such alternatives help the organization focus its competitive efforts for each industry or market in a targeted and focused manner.

Corporate-level strategy is the set of strategic alternatives from which an organization chooses as it manages its operations simultaneously across several industries and several markets. As we will discuss later, most large companies today compete in a variety of industries and markets. Thus, although they develop business-level strategies for each industry or market, they also develop an overall strategy that helps define the mix of industries and markets that are of interest to the firm.

resource deployment (*as part of strategy*) specifies how the organization will distribute its resources across the areas in which it competes

business-level strategy the set of strategic alternatives from which an organization chooses as it conducts business in a particular industry or market

corporate-level strategy the set of strategic alternatives from which an organization chooses as it manages its operations simultaneously across several industries and several markets

strategy formulation the set of processes involved in creating or determining the strategies of the organization

strategy implementation the methods by which strategies are operationalized or executed within the organization

deliberate strategy a plan chosen and implemented to support specific goals

emergent strategy pattern of action that develops over time in an organization in the absence of mission and goals or despite mission and goals

Strategy Formulation and Implementation

Drawing a distinction between strategy formulation and strategy implementation is also instructive. Strategy formulation refers to the set of processes involved in creating or determining the strategies of the organization, whereas strategy implementation refers to the methods by which strategies are operationalized or executed within the organization. The primary distinction is along the lines of content versus process: The formulation stage determines what the strategy is, and the implementation stage focuses on how the strategy is achieved.

Sometimes the processes of formulating and implementing strategies are rational, systematic, and planned. This is often referred to as a deliberate strategy—a plan chosen and implemented to support specific goals.[6] Texas Instruments (TI) excels at formulating and implementing deliberate strategies. TI uses a planning process that assigns most senior managers two distinct responsibilities: an operational, short-term responsibility and a strategic, long-term responsibility. Thus one manager may be responsible for both increasing the efficiency of semiconductor operations over the next year (operational, short term) and investigating new materials for semiconductor manufacturing in the twenty-first century (strategic, long term). TI's objective is to help managers make short-term operational decisions while keeping in mind longer-term goals and objectives.

Other times, however, organizations use an emergent strategy—a pattern of action that develops over time in an organization in the absence of mission and goals or despite mission and goals.[7] Implementing emergent strategies involves allocating resources even though an organization has not explicitly chosen its strategies. 3M has at times benefited from emergent strategies. The invention of invisible tape, for instance, provides a good example. Entrepreneurial engineers working independently took the invention to their boss, who concluded that it did not have major market potential because it was not part of an approved research and development plan. Only when the product was evaluated at the highest levels in the organization was it accepted and made part of 3M's product mix. Of course, 3M's Scotch tape became a major success despite the fact that it arose outside of the firm's established practices. 3M now counts on emergent strategies to help expand its numerous businesses.

FIGURE 5.1 USING SWOT ANALYSIS TO FORMULATE STRATEGY

Conducting a SWOT analysis is one of the most important steps in formulating strategy. Using the organization's mission as a context, managers assess internal strengths (distinctive competencies) and weaknesses as well as external opportunities and threats. The goal is then to develop good strategies that exploit opportunities and strengths, neutralize threats, and avoid weaknesses.

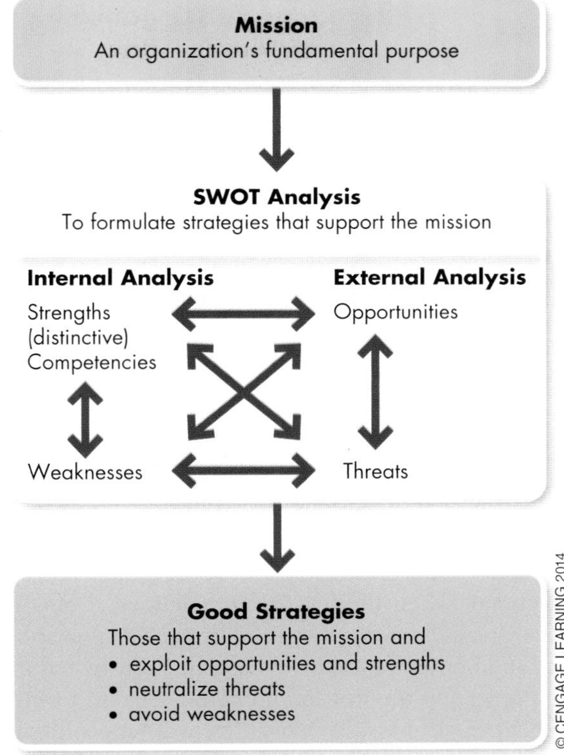

Using SWOT Analysis to Formulate Strategy

The starting point in formulating strategy is usually SWOT analysis. SWOT is an acronym that stands for strengths, weaknesses, opportunities, and threats. As shown in *Figure 5.1*, SWOT analysis is a careful evaluation of an organization's internal strengths and weaknesses as well as its environmental opportunities and threats. In SWOT analysis, the best strategies accomplish an organization's mission by (1) exploiting an organization's opportunities and strengths, while (2) neutralizing its threats, and (3) avoiding (or correcting) its weaknesses.

Evaluating an Organization's Strengths

Organizational strengths are skills and capabilities that enable an organization to conceive of and implement its strategies. Strengths may include things like a deep pool of managerial talent, surplus capital, a unique reputation and/or brand name, and well-established distribution channels.[8] Sears, for example, has a nationwide network of trained service employees who repair Sears appliances. Jane Thompson, a Sears executive, conceived of a plan to consolidate repair and home-improvement services nationwide under the well-known Sears brand name and to promote them as a general repair operation for all appliances, not just those purchased from Sears. Thus the firm capitalized on existing capabilities and the strength of its name to launch a new operation. Different strategies call on different skills and capabilities. For example, Matsushita Electric Industrial Co. has demonstrated strengths in manufacturing and selling consumer electronics under the brand name Panasonic. Matsushita's strength in electronics does not ensure success, however, if the firm decides to expand into insurance, swimming pool manufacturing, or retail. Different industries such as these require different strategies and thus different organizational strengths. SWOT analysis divides organizational strengths into two categories: common strengths and distinctive competencies.

- A common strength is an organizational capability possessed by a large number of competing firms. For example, all the major Hollywood film studios possess common strengths in lighting, sound recording, set and costume design, and makeup. *Competitive parity* exists when large numbers of competing firms are able to implement the same strategy. In this situation, organizations generally attain only average levels of performance. Thus a film company that exploits only its common strengths in choosing and implementing strategies is not likely to go beyond average performance.
- A *distinctive competence* is a strength possessed by only a small number of competing firms. Distinctive competencies are rare among a set of competitors. George Lucas's Industrial Light & Magic (ILM), for example, brought the cinematic art of special effects to new heights. Some of ILM's special effects can be produced by no other organization; these rare special effects thus comprise ILM's distinctive competence. Organizations that exploit their distinctive competencies often obtain a *competitive advantage* and attain above-normal economic performance.[9] A main purpose of SWOT analysis is to discover an

SWOT an acronym for strengths, weaknesses, opportunities, and threats

organizational strengths skills and capabilities that enable an organization to conceive of and implement its strategies

common strength an organizational capability possessed by a large number of competing firms

LEARN

organization's distinctive competencies so that the organization can choose and implement strategies that exploit its unique organizational strengths.

- An organization that possesses distinctive competencies and exploits them in the strategies it chooses can expect to obtain a competitive advantage and above-normal economic performance. However, its success will lead other organizations to duplicate these advantages. **Strategic imitation** is the practice of duplicating another firm's distinctive competence and thereby implementing a valuable strategy. Although some distinctive competencies can be imitated, others cannot. When a distinctive competence cannot be imitated, strategies that exploit these competencies generate sustained competitive advantage. A **sustained competitive advantage** is a competitive advantage that exists after all attempts at strategic imitation have ceased.[10]

> "It's my … responsibility to figure out how to get our growth goals without an acquisition."
>
> BOB MCDONALD
> CEO of Procter & Gamble[12]

"PROCTER & GAMBLE NEEDS TO SHAVE MORE INDIANS," BUSINESS WEEK, JUNE 13, 2011, P. 21.

strategic imitation the practice of duplicating another firm's distinctive competence and thereby implementing a valuable strategy

sustained competitive advantage a competitive advantage that exists after all attempts at strategic imitation have ceased

organizational weaknesses skills and capabilities that do not enable an organization to choose and implement strategies that support its mission

competitive disadvantage an organization is not implementing valuable strategies that are being implemented by competing organizations; organizations with a competitive disadvantage can expect to attain below-average levels of performance

organizational opportunities areas that may generate higher performance

organizational threats areas that increase the difficulty of an organization's performing at a high level

creativity the ability of an individual to generate new ideas or to conceive of new perspectives on existing ideas

Evaluating an Organization's Weaknesses

Organizational weaknesses are skills and capabilities that do not enable an organization to choose and implement strategies that support its mission. An organization essentially has two ways of addressing weaknesses. First, it may need to make investments to obtain the strengths required to implement strategies that support its mission. Second, it may need to modify its mission so that it can be accomplished with the skills and capabilities that the organization already possesses.

In practice, organizations have a difficult time focusing on weaknesses, in part because organization members are often reluctant to admit that they do not possess all the skills and capabilities they need. Evaluating weaknesses also calls into question the judgment of managers who chose the organization's mission in the first place and who failed to invest in the skills and capabilities needed to accomplish it. Organizations that fail either to recognize or to overcome their weaknesses are likely to suffer from competitive disadvantages. An organization has a **competitive disadvantage** when it is not implementing valuable strategies that competing organizations are implementing. Organizations with a competitive disadvantage can expect to attain below-average levels of performance.

Evaluating an Organization's Opportunities and Threats

Whereas evaluating strengths and weaknesses focuses attention on the internal workings of an organization, evaluating opportunities and threats requires analyzing an organization's environment. **Organizational opportunities** are areas that may generate higher performance. **Organizational threats** are areas that increase the difficulty of an organization's performing at a high level.

Michael Porter's "five forces" model of the competitive environment can be used to characterize the extent of opportunity and threat in an organization's environment. Porter's five forces are (1) level of competitive rivalry, (2) power of suppliers, (3) power of buyers, (4) threat of substitutes, and (5) threat of new entrants. In general, when the level of competitive rivalry, the power of suppliers and buyers, and the threat of substitutes and new entrants are all high, an industry has relatively few opportunities and numerous threats. Firms in these types of industries typically have the potential to achieve only normal economic performance. On the other hand, when the level of rivalry, the power of suppliers and buyers, and the threat of substitutes and new entrants are all low, an industry has numerous opportunities and relatively few threats. These industries hold the potential for above-normal performance for organizations in them.[11]

MANAGING CREATIVITY

Another set of cornerstones for strong conceptual skills are creativity and innovation. These concepts are distinct from one another, but they share some underlying similarities. We discuss creativity first, and then describe innovation in the next section. **Creativity** is an individual-level phenomenon and can be defined as the ability of an individual to generate new ideas or to conceive of new perspectives on existing ideas. What makes a person creative? How do people become creative? How does the creative process work? Although psychologists have not yet discovered complete answers to these questions, examining a few general patterns can help us understand the sources of individual creativity within organizations.[13]

The Creative Individual

Numerous researchers have focused their efforts on attempting to describe the common attributes of creative individuals. These attributes generally fall into three categories: background experiences, personal traits, and cognitive abilities.

Background Experiences and Creativity

Researchers have observed that many creative individuals were raised in environments in which creativity was nurtured. Mozart was raised in a family of musicians and began composing and performing music at age six. Pierre and Marie Curie, great scientists in their own right, raised a daughter, Irene, who won the Nobel Prize in chemistry. Thomas Edison's creativity was nurtured by his mother. However, people with background experiences very different from theirs also have been creative. Frederick Douglass was born into slavery in Tuckahoe, Maryland, and had very limited opportunities for education. Nonetheless, his powerful oratory and creative thinking helped lead to President Abraham Lincoln's Emancipation Proclamation, an executive order in which he outlawed slavery in the United States.

Personal Traits and Creativity Certain personal traits also have been linked to creativity in individuals. The traits shared by most creative people are openness, an attraction to complexity, high levels of energy, independence and autonomy, strong self-confidence, and a strong belief that one is, in fact, creative. Individuals who possess these traits are more likely to be creative than those who do not have them.

Cognitive Abilities and Creativity Cognitive abilities are an individual's power to think intelligently and to analyze situations and data effectively. Intelligence may be a precondition for individual creativity—although most creative people are highly intelligent, not all intelligent people are necessarily creative. Creativity also is linked with the ability to think divergently and convergently. *Divergent thinking* is a skill that allows people to see differences among situations, phenomena, or events. *Convergent thinking* is a skill that allows people to see similarities among situations, phenomena, or events. Creative people generally are skilled at both divergent and convergent thinking. Interestingly, some Japanese managers have come to question their own creative abilities. The concern is that their emphasis on group harmony may have stifled individual initiative and hampered the development of individual creativity. As a result, a few Japanese firms, including Omron Corporation, Fuji Photo, and Shimizu Corporation, have launched employee training programs intended to boost the creativity of employees.[14]

LEARN

The Creative Process

Although creative people often report that ideas seem to come to them "in a flash," individual creative activity actually tends to progress through a series of stages. These stages are illustrated in *Figure* 5.2. Not all creative activity has to follow these four stages, but much of it does.

Preparation The creative process normally begins with a period of *preparation*. To make a creative contribution to business management or business services, individuals usually must receive formal training and education in business. Formal education and training are usually the most efficient ways of becoming familiar with this vast amount of research and knowledge. This is one reason for the strong demand for undergraduate and master's level business education. Formal business education can be an effective way for an individual to get "up to speed" and begin making creative contributions quickly. Experiences that managers have on the job after their formal training has finished also can contribute to the creative process. In an important sense, the education and training of creative people never really

FIGURE 5.2 THE CREATIVE PROCESS

The creative process often follows the four-step sequence shown here. Preparation lays the foundation, while incubation allows ideas and insights to evolve. Insight occurs when the idea or insight crystalizes. Verification is then needed to test the validity of the idea or insight. The creative process does not unfold in a mechanical fashion.

© ALEXANDER RATHS/SHUTTERSTOCK.COM

The work of chemists often follows the basic creative process. Their training provides preparation. Incubation and insight yield breakthroughs, which then must be verified.

ends. It continues as long as they remain interested in the world and curious about the way things work. For example, Bruce Roth earned a Ph.D. in chemistry and then spent years working in the pharmaceutical industry learning more and more about chemical compounds and how they work in human beings.

Incubation The second phase of the creative process is *incubation*—a period of less-intense, conscious concentration during which the knowledge and ideas acquired during preparation mature and develop. A curious aspect of incubation is that it is often helped along by pauses in concentrated rational thought. Some creative people rely on physical activity such as jogging or swimming to provide a break from thinking. Others may read or listen to music. Sometimes sleep may even supply the needed pause. Bruce Roth eventually joined Warner-Lambert, an up-and-coming drug company, to help develop medication to lower cholesterol. In his spare time, Roth read mystery novels and hiked in the mountains. He later acknowledged that this was when he did his best thinking. Similarly, twice a year Bill Gates retreats to a secluded wooded cabin to reflect on trends in technology; it is during these weeks, he says, that he develops his sharpest insights into where Microsoft should be heading.[15]

Insight Usually occurring after preparation and incubation, *insight* is a spontaneous breakthrough in which the creative person achieves a new understanding of some problem or situation. Insight represents a coming together of all the scattered thoughts and ideas that were maturing during incubation. It may occur suddenly or develop slowly over time. Insight can be triggered by some external event, such as a new experience or an encounter with new data, which forces the individual to think about old issues and problems in new ways, or it can be a completely internal event in which patterns of thought finally coalesce in ways that generate new understanding. For example, one day Bruce Roth was reviewing data from some earlier studies that had found the new drug under development to be no more effective than other drugs already available. But this time he saw some statistical relationships that had not been identified previously. He knew then that he had a major breakthrough on his hands.

Verification Once an insight has occurred, *verification* determines its validity or truthfulness. For many creative ideas, verification includes scientific experiments to determine whether the insight actually leads to the results expected. Verification also may include the development of a product or service prototype. A *prototype* is one product or a very small number of products built just to see if the ideas behind the new product actually work. Product prototypes are rarely sold to the public, but they are very valuable in verifying the insights developed in the creative process. Once the new product or service is developed, verification in the marketplace is the ultimate test of the creative idea behind it. Bruce Roth and his colleagues set to work testing the new drug compound and eventually won FDA approval. The drug, named Lipitor, went on to become the largest-selling pharmaceutical in history.

Enhancing Creativity in Organizations

Managers seeking to enhance and promote creativity in their organizations can do so in a variety of ways.[16] One important method for enhancing creativity is to make it a part of the organization's culture, often through explicit goals. Firms that truly want to stress creativity, such as 3M and Rubbermaid, for example, state goals that some percentage of future revenues are to be gained from new products. This clearly communicates that creativity and innovation are valued. Best Buy recently picked four groups of salespeople in their 20s and early 30s and asked them to spend 10 weeks living together in a Los Angeles apartment complex (with expenses paid by the company and still earning their normal pay). Their job? Sit around and brainstorm new business ideas that could be rolled out quickly and cheaply.[17] Another important part of enhancing creativity is to reward creative successes, while being careful not to punish creative failures. Many ideas that seem worthwhile on paper fail to pan out in reality. If the

FIGURE 5.3 THE INNOVATION PROCESS

Organizations actively seek to manage the innovation process. These steps illustrate the general life cycle that characterizes most innovations. As with creativity, the innovation process will suffer if it is approached too mechanically and rigidly.

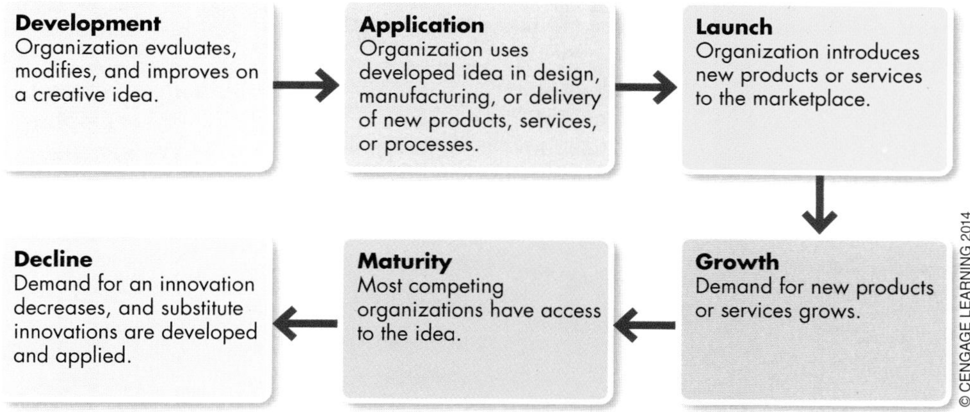

first person to come up with an idea that fails is fired or otherwise punished, others in the organization will become more cautious in their own work. As a result, fewer creative ideas will emerge.

MANAGING INNOVATION

As noted earlier, creativity and innovation are related but distinct concepts. **Innovation** is the managed effort of an organization to develop new products or services or new uses for existing products or services. Innovation is important because, without new products or services, any organization will fall behind its competition.[18]

The Innovation Process

The organizational innovation process consists of developing, applying, launching, growing, and managing the maturity and decline of creative ideas.[19] This process is depicted in *Figure* 5.3.

Innovation Development Innovation development involves the evaluation, modification, and improvement of creative ideas. Innovation development can transform a product or service with only modest potential into a product or service with significant potential. Parker Brothers, for example, decided during innovation development not to market an indoor volleyball game, but instead to sell the appealing little foam ball designed for the game separately. The firm will never know how well the volleyball game would have sold, but the Nerf ball and numerous related products generated millions of dollars in revenues for Parker Brothers.

Innovation Application Innovation application is the stage in which an organization takes a developed idea and uses it in the design, manufacturing, or delivery of new products, services, or processes. At this point, the innovation emerges from the laboratory and is transformed into tangible goods or services. One example of innovation application is the use of radar-based focusing systems in Polaroid's instant cameras. The idea of using radio waves to discover the location, speed, and direction of moving objects was first applied extensively by Allied forces during World War II. As radar technology developed during the following years, the electrical components needed became smaller and more streamlined. Researchers at Polaroid applied this well-developed technology in a new way.[20]

Application Launch Application launch is the stage at which an organization introduces new products or services to the marketplace. The important question is not "Does the innovation work?" but "Will customers want to purchase the innovative product and service?" History is full of creative ideas that did not generate enough interest among customers to be successful. Some notable "classic" innovation failures include a portable seat warmer from Sony, "New" Coke, and Polaroid's SX-70 instant camera (which cost $3 billion to develop, but never sold more than 100,000 units in a year).[21] More recently a chocolate drink introduced by Starbucks, a relatively healthy low-fat burger from McDonald's, and numerous products in the smartphone market have all done poorly and were discontinued.

innovation the managed effort of an organization to develop new products or services or new uses for existing products or services

Thus, despite development and application, new products and services can still fail at the launch phase.

Application Growth Once an innovation has been successfully launched, it then enters the stage of application growth. This is a period of high economic performance for an organization because demand for the product or service is often greater than supply. Organizations that fail to anticipate this stage may unintentionally limit their growth, as Apple did by not anticipating demand for its iMac computer.[22] At the same time, overestimating demand for a new product can be just as detrimental to performance. Unsold products can sit in warehouses for years.

Innovation Maturity After a period of growing demand, an innovative product or service often enters a period of maturity. Innovation maturity is the stage at which most organizations in an industry have access to an innovation and are applying it in approximately the same way. The technological application of an innovation during this stage of the innovation process can be very sophisticated. However, because most firms have access to the innovation, either as a result of their developing the innovation on their own or copying the innovation of others, it does not provide competitive advantage to any one of them. The time that elapses between innovation development and innovation maturity varies notably depending on the product or service. Whenever an innovation involves the use of complex skills (such as a complicated manufacturing process or highly sophisticated teamwork), moving from the growth phase to the maturity phase will take longer. In addition, if the skills needed to implement these innovations are rare and difficult to imitate, then strategic imitation may be delayed, and the organization may enjoy a period of sustained competitive advantage.

© COLOUR/SHUTTERSTOCK.COM

Innovation Decline Every successful innovation bears its own seeds of decline. Because an organization does not gain a competitive advantage from an innovation at maturity, it must encourage its creative scientists, engineers, and managers to begin looking for new innovations. This continued search for competitive advantage usually leads new products and services to move from the creative process through innovation maturity, and finally to innovation decline. Innovation decline is the stage during which demand for an innovation decreases and substitute innovations are developed and applied.

technical innovations changes in the physical appearance or performance of a product or service, or of the physical processes through which a product or service is manufactured

Forms of Innovation

Each creative idea that an organization develops poses a different challenge for the innovation process. Innovations can be radical or incremental, technical or managerial, and product or process.

Radical Versus Incremental Innovations

Radical innovations are new products, services, or technologies developed by an organization that completely replace those that already exist in an industry.[23] Incremental innovations are new products or processes that modify existing ones. Firms that implement radical innovations fundamentally shift the nature of competition and the interaction of firms within their environments. Firms that implement incremental innovations alter, but do not fundamentally change, competitive interaction in an industry.

Over the last several years, organizations have introduced many radical innovations. For example, compact disk technology replaced cassette tapes in the recording industry and now digital downloading is replacing CDs; in the video industry, DVDs have replaced videocassettes but are now being supplanted by Blu-ray DVDs and online downloading; and high-definition television is replacing traditional television technology. Whereas radical innovations like these tend to be very visible and public, incremental innovations actually are more numerous. For instance, each new generation of the iPhone and the iPad represent relatively minor changes over previous versions.

Technical Versus Managerial Innovations

Technical innovations are changes in the physical appearance or performance of a product or service, or of the physical processes through which a product or service is manufactured. Many of the most important innovations over the last several decades have been technical. For example, the serial replacement of the vacuum tube with the transistor, the transistor with the integrated circuit, and the integrated circuit with the microchip has greatly enhanced the power, ease of use, and speed of operation of a wide variety of electronic products. Not all innovations developed

FIGURE 5.4 EFFECTS OF PRODUCT AND PROCESS INNOVATION ON ECONOMIC RETURN

As the innovation process moves from development to decline, the economic return from product innovations gradually declines. In contrast, the economic return from process innovations increases during the same process.

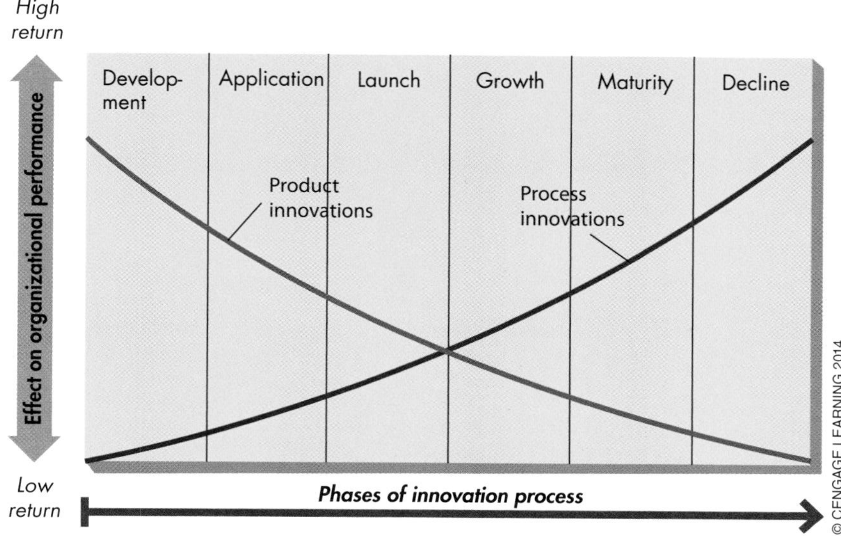

by organizations are technical, however. **Managerial innovations** are changes in the management process by which products and services are conceived, built, and delivered to customers.[24] Managerial innovations do not necessarily affect the physical appearance or performance of products or services directly. In effect, business process change or reengineering, as we discuss earlier, represents a managerial innovation.

> *"We should continue to innovate in our relationship with our employees and figure out the best things we can do for them."*
>
> LARRY PAGE
> Co-founder and CEO
> Google[25]

Product Versus Process Innovations Perhaps the two most important types of technical innovations are product innovations and process innovations. Product innovations are changes in the physical characteristics or performance of existing products or services or the creation of brand-new products or services. Process innovations are changes in the way products or services are manufactured, created, or distributed. Whereas managerial innovations generally affect the broader context of development, process innovations directly affect manufacturing.

The implementation of robotics, as we discuss earlier, is a process innovation. As *Figure 5.4* shows, the effect of product and process innovations on economic return depends on the stage of the innovation process that a new product or service occupies. At first, during development, application, and launch, the physical attributes and capabilities of an innovation most affect organizational performance. Thus, product innovations are particularly important during these beginning phases. Later, as an innovation enters the phases of growth, maturity, and decline, an organization's ability to develop process innovations, such as fine-tuning manufacturing, increasing product quality, and improving product distribution, becomes important to maintaining economic return.

Japanese organizations have often excelled at process innovation. The market for 35mm cameras was dominated by German and other European manufacturers when, in the early 1960s, Japanese organizations such as Canon and Nikon began making cameras. Some of these early Japanese products were not very successful, but these companies continued to invest in their process technology and eventually were able to increase quality and decrease manufacturing costs.[26]

managerial innovations changes in the management process by which products and services are conceived, built, and delivered to customers

The Japanese organizations came to dominate the worldwide market for 35mm cameras, and the German companies, because they were not able to maintain the same pace of process innovation, struggled to maintain market share and profitability. And, as film technology gives way to digital photography, the same Japanese firms are effectively transitioning to leadership in this market as well.

LEARN

The Failure to Innovate

To remain competitive in today's economy, organizations must be innovative. Yet, many organizations that should be innovative are not successful at bringing out new products or services or do so only after innovations created by others mature. Organizations may fail to innovate for at least three reasons.

Lack of Resources Innovation is expensive in terms of dollars, time, and energy. If a firm does not have sufficient capital to fund a program of innovation or does not currently employ the kinds of employees it needs to innovate, it may lag behind in innovation. Even highly innovative organizations cannot pursue every new product or service its employees think up. For example, numerous other commitments in the electronic instruments and computer industry prevented Hewlett-Packard from investing in Steve Jobs and Steve Wozniak's original idea for a personal computer. With infinite resources of money, time, and technical and managerial expertise, HP might have entered this market early. Because the firm did not have this flexibility, however, it had to make some difficult choices about which innovations to invest in.[27]

Failure to Recognize Opportunities Because firms cannot pursue all innovations, they need to develop the capability to carefully evaluate innovations and to select the ones that hold the greatest potential. To obtain a competitive advantage, an organization usually must make investment decisions before the innovation process reaches the mature stage. The earlier the investment, however, the greater the risk. If organizations are not skilled at recognizing and evaluating opportunities, they may be overly cautious and fail to invest in innovations that later turn out to be successful for other firms.

Resistance to Change As we discuss later, some organizations tend to resist change. Innovation means giving up old products and old ways of doing things in favor of new products and new ways of doing things. These kinds of changes can be personally difficult for managers and other members of an organization. Thus, resistance to change can slow down the innovation process.

Promoting Innovation in Organizations

A wide variety of ideas for promoting innovation in organizations has been developed over the years. Three specific ways for promoting innovation are through the reward system, through the organizational culture, and through a process called *intrapreneurship*.[28]

The Reward System A firm's reward system is the means by which it encourages and discourages certain behaviors by employees. Major components of the reward system include salaries, bonuses, and perquisites. Using the reward system to promote innovation is a fairly mechanical but, nevertheless, effective management technique. The idea is to provide financial and nonfinancial rewards to people and groups who develop innovative ideas. Once the members of an organization understand that they will be rewarded for such activities, they are more likely to work creatively. With this end in mind, Monsanto gives a $50,000 award each year to the scientist or group of scientists who develop the biggest commercial breakthrough.

It is important for organizations to reward creative behavior, but it is vital to avoid punishing creativity when it does not result in highly successful innovations. Many new product ideas will simply not work out in the marketplace because creative and innovative processes have too many uncertainties to generate positive results every time. An individual may have prepared herself to be creative, but an insight may not be forthcoming. Or managers may attempt to apply a developed innovation, only to recognize that it does not work. Indeed, some organizations operate according to the assumption that, if all their innovative efforts succeed, then they are probably not taking enough risks in research and development. At 3M, nearly 60 percent of the creative ideas suggested each year do not succeed in the marketplace.

Managers need to be careful in responding to innovative failure. If the innovative failure results from incompetence, systematic errors, or managerial sloppiness, then a firm should respond appropriately, for example, by withholding raises or reducing promotion opportunities. People who act in good faith to develop an innovation that simply does not work out, however, should not be punished for failure. If they are, they will probably not be creative in the future. A punitive reward system will discourage people from taking risks, and therefore reduce the organization's ability to obtain competitive advantages.

Organization Culture An organization's culture is the set of values, beliefs, and symbols that help guide its behavior. A strong, appropriately focused organizational culture can be used to support innovative activity. A well-managed culture can communicate a sense that innovation is valued and will be rewarded and that occasional failure in the pursuit of new ideas is not only acceptable but expected. In addition to reward systems and intrapreneurial activities, firms such as Apple, Google, Nintendo, Nokia, Sony, Walt Disney, Vodafone, and Hewlett-Packard are all known to have strong, innovation-oriented cultures that value individual creativity, risk taking, and inventiveness.[29]

Intrapreneurship in Larger Organizations In recent years, many large businesses have realized that the entrepreneurial spirit that propelled their growth becomes stagnant after they transform themselves from a small but growing concern into a larger one.[30] To help revitalize this spirit, some firms today encourage what they call "intrapreneurship." Intrapreneurs are similar to entrepreneurs, but they develop a new business in the context of a large organization. There are three intrapreneurial roles in large organizations, including the inventory, the product champion, and the sponsor.[31] To successfully use intrapreneurship to encourage creativity and innovation, the organization must find one or more individuals to perform these roles.

The *inventor* is the person who actually conceives of and develops the new idea, product, or service by means of the creative process. Because the inventor may lack the expertise or motivation to oversee the transformation of the product or service from an idea into a marketable entity, a second role comes into play. A *product champion* is usually a middle manager who learns about the project and becomes committed to it. He or she helps overcome organizational resistance and convinces others to take the innovation seriously. The product champion may have only limited understanding of the technological aspects of the innovation. Nevertheless, product champions are skilled at knowing how the organization works, whose support is needed to push the project forward, and where to go to secure the resources necessary for successful development. A *sponsor* is a top-level manager who approves of and supports a project. This person may fight for the budget needed to develop an idea, overcome arguments against a project, and use organizational politics to ensure the project's survival. With a sponsor in place, the inventor's idea has a much better chance of being successfully developed.

Several firms have embraced intrapreneurship as a way to encourage creativity and innovation. Colgate-Palmolive has created a separate unit, Colgate Venture Company, staffed with intrapreneurs who develop new products. General Foods developed Culinova as a unit to which employees can take their ideas for possible development. S.C. Johnson & Son established a $250,000 fund to support new product ideas, and Texas Instruments refuses to approve a new innovative project unless it has an acknowledged inventor, champion, and sponsor.

PHOTO BY STEPHEN BRASHEAR/GETTY IMAGES

An organization's culture can contribute to creativity and innovation. Google, for example, promotes creativity by providing employees with relaxation equipment such as climbing walls, pool tables, and comfortable lounges.

MANAGING CHANGE

The ability to effectively manage change is another important part of a manager's conceptual skills. **Organization change** is any substantive modification to some part of the organization.[32] Thus, change can involve virtually any aspect of an organization: work schedules, bases for departmentalization, span of management, machinery, organization design, people themselves, and so on. It is important to keep in mind that any change in an organization may have effects extending beyond the actual area where the change is implemented. For example, when Northrop Grumman installed a new automated production system at one of its plants, employees had to be retrained to operate new equipment, the compensation system had to be adjusted to reflect new skill levels, the span of management for supervisors had to be altered, and several jobs needed to be redesigned. Selection criteria for new employees also were changed, and a new quality

organization change any substantive modification to some part of the organization

control system was needed.[33] As you can see from this example, it is common, and often necessary, for multiple organization change activities to occur simultaneously.[34]

"Standing still is how you kill the company."
RAY DAVIS
CEO of Umpqua Holdings[40]

QUOTED IN BUSINESSWEEK, MARCH 23/30, 2009, P. 33.

Forces for Change

Why do organizations find change necessary? The basic reason is that something relevant to the organization either has changed or is likely to change in the foreseeable future. The organization therefore may have little choice but to change as well. Indeed, a primary reason for the problems that organizations often face is failure to anticipate or respond properly to changing circumstances. The forces that compel change may be external or internal to the organization.[35]

External Forces External forces for change derive from the organization's general and task environments.[36] For example, two energy crises, an aggressive Japanese automobile industry, floating currency exchange rates, and floating international interest rates—all manifestations of the international dimension of the general environment—profoundly influenced US automobile companies. New rules of production and competition forced them to dramatically alter the way they do business. In the political area, new laws, court decisions, and regulations affect organizations. The technological dimension may yield new production techniques that the organization needs to explore. The economic dimension is affected by inflation, the cost of living, and the money supply. The sociocultural dimension, reflecting societal values, determines what kinds of products or services the market will accept.

Because of its proximity to the organization, the task environment is an even more powerful force for change. Competitors influence an organization through their price structures and product lines. When American Airlines lowers the prices of its airfares, United and Delta may have little choice but to follow suit. Because customers determine what products can be sold at what prices, organizations must be concerned with consumer tastes and preferences. Suppliers affect organizations by raising or lowering prices or changing product lines. Regulators can have dramatic effects on an organization. For example, if OSHA rules that a particular production process is dangerous to workers, it can force a firm to close a plant until it meets higher safety standards. Unions can force change when they have the clout to negotiate for higher wages or if they go on strike.[37]

planned change change that is designed and implemented in an orderly and timely fashion in anticipation of future events

reactive change piecemeal response to circumstances as they develop

Internal Forces A variety of forces inside the organization may cause change. If top management revises the organization's strategy, organization change is likely to result.[38] A decision by an electronics company to enter the home computer market or a decision to increase a ten-year product sales goal by 3 percent would prompt many organization changes. Other internal forces for change may be reflections of external forces. As sociocultural values shift, for example, workers' attitudes toward their jobs also may shift—and workers may demand a change in working hours or working conditions. In such a case, even though the force is rooted in the external environment, the organization must respond directly to the internal pressure it generates.[39]

Planned Versus Reactive Change

Some change is planned in advance; other change comes about as a reaction to unexpected events. **Planned change** is change that is designed and implemented in an orderly and timely fashion in anticipation of future events. **Reactive change** is a piecemeal response to circumstances as they develop. Because reactive change may be hurried, the potential for poorly conceived and executed change is increased. Planned change usually is preferable to reactive change.[41]

Georgia-Pacific, a large forest products business, is an excellent example of a firm that went through a planned and well-managed change process. When A. D. Correll became CEO, he quickly became alarmed at the firm's high accident rate—nine serious injuries per 100 employees each year, and 26 deaths during the most recent five-year period. Although the forest products business is inherently dangerous, Correll believed that the accident rate was far too high, and he set out on a major change effort to improve things. He and other top managers developed a multistage change program intended to educate workers about safety, improve safety equipment in the plant, and eliminate a long-standing part of the firm's culture that made injuries almost a badge of courage. As a result, Georgia-Pacific achieved the best safety record in the industry, with relatively few injuries.[42]

On the other hand, Caterpillar was caught flat-footed by a worldwide recession in the construction industry, suffered enormous losses, and took several years to recover. Had managers at Caterpillar anticipated the need for change earlier, they might have been able to respond more quickly. Similarly, the importance of approaching change from a planned perspective is reinforced by the frequency of organization change. Most companies or divisions of large companies implement some form of moderate change at least every year and one or more major changes every four to five years.[43] Managers who sit back and respond only when they have to are likely to spend a lot of time hastily changing and re-changing things. A more effective approach is to anticipate forces urging change and plan ahead to deal with them.[44]

The Lewin Change Model

Kurt Lewin, a noted organizational theorist, suggested that every change requires three steps.[45] The first step is *unfreezing*—individuals who will be affected by the impending change must be led to recognize why the change is necessary. Next, the *change itself* is implemented. Finally, *refreezing* involves reinforcing and supporting the change so that it becomes a part of the system.[46] For example, one of the changes Caterpillar faced in response to the recession noted earlier involved a massive workforce reduction. The first step (unfreezing) was convincing the United Auto Workers to support the reduction because of its importance to long-term effectiveness. After this unfreezing was accomplished, 30,000 jobs were eliminated (implementation). Then Caterpillar worked to improve its damaged relationship with its workers (refreezing) by guaranteeing future pay hikes and promising no more cutbacks. As interesting as Lewin's model is, however, it lacks operational specificity. Thus, a more comprehensive perspective often is needed.

A Comprehensive Approach to Change

The comprehensive approach to change takes a systems view and delineates a series of specific steps that often leads to successful change. This expanded model is illustrated in *Figure* 5.5.

- The first step is recognizing the need for change. Reactive change might be triggered by employee complaints, declines in productivity or turnover, court injunctions, sales slumps, or labor strikes. Recognition may simply be managers' awareness that change in a certain area is inevitable. For example, managers may be aware of the general frequency of organizational change undertaken by most organizations and recognize that their organization should follow the same pattern. The immediate stimulus might be the result of a forecast indicating new market potential, the accumulation of a cash surplus for possible investment, or an opportunity to achieve and capitalize on a major technological breakthrough. Managers also might initiate change today because indicators suggest that it will be necessary in the near future.[47]

FIGURE 5.5 STEPS IN THE CHANGE PROCESS

Managers must understand how and why to implement change. A manager who follows a logical and orderly sequence, such as the one shown here, when implanting change is more likely to succeed than a manager whose change process is haphazard and poorly conceived.

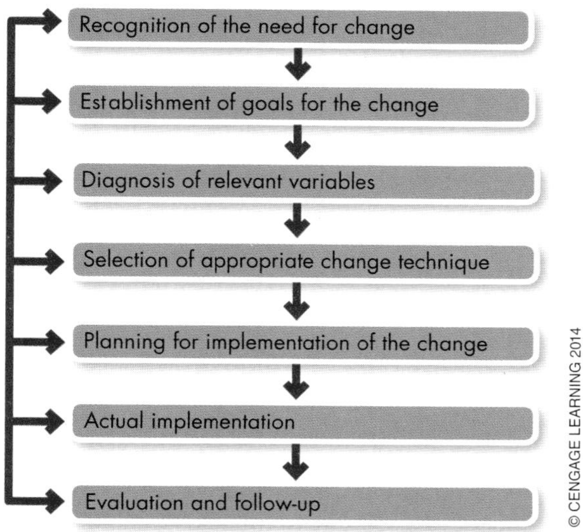

LEARN

- Managers must next set goals for the change. To increase market share, to enter new markets, to restore employee morale, to settle a strike, and to identify investment opportunities all might be goals for change.
- Third, managers must diagnose what brought on the need for change. Turnover, for example, might be caused by low pay, poor working conditions, poor supervisors, or employee dissatisfaction. Thus, although turnover may be the immediate stimulus for change, managers must understand its causes to make the right changes.
- The next step is to select a change technique that will accomplish the intended goals. If turnover is caused by low pay, a new reward system may be needed. If the cause is poor supervision, supervisors may need interpersonal skills training.
- After the appropriate technique has been chosen, its implementation must be planned. Issues to consider include the costs of the change, its effects on other areas of the organization, and the degree of employee participation appropriate for the situation.
- If the change is implemented as planned, the results should then be evaluated. If the change was intended

to reduce turnover, managers must check turnover after the change has been in effect for a while. If turnover is still too high, further changes may be necessary.[48]

LEARN

Understanding Resistance to Change

Another element in the effective management of change is understanding the resistance that often accompanies change.[49] Managers need to know why people resist change and what can be done about their resistance. When Westinghouse first provided all of its managers with personal computers, most people responded favorably. One manager, however, resisted the change to the point where he began leaving work every day at noon! It was some time before he began staying in the office all day again. Such resistance is common for a variety of reasons.[50]

Uncertainty Perhaps the biggest cause of employee resistance to change is uncertainty. In the face of impending change, employees may become anxious and nervous. They may worry about their ability to meet new job demands, they may think that their job security is threatened, or they may simply dislike ambiguity. Nabisco was once the target of an extended and confusing takeover battle, and during the entire time, employees were nervous about the impending change. The *Wall Street Journal* described them this way: "Many are angry at their leaders and fearful for their jobs. They are swapping rumors and spinning scenarios for the ultimate outcome of the battle for the tobacco and food giant. Headquarters staffers in Atlanta know so little about what's happening in New York that some call their office 'the mushroom complex,' where they are kept in the dark."[51]

Threatened Self-Interests Many impending changes threaten the self-interests of some managers within the organization. A change might diminish their power or influence within the company, so they fight it. Managers at Sears once developed a plan calling for a new type of store. The new stores would be somewhat smaller than a typical Sears store and would not be located in large shopping malls. Instead, they would be located in smaller strip centers. They would carry clothes and other "soft goods," but not hardware, appliances, furniture, or automotive products. When executives in charge of the excluded product lines heard about the plan, they raised such strong objections that the plan was cancelled.

ECHO

Different Perceptions A third reason that people resist change is due to different perceptions. A manager may make a decision and recommend a plan for change on the basis of her own assessment of a situation. Others in the organization may resist the change because they do not agree with the manager's assessment or they perceive the situation differently.[52] Executives at 7-Eleven battled this problem as they attempted to enact a major organizational change. The corporation wanted to take its convenience stores a bit "upscale" and begin selling fancy fresh foods to go, the newest hardcover novels, some gourmet products, and higher-quality coffee. But many franchisees balked because they saw this move as taking the firm away from its core blue-collar customers.

Feelings of Loss Many changes involve altering work arrangements in ways that disrupt existing social networks. Because social relationships are important, most people resist any change that might adversely affect those relationships. Other intangibles threatened by change include power, status, security, familiarity with existing procedures, and self-confidence.

Overcoming Resistance to Change

Of course, a manager should not give up in the face of resistance to change. Although there are no sure-fire cures, there are several techniques that at least have the potential to overcome resistance.[53]

Participation Participation is often the most effective technique for overcoming resistance to change. Employees who participate in planning and implementing a change are better able to understand why it is needed. Uncertainty is reduced, and self-interests and social relationships are less threatened. Having had an opportunity to express their ideas and assume the perspectives of others, employees are more likely to accept the change gracefully. A classic study of participation monitored the introduction of a change in production methods among four groups in a Virginia pajama factory.[54] The two groups that fully participated in planning and implementing the change improved significantly in their productivity and satisfaction, relative to the two groups that did not participate. As another example, the 3M Company recently attributed several million dollars in cost savings to employee participation in several organization change activities.

Education and Communication Educating employees about the need for and the expected results of an impending change should reduce their resistance. If open communication is established and maintained during the change process, uncertainty can be minimized. Caterpillar used these methods during many of its cutbacks to reduce resistance. First, it educated UAW representatives about the need for and potential value of the planned changes. Then management told all employees what was happening, when it would happen, and how it would affect them individually.

Facilitation Several facilitation procedures also are advisable. For instance, making only necessary changes, announcing those changes well in advance, and allowing time for people to adjust to new ways of doing things can help reduce resistance to change.[55] One manager at a Prudential regional office spent several months systematically planning a change in work procedures and job design. He then became too impatient and came in over the weekend with a work crew to rearrange the office layout. When employees walked in on Monday morning and saw what he had done, they were hostile, anxious, and resentful. What was a promising change became a disaster, and the manager had to scrap the entire plan.

Force-Field Analysis Although force-field analysis may sound like something out of a *Star Trek* movie, it can help overcome resistance to change. In almost any change situation, forces are acting for and against the change. To facilitate the change, managers start by listing each set of forces and then trying to tip the balance so that the forces facilitating the change outweigh those hindering the change. It is especially important to try to remove or at least minimize some of the forces acting against the change. Suppose, for example, that General Motors is considering a plant closing as part of a change. Three factors are reinforcing the change: GM needs to cut costs; it has excess capacity; and the plant has outmoded production facilities. At the same time, there is resistance from the UAW, concern for workers being put out of their jobs, and a feeling that the plant might be needed again in the future. GM might start by convincing the UAW that the closing is necessary by presenting profit and loss figures. It could then offer relocation and retraining to displaced workers. Finally, it might shut down the plant and put it in "mothballs" so that it can be renovated later. The three major factors hindering the change are thus eliminated or reduced in importance.[56]

MANAGING RISK

LEARN

A final element of a manager's conceptual skills set is the ability to manage risk. Most business activity takes place under conditions of risk. So, it is important for managers to understand the risk their business faces, assess that risk in terms of its potential consequences and benefits, and take appropriate steps to manage that risk to minimize its potential impact. We define **risk** as uncertainty about future events. **Risk management**, in turn, is the process of protecting the firm and its assets by reducing the potential consequences of risky future events.

It is important to understand the distinction between risk and the potential consequences of risky future events. No one knows what the price of oil will be in ten years, so all consumers of oil products face the same risk regarding future oil prices. However, astute managers can position themselves to be better prepared for different eventualities. For instance, suppose two competing businesses have been offered the opportunity to buy exclusive distribution rights to a new product for a fee of $500,000. One of the businesses has high debt, weak cash flow, and low cash reserves. If the firm buys the distribution rights and the product fails, the firm will have to declare bankruptcy. The other firm, has low debt, strong cash flow, and high cash reserves. While a product failure would be disappointing, this firm would be better positioned to absorb the loss. Assuming both firms are equally equipped to promote and distribute the new product, they face the same risk. However, the consequences of a product failure are quite different for the two businesses.

There are several options that managers can pursue to manage risk. These include the following:

- Understand one's own risk propensity. **Risk propensity** is the degree to which an individual is willing to take chances and make risky decisions. A manager with a high risk propensity, for example, might be expected to experiment with new ideas and gamble on new products. She might also lead the organization in new and different directions and/or be a catalyst for innovation. On the

risk uncertainty about future events

risk management the process of protecting the firm and its assets by reducing the potential consequences of risky future events

risk propensity the degree to which an individual is willing to take chances and make risky decisions

HENRIK SORENSEN

Risk management is an important function for most businesses. Floods, fire, and similar disasters are just a few of the many risks managers face today.

other hand, the same individual might jeopardize the continued well-being of the organization if the risky decisions prove to be bad ones. A manager with low risk propensity might lead to a stagnant and overly conservative organization or help the organization successfully weather turbulent and unpredictable times by maintaining stability and calm. Thus, the potential consequences of risk propensity to an organization are heavily dependent on that organization's environment.

- Understand the potential costs and benefits of potential outcomes. Managers and businesses that never take risks are unlikely to succeed. Consequently, it is important to understand the array of possible consequences that might result from a course of action and the costs and benefits associated with each.
- Reduce risk. It is also possible to reduce the consequences of risk. For instance, the riskiest approach is to never buy insurance because of the expense of monthly premiums. As long as nothing goes wrong, you come out ahead. But if problems do arise, the results can be catastrophic because of the losses incurred. At the other extreme, it is also possible to fully insure against just about any conceivable loss, thus minimizing risk. In this case, though, the monthly premiums will be extremely expensive. So, most decision makers opt for a position in which they insure against major losses but also accept some of the risk themselves (in the form of deductibles and so forth). Balancing insurance coverage with premiums and deductibles is a form of risk management.
- Share risk. Another option is to share risk, often by working with strategic partners. For instance, Shell and BP have worked together to explore for oil in remote areas of South America and Africa. If no significant oil fields are found, each firm will only lose about half of the total cost of exploration.

Managers should take special note of risk when they are making decisions. From a decision-making perspective, risk centers around the availability of information about and an understanding of the probability estimates for payoffs and costs for each outcome. Suppose, for example, that a labor contract negotiator for a company receives a "final" offer from the union right before a strike deadline. The negotiator has two alternatives: to accept or to reject the offer. The risk centers on whether the union representatives are bluffing. If the company negotiator accepts the offer, she avoids a strike but commits to a costlier labor contract. If she rejects the offer, she may get a more favorable contract if the union is bluffing, but she may provoke a strike if it is not.

Based on past experiences, relevant information, the advice of others, and her own judgment, she may conclude that there is about a 75 percent chance that union representatives are bluffing and about a 25 percent chance that they will back up their threats. Thus she can base a calculated decision on the two alternatives (accept or reject the contract demands) and the probable consequences of each. When faced with risk, managers must reasonably estimate the probabilities associated with each alternative. For example, if the union negotiators are committed to a strike if their demands are not met, and the company negotiator rejects their demands because she predicts they will not strike, her miscalculation will prove costly.

Much of what managers do—and most of the decisions they make—center around risk. Introducing a new product, adopting a new advertising campaign, agreeing to a new joint venture, signing a new contract, opening a new factory, or hiring a new assistant are each accompanied by some degree of risk. Indeed, if managers don't take risks, in all likelihood their firms will stagnate and fall behind those who do. But the astute manager can manage risk and can usually keep it within acceptable limits.

SUMMARY AND A LOOK AHEAD

After reading and studying this chapter, you should have a better understanding of conceptual skills. In particular, you should be better equipped to understand strategic thinking, as well as creativity and how it can be managed. Similarly, you should be able to describe innovation and how to manage it. Change management also should be clearer and more salient to you. Finally, you should have an appreciation of the basic issues in managing risk.

The remainder of this chapter provides opportunities for you to continue to develop and refine your conceptual skills. For instance, you will be directed to resources that allow you to visualize both effective and less-effective conceptual skills. Subsequent sections provide several opportunities for you to practice and explore conceptual skills from different perspectives. The chapter concludes with some additional assessment and interpretation data.

VISUALIZING CONCEPTUAL SKILLS

CONCEPTUAL SKILLS IN ACTION—1

Your Assignment

Consider the two BizFlix film clips for this chapter.

Charlie Wilson's War (2007) is a fictionalized account regarding Democratic Congressman Charlie Wilson (Tom Hanks) from East Texas. Wilson lives a reckless life that includes heavy drinking and chasing women. The film focuses on the Afghanistan rebellion against the Soviet troop invasion in the 1980s. Wilson becomes the unlikely champion of the Afghan cause through his role in two major congressional committees that deal with foreign policy and covert operations. Houston socialite Joanne Herring (Julia Roberts) strongly urges the intervention. CIA agent Gust Avrakotos (Philip Seymour Hoffman) helps with some details.

Inside Man (2006) is pure fiction. New York City detective Keith Frazier (Denzel Washington) leads an effort to remove Dalton Russell (Clive Owen) and his armed gang from the Manhattan Trust Bank building. Complexities set in when bank chairman Arthur Case (Christopher Plummer) seeks the help of power broker Madeline White (Jodie Foster) to prevent the thieves from getting a particular safe deposit box. This fast-paced action film goes in many directions to reach its unexpected ending.

Note how conceptual skills are shown in these two scenes.

1. In the first clip, you see how Charlie Wilson uses his conceptual (and technical) skills to process a variety of fast-moving information to analyze the "big picture" and indicate an understanding of conditions in Afghanistan. Yet, he has to double-check with his aide about how to vote as he enters the House Chamber. In what way does this represent a positive use of conceptual skills?
2. In the second clip, Detective Frazier processes information from Captain John Darius (Willem Dafoe) to assess the risks associated with contacting the gang right away. He startles Darius when he indicates that his strategy is to delay contact to give the gang a chance to become stressed. Can you suggest a way in which this could be handled differently?

CONCEPTUAL SKILLS IN ACTION—2

This exercise gives you an opportunity to think about conceptual skills that may be involved in management positions for you in the future.

Your Assignment

1. Think about conceptual skills and try to identify a scene that illustrates a positive or effective use of such skills in a movie, TV show, or a video on YouTube.
2. Now do the same for a scene that illustrates a negative or ineffective use of such skills.

Share your results with the class and discuss how the positive and negative uses of conceptual skills are shown in each clip. You also should try to suggest how the negative situation could have been changed for the better.

PRACTICING YOUR CONCEPTUAL SKILLS

PRACTICE

MANAGEMENT FUNCTIONS IN DIFFERENT ORGANIZATIONS

Management involves four basic functions, all of which require the use of conceptual skills: Planning and Decision Making, Organizing, Leading, and Controlling. This exercise will help you identify potential generalizations of management functions and conceptual skills as applied across different kinds of organizations.

Your Assignment

1. Identify one large business, one small business, one educational organization, one healthcare organization, and one government organization. Now imagine yourself in the position of a top manager in each organization.
2. Write the four functions across the top of a sheet of paper. List the names of the five organizations down the left side of the paper.
3. Now think of a situation, problem, or opportunity relevant to the intersection of each row and column on the paper. Try to think of opportunities to use conceptual skills in all 20 (five organizations, four functions) situations. For example, how might a manager in a government organization need conceptual skills to carry out the organizing function? How might a manager in a small business do likewise? How could a manager in an educational organization and in a healthcare organization use conceptual skills in carrying out the planning and decision-making function?
4. What meaningful similarities can you identify across the five columns?
5. What meaningful differences can you identify across the five columns?
6. Based on your assessment of the similarities and differences, how easy or how difficult do you think it is for a manager to move from one type of organization to another?

Choosing a New Business Startup

This exercise will help you relate conceptual skills to a decision that an entrepreneur would have to make.

Assume that you have decided to open a small business after you graduate in the community where you are attending college. Assume that you have funds to start the business without having to worry about finding investors.

Your Assignment

1. Without regard for market potential, profitability, or similar considerations, list five businesses that you might want to open and operate solely on the basis of your personal interests. For example, if you enjoy baking or bicycling, you might enjoy opening a bakery or a shop that caters to cyclists.
2. Next, list five businesses that you might want to open and operate solely on the basis of their promising market opportunity, regardless of whether they are personally attractive to you. Use the Internet to help you determine which businesses might be profitable in your community, based on factors such as population, local economic conditions, local competition, franchising opportunities, and so on.
3. Evaluate the prospects for success for each of the ten businesses (*Hint*: You might want to rank-order them).
4. Form a small group with three or four classmates and discuss your respective lists.
   (A) Look for instances where the same type of business appears on multiple lists.
   (B) Look for instances where the same business appears with similar or dissimilar prospects for success.
   (C) Discuss how important personal interest is to small business success.
   (D) Discuss how important market potential is to small business success.

Using Conceptual Skills to Understand the Behavior of Others

This exercise concerns conceptual skills that frequently must be used together to understand the behavior of others in the organization.

Human behavior is a complex phenomenon in any setting, but it is especially so in organizations. Understanding how and why people choose particular behaviors can be difficult, frustrating, but quite important. Consider, for example, the following scenario.

Lisa McLeventhal has worked in your department for several years. Until recently, she has been a "model" employee. She was always on time or early for work and stayed late whenever necessary to get her work done. She was upbeat, cheerful, and worked quite hard. She frequently said that the company was the best place she had ever worked and that you were the perfect boss.

About six months ago, however, you began to see changes in Lisa's behavior. She began to come in late occasionally, and you cannot remember the last time she agreed to work past 5:00 P.M. She also complains a lot. Other workers have started to avoid her because she is so negative. You also suspect that she may be looking for a new job.

Your Assignment

1. Assume that you have done some background checking to find out what has happened. Write a brief case (make it as descriptive as possible) with more information that explains why Lisa's behavior has changed. For example, your case could include the fact that you recently promoted someone else when Lisa may have been expecting to get the job.
2. Which diagnostic skills will assist you in understanding Lisa's changes in behavior?

3. Decide if you can resolve problems or misunderstandings with Lisa to overcome the issues that you identified in response to Question 1. For example, if you described her behavior in terms of being passed over for promotion, now describe how you think you can resolve this with Lisa.

Job Values As Perceived by Students and Employers

This exercise investigates the job values held by college students at your institution and their speculation about employers' conceptualizations of the students' job values.

Employees choose careers that match their job values. Consequently, employers need to understand employee values to recruit, manage, and motivate them. Job values are therefore important in every HR process, from job advertisements and interviews to performance appraisal to compensation planning.

Your Assignment

1. Considering what you want from your future career, complete the Job Values Survey below. In Column 2 indicate the value you place on each item in Column 1 by ranking the 14 Job Values from 1 to 14, with 1 being the most important to you and 14 being the least important.
2. When potential employers try to attract students, they should consider how much importance they think students give to each of the values. For each Job Value in Column 1, decide if you think employers believe students rank that Job Value higher than you and other students do. If so, respond with a "+" in Column 3. If you think employers believe students rank that Job Value lower than students actually do, respond with a "–" in Column 3.

JOB VALUES SURVEY		
Column 1 **Job Values**	**Column 2** **My Ranking**	**Column 3** **Do employers think students rank this higher (+) or lower (–)?**
Working conditions		
Working with people		
Employee benefits		
Challenges		
Location of job		
Self-development		
Type of work		
Job title		
Training program		
Advancement		
Salary		
Company reputation		
Job security		
Autonomy on the job		

PRACTICE

3. In small groups or a class, compute an average ranking for each value. Then discuss the results:
   (A) How much variation do you see in the job value rankings in Column 2? That is, are students' rankings quite different, moderately different, or very similar?
   (B) If there are significant differences between individuals, what impact might these differences have on the recruiting process? On the training process? On the performance evaluation and compensation process?
   (C) How much variation do you see in the responses for Column 3? Does your group or class agree on how employers perceive the values of college students?
   (D) Is there a large difference between how you think employers perceive college students and your group's or your class's reported job values? If there is a large difference, what difficulties might this create for job seekers and potential employers? How might these difficulties be reduced or eliminated?

Learning from Other Organizations

This exercise demonstrates that conceptual skills are useful in helping key managers use observations or experiences gleaned from other organizations to improve some aspect of their own organization's operations.

Your Assignment

1. Carefully recall the last time you ate in a restaurant that involved some degree of self-service, for example, a fast-food restaurant like McDonald's, a cafeteria, or a traditional restaurant with a salad bar. Recall as much as possible about the experience, and develop some ideas as to why the restaurant is organized and laid out as it is.
2. Now carefully recall the last time you purchased something in a retail outlet, for example, shoes from a shoe store, a book from a bookstore, or some software from a computer store. Again, recall as much as possible about the experience, and develop some ideas as to why the store is organized and laid out as it is.
3. Identify three or four elements of the service received at the two locations that you think most directly influenced (either positively or negatively) the quality and efficiency of the experience there.
4. Analyze the service elements from one organization and see if they can somehow be used by the other. Repeat the process for the second organization.

To Cheat or Not?

This exercise provides you with the opportunity to sharpen your conceptual skills. Think carefully and creatively about the situation before reaching a conclusion. Your instructor may ask you to work individually or in groups.

Your Assignment

Assume that two emerging technology organizations, HiTech and ChipT, enter into an agreement dealing with business in a new market. They agree to enter the market independently but to charge the same price. This is called the monopoly price because it is the price that would maximize profits to the industry if there were only one firm or, in this case, the two firms combined.

If either organization cheats by charging a lower price, it can take significant market share from the other and, as the following table shows, earn significantly more money.

		ChipT	
		Cheat (charge lower price)	Don't Cheat (charge monopoly price)
HiTech	Cheat	$5 million each	HiTech $10 million ChipT $ 3 million
	Don't cheat	ChipT $10 million HiTech $3 million	$8 million each

Discuss what could happen and what is likely to happen.

Factors Affecting Organizational Design

This exercise will encourage you to apply your conceptual skills to organization design and the factors that influence appropriate designs.

Four of the basic forms of organization design include the functional, conglomerate, divisional, and matrix approaches. Some of the factors that affect the appropriate form of design include the organization's core technology, environment, size, and life cycle.

PRACTICE

Your Assignment

1. Identify four firms that each use a different basic form of organization design.
2. Assess the technology, environment, size, and life cycle of each of the four firms.
3. Next, relate each of those situational factors to the design used by each firm. Form an opinion about the actual relationship between each factor and the design used by each firm. Do the situational factors work together in different combinations to affect organization design? For example, does a particular form of technology and certain environmental forces together influence organization design? Do you think that each firm's design is directly determined by its environment, or is the relationship you observe coincidental?
4. Prioritize the relative importance of the situational factors across the firms. Does the rank-order importance of the factors vary in any systematic way?

Can You Predict?

This exercise focuses on your conceptual and diagnostic skills; thus, you must deal with this hiring problem conceptually, without using complicated mathematical or statistical analysis.

Your Assignment

You must develop a hiring model that minimizes hiring errors. Your company, ZYX Corporation, defines "Success" as a score of 55 or greater on its performance evaluation (PE) instrument. The organization has the following additional data based on previous experience:

- The correlation between performance evaluation (PE) and a general ability test (GAT) is +0.81.
- The correlation between performance evaluation (PE) and overall undergraduate grade point averages (GPA) is +0.58.
- The correlation between performance evaluation (PE) and school quality (QLY) (biserial correlation with good = 1 and poor = 0) is +0.10 (the Pearson Product Moment correlation is +0.16).

PE	GAT	QLY	GPA
7	8	G	1.5
13	18	P	2.2
26	22	G	2.0
47	26	G	2.5
39	28	P	2.0
58	49	P	3.2
33	35	G	2.7
82	40	P	3.5
67	40	G	3.1
50	48	P	2.0
41	35	G	3.0
76	50	G	2.0
59	51	G	2.0
90	63	G	2.5
64	64	G	2.0
51	65	P	2.3
78	68	G	3.3
71	78	P	3.5
88	82	G	3.0
50	40	G	2.5

Without using complicated mathematical or statistical analysis, can you construct a model for hiring that will yield zero errors (none of either type below)?

		Actual: Failure	Actual: Success
Prediction	Success	Over Prediction Error	High Hit
	Failure	Low Hit	Under Prediction Error

See Interpretations at the end of the chapter.

The Relationship Between Quality and Financial Performance

This exercise asks you to investigate the conceptual relationship between quality and financial performance.

Among those who believe that such a relationship exists, some think that high-quality products lead to high earnings whereas others believe that only firms with high performance can afford to offer high quality. A third group believes that there is no relationship.

Your Assignment

1. View a list of recent winners of the Malcolm Baldrige Award for quality (*Hint:* Go to the National Institute of Standards and Technology site <www.baldrige.nist.gov/Contacts_Profiles.htm>). Choose three firms from the list and investigate the recent

PRACTICE

financial performance of their parent company, using earnings per share (EPS) as the measure of performance.

2. Have the winners demonstrated high performance? For example, did their EPS rise?
3. If any of the winners have shown high performance, did the high performance come before or after the award, or both before and after?
4. What conclusions do you make about the relationship between high performance and quality?

Determining Why Teams Are Successful

This exercise will give you an opportunity to practice your conceptual skills as they apply to groups or teams.

Groups and teams are becoming increasingly important in organizations, so we need to understand what makes teams successful. One way to do that is to analyze highly effective groups that exist outside the boundaries of typical business organizations, for example, a basketball team, a military squadron, a government policy group such as the president's cabinet, a student committee, and the leadership of a church or religious organization.

Your Assignment

1. Use the Internet to identify an example of a real team (a) that is not part of a normal for-profit business and (b) that you can argue is highly effective.
2. From your research, determine the reasons for the team's effectiveness. Consider team characteristics and activities, such as role structure, norms, cohesiveness, and conflict management.
3. What can a manager learn from this particular team? How can the factors that account for its success be used in a business setting?

USING YOUR CONCEPTUAL SKILLS

CREATIVITY AT KELLOGG

W. K. and John Harvey Kellogg were experimenting with ways to make health foods more appetizing and nutritious for medical patients when they accidently discovered how to make wheat flakes. W. K. Kellogg immediately saw the potential and experimented on his own. He formed the Battle Creek Toasted Corn Flake Company in 1906 and, through innovative marketing techniques, changed the way in which people thought about breakfast. Competition quickly grew, however, as companies such as General Mills and General Foods entered the market.

The Kellogg Company is a believer in creativity and innovation. It continually develops and introduces new products. Marketing innovations, beginning with the world's largest sign in 1912, are constantly being tested. Because nutrition was a major concern in the development of its first product, Kellogg was a pioneer in the nutritional labeling of its products. It introduced new packaging approaches, too, and changed its Battle Creek name to the Kellogg Company in 1922. To expand its markets, Kellogg began to grow internationally early on (Canada in 1914, Australia in 1924, and England in 1938).

During the 1950s and 1960s, Kellogg's market share grew very close to 50 percent, but in the 1970s, trouble began. The company seemed to have lost touch with its customers and, as overall demand for breakfast cereals started to decline, Quaker Oats and Nabisco began to take market share away from Kellogg. Further, health-conscious consumers began to turn away from many of its heavily sweetened brands that had been so popular. Kellogg's market share began to drop, falling to around 37 percent by 1990.

Kellogg responded with new plans. It increased advertising to shore up the overall market and to convince adults to return to eating cereal. It developed numerous healthy cereals, especially those based on oat bran. Managers began to focus on quality control to assure uniformly nutritious products. The company also moved to strengthen its foreign markets. These efforts quickly paid off, and Kellogg's market share began to climb again. Nevertheless, as the 1990s began, the competitive battle became fierce in the foreign markets, particularly Europe.

In 1999, Carlos Gutierrez became CEO of Kellogg; he was the first Latino CEO of a Fortune 500 company. He focused on higher-margin products such as Special K (which appeals to weight-conscious consumers), Kashi (targeted at the health-food set), and Nutri-Grain bars (breakfast on the go). Those creative efforts paid off and Kellogg's performance was strong. Gutierrez was named Secretary of Commerce in 2004 and left the company just as Kellogg's profits again became as soggy as its breakfast cereals.

David Mackay took over in 2006 with an eye toward pushing boundaries and exploring new things. In response to consumer groups, he announced that in 2008 Kellogg would stop advertising to children under twelve those cereals and snacks that do not meet specific nutrition guidelines. But in 2009 another challenge occurred. Grocery stores began to resist price increases on Kellogg products and started deploying more private-label goods. Kellogg continued its normal practices, however, and in early 2010 saw sales and profits increasing.

USE

Case Questions

Go Online

1. Which particular conceptual skills seem to be used most at Kellogg?
2. How have managers at Kellogg used these conceptual skills?
3. Identify opportunities and threats (strengths and weaknesses) in any overemphasis of those skills.
4. What skills do you already have that would help you be successful at Kellogg? What conceptual skills do you probably lack? What preparations would you make to have the requisite conceptual skills to assure your success?

Case References

Matthew Boyle, "Grocery stores fight back against food prices," *Fortune*, January 29, 2009 http://www.businessweek.com/magazine/content/09_06/b4118048684472.htm; Matthew Boyle, "Snap! Crackle! Pop! Cereal biz gets stale," *Fortune*, November 8, 2006 http://money.cnn.com/magazines/fortune/fortune_archive/2006/11/13/8393078/index.htm; Matthew Boyle, "The Man Who Fixed Kellogg Stale Offerings. *Fortune*, September 6, 2004 http://money.cnn.com/magazines/fortune/fortune_archive/2004/09/06/380333/index.htm; Christopher Knowlton, "Europe Cooks Up a Cereal Brawl," *Fortune*, June 3, 1991, pp. 175–179; Gary Hoover, Alta Campbell, and Patrick J. Spain (eds.) *Hoover's Handbook: Profiles of Over 500 Major Corporations* (Austin, TX: The Reference Press, 1991), p. 324.

CREATIVITY AT MERCK

Merck & Co., Inc., is the world's largest maker of prescription drugs, with about 5 percent of the market. While it shares common roots with E. Merck of Germany, they have been completely independent of one another since 1917. Merck & Co. became the world leader by having consistent sales and earnings growth brought about by innovative products. Indeed, in 1990, Merck had 18 products, each of which earned more than $100 million. To earn those products, Merck invests heavily in research and development, typically the most in the industry. Its emphasis on research can be traced to the formation of its first laboratory in 1933, where its scientists did pioneering work on vitamin B-12 and developed cortisone. During the 1940s and 1950s, five Merck scientists received Nobel Prizes.

Dr. P. Roy Vagelos, the biochemist who has been Merck's CEO since 1985, has stated that the more original thinkers Merck has, the better he likes it, because having people thinking along different lines but with similar objectives is the key to innovation and success. Vagelos is certainly qualified to be a leader in an organization with that philosophy. He graduated from Columbia's medical school and interned at Massachusetts General Hospital in Boston before heading up the biological chemistry department at Washington University in St. Louis. He came to Merck to do research and was head of research for nine years before becoming CEO.

But Merck does more than make innovative products. It is one of the best-managed companies in the world. For more than ten years *Fortune* magazine has determined the "most admired corporations" in America, and only one company has been in that group every time—Merck. Not only has it been in the group—it has dominated the ratings and been number one six times. Merck says it is successful because it attracts, develops, and keeps good people in its organization. Indeed, the promotions and merit evaluations of senior executives are affected by the number of people recruited and trained by those executives. Further, women seem able to advance successfully at Merck. One of the highest-ranking women in a Fortune 500 company was Merck's chief financial officer in 1990.

USE

In a communication to employees, Vagelos stressed the need to carefully monitor the environment and plan to respond to changes in it. He said that the trick is for Merck to anticipate environmental change and to move to take advantage of it before anybody else does. In that way, Merck would continue to be successful. According to Vagelos, "The best—really, the only—guarantee of true employment stability is a successful business."

That careful monitoring of the environment includes not just research linked to product developments but also market opportunities. Merck bought half of a Japanese drug company, Banyu, to open up that market as well as to gain access to the thinking of Japanese scientists. It has formed alliances with other drug companies to open access to new markets as well. Merck and DuPont formed a joint venture to expand the global markets for each other's products. Merck and Johnson & Johnson formed a joint venture to market products resulting from a merger of Merck with the nonprescription part of ICI Americas (the major product involved was Mylanta).

In 1994, Vagelos was replaced by Raymond V. Gilmartin after the growth of managed care had thrown the entire pharmaceutical industry into an uproar. To deal with this, Gilmartin moved to increase teamwork at Merck by streamlining and flattening the organization's structure. The streamlining involved getting rid of two noncore units: Kelco and Calgon Vestal Laboratories. In 1997, it sold its crop-protection unit and its interest in a joint venture with DuPont. Then it restructured its animal health unit, Merial, so that by the end of the 1990s it was the largest firm in veterinary pharmaceuticals. The late 1990s saw Merck introduce 15 new drugs and show strong performance.

As patents began to expire on some of Merck's blockbuster drugs, in 2005 Richard T. Clark took the reins as CEO. He narrowed the research focus and cut promotion costs by using more electronic pitches to physicians. That seemed to pay off as financial results gradually improved. Then in 2009, Merck merged with Schering-Plough and, emphasizing innovation, looked forward to continued high levels of performance.

Case Questions

1. How would you describe Vagelos's skills?
2. How have executives at Merck used conceptual skills?
3. Which particular conceptual skills seem to be used most at Merck?
4. Why are conceptual skills particularly important for a company like Merck?
5. If you were interested in a position at Merck, what preparations would you make to have the requisite conceptual skills to assure your success?

Go Online

Case References

David Ewing Duncan, "Merck in a post-blockbuster world," *Fortune*, October 20, 2009. http://money.cnn.com/2009/10/19/news/companies/merck_clark.fortune/index.htm; John Simons, "How Merck healed itself," *Fortune*, February 7, 2008. http://money.cnn.com/2008/02/04/news/companies/how_merck_healed_itself.fortune/index.htm; Amy Barrett, "Merck's plan for a comeback," *BusinessWeek*, December 16, 2005. http://www.businessweek.com/technology/content/dec2005/tc20051216_708777.htm; *Merck World*, October 1992, pp. 2–3; Kate Ballen, "America's Most Admired Corporations," *Fortune*, February 10, 1992, pp. 40–72; Alison L. Sprout, "America's Most Admired Corporations," *Fortune*, February 11, 1991, pp. 52–60.

EXTENDING YOUR CONCEPTUAL SKILLS

Your instructor may use one or more of these **Group Extensions** to provide you with yet another opportunity to develop your time-management skills. On the other hand, you may continue your development on your own by doing one or more of the **Individual Extensions**.

These **Group Extensions** are repeated exactly for each of the seven specific skills. Doing the exact **Extension** for different skills will help you to sharpen both the skills and the subtle differences between the several skills.

EXTEND

GROUP EXTENSIONS

- Form small groups of students. Have each group select an organization and a management position. Then have them identify the conceptual skills needed by a person in that position.
- Form small groups of students. Have each group identify a problem or opportunity facing a business or other organization. Then have them identify the conceptual skills needed by managers in dealing with that problem or opportunity.
- Form small groups of students. Have them identify a problem or opportunity facing a business or other organization. Assign each group to identify the conceptual skills needed by managers in dealing with that problem or opportunity.
- Form small groups of students. Assign each group one or more corporations to analyze. Have each group identify the members who serve on its board of directors and research their backgrounds. Then have the students describe the conceptual skills of those directors.
- Form small groups of students. Have each group select a job they see regularly (e.g., retail clerk, fast-food worker). Ask them to describe the conceptual skills needed on that job.

- Form small groups of students. Have students sketch the conceptual skills they would need if they were going to start a specific type of new business.
- Form small groups of students. Have each group identify examples they have recently faced that illustrate a situation that called for them to use conceptual skills.

INDIVIDUAL EXTENSIONS

- Go to the library and research a company. Characterize its level of effectiveness and identify the conceptual skills of its top executives. Share your results with the class.
- Select a highly visible manager and analyze his or her conceptual skills.
- Interview a manager from a local organization. Learn about the conceptual skills he or she needs to perform effectively.
- Think of someone you know who is a manager. Describe that person's management position in terms of the type of organization, level in the organization, and the area of management in which he or she practices. What conceptual skills does that person need to be effective?
- Plan a hypothetical change in your school focusing on the use of conceptual skills.
- Search the Internet for examples of conceptual skills in management and compare what you find with the information presented here.

YOUR CONCEPTUAL SKILLS NOW

CONCEPTUAL SKILLS ASSESSMENT

Now that you have completed Chapter 5, it is time again to assess your conceptual skills. To do so, complete the following instrument. Think about your current situation, job, or organization in which you are a member. You should respond in terms of your current situation and not by how you think you should respond or a manager should respond. If a statement doesn't currently pertain to your situation, respond in terms of what you think would currently be accurate for you in that situation.

Use this scale in your responses.

1	2	3	4	5
Not true at all	Somewhat untrue	Sometimes true Sometimes not	Somewhat true	Completely true

Total your scores and record them in the table at the end of instrument.

Given that many experts suggest the use of 360° feedback in performance appraisal, you may find it useful to obtain the views of others about your interpersonal skills. You may get a form from your instructor that is designed for others to complete, and then record their scores in the table as well. Areas where there is a large discrepancy between your views and those of others should draw your attention, and you should spend more time on developing those skills.

CONCEPTUAL SKILLS

[Note: The numbers correspond to those on the baseline assessment in Appendix A.]

____ 131. I am capable of thinking "outside the box."
____ 132. I am creative.
____ 133. I am emotionally mature.
____ 134. I am good at abstract thinking.
____ 135. I am good at analyzing problems.
____ 136. I am good at gathering information.
____ 137. I am good at identifying important information.
____ 138. I am good at identifying problems.
____ 139. I am good at solving problems.
____ 140. I am up to new challenges.
____ 141. I am willing to take risks.
____ 142. I can identify resources necessary to accomplish my tasks.
____ 143. I challenge rules and procedures.
____ 144. I deal constructively with my own failures and mistakes.
____ 145. I develop ways to evaluate how I'm doing.
____ 146. I enjoy learning new ways of doing things.
____ 147. I enjoy risks.
____ 148. I focus on performance.
____ 149. I frequently come up with fresh and imaginative approaches to a problem.
____ 150. I frequently originate change.
____ 151. I frequently take the first step to get things done.
____ 152. I generally can solve problems on my own.
____ 153. I handle change with an open mind.
____ 154. I have a good understanding of my strengths and weaknesses.
____ 155. I have high standards for myself.
____ 156. I imagine alternative solutions in solving problems.
____ 157. I initiate new ideas.
____ 158. I keep long-term and short-term goals and activities in perspective.
____ 159. I know my personal learning style and fit situations to that.
____ 160. I make forecasts to prepare for future events.
____ 161. I promote change.
____ 162. I readily take chances.
____ 163. I recognize that there is more to life than work and a job.
____ 164. I seek opportunities to test myself.
____ 165. I sell ideas.
____ 166. I set goals.
____ 167. I strive to do my best.
____ 168. I think a lot about how to get more for less.
____ 169. I try to deal with problems quickly.
____ 170. I try to learn from my mistakes.

Summary of Your Scores

Skill (max. possible score)	Your Score Now	Scores from Others	Your Score From Chapter 1
Conceptual (200)			

Interpretation of Your Scores

Compare your score with the one you reported at the beginning of Chapter 1. If there is no or only a modest improvement in your score, you should examine the same set of items from the **Managerial Skills Assessment** from Chapter 1 and compare each of them with these to see where change has and has not occurred. You should then spend more time on developing the particular skills where change either decreased or stayed the same.

INTERPRETATIONS

Goal-Setting Questionnaire

There is no further interpretation. The higher your score, the closer you are to effective goal-setting behaviors.

How Creative Are You?

Creativity is very valuable in assessing and responding to your organizational environment.

There is no further interpretation. The total indicates the extent to which you are creative. A higher score indicates greater creativity.

80 to 100	Very creative
60 to 79	Above average
40 to 59	Average
20 to 39	Below average
−100 to 19	Noncreative

Innovative Attitude Scale

The higher the total score, the more willing you are to be innovative. Your attitude toward innovation is more positive than that of people who score low. A score of 72 or greater is high, while a score of 45 or less is low. People who are not innovators have a tendency to maintain the status quo. Innovative people are entrepreneurs and individuals who like to create changes in their organizations.

INTERPRET

Personal Risk Taking

This assessment provides a general indicator of your willingness to take risks in several areas. It indicates only very general propensities, not absolute or rigid conditions.

High scores on 2, 8, 20, and 23 indicate that you are willing to incur financial risks. Items 4, 9, and 17 deal with sports risks while items 12 through 15 and 25 deal with health risks. Your willingness to incur legal risks is reflected in items 3, 10, 16, 19, and 24. Two items, 5 and 22, are specific to your role as a student while the remaining ones (1, 6, 7, 11, 18, 19, and 21) assess your general willingness to incur risk.

So, you might have a relatively high score in the financial area, indicating that you are willing to take risks that involve money, but you might have a low score in the sports and/or health area, indicating that you are unwilling to take risks that involve your physical well-being.

ENDNOTES

[1] For early discussions of strategic management, see Kenneth Andrews, *The Concept of Corporate Strategy*, rev. ed. (Homewood, Ill.: Dow Jones-Irwin, 1980); and Igor Ansoff, *Corporate Strategy* (New York: McGraw-Hill, 1965). For more recent perspectives, see Michael E. Porter, "What Is Strategy?" *Harvard Business Review*, November–December 1996, pp. 61–78; Kathleen M. Eisenhardt, "Strategy as Strategic Decision Making," *Sloan Management Review*, Spring 1999, pp. 65–74; Sarah Kaplan and Eric Beinhocker, "The Real Value of Strategic Planning," *Sloan Management Review*, Winter 2003, pp. 71–80.

[2] Dusya Vera and Mary Crossan, "Strategic Leadership and Organizational Learning," *Academy of Management Review*, 2004, vol. 29, no. 2, pp. 222–240; see also Cynthia A. Montgomery, "Putting Leadership Back Into Strategy," *Harvard Business Review*, January 2008, pp. 54–63.

[3] "The Best & Worst Managers of the Year," *BusinessWeek*, January 19, 2005, pp. 55–84.

[4] *Fortune*, July 6, 2010, p. 45.

[5] *Hoover's Handbook of American Business 2009* (Austin, Tex.: Hoover's Business Press, 2009), pp. 29–30.

[6] Gary Hamel, "Strategy as Revolution," *Harvard Business Review*, July–August 1996, pp. 69–82.

[7] Henry Mintzberg, "Patterns in Strategy Formulation," *Management Science*, October 1978, pp. 934–948; Henry Mintzberg, "Strategy Making in Three Modes," *California Management Review*, 1973, pp. 44–53.

[8] T.R Holcomb, R.M. Holmes Jr., and B.L. Connelly, "Making the Most of What You Have: Managerial Ability as a Source of Resource Value Creation," *Strategic Management Journal*, Vol. 30, No. 5, 2009, pp. 457–486.

[9] Jay Barney, "Firm Resources and Sustained Competitive Advantage," *Journal of Management*, June 1991, pp. 99–120; see also T. Russell Crook, David J. Ketchen Jr., James G. Combs, and Samuel Y. Todd, "Strategic Resources and Performance: A Meta-Analysis," *Strategic Management Journal*, 2008, Vol. 29, pp. 1141–1154.

[10] Jay Barney, "Strategic Factor Markets," *Management Science*, December 1986, pp. 1231–1241. See also Constantinos C. Markides, "A Dynamic View of Strategy," *Sloan Management Review*, Spring 1999, pp. 55–64.

[11] Michael Porter, *Competitive Strategy* (New York: Free Press, 1980).

[12] "Procter & Gamble Needs to Shave More Indians," *BusinessWeek*, June 13, 2011, p. 21.

[13] Richard W. Woodman, John E. Sawyer, and Ricky W. Griffin, "Toward a Theory of Organizational Creativity," *Academy of Management Review*, April 1993, pp. 293–321.

[14] Emily Thornton, "Japan's Struggle to be Creative," *Fortune*, April 19, 1993, pp. 129–134.

[15] "In Secret Hideaway, Bill Gates Ponders Microsoft's Future," *Wall Street Journal*, March 28, 2005, pp. A1, A13.

[16] Christina E. Shalley, Lucy L. Gilson, and Terry C. Blum, "Matching Creativity Requirements and the Work Environment: Effects on Satisfaction and Intentions to Leave," *Academy of Management Journal*, 2000, vol. 43, no. 2, pp. 215–223; see also Filiz Tabak, "Employee Creative Performance: What Makes It Happen?" *Academy of Management Executive*, 1997, vol. 11, no. 1, pp. 119–122 and Giles Hirst, Daan van Knippenberg, and Jing Zhou, "A Cross-Level Perspective on Employee Creativity: Goal Orientation, Team Learning Behavior, and Individual Creativity," *Academy of Management Journal*, Vol. 52, No. 2, 2009, pp. 280–293.

[17] "Real Life Imitates *Real World*," *BusinessWeek*, March 23/30, 2009, p. 42.

[18] Constantinos Markides, "Strategic Innovation," *Sloan Management Review*, Spring 1997, pp. 9–24; see also James Brian Quinn, "Outsourcing Innovation: The New Engine of Growth," *Sloan Management Review*, Summer 2000, pp. 13–21.

[19] L. B. Mohr, "Determinants of Innovation in Organizations," *American Political Science Review*, 1969, pp. 111–126; G. A. Steiner, *The Creative Organization* (Chicago: University of Chicago Press, 1965); R. Duncan and A. Weiss, "Organizational Learning: Implications for Organizational Design," in B. M. Staw (ed.), *Research in Organizational Behavior*, vol. 1 (Greenwich, Conn.: JAI Press, 1979), pp. 75–123; J. E. Ettlie, "Adequacy of Stage Models for Decisions on Adoption of Innovation," *Psychological Reports*, 1980, pp. 991–995.

[20] Alan Patz, "Managing Innovation in High Technology Industries," *New Management*, September 1986, pp. 54–59.

[21] "Flops," *BusinessWeek*, August 16, 1993, pp. 76–82.

[22] "Apple Can't Keep up with Demand for Newest iMac," *USA Today*, August 26, 2002, p. 3B.

[23] Willow A. Sheremata, "Centrifugal and Centripetal Forces in Radical New Product Development Under Time Pressure," *Academy of Management Review*, 2000, vol. 25, no. 2, pp. 389–408; see also Richard Leifer, Gina Colarelli O'Connor, and Mark Rice, "Implementing Radical Innovation in Mature Firms: The Role of Hobs," *Academy of Management Executive*, 2001, vol. 15, no. 3, pp. 102–113.

[24] Julian Birkinshaw, Gary Hamel, and Michael J. Mol, "Management Innovation," *Academy of Management Review*, 2008, Vol. 33, No. 4, pp. 825–845.

[25] Quoted in *Fortune*, February 6, 2012, p. 99.

[26] "Amid Japan's Gloom, Corporate Overhauls Offer Hints of Revival," *Wall Street Journal*, February 21, 2002, pp. A1, A11.

[27] Clayton M. Christensen, Stephen P. Kaufman, and Willy C. Shih, "Innovation Killers," *Harvard Business Review*, January 2008, pp. 98–107.

[28] Dorothy Leonard and Jeffrey F. Rayport, "Spark Innovation Through Empathic Design," *Harvard Business Review*, November–December 1997, pp. 102–115.

[29] "The 25 Most Innovative Companies," *BusinessWeek*, April 20, 2009, pp. 46–47.

[30] Geoffrey Moore, "Innovating Within Established Enterprises," *Harvard Business Review*, July-August 2004, pp. 87–96; see also David A. Garvin and Lynne C. Levesque, "Meeting the Challenge of Corporate Entrepreneurship," *Harvard Business Review*, October 2006, pp. 102–113.

[31] Gifford Pinchot III, *Intrapreneuring* (New York: Harper & Row, 1985).

[32] For an excellent review of this area, see Achilles A. Armenakis and Arthur G. Bedeian, "Organizational Change: A Review of Theory and Research in the 1990s," *Journal of Management*, 1999, vol. 25, no. 3, pp. 293–315.

[33] For additional insights into how technological change affects other parts of the organization, see P. Robert Duimering, Frank Safayeni, and Lyn Purdy, "Integrated Manufacturing: Redesign the Organization Before Implementing Flexible Technology," *Sloan Management Review*, Summer 1993, pp. 47–56.

[34] Joel Cutcher-Gershenfeld, Ellen Ernst Kossek, and Heidi Sandling, "Managing Concurrent Change Initiatives," *Organizational Dynamics*, Winter 1997, pp. 21–38.

[35] Michael A. Hitt, "The New Frontier: Transformation of Management for the New Millennium," *Organizational Dynamics*, Winter 2000, pp. 7–15; see also Michael Beer and Nitin Nohria, "Cracking the Code of Change," *Harvard Business Review*, May–June 2000, pp. 133–144; and Clark Gilbert, "The Disruption Opportunity," *MIT Sloan Management Review*, Summer 2003, pp. 27–32.

[36] Paul Nunes and Tim Breen, "Reinvent Your Business Before It's Too Late," *Harvard Business Review*, January–February 2011, pp. 80–87.

[37] Warren Boeker, "Strategic Change: The Influence of Managerial Characteristics and Organizational Growth," *Academy of Management Journal*, 1997, vol. 40, no. 1, pp. 152–170.

[38] Vijay Govindarajan and Chris Tumble, "The CEO's Role in Business Model Reinvention," *Harvard Business Review*, January–February 2011, pp. 108–114.

[39] Alan L. Frohman, "Igniting Organizational Change from Below: The Power of Personal Initiative," *Organizational Dynamics*, Winter 1997, pp. 39–53.

[40] Quoted in *BusinessWeek*, March 23/30, 2009, p. 33.

[41] Nandini Rajagopalan and Gretchen M. Spreitzer, "Toward a Theory of Strategic Change: A Multi-Lens Perspective and Integrative Framework," *Academy of Management Review*, 1997, vol. 22, no. 1, pp. 48–79.

[42] Anne Fisher, "Danger Zone," *Fortune*, September 8, 1997, pp. 165–167.

[43] John P. Kotter and Leonard A. Schlesinger, "Choosing Strategies for Change," *Harvard Business Review*, March–April 1979, p. 106.

[44] Clayton M. Christensen and Michael Overdorf, "Meeting the Challenge of Disruptive Change," *Harvard Business Review*, March–April 2000, pp. 67–77.

[45] Kurt Lewin, "Frontiers in Group Dynamics: Concept, Method, and Reality in Social Science," *Human Relations*, June 1947, pp. 5–41.

[46] Michael Roberto and Lynne Levesque, "The Art of Making Change Initiatives Stick," *MIT Sloan Management Review*, Summer 2005, pp. 53–62.

[47] "Time for a Turnaround," *Fast Company*, January 2003, pp. 55–61.

[48] Connie J. G. Gersick, "Revolutionary Change Theories: A Multilevel Exploration of the Punctuated Equilibrium Paradigm," *Academy of Management Review*, January 1991, pp. 10–36; see also John P. Kotter and Leonard A. Schlesinger, "Choosing Strategies for Change," *Harvard Business Review*, July–August 2008, pp. 130–141.

[49] Mel Fugate, Angelo J. Kinicki, and Gregory E. Prussia, "Employee Coping With Organizational Change: An Examination of Alternative Theoretical Perspectives and Models," *Personnel Psychology*, 2008, Vol. 61, pp. 1–36; see also Jeffrey D. Ford and Laurie W. Ford, "Decoding Resistance to Change," *Harvard Business Review*," April 2009, pp. 99–104.

[50] Clark Gilbert and Joseph Bower, "Disruptive Change," *Harvard Business Review*, May 2002, pp. 95–104.

[51] "RJR Employees Fight Distraction amid Buy-out Talks," *Wall Street Journal*, November 1, 1988, p. A8.

[52] Arnon E. Reichers, John P. Wanous, and James T. Austin, "Understanding and Managing Cynicism About Organizational Change," *Academy of Management Executive*, February 1997, pp. 48–59.

[53] For a classic discussion, see Paul R. Lawrence, "How to Deal with Resistance to Change," *Harvard Business Review*, January–February 1969, pp. 4–12, 166–176; for a more recent discussion, see Jeffrey D. Ford, Laurie W. Ford, and Angelo D'Amelio, "Resistance to Change: The Rest of the Story," *Academy of Management Review*, 2008, Vol. 33, No. 2, p. 362–377.

[54] Lester Coch and John R. P. French, Jr., "Overcoming Resistance to Change," *Human Relations*, August 1948, pp. 512–532.

[55] Benjamin Schneider, Arthur P. Brief, and Richard A. Guzzo, "Creating a Climate and Culture for Sustainable Organizational Change," *Organizational Dynamics*, Spring 1996, pp. 7–19.

[56] "Troubled GM Plans Major Tuneup," *USA Today*, June 6, 2005, pp. 1B, 2B.

CHAPTER 6

ASSESSING YOUR DIAGNOSTIC SKILLS

How Is Your Organization Managed?
Organizational Climate Questionnaire
Assessing Your Feedback Style
Organizational Structure Preferences

LEARNING ABOUT DIAGNOSTIC SKILLS

Understanding Cause and Effect
Understanding Control
The Purpose of Control
Areas of Control
Levels of Control
Responsibilities for Control
Designing Control Systems
Steps in the Control Process
Operations Control
Characteristics of Effective Control
Managing Control
Resistance to Control
Overcoming Resistance to Control
Rewarding Employees
Reinforcement Perspectives on Motivation
Popular Motivational Strategies
Using Reward Systems to Motivate Performance
Summary and a Look Ahead

VISUALIZING DIAGNOSTIC SKILLS

Diagnostic Skills in Action—1
Diagnostic Skills in Action—2

PRACTICING DIAGNOSTIC SKILLS

Relating Needs to Reality
Issues of Centralization and Decentralization
Determining Why Individuals Become Entrepreneurs
Negotiating a Franchise Agreement
Ethics in Decision Making
Using Different Methods of Power
Using Different Types of Power
Quality Relative to Price and Expectations
Diagnosing Causes of Problems
Weighing Organization Change Alternatives
Dealing With Equity and Justice Issues

USING DIAGNOSTIC SKILLS

Diagnosis at DuPont
International Training

EXTENDING YOUR DIAGNOSTIC SKILLS

Group Extensions
Individual Extensions

YOUR DIAGNOSTIC SKILLS NOW

Diagnostic Skills Assessment
Diagnostic Skills
Summary of Your Scores
Interpretation of Your Scores

INTERPRETATIONS

How Is Your Organization Managed?
Organizational Climate Questionnaire
Assessing Your Feedback Style
Organizational Structure Preferences
Mechanistic
Organic

DIAGNOSTIC SKILLS

© SELECTSTOCK

Closely related to conceptual skill is skill in diagnosing situations and events. Much like a physician diagnoses an illness based on patient symptoms, managers must frequently diagnose the causes of problems or opportunities in order to know how best to respond to them. Managers need to understand cause-and-effect relationships so they can perform their various functions better. In this chapter we explain the nature of diagnostic skills and how they are used in the critical control function in organizations. We also explore how to most effectively reward employees for their performance. Following the text section are several cases and exercises to help you further develop and master your diagnostic skills.

ASSESS

ASSESSING YOUR DIAGNOSTIC SKILLS

HOW IS YOUR ORGANIZATION MANAGED?

This self-assessment helps you define or diagnose how an organization you are familiar with is organized.

Instructions:

Focus on either an organization where you are currently working or one that you have worked for in the past. These organizations may include a private or public firm, government organization, sorority, fraternity, club, or the university you are attending.

Respond according to how you see your organization being managed by circling the letter on the scale indicting the degree to which you agree or disagree with each statement. There are no right or wrong answers.

Statements	Strongly Agree	Agree	Don't Know	Disagree	Strongly Disagree
1. If people feel they have the right approach to carrying out their job, they can usually go ahead without checking with their superior.	5	4	3	2	1
2. People in this organization don't always have to wait for orders from their superiors on important matters.	5	4	3	2	1
3. People in this organization share ideas with their superior.	5	4	3	2	1
4. Different individuals play important roles in making decisions.	5	4	3	2	1
5. People in this organization are likely to express their feelings openly on important matters.	5	4	3	2	1
6. People in this organization are encouraged to speak their minds on important matters, even if it means disagreeing with their superior.	5	4	3	2	1
7. Talking to other people about the problems someone might have in making decisions is an important part of the decision-making process.	5	4	3	2	1
8. Developing employees' talents and abilities are major concerns of this organization.	5	4	3	2	1
9. People are encouraged to make suggestions before decisions are made.	5	4	3	2	1
10. In this organization, most people can have their point of view heard.	5	4	3	2	1
11. Superiors often seek advice from their subordinates before decisions are made.	5	4	3	2	1

12. Subordinates play an active role in running this organization.	5	4	3	2	1
13. For many decisions, the rules and regulations are developed as we go along.	5	4	3	2	1
14. It is not always necessary to go through channels in dealing with important matters.	5	4	3	2	1
15. The same rules and regulations are not consistently followed by employees.	5	4	3	2	1
16. There are few rules and regulations for handling any kind of problem that may arise in making most decisions.	5	4	3	2	1
17. People from different departments are often put together in task forces to solve important problems.	5	4	3	2	1
18. For special problems, we usually set up temporary task force until we meet our objectives.	5	4	3	2	1
19. Jobs in this organization are not clearly defined.	5	4	3	2	1
20. In this organization, adapting to changes in the environment is important.	5	4	3	2	1
COLUMN TOTALS	_____	_____	_____	_____	_____
TOTAL SCORE, ALL COLUMNS _____					

Sources: Adapted from Robert T. Keller, *Type of Management System*. ©1988. Used by permission of the author.

See Interpretations at the end of the chapter.

ORGANIZATIONAL CLIMATE QUESTIONNAIRE

This exercise helps you think about the components of corporate climate and how that impacts the way in which control is exercised in the organization.

Instructions:

Think back to people at work or other organizational experiences and respond to each statement by circling the response that best fits your impression of the organization. If you have no experience to draw on, then respond to the statements by identifying those organizational characteristics you would prefer.

Statements	Strongly Agree	Slightly Agree	Don't Know	Slightly Disagree	Strongly Disagree
1. Formal communication channels are not always used.	5	4	3	2	1
2. I am not always satisfied with my role in the organization.	1	2	3	4	5
3. It's not always clear as to who has the authority to make decisions.	5	4	3	2	1

ASSESS

4. Supervisors take the responsibility for seeing that the work is done properly.	1	2	3	4	5
5. Performance, not politics, is rewarded.	5	4	3	2	1
6. My role in the organization is pretty clear to me.	5	4	3	2	1
7. Most workers do not take responsibility for their work.	1	2	3	4	5
8. I wish I could get more feedback about how well I'm doing.	1	2	3	4	5
9. Everyone has a chance to express opinions on how to do things.	5	4	3	2	1
10. My rewards usually equal my contributions.	5	4	3	2	1
11. There are rules and regulations to cover every situation.	1	2	3	4	5
12. Supervisors seldom use positive encouragement to improve performance.	1	2	3	4	5
13. Most people understand my role in the organization.	5	4	3	2	1
14. Most people do what is asked of them and do it well.	5	4	3	2	1
15. Management respects the ideas and suggestions of the workers.	5	4	3	2	1
16. People believe that each worker should solve his/her own problems.	5	4	3	2	1
17. People are not allowed to communicate informally at all levels.	1	2	3	4	5
18. There is just too much red tape at work.	1	2	3	4	5
19. Most people don't understand my role on the job.	1	2	3	4	5
20. If you perform well, you will not necessarily receive appropriate rewards.	1	2	3	4	5

Scoring:

Complete the scoring sheet below. The higher your score, the better are your skills.

Organizational Climate Questionnaire Scoring Sheet

1. *Transfer your numeric responses from the questionnaire onto this scoring sheet, and sum the categories to find your subscores and total. For example, your Communication score is the sum of your responses to Statements 1, 8, 15, and 17.*

	Communication		Role		Structure		Responsibility		Rewards		
	1.____		2.____		3.____		4.____		5.____		
	8.____		6.____		9.____		7.____		10.____		
	15.____		13.____		11.____		14.____		12.____		
	17.____		19.____		18.____		16.____		20.____		
SUBTOTALS	____	+	____	+	____	+	____	+	____	=	____

2. *Next, place an X on each of the five scales below to mark your scores that are recorded in item 1 above:*

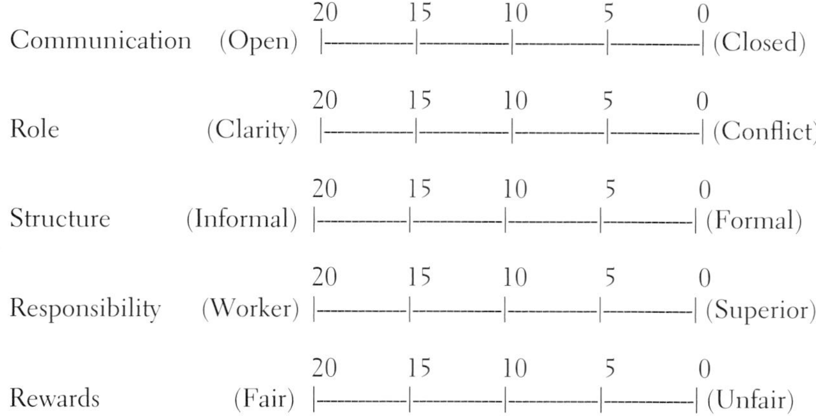

3. *Mark with an X your total score on the Organizational Climate Continuum below:*

|--------|--------|--------|--------|--------|--------|--------|--------|--------|--------|

100 90 80 70 60 50 40 30 20 10 0

Organizational Climate Continuum

Source: From Burton. *Exercises in Management*, 3E. © 1990 South-Western, a part of Cengage Learning, Inc. Reproduced by permission. www.cengage.com/permissions

See Interpretations at the end of the chapter.

ASSESSING YOUR FEEDBACK STYLE

This exercise was designed to help you understand the dynamics of performance appraisal feedback. Diagnosing performance is critical to effective management. Performance appraisal involves both diagnosis and motivation and so is critical to the effective functioning of organizations. One of the difficulties with most performance appraisal systems is that the supervisor or manager feels uncomfortable providing feedback in a one-to-one encounter. The result often is employee vagueness about what the performance appraisal really means, what it is designed to do, and how it can improve performance. The supervisor or manager fails to address those concerns because he or she did not adequately diagnose the situation. As a result, he or she lacks an understanding of how subordinates respond to performance feedback or lacks the skill necessary to provide valuable feedback.

Instructions:

Below is a list of feedback behaviors. Read the description of each behavior carefully, and then select the alternate response that best reflects the extent to which that behavior describes what you do or think you would do. Indicate your choice by circling the response. The alternative responses are as follows:

Alternative Responses

Y = *Yes, this definitely describes me.* (Y underlined)

Y = *Yes I'm fairly sure this describes me.*

? = *I'm not sure.*

N = *No, I'm fairly sure this doesn't describe me.*

N = *No, this definitely doesn't describe me.* (N underlined)

1. When communicating, I try to seek feedback from the receiver to determine if I'm being understood.	Y	Y	?	N	N
2. Whenever possible, I try to ensure that my point of view is accepted and acted upon.	Y	Y	?	N	N
3. I can easily handle and accept counterarguments to my ideas.	Y	Y	?	N	N
4. When a communication problem occurs between another person and myself, it's usually his or her fault.	Y	Y	?	N	N
5. I make sure the other person understands that I know what I am talking about.	Y	Y	?	N	N
6. If a someone comes to me with a personal problem, I try to listen objectively without being judgmental.	Y	Y	?	N	N
7. When listening to someone questioning or criticizing my procedures, I often find myself engaging in mental counterarguments—thinking about my response while the person is talking.	Y	Y	?	N	N
8. I let the other person finish an idea before intervening or finishing it for him or her.	Y	Y	?	N	N
9. When listening to someone, I find that I can easily restate (paraphrase) that person's point of view.	Y	Y	?	N	N
10. I try not to prejudge the speaker or the message.	Y	Y	?	N	N
11. Whenever I provide information to someone, I prefer using facts and data.	Y	Y	?	N	N
12. Communicating empathy for the feelings of the receiver tends to indicate weakness.	Y	Y	?	N	N
13. I try to ensure that others know how I view their actions: good, bad, strong, weak, etc.	Y	Y	?	N	N
14. In order to get people to do things properly, you have to tell them what to do.	Y	Y	?	N	N
15. When talking with someone, I like saying, "What do you think?" to introduce more acceptance of the issue.	Y	Y	?	N	N
16. If you are the boss, people expect you to tell them what to do.	Y	Y	?	N	N
17. I try to use probing, nondirective questions in discussions with individuals.	Y	Y	?	N	N
18. In providing negative feedback, I want to be certain the receiver knows how I view the situation.	Y	Y	?	N	N
19. I try to listen with empathy. I listen to what is being said as well as what I think the sender is trying to say.	Y	Y	?	N	N
20. Whenever I provide someone with feedback, I usually want to persuade them to act on it.	Y	Y	?	N	N

ASSESS

Scoring:

(1) *For the items listed, score your responses as follows:*

Item Score	Scoring
1. _____	Y = 2
3. _____	
6. _____	Y = 1
8. _____	
9. _____	? = 0
10. _____	
11. _____	N = –1
15. _____	
17. _____	N = –2
19. _____	
TOTAL _____	

(2) *For the items listed, the scoring system is reversed:*

Item Score	Scoring
2. _____	Y = –2
4. _____	
5. _____	Y = –1
7. _____	
12. _____	? = 0
13. _____	
14. _____	N = 1
16. _____	
18. _____	N = 2
20. _____	
TOTAL _____	

Source: From Vecchio. *S/G Organizational Behavior, 1E.* © 1988 South-Western, a part of Cengage Learning, Inc. Reproduced by permission. www.cengage.com/permissions

See Interpretations at the end of the chapter.

ORGANIZATIONAL STRUCTURE PREFERENCES

Instructions:

Use the following scale to indicate your level of agreement/disagreement with each of the following items:

5 – Strongly agree
4 – Agree somewhat
3 – Uncertain
2 – Disagree somewhat
1 – Strongly disagree

I prefer organizations:

_____ 1. in which there are numerous levels so that promotions can occur more easily
_____ 2. that clearly identify what I need to do to perform my job
_____ 3. in which jobs are clearly defined to eliminate conflict in accomplishing tasks
_____ 4. that have rules to identify what should and should not be done
_____ 5. in which managers make decisions without bothering me about them
_____ 6. that prescribe how things should be done and who to contact for assistance
_____ 7. in which there are clear lines of authority and communication
_____ 8. that emphasize and recognize my relation to the organization
_____ 9. in which supervisors have few people reporting to them
_____ 10. that leaves me alone to do my job
_____ 11. in which I have a fair amount of leeway to determine how to do my job
_____ 12. that involve everyone in decisions
_____ 13. in which there are few rules or written job descriptions
_____ 14. that use teams and individual activity with little or no direct supervision

_____ 15. in which information is passed informally to whomever needs it

_____ 16. that have few levels between the top and bottom of the organization

_____ 17. in which decisions are made through discussion and involvement of those affected

_____ 18. that emphasize and recognize my expertise and role in professional associations

_____ 19. in which supervisors have relatively large numbers of people reporting to them

_____ 20. that expects me to participate in the activities of the organization

Scoring:

Total your responses for items 1–10 (your score will be from 10 to 50) ... M _____
Total your responses for items 11–20 (your score will be from 10 to 50) ... O _____

Source: Adapted from Van Fleet, D. D., Van Fleet, E. W., & Seperich, G., *Agribusiness: Principles of Management*, (Clifton Park, NY: Delmar/Cengage Learning, 2013); Griffin, R. W., *Management* (Mason, OH: South-Western Cengage Learning, 2013); and Van Fleet, D. D., et al., *Behavior in Organizations* (Boston: Houghton Mifflin, 1991).

See Interpretations at the end of the chapter.

GO ONLINE to the Griffin/Van Fleet Assessment Library for online versions of these and other assessments.

LEARNING ABOUT DIAGNOSTIC SKILLS

Understanding Cause and Effect
Understanding Control
The Purpose of Control
Adaptation
Limiting the Accumulation of Error
Coping with Organizational Complexity
Minimizing Costs
Areas of Control
Levels of Control
Responsibilities for Control
Designing Control Systems
Steps in the Control Process
Establishing Standards
Measuring Performance
Comparing Performance Against Standards
Determine Need for Corrective Action
Operations Control
Preliminary Control
Screening Control
Postaction Control
Characteristics of Effective Control
Integration with Planning
Flexibility
Accuracy
Timeliness
Objectivity
Managing Control
Resistance to Control
Overcontrol
Inappropriate Focus
Rewards for Inefficiency
Too Much Accountability
Overcoming Resistance to Control
Encourage Employee Participation
Develop Verification Procedures
Rewarding Employees
Reinforcement Perspectives on Motivation
Kinds of Reinforcement in Organizations
Providing Reinforcement in Organizations
Implications of the Reinforcement Perspectives
Popular Motivational Strategies
Empowerment and Participation
Techniques and Issues in Empowerment
Alternative Forms of Work Arrangements
Using Reward Systems to Motivate Performance
Merit Reward Systems
Incentive Reward Systems
Common Team and Group Reward Systems
Other Types of Team and Group Rewards
New Approaches to Performance-Based Rewards
Summary and a Look Ahead

LEARN

Diagnostic skills enable a manager to visualize the most appropriate response to a situation. The essence of the ability to diagnose is the ability to understand and predict cause-and-effect relationships. For instance, suppose you visit your doctor because you have a fever and a sore throat. The doctor checks your temperature, examines your throat, asks you questions, and perhaps runs some lab tests. After examining the information gleaned from this examination, the doctor diagnoses the most likely cause of your illness and prescribes medicine and bed rest. The goal is for the treatment (medicine and rest) to cure the illness. In similar fashion, managers must diagnose situations such as a drop in productivity, a disruption in cash flow, an increase in employee turnover, and myriad similar problems, and decide how best to respond to them. Diagnostic skills play a role in a variety of situations across other skills, but they are especially critical in the control function in organizations and in the design, implementation, and use of reward systems to motivate employees.

UNDERSTANDING CAUSE AND EFFECT

In everyday life, we often observe events and attribute causality to them. Suppose, for example, you notice that

diagnostic skills skills that enable a manager to visualize the most appropriate response to a situation

LEARN

FIGURE 6.1 CAUSE-AND-EFFECT RELATIONSHIPS

Cause-and-effect relationships are often easy to identify. However, some relationships are not what they might appear to be. For causality to exist, the causal variable must occur before the outcome variable, a change in the causal variable must lead to a change in the outcome variable, and the change in the outcome must not have been caused by another variable.

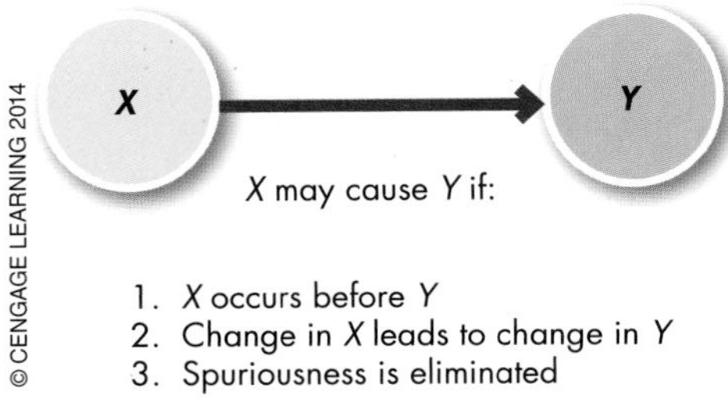

© CENGAGE LEARNING 2014

the student who sits next to you in class is often absent. You also know that she is failing the class. A logical conclusion you might draw is that her frequent absences are causing her to perform poorly. But things are often not this simple. You may have forgotten, for example, that she was attending class regularly until the first exam. As it turns out, perhaps she performed poorly on that exam. Her poor performance on the exam, in turn, destroyed her motivation and led her to stop attending class.

In general, as shown in *Figure 6.1*, three conditions must exist in order to conclude that one variable, X, causes another, Y. First, X must occur or exist before Y. We call this *temporal order*. Second, a change in X must lead to a change in Y. (The correlation can be either positive or negative. For example, an increase in pay may lead to an increase in satisfaction; the correlation between the two would be positive. However, a decrease in pay also may lead to an increase in turnover, a negative correlation.) This is called *co-variation*. And third, we must eliminate *spuriousness*—the possibility that another variable, say Z, is actually causing Y. Consider again the classmate example, noted above. Co-variation appears to exist, because she is both absent from class a lot and doing poorly in the class. If she was attending class prior to the first exam, then the exam grade may be the causal factor. But if she was not attending class earlier, then attendance may be the causal factor. As it turns out, though, one day you run into your friend at the coffee shop and ask how she is doing. After she tells you that her father has been very sick and that she has been taking care of him, you realize that both her low attendance and poor performance actually have been caused by the time demands of caring for an elderly parent. So, the presumed relationship between attendance and grades, at least in this case, was actually spurious—both are being caused by something else altogether.

control the regulation of organizational activities so that some targeted element of performance remains within acceptable limits

To relate these cause-and-effect concepts to a business setting, assume that you are the manager of a retail store. For the past few years, sales revenue at the store has been increasing about 5 percent per year and employee turnover has been relatively stable at around 12 percent per year. In looking over some current data, though, you notice two troubling things: your sales revenue appears to be dropping for the first time ever, and employee turnover is slowly but surely increasing. Because both of these factors are important to the survival of your business, you need to figure out what is going on and try to correct the problem(s). You know that a few months ago a new competitor opened down the street. After you compare prices, you realize that the new store is pricing similar products below your prices, and you see a few of your former employees working at the new store. Hence, you conclude that the new store is attracting your old customers (with lower prices) and your employees (perhaps with higher wages).

UNDERSTANDING CONTROL

Control is generally at the heart of effective diagnoses. **Control** is the regulation of organizational activities so that some targeted element of performance remains within acceptable limits. Without this regulation, organizations have no indication of how well they are performing in relation to their goals. Control, like a ship's rudder, keeps the organization moving in the proper direction. At any point in time, it compares where the organization is in terms of performance (financial, productive, or otherwise) to where it is supposed to be. Like a rudder, control provides an organization with a mechanism for adjusting its course if performance falls outside of acceptable boundaries. For example, FedEx has a performance goal of delivering 99.9 percent of its packages on time. If on-time deliveries fall to 99.6 percent, control systems will signal the problem to managers, so they can make necessary adjustments in operations to regain the target level of performance.[1] An organization without effective control procedures is not likely to reach its goals—or, if it does reach them, to know that it has. Managing control relates to diagnostic skills in that effective control requires a clear understanding of both cause and effect and what to change if control systems indicate a problem.

FIGURE 6.2 PURPOSES OF CONTROL

Control is one of the four basic management functions in organizations. The control function, in turn, has four basic purposes. Properly designed control systems can fulfill each of these purposes.

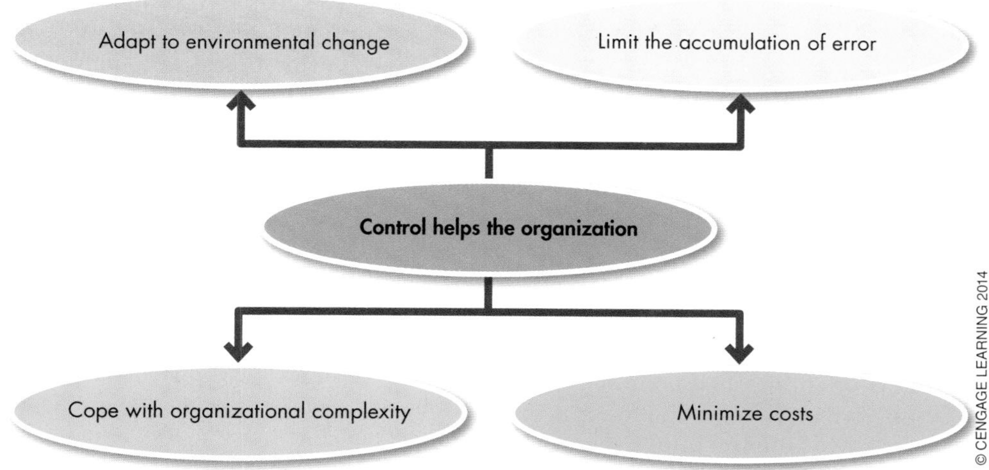

© CENGAGE LEARNING 2014

The Purpose of Control

Control provides an organization with ways to adapt to environmental change, to limit the accumulation of error, to cope with organizational complexity, and to minimize costs. These four functions of control, shown in *Figure 6.2*, are worth a closer look.

Adaptation In today's complex and turbulent business environment, all organizations contend with change. If managers could establish goals and achieve them instantaneously, they would not need control. But between the time a goal is established and the time it is reached, many things can happen in the organization and its environment to disrupt movement toward the goal—or even to change the goal itself. A properly designed control system can help managers anticipate, monitor, and respond to changing circumstances.[2] In contrast, an improperly designed system can result in organizational performance that falls far below acceptable levels. For example, Michigan-based Metalloy, a family-run metal-casting company, signed a contract to make engine-seal castings for NOK, a Japanese auto parts maker. Metalloy was satisfied when its first 5,000-unit production run yielded 4,985 acceptable castings and only 15 defective ones. NOK, however, was unhappy with this performance and insisted that Metalloy raise its standards. In short, global quality standards in most industries are such that customers demand near-perfection from their suppliers. A properly designed control system can help managers like those at Metalloy stay better attuned to rising standards.

Limiting the Accumulation of Error Small mistakes and errors do not often seriously damage the financial health of an organization. Over time, however, small errors may accumulate and become very serious. For example, Whistler Corporation, a large radar detector manufacturer, faced such rapidly escalating demand that quality essentially became irrelevant. The defect rate rose from 4 percent to 9 percent to 15 percent and eventually reached 25 percent. One day, a manager realized that 100 of the plant's 250 employees were spending all their time fixing defective units and that $2 million worth of inventory was awaiting repair. Had the company adequately controlled quality as it responded to increased demand, the problem would never have reached such proportions. Similarly, a routine quality-control inspection of a prototype of Boeing's 787 Dreamliner revealed that a fastener had not been installed correctly. Closer scrutiny then revealed that literally thousands of fasteners had been installed

ED TURNER/BOEING/UPI/NEWSCOM

incorrectly in each prototype under construction. As a result, the entire project was delayed several months. If the inspection process had been more rigorous, the error likely would have been found and corrected much earlier, rather than accumulating into a major problem for Boeing.[3]

LEARN

Coping with Organizational Complexity When a firm purchases only one raw material, produces one product, has a simple organization design, and enjoys constant demand for its product, its managers can maintain control with a very basic and simple system. But a business that produces many products from myriad raw materials and has a large market area, a complicated organization design, and many competitors needs a sophisticated system to maintain adequate control. When large firms merge, the short-term results often are disappointing. The typical reason for this is that the new enterprise is so large and complex that the existing control systems are simply inadequate. United and Continental Airlines faced this problem when they decided to merge and had to address myriad issues to transform the two firms into one.[4]

Minimizing Costs When it is practiced effectively, control also can help reduce costs and boost output. For example, Georgia-Pacific Corporation, a large wood products company, learned of a new technology that could be used to make thinner blades for its saws. The firm's control system was used to calculate the amount of wood that could be saved from each cut made by the thinner blades relative to the costs used to replace the existing blades. The results were impressive—the wood that is saved by the new blades each year fills 800 rail cars. As Georgia-Pacific discovered, effective control systems can eliminate waste, lower labor costs, and improve output per unit of input. Starbucks recently instructed its coffee shops to stop automatically brewing decaffeinated coffee after lunch. Sales of decaf plummet after lunch, and Starbucks realized that baristas were simply pouring most of it down the drain. Now, between noon and early evening they brew decaf only by the cup, and only when a customer orders it.[5] Similarly, in their quest to lower costs, many businesses are cutting back on everything from health insurance coverage to overnight shipping to business lunches for clients.

operations control focuses on the processes the organization uses to transform resources into products or services

financial control concerned with the organization's financial resources

structural control concerned with how the elements of the organization's structure are serving its intended purpose

strategic control focuses on how effectively the organization's corporate, business, and functional strategies are succeeding in helping the organization meet its goals

Areas of Control

Control can focus on any area of an organization. Most organizations define areas of control in terms of the four basic types of resources they use: physical, human, information, and financial.[6] Control of physical resources includes inventory management (stocking neither too few nor too many units in inventory), quality control (maintaining appropriate levels of output quality), and equipment control (supplying the necessary facilities and machinery). Control of human resources includes selection and placement, training and development, performance appraisal, and compensation. Organizations also attempt to control the behavior of their employees—directing them toward higher performance, for example, and away from unethical behaviors.[7]

Control of information resources includes sales and marketing forecasting, environmental analysis, public relations, production scheduling, and economic forecasting.[8] Financial control involves managing the organization's debt so that it does not become excessive, ensuring that the firm always has enough cash on hand to meet its obligations but does not have excess cash in a checking account, and ensuring that receivables are collected and bills are paid on a timely basis. In many ways, the control of financial resources is the most important area, because financial resources are related to the control of all the other resources in an organization. Too much inventory leads to storage costs; poor selection of personnel leads to termination and rehiring expenses; inaccurate sales forecasts lead to disruptions in cash flows and other financial effects. Financial issues tend to pervade most control-related activities.

Levels of Control

Just as control can be classified by area, it also can be classified by level within the organizational system. **Operations control** focuses on the processes the organization uses to transform resources into products or services.[9] Quality control is one type of operations control. **Financial control** is concerned with the organization's financial resources. Monitoring receivables to make sure customers are paying their bills on time is an example of financial control. **Structural control** is concerned with how the elements of the organization's structure are serving their intended purpose. Monitoring the administrative ratio to make sure staff expenses do not become excessive is an example of structural control. Finally, **strategic control** focuses on how effective the organization's corporate, business, and functional strategies are in helping the organization meet its goals. For example, if a corporation has been unsuccessful in implementing its strategy of diversification, its managers need to identify the reasons and either change the strategy or renew their efforts to implement it.

Responsibilities for Control

Traditionally, managers have been responsible for overseeing the wide array of control systems and concerns in organizations. They decide which types of control the organization will use, and they implement systems and take actions based on the information provided by control systems. Thus, ultimate responsibility for control rests with all managers throughout an organization. Most larger organizations also have one or more specialized managerial positions called *controller*. A controller is responsible for helping line managers with their control activities, for coordinating the organization's overall control system, and for gathering and assimilating relevant information. Many businesses that use a divisional structure have several controllers: one for the corporation and one for each division. The job of controller is especially important in organizations where control systems are complex.[11]

In addition, many organizations are beginning to use operating employees to help maintain effective control. Indeed, employee participation often is used as a vehicle for allowing operating employees an opportunity to facilitate organizational effectiveness. For example, Whistler Corporation increased employee participation in an effort to turn its quality problems around. As a starting point, the company eliminated the quality-control unit that had been responsible for checking product quality at the end of the assembly process. Next, all operating employees were told to check their own work and became responsible for correcting their own errors. As a result, Whistler eliminated its quality problems and is now highly profitable once again.

> *"Merging two airlines is unlike merging any other businesses because it's such a complex business.... There's huge technology issues, fleet issues, facilities issues, people issues."*
>
> JEFF SMISEK
> CEO of United Airlines[10]
>
> QUOTED IN BLOOMBERG BUSINESSWEEK, FEBRUARY 6–12, 2012, P. 61.

COURTESY OF THE WHISTLER GROUP

The Whistler Corporation provides a classic case of correcting quality problems. After realizing that almost half of its workforce was fixing product defects, Whistler involved its employees to participate in new methods for improving quality. As a result, quality is now at an all-time high.

DESIGNING CONTROL SYSTEMS

Given the importance of control, managers need to carefully diagnose the organizational, environmental, and operational context of the control systems they design and implement. Doing this, in turn, requires an understanding of the specific steps in the control process, the fundamental elements of operations control, and the characteristics of effective control.

Steps in the Control Process

Regardless of the type or levels of control systems an organization needs, there are four fundamental steps in any control process.[12] These are illustrated in *Figure 6.3*.

Establish Standards The first step in the control process is establishing standards. A control standard is a target against which to compare subsequent performance.[13] Employees at a Taco Bell fast-food restaurant, for example, work toward the following service standards:

1. A minimum of 95 percent of all customers will be greeted within three minutes of their arrival.

controller manager who is responsible for helping line managers with their control activities, for coordinating the organization's overall control system, and for gathering and assimilating relevant information

control standard a target against which subsequent performance will be compared

LEARN

LEARN

FIGURE 6.3 STEPS IN THE CONTROL PROCESS

Having an effective control system can help ensure that an organization achieves its goals. Implementing a control system, however, is a systematic process that generally proceeds through four interrelated steps.

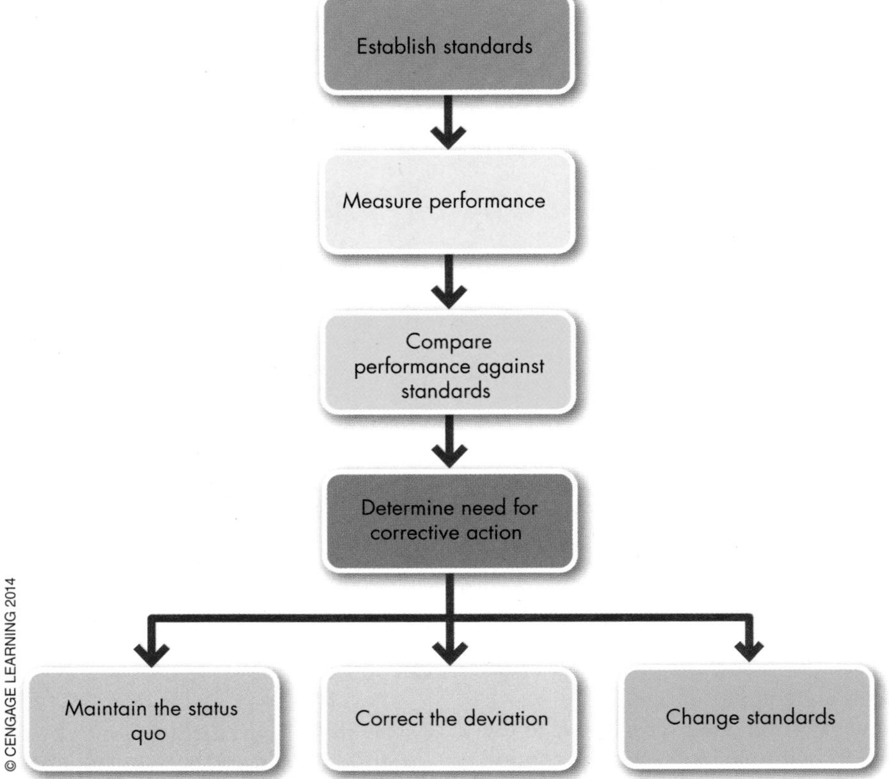

2. Preheated tortilla chips will not sit in the warmer more than 30 minutes before they are served to customers or discarded.
3. Empty tables will be cleaned within five minutes after being vacated.

Standards established for control purposes should be expressed in measurable terms. Note that standard 1 above has a time limit of three minutes and an objective target of 95 percent of all customers. In standard 3, the objective target of "all" empty tables is implied.

Control standards should also be consistent with the organization's goals. Taco Bell has organizational goals involving customer service, food quality, and restaurant cleanliness. A control standard for a retailer such as Home Depot should be consistent with its goal of increasing annual sales volume by 20 percent within five years. A hospital trying to shorten the average hospital stay for a patient will have control standards that reflect current averages. A university reaffirming its commitment to academics might adopt a standard of graduating 80 percent of its student athletes within five years of their enrollment. Control standards can be as narrow or as broad as the level of activity to which they apply and must follow logically from organizational goals and objectives. When Airbus introduced the A380, the world's largest passenger airplane, managers indicated that the firm needed to ship 270 planes in order to break even, and set a goal of delivering 18 per year. Managers also forecast that demand for very large aircraft like the A380 and Boeing's revamped 747 would exceed 1,200 planes during the next 20 years.[14]

A final aspect of establishing standards is to identify performance indicators. Performance indicators are measures of performance that provide information that is directly relevant to what is being controlled. For example, suppose an organization is following a tight schedule in building a new plant. Relevant performance indicators could be buying a site, selecting a building contractor, and ordering equipment. Monthly sales increases are not, however, directly relevant. On the other hand, if control is focused on revenue, monthly sales increases are relevant, but buying land for a new plant is less relevant.

Measure Performance The second step in the control process is measuring performance—a constant, ongoing activity for most organizations. For control to be effective, performance measures must be valid. Daily, weekly, and monthly sales figures measure sales performance, and production performance may be expressed in terms of unit cost, product quality, or volume produced. Employees' performance often is measured in terms of quality or quantity of output; but for many jobs, measuring performance is not so straightforward.

A research and development scientist at Merck, for example, may spend years working on a single project before achieving a breakthrough. A manager who takes over a business on the brink of failure may need months or even years to turn things around. Valid performance measurement, however difficult to obtain, is nevertheless vital in maintaining effective control, and performance indicators usually can be developed. The scientist's progress, for example, may be assessed partially by peer review, and the manager's success may be evaluated by her ability to convince creditors that she will eventually be able to restore profitability. As Airbus completed the design and manufacture of its A380 jumbo jet, managers recognized that delays and cost overruns had changed its breakeven point. New calculations indicated that the company would need to sell 420 planes before it would become profitable. Its annual sales, of course, remained relatively easy to measure.

> *"Closing under performing stores is a natural part of business of any smart retailer."*
>
> MARIA SCEPPAGUERICO, spokesperson for Ann Taylor[15]

USA TODAY, APRIL 13, 2009, P. 3B.

Compare Performance Against Standards The third step in the control process is comparing measured performance against established standards. Performance may be higher than, lower than, or identical to the standard. In some cases comparison is easy. The goal of each product manager at General Electric is to make the product either number one or number two (on the basis of total sales) in its market. Because this standard is clear and total sales are easy to calculate, it is relatively simple to determine whether this standard has been met. Sometimes, however, comparisons are not as clear. If performance is lower than expected, the question is how much deviation from standards to allow before taking remedial action. For example, is increasing sales by 7.9 percent close enough when the standard was 8 percent?

The timetable for comparing performance to standards depends on a variety of factors, including the importance and complexity of what is being controlled. For longer-run and higher-level standards, annual comparisons may be appropriate. In other circumstances, more frequent comparisons are necessary. For example, a business with a severe cash shortage may need to monitor its on-hand cash reserves daily. In its first year of production, Airbus did indeed deliver 18 A380s, just as it had forecast.

Determine Need for Corrective Action The final step in the control process is determining the need for corrective action. Decisions regarding corrective action draw heavily on a manager's diagnostic skills. Indeed, the ability to make the actual choice of the most effective corrective action is a critical part of effective diagnostic skills. After comparing performance against control standards, one of three actions is appropriate: maintain the status quo (do nothing), correct the deviation, or change the standards. Maintaining the status quo is preferable when performance essentially matches the standards, but it is more likely that some action will be needed to correct a deviation from the standards.

Sometimes performance that is higher than expected may cause problems for organizations. For example, when highly anticipated new video games or game systems are first introduced, the demand may be so strong that customers are placed on waiting lists. The manufacturer may be unable to increase production in the short term, though, and also knows that demand will eventually drop. At the same time, however, the firm would not want to alienate potential customers.

GOING OUT OF BUSINESS!

© ISTOCKPHOTO.COM/LILLISPHOTOGRAPHY

LEARN

LEARN

FIGURE 6.4 FORMS OF OPERATIONS CONTROL

Most organizations develop multiple control systems that incorporate all three basic forms of control. For example, the publishing company that produced this book screens inputs by hiring only qualified editors, typesetters, and printers (preliminary control). In addition, quality is checked during the transformation process, such as after the manuscript is typeset (screening control), and the outputs—printed and bound books—are checked before they are shipped from the bindery (postaction control).

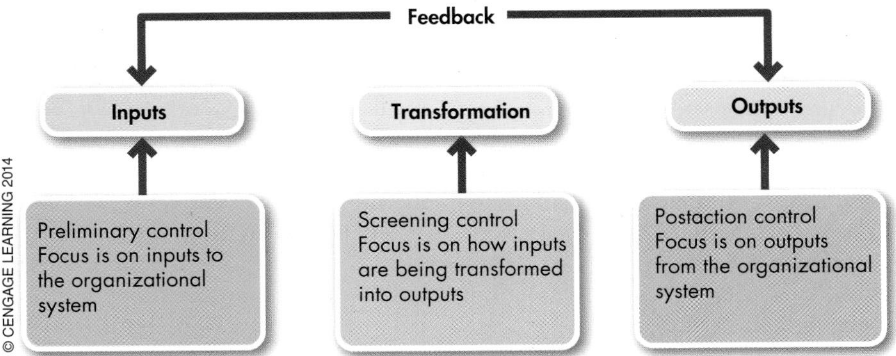

Consequently, it may decide to reduce its advertising. This may curtail demand a bit and limit customer frustration. Changing an established standard usually is necessary if it was set too high or too low at the outset. This is apparent if large numbers of employees routinely beat the standard by a wide margin or if no employees ever meet the standard. Also, standards that seemed perfectly appropriate when they were established may need to be adjusted because circumstances have since changed. As the 2008–2009 global recession began to take its toll, two major Airbus customers, Qantas and Emirates, indicated that they wanted to defer delivery of some previously ordered A380s. As a result, Airbus found it necessary to reduce its production in 2009 from 18 down to only 14. The company also indicated that the plane's breakeven point had increased, but it would not reveal the new target.

Operations Control

One of the four levels of control practiced by most organizations, operations control, is concerned with the processes the organization uses to transform resources into products or services. Given the applied nature of operations control, we will examine it in a bit more detail. As *Figure 6.4* shows, the three forms of operations control—preliminary, screening, and postaction—occur at different points in relation to the transformation processes used by the organization.

operations control concerned with the processes the organization uses to transform resources into products or services

preliminary control concentrates on the resources—financial, material, human, and information—the organization brings in from the environment

screening control focuses on meeting standards for product or service quality or quantity during the actual transformation process itself

Preliminary Control Preliminary control concentrates on the resources—financial, material, human, and information—the organization brings in from the environment. Preliminary control attempts to monitor the quality or quantity of these resources before they enter the organization. Firms like PepsiCo and General Mills hire only college graduates for their management training programs, and even then only after applicants satisfy several interviewers and selection criteria. In this way, they control the quality of the human resources entering the organization. When Sears orders merchandise to be manufactured and then sold under its own brand name, it specifies rigid standards of quality, thereby controlling physical inputs. Organizations also control financial and information resources. For example, privately held companies like Toys "R" Us and Mars limit the extent to which outsiders can buy their stock, and television networks verify the accuracy of news stories before they are broadcast.

Screening Control Screening control focuses on meeting standards for product or service quality or quantity during the actual transformation process itself. Screening control relies heavily on feedback processes. For example, in a Dell Computer assembly factory, computer system components are checked periodically as each unit is being assembled. This is done to ensure that all the components that have been assembled up to that point are working properly. The periodic quality checks provide feedback to workers so they know what, if any, corrective actions to take. Because they are useful in identifying the cause of problems, screening controls tend to be used more often than other forms of control. More and more companies are adopting screening controls because they are an effective way to promote employee participation and catch problems early in the overall transformation process. For example, Corning adopted screening controls for use in manufacturing television glass. In the past, finished television screens were inspected only after they were finished. Unfortunately, more than 4 percent of them were later returned by customers because of defects. Now the glass screens are inspected at each step in the production process, rather than at the end, and the return rate from customers has dropped to 0.03 percent.

Postaction Control Postaction control focuses on the outputs of the organization after the transformation process is complete. Corning's old system was postaction control—final inspection after the product was completed. Although Corning abandoned its postaction control system, this still may be an effective method of control, primarily if a product can be manufactured in only one or two steps or if the service is simple and routine. Although postaction control alone may not be as effective as preliminary or screening control, it can provide management with information for future planning. For example, if a quality check of finished goods indicates an unacceptably high defect rate, the production manager knows that he or she must identify the causes and take steps to eliminate them. Postaction control also provides a basis for rewarding employees. Recognizing that an employee has exceeded personal sales goals by a wide margin, for example, may alert the manager that a bonus or promotion is in order. Most organizations use more than one form of operations control. For example, Honda's preliminary control includes hiring only qualified employees and specifying strict quality standards when ordering parts from other manufacturers. Honda uses numerous screening controls in checking the quality of components during assembly of cars. A final inspection and test drive as each car rolls off the assembly line is part of the company's postaction control.[16] Indeed, most successful organizations employ a wide variety of techniques to facilitate operations control.

Characteristics of Effective Control

When designing and implementing control systems managers obviously must work to make sure those systems are as effective as possible. But what constitutes effective control? Control systems tend to be most effective when they are integrated with planning and when they are flexible, accurate, timely, and objective.

Integration with Planning Control should be linked with planning. The more explicit and precise this linkage, the more effective the control system is. The best way to integrate planning and control is to account for control as plans develop. In other words, as goals are set during the planning process, managers should pay attention to developing standards that will reflect how well the plan is realized. Managers at Champion Spark Plug Company decided to broaden the company's product line to include a full range of automotive accessories—a total of 21 new products. As part of this plan, managers decided in advance what level of sales they wanted to realize from each product for each of the next five years. They established these sales goals as standards against which to compare actual sales. Thus, by accounting for their control system as they developed the plan, managers at Champion did an excellent job of integrating planning and control.

Flexibility The control system must be flexible enough to accommodate change. Consider, for example, an organization whose diverse product line requires 75 different raw materials. The company's inventory control system must be able to manage and monitor current levels of inventory for all 75 materials. When a change in product line changes the number of raw materials needed, or when the required quantities of the existing materials change, the control system should be flexible enough to handle the revised requirements. The alternative—designing and implementing a new control system—is an avoidable expense. Champion's control system included a mechanism that automatically shipped products to major customers to keep inventories at predetermined levels. The firm had to adjust this system when one of its biggest customers decided not to stock the full line of Champion products. Because its control system was flexible, though, modifying it for the customer was relatively simple.

Accuracy Managers make a surprisingly large number of decisions based on inaccurate information. Field representatives may hedge their sales estimates to make themselves look better. Production managers may hide costs to meet their targets. Human resource managers may overestimate their minority recruiting prospects to meet affirmative action goals. In each case, the information that other managers receive is inaccurate, and the results of inaccurate information may be quite dramatic. If sales projections are inflated, a manager might cut advertising thinking it is no longer needed or increase advertising to further build momentum. Similarly, a production manager unaware of hidden costs may quote a sales price

postaction control focuses on the outputs of the organization after the transformation process is complete

LEARN

much lower than desirable. Or a human resources manager may speak out publicly on the effectiveness of the company's minority recruiting, only to find out later that these prospects have been overestimated. In each case, the result of inaccurate information is inappropriate managerial action.

LEARN

Timeliness Timeliness does not necessarily mean that something must be done quickly. Rather, it describes a control system that provides information as often as is necessary. For examples, because Champion has a wealth of historical data on its spark plug sales, it does not need information on spark plugs as frequently as it needs sales feedback for its newer products. Retail organizations usually need sales results daily in order to manage cash flow and adjust advertising and promotion. In contrast, they may require information about physical inventory only quarterly or annually. In general, the more uncertain and unstable the circumstances, the more frequently measurement is needed.

Objectivity The control system should provide information that is as objective as possible. To appreciate this, imagine the task of a manager responsible for control of his organization's human resources. He asks two plant managers to submit reports. One manager notes that morale at his plant is "okay," that grievances are "about where they should be," and that turnover is "under control." The other reports that absenteeism at her plant is running at four percent, that 16 grievances have been filed this year (compared with 24 last year), and that turnover is 12 percent. The specific information in the second report will almost always be more useful than the general information in the first. Of course, managers also need to look beyond the numbers when assessing performance. For example, a plant manager may be boosting productivity and profit margins by putting too much pressure on workers and using poor-quality materials. As a result, impressive short-run gains may be overshadowed by longer-run increases in employee turnover and customer complaints.

MANAGING CONTROL

Even when a control system has been properly designed and implemented, and even when it seems to have all of the characteristics of effective control, managers still must pay attention to how employees in the organization both utilize and respond to control. In particular, there is a tendency for people to resist control. When this occurs, there are steps managers can take to overcome—or to at least minimize—this resistance.

Resistance to Control

Managers sometimes make the mistake of assuming that the value of an effective control system is self-evident to employees. This is not always the case. Many employees resist control, especially if they feel over controlled, if they think control is inappropriately focused or rewards inefficiency, or if they are uncomfortable with accountability.

Overcontrol Occasionally, organizations try to control too many things. This becomes especially problematic when the control directly affects employee behavior. An organization that instructs its employees when to come to work, where to park, when to have morning coffee, and when to leave for the day exerts considerable control over their daily activities. Yet many organizations attempt to control not only these, but other aspects of work behavior as well. In recent years, employees' access to private email and the Internet during work hours has become an issue. Some companies have no policies governing these activities, some attempt to limit them, and some attempt to forbid this access altogether.[17] Troubles arise when employees perceive these attempts to limit their behavior as being unreasonable. A company that tells its employees how to dress, how to arrange their desks, and how to wear their hair may meet with more resistance.

Employees at Chrysler who drove non-Chrysler vehicles used to complain because they were forced to park in a distant parking lot. People felt that these efforts to control their personal behavior (what kind of car to drive) were excessive. Managers eventually removed these controls and now allow open parking. Some employees at Abercrombie & Fitch argue that the firm is guilty of overcontrol because of its strict dress and grooming requirements—for example, no necklaces or facial hair for men and only natural nail polish and earrings no larger than a dime for women. Likewise, Enterprise Rent-A-Car has a set of 30 dress-code rules

© CENGAGE LEARNING 2014

for women and 26 rules for men. The firm was recently sued by a former employee who was fired because of the color of her hair.[18]

Inappropriate Focus The control system may be too narrow, or it may focus too much on quantifiable variables and leave no room for analysis or interpretation. A sales standard that encourages high-pressure tactics to maximize short-run sales may do so at the expense of goodwill from long-term customers. Such a standard is too narrow. A university reward system that encourages faculty members to publish large numbers of articles but fails to consider the quality of the work also is focused inappropriately. Employees resist the intent of the control system by focusing their efforts only at the performance indicators being used.

Rewards for Inefficiency Imagine two operating departments that are approaching the end of their fiscal years. Department 1 expects to have $25,000 of its budget left over; department 2 is already $10,000 in the red. As a result, department 1 is likely to have its budget cut for the next year ("They had money left, so they obviously got too much to begin with"), and department 2 is likely to get a budget increase ("They obviously haven't been getting enough money"). Thus department 1 is punished for being efficient, and department 2 is rewarded for being inefficient. (No wonder departments commonly hasten to deplete their budgets as the end of the year approaches!) As with inappropriate focus, people resist the intent of this control and behave in ways that run counter to the organization's intent.

Too Much Accountability Effective controls allow managers to determine whether employees successfully discharge their responsibilities. If standards are properly set and performance is accurately measured, managers know when problems arise and which departments and individuals are responsible. People who do not want to be answerable for their mistakes or who do not want to work as hard as their boss might like therefore resist control. For example, American Express has a system that provides daily information on how many calls each of its customer-service representatives handles. If one representative typically has worked at a slower pace and handled fewer calls than other representatives, then that individual's deficient performance can more easily be pinpointed.

© CENGAGE LEARNING 2014

LEARN

Overcoming Resistance to Control

Perhaps the best way to overcome resistance to control is to create effective control to begin with. If control systems are integrated properly with organizational planning, and if the controls are flexible, accurate, timely, and objective, the organization will be less likely to overcontrol, to focus on inappropriate standards, or to reward inefficiency. Two other ways to overcome resistance are encouraging employee participation and developing verification procedures.

Encourage Employee Participation Employee participation can also help counter resistance to control. Specifically, when employees are involved with planning and implementing the control system, they are less likely to resist it. For instance, employee participation in planning, decision making, and quality control at the Chevrolet Gear and Axle plant in Detroit resulted in increased employee concern for quality and a greater commitment to meeting standards.

Develop Verification Procedures Multiple standards and information systems provide checks and balances in control and allow the organization to verify the accuracy of performance indicators. Suppose a production manager argues that she failed to meet a certain cost standard because of increased prices of raw materials. A properly designed inventory control system will either support or contradict her explanation. Suppose that an employee who was fired for excessive absences argues that he has "not been absent for a long time." An effective human resource control system should have records that show frequent and excessive absences and thus support the termination. Resistance to control declines because these verification procedures protect both employees and management. If the production manager's claim about the rising cost of raw materials is supported by the inventory control records, she will not be held solely accountable for failing to meet the cost standard, and some action probably will be taken to lower the cost of raw materials.

LEARN

REWARDING EMPLOYEES

Another area where diagnostic skills are critical is the system and process the organization uses to reward its employees. This perspective is illustrated in *Figure 6.5*. For instance, consider the cause-and-effect discussion that opened this chapter. If the "effect" we want to achieve is for employees to be motivated to perform at a high level, it becomes clear that managers need to understand the "causes" that may lead to this effect. Given that most employees expect to be rewarded for their efforts, rewards are a major causal factor in contributing to employee motivation to perform. As we saw in Chapter 5, content perspectives deal with needs, whereas process perspectives explain why people choose various behaviors to satisfy needs and how they evaluate the equity of the rewards they get for those behaviors. Using that discussion as a springboard, then, we open our discussion of rewarding employees by examining how reinforcement perspectives help maintain behavior over time.

FIGURE 6.5 USING REWARDS EFFECTIVELY

Rewards can be used most effectively if they are tied to specific outcomes the organization wants to achieve. Specifically, from a cause-and-effect perspective, rewards can serve as causal variables to affect such outcomes as productivity, performance behaviors, dysfunctional behaviors, and citizenship.

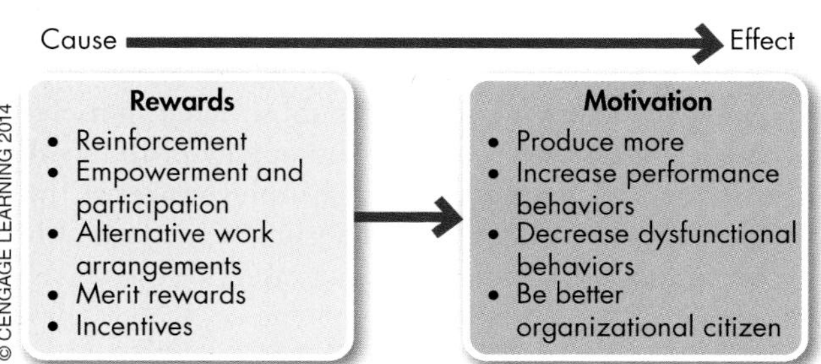

© CENGAGE LEARNING 2014

Reinforcement Perspectives on Motivation

Reinforcement perspectives explain the role of rewards as they cause behavior to change or remain the same over time. Specifically, **reinforcement theory** argues that behavior that results in rewarding consequences is likely to be repeated, whereas behavior that results in punishing consequences is less likely to be repeated.[20]

> *"We wanted to understand the root causes that were specific to our situation so that we could implement changes to improve employee morale and performance."*
>
> JAMES SCHMIDT
> CEO, Our Columbus, Ohio social services agency[19]

QUOTED IN HR MAGAZINE, JANUARY 2012, P. 31.

reinforcement theory suggests that behavior that results in rewarding consequences is likely to be repeated, whereas behavior that results in punishing consequences is less likely to be repeated

positive reinforcement a method of strengthening behavior by providing a reward or a positive outcome after a desired behavior is performed

avoidance a negative consequence that employees avoid by engaging in a desired behavior

punishment a negative consequence following undesired behavior

Kinds of Reinforcement in Organizations There are four basic kinds of reinforcement that can result from behavior—positive reinforcement, avoidance, punishment, and extinction.[21] These are summarized in *Table 6.1*. Two kinds of reinforcement strengthen or maintain behavior, whereas the other two weaken or decrease behavior.

Positive reinforcement, a method of strengthening behavior, is a reward or a positive outcome after a desired behavior is performed. When a manager observes an employee doing an especially good job and offers praise, the praise serves to positively reinforce the behavior of good work. Other positive reinforcers in organizations include pay raises, promotions, and awards. Employees who work at General Electric's customer-service center receive clothing, sporting goods, and even trips to Disney World as rewards for outstanding performance. Nucor Steel bases pay for its employees on actual productivity, and the pay workers receive each week reflects their performance that week. The other method of strengthening desired behavior is through **avoidance**. For example, an employee may come to work on time to avoid a reprimand. In this instance, the employee is motivated to perform the behavior of punctuality to avoid an unpleasant consequence that is likely to follow tardiness.

Punishment is used by some managers to weaken undesired behaviors. When an employee is loafing, coming to work late, doing poor work, or interfering with the work of others, the manager might resort to reprimands, discipline, or fines. The logic is that the unpleasant consequence will reduce the likelihood that the employee will choose that particular behavior again. Given the counterproductive side effects of punishment (such as resentment and hostility), it is often advisable to use the other kinds of reinforcement if at all possible.

A. CHEDERROS

Punishment is occasionally necessary in organizations. Managers should be careful, however, to carry out punishment in an appropriate manner. This manager appears to be going overboard!

Extinction also can be used to weaken behavior, especially behavior that has previously been rewarded. Extinction occurs when a behavior is repeated because it is rewarded, but then it stops when the reward is removed. When an employee tells an off-color joke and the boss laughs, the laughter reinforces the behavior and the employee may continue to tell off-color jokes. By simply ignoring this behavior and not reinforcing it, the boss can cause the behavior to subside and eventually become "extinct."

Providing Reinforcement in Organizations

Not only is the kind of reinforcement important, but so is when or how often it occurs. Various strategies are possible for providing reinforcement. These are also listed in *Table 6.1*. The fixed-interval schedule provides reinforcement at fixed intervals of time, regardless of behavior. A good example of this schedule is the weekly or monthly paycheck. This method provides the least incentive for good work because employees know they will be paid regularly regardless of their efforts. A variable-interval schedule also uses time as the basis for reinforcement, but the time interval varies from one reinforcement to the next. This schedule is appropriate for praise or other rewards based on visits or inspections. When employees do not know when the boss is going to drop by, they tend to maintain a reasonably high level of effort all the time.

A fixed-ratio schedule gives reinforcement after a fixed number of behaviors, regardless of the time that elapses between behaviors. This results in an even higher level of effort. For example, when Sears is recruiting new credit card customers, salespersons get a small bonus for every fifth application returned from their department. Under this arrangement, motivation will be high because each application gets the person closer to the next bonus. The variable-ratio schedule, the most powerful schedule in terms of maintaining desired behaviors, varies the number of behaviors needed for each reinforcement. A supervisor who praises an employee for her second order, the seventh order after that, the ninth after that, then the fifth, and then the third is using a variable-ratio schedule. The employee is motivated to increase the frequency of the desired behavior because each performance increases the probability of receiving a reward. Of course, a variable-ratio schedule is difficult (if not impossible) to use for formal rewards such as pay because it would be too complicated to keep track of who was rewarded when.

LEARN

extinction occurs when a behavior is repeated because it is rewarded but then stops when the reward is removed

fixed-interval schedule provides reinforcement at fixed intervals of time, regardless of behavior

variable-interval schedule uses time as the basis for reinforcement, but the time interval varies from one reinforcement to the next

fixed-ratio schedule gives reinforcement after a fixed number of behaviors, regardless of the time that elapses between behaviors

variable-ratio schedule varies the number of behaviors needed for each reinforcement

TABLE 6.1 ELEMENTS OF REINFORCEMENT THEORY

Arrangement of the Reinforcement Contingencies	
1. Positive Reinforcement. Strengthens behavior by providing a desirable consequence.	3. Punishment. Weakens behavior by providing an undesirable consequence.
2. Avoidance. Strengthens behavior by allowing escape from an undesirable consequence.	4. Extinction. Weakens behavior by ignoring it.
Schedules for Applying Reinforcement	
1. Fixed-Interval. Reinforcement is applied at fixed time intervals, regardless of behavior.	3. Fixed-Ratio. Reinforcement is applied after a fixed number of behaviors, regardless of time.
2. Variable-Interval. Reinforcement is applied at variable time intervals.	4. Variable-Ratio. Reinforcement is applied after a variable number of behaviors.

© CENGAGE LEARNING 2014

LEARN

Managers who want to use reinforcement theory to motivate their employees generally do so with a technique called **behavior modification**, or **OB Mod**.[22] An OB Mod program starts by specifying behaviors that are to be increased (such as producing more units) or decreased (such as coming to work late). These target behaviors are then tied to specific forms or kinds of reinforcement. Although many organizations (such as Procter & Gamble and Ford) have used OB Mod, the best-known application was at Emery Air Freight (now a part of DHL). Management felt that the containers used to consolidate small shipments into fewer, larger shipments were not being packed efficiently. Through a system of self-monitored feedback and rewards, Emery increased container usage from 45 percent to 95 percent and saved more than $3 million during the first three years of the program.[23]

Implications of the Reinforcement Perspectives Reinforcement in organizations can be a powerful force for maintaining employee motivation. Of course, for reinforcement to be truly effective, managers need to use it in a manner consistent with the various types and schedules of reinforcement discussed above. In addition, managers must understand that they may be inadvertently motivating undesired or dysfunctional behaviors. For instance, if an employee routinely comes to work late but experiences no consequences, both that worker and others will see that it is all right to be late for work.

Popular Motivational Strategies

Although the reinforcement perspective and the various theories discussed in Chapter 5 provide a solid explanation for motivation, managers must still use various techniques and strategies to actually apply them. Among the most popular motivational strategies today are empowerment and participation and alternative forms of work arrangements. Various forms of performance-based reward systems, discussed in the next section, also reflect efforts to boost motivation and performance.

behavior modification (OB Mod) an integrated procedure for using reinforcement theory

empowerment the process of enabling workers to set their own work goals, make decisions, and solve problems within their spheres of responsibility and authority

participation the process of giving employees a voice in making decisions about their own work

Empowerment and Participation Empowerment and participation represent important methods that managers can use to enhance employee motivation. **Empowerment** is the process of enabling workers to set their own work goals, make decisions, and solve problems within their spheres of responsibility and authority. **Participation** is the process of giving employees a voice in making decisions about their own work. Thus empowerment is a somewhat broader concept that promotes participation in a wide variety of areas, including but not limited to work itself, work context, and work environment.[24]

The role of participation and empowerment in motivation can be expressed in terms of both content perspectives and expectancy theory. Employees who participate in decision making may be more committed to executing decisions properly. Furthermore, the successful process of making a decision, executing it, and then seeing the positive consequences can help satisfy one's need for achievement, provide recognition and responsibility, and enhance self-esteem. Simply being asked to participate in organizational decision making also may enhance an employee's self-esteem. In addition, participation should help clarify expectancies; that is, by participating in decision making, employees may better understand the linkage between their performance and the rewards they want most.

> *"My job as a leader is to make sure everybody in the company has great opportunities, and that they feel they're having a meaningful impact and are contributing to the good of society."*
>
> LARRY PAGE
> co-founder and CEO
> Google[25]
>
> QUOTED IN FORTUNE, FEBRUARY 6, 2012, P. 99.

At one level, employees can participate in addressing questions and making decisions about their own job. Instead of just telling them how to do their job, for example, managers can ask employees to make their own decisions about how to do it. Based on their own expertise and experience with their tasks, workers might be able to improve their own productivity. In many situations, they might also be well qualified to make decisions about what materials to use, what tools to use, and so forth.

It also might be helpful to let workers make decisions about administrative matters, such as work schedules. If jobs are relatively independent of one another, employees might decide when to change shifts, take breaks, go to lunch, and so forth. A work group or team also might be able to schedule vacations and days off for its members. Many companies are giving employees opportunities to participate in broader issues of product quality. Such participation has become a hallmark of successful Japanese and other international firms, and many US companies have followed suit.

LEARN

Techniques and Issues in Empowerment In recent years, many organizations have actively sought ways to extend participation beyond the traditional areas. Simple techniques, such as suggestion boxes and question-and-answer meetings, allow a certain degree of participation, for example. The basic motive has been to better capitalize on the assets and capabilities inherent in all employees. Thus, many managers prefer the term *empowerment* to *participation* because of its more comprehensive character.

One method used to empower workers is the use of work teams, as discussed in Chapter 5. Such teams are collections of employees empowered to plan, organize, direct, and control their own work. Their supervisor, rather than being a traditional "boss," plays more the role of a coach. The other method for empowerment is to change the team's overall method of organizing. The basic pattern is for an organization to eliminate layers from its hierarchy, and thereby become much more decentralized. Power, responsibility, and authority are delegated as far down the organization as possible, placing the control over work squarely in the hands of those who actually do it.[26]

Regardless of the specific technique or method used, however, empowerment will enhance organizational effectiveness only if certain conditions exist. First of all, the organization must be sincere in its efforts to spread power and autonomy to lower levels of the organization. Token efforts to promote participation in only a few areas are not likely to succeed. Second, the organization must be committed to maintaining participation and empowerment. Workers will be resentful if they are given more control, only later to have it reduced or taken away altogether. Third, workers must truly believe that they and their managers are working together in their joint best interests. In some factory settings, for instance, high-performing workers routinely conceal the secrets of their high output. They fear that if management learns those secrets, it will use them to raise performance expectations.[27] In addition, the organization must be systematic and patient in its efforts to empower workers. Turning over too much control too quickly can spell disaster. Finally, the organization must be prepared to increase its commitment to training. Employees given more freedom in how they work likely will need additional training to help them exercise that freedom most effectively.[28]

Alternative Forms of Work Arrangements Many organizations today are also experimenting with a variety of alternative work arrangements. These arrangements generally are intended to enhance employee motivation and performance by providing employees with greater flexibility in how and when they work. Among the more popular alternative work arrangements are variable work schedules, flexible work schedules, job sharing, and telecommuting.[29]

- *Variable work schedules.* Although there are many exceptions, of course, the traditional work schedule starts at 8:00 or 9:00 in the morning and ends at 5:00 in the evening, five days a week (and, of course, many managers and other professionals work additional hours outside of these times). Unfortunately, this schedule makes it difficult to attend to routine personal business—going to the bank, seeing a doctor or dentist for a routine checkup, having a parent-teacher conference, getting an automobile serviced, and so forth. At a surface level, then, employees locked into this sort of arrangement may find it necessary to take a sick day or a vacation day to handle these activities. At a more unconscious level, some people may also feel so powerless and constrained by their job schedule as to feel increased resentment and frustration. To help counter these problems, some businesses use variable work schedules, which deviate from the traditional work schedule. One such deviation is the compressed work schedule, with which employees work a full 40-hour week in fewer than the traditional five days.[30] One approach involves working 10 hours a day for four days, leaving an extra day off. Another alternative is for employees to work slightly less than 10 hours a day, but to complete the 40 hours by lunchtime on Friday. And a few firms have tried having employees work 12 hours a day for three days, followed by four days off. Organizations that have used these forms of compressed workweeks include John Hancock, BP Amoco, and Philip Morris. One problem with this schedule is that when employees put in too much time in a single day, they tend to get tired and perform at a lower level later in the day. A schedule that some organizations today are beginning to use is what they call a "nine-eighty" schedule. Under this arrangement, an employee works a traditional schedule one week and a compressed schedule the next, getting every other Friday off. In other words, they work 80 hours (the equivalent of two weeks of full-time work) in nine days. By alternating the regular and compressed schedules across half of its workforce, the organization can be fully staffed at all times, while still giving employees two full days off each month. Shell Oil and BP Amoco Chemicals are two of the firms that currently use this schedule.

variable work schedules deviation from the traditional work schedule that starts at 8:00 or 9:00 in the morning and ends at 5:00 in the evening, five days a week

compressed work schedule working a full 40-hour week in fewer than the traditional five days

LEARN

- *Flexible work schedules.* Another alternative work arrangement is **flexible work schedules**, sometimes called flextime. Flextime gives employees more personal control over the times they work. The workday is broken down into two categories: flexible time and core time. All employees must be at their workstation during core time, but they can choose their own schedules during flexible time. Thus one employee may choose to start work early in the morning and leave in mid afternoon, another to start in the late morning and work until late afternoon, and still another to start early in the morning, take a long lunch break, and work until late afternoon. Organizations that have used the flexible work schedule method for arranging work include Hewlett-Packard, Microsoft, Texas Instruments, and NetFlix.
- *Job sharing.* Yet another useful alternative work arrangement is job sharing. In **job sharing**, two part-time employees share one full-time job. One person may perform the job from 8:00 A.M. to noon and the other, from 1:00 P.M. to 5:00 P.M. Job sharing may be desirable for people who want to work only part time or when job markets are tight. For its part, the organization can accommodate the preferences of a broader range of employees and may benefit from the talents of more people.
- *Telecommuting.* An increasingly popular approach to alternative work arrangements is **telecommuting**—allowing employees to spend part of their time working offsite, usually at home. By using email, the Internet, and other forms of information technology, many employees can maintain close contact with their organization and get as much work done at home as they do at the office. The increased power and sophistication of modern communication technology is making telecommuting easier and easier. One recent study found that nearly 40 percent of the US workforce (33 million workers) are in jobs that allow for partial or complete telecommuting. Nearly half of AT&T's employees have received mobile and remote access technologies that provide them with the flexibility to work from various locations. And 40 percent of IBM's employees currently telecommute. (In the case of IBM, not only are employees more satisfied with the arrangement, but the firm has saved close to $2.9 billion in office space expenses.)[31]

flexible work schedules gives employees more personal control over the times they work

job sharing two part-time employees share one full-time job

telecommuting allowing employees to spend part of their time working offsite, usually at home

reward system the formal and informal mechanisms by which employee performance is defined, evaluated, and rewarded

merit pay pay awarded to employees on the basis of the relative value of their contributions to the organization

© TODD WARNOCK

Job sharing is when two people share one job. This woman has just come to work in the afternoon and is getting some work for her job share "partner" who was in during the morning.

Using Reward Systems to Motivate Performance

Aside from these types of motivational strategies, an organization's reward system is its most basic tool for managing employee motivation. An organizational **reward system** is the formal and informal mechanisms by which employee performance is defined, evaluated, and rewarded. Of course, rewards that are tied specifically to performance have the greatest impact on enhancing both motivation and actual performance. Performance-based rewards play a number of roles and address a variety of purposes in organizations. The major purposes involve the relationship of rewards to motivation and to performance. Specifically, organizations want employees to perform at relatively high levels and need to make it worth their effort to do so. When rewards are associated with higher levels of performance, employees presumably will be motivated to work harder to achieve those awards. At that point, their own self-interests coincide with the organization's interests. Performance-based rewards also are relevant regarding other employee behaviors, such as retention and citizenship.

Merit Reward Systems Merit reward systems are among the most fundamental forms of performance-based rewards.[32] **Merit pay** generally refers to pay awarded to employees on the basis of the relative value of their contributions to the organization. Employees who make greater contributions are given higher pay than those who make lesser contributions. **Merit pay plans**, then, are compensation plans that formally base at least some meaningful portion of compensation on merit. The most general form of merit pay plan is to provide annual salary increases to individuals in the organization based on their relative merits. Merit, in turn, is usually determined or defined based on the individual's performance and overall contributions to the organization. For example, an organization using a traditional merit pay plan might instruct its supervisors to give all employees an average pay raise of, say, 4 percent. But the individual supervisor is further instructed to differentiate among high, average, and low performers. Under a simple system, for example, a manager might give the top 25 percent of her employees a 6 percent pay raise, the middle 50 percent a 4 percent or average pay raise, and the bottom 25 percent a 2 percent pay raise.

Incentive Reward Systems Incentive reward systems are among the oldest forms of performance-based rewards. For example, some companies were using individual piece-rate incentive plans more than 100 years ago.[33] Under a piece-rate incentive plan, the organization pays an employee a certain amount of money for every unit she or he produces. For example, an employee might be paid $1 for every dozen units of products that are successfully completed. But such simplistic systems fail to account for such facts as minimum wage levels and rely heavily on the assumptions that performance is totally under an individual's control and the individual employee does a single task continuously throughout his or her work time. Thus, most organizations today that try to use incentive compensation systems use more sophisticated methods.

- *Incentive pay plans.* Generally speaking, individual incentive pay plans reward individual performance on a real-time basis. In other words, rather than getting an increase in base salary at the end of the year, an individual instead receives some level of salary increase or financial reward tied to outstanding performance, and the increase or reward is granted close to when that performance occurred. Individual incentive systems are most likely to be used in cases in which performance can be objectively assessed in terms of number of units of output or similar measures, rather than on a subjective assessment of performance by a superior. The WD-40 Company uses an individual incentive plan for almost its entire workforce. The firms' managers credit the incentive plan with motivating high levels of employee performance during the 2008–2010 recession that enabled the firm to achieve record profits.[34]

Some variations on a piece-rate system, described earlier, are still fairly popular. Although many of these still resemble the early plans in most ways, a well-known piece-rate system at Lincoln Electric illustrates how an organization can adapt the traditional model to achieve better results. For years, Lincoln's employees were paid individual incentive payments based on their performances. However, the amount of money shared (or the incentive pool) was based on the company's profitability. There also was a well-organized system whereby employees could make suggestions for increasing productivity. There was motivation to do this because the employees received one-third of the profits. (Another third went to the stockholders, and the last share was retained for improvements and seed money.) Thus, the pool for incentive payments was determined by profitability, and an employee's share of this pool was a function of his or her base pay and rated performance based on the piece-rate system. Lincoln Electric was most famous, however, for stories about production workers receiving a year-end bonus payment that equaled their yearly base pay.[35] In recent years, Lincoln has partially abandoned its famous system for business reasons, but it still serves as a benchmark for other companies seeking innovative piece-rate pay systems.

Perhaps the most common form of individual incentive is sales commission paid to people engaged in sales work. For example, sales representatives for consumer products firms and retail sales agents may be compensated under this type of commission system. In general, the person might receive a percentage of the total volume of attained sales as her or his commission for a period of time. Some sales jobs are based entirely on commission, whereas others use a combination of base minimum salary with additional commission as an incentive. Notice that these plans put a considerable amount of the salespersons' earnings "at risk." The companies using these plans often have drawing accounts to allow the salesperson to live during lean periods. The person then "owes" this money back to the organization. If the person does not perform well, he or she will not be paid much. The portion of salary based on commission is not guaranteed, and it is paid only if sales reach some target level.

- *Other forms of incentive.* Occasionally organizations use other forms of incentives to motivate people. For example, a nonmonetary incentive, such as additional time off or a special perk, might be a useful incentive. For example, a company might establish a sales contest in which the sales group that attains the highest level of sales increase over a specified period of time will receive an extra week of paid vacation, perhaps even at an arranged place, such as a tropical resort or a ski lodge.[36]

piece-rate incentive plan the organization pays an employee a certain amount of money for every unit she or he produces

incentive pay plans individual incentive plans reward individual performance on a real-time basis

LEARN

A major advantage of incentives relative to merit systems is that incentives are typically a one-shot reward and do not accumulate by becoming part of the individual's base salary. Stated differently, an individual whose outstanding performance entitles him or her to a financial incentive gets the incentive only one time, based on that level of performance. If the individual's performance begins to erode in the future, then the individual may receive a lesser incentive or perhaps no incentive in the future. As a consequence, his or her base salary remains the same or is perhaps increased at a relatively moderate pace; he or she receives one-time incentive rewards as recognition for exemplary performance. Furthermore, because these plans, by their very nature, focus on one-time events, it is much easier for the organization to change the focus of the incentive plan. At a simple level, for example, an organization can set up an incentive plan for selling one product during one quarter, but then shift the incentive to a different product the next quarter, as the situation requires. Automobile companies such as Ford and GM routinely do this by reducing sales incentives for models that are selling very well and increasing sales incentives for models that are selling below expectations or are about to be discontinued.

The merit compensation and incentive compensation systems deal primarily with performance-based reward arrangements for individuals. A different set of performance-based reward programs are targeted for teams and groups. These programs are particularly important for managers to understand, given the widespread trends toward team- and group-based methods of work and organizations.[37]

Common Team and Group Reward Systems

There are two commonly used types of team and group reward systems. One type used in many organizations is an approach called gainsharing. Gainsharing programs are designed to share the cost savings from productivity improvements with employees. The underlying assumption of gainsharing is that both the employees and the employer have the same goals and thus should share appropriately in incremental economic gains.[38]

In general, organizations that use gainsharing start by measuring team- or group-level productivity. It is important that this measure be valid and reliable, and that it truly reflect current levels of performance by the team or group. The team or work group is given the charge of attempting to lower costs and otherwise improve productivity through measures that its members develop and its manager approves. Resulting cost savings or productivity gains that the team or group is able to achieve are then quantified and translated into dollar values. A predetermined formula is then used to allocate these dollar savings between the employer and the employees themselves. A typical formula for distributing gainsharing savings is to provide 25 percent to the employees and 75 percent to the company. One specific type of gainsharing plan is an approach called the Scanlon plan. This approach was developed by Joseph Scanlon in 1927. The **Scanlon plan** has the same basic strategy as gainsharing plans, in that teams or groups of employees are encouraged to suggest strategies for reducing costs. However, the distribution of these gains usually is tilted much more heavily toward employees, with employees usually receiving between two-thirds and three-fourths of the total cost savings that the plan achieves. Furthermore, the distribution of cost savings resulting from the plan is given not just to the team or group that suggested and developed the ideas, but across the entire organization.

gainsharing programs designed to share the cost savings from productivity improvements with employees

Other Types of Team and Group Rewards

Although gainsharing and Scanlon-type plans are among the most popular group incentive reward systems, some organizations use other systems. Some companies, for example, use true incentives at the team or group level. Just as with individual incentives, team or group incentives tie rewards directly to performance increases. And, like individual incentives, team or group incentives are paid as they are earned rather than added to employees' base salary. The incentives are distributed at the team or group level, however, rather than at the individual level. In some cases, the distribution may be based on the existing salary of each employee, with incentive bonuses given on a proportionate basis. In other settings, each member of the team or group receives the same incentive pay.

Some companies also use nonmonetary rewards at the team or group level—most commonly in the form of prizes and awards. For example, a company might designate the particular team in a plant or subunit of the company that achieves the highest level of productivity increase, the highest level of reported customer satisfaction, or a similar index of performance. The reward itself might take the form of additional time off, as described earlier in this chapter, or a tangible award, such as a trophy or plaque. The idea is that the reward is at the team level and serves as recognition of exemplary performance by the entire team.

Other kinds of team or group-level incentives go beyond the contributions of a specific work group. These are generally organization-wide kinds of incentives. One long-standing method for this approach is profit sharing. In a profit-sharing approach, at the end of the year some portion of the company's profits is paid into a profit-sharing pool that is then distributed to all employees. Either this amount is distributed at that time, or it is put into an escrow account and payment is deferred until the employee retires.

The basic rationale behind profit-sharing systems is that everyone in the organization can expect to benefit when the company does well. But, during bad economic times, when the company is achieving low or perhaps no profits, then no profits are shared. This sometimes results in negative reactions from employees, who may have come to feel that profit sharing is a part of their annual compensation.

Employee stock ownership plans (ESOPs) also represent a group-level reward system that some companies use. Under the employee stock ownership plan, employees are gradually given a major stake in ownership of a corporation. The typical form of this plan involves the company taking out a loan, which is then used to buy a portion of its own stock in the open market. Over time, company profits are used to pay off this loan. Employees, in turn, receive a claim on ownership of some portion of the stock held by the company, based on their seniority and perhaps on their performance. Eventually, each individual becomes an owner of the company. One recent study found that 20 percent of employees in the private sector—25 million Americans—reported owning stock in their companies, with 10 percent holding stock options.[39]

© ISTOCKPHOTO.COM/NEUSTOCKIMAGES

Prizes and awards are often an effective means of rewarding top performers. This person is being recognized for having the largest performance improvement in her department.

New Approaches to Performance-Based Rewards Some organizations recognize that they can leverage the value of the incentives that they offer to their employees and to groups in their organization by allowing those individuals and groups to have a say in how rewards are distributed. For example, at the extreme, a company could grant salary increase budgets to work groups and then allow the members of those groups themselves to determine how the rewards are going to be allocated among the various members of the group. This strategy would appear to hold considerable promise if everyone understands the performance arrangements that exist in the work group and everyone is committed to being fair and equitable. Unfortunately, it can create problems if people in a group feel that rewards are not being distributed fairly.[40]

Organizations are becoming innovative in the incentive programs they offer. For example, some now offer stock options to all their employees, rather than just to top executives. In addition, some firms are looking into ways to purely individualize reward systems. For instance, a firm might offer one employee a paid three-month sabbatical every two years in exchange for a 20 percent reduction in salary. Another employee in the same firm might be offered a 10 percent salary increase in exchange for a 5 percent reduction in company contributions to the person's retirement account. Corning, General Electric, and Microsoft are among the firms closely studying this option.[41]

Regardless of the method used, however, managers need to effectively communicate what rewards are being distributed and explain the basis for the distribution. For example, if incentives are being distributed on the basis of perceived individual contributions to the organization, then members of the organization should be informed of that fact. This will presumably better enable them to understand the basis on which pay increases and other incentives and performance-based rewards have been distributed.

SUMMARY AND A LOOK AHEAD

After reading and studying this chapter, you should have a better understanding of diagnostic skills. In particular, you should be better equipped to understand cause-and-effect relationships. You should understand the control process, as well as how to most effectively design and manage control systems. You also should have a more complete understanding of how reinforcement, various motivational strategies, and reward systems can serve to have positive effects on employee performance and other behaviors.

The remainder of this chapter provides opportunities for you to continue to develop and refine your own diagnostic skills. For instance, you will be directed to resources where you can visualize both effective and less-effective diagnostic skills. Subsequent sections provide several different opportunities for you to practice and explore diagnostic skills from different perspectives. The chapter concludes with additional assessment and interpretation data.

VISUALIZING DIAGNOSTIC SKILLS

DIAGNOSTIC SKILLS IN ACTION—1

Your Assignment

Consider the two BizFlix film clips for this chapter.

Rendition (2007) deals with terrorism and torture. After a terrorist bomb kills an American envoy overseas, an investigation leads to Anwar El-Ibrahimi (Omar Metwally) who has been living in the United States and is married to an American. When he lands in Washington, D.C., from Cape Town, South Africa, US government operatives suddenly whisk him from his flight. He is a suspected terrorist whom the government sends to North Africa for torture and interrogation (extraordinary rendition). Douglas Freeman (Jake Gyllenhaal), a CIA analyst, becomes involved. He reacts negatively to the torture techniques and urges El-Ibrahimi's release. The story has other complications in the form of El-Ibrahimi's pregnant wife at home who desperately works for her husband's safe return.

Played (2006) is about the London underworld and its criminal underground. One of those criminals, Ray Burns (Mick Rossi), does prison time for a crime he did not commit. After serving eight years, he is released and focuses his attention on getting even with his enemies. This fast-moving film peers deeply into London's criminal world, which includes some crooked London police, especially Detective Brice (Vinnie Jones). The film's unusual ending reviews all major parts of the plot.

Note how diagnostic skills are shown in these two clips.

1. The first clip is an edited composite taken from different parts of the film. This scene opens with a night shot of the Washington Monument. Congressional aide Alan Smith's (Peter Sarsgaard) voice-over says, "She called you?" The scene ends after Senator Hawkins (Alan Arkin) tells Alan to back off and leaves for a meeting. What diagnostic skills does Senator Hawkins display?
2. The second clip starts with a close-up of a photograph of an ape that Riley (Patrick Bergin) carefully examines. Detective Brice calls him and carefully outlines how he has diagnosed a situation whereby Riley can rob a location to obtain heroin. Riley then recruits Ray Burns to perform the actual robbery. The scenes end after Ray Burns accepts Riley's offer. He walks away while saying, "All right. Let's rock and roll, man. All right. Thanks, Riley." Riley says, "Thank you, Ray." Do you feel that Brice's diagnosis is sufficient for such an endeavor (overlooking the fact that it is criminal)? Why or why not?

DIAGNOSTIC SKILLS IN ACTION—2

This exercise gives you an opportunity to think about diagnostic skills that may be involved in management positions in your future.

Your Assignment

1. Think about the diagnostic skills covered in this chapter and try to identify a scene that illustrates a positive or effective use of such skills in a movie, a TV show, or a video on YouTube.
2. Now do the same for a scene that illustrates a negative or ineffective use of those same skills.

Share your results with the class and discuss how the positive and negative uses of diagnostic skills are shown in each clip. Try to suggest how the negative situation could have been changed for the better.

PRACTICING DIAGNOSTIC SKILLS

RELATING NEEDS TO REALITY

This exercise enables you to develop your diagnostic skills by relating need theory to reality in a personal way.

Your Assignment

1. Prepare a list of approximately 15 things that you want from life. These can be very specific ("a nice house") or very general ("a feeling of helping others"). Try to include some things you want right now and other things that you want later in life.
2. Classify each item from your "wish list" in terms of the need or needs it might satisfy this theoretical categorization—physiological/survival, safety/security, social/belongingness, esteem/recognition, self-actualization/"being the best you can be."
3. After your instructor organizes the class into groups of three, spend a few minutes in the group discussing each person's list and its classification according to needs.
4. After your instructor reconvenes the entire class, discuss the extent to which this theory can serve as a useful framework for classifying individual needs. Students who found that their needs could be categorized neatly or those who found little correlation between their needs and theoretical categories are especially encouraged to share their results.
5. As a result of this exercise, do you now place more or less trust in this need theory as a viable management tool?
6. Think of a way(s) that managers could use some form of this exercise in an organizational setting to enhance employee motivation.

PRACTICE

ISSUES OF CENTRALIZATION AND DECENTRALIZATION

This exercise enables you to develop your diagnostic skills as they relate to issues of centralization and decentralization. Managers often need to change the degree of centralization or decentralization in their organization.

Begin this exercise by reflecting on two very different scenarios. In Scenario A, assume you are the top manager in a large organization that has a long and well-known history of being centralized. For valid reasons beyond the scope of this exercise, assume you have made a decision to make the firm much more decentralized.

In Scenario B, assume the exact opposite situation. That is, you are the top manager of a firm that has always been decentralized but has now decided to become more centralized.

Your Assignment

1. What are the impacts of each scenario to the companies?
2. Make a list of the major barriers you see to implementing decentralization in Scenario A.
3. Make a list of the major barriers you see to implementing centralization in Scenario B.
4. Which scenario do you think would be easiest to implement? That is, is it likely easier to move from centralization to decentralization or from decentralization to centralization? Explain your answer.
5. Given a choice of starting your own career in a firm that is either highly centralized or highly decentralized, which do you think you would prefer? Why?

DETERMINING WHY INDIVIDUALS BECOME ENTREPRENEURS

This exercise provides an opportunity to use diagnostic skills in analyzing your own personal background to determine whether you are likely to choose an entrepreneurial career.

Scholars of entrepreneurship are concerned with understanding why some individuals choose to start a new business whereas others do not. Investigators have surveyed thousands of entrepreneurs and non-entrepreneurs in an attempt to discover factors that can distinguish between the two groups. Hundreds of studies have been conducted and some consensus has emerged. Judging on the basis of numerous studies, entrepreneurship is more likely when an individual:

- is the parent, child, spouse, or sibling of an entrepreneur
- is an immigrant to the United States or the child of an immigrant
- is a parent
- is a member of the Jewish or Protestant faith
- holds a professional degree in a field such as medicine, law, or engineering
- has recently experienced a life-changing event, such as getting married, having a child, moving to a new city, or losing a job

Your Assignment

1. Choose one of the categories listed above and explain why this factor might make an individual more likely to become a business owner.
2. From the categories listed above, choose one that is true of yourself (don't choose the same category that you chose in Question 1). In your opinion, does that factor make it more likely that you will become an entrepreneur? Why or why not?
3. If none of the categories above applies to you, tell whether that fact makes it less likely that you will become an entrepreneur, and explain why.

NEGOTIATING A FRANCHISE AGREEMENT

This exercise provides an opportunity to develop your diagnostic skills by visualizing and analyzing a situation from two points of view so you can develop a rational solution or decision.

Your Assignment

1. Assume that you are the owner of a rapidly growing restaurant chain. In order to continue your current level of growth, you are considering selling franchises for new restaurants.
   (A) Outline the major points of most concern to you for including in a franchising agreement.
   (B) Note the characteristics you would look for in potential franchisees.
2. Assume that you are an individual investor looking to buy a franchise in a rapidly growing restaurant chain.
   (A) Outline the major factors that might determine which franchise you elect to buy.
   (B) Note the characteristics you would look for in a potential franchiser.
3. Now form groups of four. Randomly select one member of the group to play the role of the franchiser, with the other three members playing the roles of potential franchisees. Role-play a negotiation meeting. The franchiser should stick as closely as possible to the major points developed in Step 1 above. Similarly, the potential franchisees should try to adhere to the points they developed in Step 2 above.
4. Did doing both Step 1 and Step 2 in advance help or hinder your negotiations?
5. Can a franchising agreement be so one-sided as to damage the interests of both parties? How so?

ETHICS IN DECISION MAKING

This exercise will help you develop your diagnostic and decision-making skills by applying them to an ethical business dilemma.

As businesses, industries, societies, and technologies become more complex, ethical dilemmas become more puzzling. Consider, for example, the ethical dilemmas related to the online publication of music. The growth of file-sharing programs and fast Internet connections, the desire of many businesses and customers to bypass intermediaries, and changing societal definitions of "theft" all contribute to this difficult situation.

In 2001 Napster, the most popular file-sharing program at that time, was shut down by a lawsuit from the Recording Industry Association of America, which represented music publishers and distributors. After Napster's demise, many legal music distribution sites came online, including iTunes, buy.com, P3.com, and even WalMart.com. However there are still many distributors that spread mainly illegal content.

Your Assignment

Use the Internet to investigate up-to-date information about online music publishing, and then answer the following questions.

1. Consider each of the stakeholders in the online music publishing industry—recording artists, recording companies, consumers, online file-sharing companies such as Grokster, and legitimate websites such as iTunes. Analyze the ethical problems within the online music industry today from the point of view of each party.
2. What would be the best outcome for each party?
3. Is there any way to satisfy the needs of all the stakeholders? If yes, explain how this can be accomplished. If no, explain why a mutually beneficial solution will not be possible.
4. What impact did your personal ethics have on your answer to Question 3?

USING DIFFERENT METHODS OF POWER

A situation that managers often face is whether to use power (and if so, which type of power) to solve a problem. This exercise helps you develop your diagnostic skills as they relate to using different types of power in different situations.

Several methods of using power have been identified, including the following:

- *Legitimate request.* The manager's requests are granted because the subordinate recognizes that the organization has given the manager the right to make the request. Most day-to-day interactions between manager and subordinate are of this type.
- *Instrumental compliance.* In this form of exchange, a subordinate complies to get the reward that the manager controls. Suppose a manager asks a subordinate to do something outside the range of the subordinate's normal duties, such as working extra hours on the weekend, terminating a relationship with a long-standing buyer, or delivering bad news. The subordinate complies and, as a direct result, reaps praise and a bonus from the manager. The next time the subordinate is asked to perform a similar activity, that subordinate will recognize that compliance will be instrumental in her getting more rewards. Hence, the basis of instrumental compliance is clarifying important performance-reward contingencies.
- *Coercion.* This form of power is used when the manager suggests or implies that the subordinate will be punished, fired, or reprimanded if he does not do something.
- *Rational persuasion.* This form of power is used when the manager can convince the subordinate that compliance is in the subordinate's best interest. For example, a manager might argue that the subordinate should accept a transfer because it would be good for the subordinate's career. In some ways, rational persuasion is like reward power, except that the manager does not really control the reward.
- *Personal identification.* This use of power occurs when a manager who recognizes that she has referent power over a subordinate can shape the behavior of that subordinate by engaging in desired behaviors. The manager consciously becomes a model for the subordinate and exploits personal identification.
- *Inspirational appeal.* This use of power occurs when a manager can induce a subordinate to do something consistent with a set of higher ideals or values through inspirational appeal. For example, a plea for loyalty represents an inspirational appeal.

Your Assignment

1. Give a specific example of each of the six methods of using power. Can you cite a personal example of having used or witnessed the use of any of these methods?
2. Is a manager more likely to use a single type of power or multiple forms of power at the same time?
3. What are some other methods and approaches to using power?
4. Describe some of the dangers and pitfalls associated with using power.

USING DIFFERENT TYPES OF POWER

Diagnostic skills help a manager visualize appropriate responses to a situation. One situation that leaders often face is deciding the type of power to use in response to different situations. Types of power include legitimate (from a position in an organization), reward (controls rewards), coercive (control punishment or removal of rewards), expert (based on knowledge and skill), and referent (based on personal identification, imitation, and charisma).

The president of the United States is one of the most powerful leaders in the world. His formal speeches are carefully crafted statements that address specific concerns, but they also are deliberately loaded with language that invokes the power of the office. The annual State of the Union address is often the most detailed and polished public speech given by the president in a year. So it is natural that the State of the Union address would contain many references to the various types of power wielded by the president.

Your Assignment

Read a transcript of a president's State of the Union address. Then answer the following questions. (*Hint:* Do an Internet search.)

1. What types of power is the president using in this speech? Give specific examples of each type. For example, (1) George W. Bush's 2007 speech, "I congratulate the Democrat majority." (2) Barack Obama's 2011 speech, "Now it's our turn. We know what it takes to compete for the jobs and industries of our time. We need to out-innovate, out-educate, and out-build the rest of the world."
2. In addition to this speech, list some of this president's other actions or words that, in your opinion, tend to give him more power. List some actions or words you think reduce his power.
3. Does this speech inspire you to be a follower of this president? Why or why not?

PRACTICE

QUALITY RELATIVE TO PRICE AND EXPECTATIONS

The quality of a product or service is relative to price and expectations. This exercise shows that a manager's diagnostic skills—the ability to visualize responses to a situation—can be useful in helping position quality relative to price and expectations.

Your Assignment

1. Think of a recent occasion when you purchased tangible products (for example, clothing, electronic equipment, luggage, or professional supplies), one of which (A) you came to feel was of especially high quality, and (B) you felt had low or poor quality.
2. Next, recall experiences involving the purchase of services rather than products (for example, airline trip, haircut, dry cleaning, oil change for your car), one of which (A) you came to feel was of especially high quality, and (B) you felt was of low or poor quality.
3. Finally, recall experiences in which both products and services were involved and there was a disparity between the quality of the product and that of the service; that is, a poor-quality product accompanied by outstanding service, or a high-quality product accompanied by mediocre service. Examples might include having questions answered by someone about a product you were buying, or returning a defective or broken product for a refund or warranty repair, a meal in a restaurant, or shopping for any product where you required extensive assistance from the sales staff.
4. Using the six examples identified above, assess the extent to which the quality you associated with each was a function of price and of your expectations.
5. For those products and services that you rated as poor or only adequate, could their quality be improved without greatly affecting price? If so, how?
6. Can high-quality service offset a product that is of poor or only adequate quality?

7. Can outstanding product quality offset service that is poor or barely adequate?
8. How should a manager go about diagnosing the quality-price relationship for a product or service?

DIAGNOSING CAUSES OF PROBLEMS

This exercise helps demonstrate the relationship between diagnostic skills and the control function of management.

Assume you are the manager of a popular, locally owned restaurant that competes with chains such as Chili's, Bennigan's, and Applebee's. You have been able to maintain your market share even with increased competition from these outlets by providing exceptional service. Recently, though, you have become aware of three trends that concern you. First, your costs are increasing. Monthly charges for food purchases seem to be growing at an exceptionally rapid pace. Second, customer complaints are also increasing. Although the actual number of complaints is still quite small, complaints are nevertheless increasing. And, finally, turnover among your employees is increasing. Although turnover in the restaurant business is usually very high, the recent increase at your restaurant is in marked contrast to your historical pattern of turnover.

PRACTICE

Your Assignment

1. Diagnose the problem by identifying as many potential causes as possible for the increases in each of the three problem areas: food costs, customer complaints, and employee turnover.
2. Group the causes into two categories: more likely and less likely.
3. Develop at least one potential action that you might take to address each cause.

WEIGHING ORGANIZATION CHANGE ALTERNATIVES

This exercise will help you learn how diagnostic skills help a manager to visualize the most appropriate response to a situation. These skills are especially important during a period of organization change, and change is exactly what you are suddenly facing.

Assume that you are the general manager of a hotel located on a tropical island. Situated along a beautiful stretch of beach, the hotel is one of six large resorts in the immediate area. It is also one of the oldest on the island. The hotel has been operated for several years as a franchise unit of a large international hotel chain (as are all of the other hotels on the island), and that franchise is owned by a group of foreign investors.

For the last few years the hotel's owners have been taking most of the profits for themselves and putting relatively little back into the hotel. They have also let you know that their business is not in good financial health—the money earned from your hotel is being used to offset losses they are incurring elsewhere. In contrast, most of the other nearby hotels have recently been refurbished, and plans have just been announced to build two new hotels in the near future.

A team of executives from franchise headquarters has just visited your hotel. They expressed considerable disappointment in the property, noting that it has not kept pace with the other resorts on the island. They also informed you that if the property is not brought up to their standards, the franchise agreement will be revoked when it comes up for review next year.

You see this move as potentially disastrous because you would lose the franchisor's brand name, access to its reservation system, and so forth. Sitting alone in your office, you have identified several alternatives that seem viable:

- Try to convince the owners to remodel the hotel. You estimate it will cost $10 million to meet the franchisor's minimum standards and another $10 million to compete with the other top resorts on the island.
- Try to convince the franchisor to give you more time and more options for upgrading the facility.
- Allow the franchise agreement to terminate and try to succeed as an independent hotel.
- Assume that the hotel will fail, and start looking for another job. You have a good reputation, although you may have to start at a lower level (maybe assistant manager) with another firm.

Your Assignment

1. Rank-order the above four alternatives in terms of their potential success. Make assumptions as appropriate.
2. Identify other alternatives not noted above.
3. Can any alternatives be pursued simultaneously?
4. Develop an overall strategy for saving the hotel while protecting your own interests.

DEALING WITH EQUITY AND JUSTICE ISSUES

This exercise will provide you with insights into how diagnostic skills are used when managers attempt to deal with the critical issues of equity and justice in the workplace.

Assume you are a manager of a group of professional employees in the electronics industry. Ray Lambert, one of your employees, asks to meet with you. The company has just announced an opening for a team leader position in your group, and you know that Ray wants the job. You are unsure as to how to proceed. Ray feels that he has earned the opportunity on the basis of his consistent efforts, but you see things a bit differently. Since you hired him about ten years ago, he has been a solid but not an outstanding employee. As a result, he has consistently received average performance evaluations, pay increases, and so forth. He actually makes somewhat less today than a couple of other people with less tenure in the group because they have had stronger performance records.

You really want to appoint another employee, Margot Sylvant, to the job. She has worked for the firm only six years, but during that time she has consistently been your top performer. You want to reward her performance and you think that she will do an excellent job. On the other hand, you don't want to lose Ray, a solid member of the group.

Your Assignment

1. Itemize the inputs (time and effort) and outputs (performance) of Ray and Margot.
2. How are Ray and Margot likely to see the situation?
3. Outline a conversation with Ray in which you will convey your decision to hire Margot.
4. What advice might you offer Margot about interacting with Ray in her new job?
5. What other rewards might you offer Ray to keep him motivated?

USING DIAGNOSTIC SKILLS

USE

DIAGNOSIS AT DUPONT

Today DuPont is the second-largest chemical company in the United States, second only to its long-time rival, Dow. Members of the DuPont family served as the top executives and managed the company as a family business until the early 1970s. However, DuPont eventually became a professionally managed corporation with a strong divisional structure based on products. DuPont also began to expand its operations into paints, dyes, artificial fibers, and plastics and from there into all forms of chemistry.

DuPont, however, has been struggling for a quarter of a century. It developed six principal business segments: industrial products, fibers, polymers, petroleum, coal, and diversified businesses. Then it purchased Conoco in 1981, suggesting a change in direction. DuPont's performance during the 1980s slipped from excellent to average, and the company seemed not to be as successful at diagnosing and anticipating cyclical impacts as it had in the past. Four different CEOs battled to diagnose these problems and to keep the firm on a steady growth course with varying degrees of success. In addition, DuPont became known as the number-one corporate polluter in the United States because of problems with both emissions from its plants and its disposal of hydrochloric acid. Nevertheless, by the end of the 1980s, total sales had nearly tripled while the total number of employees stayed almost the same.

Then came the 1990s. As a result of a joint research project, Battelle filed suit charging that DuPont had deliberately misappropriated Battelle's trade secrets. A major fungicide, Benlate, proved a disappointment and was eventually withdrawn from the market as it ended up damaging some crops. By the end of 1992, DuPont's net income had fallen for two years and return on equity had dropped. DuPont diagnosed the situation and began making strategic and tactical plans to rectify it.

Top management was reorganized, managerial and supervisory positions were eliminated, early retirements were pushed, and whole levels of management disappeared. Decision making was decentralized further than before, cutting the red tape with which customers had to deal. The company spun off pharmaceuticals into a joint venture with Merck & Company, slashed yearly operating costs, and made efforts to reduce DuPont's problems with pollution. It kept research and development expenditures high and developed joint projects to encourage innovation. It also emphasized closer contact with customers. Further, it cut weak businesses, particularly those that lacked strong market shares or potential such as its acrylics products business. Lastly, it expanded the company's global role by developing offshore businesses.

A decade of reinventing itself did not improve things, however. Merger talks with Monsanto went nowhere. Conoco, including pharmaceuticals and DuPont's core business of nylon and textiles, was sold in 1998. In 1999 Pioneer was bought, which meant that DuPont was entering an entirely new business, seed production, in which it had no experience. All of this shuffling and reshuffling may have set the stage for DuPont eventually to reemerge as the dominant business it once was, but from 1998 through 2008, its stock price fell by half. The bottom year was 2008, which saw two more restructurings and thousands of employee layoffs. The company's new CEO, Ellen Kullman, has been using her extensive experience to help diagnose the current situation and to develop strong, clear plans to make DuPont great again.

Case Questions

Go Online

1. Why did DuPont seem to have so much trouble diagnosing its problems?
2. What diagnostic skills would seem to be the most important at DuPont? Why?

3. What seem to be the strengths and weaknesses of DuPont employees? Why?
4. What diagnostic skills do you have for working in a managerial position in one of DuPont's businesses? What preparations would you need to make to have the requisite diagnostic skills for success there?

Case References

Carol J. Loomis, "Ellen Kullman's quest to make DuPont great again," *Fortune*, April 15, 2010 http://money.cnn.com/2010/04/14/news/companies/kullman_dupont.fortune/index.htm; Geoff Colvin, "The sustainability exec: DuPont's Linda Fisher," *Fortune*, November 12, 2009 http://money.cnn.com/2009/11/10/news/companies/dupont_fisher_sustainability.fortune/index.htm; Andy Serwer, "Oil's fall soups up DuPont," *Fortune*, September 26, 2006 http://money.cnn.com/2006/09/26/commentary/streetlife.fortune/index.htm; Joseph Weber, "DuPont: The Wollard Years," *BusinessWeek*, August 31, 1992, pp. 70–71; Zachary Schiller and Janet Bamford, "A Tooth-and-Nail Fight Over Plastics," *BusinessWeek*, May 4, 1992, p. 35.

INTERNATIONAL TRAINING

As the global economy becomes more integrated and organizations more global, training in international business has steadily increased. That training is necessary in many situations such as when a German manager for an American company in Europe is relocated to run a plant in China. International training is useful not just for dealing with issues around the globalization of business but also for dealing with diversity in organizations at home. In 1990, for instance, a Digital Equipment Corporation plant in Boston had 350 employees from 44 countries who spoke 19 languages. The plant printed announcements in English, Chinese, French, Spanish, Portuguese, Vietnamese, and Haitian Creole. And with many foreign corporations making direct investments in US companies, many Americans find that their supervisors are from other countries. Language and cultural training can help to ease problems in all such situations.

Research suggests that the ability to communicate effectively both orally and in writing as well as the mastery of at least one foreign language and its culture are fundamental to successful international management. Businesses are training people in these fundamentals and business school training is increasing outside the United States. The London Business School; INSEAD (L'Institut Européen d'Administration des Affaires) in Fontainebleau, France; the Hong Kong UST Business School; the Indian School of Business; the International Management Institute in Geneva, Switzerland; and the International Management Development Institute in Lausanne, Switzerland, all have far more applicants than they are able to accept. This is also true in business programs at Bocconi University in Italy and in Spain's top-rated business programs.

When international managers do not succeed, it is seldom because they lack technical knowledge. Their lack of success is more frequently due to an inability to understand and adapt to an unfamiliar culture—a lack of skills. Doing business requires specialized language knowledge of labor laws, tax codes, legal constraints, and accounting concepts. Understanding such differences involves diagnostic skills. While one key component to such adaptation is the ability to communicate in the language of that culture, understanding culture goes beyond understanding language. Some cultures, for instance, put great emphasis on punctuality while others are far more casual about time. In some cultures it is considered bad taste to "get right to business" before exchanging social pleasantries. In the United States, managers generally "make" decisions, while in many other cultures, managers "take" decisions—obtain decisions from others in a more highly participative manner. Being able to correctly diagnose the situation is vitally important and the skill involved can be improved through training.

Organizations that recognize the importance of international and cross-cultural training are reaping the benefits of such training. A recent study found that 69 percent of companies surveyed used cross-cultural training for those moving to overseas assignments. This type of training is expensive, however. One- or two-day cross-cultural workshops can cost as much as $5,000 or more per family being relocated. Nevertheless, many companies find it highly valuable and well worth the cost. For example, of 800 employees receiving cross-cultural training before being sent to Saudi Arabia, Shell Oil found that only three returned to the United States early, a considerable improvement over its past experience. At SC Johnson Wax, the use of training has reduced the failure rate for overseas managers to less than 2 percent, again a significant improvement.

Case Questions

Go Online

1. In what way does this case suggest that the skill set for success in management is changing?
2. How should companies respond to this change?
3. What might be the costs and benefits of international training?
4. Which particular diagnostic skills seem to be important for overseas assignments?
5. If you were interested in working for an international company in an overseas location, which of your skills would be compatible? What skills do you think you would lack? How would you go about acquiring those essential skills?

Case References

Gretchen Lang, "Cross-cultural training: How much difference does it really make?" *New York Times*, January 24, 2004 http://www.nytimes.com/2004/01/24/news/24iht-rcross_ed3_.html; Rita Bennett, Anne Aston, and Tracy Colquhoun (2000). "Cross-cultural training: A critical step in ensuring the success of international assignments," *Human Resource Management*, 39 (2–3), 239–250; Noel J. Shumsky, "Justifying the Intercultural Training Investment," *The Journal of European Business*, September 1, 1992, pp. 38–43; Shari Caudron, "Training Ensures Success Overseas," *Personnel Journal*, December 1, 1991, pp. 27–31; Kenneth Labich, "What Our Kids Must Learn," *Fortune*, January 27, 1992, pp. 64–66.

EXTEND

EXTENDING YOUR DIAGNOSTIC SKILLS

Your instructor may use one or more of these **Group Extensions** to provide you with yet another opportunity to develop your time-management skills. On the other hand, you may continue your development on your own by doing one or more of the **Individual Extensions**. These **Group Extensions** are repeated exactly for each of the seven specific skills. Doing the same **Extension** for different skills will help you to sharpen both the skills and understand the subtle differences between the several skills.

GROUP EXTENSIONS

- Form small groups of students. Have each group select an organization and a management position. Then have them identify the diagnostic skills needed by a person in that position.

- Form small groups of students. Have each group identify a problem or opportunity facing a business or other organization. Then have them identify the diagnostic skills needed by managers in dealing with that problem or opportunity.
- Form small groups of students. Have them identify a problem or opportunity facing a business or other organization. Assign each group to identify the diagnostic skills needed by managers in dealing with that problem or opportunity.
- Form small groups of students. Assign each group one or more corporations to analyze. Have each group identify the members who serve on its board of directors and research their backgrounds. Then have the students describe the diagnostic skills of those directors.
- Form small groups of students. Have each group select a job they see regularly (e.g., retail clerk, fast-food worker). Ask them to describe the diagnostic skills needed on that job.
- Form small groups of students. Have students sketch the diagnostic skills they would need if they were going to start a specific type of new business.
- Form small groups of students. Have each group identify examples they have recently faced that illustrate a situation that called for them to use diagnostic skills.

INDIVIDUAL EXTENSIONS

- Go to the library and research a company. Characterize its level of effectiveness and identify the diagnostic skills of its top executives. Share your results with the class.
- Select a highly visible manager and analyze his or her diagnostic skills.
- Interview a manager from a local organization. Learn about the diagnostic skills he or she needs to perform effectively.
- Think of someone you know who is a manager. Describe that person's management position in terms of the type of organization, level in the organization, and the area of management in which he or she practices. What diagnostic skills does that person need to be effective?
- Plan a hypothetical change in your school focusing on the use of diagnostic skills.
- Search the Internet for examples of diagnostic skills in management and compare what you find with the information presented here.

YOUR DIAGNOSTIC SKILLS NOW

DIAGNOSTIC SKILLS ASSESSMENT

Now that you have completed Chapter 6, it is time again to assess your diagnostic skills. To do so, complete the following instrument. Think about your current situation, job, or organization of which you are a member. You should respond in terms of your current situation and not by how you think you should respond or a manager should respond. If a statement doesn't pertain to your current situation, respond in terms of what you think would be accurate for you in that situation.

Use this scale in your responses.

1	2	3	4	5
Not true at all	Somewhat untrue	Sometimes true Sometimes not	Somewhat true	Completely true

Total your scores and record them in the table at the end of instrument.

Given that many experts suggest the use of 360° feedback in performance appraisal, you may find it useful to obtain the views of others about your diagnostic skills. You may get a form from your instructor that is designed for others to complete about you, and then record their scores in the table as well. Areas where there is a large discrepancy between your views and those of others should draw your attention and you should spend more time on developing those skills.

DIAGNOSTIC SKILLS

[**Note: The numbers correspond to those on the baseline assessment in Appendix A.**]

____ 171. I act independently when it is necessary.
____ 172. I adapt quickly to new situations.
____ 173. I am able to visualize the major aspects of problems.
____ 174. I am prepared to bend the rules if necessary.
____ 175. I am systematic and methodical.
____ 176. I am willing to compromise to get agreement.
____ 177. I analyze facts before making decisions.
____ 178. I approach problems by first trying to determine the root cause(s).
____ 179. I ask questions about difficult problems before trying to solve them.
____ 180. I assure that those in my group have the resources needed to succeed.
____ 181. I break problems down into their component parts to better solve them.
____ 182. I define the problem before trying to solve it.
____ 183. I develop potential solutions to problems.
____ 184. I diagnose causes of poor performance before acting to correct it.
____ 185. I focus on questions and problems important to the organization.
____ 186. I frequently have ideas about how to improve group activities.
____ 187. I generally can quickly identify key issues.
____ 188. I identify easy tasks and get them out of the way before tackling more difficult ones.
____ 189. I identify limits to solutions to help overcome them.
____ 190. I like a challenging climate to work in.
____ 191. I like to get the details right.
____ 192. I pitch in and lead by example.
____ 193. I seek to understand the symptoms of a problem in order to develop solutions.
____ 194. I try to focus group discussions on the problem at hand.
____ 195. I try to get divergent views on a problem and its solution.
____ 196. I try to get others to develop potential solutions to problems.

____ 197. I try to help others understand and solve problems.
____ 198. I try to take advantage of opportunities as they arise.
____ 199. I use information from my communication networks in analyzing problems.
____ 200. I usually "look before I leap."

Summary of Your Scores

Skill (max. possible score)	Your Score Now	Scores from Others	Your Score From Chapter 1
Diagnostic (150)			

Interpretation of Your Scores

Compare your score with the one you reported at the beginning of Chapter 1. If there is no or only a modest improvement in your score, you should examine the same set of items from the **Managerial Skills Assessment** from Chapter 1 and compare each of them with these to see where change has and has not occurred. You should then spend more time on developing the particular skills where change either decreased or stayed the same.

INTERPRETATIONS

HOW IS YOUR ORGANIZATION MANAGED?

Compare your Total Score with the totals in the table below. High scores indicate a highly organic and participative organization. Low scores are associated with a mechanistic or bureaucratically managed organization.

Bureaucratic System 1				Mixed Systems 2 and 3				Organic System 4	
0–9	10–19	20–29	30–39	40–49	50–59	60–69	70–79	80–89	90–100

ORGANIZATIONAL CLIMATE QUESTIONNAIRE

INTERPRET

You were told to think back to work or other organizational experiences and respond to each statement by circling the response that best fits your impression of the organization. You then totaled your scores.

The higher your score on Communication, the more open the organization is to communication exchanges throughout the organization. The higher your score on Role, the clearer roles are in the organization. The higher your score on Structure, the more informal the organization is. The higher your score on Responsibility, the more lower level members of the organization assume responsibility for getting the tasks accomplished.

The higher your score on Rewards, the fairer the organizational reward system is. And, finally, the higher your total scores, the more favorable the organization's climate is and the more control is dispersed and shared throughout the organization rather than being held exclusively in the hands of upper management.

ASSESSING YOUR FEEDBACK STYLE

The score on Part 1 indicates, or is suggestive of, your tendency to use the problem-solving method in providing feedback to others. Your score on Part 2 indicates your preference for the tell-and-sell method of providing feedback. Each of us has the ability to use both methods. Based on your score, which method do you prefer?

Two approaches to performance appraisal were noted by Maier, who described the objectives, assumptions, employee reactions, and supervisor skills associated with each method. The tell-and-sell method, which is the more commonly applied of the two, has two objectives: (1) to communicate evaluation and (2) to persuade the employee to improve. It is based on four assumptions: (a) the employee desires to correct weaknesses if he or she knows them, (b) any person can improve if she or he so chooses, (c) a superior is qualified to evaluate a subordinate, and (d) people profit from criticism and appreciate help. The skills required on the part of the supervisor are sales skills and patience. The employee usually reacts in three ways: (1) suppressed defensive behavior, (2) attempts to cover hostility, and (3) little change in performance.

The objective of the problem-solving method is to stimulate growth and development in the employee. It is based on three assumptions: (a) growth can occur without correcting faults, (b) discussing job problems leads to improved performance, and (c) discussion develops new ideas and mutual interests. The skills required of the supervisor are: (1) listening and reflecting feelings, (2) reflecting ideas, (3) using exploratory questions, and (4) summarizing. The reaction is often problem-solving behavior and employee commitment to the changes or objectives discussed because they are his or her ideas.

ORGANIZATIONAL STRUCTURE PREFERENCES

This assessment suggests your relative preference for a mechanistic versus organic organizational structure. Your M score indicates your relative preference for mechanistic organizations and your O score indicates your relative preference for organic organizations.

Some of the characteristics of each type of organization are shown below.

Mechanistic

1. Tasks are specialized and rigidly defined.
2. Roles (rights, obligations, and technical methods) are precisely defined.
3. The structure of control, authority, and communication is hierarchical.
4. Communication is primarily vertical and is in the form of instructions from superiors and requests for decisions from subordinates.
5. Loyalty and obedience are required.
6. Importance and prestige is associated with the organization and its members.

Organic

1. Tasks are interdependent and flexible.
2. Roles are general.
3. The structure of control, authority, and communication is based on networks.
4. Communication is both vertical and horizontal and takes the form of information and advice.
5. Organizational commitment is valued over loyalty or obedience.
6. Importance and prestige are associated with expertise and professional associations.

ENDNOTES

[1] For a complete discussion of how FedEx uses control in its operations, see "The FedEx Edge," *Fortune*, April 3, 2006, pp. 77–84.

[2] William Taylor, "Control in an Age of Chaos," *Harvard Business Review*, November–December 1994, pp. 64–70.

[3] "Fastener Woes to Delay Flight of First Boeing 787 Jets," *The Wall Street Journal*, November 5, 2008, p. B1.

[4] "Marriage at 30,000 Feet," *Bloomberg Businessweek*, February 6–12, 2012, pp. 58–63.

[5] "Starbucks Brews Up New Cost Cuts By Putting Lid on Afternoon Decaf," *The Wall Street Journal*, January 28, 2009, p. B1.

[6] Mark Kroll, Peter Wright, Leslie Toombs, and Hadley Leavell, "Form of Control: A Critical Determinant of Acquisition Performance and CEO Rewards," *Strategic Management Journal*, 1997, vol. 18, no. 2, pp. 85–96.

[7] For an example, see Donald Lange, "A Multidimensional Conceptualization of Organizational Corruption Control," *Academy of Management Review*, 2008, Vol. 33, No. 3, pp. 710–729.

[8] Karynne Turner and Mona Makhija, "The Role of Organizational Controls in Managing Knowledge," *Academy of Management Review*, 2006, vol. 31, no. 1, pp. 197–217.

[9] Sim Sitkin, Kathleen Sutcliffe, and Roger Schroeder, "Distinguishing Control from Learning in Total Quality Management: A Contingency Perspective," *Academy of Management Review*, 1994, vol. 19, no. 3, pp. 537–564.

[10] Quoted in *Bloomberg Businessweek*, February 6–12, 2012, p. 61.

[11] Robert Lusch and Michael Harvey, "The Case for an Off-Balance-Sheet Controller," *Sloan Management Review*, Winter 1994, pp. 101–110.

[12] Edward E. Lawler III and John G. Rhode, *Information and Control in Organizations* (Pacific Palisades, Calif.: Goodyear, 1976).

[13] Charles W. L. Hill, "Establishing a Standard: Competitive Strategy and Technological Standards in Winner-Take-All Industries," *Academy of Management Executive*, 1997, vol. 11, no. 2, pp. 7–16.

[14] "Airbus Clips Superjumbo Production," *The Wall Street Journal*, May 7, 2009, p. B1.

[15] *USA Today*, April 13, 2009, p. 3B.

[16] "An Efficiency Guru Refits Honda to Fight Auto Giants," *The Wall Street Journal*, September 15, 1999, p. B1.

[17] "Workers, Surf at Your Own Risk," *BusinessWeek*, June 12, 2000, pp. 105–106.

[18] "Enterprise Takes Idea of Dressed for Success to a New Extreme," *The Wall Street Journal*, November 20, 2002, p. B1.

[19] Quoted in *HR Magazine*, January 2012, p. 31.

[20] B. F. Skinner, *Beyond Freedom and Dignity* (New York: Knopf, 1971). See also Raymond A. Noe, Michael J. Tews, and Alison McConnell Dachner, "Learner Engagement: A New Perspective for Enhancing Our Understanding of Learner Motivation and Workplace Learning," in *The Academy of Management Annals 2010* (James P. Walsh and Arthur P. Brief, Editors) Taylor and Francis, Philadelphia Pennsylvania, 2010, pp. 279–316.

[21] Fred Luthans and Robert Kreitner, *Organizational Behavior Modification and Beyond: An Operant and Social Learning Approach* (Glenview, Ill.: Scott, Foresman, 1985).

[22] W. Clay Hamner and Ellen P. Hamner, "Behavior Modification on the Bottom Line," *Organizational Dynamics*, Spring 1976, pp. 2–21.

[23] "At Emery Air Freight: Positive Reinforcement Boosts Performance," *Organizational Dynamics*, Winter 1973, pp. 41–50; for a recent update, see Alexander D. Stajkovic and Fred Luthans, "A Meta-Analysis of the Effects of Organizational Behavior Modification on Task Performance, 1975–95," *Academy of Management Journal*, 1997, vol. 40, no. 5, pp. 1122–1149.

[24] David J. Glew, Anne M. O'Leary-Kelly, Ricky W. Griffin, and David D. Van Fleet, "Participation in Organizations: A Preview of the Issues and Proposed Framework for Future Analysis," *Journal of Management*, 1995, vol. 21, no. 3, pp. 395–421.

[25] Quoted in *Fortune*, February 6, 2012, p. 99.

[26] Robert E. Quinn and Gretchen M. Spreitzer, "The Road to Empowerment: Seven Questions Every Leader Should Consider," *Organizational Dynamics*, Autumn 1997, pp. 37–47.

[27] "On Factory Floors, Top Workers Hide Secrets to Success," *The Wall Street Journal*, July 1, 2002, pp. A1, A10.

[28] Russ Forrester, "Empowerment: Rejuvenating a Potent Idea," *Academy of Management Executive*, 2000, vol. 14, no. 3, pp. 67–77.

[29] Baxter W. Graham, "The Business Argument for Flexibility, *HRMagazine*, May 1996, pp. 104–110.

[30] A. R. Cohen and H. Gadon, *Alternative Work Schedules: Integrating Individual and Organizational Needs* (Reading, Mass.: Addison Wesley, 1978). See also Ellen Ernst Kossek and Jesse S. Michel, "Flexible Work Schedules," in Sheldon Zedeck, (Ed.), *Handbook of Industrial and Organizational Psychology* (American Psychological Association: Washington, D.C., 2010).

[31] "How Telecommuting Lets Workers Mobilize for Sustainability," GreenBiz.com, February 17, 2011; "Study: Telecommuting can Save American Households $1.7 Billion per Year," SmartPlanet.com, March 16, 2011.

[32] Barry Gerhart, Sara L. Rynes, Ingrid Smithey Fulmer, "Pay and Performance: Individuals, Groups, and Executives," in *The Academy of Management Annals 2009* (James P. Walsh and Arthur P. Brief, Editors) Taylor and Francis, Philadelphia Pennsylvania, 2009, pp. 251–316. See also Joseph J. Martocchio, "Strategic Reward and Compensation Plans," in Sheldon Zedeck, (Ed.), *Handbook of Industrial and Organizational Psychology* (American Psychological Association: Washington, D.C., 2010).

[33] Daniel Wren, *The Evolution of Management Theory*, 4th ed. (New York: Wiley, 1994).

[34] Eric Krell, "All for Incentives, Incentives for All," *HR Magazine*, January 2011, pp. 34–38.

[35] C. Wiley, "Incentive Plan Pushes Production," *Personnel Journal*, August 1993, p. 91.

[36] "When Money Isn't Enough," *Forbes*, November 18, 1996, pp. 164–169.

[37] Jacquelyn DeMatteo, Lillian Eby, and Eric Sundstrom, "Team-Based Rewards: Current Empirical Evidence and Directions for Future Research," in L. L. Cummings and Barry Staw (eds.), *Research in Organizational Behavior*, vol. 20 (Greenwich, Conn.: JAI, 1998), pp. 141–183.

[38] Theresa M. Welbourne and Luis R. Gomez-Mejia, "Gainsharing: A Critical Review and a Future Research Agenda," *Journal of Management*, 1995, vol. 21, no. 3, pp. 559–609.

[39] "A Statistical Profile of Employee Ownership," The National Center for Employee Ownership, March 2010.

[40] Steve Kerr, "The Best-Laid Incentive Plans," *Harvard Business Review*, January 2003, pp. 27–40.

[41] "Now It's Getting Personal," *BusinessWeek*, December 16, 2002, pp. 90–92.

CHAPTER 7

ASSESSING YOUR COMMUNICATION SKILLS

A Communication Skills Survey
Becoming Aware of Your Communication Style
Feedback Skills Questionnaire
Gender Differences in Communication

LEARNING ABOUT COMMUNICATION SKILLS

The Meaning of Communication
- *The Role of Communication in Management*
- *The Communication Process*

Forms of Communication in Organizations
- *Interpersonal Communication*
- *Communication in Networks and Work Teams*
- *Organizational Communication*
- *Electronic Communication*

Informal Communication in Organizations
- *The Grapevine*
- *Management by Wandering Around*
- *Nonverbal Communication*

Managing Organizational Communication
- *Barriers to Communication*
- *Improving Communication Effectiveness*

Summary and a Look Ahead

VISUALIZING COMMUNICATION SKILLS

Communication Skills in Action—1
Communication Skills in Action—2

PRACTICING COMMUNICATION SKILLS

Alone or Together?
"Best/Worst" Presentations
Can You Communicate Accurately?
Communicating a Change in Strategy
Ethical Issues
Communicating Human Resource Information
Communication in International Business
Announcing Unpopular Decisions
Slide Presentation
Communicating Across Time Zones

USING COMMUNICATION SKILLS

Japan and America—Alike but Different
Workplace Violence

EXTENDING YOUR COMMUNICATION SKILLS

Group Extensions
Individual Extensions

YOUR COMMUNICATION SKILLS NOW

Communication Skills Assessment
Communication Skills
- *Summary of Your Scores*
- *Interpretation of Your Scores*

INTERPRETATIONS

A Communication Skills Survey
Becoming Aware of Your Communication Style
Feedback Skills Questionnaire
Gender Differences in Communication

Communication Skills

DMITRIY SHIRONOSOV

As noted several times earlier in the book, communication skills overlap or interact with numerous other skills and so merit particular attention. This chapter focuses on helping you develop your own communication skills. We start with an overall view of communication, and then provide detailed text material to help you learn more about it. We discuss various barriers to communication and recommend ways to overcome those barriers. Following the text section there are several cases and exercises to help you further develop and master effective communication skills.

ASSESS

ASSESSING YOUR COMMUNICATION SKILLS

A COMMUNICATION SKILLS SURVEY

This survey will help you to understand the characteristics of a good communicator while gaining insights into your own communication skills.

Instructions:

Think back to work or other organizational experiences and respond to each statement below by circling the response that best fits your attitudes and behaviors.

Statements	Strongly Agree	Slightly Agree	Not Sure	Slightly Disagree	Strongly Disagree
1. When responding, I try to use specific details or examples.	5	4	3	2	1
2. I tend to talk more than others.	1	2	3	4	5
3. If the other person seems not to understand me, I try to speak more slowly and more distinctly.	5	4	3	2	1
4. I tend to forget that some words have many meanings.	1	2	3	4	5
5. When I give feedback, I respond to the facts and keep the feelings out of it.	1	2	3	4	5
6. I am not embarrassed by periods of silence when I'm talking to someone.	5	4	3	2	1
7. I concentrate hard to avoid distracting nonverbal cues.	5	4	3	2	1
8. Listening and hearing are the same things.	1	2	3	4	5
9. I make sure the person wants feedback before I give it.	5	4	3	2	1
10. I avoid saying, "Good," "Go on," etc., while the other person is speaking.	5	4	3	2	1
11. I try to delay giving feedback so I can have more time to think it through.	1	2	3	4	5
12. I enjoy using slang and quaint local expressions.	1	2	3	4	5
13. My feedback focuses on how the other person can use my ideas.	5	4	3	2	1
14. Body language is important for speakers, not listeners.	1	2	3	4	5
15. I use technical jargon only when talking to experts.	5	4	3	2	1
16. When someone is wrong, I make sure he knows it.	1	2	3	4	5

ASSESS

17. I try to express my ideas in general, overall terms.	1	2	3	4	5
18. When I'm listening, I try not to be evaluative.	5	4	3	2	1

Scoring:

Complete the scoring sheet below. The higher your score, the better are your skills.

Communication Skills Survey Scoring Sheet

(1) *Transfer your numeric responses from the survey onto this scoring sheet, and sum the categories and total. For instance, your Feedback Skill score is the sum of your responses to Statements 1, 5, 9, 11, 13, and 16.*

	Feedback Skill		Listening Skill		Articulation Skill		
	1.____		2.____		3.____		
	5.____		6.____		4.____		
	9.____		8.____		7.____		
	11.____		10.____		12.____		
	13.____		14.____		15.____		
	16.____		18.____		17.____		
Totals	____	+	____	+	____	=	____

(2) *Place an X on each of the three continuums below to mark your subtotals.*

Feedback Skills (high) |---------|---------|---------|---------|---------|---------| (low)

Listening Skills (high) |---------|---------|---------|---------|---------|---------| (low)

Articulation Skills (high) |---------|---------|---------|---------|---------|---------| (low)

30 25 20 15 10 5 0

(3) *Place an X on the Communication Skills Continuum below to mark your total score.*

|--------|--------|--------|--------|--------|--------|--------|--------|--------|--------|

100 90 80 70 60 50 40 30 20 10 0

Organizational Climate Continuum

Source: From Burton. *Exercises in Management*, 3E. © 1990 South-Western, a part of Cengage Learning, Inc. Reproduced by permission. www.cengage.com/permissions

See Interpretations at the end of the chapter.

BECOMING AWARE OF YOUR COMMUNICATION STYLE

Communication pervades all managerial activities and encompasses much of a manager's time. Your communication style has a tremendous influence on how effectively you are able to communicate. This self-assessment helps you to become aware of your current communication style.

Instructions:

Assess how true each of the following statements is of you. For each statement, rate yourself according to the following scale:

Rating Scale
5 – Definitely true of me
4 – Probably true of me
3 – Neither true or not true; undecided
2 – Probably not true of me
1 – Definitely not true of me

_____ 1. I can be impulsive.
_____ 2. I get angry easily.
_____ 3. I get frustrated when arguing with others.
_____ 4. Others say that I am a poor listener.
_____ 5. I have low tolerance for disagreement.
_____ 6. I interrupt frequently.
_____ 7. I speak more than others in most conversations.
_____ 8. Other people say that I can be impatient.
_____ 9. I stand close to others when talking to them.
_____ 10. I tend to react instantly to negative situations.
_____ 11. I tend to speak in a loud voice.
_____ 12. Others say that I do not listen well.
_____ 13. I tend to stand or sit erectly when talking to others.
_____ 14. I tend to talk fast.
_____ 15. I tend to use piercing eye contact.
_____ 16. Others say that I don't show appreciation.
_____ 17. I use "you" statements—you should do this, you ought to know that.
_____ 18. I would prefer that everyone be like me.
_____ 19. Other people say that I have difficulty seeing their points of view.
_____ 20. When expressing my view, I frequently point or shake a finger.
_____ 21. I frequently think that people don't consider my feelings.
_____ 22. I often indicate agreement even though I don't really agree.
_____ 23. I am reluctant to express my own wants and feelings.
_____ 24. Others say that I don't speak up when I should.
_____ 25. I don't seem to get what I want in discussions.
_____ 26. I tend to avoid eye contact especially when a disagreement occurs.
_____ 27. I am hesitant to make my views known.
_____ 28. Other people say that I speak softly.
_____ 29. I generally let others make decisions for me.
_____ 30. I smile and nod in agreement when listening to others.
_____ 31. I spend a lot of time asking for advice or assistance.
_____ 32. Others say that I apologize a great deal.
_____ 33. I try to understand both sides of issues to avoid conflict.
_____ 34. I generally don't get the credit I deserve.
_____ 35. I usually have a slumped or very relaxed body posture when talking to others.
_____ 36. Others say that I ask permission unnecessarily.

_____ 37. I tend to say "You should do it" a lot.
_____ 38. I avoid confrontations.
_____ 39. Other people say that I don't want to "make waves."
_____ 40. When talking I speak in a low volume.
_____ 41. I try to maintain good eye contact with the person whom I am talking.
_____ 42. I ask about the feelings of others.
_____ 43. I try to express my feelings clearly.
_____ 44. Others say that I am even tempered.
_____ 45. I confront problems at the time they happen.
_____ 46. I listen well without interrupting.
_____ 47. I speak in a calm way without raising my voice even when disagreements occur.
_____ 48. Other people say that I have a sense of humor.
_____ 49. I use "I" statements a lot—I understand or I'll try.
_____ 50. I generally have a relaxed body posture when talking with others.
_____ 51. I try to express myself directly and honestly about my wants and feelings.
_____ 52. Others say that I am action-oriented.
_____ 53. I try to determine what alternatives or options exist in resolving disagreements.
_____ 54. I don't let negative feelings build up.
_____ 55. I try not to be judgmental.
_____ 56. Others say that I am flexible or versatile in adjusting to changing conditions.
_____ 57. I try to be realistic in my expectations.
_____ 58. I tend to vary the rate at which I talk.
_____ 59. Other people say that I do not allow others to abuse or manipulate me.
_____ 60. When speaking I tend to use open, natural gestures.

Scoring:

Total for items 1–20 _____ = your G score
Total for items 21–40 _____ = your P score
Total for items 41–60 _____ = your S score

Sources: Adapted from Wayne Weiten, Dana S. Dunn, and Elizabeth Yost Hammer. 2011. *Psychology Applied to Modern Life*, 10th ed.; Belmont, CA: Wadsworth Publishing; Ruth Sherman, Women's Business Center at www.au.af.mil/au/awc/awcgate/sba/comm_style.htm (accessed January 18, 2012); John Jackson and Lorraine Bosse-Smith. 2008. *Leveraging Your Communication Style*. Nashville, TN: Abingdon Press; Christopher L. Heffner, The CEDA Meta-Profession Project at www.cedanet.com/meta/communication_styles.htm (accessed January 25, 2012); and Serenity Online Therapy at serenityonlinetherapy.com/assertiveness.htm (accessed January 23, 2012).

See Interpretations at the end of the chapter.

FEEDBACK SKILLS QUESTIONNAIRE

Performance feedback is critical to effective organizational functioning and is one of the most important forms of communication a manager employs. This assessment will provide you with an indication of your skill in providing performance feedback.

Instructions:

Using the following scale, in the spaces at the left of each item indicate the degree to which you agree or disagree that the statement is like you. Mark your answers as accurately and frankly as possible. Try not to guess how feedback should be provided.

ASSESS

For each statement, rate yourself according to the following scale:

Rating Scale
5 – Definitely true of me
4 – Probably true of me
3 – Neither true or not true; undecided
2 – Probably not true of me
1 – Definitely not true of me

_____ 1. I try to get right to the point rather than "beating around the bush."
_____ 2. I focus on what the person has done rather than on characteristics of the person.
_____ 3. I express my appreciation for work well done.
_____ 4. I say things like "there are errors in your work" rather than "you need to check your work more carefully."
_____ 5. I focus on facts and observations rather than opinions.
_____ 6. I provide both positive and constructive feedback but not in the same sentence.
_____ 7. When giving negative feedback, I try to get the person to acknowledge the concern and suggest how improvements could be made.
_____ 8. I ask the person to provide their own evaluation first.
_____ 9. I generally first ask whether the other person wants feedback.
_____ 10. When giving positive or negative feedback, I try to establish goals for the future.
_____ 11. I ask the person to indicate what I have said to assure that he or she understood me.
_____ 12. I express concern when performance is below expectations.
_____ 13. I provide feedback as soon as I can after the behavior has occurred.
_____ 14. I always use face-to-face meetings when providing feedback.
_____ 15. When giving positive or negative feedback, I provide specific information rather than making general statements such as "your work is excellent" or "your work needs improvement."

Scoring:
Compute your Feedback Skill score by adding the values you indicated on the 15 items above: _____

Sources: Adapted from Elaine D. Pulakos. 2004. *Performance Management.* Alexandria, VA: SHRM Foundation; Marty Brounstein, Giving Constructive Feedback. www.dummies.com/how-to/content/giving-constructive-feedback.html (accessed January 18, 2012); Kenneth N. Wexley. 1986. Appraisal Interview. In R. A. Berk (Ed.), *Performance Assessment.* Baltimore: Johns Hopkins University Press, 167–185; Van Fleet, D. D., Peterson, T. O., & Van Fleet, E. W. 2005. Closing the Performance Feedback Gap With Expert Systems. *Academy of Management Executive,* 19(3): 38–53; Susan M. Heathfield, Provide Feedback that Has an Impact. humanresources.about.com/cs/communication/ht/Feedbackimpact.htm (accessed January 18, 2012).

See Interpretations at the end of the chapter.

GENDER DIFFERENCES IN COMMUNICATION

With substantial numbers of women in the workforce, communication between men and women has increased, and will continue to do so. The following assessment surveys your beliefs and values about communication differences between men and women.

Instructions:
Mark each statement as either True or False. Even if it may be difficult to make a decision on some items, force yourself to make a choice.

True/False

_____ 1. Men and women communicate differently.
_____ 2. Men interrupt more than women.
_____ 3. Males and females have very different language skills.
_____ 4. Men are more aggressive and can throw things further.
_____ 5. Men's and women's brains are hardwired differently when it comes to language.
_____ 6. Females talk more than males.
_____ 7. Females are more verbally skilled than males.
_____ 8. Females use language cooperatively, because they prefer harmony and equality.
_____ 9. Females seek to connect with others, while males use language with the intention of accomplishing things.
_____ 10. Males are more direct and not as polite in communicating.

Source: Adapted from Y. K. Fulbright, 2011. "Male-Female Communication: Debunking the Mars-Venus Myth." *The Huffington Post* at www.huffingtonpost.com (accessed November 7, 2011); D. Cameron (2007). *The Myth of Mars and Venus*. Oxford University Press; and S. Poole, (October 19, 2007); *The Guardian* at www.guardian.co.uk (accessed November 7, 2011).

See Interpretations at the end of the chapter.

GO ONLINE to the Griffin/Van Fleet Assessment Library for online versions of these and other assessments.

LEARN

LEARNING ABOUT COMMUNICATION SKILLS

The Meaning of Communication
The Role of Communication in Management
The Communication Process
Forms of Communication in Organizations
Interpersonal Communication
Oral Communication
Written Communication
Choosing the Right Form
Communication in Networks and Work Teams
Organizational Communication
Vertical Communication
Horizontal Communication
Electronic Communication
Information Systems
Personal Electronic Technology
Informal Communication in Organizations
The Grapevine
Management by Wandering Around
Nonverbal Communication
Managing Organizational Communication
Barriers to Communication
Individual Barriers
Organizational Barriers
Improving Communication Effectiveness
Individual Skills
Organizational Skills
Summary and a Look Ahead

A typical day for a manager includes sending, reading, and replying to emails, texts, telephone calls, and print correspondence; attending meetings; reading about current events online; and having private conversations with others.[1] Each of these activities involves communication. In fact, most managers typically spend more than half their time on some form of communication. Because communication always involves two or more people, other behavioral processes, such as motivation, leadership, and group and team interactions all come into play. Top executives, in particular, must handle communication effectively if they are to be true leaders. Hence, all managers must strive to develop and refine their communication skills.

communication the process of transmitting information from one person to another

effective communication the process of sending a message in such a way that the message received is as close in meaning as possible to the message intended

THE MEANING OF COMMUNICATION

Imagine three managers working in an office building. The first is alone and is yelling to a subordinate for help. No one appears, but he continues to yell. The second is talking to a subordinate on a cell phone, but a poor signal causes the subordinate to misunderstand some important numbers the manager gives her. As a result, the subordinate sends 1,500 crates of eggs to 150 Fifth Street instead of 150 crates of eggs to 1500 Fifteenth Street. The third manager is talking in her office with a subordinate who clearly hears and understands what is being said. Each of these managers is attempting to communicate, but with different results.

Communication is the process of transmitting information from one person to another. Did any of our three managers communicate? The last did, and the first did not. What about the second? In fact, she did communicate; she transmitted information, and information was received. The problem was that the message transmitted and the message received were not the same. The words spoken by the manager were distorted by static and noise. **Effective communication**, then, is the process of sending a message in such a way that the message received is as close in meaning as possible to the message intended. Although the second manager engaged in communication, it was not effective. From one perspective, then, the proper use of communication skills will enhance the probability that a general communication exchange will be effective.

Our definition of effective communication is based on the ideas of meaning and consistency of meaning. Meaning is the idea that the individual who initiates the communication exchange wishes to convey. In effective communication, the meaning is transmitted in such a way that the receiving person understands it. For example, consider these messages:

1. The high today will be 95 degrees.
2. It will be hot today.
3. Ceteris paribus.
4. X16**q zabb& 37.

You generally understand the meaning of the first statement. The second statement may seem clear at first, but it is somewhat less clear than the first statement because hot is a relative condition, and the word can mean different things to different people. Fewer still understand the third statement, because it is written in Latin. No one will understand the last statement because it is written in a secret code!

The Role of Communication in Management

We noted earlier the variety of activities that fill a manager's day. Meetings, telephone calls, and correspondence are all a necessary part of every manager's job—and all clearly involve communication. To better understand the linkages between communication and management, recall the variety of roles that managers must fill. Each of the ten basic managerial roles discussed in Chapter 1 (see *Table 1.1*) would be impossible to fill without communication.[2] Interpersonal roles involve interacting with supervisors, subordinates, peers, and others outside the organization. Decisional roles require managers to seek out information to use in making decisions and then communicate those decisions to others. Informational roles focus specifically on acquiring and disseminating information.

Communication also relates directly to the basic management functions of planning, organizing, leading, and controlling. These connections, in turn, also highlight the interdependence of communication skills with other key skills already discussed such as diagnostic, conceptual, time management, and interpersonal skills. Environmental scanning, integrating planning-time horizons, and decision making, for example, all necessitate communication. Delegation, coordination, and organization change and development do as well. Developing reward systems and interacting with subordinates as a part of the leading function would be impossible without some form of communication. And communication is essential to establishing standards, monitoring performance, and taking corrective actions as a part of control. Clearly, then, communication is a pervasive part of virtually all managerial activities.[3]

The Communication Process

Figure 7.1 illustrates how communication generally takes place between people. The process of communication begins when one person (the sender) wants

LEARN

FIGURE 7.1 THE COMMUNICATION PROCESS

Noise can disrupt the communication process at any step. Managers must therefore understand that a conversation in the next office, a fax machine out of paper, a disabled email network, or the receiver's worries may all hinder the manager's best attempts to communicate. The numbers indicate the sequence in which steps take place.

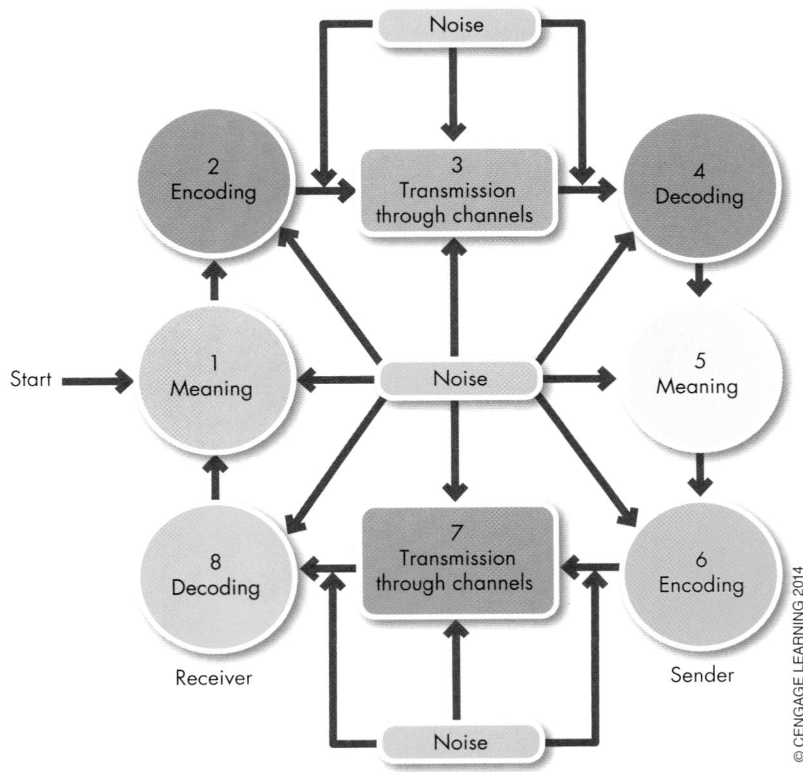

LEARN

to transmit a fact, idea, opinion, or other information to someone else (the receiver). This fact, idea, or opinion has meaning to the sender, whether it be simple and concrete or complex and abstract. For example, Linda Porter, a marketing representative at Canon, recently landed a new account and wanted to tell her boss about it. This fact and her motivation to tell her boss represented meaning.

> "Some people believe you should say something just once. But I think you get a message across by communicating it every day."
>
> JIM SINEGAL
> co-founder and CEO of Costco Wholesale[4]

FORTUNE, JULY 6, 2010, P. 44.

The next step is to encode the meaning into a form appropriate to the situation. The encoding might take the form of words, facial expressions, gestures, or even artistic expressions and physical actions. For example, the Canon representative might have said, "I just landed the Acme account," "We just got some good news from Acme," "I just spoiled Xerox's day," "Acme just made the right decision," or any number of other things. She actually chose the second message. Clearly, the encoding process is influenced by the content of the message, the familiarity of sender and receiver, and other situational factors.

After the message has been encoded, it is transmitted through the appropriate channel or medium. The channel by which this encoded message is being transmitted to you is the printed page. Common channels in organizations include meetings, email, memos, letters, reports, and telephone calls. Linda Porter might have written her boss a note, sent him an email, called him on the telephone, or dropped by his office to convey the news. Because both she and her boss were out of the office when she got the news, she called and left a message for him on his voicemail.

After the message is received, it is decoded back into a form that has meaning for the receiver. As noted earlier, the consistency of this meaning can vary dramatically. Upon hearing about the Acme deal, the sales manager at Canon might have thought, "This will mean a big promotion for both of us," "This is great news for the company," or "She's blowing her own horn too much again." His actual feelings were closest to the second statement.

REUTERS/ROBERT SORBO RSS

Jim Sinegal

In many cases, the meaning prompts a response, and the cycle is continued when a new message is sent by the same steps back to the original sender. The manager might have called the sales representative to offer congratulations, written her a personal note of praise, offered praise in an email, or sent a formal letter of acknowledgment. Linda's boss wrote her a personal note.

"Noise" may disrupt communication anywhere along the way. Noise can be the sound of someone coughing, a truck driving by, or two people talking close at hand. It can also include disruptions such as a letter lost in the mail, a dead telephone line, an interrupted cell phone call, an email misrouted or infected with a virus, or one of the participants in a conversation being called away before the communication process is completed. If the note written by Linda's boss had gotten lost, she might have felt unappreciated. As it was, his actions positively reinforced not only her efforts at Acme but also her effort to keep him informed. Another form of noise might be difficulties in understanding messages due to language barriers.

FORMS OF COMMUNICATION IN ORGANIZATIONS

Managers need to understand several kinds of communication that are common in organizations today.[5] Mastering communication skills requires that managers understand interpersonal communication, communication in networks and teams, organizational communication, and electronic communication.

Interpersonal Communication

Interpersonal communication generally takes one of two forms: oral or written. As we will see, each has clear strengths and weaknesses.

Oral Communication Oral communication takes place in conversations, group discussions, telephone calls, and other situations in which the spoken word is used to express meaning. One classic study (conducted before the advent of email) demonstrated the importance of oral communication by finding that most managers spend between 50 and 90 percent of their time talking to people.[6] Oral communication is prevalent for several reasons. The primary advantage of oral communication is that it promotes prompt feedback and interchange in the form of verbal questions or agreement, facial expressions, and gestures. Oral communication is also easy (all the sender needs to do is talk), and it can be done with little preparation (though careful preparation is advisable in certain situations). The sender does not need pencil and paper, a printer, or other equipment. In another survey, 55 percent of the executives sampled felt that their own written communication skills were fair or poor, so they chose oral communication to avoid embarrassment![7]

However, oral communication also has drawbacks. It may suffer from problems of inaccuracy if the speaker chooses the wrong words to convey meaning or leaves out pertinent details, if noise disrupts the process, or if the receiver forgets part of the message.[8] In a two-way discussion, there is seldom time for a thoughtful, considered response or for introducing many new facts, and there is no permanent record of what has been said. In addition, although most managers are comfortable talking to people individually or in small groups, fewer enjoy speaking to larger audiences.[9]

Written Communication "Putting it in writing" in a letter, report, memorandum, handwritten note, or email can solve many of the problems inherent in oral communication. Nevertheless, and perhaps surprisingly, written communication is not as common as one might imagine, nor is it a mode of communication much respected by managers. One sample of managers indicated that only 13 percent of the printed mail they received was of immediate use to them.[10] More than 80 percent of the managers who responded to another survey indicated that the written communication they received was of fair or poor quality.[11]

The biggest single drawback of traditional forms of written communication is that they inhibit feedback and interchange. When one manager sends another manager a letter, it must be written or dictated, printed, mailed, received, routed, opened, and read. If there is a misunderstanding, it may take several days for it to be recognized, let alone rectified. Although the use of email is, of course, much faster, both sender and receiver must still have access to a computer or other device, and the receiver must open and read the message for it to actually be received. A phone call could settle the whole matter in just a few minutes. Thus written communication often inhibits feedback and interchange and is usually more difficult and time consuming than oral communication.

Of course, written communication offers some advantages. It is often quite accurate and provides a permanent record of the exchange. The sender can take the time to collect and assimilate the information and can draft and revise it before it is transmitted. The receiver can take the time to read it carefully and can refer to it repeatedly, as needed. For these reasons, written communication is generally preferable when important details are involved. At times, it is important to one or both parties to have a written record available as evidence of exactly what took place. Julie Regan, founder of Toucan-Do, an importing company based in Honolulu, relies heavily on formal business letters in establishing contacts and buying merchandise from vendors in Southeast Asia. She believes that such letters give her an opportunity to think through what she wants to say, tailor her message to each individual, and avoid later misunderstandings.

Choosing the Right Form Which form of interpersonal communication should the manager use? The best medium will be determined by the situation. Oral communication or email often is preferred when the message is personal, nonroutine, and brief. More formal written communication is usually best when the message is more impersonal, routine, and longer. And, given the prominent role that emails have played in several recent court cases, managers should always use discretion when sending messages electronically.[12] For example, private emails made public during legal proceedings have played major roles in litigation involving Enron, Tyco, WorldCom, and Morgan Stanley.[13]

The manager can also combine media to capitalize on the advantages of each. For example, a quick telephone call to set up a meeting is easy and gets an immediate response. Following up the call with a reminder email or handwritten note helps ensure that the recipient will

LEARN

oral communication takes place in conversations, group discussions, telephone calls, and other situations in which the spoken word is used to express meaning

written communication relies on written media such as letters, memos, reports, emails, and web posting to convey meaning

LEARN

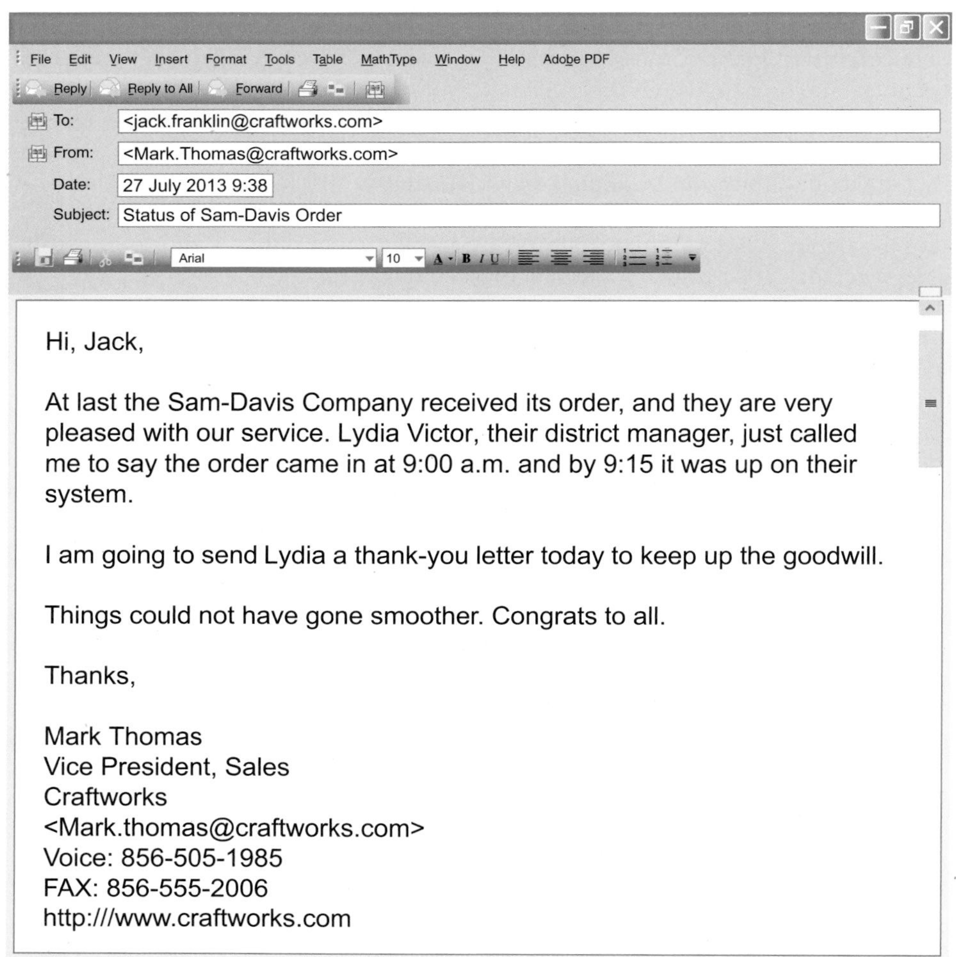

File Edit View Insert Format Tools Table MathType Window Help Adobe PDF

Reply Reply to All Forward

To: <jack.franklin@craftworks.com>

From: <Mark.Thomas@craftworks.com>

Date: 27 July 2013 9:38

Subject: Status of Sam-Davis Order

Arial 10

Hi, Jack,

At last the Sam-Davis Company received its order, and they are very pleased with our service. Lydia Victor, their district manager, just called me to say the order came in at 9:00 a.m. and by 9:15 it was up on their system.

I am going to send Lydia a thank-you letter today to keep up the goodwill.

Things could not have gone smoother. Congrats to all.

Thanks,

Mark Thomas
Vice President, Sales
Craftworks
<Mark.thomas@craftworks.com>
Voice: 856-505-1985
FAX: 856-555-2006
http:///www.craftworks.com

remember the meeting, and it provides a record of the meeting's having been called. Electronic communication, discussed more fully later, blurs the differences between oral and written communication and can help each be more effective.

> "I'm not a big emailer. I prefer face-to-face whenever possible."
>
> A.G. LAFLEY, former Procter & Gamble chairman[14]
>
> FORTUNE, DECEMBER 12, 2005, UNNUMBERED LEADERSHIP INSERT.

Communication in Networks and Work Teams

communication network the pattern through which the members of a group or team communicate

Although communication among team members in an organization is clearly interpersonal in nature, substantial research also focuses specifically on how people in networks and work teams communicate with one another. A **communication network** is the pattern through which the members of a group or team communicate. Researchers studying group dynamics have discovered several typical networks in groups and teams consisting of three, four, and five members. Representative networks among members of five-member teams are shown in *Figure 7.2*.[15]

In the wheel, or X, pattern, all communication flows through one central person, who is probably the group's leader. In a sense, the wheel is the most centralized network because one person receives and disseminates all information. The Y pattern is slightly less centralized—two people are close to the center. The chain pattern offers a more even flow of information among members,

FIGURE 7.2 COMMUNICATION IN NETWORKS AND WORK TEAMS

Research on communication networks has identified five basic networks for five-person groups and teams. These networks vary in terms of information flow, position of the leader, and effectiveness for different types of tasks. Managers might strive to create centralized networks when group or team tasks are simple and routine. Alternatively, managers can foster decentralized groups when group tasks are complex and nonroutine.

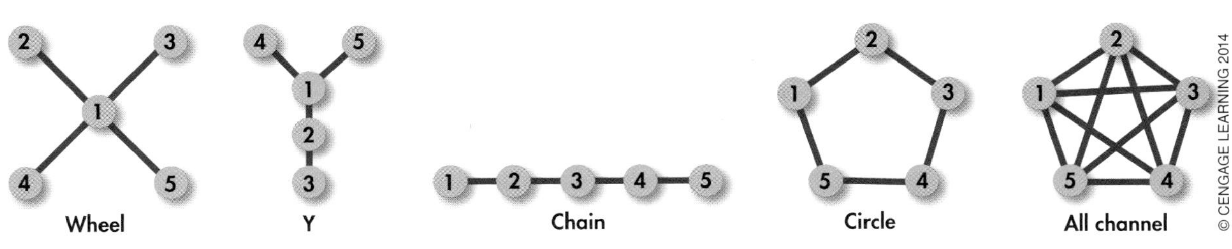

although two people (the ones at each end) interact with only one other person. This path is closed in the circle pattern. Finally, the all-channel network pattern, the most decentralized, allows a free flow of information among all group members. Everyone participates equally, and the group's leader, if there is one, is not likely to have excessive power.

Research conducted on networks suggests some interesting connections between the type of network and group performance. For example, when the group's task is relatively simple and routine, centralized networks tend to perform with greatest efficiency and accuracy. The dominant leader facilitates performance by coordinating the flow of information. When a group of accounting clerks is logging incoming invoices and distributing them for payment, for example, one centralized leader can coordinate things efficiently. When the task is complex and nonroutine, such as making a major decision about organizational strategy, decentralized networks tend to be most effective because open channels of communication permit more interaction and a more efficient sharing of relevant information. Managers should recognize the effects of communication networks on group and organizational performance and should try to structure networks accordingly.

Organizational Communication

Still other forms of communication in organizations are those that flow among and between organizational units or groups. Each of these involves oral or written communication, but each also extends to broad patterns of communication across the organization.[16] As shown in *Figure 7.3*, two of these forms of communication follow vertical and horizontal linkages in the organization.

Vertical Communication Vertical communication is communication that flows up and down the organization, usually along formal reporting lines—that is, it is the communication that takes place between managers and their superiors and subordinates. Vertical communication may involve only two people, or it may flow through several different organizational levels.

Upward communication consists of messages from subordinates to superiors. This flow is usually from subordinates to their direct superior, then to that person's direct superior, and so on up the hierarchy. Occasionally, a message might bypass a particular superior. The typical content of upward communication is requests, information that the lower-level manager thinks is of importance to the higher-level manager, responses to requests from the higher-level manager, suggestions, complaints, and financial information. Research has shown that upward communication is more subject to distortion than is downward communication. Subordinates are likely to withhold or distort information that makes them look bad. The greater the degree of difference in status between superior and subordinate and the greater the degree of distrust, the more likely the subordinate is to suppress or distort information.[17] For example, subordinates might choose to withhold information about problems from their boss if they think the news will make him angry and if they think they can solve the problem themselves without his ever knowing about it.

Downward communication occurs when information flows down the hierarchy from superiors to subordinates. The typical content of these messages

vertical communication
communication that flows up and down the organization, usually along formal reporting lines

FIGURE 7.3 FORMAL COMMUNICATION IN ORGANIZATIONS

Formal communication in organizations follows official reporting relationships or prescribed channels. For example, vertical communication, shown here with the solid lines, flows between levels in the organization and involves subordinates and their managers. Horizontal communication, shown with dashed lines, flows between people at the same level and usually is used to facilitate coordination.

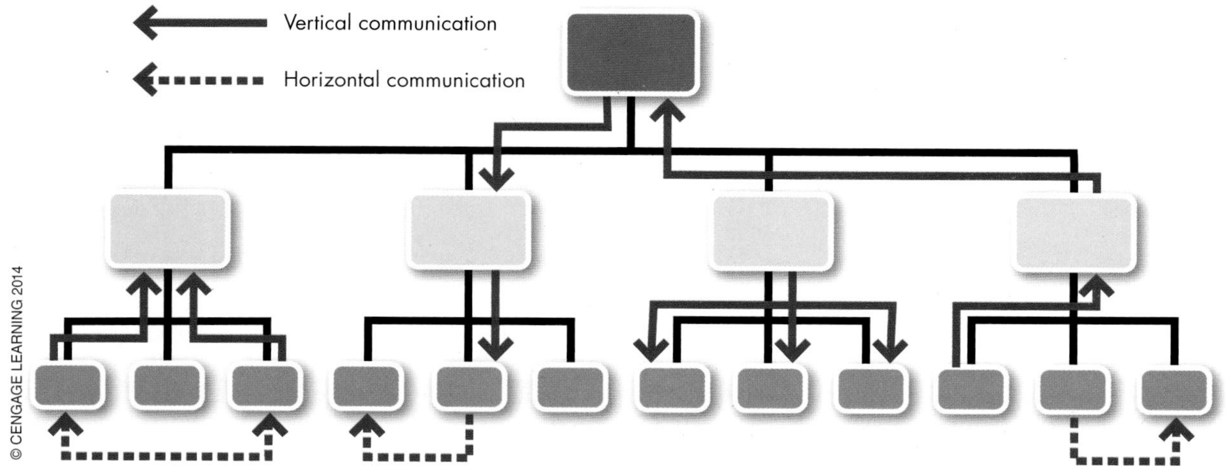

© CENGAGE LEARNING 2014

is directives on how something is to be done, the assignment of new responsibilities, performance feedback, and general information that the higher-level manager thinks will be of value to the lower-level manager. Vertical communication can and usually should be two-way in nature. In other words, give-and-take communication with active feedback is generally likely to be more effective than one-way communication.[18]

Horizontal Communication Whereas vertical communication involves a superior and a subordinate, **horizontal communication** involves colleagues and peers at the same level of the organization. For example, an operations manager might communicate to a marketing manager that inventory levels are running low and that projected delivery dates should be extended by two weeks. Horizontal communication probably occurs more among managers than among nonmanagers.

This type of communication serves a number of purposes.[19] It facilitates coordination among interdependent units. For example, a manager at Motorola was once researching the strategies of Japanese semiconductor firms in Europe. He found a great deal of information that was relevant to his assignment. He also uncovered some additional information that was potentially important to another department, so he passed it along to a colleague in that department, who used it to improve his own operations. Horizontal communication also can be used for joint problem solving, as when two plant managers at Northrop Grumman get together to work out a new method to improve productivity. Finally, horizontal communication plays a major role in work teams with members drawn from several departments.

horizontal communication involves colleagues and peers at the same level of the organization

Electronic Communication

Finally, as already noted, electronic communication has taken on much greater importance for managers in recent times. Both formal information systems and personal information technology have reshaped how managers communicate with one another.

Information Systems Most larger businesses manage at least a portion of their organizational communication through information systems. Some firms go so far as to create a position for a chief information officer, or CIO. General Mills, Xerox, and Burlington Industries all have such a position. The CIO is responsible for determining the information-processing needs and requirements of the organization and then putting in place systems that facilitate smooth and efficient organizational communication.

Part of the CIO's efforts also involves the creation of one or more formal information systems linking all relevant managers, departments, and facilities in the organization. Most enterprise resource-planning systems play this role very effectively. In the absence of such a system, a marketing manager, for example, may need to call a warehouse manager to find out how much of a particular product is in stock before promising shipping dates to a customer. An effective formal information system allows the marketing manager to get the information more quickly, and probably more accurately, by plugging directly into a computerized information system.

Personal Electronic Technology In recent years, the nature of organizational communication has changed dramatically, mainly due to breakthroughs in personal electronic communication technology, and the future promises even more change. Electronic typewriters and photocopying machines were early breakthroughs. The photocopier, for example, made it possible for a manager to have a typed report distributed to large numbers of other people in an extremely short time. Personal computers have accelerated the process even more. Email networks, the Internet, corporate intranets, social-networking sites, wireless communication systems, and other breakthroughs are carrying communication technology even further.

It is also becoming common to have teleconferences in which managers stay at their own locations (such as offices in different cities) but are seen on computer monitors as they "meet." A manager in New York can keyboard a letter or memorandum at her personal computer and via email deliver it to hundreds or even thousands of colleagues around the world in a matter of seconds. Managers can also retrieve highly detailed information with ease from large electronic databanks. This has all given rise to a new version of an old work arrangement—the cottage industry. In the cottage industry, people worked at home (in their "cottage") and periodically brought the products of their labors in to the company. Telecommuting is the label given to the new electronic cottage industry. In telecommuting, people work at home on their computers and transmit their work to their companies via telephone lines or cable modems.

Cellular telephones and facsimile machines have made it even easier for managers to communicate with business associates. Many now use cell phones to make calls while commuting to and from work, and they carry their phones with them so that they can receive calls throughout the day. Facsimile machines and scanners make it easy for people to use written communication media and get rapid feedback. And even newer personal computing devices, such as BlackBerries, iPhones, and iPads are further revolutionizing how people communicate with one another.

Psychologists, however, are beginning to associate some problems with these communication advances. For one thing, managers who seldom work in their "real" offices are likely to fall behind in their fields. They also miss much of the informal communication that takes place. Thus, they may be victims of organizational politics because they are not present to keep in touch with and protect themselves from what is going on. Moreover, the use of electronic communication at the expense of face-to-face meetings and conversations makes it hard to build a strong culture, develop solid working relationships, and create a mutually supportive atmosphere of trust and cooperation.[20] Finally, electronic communication is also opening up new avenues for dysfunctional employee behavior, such as the passing of lewd or offensive materials to others. For example, the *New York Times* once fired almost 10 percent of its workers at one of its branch offices for sending inappropriate emails at work.[21]

© IMAGE SOURCE

Teleconferencing is becoming increasingly common in today's businesses. Cost and distance, as well as the availability of new technology like Skype, are some of the causes for this trend.

INFORMAL COMMUNICATION IN ORGANIZATIONS

The forms of organizational communication discussed in the previous section all represent planned and relatively formal communication mechanisms. However, in many cases some of the communication that takes place in an organization transcends these formal channels and instead follows any of several informal methods. Effective communication skills include not

LEARN

FIGURE 7.4 INFORMAL COMMUNICATION IN ORGANIZATIONS

Informal communication in organizations may or may not follow official reporting relationships or prescribed channels. It may flow across different levels and different departments or work units, and it may or may not have anything to do with official organizational business.

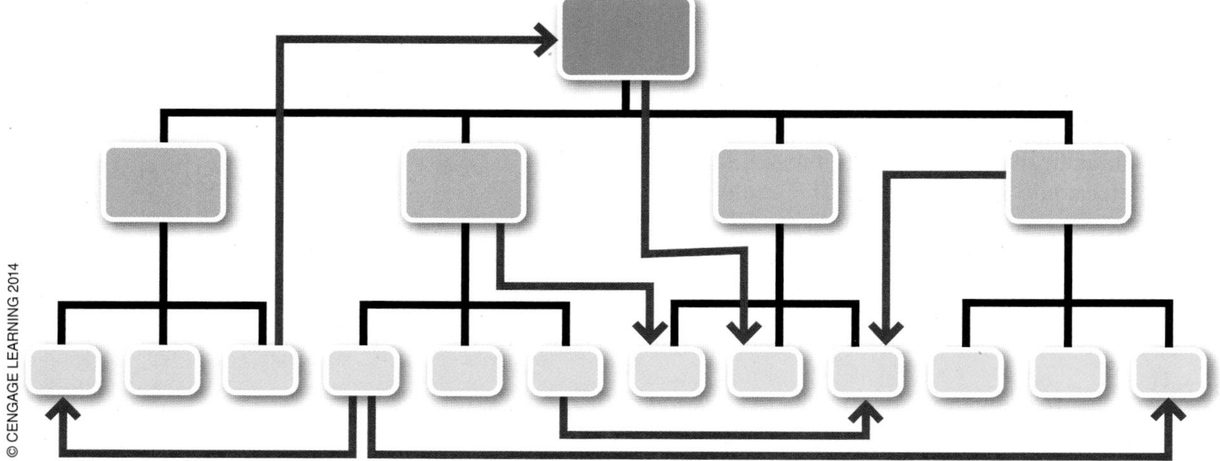

© CENGAGE LEARNING 2014

only mastering the formal mechanisms discussed earlier but also understanding these informal methods. *Figure 7.4* illustrates numerous examples of informal communication. Common forms include the grapevine, management by wandering around, and nonverbal communication.

The Grapevine

The grapevine is an informal communication network that can permeate an entire organization. Grapevines are found in all organizations except the very smallest, but they do not always follow the same patterns as, nor do they necessarily coincide with, formal channels of authority and communication. Research has identified several kinds of grapevines.[22] The two most common are illustrated in *Figure 7.5*. The *gossip chain* occurs when one person spreads the message to many other people. Each one, in turn, may either keep the information confidential or pass it on to others. The gossip chain is likely to carry personal information. The other common grapevine is the *cluster chain,* in which one person passes the information to a selected few individuals. Some of the receivers pass the information to a few other individuals; the rest keep it to themselves.

grapevine an informal communication network that can permeate an entire organization

There is some disagreement about the accuracy of information carried by the grapevine, but research increasingly finds it to be fairly accurate, especially when the information is based on fact rather than speculation. One study found that the grapevine may be between 75 percent and 95 percent accurate.[23] That same study found that informal communication is increasing in many organizations for two basic reasons. One contributing factor is the recent increase in merger, acquisition, and takeover activity. Because such activity can greatly affect the people within an organization, it follows that they may spend more time talking about it.[24] The second contributing factor is that as more and more corporations move facilities from inner cities to suburbs, employees tend to talk less and less to others outside the organization and more and more to one another. More recently, another study looked at the effects of the 2009–2010 recession and large-scale job losses on informal communication. More than half of the survey participants reported a sharp increased in gossip and rumors in their organizations. The same survey also reported an increase in the amount of eavesdropping in the majority of those businesses surveyed.[25] Interestingly, virtually all of the research on grapevines was conducted before the advent of email. It would seem likely that email has both increased the penetration of the grapevine throughout the organization. It may have increased accuracy as well, because people can forward actual messages rather than having to recall details and then verbalize the details.

Attempts to eliminate the grapevine are fruitless, but fortunately, the manager does have some control over it. By maintaining open channels of communication and

FIGURE 7.5 COMMON GRAPEVINE CHAINS IN ORGANIZATIONS

The two most common grapevine chains in organizations are the gossip chain (in which one person communicates messages to many others) and the cluster chain (in which many people pass messages to a few others).

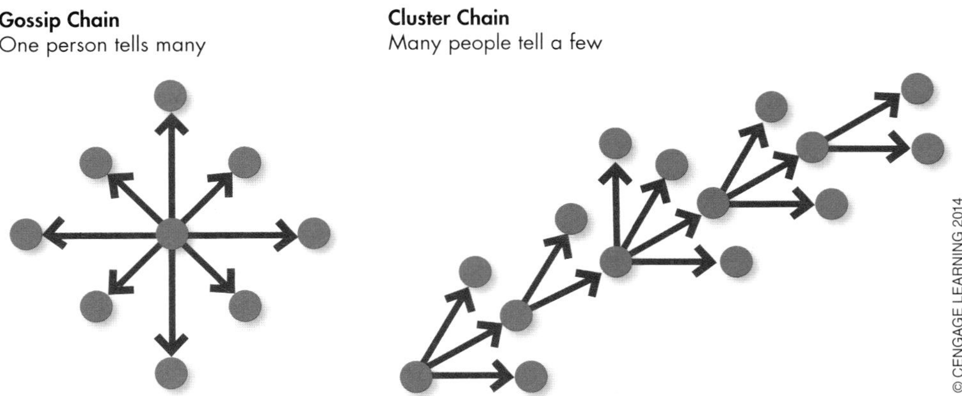

responding vigorously to inaccurate information, the manager can minimize the damage the grapevine can do. The grapevine actually can be an asset. By learning who the key people in the grapevine are, for example, the manager can partially control the information they receive and use the grapevine to sound out employee reactions to new ideas, such as a change in human resource policies or benefit packages. The manager also can get valuable information from the grapevine and use it to improve decision making.[26]

Management by Wandering Around

Another increasingly popular form of informal communication is called, interestingly enough, management by wandering around.[27] The basic idea is that some managers keep in touch with what is going on by wandering around and talking with people—immediate subordinates, subordinates far down the organizational hierarchy, delivery people, customers, or anyone else who is involved with the company. Bill Marriott, for example, frequently visits the kitchens, loading docks, and custodial work areas whenever he tours a Marriott hotel. He claims that, by talking with employees throughout the hotel, he gets new ideas and has a better feel for the entire company. And, when United Airlines CEO Jeff Smisek travels, he makes a point of talking to flight attendants and other passengers to gain continuous insights into how the business can be run more effectively.

A related form of organizational communication that really has no specific term is the informal interchange that takes place outside the normal work setting. Employees attending the company picnic, playing on the company softball team, or taking fishing trips together will almost always spend part of their time talking about work. For example, Texas Instruments engineers at TI's Lewisville, Texas, facility often frequent a local bar in town after work. On any given evening, they talk about the Dallas Cowboys, the newest government contract received by the company, the weather, their boss, the company's stock price, local politics, and problems at work. There is no set agenda, and the key topics of discussion vary from group to group and from day to day. Still, the social gatherings serve an important role. They promote a strong culture and enhance understanding of how the organization works.

Nonverbal Communication

Nonverbal communication is a communication exchange that does not use words or uses words to carry more meaning than the strict definition of the words themselves. Nonverbal communication is a powerful but little-understood form of communication in organizations. It often relies on facial expressions, body movements, physical contact, and gestures. One study found that as much as 55 percent of the content of a message is transmitted by facial expressions and body posture and that another 38 percent derives from inflection and tone. Words themselves account for only 7 percent of the content of the message.[28]

management by wandering around practice of keeping in touch with what is going on by wandering around and talking with people

nonverbal communication a communication exchange that does not use words or uses words to carry more meaning than the strict definition of the words themselves

© MICHAL KOWALSKI/SHUTTERSTOCK.COM

Nonverbal communication can convey a great deal of information. For instance, the exchange shown here clearly reflects a lot of nonverbal communication.

Research has identified three kinds of nonverbal communication practiced by managers—images, settings, and body language.[29] In this context, images are the kinds of words people elect to use. "Damn the torpedoes, full speed ahead" and "Even though there are some potential hazards, we should proceed with this course of action" may convey the same meaning. Yet the person who uses the first expression may be perceived as a maverick, a courageous hero, an individualist, or a reckless and foolhardy adventurer. The person who uses the second might be described as aggressive, forceful, diligent, or narrow minded and resistant to change. At a recent meeting of Walmart executives, former CEO Lee Scott announced that "I can tell everyone what color underwear they're wearing." His meaning? There was a political issue dividing the group, and Scott wanted those in attendance to know that he was aware of which executives were on each side of the issue.[30] In short, our choice of words conveys much more than just the strict meaning of the words themselves.

The setting for communication also plays a major role in nonverbal communication. Boundaries, familiarity, the home turf, and other elements of the setting are all important. Much has been written about the symbols of power in organizations. The size and location of an office, the kinds of furniture in the office, and the accessibility of the person in the office all communicate useful information. For example, when H. Ross Perot ran EDS, he positioned his desk so that it was always between him and a visitor. This kept him in charge. When he wanted a less formal dialogue, he moved around to the front of the desk and sat beside his visitor. Michael Dell of Dell Computer has his desk facing a side window so that, when he turns around to greet a visitor, there is never anything between them.

A third form of nonverbal communication is body language.[31] The distance we stand from someone as we speak has meaning. In the United States, standing very close to someone you are talking to generally signals either familiarity or aggression. The English and Germans stand farther apart than Americans do when talking, whereas the Arabs, Japanese, and Mexicans stand closer together.[32] Eye contact is another effective means of nonverbal communication. For example, prolonged eye contact might suggest either hostility or romantic interest. Other kinds of body language include body and hand movement, pauses in speech, and mode of dress.

The manager should be aware of the importance of nonverbal communication and recognize its potential impact. Giving an employee good news about a reward with the wrong nonverbal cues can destroy the reinforcement value of the reward. Likewise, reprimanding an employee but providing inconsistent nonverbal cues can limit the effectiveness of the sanctions. The tone of the message, where and how the message is delivered, facial expressions, and gestures can all amplify or weaken the message or change the message altogether.

MANAGING ORGANIZATIONAL COMMUNICATION

In view of the importance and pervasiveness of communication in organizations, it is vital for managers to understand how to manage the communication process.[33] Managers should understand how to maximize the potential benefits of communication and minimize the potential problems. We begin our discussion of communication management by considering the factors that might disrupt effective communication and how to deal with them.

Barriers to Communication

Several factors may disrupt the communication process or serve as barriers to effective communication.[34] As shown in *Table 7.1*, these may be divided into two classes: individual barriers and organizational barriers.

Individual Barriers Several individual barriers may disrupt effective communication. One common problem is conflicting or inconsistent signals. A manager is

TABLE 7.1 BARRIERS TO EFFECTIVE COMMUNICATION

Individual Barriers	Organizational Barriers
Conflicting or inconsistent signals	Semantics
Credibility about the subject	Status or power differences
Reluctance to communicate	Different perceptions
Poor listening skills	Noise
Predispositions about the subject	Overload
	Language differences

© CENGAGE LEARNING 2014

sending conflicting signals when she says on Monday that things should be done one way, but then prescribes an entirely different procedure on Wednesday. Inconsistent signals are being sent by a manager who says that he has an "open door" policy and wants his subordinates to drop by, but keeps his door closed and becomes irritated when someone stops in.

© RUBBERBALL/ALAMY

Another barrier is lack of credibility. Credibility problems arise when the sender is not considered a reliable source of information. He may not be trusted or may not be perceived as knowledgeable about the subject at hand. When a politician is caught withholding information or when a manager makes a series of bad decisions, the extent to which he or she will be listened to and believed thereafter diminishes. In extreme cases, people may talk about something they obviously know little or nothing about.

Some people are simply reluctant to initiate a communication exchange. This reluctance may occur for a variety of reasons. A manager may be reluctant to tell subordinates about an impending budget cut because he knows they will be unhappy about it. Likewise, a subordinate may be reluctant to transmit information upward for fear of reprisal or because it is felt that such an effort would be futile.

Poor listening habits can be a major barrier to effective communication. Some people are simply poor listeners. When someone is talking to them, they may be daydreaming, looking around, reading, or listening to another conversation. Because they are not concentrating on what is being said, they may not comprehend part or all of the message. They may even think that they really are paying attention, only to realize later that they cannot remember parts of the conversation.

Receivers may also bring certain predispositions to the communication process. They may already have their minds made up, firmly set in a certain way. For example, a manager may have heard that his new boss is unpleasant and hard to work with. When she calls him in for an introductory meeting, he may go into that meeting predisposed to dislike her and discount what she has to say.

LEARN

Organizational Barriers Other barriers to effective communication involve the organizational context in which the communication occurs. Semantic problems arise when words have different meanings for different people. Words and phrases such as *profit*, *increased output*, and *return on investment* may have positive meanings for managers but less positive meanings for workers.

Communication problems also may arise when people of different power or status try to communicate with each other. The company president may discount a suggestion from an operating employee, thinking, "How can someone at that level help me run my business?" Or, when the president goes out to inspect a new plant, workers may be reluctant to offer suggestions because of their lower status. The marketing vice president may have more power than the human resource vice president and consequently may not pay much attention to a staffing report submitted by the human resource department.

If people perceive a situation differently, they may have difficulty communicating with one another. When two managers observe that a third manager has not spent much time in her office lately, one may believe that she has been to several important meetings, and the other may think she is "hiding out." If they need to talk about her in some official capacity, problems may arise because one has a positive impression and the other, a negative impression.

Environmental factors also may disrupt effective communication. As mentioned earlier, noise may affect communication in many ways. Similarly, overload may be a problem when the receiver is being sent more information than he or she can effectively handle. Many managers report getting so many email messages each

LEARN

day that they sometimes feel overwhelmed.[36] And, when the manager gives a subordinate many jobs on which to work and at the same time, the subordinate is being told by family and friends to do other things, overload may result and communication effectiveness diminishes.

Finally, as businesses become more and more global, different languages can create problems. To counter this problem, some firms are adopting an "official language." For example, when the German chemical firm Hoechst merged with the French firm Rhone-Poulenc, the new company adopted English as its official language. Indeed, English is increasingly becoming the standard business language around the world.[37]

> "...a synergy-related headcount adjustment goal,"
> wording used in a Nokia press to announce the reduction of 9,000 jobs[35]

QUOTE FROM NOKIA PRESS ANNOUNCEMENT

Improving Communication Effectiveness

Considering how many factors can disrupt communication, it is fortunate that managers can resort to several techniques for improving communication effectiveness.[38] As shown in *Table 7.2*, these techniques include both individual and organizational skills.

Individual Skills The single most important individual skill for improving communication effectiveness is being a good listener.[39] Being a good listener requires that the individual be prepared to listen, not interrupt the speaker, concentrate on both the words and the meaning being conveyed, be patient, and ask questions as appropriate.[40] So important are good listening skills that companies such as Delta, IBM, and Boeing conduct programs to train their managers to be better listeners. *Figure 7.6* illustrates the characteristics of poor listeners versus good listeners.

In addition to being a good listener, several other individual skills can promote effective communication. Feedback, one of the most important, is facilitated by two-way communication. Two-way communication allows the receiver to ask questions, request clarification, and express opinions that let the sender know whether he or she has been understood. In general, the more complicated the message, the more useful two-way communication is. In addition, the sender should be aware of the meanings that different receivers might attach to various words. For example, when addressing stockholders, a manager might use the word *profits* often. When addressing labor leaders, however, she may choose to say *profits* less often.

Furthermore, the sender should try to maintain credibility. This can be accomplished by not pretending to be an expert when one is not, by "doing one's homework" and checking facts, and by otherwise being as accurate and honest as possible. The sender also should try to be sensitive to the receiver's perspective. A manager who must tell a subordinate that she has not been recommended for a promotion should recognize that the subordinate most likely will be frustrated and unhappy. The content of the message and its method of delivery should be chosen accordingly. The manager also should be primed to accept a reasonable degree of hostility and bitterness without getting angry in return.[41]

Finally, the receiver should also try to be sensitive to the sender's point of view. Suppose that a manager has just received some bad news—for example, he is told that his position is being eliminated next year. The people around him should understand that he may be disappointed, angry, or even depressed for a while. Thus, they might make a special effort not to take offense if he snaps at them, and they might look for signals that he needs someone to talk to.[42]

TABLE 7.2 OVERCOMING BARRIERS TO COMMUNICATION

Individual Skills	Organizational Skills
Develop good listening skills	Follow up
Encourage two-way communication	Understand the richness of media
Be aware of language and meaning	
Maintain credibility	
Be sensitive to receiver's perspective	
Be sensitive to sender's perspective	

© CENGAGE LEARNING 2014

Organizational Skills Two useful organizational skills can also enhance communication effectiveness for both the sender and the receiver—following up and understanding the richness of different media. Following up simply involves checking at a later time to be sure that a message has been received and understood. After a manager mails a report to a colleague, she might call a few days later to make sure the report has arrived. If it has, the manager might ask whether the colleague has any questions about it.

Both parties also should understand the richness associated with different media. When a manager is going

FIGURE 7.6 MORE AND LESS EFFECTIVE LISTENING SKILLS

Effective listening skills are a vital part of communication in organizations. There are several barriers that can contribute to poor listening skills by individuals in organizations. Fortunately, there are also several practices for improving listening skills.

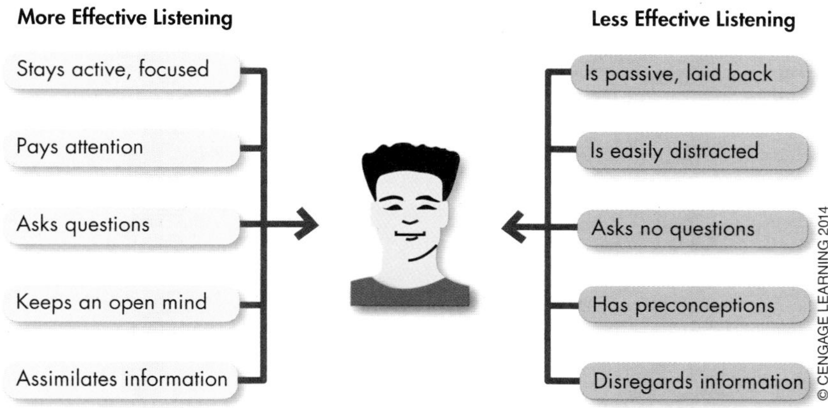

VISUALIZE

to lay off a subordinate temporarily, he or she should deliver the message in person. A face-to-face channel of communication gives the manager an opportunity to explain the situation and answer questions. When the purpose of the message is to grant a pay increase, written communication may be appropriate because it can be more objective and precise. The manager could then follow up the written notice with personal congratulations.

SUMMARY AND A LOOK AHEAD

After reading and studying this chapter, you should now have a better understanding of communication skills. Specifically, you should have a clear understanding of the meaning of communication, understand what makes communication effective, and know the basic communication process. You should also have a clearer understanding of the strengths and weaknesses of different forms of communication. In addition, you should have a stronger understanding of various forms of informal communication. Finally, you should be able to identify the primary barriers to effective communication and how to best overcome those barriers.

The remainder of this chapter provides opportunities for you to continue to develop and refine your own interpersonal skills. For instance, you will be directed to resources where you can visualize both effective and less effective interpersonal skills. Subsequent sections provide several different opportunities for you to practice and explore interpersonal skills from different perspectives. The chapter concludes with some additional assessment and interpretation data.

VISUALIZING COMMUNICATION SKILLS

COMMUNICATION SKILLS IN ACTION—1

Your Assignment

Consider the two BizFlix film clips for this chapter.

Baby Mama (2008) is a comedy. Kate Holbrook (Tina Fey), single and in her late thirties, is successful in her career, but childless. She loves children and wants a child but does not want to take chances with a pregnancy at her age. Kate enlists the help of Angie Ostrowiski (Amy Poehler) from South Philadelphia to act as her surrogate mother. Former attorney, now Super Fruity fruit smoothies' owner Rob Ackerman (Greg Kinnear) enters the scene and begins dating Kate. Angie becomes pregnant but it is not clear whether the child is Kate's or Angie's. Complex, intertwined relationships and social interactions develop.

Because I Said So (2007) involves mother–daughter communication at several levels. Meet Daphne Wilder (Diane Keaton)—your typical meddling, overprotective, and divorced mother of three daughters. Two of her three beautiful daughters have married. That leaves Millie (Mandy Moore) as the focus of Daphne's undivided attention and compulsive behavior to find Millie a mate. Daphne places some online advertising, screens the applicants, and submits those she approves to Millie. Along the way, Daphne meets Joe (Stephen Collins), the father of one applicant.

Note how communication skills are shown in these two clips.

1. The first clip starts with a shot of Kate and Rob seated at a table in a vegan restaurant. The vegan waiter (Jon Glaser) approaches the table and introduces himself. They soon discover that a vegan restaurant is the wrong place to be and the film cuts to the two of them at a walk-up cheesesteak sandwich shop. She orders hers and the scene ends with him saying, "Yeah, I'll have the same." What communication skills (or lack thereof) are shown in this clip?
2. The second clip starts as Daphne answers her cell phone and says the person has the wrong number. The clip then follows the frantic rearrangement of the sofa, which ends up in the same place it started, as Daphne and Millie argue about Millie taking a call from Jason who is asking her for a date. The scene ends as Millie screams "and don't say great too much." Do you feel that these two are really communicating? Why or why not?

COMMUNICATION SKILLS IN ACTION—2

This exercise gives you an opportunity to think about communication skills that may be involved in management positions for you in the future.

Your Assignment

1. Think about communication skills and try to identify a scene that illustrates a positive or effective use of such skills in a movie, a TV show, or a video on YouTube.
2. Now do the same for a scene that illustrates a negative or ineffective use of those same skills.

Share your results with the class and discuss how the positive and negative use of communication skills is shown in each clip. You should also try to suggest how the negative situation could have been changed for the better.

PRACTICING COMMUNICATION SKILLS

ALONE OR TOGETHER?

The purpose of this exercise is to provide an opportunity to examine both individual and group communication skills. Everyone will participate individually and then as a member of a group.

Your Assignment

1. Your instructor will identify a category. In 30 seconds—and with no interaction among classmates—write down as many items as you can that belong in that category.
2. Your instructor will then organize the class into small groups. Group members will exchange lists and proceed as follows:
   (A) Write the total number of items at the top of the list that you received from another classmate. (*Note:* Any disputes as to whether an item fits into the category will be decided by the instructor.)
   (B) As a group, sum the individual totals for a group total.
   (C) Divide the group total by the number of group members. Report this "average individual score" to your instructor.
3. Now your instructor will identify a different category. Again, in 30 seconds the group should list as many items as it can for that category. The total number of items generated by the group is then reported to your instructor as your "group score."
4. For each group, your instructor will put both the individual and group scores on the board as the basis for discussion.

"BEST/WORST" PRESENTATIONS

Success in business today can often be either accelerated or hindered by one's ability to prepare and deliver effective presentations. Presentations may vary greatly in style and sophistication according to a variety of factors. These include (A) the presenter's relationship with the audience—peers or high-level management, in-house group or outsiders such as customers or suppliers or financiers; (B) audience size—individual, departmental, company-wide, national; (C) technicality and audience expectation—blue-collar or white-collar, technical background; and (D) what is at stake for the presenter—his or her future, a need for cooperation or votes or dollars. One way to learn presentation Do's and Do Not's is to observe effective and ineffective presentations. This exercise will help you analyze some of the Do's in other people's presentations.

Your Assignment

1. Organize into small groups.
   (A) Each group member should describe the "Best Presentation I Ever Saw." Also share any details that you may know about influences such as those mentioned above in the introduction to this exercise (audience relationship, audience size, technicality, what is at stake for presenter).
   (B) The group will develop a list of those things that make a presentation "best."
   (C) Repeat A and B for the "Worst Presentation I Ever Saw."
2. Your instructor will reconvene the class so that the groups can share their lists.
   (A) Look for similarities and differences among the lists.
   (B) Discuss the importance of each item.
   (C) Discuss which of the factors mentioned above in the introduction to this exercise may have influenced the original presentations that students are recalling in their lists.

CAN YOU COMMUNICATE ACCURATELY?

This assignment provides an interesting opportunity to see how communication skills can be sharpened through the use of feedback.

Your Assignment

1. Your instructor will ask for two volunteers. One volunteer will leave the room but will be called back later in the exercise.
2. The second volunteer will be given a card with a geometric figure on it. He or she will go to the front of the room and, while turned to face the wall instead of the class, will describe the figure in detail. The class must remain silent, asking no questions and making no comments or noises, while each participant attempts to draw the figure described.
3. Afterwards, the instructor will show the figure to the class, using a slide or a drawing large enough for all to see. How long did this take, and how many participants were able to reproduce the figure accurately during that time period?
4. The first volunteer is called back into the room and given a card with a different figure on it.
5. He or she is told to go to the front of the class, face the class, and describe the figure. The class can ask questions, and the volunteer can answer them and elaborate on his or her description.
6. As before, your instructor will then reveal the figure to the class. How long did this take, and how many participants were able to reproduce the figure accurately during this time period?
7. Compare the results of the two methods of communicating with the class. Did one method produce superior results? Did that method cost more time or less time?

COMMUNICATING A CHANGE IN STRATEGY

Communicating a decision to change is an important part of management and requires strong communication skills.

Assume that you are the CEO of a large discount retailer. You have decided that your firm needs to change its strategy to survive. Specifically, you want the firm to move away from discount retailing and into specialty retailing. To do so, you will need to close 400 of your 1,200 discount stores within the next year. You also will need to increase the expansion rate of your two existing specialty chains and launch one new chain. Your tentative plans call for opening 300 new specialty stores in one business and 150 stores in the other business next year. You also want to finalize the basic concept for the new chain and to have 10 stores open next year as well. Finally, although you will be able to transfer some discount store employees to specialty retail jobs, a few hundred people will lose their jobs.

Your Assignment

1. Develop a press release that outlines these goals (You may need to go online or to the library to determine a good format for a press release.)
2. Determine the best way to communicate the goals to your employees.
3. Develop a contingency plan for dealing with problems that arise after these new goals are communicated.

ETHICAL ISSUES

This exercise will help you develop your communication skills and understand the importance of clarity and tact when communicating about sensitive subjects, such as ethical issues.

Scenario 1: Assume that, after two years of experience in corporate marketing with a national cell phone provider, you are hired by a competing firm. Your new boss, the marketing vice president, asks you to provide specific details about your former employer's customers. He intends to use that information to "steal" those customers by, for example, offering them a lower price. You signed a nondisclosure agreement with your first employer that forbids you to reveal that information. In addition, you personally have strong ethical concerns.

Scenario 2: Assume that, after two years of experience in corporate marketing with a national cell phone provider, you are hired by a competing firm. Your new boss, the marketing vice president, asks you to contact some of your former colleagues. He intends to use that information to "steal" those employees by, for example, offering them a higher salary. As far as you know, there are no legal concerns with this request but you are unsure about the ethical implications. When you questioned your boss, he replied, "Don't worry about it. Everybody does it; it's no big deal." You want to keep your new job but feel compelled to respond.

PRACTICE

Your Assignment

1. With Scenario 1 in mind, compose a written response to your boss, outlining your position. While you may mention legal consequences, be sure to emphasize the ethical issues. To persuade your boss to change his mind, you will need to address his statement and the underlying reasons for his request.
2. With Scenario 2 in mind, compose a written response to your boss, outlining your position. To persuade your boss to change his mind, you will need to address his statement and the underlying reasons for his request.
3. What do you think the likely outcome would be for each scenario? What would be the ultimate consequences for you, your boss, and your company?
4. While Scenarios 1 and 2 are similar, there is an important difference: the certainty that an action is unethical versus uncertainty about an action's ethical implications. How does that difference affect your communication?

COMMUNICATING HUMAN RESOURCE INFORMATION

Communication skills are especially important in the human resource area because people are the domain of Human Resource Management. This exercise provides an opportunity to see how communication can foster good relationships between management and employees.

Many companies provide various benefits to their workers, including such options as pay for time not worked, insurance coverage, pension plans, and so forth. These benefits are often very costly to the organization. For example, benefits often equal about another one-third of what employees are paid in wages and salaries. In some countries, such as Germany, the figures are even higher.

Yet many employees often fail to appreciate the actual value of the benefits their employers provide; they underestimate the dollar value of their benefits. And when comparing their income to that of others, or when comparing alternative job offers, many people focus almost entirely on direct compensation—wages and salaries paid directly to the individual. For example, an individual who has two offers, one for $20,000 a year and another for $22,000, is likely to choose the second offer without considering that the first offer has sufficiently more attractive benefits to make the total compensation packages equivalent.

Your Assignment

1. Why do you think most people focus on direct compensation (wages and salaries) when assessing their compensation?
2. If you were the HR manager for a firm, how would you go about communicating the value of benefits to your employees?
3. Suppose an employee comes to you and says that he is thinking about leaving for a "better job." You then learn that he is defining "better" only in terms of higher pay. How might you help him compare total compensation?
4. Some firms today are cutting their benefits. How would you communicate a benefit cut to your employees?

COMMUNICATION IN INTERNATIONAL BUSINESS

International business has grown dramatically in recent years, resulting in more and more businesses needing to communicate periodically with one another in various operations scattered in far-flung locations around the globe. This exercise will help sensitize you to some of the issues and complexities involved in communication in international business.

Assume that you have just been hired as a communication consultant by a small but rapidly growing international business. The business has operations in New York, Paris, Munich, Tokyo, Hong Kong, and Rio de Janeiro. The owner of the business is frustrated because managers in different locations are having trouble maintaining contact with one another. This has led to several mistakes and missed opportunities. Your task is to determine how to improve inter-organizational communication in the business.

Your Assignment

1. Look at a map and find the various locations where the business has operations. You may also need to do some research into each location.
2. Develop a list of every problem that managers in each city may face when attempting to communicate with the others.
3. Identify one or more ways managers could overcome each of these problems.

ANNOUNCING UNPOPULAR DECISIONS

This exercise allows you to practice your communication skills in writing memos to motivate individuals or groups to accept decisions that they dislike.

Assume you supervise a group of six employees who work in an indoor facility in a relatively isolated location. The company you work for has recently adopted an ambiguous policy regarding smoking. Essentially, the policy states that all company work sites are to be smoke-free unless the employees at a specific site choose differently and at the discretion of the site supervisor.

Four members of the work group that you supervise are smokers. They have come to you with the argument that, because they constitute the majority, they should be allowed to smoke at work. The other two members of the group, both nonsmokers, have heard about this proposal and have also discussed the situation with you. They argue that the health-related consequences of secondary smoke should outweigh the preferences of the majority.

To compound the problem, your boss wrote the new policy and has been quite defensive about it when numerous other individuals criticized it. So you know that the boss will get very angry if you also raise concerns about the policy rather than just going along with it.

Finally, you are personally indifferent about the issue. You do not smoke, but members of your family do. Secondary smoke does not bother you, and you don't have a strong opinion about it. Still, you have to make a decision. As you see the situation, your choices are to: (A) mandate a smoke-free environment, (B) continue to allow smoking in the facility, or (C) ask your boss to clarify the policy.

Your Assignment

1. Prepare an outline that you will use to announce to the four smokers that you have chosen Option A.
2. Prepare an outline that you will use to inform the two nonsmokers that you have chosen Option B.
3. Assume that you have chosen Option C. Prepare an outline that you will use when you meet with your boss.
4. Are there other alternatives?
5. How would you handle your decision if you were actually the group supervisor?

PRACTICE

SLIDE PRESENTATION

The ability to prepare and deliver effective presentations is often critical to a manager's success in business today. Indeed, some companies require job applicants to make a presentation—which often is a slide presentation that the applicant carries in a laptop computer—as part of their job interviews. This exercise assumes that you have never prepared a slide presentation, and therefore gives you an opportunity to make a few simple slides that will also demonstrate how fonts and colors affect readability.

Your Assignment

Using the following instructions to demonstrate the readability of different fonts and colors, prepare nine PowerPoint© slides, each of which contains a list of the seven major skills covered in this book:

SLIDE 1: Use the Times Roman font for the list of seven major skills.
SLIDE 2: Use the Verdana font for the list of seven major skills.
SLIDE 3: Copy Slide 1 but type the odd-numbered skills in all-capital letters.
SLIDE 4: Copy Slide 2 but type the odd-numbered skills in all-capital letters
SLIDE 5: Copy Slide 1 but change every other word to italics.
SLIDE 6: Copy Slide 2 but change every other word to italics.
SLIDE 7: Copy Slide 1 but use three colors for each odd-numbered skill.
SLIDE 8: Copy Slide 2 but use three colors for each odd-numbered skill.
SLIDE 9: Look at each of those slides and then prepare one final slide that you feel is easy to read.

Compare the results of the slides. Did one method produce superior results? What are the implications for management presentations?

COMMUNICATING ACROSS TIME ZONES

International managers face additional communication challenges due to differences in language, time zones, and so forth. As a way to sharpen your communication skills, this exercise examines the impact of different time zones on business activities.

Assume that you are a manager in a large multinational firm. Your office is in San Francisco. You need to arrange a conference call with several other managers to discuss an upcoming strategic change by your firm. The other managers are located in New York, London, Rome, Moscow, Tokyo, Singapore, and Sydney.

Your Assignment

1. Determine the time differential in each city. When it is 10:00 A.M. in San Francisco, what time is it in each of the other locations that you will need to call?
2. Assuming that people in each city have a "normal" workday of 8:00 A.M. to 5:00 P.M., determine the optimal time for your conference call. That is, what time can you place to call so as to minimize the number of people who are inconvenienced?
3. Assume that you need to visit each office in person, spending one full day in each city. Use the Internet to review airline schedules, take into account differences in time zones, and develop an itinerary.

USING COMMUNICATION SKILLS

USE

JAPAN AND AMERICA—ALIKE BUT DIFFERENT

The United States and Japan are strong trading partners. Consumers in each country freely buy the same products and services. Japanese consumers wear US clothing and eat US fast food while Americans drive Japanese cars and use Japanese electronic products.

With these similarities in buying and consuming behavior, it seems reasonable that the Americans and the Japanese would see each other as mostly alike and that business communication would be easy. That is not the case. Cultural differences are so great and centuries of misunderstanding are so strong that differences in perceptions and attitudes between the two countries are a problem. Plus, communication styles also differ significantly. Japanese communication is not particularly unique, it is subjective, emotional, and polite or tacit in nature, but Americans perceive it to be vague and indirect, which could lead to difficulties in understanding.

In the United States, one survey found that only 13 percent of Americans believe they know a lot about Japan. Another 42 percent indicated they know a little, but 45 percent said they did not know much at all about Japan. When Japanese were asked the same question about Americans, 5 percent said they knew a lot, 42 percent said they knew a little, and more than half (51 percent) said that they did not know very much. Thus, in each country most of those surveyed felt that they knew little about the other country.

However, Americans and Japanese do hold some similar perceptions about the other. For example, each admires the degree of scientific and technical accomplishment in the other country, and respect for family life is about the same. Each also sees the other as being relatively friendly and nonviolent. Indeed, in a recent poll, a record 80 percent of the American public said Japan was a dependable country. This is a considerable shift in attitudes toward Japan, as only 60 percent of Americans indicated trust of Japan in a similar poll in 1998.

But the differences between the two populations far outweigh the similarities. The Japanese have much higher admiration for Americans for their form of government (63 percent), role in world leadership (84 percent), freedom of expression (89 percent), variety of lifestyles (86 percent), leisure time (88 percent), and treatment of women (68 percent) than Americans do for the Japanese (23, 31, 27, 25, 15, and 20 percent, respectively). Similarly, Americans admire the Japanese for their industriousness (88 percent) and educational institutions (71 percent) much more than the Japanese admire Americans for the same characteristics (27 and 48 percent, respectively). Moreover, Americans see Japanese as being extremely competitive, not lazy at all, extremely hard working, very crafty, and quite well educated, whereas Japanese people see Americans as being moderately competitive, somewhat lazy, not very hard working, not very crafty, and somewhat poorly educated.

Finally, Americans and Japanese see some trade issues differently. Americans feel that they do not do as well in Japan because of trade restrictions, but the Japanese counter that it is because of lower quality. Specifically two-thirds of Americans believe that Japan unfairly keeps US products out of its country, while only one-third of the Japanese feel this same way. And half of the Japanese feel that US firms do so poorly in Japan primarily because their products are not as good as those made by Japanese firms. Only 22 percent of Americans hold this same opinion.

Case Questions

1. What information in this case came as a surprise to you? Why?
2. What skills would be needed for a US manager doing business in Japan? For a Japanese manager doing business in the United States?

Go Online

3. Which of the above skills do you think you already possess? Which skills do you think would be the most difficult for you to develop?

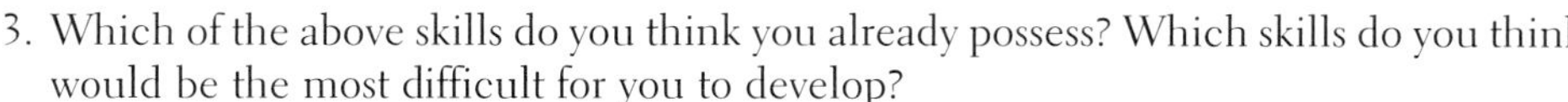

4. If you were working in a US corporation and were assigned to a post in Japan, what preparations would you make to avoid or reduce communication problems?

Case References

Editorial, "In Japan We Trust,' *The Japan Times*, Sunday, June 21, 2009, http://search.japantimes.co.jp/cgi-bin/ed20090621a1.html; Michael Haugh, "Japanese and Non-Japanese Perceptions of Japanese Communication," *New Zealand Journal of Asian Studies*, 5: 1, June, 2003, pp. 156–177; "Hey, Japan! Here's a Survey!" *Industry Week*, February 17, 1992, pp. 58–60; "Japan in the Mind of America," *Time*, February 10, 1992, pp. 16–20; "America in the Mind of Japan," *Time*, February 10, 1992, pp. 20–23.

WORKPLACE VIOLENCE

In the last quarter of the 20th century, workplace violence increased rapidly—so much so that it has become commonplace in America. From 1997 to 2007, for example, the most recent year for which data are available, more than 7,000 occupational homicides occurred nationwide, according to the United States Bureau of Labor Statistics. Most involved robberies, but more than 1,000 involved work associates. Dismissed workers, overstressed employees, and dissatisfied customers are turning to verbal assaults, fistfights, pistol whippings, knives, and even guns to settle real and imagined grievances.

Many of the violent workers are middle-aged white males who feel that their years of service are being ignored to make room for younger, less-qualified, and perhaps even minority personnel. They may live alone, have moved recently, or have experienced a separation, divorce, or death. Their work is their primary social attachment and provides what little meaning they have in their lives. In America, with an increased divorce rate, increased mobility, and loss of church or neighborhood belongingness, many people fit this description. The movement of jobs offshore and the poor economic conditions we continue to experience only exacerbate the potential for violence.

Under the Occupational Safety and Health Act of 1970 (Section 5(a)(1), the US government requires organizations to furnish a place of employment "free from recognized hazards" that may cause death or serious physical harm to employees. So managers must take reasonable steps to assure that employees, customers, and business associates are protected. Managers must examine safety and security programs to make sure that they can adequately protect their assets. Labor disputes, particularly if they are acrimonious, may incite some striking workers to sabotage or vandalize property. To avoid violence, managers should use consistent, sympathetic communication when informing individuals that they are being terminated. The most important step managers can take is to develop and practice communication policies designed to defuse volatile situations before they reach the point of violence. Threats and intimidation should be prohibited. Reports of potential violence should be investigated promptly. Outlets should be provided for personnel to vent their feelings and frustrations. An emergency plan to deal with violence should it arise needs to be developed, including ways in which to secure the premises.

Communication is a key to dealing with workplace violence. Human resource (HR) professionals within an organization generally are the most qualified to provide the skills necessary to deal with it. They can help to develop programs for assisting laid-off individuals, such as outplacement and counseling services, re-training programs, and other forms of assistance that can greatly reduce the risk of workplace violence. Unfortunately, many organizations cut their human resource departments as one of the first steps in cost reduction, downsizing, or other restructuring programs.

USE

Case Questions

Go Online

1. This case refers to defusing volatile situations before they reach the point of violence. How might that be done? What skills would be needed to do this?
2. What communication skills are necessary to report potential incidents of workplace violence?
3. What communication skills are needed to handle a situation after a violent incident has occurred?
4. Which communication skills do you think most employees and/or managers lack for dealing with workplace violence? Why?
5. Are your skills up to the task? If you experience or observe a potentially violent encounter at work, are you be able to communicate with the problem employee without making the situation worse?
6. Even now, while in school or your current job, what can you do to begin improving your skills for dealing with potential workplace violence?

Case References

David D. Van Fleet and Ella W. Van Fleet, *The Violence Volcano: Reducing the Risk of Workplace Violence*, Charlotte, NC: Information Age Publishing, 2010; "Recession fuels worries of U.S. workplace violence," April 22, 2009, uk.reuters.com/article/marketsNewsUS/idUKN215017452 0090422?pageNumber=3; Christine Woolsey, "Workplace Security Plans Worth Employing," *Business Insurance*, June 6, 1994, pp. 14–15; Roberta Maynard, "Avoiding Worker Violence over Terminations," *Nation's Business*, May 1994, p. 13; Daniel Weisberg, "Preparing for the Unthinkable," *Management Review*, March 1994, pp. 58–61; Jenny C. McCune, "The Age of Rage," *Small Business Reports*, March 1994, pp. 35–41.

EXTENDING YOUR COMMUNICATION SKILLS

Your instructor may use one or more of these **Group Extensions** to provide you with more opportunities to develop your time-management skills. On the other hand, you may continue your development on your own by doing one or more of the **Individual Extensions**.

These **Group Extensions** are repeated exactly for each of the seven specific skills. Doing the exact **Extension** for different skills will help you to sharpen both the skills and the subtle differences between the several skills.

GROUP EXTENSIONS

- Form small groups of students. Have each group select an organization and a management position. Then have them identify the communication skills needed by a person in that position.
- Form small groups of students. Have each group identify a problem or opportunity facing a business or other organization. Then have them identify the communication skills needed by managers in dealing with that problem or opportunity.
- Form small groups of students. Have each group identify a problem or opportunity facing a business or other organization. Assign each group to identify the communication skills needed by managers in dealing with that problem or opportunity.
- Form small groups of students. Assign each group one or more corporations to analyze. Have them identify the members who serve on its board of directors and research their backgrounds. Then have the students describe the communication skills of those directors.
- Form small groups of students. Have each group select a job they see regularly (e.g., retail clerk, fast-food worker). Ask them to describe the communication skills needed on that job.
- Form small groups of students. Have students sketch the communication skills they would need if they were going to start a specific type of new business.
- Form small groups of students. Have each group identify recent examples illustrating a situation that called for them to use communication skills.

INDIVIDUAL EXTENSIONS

- Go to the library and research a company. Characterize its level of effectiveness and identify the communication skills of its top executives. Share your results with the class.
- Select a highly visible manager and analyze his or her communication skills.
- Interview a manager from a local organization. Learn about what communication skills he or she needs to perform effectively.
- Think of someone you know who is a manager. Describe that person's management position in terms of the type of organization, level in the organization, and the area of management in which he or she practices. What communication skills does that person need to be effective?

- Plan a hypothetical change in your school focusing on the use of communication skills.
- Search the Internet for examples of communication skills in management and compare what you find with the information presented here.
- Tom Peters, a famous management guru, is purported to have said: "Communication is everyone's panacea for everything." What does that mean to you?

YOUR COMMUNICATION SKILLS NOW

COMMUNICATION SKILLS ASSESSMENT

Now that you have completed Chapter 7, it is time again to assess your communication skills. To do so, complete the following instrument. Think about your current situation, job, or organization in which you are a member. You should respond in terms of your current situation and not by how you think you should respond or a manager should respond. If a statement doesn't pertain to your current situation, respond in terms of what you think would be accurate for you in that situation.

Use this scale in your responses.

1	2	3	4	5
Not true at all	Somewhat untrue	Sometimes true Sometimes not	Somewhat true	Completely true

Total your scores and record them in the table at the end of instrument.

Given that many experts suggest the use of 360° feedback in performance appraisal, you may find it useful to obtain the views of others about your interpersonal skills. You may get a form from your instructor that is designed for others to complete about you and then record their scores in the table as well. Areas where there is a large discrepancy between your views and those of others should draw your attention and you should spend more time developing those skills.

COMMUNICATION SKILLS

[Note: The numbers correspond to those on the baseline assessment in Appendix A.]

____ 201. I accurately perceive nonverbal messages.
____ 202. I actively seek advice from others.
____ 203. I am an easy person to work with.
____ 204. I am an excellent communicator.
____ 205. I am aware of my emotional reactions to what is being said in a conversation.
____ 206. I am aware of emotional reactions of others to what is being said in a conversation.
____ 207. I am capable of editing written documents.
____ 208. I am clear and understandable in oral communication.
____ 209. I am good at expressing my ideas.
____ 210. I am good at negotiating.
____ 211. I am good at persuasion.
____ 212. I am good at reporting information.

_____ 213. I am good at teaching.
_____ 214. I ask for additional explanation if I don't understand something someone says.
_____ 215. I can accurately describe my feelings.
_____ 216. I can be forceful and persuasive in oral communication.
_____ 217. I can facilitate group discussions.
_____ 218. I can interview others fairly well.
_____ 219. I can prepare written reports easily and quickly.
_____ 220. I can provide appropriate feedback.
_____ 221. I can relate well to different types of people.
_____ 222. I can speak effectively in front of a group.
_____ 223. I can work alone or with others.
_____ 224. I coach others to help them.
_____ 225. I contribute to understanding by asking questions.
_____ 226. I counsel others to assist them.
_____ 227. I deal calmly with difficult situations.
_____ 228. I do not become defensive when I am being criticized.
_____ 229. I encourage those around me to feel free to air their feelings, even strong ones.
_____ 230. I enjoy being part of a group.
_____ 231. I enjoy being with others.
_____ 232. I find it easy to express my feelings.
_____ 233. I find it easy to see things from another's point of view.
_____ 234. I generally find what others have to say interesting.
_____ 235. I generally get my point across when talking.
_____ 236. I generally listen without interrupting.
_____ 237. I keep others up-to-date about information and change.
_____ 238. I let others know if they will be affected by something I am doing.
_____ 239. I listen attentively.
_____ 240. I listen more than talk when I'm with others.
_____ 241. I listen to disagreements among others.
_____ 242. I listen to the concerns of others.
_____ 243. I listen to the views and ideas of others.
_____ 244. I listen to what the team wants to do.
_____ 245. I listen well in group situations.
_____ 246. I make a good impression when I give a presentation.
_____ 247. I make my views known without being pushy about it.
_____ 248. I make sure that people experience no "surprises" from me.
_____ 249. I provide clear, specific feedback.
_____ 250. I provide feedback linked to particular performance or behavior.
_____ 251. I seldom get into arguments.
_____ 252. I set an example for how hard people in my organization should work.
_____ 253. I speak effectively.
_____ 254. I state my views clearly and concisely when speaking with others.
_____ 255. I strive to be in communication networks so that I am aware of important information.
_____ 256. I teach others how to do tasks.

____ 257. I tend to be good with words.
____ 258. I tend to provide a lot of information to others.
____ 259. I try to give others a chance to say what they think.
____ 260. I try never to be too busy to listen to the problems and concerns of others.
____ 261. I try to clearly explain the desired results when assigning tasks.
____ 262. I try to find out what others think before reaching conclusions.
____ 263. I try to give feedback that will help people solve their own problems.
____ 264. I try to identify the "real" message in communication from others.
____ 265. I try to provide feedback on problems rather than personal characteristics.
____ 266. I try to put myself in the other person's shoes when I talk to them.
____ 267. I try to respond to people in a helpful way.
____ 268. I use correct grammar.
____ 269. I welcome the views of others.
____ 270. I write clearly and concisely.

Summary of Your Scores

Skill (max. possible score)	**Your Score Now**	**Scores from Others**	**Your Score From Chapter 1**
Communication (350)			

Interpretation of Your Scores

Compare your score with the one you reported at the beginning of Chapter 1. If there is no or only a modest improvement in your score, you should examine the same set of items from the **Managerial Skills Assessment** from Chapter 1 and compare each of them with these to see where change has and has not occurred. You should then spend more time on developing the particular skills where change either decreased or stayed the same.

INTERPRETATIONS

INTERPRET

A COMMUNICATION SKILLS SURVEY

There is no further interpretation. The column totals indicate the extent to which each type of communication is used effectively. A higher score indicates better skills.

BECOMING AWARE OF YOUR COMMUNICATION STYLE

Developing an awareness of your communication style can help you understand how others see you. You may also be aware that you can change or alter your style to best fit the particular circumstances.

This assessment uses three basic communication styles:

- Aggressive: your G scores indicate this (total for items 1–20)
- Passive: your P scores indicate this (total for items 21–40)
- Assertive: your S scores indicate this (total for items 41–60)

A brief description of each of these follows.

Aggressive communication is a style that focuses on the "self" rather than "others" or "issues." Aggressive communicators may be abrupt, domineering, and even abusive. This style tends to alienate others and, hence, does not lead to long-term positive relationships. Aggressive communicators look to assign blame and generally deny their own shortcomings.

Passive communication is an avoidance style. Passive communicators tend not to respond to negative situations, instead "swallowing" their emotions. Their feelings tend to build up over time and can lead to explosive outbursts and/or violence. These individuals may become dependent on others and even promote the "causes" of others.

Assertive communication is a style that focuses on openness in the expression of feelings. Assertive communicators understand the wants and feelings of both themselves and others. These individuals tend to make informed decisions quickly, especially in emergency situations.

FEEDBACK SKILLS QUESTIONNAIRE

The total of the scores on the 15 items is your Feedback Skill Score. Scores range from 15 to 75.

Higher scores indicate better skill in providing feedback to others.

GENDER DIFFERENCES IN COMMUNICATION

The following answers are based on Y. K. Fulbright, (2011). "Male-Female Communication: Debunking the Mars-Venus Myth." *The Huffington Post* at www.huffingtonpost.com (accessed November 7, 2011); D. Cameron (2007). *The Myth of Mars and Venus.* Oxford University Press; and S. Poole, (October 19, 2007). *The Guardian* at http://www.guardian.co.uk (accessed November 7, 2011).

1. Men and women communicate differently.

   Studies show a 99.7% overlap in the way men and women communicate. Cameron suggests that women smile more and spell better, but that makes only a moderate difference in the way they communicate.

2. Men interrupt more than women.

   Women interrupt just as much as men do. Cameron suggests that when and how people interrupt is about power and social relationships, not about gender.

3. Males and females have very different language skills.

   According to most recent research, the language skills of men and women are nearly identical.

4. Men are more aggressive and can throw things farther.

   Yes, but there is more variability within the groups than between them. Some women can clearly out throw men, so even though the average may be greater for men, it has little practical value.

5. Men's and women's brains are wired differently when it comes to language.

   There does seem to be some evidence that neurological differences between men and women exist. However, Cameron argues that this has had little impact on how men and women communicate.

6. Females talk more than males.

   This is not true. When 56 research studies were reviewed, men talked more than women in 34 of the studies and women talked more than men in only two. Recent research reports that both genders speak almost the exact number of words daily.

7. Females are more verbally skilled than males.

   A 2005 meta-analysis by Janet Shibley Hyde ("The Gender Similarities Hypothesis," *American Psychologist*, September 2005, Vol. 60, No. 6, pp. 581–592) found a moderate effect size favoring women, but it also found that there was a near zero effect for reading comprehension, vocabulary, and verbal reasoning.

8. Females use language cooperatively, because they prefer harmony and equality.

   While Hyde's meta-analysis found a moderate effect size for women for smiling during conversations and small effect sizes for them in certain other areas of speech, the evidence does not necessarily support the view that these differences are genetic in nature.

9. Females seek to connect with others, while males use language with the intention of accomplishing things.

   When men and women are performing the same activities or roles, no differences have been observed. The differences that have been reported indicate that the genders may differ when they are engaged in different activities or are playing different roles.

10. Males are more direct and not as polite in communicating.

    Again, Hyde's meta-analysis found only a small effect size favoring males when it came to assertive speech. And, as noted earlier, there is as much if not more variation within each gender than there is when you compare across gender.

For other research on this topic see:

Gray, J. (1992). *Men Are from Mars, Women Are from Venus: A Practical Guide for Improving Communication and Getting What You Want in Your Relationships*, NY: HarperCollins Publishers.

Hirshman, L. (1994). "Female–male differences in conversational interaction." *Language in Society*, 23: 427–442

Tannen, D. (1990). *You Just Don't Understand: Women and Men in Conversation.* NY: William Morrow.

Thorne, B. (1993) *Gender Play: Girls and Boys in School.* New Brunswick, NJ: Rutgers University Press.

ENDNOTES

[1] Henry Mintzberg, *The Nature of Managerial Work* (New York: Harper & Row, 1973).

[2] *Ibid.*

[3] Batia M. Wiesenfeld, Sumita Charan, and Raghu Garud, "Communication Patterns as Determinants of Organizational Identification in a Virtual Organization," *Organization Science*, 1999, vol. 10, no. 6, pp. 777–790.

[4] *Fortune*, July 6, 2010, p. 44.

[5] Bruce Barry and Ingrid Fulmer, "The Medium and the Message: The Adaptive Use of Communication Media in Dyadic Influence," *Academy of Management Review*, 2004, vol. 29, no. 2, pp. 272–292.

[6] Mintzberg, *The Nature of Managerial Work.*

[7] Reid Buckley, "When You Have to Put It to Them," *Across the Board*, October 1999, pp. 44–48.

[8] "'Did I Just Say That?!' How to Recover from Foot-in-Mouth," The *Wall Street Journal*, June 19, 2002, p. B1.

[9] "Executives Who Dread Public Speaking Learn to Keep Their Cool in the Spotlight," The *Wall Street Journal*, May 4, 1990, pp. B1, B6.

[10] Mintzberg, *The Nature of Managerial Work.*

[11] Buckley, "When You Have to Put It to Them."

[12] "Watch What You Put in That Office Email," *BusinessWeek*, September 30, 2002, pp. 114–115.

[13] Nicholas Varchaver, "The Perils of E-mail," *Fortune*, February 17, 2003, pp. 96–102; "How a String of E-Mail Came to Haunt CSFB and Star Banker," The *Wall Street Journal*, February 28, 2003, pp. A1, A6; "How Morgan Stanley Botched a Big Case by Fumbling Emails," The *Wall Street Journal*, May 16, 2005, pp. A1, A10.

[14] *Fortune*, December 12, 2005, unnumbered leadership insert.

[15] A. Vavelas, "Communication Patterns in Task-Oriented Groups," *Journal of the Accoustical Society of America*, 1950, vol. 22, pp. 725–730; Jerry Wofford, Edwin Gerloff, and Robert Cummins, *Organizational Communication* (New York: McGraw-Hill, 1977).

[16] Nelson Phillips and John Brown, "Analyzing Communications in and Around Organizations: A Critical Hermeneutic Approach," *Academy of Management Journal*, 1993, vol. 36, no. 6, pp. 1547–1576.

[17] Walter Kiechel III, "Breaking Bad News to the Boss," *Fortune*, April 9, 1990, pp. 111–112.

[18] Mary Young and James Post, "How Leading Companies Communicate with Employees," *Organizational Dynamics*, Summer 1993, pp. 31–43.

[19] For one example, see Kimberly D. Elsbach and Greg Elofson, "How the Packaging of Decision Explanations Affects Perceptions of Trustworthiness," *Academy of Management Journal*, 2000, vol. 43, no. 1, pp. 80–89.

[20] Kristin Byron, "Carrying Too Heavy a Load? The Communication and Miscommunication of Emotion by Email," *Academy of Management Review*, 2008, Vol. 33, No. 2, pp. 309–327.

[21] "Those Bawdy E-Mails Were Good for a Laugh—Until the Ax Fell," The *Wall Street Journal*, February 4, 2000, pp. A1, A8.

[22] Keith Davis, "Management Communication and the Grapevine," *Harvard Business Review*, September–October 1953, pp. 43–49.

[23] "Spread the Word: Gossip Is Good," The *Wall Street Journal*, October 4, 1988, p. B1.

[24] David M. Schweiger and Angelo S. DeNisi, "Communication with Employees Following a Merger: A Longitudinal Field Experiment," *Academy of Management Journal*, March 1991, pp. 110–135.

[25] "Job Fears Make Offices All Fears," The *Wall Street Journal*, January 20, 2009, p. B7.

[26] Nancy B. Kurland and Lisa Hope Pelled, "Passing the Word: Toward a Model of Gossip and Power in the Workplace," *Academy of Management Review*, 2000, vol. 25, no. 2, pp. 428–438.

[27] Tom Peters and Nancy Austin, *A Passion for Excellence* (New York: Random House, 1985).

[28] Albert Mehrabian, *Non-verbal Communication* (Chicago: Aldine, 1972).

[29] Michael B. McCaskey, "The Hidden Messages Managers Send," *Harvard Business Review*, November–December 1979, pp. 135–148.

[30] Suzanne Kapner, "Changing of the Guard at Wal-Mart," *Fortune*, March 2, 2009, pp. 68–76.

[31] David Givens, "What Body Language Can Tell You That Words Cannot," *U.S. News & World Report*, November 19, 1984, p. 100.

[32] Edward J. Hall, *The Hidden Dimension* (New York: Doubleday, 1966).

[33] For a detailed discussion of improving communication effectiveness, see Courtland L. Bovee, John V. Thill, and Barbara E. Schatzman, *Business Communication Today*, 7th ed. (Upper Saddle River, N.J.: Prentice Hall, 2003).

[34] Otis W. Baskin and Craig E. Aronoff, *Interpersonal Communication in Organizations* (Glenview, Ill.: Scott, Foresman, 1980).

[35] *BusinessWeek*, December 22, 2008, p. 15.

[36] "You Have (Too Much) E-Mail," *USA Today*, March 12, 1999, p. 3B.

[37] Justin Fox, "The Triumph of English," *Fortune*, September 18, 2000, pp. 209–212.

[38] Joseph Allen and Bennett P. Lientz, *Effective Business Communication* (Santa Monica, Calif.: Goodyear, 1979).

[39] "Making Silence Your Ally," *Across the Board*, October 1999, p. 11.

[40] Boyd A. Vander Houwen, "Less Talking, More Listening," *HRMagazine*, April 1997, pp. 53–58.

[41] For a discussion of these and related issues, see Eric M. Eisenberg and Marsha G. Witten, "Reconsidering Openness in Organizational Communication," *Academy of Management Review*, July 1987, pp. 418–426.

[42] For a recent illustration, see Barbara Kellerman, "When Should a Leader Apologize—and When Not?" *Harvard Business Review*, April 2006, pp. 72–81.

CHAPTER 8

ASSESSING YOUR DECISION-MAKING SKILLS

Decision-Making Styles
Internal-External Control Sampler
Problem-Solving Style Questionnaire
Your Decision-Making Style

LEARNING ABOUT DECISION-MAKING SKILLS

The Decision-Making Context
Kinds of Decisions
Conditions for Making Decisions
Rational Decision Making
Recognizing and Defining the Decision Situation
Identifying Alternatives
Evaluating Alternatives
Selecting an Alternative
Implementing the Chosen Alternative
Following Up and Evaluating the Results
Behavioral Processes and Decision Making
The Administrative Model
Coalitions and Decision Making
Intuition
Escalation of Commitment
Risk Propensity and Decision Making
Ethics and Decision Making
Participative and Group Decision Making
Employee Participation and Involvement
Group and Team Decision Making
How Much Participation Should Be Allowed?
Making Decisions for Contingencies and During Crisis
Summary and a Look Ahead

VISUALIZING DECISION-MAKING SKILLS

Decision-Making Skills in Action—1
Decision-Making Skills in Action—2

PRACTICING YOUR DECISION-MAKING SKILLS

Making Career Choices
Choosing Team Members
Decision Making and Communication
Examining One Component of an Organization's Control System
Cost Reduction Decisions
Evaluating Training
Individual vs. Nominal Group Decision Making
Journaling and Affinity Diagrams in Decision Making
Designing a New Organization
Decision Making and Communicating in a Small Business

USING YOUR DECISION-MAKING SKILLS

Decisions, Decisions, Decisions
Lufthansa

EXTENDING YOUR DECISION-MAKING SKILLS

Group Extensions
Individual Extensions

YOUR DECISION-MAKING SKILLS NOW

Decision-Making Skills Assessment
Decision-Making Skills
Summary of Your Scores
Interpretation of Your Scores

INTERPRETATIONS

Decision-Making Styles
Internal-External Control Sampler
Problem-Solving Style Questionnaire
Your Decision-Making Style

Decision-Making Skills

© ISTOCKPHOTO.COM/STEVE COLE

As introduced in Chapter 1, decision-making skills refer to the manager's ability to correctly recognize and define problems and opportunities and to then select an appropriate course of action to solve problems and capitalize on opportunities. This chapter focuses on helping you develop your own decision-making skills. We start with four different decision-making assessments, and then provide detailed text material to help you learn more about this important skill. Following the text section are several cases and exercises to help you further develop and master effective managerial decision making.

ASSESS

ASSESSING YOUR DECISION-MAKING SKILLS

DECISION-MAKING STYLES

Decision making is clearly important. However, individuals differ in their decision-making style, or the way they approach decisions. The following assessment is designed to help you understand your personal decision-making style.

Instructions:
Respond to the following statements by indicating the extent to which each one describes you. Circle the response that best represents your self-evaluation.

1. Overall, I'm _____ to act.
   (a) quick (b) moderately fast (c) slow
2. I spend ____ amount of time making important decisions as/than I do making less important ones.
   (a) about the same (b) a greater (c) a much greater
3. When making decisions, I _____ go with my first thought.
   (a) usually (b) occasionally (c) rarely
4. When making decisions, I'm _____ concerned about making errors.
   (a) rarely (b) occasionally (c) often
5. When making decisions, I _____ recheck my work more than once.
   (a) rarely (b) occasionally (c) usually
6. When making decisions, I gather _____ information.
   (a) little (b) some (c) lots of
7. When making decisions, I consider _____ alternatives.
   (a) few (b) some (c) lots of
8. I usually make decisions _____ before the deadline.
   (a) way (b) somewhat (c) just
9. After making a decision, I _____ look for other alternatives, wishing I had waited.
   (a) rarely (b) occasionally (c) usually
10. I _____ regret having made a decision.
    (a) rarely (b) occasionally (c) often

Source: Adapted from Robert N. Lussier, *Supervision: A Skill-Building Approach*, Second Edition, pp. 122–123, ©1994 by Richard D. Irwin, Inc. Reproduced with permission of The McGraw-Hill Companies.

See Interpretations at the end of the chapter

INTERNAL-EXTERNAL CONTROL SAMPLER

A manager's decision making is shaped to a large extent by his or her locus of control. Julian E. Rotter developed a forced-choice 29-item scale for measuring an individual's degree of internal (I) and external (E) control. This I-E test is widely used. The following are sample items taken from an earlier version of the test.

Instructions: *For each set of items below, circle the statement that you more strongly believe.*

Circle the item in Column 1 or Column 2.	
1. Promotions are earned through hard work and persistence.	1. Making a lot of money is largely a matter of getting the right breaks.
2. In my experience I have noticed that there is usually a direct connection between how hard I study and the grades I get.	2. Many times the reactions of teachers seem haphazard to me.
3. The number of divorces indicates that more and more people are not trying to make their marriages work.	3. Marriage is largely a gamble.
4. When I am right, I can convince others.	4. It is silly to think that one can really change another person's basic attitudes.
5. In our society a man's future earning power is dependent upon his ability.	5. Getting promoted is really a matter of being a little luckier than the next guy.
6. If one knows how to deal with people they are really quite easily led.	6. I have little influence over the way other people behave.
7. In my case the grades I make are the results of my own efforts; luck has little or nothing to do with it.	7. Sometimes I feel that I have little to do with the grades I get.
8. People like me can change the course of world affairs if we make ourselves heard.	8. It is only wishful thinking to believe that one can really influence what happens in society at large.
9. I am the master of my fate.	9. A great deal that happens to me is probably a matter of chance.
10. Getting along with people is a skill that must be practiced.	10. It is almost impossible to figure out how to please some people.

Scoring:

Count the number of statements you circled in Column 1: _____ *(0-10)*
Count the number of statements you circled in Column 2: _____ *(0-10)*
Interpret your score: The higher your score in Column 1, the more you tend to have an *internal* *locus of control. The higher your score in Column 2, the more you tend to have an* *external* *locus of control.*

Source: Julian E. Rotter, "External Control and Internal Control," *Psychology Today*, 5, no. 1 (June 1971), p. 42. Reprinted with permission from *Psychology Today* magazine, ©1971 PT PARTNERS, L.P.

See Interpretations at the end of the chapter.

PROBLEM-SOLVING STYLE QUESTIONNAIRE

One of the critical skills needed by all managers is the ability to solve problems. One of the underlying characteristics of problem solving is how the managers prefer to gather and evaluate information. This self-assessment will aid you in determining your preferred problem-solving style.

Instructions:

Indicate the response that usually describes your concerns and behaviors. There are no right or wrong answers to the questions. For each question, indicate which of the two alternative statements is more characteristic of you. Some statements may seem to be equally characteristic or uncharacteristic of you. While we anticipated this, try to choose the statement that is relatively more characteristic of what you do or feel in your everyday life. You will be working with pairs of statements and will have 5 points to distribute among the statements. Points may be divided between each A and B statement in any of the following combination pairs.

- *If A is completely characteristic of you and B is completely uncharacteristic, write a 5 on your answer sheet under A and a 0 under B.* A B 5 0
- *If A is considerably more characteristic of you and B is somewhat characteristic, write a 4 on your answer sheet under A and a 1 under B.* A B 4 1
- *If A is only slightly more characteristic of you than B, write a 3 on your answer sheet under A and a 2 under B.* A B 3 2
- *Each of the above three combinations may be used in reverse under. For example, should you feel that B is slightly more characteristic of you than A, write a 2 on your answer sheet under A and a 3 under B (and so on, for A=1, B=4; or A=0 and B=5).* A B 2 3

Be sure that the numbers you assign to each pair sum to 5 points. Relate each question in the index to your own behavior. Remember, there is no right or wrong answer. Attempts to give a "correct" response merely distort the meaning of your answers and render the inventory's results valueless.

Questions	Score
1. Are you more (A) pragmatic (B) idealistic	A | B
2. Are you more impressed by (A) standards (B) sentiments	A | B
3. Are you more interested in that which (A) convinces you by facts (B) emotionally moves you	A | B
4. It is worse to (A) be practical (B) have a boring routine	A | B
5. Are you more attracted to (A) a person with common sense (B) a creative person	A | B
6. In judging others, are you more swayed by (A) the rules (B) the situation	A | B
7. Are you more interested in (A) what has happened (B) what can happen	A | B
8. Do you more often have (A) presence of mind (B) warm emotions	A | B
9. Are you more frequently (A) a realistic sort of person (B) an imaginative sort of person	A | B
10. Are you more (A) faithful (B) logical	A | B
11. Are you more (A) action oriented (B) creation oriented	A | B
12. Which guides you more (A) your brain (B) your heart	A | B

13. Do you take pride in your
    (A) realistic outlook
    (B) imaginative ability
    A | B
14. Which is more of a personal compliment
    (A) you are consistent in reasoning
    (B) you are considerate of others
    A | B
15. Are you more drawn to
    (A) basics
    (B) implications
    A | B
16. It is better to be
    (A) fair
    (B) sentimental
    A | B
17. Would you rather spend time with
    (A) realistic people
    (B) idealistic people
    A | B
18. Would you describe yourself as
    (A) hard
    (B) soft
    A | B
19. Would your friends say that you are
    (A) someone who is filled by new ideas
    (B) someone who is a realist
    A | B
20. It is better to be called a person who shows
    (A) feelings
    (B) reasonable consistency
    A | B

Scoring:

(1) *In the appropriate columns below, enter the numbers for your responses to each of the 20 questions. Then add down each column to obtain a total for score A and score B.*

Questions	Column I A	Column II B
1.	______	______
3.	______	______
5.	______	______
7.	______	______
9.	______	______
11.	______	______
13.	______	______
15.	______	______
17.	______	______
19.	______	______
Total	______	______
	S	N

Questions	Column III A	Column IV B
2.	______	______
4.	______	______
6.	______	______
8.	______	______
10.	______	______
12.	______	______
14.	______	______
16.	______	______
18.	______	______
20.	______	______
Total	______	______
	T	F

(2) *Compare the totals for Columns I and II. If your highest point total is for A or if your two totals are equal, circle the letter "S." If your highest point total is for B, circle the letter "N."*

(3) *Compare the totals for Columns III and IV. If your highest point total is for A, circle the letter "T." If your highest point total is for B or if the total score for A and B are equal, circle the letter "T."*

Source: From Hellriegel/Slocum/Woodman. Organizational Behavior, 6E. © 1992 South-Western, a part of Cengage Learning, Inc. Reproduced by permission. www.cengage/com/permissions

See Interpretations at the end of the chapter.

ASSESS

YOUR DECISION-MAKING STYLE

Decision making is clearly an important skill for managers. The degree of preparation, the extent to which people rely on information and structure, and the influences on those decision-making patterns often is dictated by the style people tend to use most frequently. The Decision Style Inventory (Rowe, Mason, Dickel, Mann and Mockler, 1994) utilizes a simple questionnaire to determine which style is dominant. The technique focuses on how we prefer to gather and use information among other things. Once we know and understand ourselves, we can begin to understand the style of others.

Instructions:

Complete the following questionnaire. Read each question on the left-hand side and score each response on the same line according to which alternative you rate the closest to the way you think or feel. Each question is answered by assigning values as follows:

8	4	2	1
Most like me			*Least like me*

For example, in the first question an individual may want to assign an 8 to "be recognised for my work," a 4 to "have a position with status," a 2 to "feel secure," and a 1 to "be outstanding in my field." Remember that each score can be assigned only once to each question. In other words, all four numbers (8, 4, 2, 1) must be used for each question; but do not repeat any of these four numbers for any one question. Thus, using two 8s or two 2s would not be a correct response to any given question. An interpretation of the scores will be provided later.

There are no right or wrong answers. Each person is different and will, therefore, score the questions differently. Generally the first answer that comes to mind is the best to put down. Your score reflects how you see yourself, not what you believe is correct or desirable, as related to your work situation. It covers typical decisions that you make in your work environment.

ASSESS

Question	Column	1	Column	2	Column	3	Column	4
1 My prime objective is to:	Have a position with status		Be the best in my field		Achieve recognition for my work		Feel secure in my job	
2 I enjoy jobs that:	Are technical and well defined		Have considerable variety		Allow independent action		Involve people	
3 I expect people working for me to be:	Productive and Fast		Highly capable		Committed and responsive		Receptive to suggestions	
4 In my job, I look for:	Practical results		The best solutions		New approaches or ideas		A good working environment	
5 I communicate best with others:	In a direct, one to one basis		In writing		By having a group discussion		In a formal meeting	
6 In my planning I emphasize:	Current problems		Meeting objectives		Future goals		Developing people's careers	
7 When faced with solving a problem, I:	Rely on proven approaches		Apply careful analysis		Look for creative approaches		Rely on my feelings	
8 When using information I prefer:	Specific facts		Accurate and complete data		Broad coverage of many options		Limited data that is easily understood	
9 When I am not sure about what to do, I:	Rely on intuition		Search for facts		Look for a possible compromise		Wait before making a decision	
10 Whenever possible, I avoid:	Long debates		Incomplete work		Using numbers or formulas		Conflict with others	
11 I am especially good at:	Remembering dates and facts		Solving difficult problems		Seeing many possibilities		Interacting with others	
12 When time is important, I:	Decide and act quickly		Follow plans and priorities		Refuse to be pressured		Seek guidance or support	
13 In social settings I generally:	Speak with others		Think about what is being said		Observe what is going on		Listen to the conversation	
14 I am good at remembering:	People's names		Places we met		People's faces		People's personality	
15 The work I do provides me:	The power to influence others		Challenging assignments		Achieving my personal goals		Acceptance by the group	
16 I work well with those who are:	Energetic and ambitious		Self confident		Open minded		Polite and trusting	
17 When under stress, I:	Become anxious		Concentrate on the problem		Become frustrated		Am forgetful	
18 Others consider me:	Aggressive		Disciplined		Imaginative		Supportive	
19 My decisions typically are:	Realistic and direct		Systematic or abstract		Broad and flexible		Sensitive to the needs of others	
20 I dislike:	Losing control		Boring work		Following rules		Being rejected	
	Column 1 Total		**Column 2 Total**		**Column 3 Total**		**Column 4 Total**	

Scoring:

When you have finished scoring all the questions, total all four columns. Then write your scores for each column in the corresponding boxes on the grid below:

Column 2 Total: ______ **ANALYTICAL**	Column 3 Total: ______ **CONCEPTUAL**	(Columns 2 + 3) ______ **THINKING**
Column 1 Total: ______ **DIRECTIVE**	Column 4 Total: ______ **BEHAVIORAL**	(Columns 1 + 4) ______ **ACTING**
(Columns 2 + 1) ______ **TASK ORIENTED**	(Columns 3 + 4) ______ **PEOPLE ORIENTED**	

Source: Adapted from a learning activity designed by Sharon Gerstmeier (Strategic Learning Partnerships), 1994, based on work by Rowe, Mason, Dickel, Mann & Mockler, Decision Style Inventory, Rowe AJ., Mason, RO., Dickel, KE., (1993) Strategic Management: A Methodological Approach. Copyright © 1983 by Alan J. Rowe.

See Interpretation at the end of the chapter.

GO ONLINE to the Griffin/Van Fleet Assessment Library for online versions of these and other assessments.

LEARNING ABOUT DECISION-MAKING SKILLS

The Decision-Making Context
- *Kinds of Decisions*
- *Conditions for Making Decisions*

Rational Decision Making
- *Recognizing and Defining the Decision Situation*
- *Identifying Alternatives*
- *Evaluating Alternatives*
- *Selecting an Alternative*
- *Implementing the Chosen Alternative*
- *Following Up and Evaluating the Results*

Behavioral Processes and Decision Making
- *The Administrative Model*
- *Coalitions and Decision Making*
- *Intuition*
- *Escalation of Commitment*
- *Risk Propensity and Decision Making*
- *Ethics and Decision Making*

Participative and Group Decision Making
- *Employee Participation and Involvement*
- *Group and Team Decision Making*
  - Forms of Group and Team Decision Making
  - Advantages of Group and Team Decision Making
  - Disadvantages of Group and Team Decision Making
  - Managing Group and Team Decision Making

How Much Participation Should Be Allowed?

Making Decisions for Contingencies and During Crisis

Summary and a Look Ahead

Decision-making skills refer to the manager's ability to accurately recognize and define problems and opportunities and then to select an appropriate course of action to solve problems and capitalize on opportunities. This chapter will help you better understand how managers make decisions and provide some guidance on increasing the likelihood of a good decision. We will discuss the rational approach to decision making and then describe several behavioral forces and processes that often limit or constrain rationality. We'll also examine participative and group decision making and discuss decision making during crises. As you develop an understanding of these various perspectives on decision making, you should anticipate that your own decision-making skills will improve. To begin, we'll introduce some definitions and provide the context for managerial decision making.

THE DECISION-MAKING CONTEXT

As you begin to develop an understanding of decision making, it is important to recognize that *decision making* can refer to either a specific act or a general process. **Decision making** is the act of choosing one alternative from among a set of alternatives. The decision-making process, however, is much more than this. One step of the process, for example, involves the decision maker recognizing that a decision is necessary and identifying the set of feasible alternatives before selecting one. Hence, the **decision-making process** includes recognizing and defining the nature of a decision situation, identifying alternatives, choosing the "best" alternative, and putting it into practice.[1] Further, as part of the decision-making process the manager often must decide who will make the decision. Hence, a manager needs to understand how to both make the "best" decision him or herself but also how to most effectively manage decision-making processes that may involve other people.

The word *best*, of course, implies effectiveness. Effective decision making requires that the decision maker understand the situation driving the decision. Most people would consider an effective decision to be one that optimizes some set of factors, such as profits, sales, employee welfare, and market share. In some situations, though, an effective decision may be one that minimizes loss, expenses, or employee turnover. It may even mean selecting the best method for going out of business, laying off employees, or terminating a strategic alliance. During the 2008–2010 recession, for example, the most effective decisions included those involving cutting costs, minimizing losses, reallocating resources, and so forth.

decision-making skills the manager's ability to accurately recognize and define problems and opportunities and to then select an appropriate course of action to solve problems and capitalize on opportunities

decision making the act of choosing one alternative from among a set of alternatives

decision-making process recognizing and defining the nature of a decision situation, identifying alternatives, choosing the "best" alternative, and putting it into practice

© ISTOCKPHOTO.COM/WENDELLANDCAROLYN

© KIM KARPELES/ALAMY

Decisions often involve trying to achieve an optimal solution. For instance, retailers may decide to both close existing stores and open new ones as situations change.

Learning that the firm is earning higher-than-projected profits, for example, requires a subsequent decision. Should the extra funds be used to increase shareholder dividends, reinvest in current operations, or expand into new markets?

Of course, it may take a long time before a manager knows if the right decision was made. For example, in late 2008 and early 2009 government leaders made the decision to invest billions of dollars in failing financial institutions and other businesses. It will be years—or perhaps decades—before economists and other experts will know if those were sound decisions or if the United States would have been better off allowing those businesses to fail.

Kinds of Decisions

Managers must make many different types of decisions. In general, however, most decisions fall into one of two categories: programmed and nonprogrammed.[2] A **programmed decision** is one that is relatively structured or recurs with some frequency (or both). Starbucks uses programmed decisions to purchase new supplies of coffee beans, cups, and napkins. Likewise, the Green Bay Ford dealer made a decision that he will sponsor a youth soccer team each year. Thus, when the soccer club president calls, the dealer already knows what he will do. Many decisions regarding basic operating systems and procedures and standard organizational transactions are of this variety and can, therefore, be programmed.[3]

Nonprogrammed decisions, on the other hand, are relatively unstructured and occur much less often. Disney's decision to buy Pixar and United and Continental's decision to merge were both nonprogrammed decisions. Managers faced with such decisions must treat each one as unique, investing enormous amounts of time, energy, and resources into exploring the situation from all perspectives. Intuition and experience are major factors in nonprogrammed decisions. Most of the decisions made by top managers involving strategy (including mergers, acquisitions, and takeovers) and organization design are nonprogrammed. So are decisions about new facilities, new products, labor contracts, and legal issues.

We should also note that managers make decisions about both problems and opportunities. For example, deciding how to cut costs by 10 percent reflects a problem—an undesirable situation that requires a solution. But decisions are also necessary in situations of opportunity.

> *"The big decision we made was that we divested [Aston Martin, Jaguar, Land Rover, Volvo, Mazda] to have a laser focus on the Ford and Lincoln brands."*
>
> ALAN MULALLY
> Ford CEO[4]

"HOW MULALLY HELPED TURN FORD AROUND," USA TODAY, JULY 18, 2011, P. 2B.

programmed decisions decisions that are relatively structured or recur with some frequency (or both)

nonprogrammed decisions decisions that are relatively unstructured and occur much less often

Conditions for Making Decisions

Just as there are different kinds of decisions, there are also different conditions under which

FIGURE 8.1 DECISION-MAKING CONDITIONS

Most major decisions in organizations today are made under conditions of uncertainty. Managers making decisions in these circumstances must be sure to learn as much as possible about the situation and approach the decision from a logical and rational perspective.

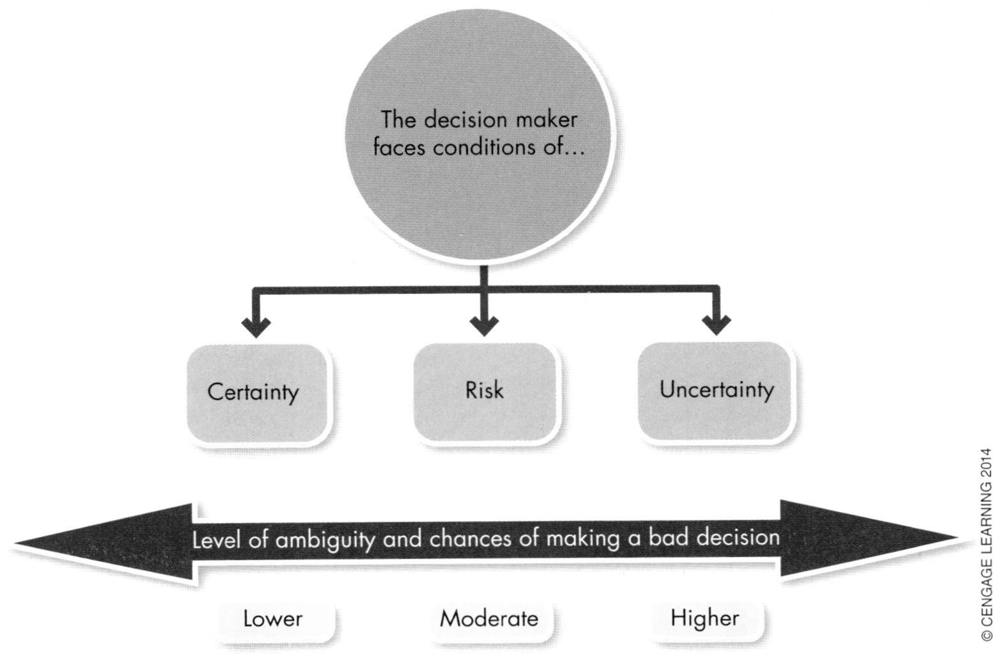

decisions are made. Managers sometimes have an almost perfect understanding of conditions surrounding a decision, but at other times they have few clues about those conditions. In general, as shown in *Figure 8.1*, the circumstances that exist for the decision maker are conditions of certainty, risk, or uncertainty.[5]

When the decision maker knows with reasonable certainty what the alternatives are and what conditions are associated with each alternative, a state of certainty exists. Suppose, for example, that managers at Singapore Airlines make a decision to buy five new jumbo jets. Their next decision is from whom to buy them. Because there are only two companies in the world that make jumbo jets, Boeing and Airbus, Singapore Airlines knows its options exactly. Each supplier has proven products and will negotiate prices and delivery dates. The airline thus knows the alternative conditions associated with each. There is little ambiguity and relatively little chance of making a bad decision.

Few organizational decisions, however, are made under conditions of true certainty. The complexity and turbulence of the contemporary business world make such situations rare. Even the airplane purchase decision we just considered has less certainty than it appears. The aircraft companies may not be able to guarantee delivery dates, so they may write cost-increase or inflation clauses into contracts. Thus the airline may be only partially certain of the conditions surrounding each alternative.

A more common decision-making condition is a state of risk. Under a state of risk, the availability of each alternative and its potential payoffs and costs are all associated with probability estimates.[6] Suppose, for example, that a labor contract negotiator for a company receives a "final" offer from the union right before a strike deadline. The negotiator has two alternatives: to accept or to reject the offer. The risk centers on whether the union representatives are bluffing. If the company negotiator accepts the offer, she avoids a strike but commits to a relatively costlier labor contract. If she rejects the contract, she may get a more favorable contract if the union is bluffing, but she may provoke a strike if it is not.

On the basis of past experiences, relevant information, the advice of others, and her own judgment, she may conclude that there is about a 75 percent chance that union representatives are bluffing and about a

state of certainty situation in which the decision maker knows with reasonable certainty what the alternatives are and what conditions are associated with each alternative

state of risk situation in which the availability of each alternative and its potential payoffs and costs are all associated with probability estimates

LEARN

© CLERKENWELL

These people represent different sides of a negotiation involving management and labor. Each must make critical decisions as they negotiate a new labor contract.

25 percent chance that they will back up their threats. Thus she can base a calculated decision on the two alternatives (accept or reject the contract demands) and the probable consequences of each. When making decisions under a state of risk, managers must reasonably estimate the probabilities associated with each alternative. For example, if the union negotiators are committed to a strike if their demands are not met, and the company negotiator rejects their demands because she guesses they will not strike, her miscalculation will prove costly.

As indicated in *Figure 8.1*, decision making under conditions of risk is accompanied by moderate ambiguity and chances of a bad decision. For instance, like many other automobile companies, Ford laid off thousands of workers during 2008. But toward the end of the year, Ford executives noted that as fuel prices were dropping, demand for its new F-150 pickup was increasing. So, the firm rehired 1,000 of its former workers to help build more pickups. The risk was that if gas prices had surged unexpectedly and/or demand for the F-150 had cooled, Ford would have been in the embarrassing position of having recalled workers and then once again terminating them. But the upside was that if Ford's assessments were correct, the firm would generate new revenues and more profits.[7] In the end, Ford's decision proved to be the correct one as demand continued to increase.[8]

state of uncertainty situation in which the decision maker does not know all the alternatives, the risks associated with each, or the likely consequences of each alternative

rational model of decision making a prescriptive approach that tells managers how they should make decisions; it rests on the assumptions that managers are logical and rational and that they make decisions that are in the best interests of the organization

Most of the major decision making in contemporary organizations is done under a **state of uncertainty**. The decision maker does not know all the alternatives, the risks associated with each, or the likely consequences of each alternative. This uncertainty stems from the complexity and dynamism of contemporary organizations and their environments. The emergence of the Internet as a significant force in today's competitive environment has served to increase both revenue potential and uncertainty for most managers.

To make effective decisions in these circumstances, managers must acquire as much relevant information as possible and approach the situation from a logical and rational perspective. Intuition, judgment, and experience always play major roles in the decision-making process under conditions of uncertainty. Even so, uncertainty is the most ambiguous condition for managers and the one most prone to error.[9] Indeed, many of the problems associated with the downfall of Arthur Andersen resulted from the firm's apparent difficulties in responding to ambiguous and uncertain decision parameters regarding the firm's moral, ethical, and legal responsibilities.[10]

RATIONAL DECISION MAKING

The **rational model of decision making** is a prescriptive approach that tells managers how they should make decisions. It assumes that managers are logical and rational and that they make decisions that are in the best interests of the organization. (As we see later, these conditions rarely, if ever, actually exist.) Specifically, the rational model makes the following assumptions:

1. Decision makers have complete information about the decision situation and possible alternatives.
2. Decision makers can effectively eliminate uncertainty to achieve a decision condition of certainty.
3. Decision makers evaluate all aspects of the decision situation logically and rationally.

A manager who wants to approach a decision rationally and logically should try to follow the steps in rational decision making shown in *Figure 8.2*. These steps help the decision maker to focus on facts and logic and help guard against inappropriate assumptions and pitfalls.

FIGURE 8.2 THE RATIONAL MODEL OF DECISION MAKING

The classical model of decision making assumes that managers are rational and logical. It attempts to prescribe how managers should approach decision situations.

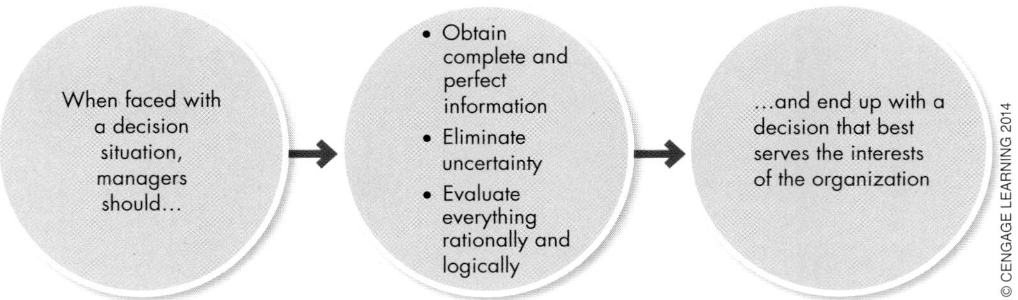

Recognizing and Defining the Decision Situation

The first step in rational decision making is to recognize that a decision is necessary—that is, there must be some stimulus or spark to initiate the process. For many decisions and problem situations, the stimulus may occur without any warning. When equipment malfunctions, the manager must decide whether to repair or replace it. Or, when a major crisis erupts, as described in Chapter 3, the manager must decide how to deal with it quickly. As we already noted, the stimulus for a decision may be either positive or negative. A manager who must decide how to invest surplus funds, for example, faces a positive decision situation. A negative financial stimulus could involve having to trim budgets because of cost overruns.

Inherent in problem recognition is the need to define precisely what the problem is. The manager must develop a complete understanding of the problem, its causes, and its relationship to other factors. This understanding comes from careful analysis and thoughtful consideration of the situation. Consider the current situation in the international air travel industry. Because of the growth of international travel related to business, education, and tourism, global carriers like Singapore Airlines, KLM, JAL, British Airways, American Airlines, and others need to increase their capacity for international travel. Because most major international airports are already operating at or near capacity, adding a significant number of new flights to existing schedules is not feasible. As a result, the most logical alternative is to increase capacity on existing flights. Thus Boeing and Airbus, the world's only manufacturers of large commercial aircraft, recognized an important opportunity and defined their decision situation as how to best respond to the need for increased global travel capacity.[11]

Identifying Alternatives

Once the decision situation has been recognized and defined, the second step is to identify alternative courses of effective action. Developing both obvious, standard alternatives and creative, innovative alternatives is generally useful.[12] In general, the more important the decision, the more attention is directed to developing alternatives.[13] If the decision involves a multimillion-dollar relocation, a great deal of time and expertise will be devoted to identifying the best locations. J.C. Penney spent two years searching before selecting the Dallas–Fort Worth area for its new corporate headquarters. If the problem is to choose a color for the company's softball team uniforms, less time and expertise will be brought to bear.

Although managers should seek creative solutions, they also must recognize that various constraints often limit their alternatives. Common constraints include legal restrictions, moral and ethical norms, authority constraints, and constraints imposed by the power and authority of the manager, available technology, economic considerations, and unofficial social norms. Boeing and Airbus identified three alternatives to address the decision situation of increasing international airline travel capacity: They could develop new large planes independently, they could collaborate in a joint venture to create a single new large plane, or they could modify their largest existing planes to increase their capacity.

Evaluating Alternatives

The third step in the decision-making process is evaluating each of the alternatives. *Figure* 8.3 presents a decision tree that can be used to judge different alternatives. The figure suggests that managers evaluate each alternative in terms of its *feasibility*, its *satisfactoriness*, and

FIGURE 8.3 EVALUATING ALTERNATIVES IN THE DECISION-MAKING PROCESS

Managers must thoroughly evaluate all the alternatives, which increases the chances that the alternative finally chosen will be successful. Failure to evaluate an alternative's feasibility, satisfactoriness, and consequences can lead to a wrong decision.

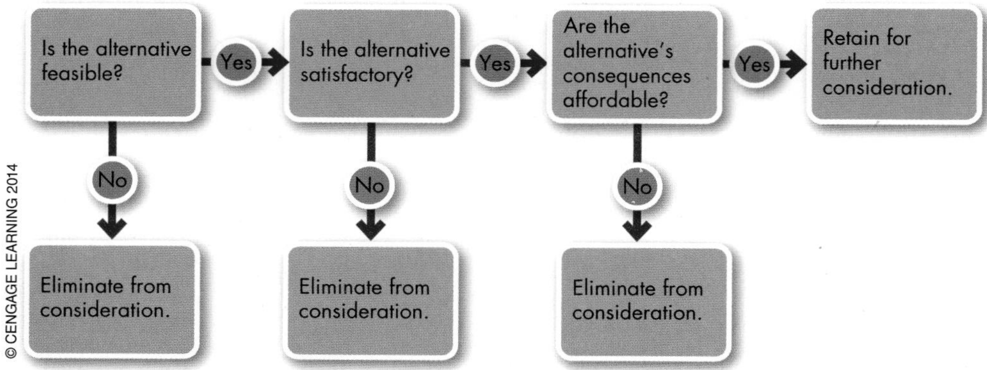

its *consequences*. The first question to ask is whether an alternative is feasible. Is it within the realm of probability and practicality? For a small, struggling firm, an alternative requiring a huge financial outlay is probably out of the question. Other alternatives may not be feasible because of legal barriers. And limited human, material, and information resources may make other alternatives impractical.

> "We don't think that [building the A380] is a very smart thing to do."
> RANDY BAESLER
> Boeing executive[14]

WALL STREET JOURNAL, MAY 27, 2005, P. A1.

When an alternative has passed the test of feasibility, the manager must next determine how well it satisfies the conditions of the decision situation. For example, a manager searching for ways to double production capacity might initially consider purchasing an existing plant from another company. If a more detailed analysis reveals that the new plant would increase production capacity by only 35 percent, this alternative may not be satisfactory.

Finally, when an alternative has proven both feasible and satisfactory, its probable consequences must still be assessed. To what extent will a particular alternative influence other parts of the organization? What financial and nonfinancial costs will be associated with such influences? For example, a plan to boost sales by cutting prices may disrupt cash flows, require a new advertising program, and alter the behavior of sales representatives because it requires a different commission structure. The manager, then, must put "price tags" on the consequences of each alternative. Even an alternative that is both feasible and satisfactory must be eliminated if its consequences are too expensive for the total system. Airbus felt it would be at a disadvantage if it tried to simply enlarge its existing planes, because the Boeing 747 was already the largest aircraft being made and it could easily be expanded to remain the largest. Boeing, meanwhile, was seriously concerned about the risk inherent in building a new and even larger plane, even if it shared the risk with Airbus as a joint venture.

Selecting an Alternative

Even though many alternatives fail to pass the triple tests of feasibility, satisfactoriness, and affordable consequences, two or more alternatives may remain. Choosing the best of these is the real crux of decision making. One approach is to choose the alternative with the optimal combination of feasibility, satisfactoriness, and affordable consequences. Even though most situations do not lend themselves to objective, mathematical analysis, the manager can often develop subjective estimates and weights for choosing an alternative.

Optimization also is a frequent goal. Because a decision is likely to affect several individuals or units, any feasible alternative will probably not maximize all of the relevant goals. Suppose that the manager of the Kansas City Royals needs to select a new outfielder for the upcoming baseball season. Bill hits 0.350 but has difficulty catching fly balls; Joe hits only 0.175 but is outstanding in the field; and Sam hits 0.290 and is a solid, but not an outstanding, fielder. The manager probably would select Sam because of the optimal balance of hitting and fielding.

Decision makers should also remember, though, that finding multiple acceptable alternatives may be

© DR_FLASH/SHUTTERSTOCK.COM

© LUKICH/SHUTTERSTOCK.COM

© THOR JORGEN UDVANG/SHUTTERSTOCK.COM

Airbus and Boeing recently faced the same situation but arrived at very different decisions. Airbus decided to design and launch the A380. Boeing, meanwhile, decided to redesign the venerable 747 and introduce the new 787.

possible; in other words, selecting just one alternative and rejecting all the others might not be necessary. For example, the Royals' manager might decide that Sam will start each game, Bill will be retained as a pinch hitter, and Joe will be retained as a late-inning defensive substitute. In many hiring decisions, managers rank the candidates remaining after evaluation. If the top candidate rejects the offer, it may be automatically extended to the number-two candidate and, if necessary, to the remaining candidates in order. For the reasons noted earlier, Airbus proposed a joint venture with Boeing. Boeing, meanwhile, decided that its best course of action was to modify its existing 747 to increase its capacity. As a result, Airbus then decided to proceed on its own to develop and manufacture a new jumbo jet. Boeing, however, also decided that in addition to modifying its 747 it would also develop a new plane to offer as an alternative, albeit one not as large as the 747 or the proposed Airbus plane.

LEARN

Implementing the Chosen Alternative

After an alternative has been selected, the manager must put it into effect. In some decision situations, implementation is easy; in others, it is more difficult. In the case of an acquisition, for example, managers must decide how to integrate all the activities of the new business, including purchasing, human resource practices, and distribution, into an ongoing organizational framework. For example, when United and Continental decided to merge managers estimated that it would take almost two years to integrate the two firms into a single one.

Managers also must consider people's resistance to change when implementing decisions. The reasons for such resistance include insecurity, inconvenience, and fear of the unknown. When J.C. Penney decided to move its headquarters from New York to Texas, many employees decided to resign rather than relocate. Managers should anticipate potential resistance at various stages of the implementation process. Managers should also recognize that even when all alternatives have been evaluated as precisely as possible and the consequences of each alternative weighed, unanticipated consequences are still likely. Any number of factors—unexpected cost increases, a less-than-perfect fit with existing organizational subsystems, or unpredicted effects on cash flow or operating expenses, for example—could develop after implementation has begun. Boeing set its engineers to work expanding the capacity of its 747 from 416 passengers to as many as 520 passengers by adding 30 feet to the plane's body. The company also has been developing its new plane intended for international travel, the Boeing 787 Dreamliner. Airbus engineers, meanwhile, spent years developing and constructing its new jumbo jet, the A380, equipped with escalators and elevators, and capable of carrying 655 passengers. Airbus's development costs were estimated to be more than $12 billion.

LEARN

Following Up and Evaluating the Results

The final step in the decision-making process requires that managers evaluate the effectiveness of their decision—that is, they make sure that the chosen alternative has served its original purpose. If an implemented alternative appears not to be working, the manager can respond in several ways. Another previously identified alternative (the second or third choice, for instance) could be adopted. Or the manager might recognize that the situation was not correctly defined to begin with and start the process all over again. Finally, the manager might decide that the original alternative is in fact appropriate but has not yet had time to work or should be implemented in a different way.[15]

Failure to evaluate a decision's effectiveness may have serious consequences. The Pentagon once spent $1.8 billion and eight years developing the Sergeant York anti-aircraft gun. From the beginning, tests revealed major problems with the weapon system, but not until it was in its final stages, when it was demonstrated to be completely ineffective, was the project scrapped.

At this point, both Boeing and Airbus are still learning about the consequences of their decisions. Airbus's A380 has been placed in commercial service. However, the plane has suffered numerous mechanical problems. Moreover, because the 2008–2010 recession dealt a blow to large international airlines, some of them—such as Qantas Airways and Emirates Airlines—deferred or cancelled orders for the plane. Airbus estimated that it needs to sell 420 A380s before it starts making a profit. Current projections suggest that sales of the plane may not hit that target until at least 2020.[16] Meanwhile, it appeared for a while that Boeing's commitment to the new 787 might prove to be the best decision of all. A key element of the new plane is that it is much more fuel-efficient than other international airplanes. Given the dramatic surge in fuel costs in recent years, a fuel-efficient option like the 787 will presumably be an enormous success. However, the 787 suffered from numerous manufacturing problems, and delivery of the plane was delayed for several years. While the first 787 was scheduled for delivery in 2008, it wasn't actually delivered until late 2011. Hence, the real impact of the new plane will not be known for a few more years.[17]

administrative model describes how decisions often actually are made; argues that managers (1) use incomplete and imperfect information, (2) are constrained by bounded rationality, and (3) tend to "satisfice" when making decisions

bounded rationality decision makers are limited by their values and unconscious reflexes, skills, and habits

BEHAVIORAL PROCESSES AND DECISION MAKING

If managers approached all decision situations as logically as described in the previous section, more decisions might prove to be successful. Yet managers often make decisions with little consideration for logic and rationality. Some experts have estimated that US companies use rational decision-making techniques less than 20 percent of the time.[18] And, even when organizations try to be logical, they sometimes fail. For example, when Starbucks opened its first coffee shops in New York, it relied on scientific marketing research, taste tests, and rational deliberation in making a decision to emphasize drip over espresso coffee. However, that decision proved wrong, as New Yorkers strongly preferred the same espresso-style coffees that were Starbucks' mainstays in the West. Hence, the firm had to quickly reconfigure its stores to better meet customer preferences.

On the other hand, sometimes when a decision is made with little regard for logic, it can still turn out to be correct.[19] An important ingredient in how these forces work is the behavioral aspect of decision making. The administrative model better reflects these subjective considerations. Other behavioral aspects include political forces, intuition and escalation of commitment, risk propensity, and ethics.

The Administrative Model

Herbert A. Simon was one of the first experts to recognize that managers do not always make decisions with rationality and logic.[20] Simon was subsequently awarded the Nobel Prize in economics. Rather than prescribing how decisions should be made, his view of decision making, now called the **administrative model**, describes how decisions often actually are made. The model holds that managers (1) use incomplete and imperfect information, (2) are constrained by bounded rationality, and (3) tend to "satisfice" when making decisions.

Bounded rationality suggests that decision makers are limited by their values and unconscious reflexes, skills, and habits. They also are limited by less-than-complete information and knowledge. Bounded rationality partially explains how US auto executives allowed Japanese automakers to get such a strong foothold in the US domestic market. For years, executives at GM, Ford, and Chrysler compared their companies' performances only to one another's and ignored foreign imports. They did not acknowledge the foreign "threat" until the domestic auto market had been changed forever. If managers had gathered complete information from the beginning, they might have been better able to thwart their foreign competitors. Essentially, then, the concept of bounded rationality suggests that although people try to be rational decision makers, their rationality has limits.

Another important part of the administrative model is satisficing. This concept suggests that rather than conducting an exhaustive search for the best possible alternative, decision makers tend to search only until they identify an alternative that meets some minimum standard of sufficiency. A manager looking for a site for a new plant, for example, may select the first site she finds that meets basic requirements for transportation, utilities, and price, even though further search might yield a better location. People satisfice for a variety of reasons. Managers may simply be unwilling to ignore their own motives (such as reluctance to spend time making a decision) and therefore not be able to continue searching after identifying a minimally acceptable alternative. The decision maker may be unable to weigh and evaluate large numbers of alternatives and criteria. Also, subjective and personal considerations often intervene in decision situations.

Because of the inherent imperfection of information, bounded rationality, and satisficing, the decisions made by a manager may or may not actually be in the best interests of the organization. A manager may choose a particular location for the new plant because it offers the lowest land prices, an excellent workforce, and the best availability of utilities and transportation. Or she may choose the location because it is located in a community where she wants to live.

In summary, then, the rational and administrative models paint quite different pictures of decision making. Which is more correct? Actually, each can be used to better understand how managers make decisions. The rational model is prescriptive: It explains how managers can at least attempt to be more rational and logical in their approaches to decisions. Managers can use the administrative model to develop a better understanding of their inherent biases and limitations.[21] In the following sections, we describe more fully other behavioral forces that can influence decisions.

© YURI ARCURS I DREAMSTIME.COM

Coalitions and Decision Making

Coalitions also can play a major role how decisions are made. A coalition is an informal alliance of individuals or groups formed to achieve a common goal. This common goal is often a preferred decision alternative. For example, coalitions of stockholders sometimes band together to force a board of directors to make a certain decision.

When General Motors decided to launch Saturn as a new automobile company, the idea had the full backing and support of GM CEO Roger Smith. Saturn was to have its own factories, design teams, and dealer networks and was to compete directly with high-quality foreign imports like Toyota and Honda. Just as the first Saturn cars were being introduced, however, Smith retired. As it turned out, there was a coalition of senior GM executives who had opposed the Saturn concept but had been unable to do anything about it because Smith was such a powerful product champion. When Smith left GM, though, the coalition managed to divert resources intended for Saturn to other GM brands. As a result, new Saturn products were delayed, the brand received weak marketing support, and it never lived up to expectations.[22]

The impact of coalitions can be either positive or negative. They can help astute managers get the organization on a path toward effectiveness and profitability, or they can strangle well-conceived strategies and decisions. Managers must recognize when to use coalitions, how to assess whether coalitions are acting in the best interests of the organization, and how to constrain their dysfunctional effects.[23]

Intuition

Another important decision process that goes beyond logic and rationality is intuition. Intuition is an innate belief about something, without conscious consideration. Managers sometimes decide to do something because it "feels right" or they have a "hunch." This feeling usually is not arbitrary, however. Rather, it is based on years of experience and practice in making

satisficing decision makers tend to search only until they identify an alternative that meets some minimum standard of sufficiency rather than conducting an exhaustive search for the best possible alternative

coalition an informal alliance of individuals or groups formed to achieve a common goal

intuition an innate belief about something, without conscious consideration

LEARN

JUSTIN SULLIVAN/GETTY IMAGES

When General Motors launched Saturn, it was hailed as a new US automobile company that would use Japanese methods and techniques to better compete with Toyota, Honda, and Nissan. However, a coalition of GM executives opposed to the concept managed to weaken Saturn, and it was eventually closed.

decisions in similar situations.[24] An inner sense may help managers make an occasional decision without going through a full-blown rational sequence of steps. Of course, all managers, but most especially inexperienced ones, should be careful not to rely too heavily on intuition. If rationality and logic are continually flouted for "what feels right," the odds are that disaster will strike one day.

> *"Nothing is more difficult, and therefore more precious, than to be able to decide."*
> Napoleon[25]

FORTUNE, JUNE 27, 2005, P. 55.

Escalation of Commitment

Another important behavioral process that influences decision making is **escalation of commitment** to a chosen course of action. In particular, decision makers sometimes make decisions and then become so committed to the courses of action suggested by those decisions that they stay with them, even when the decisions appear to have been wrong.[26] For example, when people buy stock in a company, they sometimes refuse to sell it even after repeated drops in price. They chose a course of action—buying the stock in anticipation of making a profit—and then stay with it even in the face of increasing losses. Moreover, after the value drops, they rationalize that they can't sell now because they will lose money.

escalation of commitment adhering to a decision beyond a point after it has become clear that it is wrong

For years Pan American World Airways ruled the skies and used its profits to diversify into real estate and other businesses. But, with the advent of deregulation, Pan Am began to struggle and lose market share to other carriers. When Pan Am managers finally realized how ineffective its airline operations had become, experts today point out that the "rational" decision would have been to sell off the remaining airline operations and concentrate on the firm's more profitable businesses. But, because they still saw the company as being first and foremost an airline, they instead began to slowly sell off the firm's profitable holdings to keep the airline flying. Eventually, the company was left with nothing but an ineffective and inefficient airline. Managers then had to sell off its more profitable routes before eventually being taken over by Delta. Had Pan Am managers made the more rational decision years earlier, chances are the firm could still be a profitable enterprise today, albeit one with no involvement in the airline industry.[27]

In contrast, a group of investors licensed the use of Hard Rock logos and trademarks for a large theme park—Hard Rock Park—to be built in South Carolina. After six years of planning and construction and an investment of more than $400 million, the park opened in Myrtle Beach to dismal reviews and poor attendance. Rather than increasing their investment and trying to increase attendance, owners decided after only nine months to shut the park down and sell off its assets.[28]

Thus, decision makers must walk a fine line. On the one hand, they must guard against sticking too long with an incorrect decision. To do so can bring about financial decline. On the other hand, managers should not bail out of seemingly incorrect decisions too soon, as Adidas once did. Adidas had dominated the market for professional athletic shoes. It subsequently entered the market for amateur sports shoes and did well there also. But managers interpreted a sales slowdown as a sign that the boom in athletic shoes was over. They thought that they had made the wrong decision and ordered drastic cutbacks. The market took off again with Nike at the head of the pack, and Adidas fell far behind. New managers have changed the way Adidas makes decisions, and the firm is again on its way to becoming a force in the athletic shoe and apparel markets.

RANDALL HILL/MYRTLE BEACH SUN NEWS/MCT VIA GETTY IMAGES

Escalation of commitment can lead to financial ruin. Investors in a poorly conceived Hard Rock theme park in South Carolina avoided this mistake by shuttering the park soon after it became apparent that it was doomed to failure.

Risk Propensity and Decision Making

The behavioral element of risk propensity is the extent to which a decision maker is willing to gamble when making a decision. Some managers are cautious about every decision they make. They try to adhere to the rational model and are extremely conservative in what they do. Such managers are more likely to avoid mistakes, and they infrequently make decisions that lead to big losses. Other managers are extremely aggressive in making decisions and are willing to take risks.[29] They rely heavily on intuition, reach decisions quickly, and often risk big investments on their decisions. As in gambling, these managers are more likely than their conservative counterparts to achieve big successes with their decisions; they are also more likely to incur greater losses.[30] The organization's culture is a prime ingredient in fostering different levels of risk propensity.

Ethics and Decision Making

As we introduce in Chapter 2, individual ethics are personal beliefs about right and wrong behavior. Decision making involves ethics in a number of ways. For example, suppose that, after careful analysis, a manager realizes that his company could save money by closing his own department and subcontracting with a supplier for the same services. But to recommend this course of action would result in the loss of several jobs, including his own. His own ethical standards will clearly shape how he proceeds.[31] Indeed, each component of managerial ethics (relationships of the firm to its employees, of employees to the firm, and of the firm to other economic agents) involves a wide variety of decisions, all of which are likely to have an ethical component. Managers must remember that, just as behavioral processes such as politics and risk propensity affect the decisions they make, so, too, do their own ethical beliefs.[32]

PARTICIPATIVE AND GROUP DECISION MAKING

While managers may make decisions themselves, they often manage decision-making processes by empowering subordinates and/or groups to make decisions. We first examine employee participation and involvement and then turn to group decision making.

Employee Participation and Involvement

Participation occurs when employees have a voice in decisions about their own work. (One important model that can help managers determine the optimal level of employee participation, Vroom's decision tree approach, is discussed later). Empowerment is the process of enabling workers to set their own work goals, make decisions, and solve problems within their spheres of responsibility and authority. Thus, empowerment is a somewhat broader concept that promotes participation in a wide variety of areas, including but not limited to work itself, work context, and work environment.[33]

At one level, employees can participate in addressing questions and making decisions about their own jobs. Instead of just telling them how to do their jobs, for example, managers can ask

risk propensity the extent to which a decision maker is willing to gamble when making a decision

participation occurs when employees have a voice in decisions about their own work

empowerment the process of enabling workers to set their own work goals, make decisions, and solve problems within their spheres of responsibility and authority

LEARN

employees to make their own decisions about how to do them. Based on their own expertise and experience with their tasks, workers might be able to improve their own productivity. In many situations, they also might be well qualified to make decisions about what materials to use, what tools to use, and so forth.

LEARN

It might also help to let workers make decisions about administrative matters, such as work schedules. If jobs are relatively independent of one another, employees might decide when to change shifts, take breaks, go to lunch, and so forth. A work group or team also might be able to schedule vacations and days off for all of its members. Furthermore, employees are getting increasing opportunities to participate in broader issues of product quality. Involvement of this type has become a hallmark of successful Japanese and other international firms, and many US companies have followed suit.

Regardless, however, empowerment only enhances organizational effectiveness if certain conditions exist. First, the manager must be sincere in his or her efforts to spread power and autonomy to subordinates. Token efforts to promote participation in just a few areas are unlikely to succeed. Second, the manager must be committed to maintaining participation and empowerment. Workers will be resentful if they are given more control only to later have it reduced or taken away altogether. Third, the manager must be systematic and patient in his or her efforts to empower workers. Turning over too much control too quickly can spell disaster. Finally, the manager must be prepared to increase the company's commitment to training. Employees who are given more freedom concerning how they work are likely to need additional training to help them exercise that freedom effectively.

Group and Team Decision Making

In more and more organizations today, important decisions are made by groups and teams rather than by individuals. Examples include the executive committee of Abercrombie & Fitch, product design teams at Texas Instruments, and marketing planning groups at Red Lobster. Managers typically can choose whether to have individuals or groups and teams make a particular decision. Further, they often may find themselves part of a group or team charged with making decisions. Thus, knowing about forms of group and team decision making and their advantages and disadvantages is important.[34]

interacting groups and teams the most common form of decision-making group; an existing or a newly designated group or team is asked to make a decision

Delphi group used to form a decision from a consensus of expert opinion

Forms of Group and Team Decision Making

The most common methods of group and team decision making are interacting groups, Delphi groups, and nominal groups. Increasingly, these methods of group decision making are being conducted online.[35]

Interacting groups and teams are the most common form of decision-making group. The format is simple—either an existing or a newly designated group or team is asked to make a decision. Existing groups or teams might be functional departments, regular work teams, or standing committees. Newly designated groups or teams can be ad hoc committees, task forces, or newly constituted work teams. The group or team members talk among themselves, argue, agree, argue some more, form internal coalitions, and so forth. Finally, after some period of deliberation, the group or team makes its decision. An advantage of this method is that the interaction among people often sparks new ideas and promotes understanding. A major disadvantage, though, is that political processes can play too big a role.

A **Delphi group** is sometimes used to develop a consensus of expert opinion. Developed by the Rand Corporation, the Delphi procedure solicits input from a panel of experts who contribute individually. Their opinions are combined and, in effect, averaged. Assume, for example, that the problem is to establish an expected date for a major technological breakthrough in converting coal into usable energy. The first step in using the Delphi procedure is to obtain the cooperation of a panel of experts. For this situation, experts might include various research scientists, university researchers, and executives in a relevant energy industry. At first, the experts are asked to anonymously predict a time frame for the expected breakthrough. The persons coordinating the Delphi group collect the responses, average them, and ask the experts for another prediction. In this round, the experts who provided unusual or extreme predictions may be asked to justify them. These explanations may then be relayed to the other experts. When the predictions stabilize, the average prediction is taken to represent the decision of the group of experts. The time, expense, and logistics of the Delphi technique rule out its use for routine, everyday decisions, but it has been successfully used for forecasting technological breakthroughs at Boeing, market potential for new products at General Motors, research and development patterns at Eli Lilly, and future economic conditions by the US government.[36] Moreover, the Delphi method originally relied on paper-and-pencil responses obtained and shared through the mail; modern communication technologies such as email and the Internet have enabled Delphi users to get answers much more quickly than in the past.

TABLE 8.1 ADVANTAGES AND DISADVANTAGES OF GROUP AND TEAM DECISION MAKING

Advantages	Disadvantages
1. More information and knowledge are available.	1. The process takes longer than individual decision making, so it is costlier.
2. More alternatives are likely to be generated.	2. Compromise decisions resulting from indecisiveness may emerge.
3. More acceptance of the final decision is likely.	3. One person may dominate the group.
4. Enhanced communication of the decision may result.	4. Groupthink may occur.
5. Better decisions generally emerge.	

© CENGAGE LEARNING 2014

LEARN

Another useful group and team decision-making technique that managers occasionally use is the nominal group. Unlike the Delphi method, in which group members do not see one another, nominal group members are brought together in a face-to-face setting. The members represent a group in name only, however; they do not talk to one another freely like the members of interacting groups. Nominal groups are used most often to generate creative and innovative alternatives or ideas. To begin, the manager assembles a group of knowledgeable experts and outlines the problem to them. The group members are then asked to individually write down as many alternatives as they can think of. The members then take turns stating their ideas, which are recorded on a flip chart or board at the front of the room. Discussion is limited to simple clarification. After all alternatives have been listed, a more open discussion takes place. Group members then vote, usually by rank-ordering the various alternatives. The highest-ranking alternative represents the decision of the group. Of course, the manager in charge may retain the authority to accept or reject the group decision.[37]

Advantages of Group and Team Decision Making The advantages and disadvantages of group and team decision making relative to individual decision making are summarized in *Table 8.1*. One advantage is simply that more information is available in a group or team setting—as suggested by the old axiom, "Two heads are better than one." A group or team represents a variety of educational backgrounds, experiences, and perspectives. Partly as a result of this increased information, groups and teams typically can identify and evaluate more alternatives than can one person.[38] The people involved in a group or team decision understand the logic and rationale behind it, are more likely to accept it, and are equipped to communicate the decision to their work group or department.[39]

Disadvantages of Group and Team Decision Making Perhaps the major drawback of group and team decision making is the additional time and hence, the greater expense involved. The increased time stems from interaction and discussion among group or team members. If a given manager's time is worth $50 an hour, and if the manager spends two hours making a decision, the decision "costs" the organization $100. For the same decision, a group of five managers might require three hours of time. At the same $50-an-hour rate, the decision "costs" the organization $750. Assuming the group or team decision is better, the additional expense may be justified, but the fact remains that group and team decision making is more costly.

Group or team decisions also may represent undesirable compromises.[40] For example, hiring a compromise top manager (someone who is acceptable to everyone but who is no one's top choice) may be a bad decision in the long run because he or she may not be able to respond adequately to various subunits in the organization nor have everyone's complete support. Sometimes one individual dominates the group process to the point where others cannot make a full contribution. This dominance may stem from a desire for power or from a naturally dominant personality. The problem is that what appears to emerge as a group decision may actually be the decision of one person.

Finally, a group or team may succumb to a phenomenon known as "groupthink." Groupthink occurs when the desire for consensus and cohesiveness overwhelms the goal of reaching the best possible decision.[41] Under the influence of groupthink, the group may arrive at decisions that are made not in the best interests of either the group or the organization, but rather to avoid conflict among group members.

nominal group used most often to generate creative and innovative alternatives or ideas

groupthink occurs when the desire for consensus and cohesiveness overwhelms the goal of reaching the best possible decision

BOB PEARSON/AFP/GETTY IMAGES

One of the most clearly documented examples of groupthink involved the space shuttle *Challenger* disaster. As NASA was preparing to launch the shuttle, numerous problems and questions arose. At each step of the way, however, decision makers argued that there was no reason to delay and that everything would be fine. Shortly after its launch, the shuttle exploded, killing all seven crew members.

Managing Group and Team Decision-Making Processes Managers can do several things to help promote the effectiveness of group and team decision making. One is simply being aware of the pros and cons of having a group or team make the decision. Time and cost can be managed by setting a deadline by which the decision must be made final. Dominance can be at least partially avoided if a special group is formed just to make the decision. An astute manager, for example, should know who in the organization may try to dominate and can either avoid putting that person in the group or put several strong-willed people together.

To avoid groupthink, each member of the group or team should critically evaluate all alternatives. So that members present divergent viewpoints, the leader should not make his or her own position known too early. At least one member of the group or team might be assigned the role of devil's advocate. And, after reaching a preliminary decision, the group or team should hold a follow-up meeting wherein divergent viewpoints can be raised again if any group members wish to do so.[42] Gould Paper Corporation used these methods by assigning managers to two different teams. The teams then spent an entire day in a structured debate presenting the pros and cons of each side of an issue to ensure the best possible decision.

Vroom's decision tree approach uses decision trees to determine the degree to which subordinates should be encouraged to participate in decision making based on characteristics of the situation

HOW MUCH PARTICIPATION SHOULD BE ALLOWED?

Generally speaking a manager usually will be able to decide how much participation to allow in making decisions. A useful framework for helping make this decision is Vroom's decision tree approach. The earliest version of this model was proposed by Victor Vroom and Philip Yetton and later revised and expanded by Vroom and Arthur Jago.[43] Vroom refined the original model again in 2000.[44] Even if a manager does not use the full model, the situational factors it describes are still useful to consider.

Vroom's decision tree approach assumes that the degree to which subordinates should be encouraged to participate in decision making depends on the characteristics of the situation. In other words, no one decision-making process is best for all situations. After evaluating a variety of problem attributes (characteristics of the problem or decision), the leader determines an appropriate decision style that specifies the amount of subordinate participation.

Vroom's current formulation suggests that managers use one of two different decision trees.[45] To do so, the manager first assesses the situation in terms of several factors. This assessment involves determining whether the given factor is "high" or "low" for the decision that is to be made. For instance, the first factor is decision significance. If the decision is extremely important and may have a major impact on the organization (such as choosing a location for a new plant), its significance is high. But if the decision is routine, and its consequences not terribly important (such as selecting a logo for the firm's softball team uniforms), its significance is low. This assessment guides the manager through the paths of the decision tree to a recommended course of action. One decision tree is to be used when the manager is primarily interested in making the decision as timely as possible; the other is to be used when time is less critical, and the manager wants to help subordinates improve and develop their own decision-making skills.

The two decision trees are shown in *Figures* 8.4 and 8.5. The problem attributes (situational factors) are arranged along the top of the decision tree. To use the model, the decision-maker starts at the left side of the diagram and assesses the first problem attribute (decision significance). The answer determines the path to the second node on the decision tree, where the next attribute (importance of commitment) is assessed.

FIGURE 8.4 VROOM'S TIME-DRIVEN DECISION TREE

Managers should use this matrix for situations where time is of the highest importance in making a decision. The matrix operates like a funnel. You start at the left with a specific decision problem in mind. The column headings denote situational factors that may or may not be present in that problem. You progress by selecting high or low (H or L) for each relevant situational factor. Proceed down the funnel, judging only those situational factors for which a judgment is called, until you reach the recommended process.

PROBLEM STATEMENT	Decision Significance	Importance of Commitment	Leader Expertise	Likelihood of Commitment	Group Support	Group Expertise	Team Competence	
	H	H	H	H	—	—	—	**Decide**
	H	H	H	L	H	H	H	**Delegate**
	H	H	H	L	H	H	L	**Consult (group)**
	H	H	H	L	H	L	—	**Consult (group)**
	H	H	H	L	L	—	—	**Consult (group)**
	H	H	L	H	H	H	H	**Facilitate**
	H	H	L	H	H	H	L	**Consult (individually)**
	H	H	L	H	H	L	—	**Consult (individually)**
	H	H	L	H	L	—	—	**Consult (individually)**
	H	H	L	L	H	H	H	**Facilitate**
	H	H	L	L	H	H	L	**Consult (group)**
	H	H	L	L	H	L	—	**Consult (group)**
	H	H	L	L	L	—	—	**Consult (group)**
	H	L	H	—	—	—	—	**Decide**
	H	L	L	—	H	H	H	**Facilitate**
	H	L	L	—	H	H	L	**Consult (individually)**
	H	L	L	—	H	L	—	**Consult (individually)**
	H	L	L	—	L	—	—	**Consult (individually)**
	L	H	—	H	—	—	—	**Decide**
	L	H	—	L	—	—	H	**Delegate**
	L	H	—	L	—	—	L	**Facilitate**
	L	L	—	—	—	—	—	**Decide**

Source: Adapted and reprinted from *Organizational Dynamics*, Vol. 28, no. 4, Victor H. Vroom, "Leadership and the Decision-Making Process," pp. 82–94, Copyright 2000, with permission from Elsevier.

This process continues until a terminal node is reached. In this way, the manager identifies an effective decision-making style for the situation.

The various decision styles reflected at the ends of the tree branches represent different levels of subordinate participation that the manager should attempt to adopt in a given situation. The five styles are defined as follows:

- *Decide*: The manager makes the decision alone and then announces or "sells" it to the group.
- *Delegate*: The manager allows the group to define for itself the exact nature and parameters of the problem and to then develop a solution.
- *Consult (Individually)*: The manager presents the program to group members individually, obtains their suggestions, and then makes the decision.
- *Consult (Group)*: The manager presents the problem to group members at a meeting, gets their suggestions, and then makes the decision.
- *Facilitate*: The manager presents the problem to the group at a meeting, defines the problem and its boundaries, and then facilitates group member discussion as members make the decision.

Vroom's decision tree approach represents a very focused but quite complex perspective on leadership. To

FIGURE 8.5 VROOM'S DEVELOPMENT-DRIVEN DECISION TREE

A leader should use this matrix when he or she is more interested in developing employees than in making the decision as quickly as possible. Just as with the time-driven tree shown in Figure 8.4, the leader assesses up to seven situational factors. These factors, in turn, funnel the leader to a recommended process for making the decision.

PROBLEM STATEMENT	Decision Significance	Importance of Commitment	Leader Expertise	Likelihood of Commitment	Group Support	Group Expertise	Team Competence	
	H	H	—	H	H	H	H	**Decide**
							L	**Facilitate**
						L	—	**Consult (group)**
					L	—	—	
				L	H	H	H	**Delegate**
							L	**Facilitate**
						L	—	
					L	—	—	**Consult (group)**
		L	—	—	H	H	H	**Delegate**
							L	**Facilitate**
						L	—	**Consult (group)**
					L	—	—	
	L	H	—	H	—	—	—	**Decide**
				L	—	—	—	**Delegate**
		L	—	—	—	—	—	**Decide**

Source: Adapted and reprinted from *Organizational Dynamics*, Vol. 28, no. 4, Victor H. Vroom, "Leadership and the Decision-Making Process," pp. 82–94, Copyright 2000, with permission from Elsevier.

compensate for this difficulty, Vroom developed expert-system software to help managers assess a situation accurately and quickly and then make an appropriate decision regarding employee participation. Many firms, including Halliburton Company, Litton Industries, and Borland International, have provided their managers with training in how to use the various versions of this model.

MAKING DECISIONS FOR CONTINGENCIES AND DURING CRISIS

contingency planning the process of making decisions in advance regarding alternative courses of action to be taken if an intended course of action is unexpectedly disrupted or rendered inappropriate

crisis management the set of procedures the organization uses in the event of a disaster or other unexpected calamity

Managers also must be adept at making decisions related to contingencies and during crisis. **Contingency planning** is the process of making decisions in advance regarding alternative courses of action to be taken if an intended course of action is unexpectedly disrupted or rendered inappropriate.[46] **Crisis management**, a related concept, is the set of procedures the organization uses in the event of a disaster or other unexpected calamity. Some elements of crisis management may be orderly and systematic, whereas others may be more ad hoc and develop as events unfold.

An excellent example of widespread contingency planning occurred during the late 1990s in anticipation of what was popularly known as the "Y2K bug." Concerns about the impact of technical glitches in computers stemming from their internal clocks' changing from 1999 to 2000 resulted in contingency planning for most organizations. Many banks and hospitals, for example, had extra staff available; some organizations created backup computer systems; and some even stockpiled inventory in case they could not purchase new products or materials.[48]

The devastating hurricanes that hit the Gulf Coast in 2005—Katrina and Rita—dramatically underscored the importance of effective crisis management. For example, inadequate and ineffective responses by the Federal Emergency Management Agency (FEMA)

LEARN

illustrated to many people that organization's weaknesses in coping with crises. On the other hand, some organizations responded much more effectively. Walmart began ramping up its emergency preparedness on the same day that Katrina was upgraded from a tropical depression to a tropical storm. In the days before the storm struck, Walmart stores in the region were supplied with powerful generators and large supplies of dry ice so they could reopen as quickly as possible after the storm had passed. In neighboring states, the firm also had scores of trucks standing by crammed with both emergency-related inventory for its stores and emergency supplies it was prepared to donate—bottled water, medical supplies, and so forth. And Walmart often beat FEMA by several days in delivering those supplies.[49]

> "We are professional crisis managers in the airline business, and we're good at it."
>
> JEFF SMISEK
> United CEO[47]

FORTUNE, MAY 2, 2011, P. 54.

Seeing the consequences of poor crisis management after the terrorist attacks of September 11, 2001, and the 2005 hurricanes, many firms today are actively working to create new and better crisis-management plans and procedures. For example, both Reliant Energy and Duke Energy rely on computer trading centers where trading managers actively buy and sell energy-related commodities. If a terrorist attack or natural disaster such as a hurricane were to strike their trading centers, they would essentially be out of business. Prior to September 11, 2001, each firm had relatively vague and superficial crisis plans. Now they and most other companies have much more detailed and comprehensive plans in the event of another crisis. Both Reliant and Duke, for example, have created secondary trading centers at other locations. In the event of a shutdown at their main trading centers, these firms can quickly transfer virtually all their core trading activities to their secondary centers within 30 minutes or less.[50] Unfortunately, however, because it is impossible to forecast the future precisely, no organization can ever be perfectly prepared for all crises. Indeed, one element of the recent BP oil spill in the Gulf of Mexico that was surprising to many people was that the firm did not have a crisis plan in place to cap the spill immediately.[51]

The mechanics of contingency planning are shown in *Figure 8.6*. In relation to an organization's other plans, contingency planning comes into play at four action points. At action point 1, management develops the basic plans of the organization. These may include strategic, tactical, and operational plans. As part of this development process, managers usually consider various contingency events. Some management groups even assign someone the role of devil's advocate to ask, "But what if. . ." about each course of action. A variety of contingencies is usually considered.

At action point 2, the plan that management chooses is put into effect. The most important contingency events also are defined. The contingency-planning process considers only events that are likely to occur and whose effects will have a substantial impact on the organization. Next, at action point 3, the company specifies certain indicators or signs that suggest that a contingency event is about to take place. A bank manager might decide that a 2 percent drop in interest rates should be considered a contingency event. An indicator might be two consecutive months with

FIGURE 8.6 CONTINGENCY PLANNING

Most organizations develop contingency plans. These plans specify alternative courses of action to take if an intended plan is unexpectedly disrupted or rendered inappropriate.

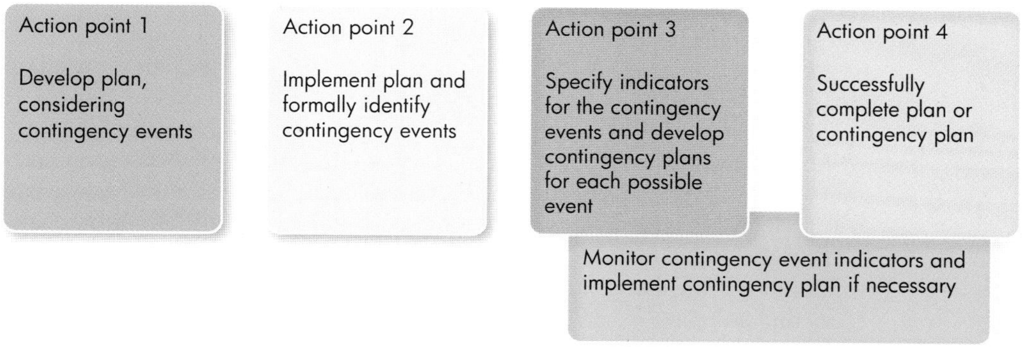

© CENGAGE LEARNING 2014

a drop of 0.5 percent in each. As indicators of contingency events are being defined, the contingency plans themselves should also be developed. Examples of contingency plans for various situations are delaying plant construction, developing a new manufacturing process, and cutting prices.

After this stage, the managers of the organization monitor the indicators identified at action point 3. If the situation dictates, a contingency plan is implemented. Otherwise, the primary plan of action continues in force. Finally, action point 4 marks the successful completion of either the original plan or a contingency plan.

Contingency planning is becoming increasingly important for most organizations, especially for those operating in particularly complex or dynamic environments. Few managers have such an accurate view of the future that they can anticipate and plan for everything. Contingency planning is a useful technique for helping managers cope with uncertainty and change. Crisis management, by its very nature, however, is more difficult to anticipate. But organizations that have a strong culture, strong leadership, and a capacity to deal with the unexpected stand a better chance of successfully weathering a crisis than do other organizations.[52]

SUMMARY AND A LOOK AHEAD

After reading and studying this chapter, you should have a better understanding of decision-making skills. Specifically, you should understand the kinds of decisions and the different contexts in which decisions are made. You also should be familiar with the steps in rational decision making and have a stronger understanding of numerous behavioral processes that can influence decision making. In addition, you should have greater insights into participation and group decision making and how to decide how much participation to allow. Finally, you should understand the basic elements of making decisions for different contingencies and during crisis situations.

The remainder of this chapter provides opportunities for you to continue to develop and refine your own decision-making skills. For instance, you will be directed to resources where you can visualize both effective and less effective decision-making skills. Subsequent sections provide opportunities for you to practice and explore decision-making skills from different perspectives. The chapter concludes with additional assessment and interpretation data.

VISUALIZING DECISION-MAKING SKILLS

DECISION-MAKING SKILLS IN ACTION—1

Your Assignment

Consider the two BizFlix film clips for this chapter.

The Emperor's Club (2002) is about how one person can make a difference. William Hundert (Kevin Kline), a professor at the exclusive Saint Benedict's Academy for Boys, believes in teaching his students about living a principled life. He also wants them to learn his beloved classical literature. A new student, Sedgewick Bell (Emile Hirsch), challenges Hundert's principled ways. Bell's behavior during the 73rd annual Mr. Julius Caesar Contest causes Hundert to suspect that Bell leads a less-than-principled life, a suspicion confirmed years later during a reenactment of the competition.

Field of Dreams (1989) is a baseball movie that's about a lot more than just baseball. Ray Kinsella (Kevin Costner) hears a voice while working in his Iowa cornfield that says, "If you build it, he will come." Ray concludes that "he" is legendary "Shoeless Joe" Jackson (Ray Liotta), a 1919 Chicago White Sox player suspended for rigging the 1919 World Series. With the support of his wife Annie (Amy Madigan), Ray jeopardizes his farm by replacing some corn fields with a modern baseball diamond. "Shoeless Joe" soon arrives, followed by the rest of the suspended players. This charming fantasy film, based on W. P. Kinsellas's novel *Shoeless Joe*, shows the rewards of pursuing a dream.

Note how decision-making skills are shown in these two clips.

1. The first clip starts with Mr. Hundert as the honored guest of his former student Sedgewick Bell (Joel Gretsch) at Bell's estate, as Hundert confronts Bell for cheating during a competition just ended. Bell won the competition, but Hundert noticed that Bell was wearing an earpiece. This scene appears at the end of the film. It is an edited version of the competition reenactment. Bell announced his candidacy for the US Senate just before he spoke with Hundert in the bathroom. In his announcement, he carefully described his commitment to specific values he would pursue if elected. What specific decisions does this clip show?
2. The second clip is part of the "People Will Come" sequence toward the end of the film. By this time in the story, Ray has met Terrence Mann (James Earl Jones). They have traveled together from Boston to Minnesota to find A. W. "Moonlight" Graham (Burt Lancaster). At this point, the three are at Ray's Iowa farm. This scene follows Mark's (Timothy Busfield) arrival to discuss the foreclosure of Ray and Annie's mortgage. Mark, who is Annie's brother, cannot see the players on the field. Ray and Annie's daughter Karin (Gaby Hoffmann) proposes that people will come to Iowa City and buy tickets to watch a baseball game. Mark does not understand her proposal. Ray then makes a momentous decision. Do you feel that Ray had sufficient information to make an informed decision? Why or why not?

PRACTICE

DECISION-MAKING SKILLS IN ACTION—2

This exercise gives you an opportunity to think about decision-making skills that may be involved in management positions for you in the future.

Your Assignment

1. Think about the decision-making skills covered in this chapter and try to identify a scene that illustrates a positive or effective use of such skills in a movie, a TV show, or a video on YouTube.
2. Now do the same for a scene that illustrates a negative or ineffective use of those same skills.

Share your results with the class and discuss how the positive and negative uses of decision-making skills are shown in each clip. You should also try to suggest how the negative situation could have been changed for the better.

PRACTICING YOUR DECISION-MAKING SKILLS

MAKING CAREER CHOICES

This exercise gives you practice in using decision-making skills to define problems and opportunities to choose an appropriate course of action that will capitalize on opportunities; in this case, it is choosing a career.

Job seekers must thoroughly understand their own abilities, preferences, and goals to make appropriate career choices. This particularly applies to recent college graduates who are preparing to enter a career field that is largely unknown to them. Fortunately, a variety of sources of information are available to help. The Bureau of Labor Statistics maintains data about occupations, employment prospects, compensation, working conditions, and many other issues of interest to job seekers. The information is available by industry, occupation, employer type, and region.

Your Assignment

1. Conduct an online search of the Department of Labor's National Compensation Survey, beginning at <http://www.bls.gov/ncs/home.htm> (or search online for the survey's title). Then select "Multiple occupations for one geographic area." Next choose either "National" or a particular state or metropolitan area if your career plans are focused on a specific geographic area. Find the detailed data related to the occupation that you think will be your most likely career choice upon graduation. Make a note of the "Annual Mean Wage" for that occupation in that location.
2. Locate detailed data about two other occupations that you might consider, and record the annual mean wage for them. Judging purely on the basis of salary information, which of the three occupations would be the most desirable?
3. Access job descriptions for various occupations at <www.bls.gov/oco> and click on the link for the "A–Z Index." Or go directly to <www.bls.gov/oco/ooh_index.htm> and read the descriptions for each of your three choices. Judging purely on the basis of job characteristics, which occupation would be best for you?
4. Is there a conflict between your answers to questions 2 and 3? If so, how will you resolve it?
5. Are there any job characteristics that you desire strongly enough to sacrifice pay in order to have them? What are those characteristics? What are the limits, if any, on your willingness to sacrifice pay?

PRACTICE

CHOOSING TEAM MEMBERS

This exercise helps to build your decision-making skills by giving you practice in selecting members for a cross-functional team.

Assume you are the vice president of marketing and customer support for a medium-sized firm that creates and sells accounting software to businesses. Most of your clients are service firms with annual sales of $1 to $10 million. Your company is preparing to launch a new product, an add-on to your current software that will allow customers to use your system to manage their human resources expenses and scheduling.

The new-product release team is being formed now. It will work autonomously with only minor oversight from you. Its responsibilities will include preparing a marketing campaign to inform current and potential customers about the new product, answering customer questions about how to use the product, and shipping the product to purchasers. Thus far, the team includes one member who helped to write the software code, one finance person, and one member from the logistics department who will be in charge of distribution of the finished product. While each of these members performs an important function on the team, you believe that the two members still to be chosen will be the most crucial factors in the creation of a positive group experience.

Your Assignment

1. From the employee list that follows these questions, choose two additional members to complete the team—one from marketing and one from customer service. As you choose members, keep these four goals in mind:

   (A) You want the new-product launch to be effective and meet sales targets.

   (B) You want the group's tasks to be performed quickly and efficiently.

(C) You want the group to function smoothly as a team, with cohesiveness and not too much conflict.

(D) You anticipate that your company will soon have more new product launches so you want to use this launch as an opportunity to train and develop workers for the future.

(NOTE: You may find it helpful to construct a simple 4 (goals) × 7 (people) table to record your evaluations.)

2. Look back upon your decision-making process. What qualities were most important for you as you made your choices? Did you look for the same qualities for both positions? Explain.
3. How did you cope with making choices guided by four differing goals? For example, were you forced to make trade-offs among your four goals?
4. Are you satisfied that the group will meet your four goals? Explain why or why not.
5. What did you learn about the importance of group composition? How could managers benefit from what you learned?

Employees Eligible For The Team:

Sampat Sengupta, age 61, has an M.B.A. and 40 years of experience in customer service in the IT industry. He has never married; his career has been the most important part of his life. Sampat joined your company five years ago, following the acquisition of his previous employer and the subsequent closing of its operations. At his previous job, he was head of the customer service group of a much larger company. He makes many innovative suggestions for improving customer service at your firm, including a recent reorganization of the department that saved the company thousands of dollars. Sampat resents working for someone like Whitney Armstrong, who has less business-related education and experience than he does. In your opinion, his customer service knowledge is extensive and his job performance is far above average. He works longer hours and engages in more professional activities outside of work than anyone else at your company. Sampat is asking to work on the launch team and suggests that you name him as head of the team.

Whitney Armstrong, age 53, is the head of customer support, has a Ph.D. in computer science, and is the most senior candidate. She has been with the company since it was founded 14 years ago and is a personal friend of many of the senior staff. After beginning her career in the technology group, Whitney did not continue to update her programming skills. About 10 years ago, she moved into customer support, where she became friendly with many of the customers. Her performance as head of customer support has been average, in your opinion. She gets along well with everyone but allows her employees to get away with sloppy, slow work. Whitney is extroverted and agreeable; she hates to say, "No." Often she is overly optimistic about how much she can do and therefore takes on too many tasks. Whitney assumes that, due to her position as head of customer support, she has a right to a place on the launch team.

Collin Barnett, a 45-year-old with a bachelor's degree in English, is in charge of marketing communications with customers. Before moving into marketing 10 years ago, he was an average performer for 10 years in customer service. Of all your marketing staff, Collin has the most experience with and knowledge of customers. He is extremely outgoing and positive. He often can be found in the employee lounge, telling jokes or chatting about sports. He is friends with everyone in the company and volunteers to arrange employee social events. His Christmas parties and picnics are always well attended and enjoyable. In your opinion, Collin's performance otherwise is just barely average. In other words, he is one of the least productive workers but everyone enjoys working with him. As a result of his work friendships, he often is asked to do less than his coworkers. Even so, his work is often of good quality. Collin has enjoyed working on cross-functional teams in the past because it allows him to work with friends he otherwise does not see often.

Jalia Murphy, 36 years old, has a bachelor's degree in public relations. She began working for your company about six years ago after a failed attempt to start her own PR firm. She is your creative marketing superstar. Every one of her advertising campaigns has been highly successful, and she even won a local Chamber of Commerce award a year ago, a first for your company. She excels at ad concepts and design, but her leadership skills are weak. Jalia usually chooses to communicate by email or phone and is uncomfortable speaking in front of a group. She works from home two days each week, explaining that she needs peace and quiet to "work the magic." She is emotionally mature and is often the person that other employees turn to when they are having personal problems. She has helped to resolve more than one work conflict simply by listening to each person and offering suggestions. Jalia has expressed her interest in designing the marketing campaign for the launch team, but not the other tasks.

Marilee West, a 30-year-old with a high-school diploma, is part of your customer service group. A single mother, she is ambitious and has worked hard to move up from a clerical position to a higher-paying, professional one. She is intensely loyal to your company and is also a conscientious worker, reliably completing every task well and on time. Unfortunately, her relationship with her supervisor, Whitney Armstrong, is not very good right now. Whitney has asked Marilee to shift her work schedule into the evening hours and Marilee refused, saying that her family time came first. On the whole, however, Marilee is well liked by her coworkers. Because she is so efficient, she often has time to help others complete their tasks. In your opinion, Marilee is invaluable to the customer service group. She is also eager to work on the launch team in order to expand her skills.

Alandra Pacheco, a 28-year-old, is the newest hire in the marketing department. She is attending night school while finishing her undergraduate degree in marketing. She came to your company one year ago as a summer intern and did so well that she was offered a full-time job. While she still has a lot to learn about marketing, she is bright and determined. Prior to working for your company, Alandra was a sales associate in a department store, where she learned customer service skills and developed an interest in marketing. Outside of work, she is active in a community organization that supports adult immigrants in learning English. Her fluency in Spanish is an asset in dealing with your Spanish-speaking customers. Thus far, Alandra's work has been average, but you believe she will improve with further education and experience. She is cooperative and willing to try anything that she is asked to do but hesitant to put forth her own ideas. She lacks confidence and seems to just go along with whatever others say. When you spoke to Alandra about the team, she replied, "It sounds like a good opportunity for me, but I don't know that I will have anything valuable to contribute."

Parker Goldman, the youngest member of the team at age 24, is a natural computer whiz who began working as a programmer for your company while still in high school. However, when he began college, he realized he had a passion for working with others and therefore switched from computers to marketing. He finished his B.B.A. and joined the marketing department two years ago. In your opinion, Parker is the most intelligent candidate and has the best technical skills. His performance in the marketing department has been above average, and other marketing staffers have begun to turn to him for advice. Parker is enthusiastic, ambitious, and positive, yet he is often not very tactful with others who are not as clever or skilled as he is. You saw an email on his computer from a headhunter offering a salary increase, thus you fear that Parker may not stay with your company for long. When you asked him if he wanted to be on the team, Parker said it sounded "cool," but he says that about most tasks.

DECISION MAKING AND COMMUNICATION

Decision making and communication are highly interrelated. This exercise will give you insights into some of those interrelations.

Your Assignment

1. Identify a decision that you will need to make sometime in the future. If you work in a managerial position, you may select a real problem or issue to address; for example, the selection or termination of an employee, the allocation of pay raises, or the selection of someone for a promotion. If you do not work in a managerial position, you may instead select an upcoming decision related to your academic work; for example, what major to select, whether to attend summer school or to get a job, which job to select, or whether to live on or off campus next year. Be sure to select a decision that has not yet been made.
2. On a sheet of paper, list the kinds of information that you will most likely use in making your decision. Beside each one, make notes as to where you can obtain the information, in what form it will be presented, its reliability, and other relevant characteristics of the information.
3. Next, assume that you have used the information obtained above and have made your decision. On the other side of the paper, list the various communication consequences that come with your decision. For example, if your choice involves an academic major, you may need to inform your advisor and your family. If your choice involves the managerial decision to promote someone, you will need to inform that person and others. List as many consequences as you can.
4. Beside each consequence, make notes as to how you would communicate with each party, the timeliness of your communication, and any other factors that seem to be relevant.
5. What behavioral forces might play a role in your decision?

PRACTICE

EXAMINING ONE COMPONENT OF AN ORGANIZATION'S CONTROL SYSTEM

This exercise asks you to use your decision-making skills in developing a plan for strengthening one of an organization's control systems.

Organizations use a wide variety of methods for control. One control system is the corporate board of directors, a group of individuals often chosen by the firm's CEO or by other directors. Boards of directors are especially important in strategic control. They have the responsibility of ensuring that the corporation is achieving its strategic goals while acting ethically, of overseeing the performance of the CEO and other members of the top-management team, and of looking out for the interests of shareholders. Yet the recent corporate scandals at Enron, WorldCom, and other firms have shown that some boards provide inadequate control.

The United States Securities and Exchange Commission (SEC) has put forth proposals for a number of reforms it hopes will enhance the control power of boards. Some of its recommendations focus on board composition. If boards do not contain the right number and kind of directors, the SEC claims, they are less likely to be effective. The SEC recommends that firms apply the following guidelines:

- Keep the size of the board to one dozen or fewer directors so that each has a more personal stake in the process.
- To increase objectivity, choose outside directors for the most part. Outside directors are not employees of the firm, are not related to any employees, and are not involved in significant business dealings with the CEO or the firm.
- Require directors to hold significant amounts of company stock, to align their interests more closely with those of stockholders.

- Choose several experts in corporate accounting or finance, especially on the audit and compensation committees.
- To ensure that directors have sufficient time for this board, do not choose directors who serve on more than three boards.

Your Assignment

1. Choose an organization that interests you, and use the Internet to research its board of directors. (*Hint:* Company websites are a good place to start.) Then search the Internet for biographies of the individual directors.
2. In which of the five areas mentioned by the SEC is this firm's board of directors acceptable? In which of the five areas is this firm's board not acceptable?
3. What are some probable consequences for organizational control? Consider both positive and negative consequences.
4. If you were a decision-maker in charge of selecting board members, what would you do to increase the effectiveness of the board?

COST REDUCTION DECISIONS

This exercise will help you develop your own decision-making skills while also helping you to better understand the importance of interdependence among units in organizations.

Assume that you are the vice president of a large American company that designs and manufactures sunglasses. Because of the rise in consumer demand, the firm has grown substantially in recent years. At the same time, this growth has not gone unnoticed, enticing several competitors to enter the market in the last two years. Therefore, your CEO has instructed you to find a way to cut costs by 10 percent so prices can be cut by that same amount. She feels this tactic is necessary to retain your market share in the face of new competition.

You have looked closely at the situation and have determined three different ways to accomplish this cost reduction:

- Begin buying slightly lower-grade materials, such as plastic and glass.
- Lay off a portion of your workforce and then pressure the remaining workers to be more productive. As part of this same option, future growth in manufacturing capacity will be outsourced to developing countries, where workers are paid a lower wage than US workers.
- Replace existing manufacturing equipment with newer, more efficient equipment. Although this will require a substantial up-front investment, you are certain it will result in lower production costs.

Your Assignment

1. Carefully examine the three alternatives and list the pluses and minuses for each one.
2. In what ways might each alternative effort affect other parts of the organization?
3. Which is the most costly option in terms of impact on other parts of the organization (not absolute dollars)? Which is the least costly?
4. What are the primary obstacles that you may face regarding each of the three alternatives?
5. Can you think of other alternatives that might accomplish the cost-reduction goal?

EVALUATING TRAINING

This exercise provides you with the opportunity to sharpen your skills in interpreting information to make a decision.

Your Assignment

Your instructor will organize the class into small groups to discuss each of the following questions. Each group should try to reach a consensus to share with the entire class. Think carefully and creatively about the question and, if you feel that more information would be helpful, identify what that information might be.

1. As plant manager you have been asked to identify a training and development program to which you can send subordinate managers. Published information about two programs under consideration states:

   Program A – More than half of the attendees of this program have soon afterward become top executives for their companies.

   Program B – Most attendees continue to receive rapid promotions in their companies.

   What can you conclude from this?

2. As a member of the Executive Committee, you have received a report from the executive in charge of the training program. The report states (in vastly reduced form):

   "We felt that our lower-level managers were not sufficiently human-relations oriented. We set up a program to train them in human relations. It took one hour a week (after work) for six weeks. At the end of the program, we gave the participants a test and found that they were now quite knowledgeable about human relations. This is just an example of how wisely and effectively your Training Division is spending your money."

   What is your reaction to this report? Why?

3. Later in the same report, it states:

   "To evaluate our programs, we always ask the participants to answer a few questions before they leave. One is 'Did you learn anything in this program?' and another is 'Did you enjoy the program?' Since we always get at least a two-thirds affirmative response and frequently ninety or so percent affirmative responses to each of these questions, we conclude that the programs are a tremendous success."

   Do you agree with this assessment? Why or why not?

4. As a training director for ML&T Company, you come across a report that suggests a highly successful approach to training. While most of the evidence to support that view comes form anecdotal quotes from participants, the results of a statistically significant study are presented in an appendix. The study compares the basic results for a group that went through this successful training with a group that had not gone through it. A five-point Likert scale (1 2 3 4 5) was used.

   - Trained group: Number = 522 Mean = 3.3472 Standard Deviation = 1.5369
   - Untrained group: Number = 496 Mean = 3.1498 Standard Deviation = 1.6431
   - A t-test of the significance between means shows that this difference is significant at the 5% level ($t = 1.96$).

   Would you adopt the training program based on these findings? Why or why not?

PRACTICE

INDIVIDUAL VS. NOMINAL GROUP DECISION MAKING

This exercise will enable you to compare individual decision making with decision making conducted through the use of nominal groups.

Individual decision making has some advantages over group decision making, such as speed, simplicity, and lack of conflict. However, there are times when these advantages are outweighed by other considerations. Innovation, in particular, is lower when an individual makes a decision. Nominal groups are especially well suited for fostering creativity because more input from more diverse individuals can generate more varied alternative courses of action. Individuals have the freedom to list as many creative alternatives as they can without worrying about criticism or political pressure. Thus, nominal groups foster creativity by combining techniques for improving both individual and group innovation.

Assume that you and your classmates are the top administrators of a state-run university with about 15,000 students. Over the last three years, the university has received an increasing number of applicants, but its staff and physical facilities have remained at the same level. The university is currently facing a problem: students and their families are pressuring the university to admit more applicants. The state legislature, which provides more than half of the university's funds, is responding to this pressure by asking the university to increase enrollment by at least 3,000 students, or 20 percent.

Your Assignment

1. Individually, write down as many creative responses as you can to the problem. Do not worry about whether the alternatives you are generating are practical. In fact, try to list as many different, even "far-out" responses as you can.
2. All students share their lists with the entire class. No one, under any circumstances, should reveal whether you think any idea is "good" or "bad." Ask other students questions about their suggestions only for purposes of clarification.
3. After all the individual ideas are listed and clarified, add to the list any additional ideas developed by the class during this process.
4. As a class, choose (by voting) the three actions that you think are most likely to resolve the problem to the satisfaction of the interested parties.
5. Did the nominal-group technique generate more attractive alternatives than those you generated on your own?
6. In your opinion, are the three alternatives chosen by class vote "better" solutions than those you thought of on your own? Explain your answer.
7. Give some suggestions about what types of decisions in organizations could be made effectively through nominal-group decision making. When should it *not* be used?

JOURNALING AND AFFINITY DIAGRAMS IN DECISION-MAKING

This exercise gives you practice using journaling and affinity diagrams for effective decision making. These techniques will help expand and improve decision making in many areas of your life, both personal and professional.

The chemist Linus Pauling, winner of Nobel Prizes in both Chemistry and Peace, said, "The best way to have a good idea is to have a lot of ideas." Journaling is one technique to increase the quantity of ideas generated in response to a decision situation. Affinity diagrams help you interpret and organize a quantity of diverse ideas. You can use affinity diagrams alone or in conjunction with journaling or other idea-generation techniques. The diagrams are particularly useful in decision situations that involve lots of ideas, where the ideas are very different from each other and the relationships between the ideas are not well understood, and where the underlying questions seem overwhelming or too complex to analyze rationally.

Assume that graduation day is approaching and you must decide where to live. Your options are broad and the decision will be for at least five years but would not necessarily commit you for the rest of your life. You could choose to live in an urban, suburban, or rural community. You could choose a large or small community, various regions of the country or world, and many different types of social and economic settings.

Your Assignment

1. Have on hand at least 50 index cards, sticky notes, or small slips of paper. Set aside 30 minutes or so of quiet time to think about the qualities you desire for your future hometown. Relax and visualize your ideal community, and then use the cards or slips of paper to jot down the qualities that you desire. For example, your ideas might include "ethnic diversity" or "upscale suburb." Allow the answers to just come to you, without forcing your thinking along any one path. Don't edit yourself or criticize your thoughts at this point in the process. It's OK to have some ideas that don't seem rational, that are duplicates, that seem to be in conflict, or that even seem meaningless. Try to work quickly and without interruption to generate at least 25 ideas. Stop only when you feel that you have exhausted your supply of ideas. This process is one way to use the technique known as "journaling."
2. Lay out the cards so you can see all of them, and then read them. Next, group the cards according to similar ideas. Gradually, as you rearrange them, patterns of ideas will emerge. Again, try not to be critical or rational; simply consider the relationships between the ideas. Keep moving the cards into different combinations until you find a set of groups that "feels right."
3. Then assign each of these groups a theme that identifies the common element; for example, you could group "green housing," "good public transportation," and "vegetarian restaurants" into a theme called "environmentally conscious." Or "good public transportation," "short commute to work," and "walk to restaurants and stores" could be grouped as a "convenience" theme. The finished project—a grouping of a diverse set of ideas into related themes—is called an "affinity diagram."
4. Answer the following questions about your experience in steps 1 and 2 above.
   (A) Did the techniques of journaling and affinity diagramming help you to generate more ideas and to better see the connections between ideas? If so, explain how. If not, what technique(s) would have worked better?
   (B) Note that both of these techniques explicitly encourage the behavioral aspects of decision making, especially intuition. Do you think this is appropriate when making this type of decision, or would a more rational approach be more effective?
   (C) How might a manager use these techniques at work? What situations would not be appropriate for the use of these techniques?

PRACTICE

DESIGNING A NEW ORGANIZATION

This exercise will give you some practice in making decisions associated with organization design.

Assume that you have decided to open a casual sportswear business in your local community. Your products will be athletic caps, shirts, shorts, and sweats emblazoned with the logos of the local college and high schools. You are a talented designer, and you have developed some ideas that will make your products unique and very popular. You also have inherited enough money to get your business up and running and to cover about one year of living expenses so that you do not need to pay yourself a salary the first year.

You intend to buy sportswear in various sizes and styles from other suppliers. Your firm will then use silkscreen processes to add the logos and other decorative touches to the products. Local clothing store owners have seen samples of your products and have expressed a keen interest in selling them. You know that you will also need to service accounts and keep your customers happy.

You are now trying to determine how many people you need to get your business going and how to most effectively group them into an organization. You realize that you can start out quite small and then expand as sales warrant; but you worry that, if you are continually adding people and rearranging your organization, confusion and inefficiency will result.

Your Assignment

1. For each of the following three scenarios, decide how to best design your organization. Sketch a basic organization chart to show your thoughts.
   - *Scenario 1:* You will sell the products yourself, starting with a workforce of five individuals.
   - *Scenario 2:* You will oversee production (not doing sales) and will start with a workforce of nine individuals.
   - *Scenario 3:* You will not handle any one function yourself but will instead oversee the entire operation, starting with a workforce of fifteen individuals.
2. Form small groups of four to five people each. Compare your various organization charts, focusing on similarities and differences.
3. Working in the same groups, assume that five years have passed and your business has become a success. You have a large plant for making your products, and you are shipping them to 15 states. You employ almost 500 workers. Create an organization design that you think best fits this organization.
4. After completing the above exercises, answer the following questions:
   (A) How clear or ambiguous were the decisions about organization design?
   (B) What are your thoughts about starting out large to maintain stability as opposed to starting small and then growing?
   (C) What basic factors did you consider in choosing a design for your organization?

PRACTICE

DECISION MAKING AND COMMUNICATING IN A SMALL BUSINESS

This exercise will help you understand some of the complexities of decision making and communicating in smaller businesses, which, some entrepreneurs argue, is even more important than in large organizations.

Assume that you are the owner/manager of a small retail chain that sells moderately priced apparel for professional men and women. You have ten stores located in the Midwest. Each store has a general manager responsible for the overall management of that specific store, and one assistant manager. In addition, your corporate office is staffed by an HR manager, an advertising specialist, and two buyers. In the past, local managers had complete control over their individual stores. As a result, each store has a different layout, a different culture, and different policies and procedures.

You have decided to begin opening more stores at a rapid pace. To expedite this process, you want to standardize your stores. Unfortunately, many of your current managers will be unhappy with this decision because they will see it as a loss of authority and managerial discretion. Nevertheless, you believe these changes are important for achieving standardization in all areas.

Your plans are to remodel all stores to fit a standard layout. You also intend to develop a policy and operations manual for each store. This manual will specify exactly how each store will be managed. You plan to inform your managers of this plan first in a memo and then in a follow-up meeting to discuss questions and concerns.

Your Assignment

1. Make a list of the primary objections you anticipate.
2. Draft a memo the store managers that explains your intentions.
3. Outline an agenda for the meeting in which you plan to address the managers' questions and concerns.
4. Do you think that the managers should have been involved in the decision? Why or why not?
5. How might you have handled this differently?

USING YOUR DECISION-MAKING SKILLS

USE

DECISIONS, DECISIONS, DECISIONS

Frank and Charles Seiberling began making rubber for bicycle tires in 1898 but quickly moved to making tires for all kinds of vehicles, including airplane tires in 1909 when there were only 100 planes in the United States. By 1916 the Seiberlings' firm was the largest tire maker in the United States and soon was leading the world. Poor financial management of this expansion, however, led to major problems. Goodyear bought out the Seiberling brothers after World War I, with Paul Litchfield heading production (and the company) for more than 30 years. Goodyear is still a leading tire maker, but France's Michelin and Japan's Bridgestone also are strong players in the industry.

As competition increased, Goodyear's dominance began to shrink. As a result, during the 1980s Goodyear began substantial restructuring. It sold Goodyear Farms in Arizona; began making off-brand tires under the Kelly-Springfield, Lee, and Atlas names; and dropped thousands of employees from the payroll. That was not enough, however.

Goodyear had incurred a large debt to stave off a takeover attempt in 1986. American car sales were down. Further, it owned an oil pipeline, which, although completed by 1989, was consuming cash and operating at less than capacity. Net income per share dropped every year from 1987 through 1991. Then the board hired the retired CEO of Rubbermaid Inc., Stanley Gault, to try to turn Goodyear around.

Gault is described as a blizzard of activity who manages without having to give direct orders. He believes in organizations built upon trust, prefers people to call him by his first name, and regularly visits tire stores on Saturdays. He made a series of decisions designed to reduce costs and increase sales. He installed closed-circuit television so that workers can keep abreast of the company's financial position and played videotapes of his quarterly question-and-answer meetings at corporate headquarters. To hold down costs, he removed light bulbs from most of the lamps in his office, replaced company limousines with sedans, and sold three of the five corporate jets. He introduced new products, sold new stock, and opened new channels of distribution such as using the Sears network of stores. All of this seemed to work. Gault was named CEO of the year by a leading trade publication. Sales and profits were up in 1992 and Goodyear's prospects for the future looked bright.

But turbulent times were ahead. Revenues bounced up and down through 2003 and then strong growth continued until 2008 and 2009. To focus and strengthen its operations, in 2005 Goodyear decided to sell its North American operations that produced tires specifically for farm and tractor use, its Wingtack adhesive resins business, and an Indonesian rubber plantation. Goodyear decided to adopt a business management strategy developed by Motorola known as Six Sigma. Six Sigma uses a commitment to excellence, customer satisfaction, process improvement, and fact-based decision making. Employees are given greater discretion to make decisions. They add value through increased productivity, creativity, and improved decision making.

The year 2006 saw solid earnings despite a decision to exit some segments of the private label tire market. That year also saw a major strike and soaring raw material prices. CEO Robert Keegan moved to cut costs, and in 2007 Goodyear sold its engineered-products business to focus its strategic decision making. The company also made the decision to change the ways in which tires are sold with better displays intended to appeal to women.

Case Questions

Go Online

1. What roles has decision making played at Goodyear?
2. Describe the decision-making skills of management at Goodyear.
3. Can you identify weaknesses that may be caused by an emphasis on those skills?
4. How would you go about assuring that you have the sort of skills for jobs like those at Goodyear?

USE

Case References

Lisa LaMotta, "Goodyear bounces back," *Forbes*, April 25, 2008 http://www.forbes.com/2008/04/25/goodyear-tires-earnings-markets-equity-cx_lal_0425markets19.html; Telis Demos, "Money losers," *Fortune*, July 9, 2007 http://money.cnn.com/galleries/2007/fortune/0707/gallery.global500_losers.fortune/11.html; Matthew Boyle, "Goodyear rolls out softer sell for tires," *Fortune*, February 14, 2006 http://money.cnn.com/2006/02/14/news/companies/pluggedin_fortune/index.htm; "CEO of the Year: Stanley Gault of Goodyear," *Financial World*, March 31, 1992, p. 26; Peter Nulty, "The Bounce is Back at Goodyear," *Fortune*, September 7, 1992, pp. 70–72.

LUFTHANSA

Deutsche Lufthansa AG, more popularly known simply as Lufthansa, is the government-owned airline of Germany. Lufthansa has an excellent on-time record, is one of the world's largest airlines, and is one of the world's largest air cargo carriers. Because the German government owns Lufthansa, the airline has never had to worry too much about profitability. Moreover, because European airline activity has been so heavily regulated, there were relatively few competitive measures the airline could take. Thus, for years Lufthansa carried out its mission as efficiently as it could while functioning in a relatively protected and insulated environment.

Around 1990, however, things began to change. For one thing, the German government, strapped for cash by the financial pressures of its reunification program, mandated better financial performance by Lufthansa. Indeed, there was even talk of privatizing the airline. Further, the opening of the European market in 1992 following deregulation increased competition among all European airlines.

To fight back, Lufthansa brought in a new CEO, Juergen Weber. Weber quickly realized that the airline had to cut its costs if it were to remain competitive. Indeed, analyses revealed that Lufthansa had the lowest profit margins of any major European carrier. Weber decided to start with labor, announcing plans to cut 7,000 jobs. Workers affected by the cuts were represented by two unions, the German Corporate Employees Union (DAG) and the Public Workers' Union (OTV). The two unions had quite different responses to Weber's plan.

The OTV, representing flight attendants and ground-services staff, decide to take a hard line. It demanded that Lufthansa first trim management and administrative payrolls. Moreover, the union threatened strikes and/or work slowdowns if its demands were not met. The DAG, however, which represents pilots, engineers, and technicians, took a more conciliatory stance. Like the OTV, the DAG urged that Lufthansa cut administrative costs; but the DAG also volunteered to take an 8 percent wage cut and to increase work hours from 37.5 hours per week to 40 hours per week.

Both unions were concerned about a new airline that Lufthansa was planning to start. Lufthansa wanted to keep its current organization for international flights but intended to create an entirely new airline called Lufthansa Express for all domestic flights. Lufthansa Express would pay lower wages and provide fewer benefits for its workers. While a few planes actually had the word "Express" painted on them, the separate airline never got off the ground.

Throughout the 2000s, Lufthansa's executives decided to use mergers, acquisitions, and joint arrangements to keep the airline strong. As a result, in 2000 it partnered with Air One, an Italian airline. In 2004 Lufthansa became a launch customer for Boeing's Internet connectivity service, Connexion, by Boeing. In 2005, Swiss International Air Lines (SWISS) merged with Lufthansa and then entered into a partnership with JetBlue, a US low-cost carrier. In 2008 Lufthansa bought control of Brussels Airlines and British Midland International (BMI). Despite rough times in 2001–2002 and a major strike in 2008, air traffic and revenues were up for 2010. Lufthansa seemed to be flying high.

USE

Case Questions

1. How has decision making been a part of Lufthansa's continued success?
2. Would that be true for a private German or US airline? Why or why not?
3. Describe the decision-making skills of management at Lufthansa.
4. Which of the decision-making skills in Question 3 above are probably more important, and which are less important, for managing in a US airline?
5. If you were interested in a position in the Lufthansa organization, what preparations would you make to have the requisite decision-making skills for success?

Go Online

Case References

Cornelius Rahn, "Lufthansa Targets 2010 Earnings Growth on Traffic," *BusinessWeek*, March 11, 2010 http://www.businessweek.com/news/2010-03-11/lufthansa-targets-2010-earnings-growth-on-traffic-increase.html; Marc Gunther, "Nothing blue about JetBlue," *Fortune*, September 3, 2009 http://money.cnn.com/2009/09/03/news/companies/jetblue_airways_airline.fortune/index.htm; Ken Stier, "The not-so-friendly skies of Europe," *Fortune*, May 25, 2006 http://money.cnn.com/magazines/fortune/fortune_archive/2006/05/15/8376910/index.htm; "Even Lufthansa is Carrying Too Much Baggage," *BusinessWeek*, September 7, 1992, p. 80; "Steering a Supertanker," Interavia Aerospace Review, January 1992, p. 64.

EXTENDING YOUR DECISION-MAKING SKILLS

Your instructor may use one or more of these **Group Extensions** to provide you with yet another opportunity to develop your decision-making skills. On the other hand, you may continue your development on your own by doing one or more of the **Individual Extensions**.

These **Extensions** are repeated exactly for each of the seven specific skills. Doing the exact **Extension** for different skills will help you to sharpen both the skills and the subtle differences between the several skills.

GROUP EXTENSIONS

- Form small groups of students. Have each group select an organization and a management position. Then have them identify the decision-making skills needed by a person in that position.
- Form small groups of students. Have each group identify a problem or opportunity facing a business or other organization. Then have them identify the decision-making skills needed by managers in dealing with that problem or opportunity.
- Form small groups of students. Assign each group one or more corporations to analyze. Have them identify the members who serve on its board of directors and research their backgrounds. Then have the students describe the decision-making skills of those directors.
- Form small groups of students. Have each group select a job they see regularly (e.g., retail clerk, fast-food worker). Ask them to describe the decision-making skills needed on that job.
- Form small groups of students. Have students sketch the decision-making skills they would need if they were going to start a specific type of new business.
- Form small groups of students. Have each group identify examples they have recently faced that illustrate a situation that called for them to use decision-making skills.

EXTEND

INDIVIDUAL EXTENSIONS

- Go to the library and research a company. Characterize its level of effectiveness and identify the decision-making skills of its top executives. Share your results with the class.
- Select a highly visible manager and analyze his or her decision-making skills.
- Interview a manager from a local organization. Learn about what decision-making skills he or she needs to perform effectively.
- Think of someone you know who is a manager. Describe that person's management position in terms of the type of organization, level in the organization, and the area of management in which he or she practices. What decision-making skills does that person need to be effective?
- Plan a hypothetical change in your school focusing on the use of decision-making skills.
- Search the Internet for examples of decision-making skills in management and compare what you find with the information presented here.

- Bob Woodward, the well-known political correspondent, is purported to have said: "When you see how the president makes political or policy decisions, you see who he is. The essence of the presidency is decision making." What do you think this means, and how can you use it to improve your own decision making?

YOUR DECISION-MAKING SKILLS NOW

DECISION-MAKING SKILLS ASSESSMENT

Now that you have completed Chapter 8, it is time again to assess your decision-making skills. To do so, complete the following instrument. Think about your current situation, job, or organization to which you belong. Respond in terms of your current situation and not by how you think you should respond or a manager should respond. If a statement does not pertain to your situation, respond in terms of what you think would be accurate for you in that situation.

Use this scale in your responses.

1	**2**	**3**	**4**	**5**
Not true at all	Somewhat untrue	Sometimes true Sometimes not	Somewhat true	Completely true

Total your scores and record them in the table at the end of instrument.

Given that many experts suggest the use of 360° feedback in performance appraisal, you may find it useful to obtain the views of others about your interpersonal skills. You may get a form from your instructor for others to complete and then record their scores in the table as well. Areas where there is a large discrepancy between your views and those of others should draw your attention and you should spend more time on developing those skills.

DECISION-MAKING SKILLS

[**Note: The numbers correspond to those on the baseline assessment in Appendix A.**]

____ 271. I accept responsibility for my actions.

____ 272. I always plan how deadlines are going to be met.

____ 273. I am able to deal with ambiguous and uncertain assignments.

____ 274. I am prepared to let others take the lead.

____ 275. I avoid making rash decisions.

____ 276. I can act decisively when necessary.

____ 277. I can handle conflict.

____ 278. I can handle tasks that involve large amounts of information.

____ 279. I can manage groups.

____ 280. I consider alternatives before making decisions.

____ 281. I delegate to get things done.

____ 282. I do not avoid making difficult decisions.

_____ 283. I do what I say.
_____ 284. I don't get involved in the details.
_____ 285. I generally feel that I have made right decisions.
_____ 286. I generally make decisions that are logical and rational.
_____ 287. I have an ability to cut through red tape.
_____ 288. I involve others in making decisions.
_____ 289. I involve others in planning.
_____ 290. I make decisions with others.
_____ 291. I make things happen.
_____ 292. I make timely decisions.
_____ 293. I rarely hesitate when making decisions.
_____ 294. I readily delegate tasks.
_____ 295. I seek good input before making decisions.
_____ 296. I set difficult goals for myself.
_____ 297. I take full responsibility for my decisions.
_____ 298. I try to make clear to others why I make the decisions that I do.
_____ 299. I usually make sound decisions even under pressure.
_____ 300. I weigh my options carefully when making decisions.

Summary of Your Scores

Skill (max. possible score)	Your Score Now	Scores from Others	Your Score From Chapter 1
Decision making (150)			

Interpretation of Your Scores

Compare your score with the one you reported at the beginning of Chapter 1. If there is no or only a modest improvement in your score, you should examine the same set of items from the **Managerial Skills Assessment** from Chapter 1 and compare each of them with these to see where change has and has not occurred. You should then spend more time on developing the particular skills where change either decreased or stayed the same.

INTERPRET

INTERPRETATIONS

DECISION-MAKING STYLES

Generally there are three decision-making styles: reflexive, consistent, and reflective. You can determine your style by totaling the numbers assigned to each response where (a) = 1, (b) = 2, and (c) = 3 and then comparing your totals to the following scale: 10–16, reflexive; 17–23, consistent; and 24–30, reflective.

Reflexive decision makers like to make quick decisions without taking the time to get all the information they may need and without considering all the alternatives. They are decisive, however, and do not procrastinate. Students who tend to be reflexive should be cautioned to slow down a bit.

Consistent decision makers are more balanced with a mix of both reflexive and reflective styles. Therefore, they tend to have the best record for making good decisions.

Reflective decision makers tend to take plenty of time to make decisions, gathering considerable information and analyzing several alternatives. While they do not make hasty decisions, they can procrastinate, waste resources searching for information, and be viewed as wishy-washy and indecisive. Students who tend to be reflective should be advised to speed up their decision processes.

INTERNAL-EXTERNAL CONTROL SAMPLER

Locus of control is the degree to which a person believes that behavior has a direct impact on its consequences.

A person with an internal locus of control believes that each person is in control of his or her life so that success or failure results from one's own behavior and decisions. Internals want to participate, prefer decentralized organizations, want freedom and autonomy to perform their jobs, and like reward systems based on individual performance.

A person with an external locus of control thinks that forces beyond his or her control dictate what happens to him or her. So those with an external locus of control believe that success or failure results from fate, chance, luck, or the behavior of others. Externals prefer centralized organizations, structured jobs, and reward systems based on seniority.

Most successful top managers appear to have an internal locus of control.

PROBLEM-SOLVING STYLE QUESTIONNAIRE

The letter "S" under column I-A refers to *sensation*. The letter "N" under column II-B refers to *intuitive*. The letter "T" under column III-A refers to *thinking*, and the letter "F" under column IV-B refers to *feeling*.

The first two columns identify your sensation-intuitive scores. Generally, people have preferred one of these two styles for gathering information. The following table presents a summary of characteristics about these two styles.

Comparisons of Sensation and Intuitive Types of People

Characteristic	Sensation Type	Intuitive Type
Focus	Details, practical, action, get things done quickly	Patterns, innovation, ideas, long-range planning
Time orientation	Present, lives life as it is	Future achievement, change, rearrange
Work environment	Pays attention to detail, patient with details and does not make factual errors, not risk-takers	Looks at the "big picture," patient with complexity, risk-takers
Strengths	Pragmatic, results-oriented, objective, competitive	Original, imaginative, creative, idealistic
Possible weaknesses	Impatient when projects get delayed, decides issues too quickly, lacks long-range perspective, can oversimplify a complex task	Lacks follow-through, makes errors of fact, impractical, takes people's contributions for granted

The next two columns represent the thinking-feeling scores. People generally prefer to evaluate information based on one of these two styles. The table below summarizes the characteristics about these two styles.

	Comparisons of Thinking and Feeling Types of People	
Characteristic	Thinking Type	Feeling Type
Focus	Logic of situation, truth, organization principles	Human values and needs, harmony, feelings, emotions
Time orientation	Past, present, future	Past
Work Environment	Businesslike, impersonal, treats others fairly, well organized	Naturally friendly, personal, harmony, care and concern for others
Strengths	Good at putting things in logical order; tends to be firm and tough-minded, rational, objective; predicts logical results	Enjoys pleasing people, sympathetic, loyal, draws out feelings in others, takes interest in person behind the job or idea
Possible Weaknesses	Overly analytical, unemotional, too serious, rigid, verbose	Sentimental, postpones unpleasant tasks, avoids conflict

YOUR DECISION-MAKING STYLE

Every person has a characteristic way of making decisions. This assessment uses four categories—analytical, conceptual, behavioral, and directive. Some characteristics of each of those are:

- Analytical (thinking–task): capacity for abstract; logical thinking; high tolerance for ambiguity; searches out and verifies large amounts of data; identifies and questions underlying assumptions; task oriented; performance is achieved by analysis, planning, and forecasting.
- Conceptual (thinking–people): creative capacity; broad "systems thinkers"; high tolerance for ambiguity and complexity; values quality; shares values with colleagues; high need for achievement; requires praise and constructive feedback; needs freedom; people oriented; performance is achieved by exploring options and creativity.
- Behavioral (acting–people): personal; focuses on individual; low tolerance for ambiguity; characterized as supportive and participative; people oriented; good listeners; prefers "soft" data to "hard" data; people and social concerns oriented.
- Directive (acting–task): focuses on short-term results; appetite for control; low tolerance for ambiguity; implements operational objectives systematically and efficiently; efficiency oriented; facts are reality; communicates through numbers and facts; seeks to establish structure in work; task oriented.

The styles scores and their meanings can be interpreted as follows:

	Least Preferred	Backup	Dominant	Very Dominant
Directive	20–67	68–81	82–89	90–160
Analytical	20–82	83–96	97–104	105–160
Conceptual	20–72	73–86	87–94	95–160
Behavioral	20–47	48–61	62–69	70–160

For comparative purposes, here are some typical scores:

	D	A	C	B
Average	75	90	80	55
Admirals	[59]	(102)	(92)	[47]
Senior Executives	(70)	90	93	[47]
Police Chiefs	71	90	81	58
Financial Planners	75	(100)	74	51
Strategic Planners	[62]	[81]	**(100)**	57
Male Managers	74	89	83	54
Female Managers	75	88	74	(64)

[ ] = Least Preferred

( ) = Dominant

( ) = Very Dominant

Source: Adapted from a PowerPoint® presentation by William Benjamin Martz, Jr., posted online at http://www.uccs.edu/~wmartz/buad100/DECSTYLE.PPT", adapted from Managing with style, Alan Rowe and R. O. Mason, Jossey-Bass, 1987.

ENDNOTES

[1] E. Frank Harrison, *The Managerial Decision Making Process*, 5th ed. (Boston: Houghton Mifflin, 1999). See also Elke U. Weber and Eric J. Johnson, "Mindful Judgment and Decision Making," in *Annual Review of Psychology* 2009 (Susan T. Fiske, Daniel L. Schacter, and Robert Sternberg, Editors) Annual Reviews, Palo Also California, 2009, pp. 53–86.

[2] George P. Huber, *Managerial Decision Making* (Glenview, Ill.: Scott, Foresman, 1980).

[3] For an example, see Paul D. Collins, Lori V. Ryan, and Sharon F. Matusik, "Programmable Automation and the Locus of Decision-Making Power," *Journal of Management*, 1999, vol. 25, pp. 29–53.

[4] "How Mulally Helped Turn Ford Around," *USA Today*, July 18, 2011, p. 2B.

[5] Huber, *Managerial Decision Making*. See also David W. Miller and Martin K. Starr, *The Structure of Human Decisions* (Englewood Cliffs, N.J.: Prentice-Hall, 1976); Alvar Elbing, *Behavioral Decisions in Organizations*, 2nd ed. (Glenview, Ill: Scott, Foresman, 1978).

[6] Rene M. Stulz, "Six Ways Companies Mismanage Risk," *Harvard Business Review*," March 2009, pp. 86–94.

[7] "Ford Lays Bet On New Truck By Rehiring 1,000 Workers," *Wall Street Journal*, October 31, 2008, pp. B1, B2.

[8] "High-End Pickup Sales Power Forward," *USA Today*, February 6, 2012, p. B1.

[9] Gerard P. Hodgkinson, Nicola J. Bown, A. John Maule, Keith W. Glaister, and Alan D. Pearman, "Breaking the Frame: An Analysis of Strategic Cognition and Decision Making Under Uncertainty," *Strategic Management Journal*, 1999, vol. 20, pp. 977–985.

[10] "Andersen's Fall from Grace Is a Tale of Greed and Miscues," *Wall Street Journal*, June 7, 2002, pp. A1, A6.

[11] Jerry Useem, "Boeing vs. Boeing," *Fortune*, October 2, 2000, pp. 148–160; "Airbus Prepares to 'Bet the Company' as It Builds a Huge New Jet," *Wall Street Journal*, November 3, 1999, pp. A1, A10.

[12] Robert C. Litchfield, "Brainstorming Reconsidered: A Goal-Based View," *Academy of Management Review*, 2008, Vol. 33, No. 3, pp. 649–668.

[13] Paul Nutt, "Expanding the Search for Alternatives During Strategic Decision-Making," *Academy of Management Executive*, 2004, vol. 18, no. 4, pp. 13–22.

[14] *Wall Street Journal*, May 27, 2005, p. A1.

[15] Paul J.H. Schoemaker and Robert E. Gunther, "The Wisdom of Deliberate Mistakes," *Harvard Business Review*, June 2006, pp. 108–115.

[16] "Airbus Clips Superjumbo Production," *Wall Street Journal*, May 7, 2009, p. B1.

[17] "Accommodating the A380," *Wall Street Journal*, November 29, 2005, p. B1; "Boeing Roars Ahead," *BusinessWeek*, November 7, 2005, pp. 44–45; "Boeing's New Tailwind," *Newsweek*, December 5, 2005, p. 45.

[18] "The Wisdom of Solomon," *Newsweek*, August 17, 1987, pp. 62–63.

[19] "Making Decisions in Real Time," *Fortune*, June 26, 2000, pp. 332–334. See also Eugene Sadler-Smith and Erella Shefy, "The Intuitive Executive: Understanding and Applying 'Gut Feel' in Decision-Making," *Academy of Management Executive*, 2004, vol. 18, no. 4, pp. 76–91 and Don A. Moore and Francis J. Flynn, "The Case of Behavioral Decision Research in Organizational Behavior," in James P. Walsh and Arthur P. Brief, *The Academy of Management Annals*, Volume 2 (London: Routledge, 2008), pp. 399–432.

[20] Herbert A. Simon, *Administrative Behavior* (New York: Free Press, 1945). Simon has refined and updated his ideas in Herbert A. Simon, *Administrative Behavior*, 3rd ed. (New York: Free Press, 1976), and Herbert A. Simon, "Making Management Decisions: The Role of Intuition and Emotion," *Academy of Management Executive*, February 1987, pp. 57–63.

[21] Patricia Corner, Angelo Kinicki, and Barbara Keats, "Integrating Organizational and Individual Information Processing Perspectives on Choice," *Organization Science*, August 1994, pp. 294–302.

[22] "Lessons From Saturn's Fall," *BusinessWeek*, March 2, 2009, p. 25.

[23] Kimberly D. Elsbach and Greg Elofson, "How the Packaging of Decision Explanations Affects Perceptions of Trustworthiness," *Academy of Management Journal*, 2000, vol. 43, pp. 80–89.

[24] Kenneth Brousseau, Michael Driver, Gary Hourihan, and Rikard Larsson, "The Seasoned Executive's Decision-Making Style," *Harvard Business Review*, February 2006, pp. 111–112; see also Erik Dane and Michael G. Pratt, "Exploring Intuition and its Role in Managerial Decision Making," *Academy of Management Review*, 2007, Vol. 32, No. 1, pp. 33–54.

[25] *Fortune*, June 27, 2005, p. 55.

[26] Barry M. Staw and Jerry Ross, "Good Money After Bad," *Psychology Today*, February 1988, pp. 30–33; D. Ramona Bobocel and John Meyer, "Escalating Commitment to a Failing Course of Action: Separating the Roles of Choice and Justification," *Journal of Applied Psychology*, 1994, vol. 79, pp. 360–363.

[27] Mark Keil and Ramiro Montealegre, "Cutting Your Losses: Extricating Your Organization When a Big Project Goes Awry," *Sloan Management Review*, Spring 2000, pp. 55–64.

[28] "Closing Time for a Rock Theme Park," *Wall Street Journal*, January 7, 2009, p. B1.

[29] Gerry McNamara and Philip Bromiley, "Risk and Return in Organizational Decision Making," *Academy of Management Journal*, 1999, vol. 42, pp. 330–339.

[30] For an example, see Brian O'Reilly, "What It Takes to Start a Startup," *Fortune*, June 7, 1999, pp. 135–140.

[31] Martha I. Finney, "The Catbert Dilemma—The Human Side of Tough Decisions," *HRMagazine*, February 1997, pp. 70–78.

[32] Ann E. Tenbrunsel and Kristen Smith-Crowe, "Ethical Decision Making: Where We've Been and Where We're Going," in James P. Walsh and Arthur P. Brief, *The Academy of Management Annals*, Volume 2 (London: Routledge, 2008), pp. 545–607.

[33] David J. Glew, Anne M. O'Leary-Kelly, Ricky W. Griffin, and David D. Van Fleet, "Participation in Organizations: A Preview of the Issues and Proposed Framework for Future Analysis," *Journal of Management*, 1995, vol. 21, no. 3, pp. 395–421; for a recent update, see Russ Forrester, "Empowerment: Rejuvenating a Potent Idea," *Academy of Management Executive*, 2002, vol. 14, no. 1, pp. 67–78.

[34] Edwin A. Locke, David M. Schweiger, and Gary P. Latham, "Participation in Decision Making: When Should It Be Used?" *Organizational Dynamics*, Winter 1986, pp. 65–79; Nicholas Baloff and Elizabeth M. Doherty, "Potential Pitfalls in Employee Participation," *Organizational Dynamics*, Winter 1989, pp. 51–62.

[35] "The Art of Brainstorming," *BusinessWeek*, August 26, 2002, pp. 168–169.

[36] Andre L. Delbecq, Andrew H. Van de Ven, and David H. Gustafson, *Group Techniques for Program Planning* (Glenview, Ill.: Scott, Foresman, 1975); Michael J. Prietula and Herbert A. Simon, "The Experts in Your Midst," *Harvard Business Review*, January–February 1989, pp. 120–124.

[37] For an extension of the nominal group method, see Kevin P. Coyne, Patricia Gorman Clifford, and Renee Dye, "Breakthrough Thinking From Inside the Box," *Harvard Business Review*, December 2007, pp. 71–80.

[38] Norman P. R. Maier, "Assets and Liabilities in Group Problem Solving: The Need for an Integrative Function," in J. Richard Hackman, Edward E. Lawler III, and Lyman W. Porter (eds.), *Perspectives on Business in Organizations*, 2nd ed. (New York: McGraw-Hill, 1983), pp. 385–392.

[39] Anthony L. Iaquinto and James W. Fredrickson, "Top Management Team Agreement About the Strategic Decision Process: A Test of Some of Its Determinants and Consequences," *Strategic Management Journal*, 1997, vol. 18, pp. 63–75.

[40] Richard A. Cosier and Charles R. Schwenk, "Agreement and Thinking Alike: Ingredients for Poor Decisions," *Academy of Management Executive*, February 1990, pp. 69–78.

[41] Irving L. Janis, *Groupthink*, 2nd ed. (Boston: Houghton Mifflin, 1982).

[42] *Ibid.*

[43] Victor H. Vroom and Philip H. Yetton, *Leadership and Decision Making* (Pittsburgh: University of Pittsburgh Press, 1973); Victor H. Vroom and Arthur G. Jago, *The New Leadership* (Englewood Cliffs, N.J.: Prentice-Hall, 1988).

[44] Victor Vroom, "Leadership and the Decision-Making Process," *Organizational Dynamics*, Spring 2000.

[45] Vroom and Jago, *The New Leadership*.

[46] K. A. Froot, D. S. Scharfstein, and J. C. Stein, "A Framework for Risk Management," *Harvard Business Review*, November–December 1994, pp. 91–102.

[47] *Fortune*, May 2, 2011, p. 54.

[48] "How the Fixers Fended off Big Disasters," *Wall Street Journal*, December 23, 1999, pp. B1, B4.

[49] "At Wal-Mart, Emergence Plan Has Big Payoff," *Wall Street Journal*, September 12, 2005, pp. B1, B3.

[50] "Next Time," *USA Today*, October 4, 2005, pp. 1B, 2B; see also Judith A. Clair and Ronald L. Dufresne, "How Companies Can Experience Positive Transformation from a Crisis," *Organizational Dynamics*, 2007, Vol. 36, No. 1, pp. 63–77.

[51] "Trial to Put BP Oil Spill in Perspective," *USA Today*, February 27, 2012, pp. 1B, 2B.

[52] Michael Watkins and Max Bazerman, "Predictable Surprises: The Disasters You Should Have Seen Coming," *Harvard Business Review*, March 2003, pp. 72–81.

9

Assessing Your Technical Skills

PBS (Power Bases Score) Questionnaire
Defining Quality and Productivity
Understanding Control
Are You Technically Oriented?

Learning About Technical Skills

Technology, Product and Service, Industry, and Business Knowledge
Accounting and Financial Management Techniques
- *Budgets*
- *Financial Statements*
- *Ratio Analysis*

Forecasting Techniques
- *Sales and Revenue Forecasting*
- *Technological Forecasting*
- *Other Types of Forecasting*
- *Forecasting Techniques*

Other Planning Techniques
- *Linear Programming*
- *Breakeven Analysis*
- *Simulations*
- *PERT*

Decision-Making Tools
- *Payoff Matrices*
- *Decision Trees*
- *Other Techniques*

Summary and a Look Ahead

Visualizing Technical Skills

Technical Skills in Action—1
Technical Skills in Action—2

Practicing Your Technical Skills

Applying Technical Skills to Budgeting
Using Your Technical Skills on the Internet
Getting Organized
Using the Internet to Obtain Data
Identifying Technical Skills Related to Quality and Productivity
Span of Management
Using SWOT to Evaluate Work-Life Strengths and Weaknesses
Identifying Technical Skills Needed in Different Organizations
Impact of Organizational Strategy on Structure

Using Your Technical Skills

Perrier Keeps Flowing
Restaurant Operations

Extending Your Technical Skills

Group Extensions
Individual Extensions

Your Technical Skills Now

Technical Skills Assessment

Interpretations

PBS (Power Bases Score) Questionnaire
Defining Quality and Productivity
Understanding Control
Are You Technically Oriented?

Technical Skills

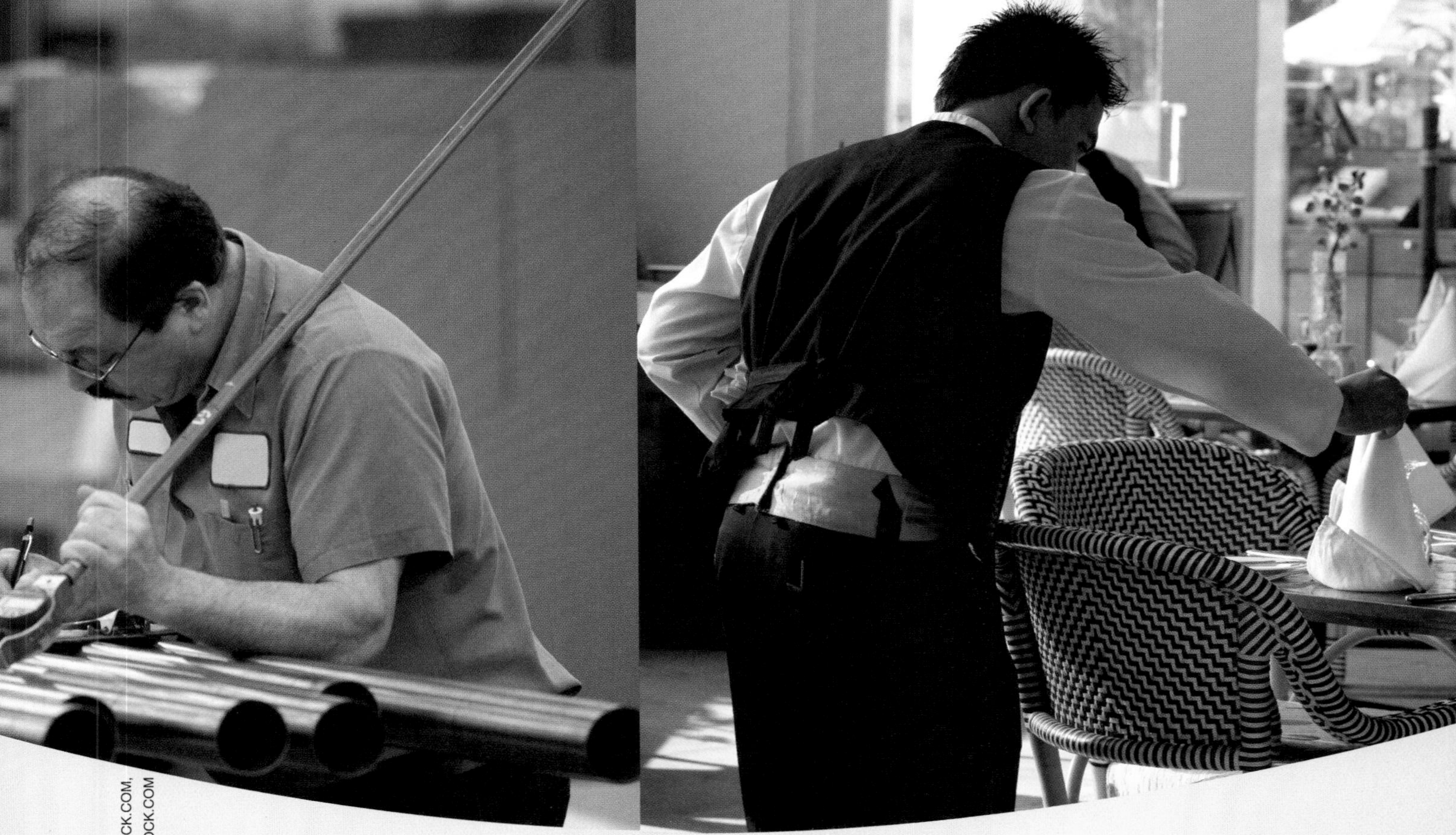

© CHRISTIAN DELBERT/SHUTTERSTOCK.COM, ERWINOVA/SHUTTERSTOCK.COM

Decision-making skills, discussed in the previous chapter, frequently also involve technical knowledge and skill. Technical skills are also often required in conjunction with the other core management skills. This chapter, then, focuses on helping you develop your own technical skills. We start with a general discussion of business and organization knowledge and then provide more detailed material regarding technical skills and decision-making tools. Following the text section, several cases and exercises will help you further develop and master technical skills.

ASSESS

ASSESSING YOUR TECHNICAL SKILLS

PBS (POWER BASES SCORE) QUESTIONNAIRE

Organizations generally use six kinds of power: Legitimate, Reward, Coercive, Referent, Expert, and Relations. This self-test tells you the extent to which you use or would use each kind of power.

Instructions:

For each of the 30 items below, please indicate the degree to which each statement describes you. Please make your assessment as objectively and factually based as you can, without considering what you think the "best" answer is. If your work experience is limited, please indicate what you think you would do in a job. Using the following scale, write the appropriate number from 1 to 7 in the blanks in the left-hand column.

Very little extent		Little extent	Some extent		Great extent	Very great extent
1	2	3	4	5	6	7

To what extent do you or would you:

_____ 1. Know a great deal about how to do your job and others' jobs?
_____ 2. Warrant people's trust and respect?
_____ 3. Expect others to do what you suggest because you're the boss?
_____ 4. Make yourself available to talk about non-job related matters?
_____ 5. Behave in ways that others would like to behave?
_____ 6. Influence how much of a pay increase others receive?
_____ 7. Serve as a source of information and advice on job-related issues?
_____ 8. Pull "rank" in asking others to do a task?
_____ 9. Demonstrate behavior that others really respect?
_____ 10. Have an impact on promotions in your organization?
_____ 11. Express interest in talking with others about things not related to the job?
_____ 12. Make people feel uncomfortable when they have made an error or broken a rule?
_____ 13. Have knowledge that is important to others in performing their jobs?
_____ 14. Criticize others and their work?
_____ 15. Assume that subordinates have a duty to follow your requests?
_____ 16. Reprimand people for making mistakes?
_____ 17. Provide answers to others about how to do a job better?
_____ 18. Have a say about the size of a pay increase or a promotion that others might receive?
_____ 19. Act in a manner that others admire and aspire to be like?
_____ 20. Make yourself available to listen to others' concerns?
_____ 21. Use your position (or authority) to get people to do their tasks?
_____ 22. Give out penalties or write reports for someone's personnel file for doing a poor job?
_____ 23. Recognize good performance in a way that is meaningful to people?

_____ 24. Rely on friendship to get work done?
_____ 25. Publicly criticize people when they have made a mistake?
_____ 26. Demonstrate characteristics and behavior that others admire?
_____ 27. Let people have a day off or similar benefit for doing a good job?
_____ 28. Teach people how to do their jobs more effectively?
_____ 29. Believe you have the right to make decisions that affect others on the job?
_____ 30. Depend on good interpersonal relations between yourself and others?

Scoring:
In the numbered spaces below that correspond to the numbered statements from the PBS, record your answers, using a scale of 1 to 7. Then add the total in each column to determine the extent to which each power base is used. A higher score means the power base is used more. The numbers in the last row are the mean scores for each power base from a national sample of managers. They can be used for comparison, but do not necessarily represent a best score.

	Power Bases					
	Referent	Expert	Relations	Legitimate	Reward	Coercive
	2. ____	1. ____	4. ____	3. ____	6. ____	12. ____
	5. ____	7. ____	11. ____	8. ____	10. ____	14. ____
	9. ____	13. ____	20. ____	15. ____	18. ____	16. ____
	19. ____	17. ____	24. ____	21. ____	23. ____	22. ____
	26. ____	28. ____	30. ____	29. ____	27. ____	25. ____
Sums:	______	______	______	______	______	______
National Survey Mean:	23.75	24.50	24.05	18.70	29.60	13.40

Power Bases: Referent (based on personal identification, imitation, and charisma), Expert (based on knowledge and skill), Relations (friendly relationship between two people), Legitimate (from a position in an organization), Reward (controls rewards), and Coercive (controls punishment or removal of rewards).

Source: W. Alan Randolph and Richard S. Blackburn, Managing Organizational Behavior (Homewood, IL: Irwin, 1989), pp. 412–413. This survey of Power Bases was developed by W. Alan Randolph and Barry Z. Posner for use in assessing how people use their bases of power. Questionnaire and scoring ©1987 W. Alan Randolph and Barry Z. Posner. Reprinted with permission.

See Interpretations at the end of the chapter.

DEFINING QUALITY AND PRODUCTIVITY

Quality is a complex term whose meaning has no doubt changed over time. The following assessment surveys your ideas about and approaches to quality.

Instructions:
You will agree with some of the statements and disagree with others. In some cases, making a decision may be difficult, but you should force yourself to make a choice. Record your answers next to each statement according to the following rating scale:

Rating Scale
4 – Strongly Agree
3 – Slightly Agree
2 – Somewhat Disagree
1 – Strongly Disagree

ASSESS

_____ 1. Quality refers to a product's or a service's ability to fulfill its primary operating characteristics, such as providing a sharp picture of a television set.
_____ 2. Quality is an absolute, measurable aspect of a product or service.
_____ 3. The concept of quality includes supplemental aspects of a product or service, such as the remote control for a television set.
_____ 4. Productivity and quality are inversely related so that, to get one, you must sacrifice the other.
_____ 5. The concept of quality refers to the extent to which a product's design and operating characteristics conform to certain set standards.
_____ 6. Productivity refers to what is created relative to what it takes to create it.
_____ 7. Quality means that a product will not malfunction during a specified period of time.
_____ 8. Quality refers only to products; it is immeasurable for services.
_____ 9. The length of time that a product or service will function is what is known as quality.
_____ 10. Everyone uses exactly the same definition of quality.
_____ 11. Quality refers to the repair ease and speed of a product or service.
_____ 12. Being treated courteously has nothing to do with the quality of anything.
_____ 13. How a product looks, feels, tastes, or smells is what is meant by quality.
_____ 14. Price, not quality, is what determines the ultimate value of services.
_____ 15. Quality refers to what customers think of a product or service.
_____ 16. Productivity and quality cannot both increase at the same time.

Source: From Van Fleet, Contemporary Management, 3e © 1994 South-Western, a part of Cengage Learning, Inc. Reproduced by permission. www.cengage.com/permissions

See Interpretations at the end of the chapter.

UNDERSTANDING CONTROL

Control is an area that relies heavily on technical skills. Control systems must be constructed carefully for all organizations, regardless of their specific goals. The following assessment surveys your ideas about and approaches to control.

Instructions:

You will agree with some of the following statements and disagree with others. In some cases, making a decision may be difficult, but you should force yourself to make a choice. Record your answer (1-2-3-4) next to each statement according to the following scale:

Rating Scale

4 Strongly Agree   3 Slightly Agree   2 Somewhat Disagree   1 Strongly Disagree

_____ 1. Effective controls must be unbending if they are to be used consistently.
_____ 2. The most objective form of control is one that uses measures such as stock prices and rate of return on investment (ROI).
_____ 3. Control is restrictive and should be avoided if at all possible.
_____ 4. Controlling through rules, procedures, and budgets should not be used unless measurable standards are difficult or expensive to develop.
_____ 5. Overreliance on measurable control standards is seldom a problem for business organizations.

ASSESS

_____ 6. Organizations should encourage the development of individual self-control.

_____ 7. Organizations tend to try to establish behavioral controls as the first type of control to be used.

_____ 8. The easiest and least costly form of control is output or quantity control.

_____ 9. Short-run efficiency and long-run effectiveness result from the use of similar control standards.

_____ 10. Controlling by taking into account return on investment (ROI) and by using stock prices in making control decisions are ways of ensuring that a business organization is responding to its external market.

_____ 11. Self-control should be relied on to replace other forms of control.

_____ 12. Controls such as return on investment (ROI) are more appropriate for corporations and business units than for small groups or individuals.

_____ 13. Control is unnecessary in a well-managed organization.

_____ 14. The use of output or quantity controls can lead to unintended or unfortunate consequences.

_____ 15. Standards of control do not depend on which constituency is being considered.

_____ 16. Controlling through the use of rules, procedures, and budgets can lead to rigidity and to a loss of creativity in an organization.

_____ 17. Different forms of control cannot be used at the same time. An organization must decide how it is going to control and then stick to that method.

_____ 18. Setting across-the-board output or quantity targets for divisions within a company can lead to destructive results.

_____ 19. Control through rules, procedures, and budgets is generally not very costly.

_____ 20. Reliance on individual self-control can lead to problems with integration and communication.

Source: From Hill / Jones. STRATEGIC MANAGEMENT, 4/E TXT, 4E © 1998 South-Western, a part of Cengage Learning, Inc. Reproduced by permission. www.cengage.com/permissions

See Interpretations at the end of the chapter.

ARE YOU TECHNICALLY ORIENTED?

People tend to think about problems differently. Some are more technical while others are more intuitive. The following questions are designed to provide feedback on your preferences in problem solving.

Instructions:

Answer each question as accurately as you can. This is a forced-choice test, so choose the option you like best (or dislike least), but be sure to answer each one.

1. When I solve problems, my basic approach is
   (A) logical, rational
   (B) intuitive

2. If I were to write books, I would prefer to write
   (A) fiction
   (B) nonfiction

3. When I read, I am looking for
   (A) main ideas
   (B) specific facts and details

4. When I read, the stores I prefer are
   (A) realistic
   (B) fantasy
5. While I study or read,
   (A) I listen to music on the radio
   (B) I must have silence
6. I prefer to learn
   (A) through ordering and planning
   (B) through free exploration
7. I prefer to organize things
   (A) sequentially
   (B) in terms of relationships
8. The statement that best describes my moods is
   (A) almost no mood changes
   (B) frequent mood changes
9. I enjoy clowning around.
   (A) yes
   (B) no
10. I would describe myself as
    (A) generally conforming
    (B) generally nonconforming
11. I am absent-minded
    (A) frequently
    (B) virtually never
12. The type of assignment that I like best is
    (A) well structured
    (B) open ended
13. I find it more preferable to
    (A) produce ideas
    (B) draw conclusions
14. The following is more fun for me:
    (A) dreaming
    (B) planning realistically
15. I find it more exciting to
    (A) invent something new
    (B) improve on something already in existence
16. The type of story that I prefer is
    (A) fair
    (B) sentimental
17. I prefer the following:
    (A) cats
    (B) dogs
18. I prefer the following activity:
    (A) creating stories
    (B) analyzing stories
19. I find it easier to think when I am
    (A) sitting up straight
    (B) lying down

20. I would prefer to be
    (A) a music composer
    (B) a music critic
21. If someone wanted to hypnotize me,
    (A) I think I could be hypnotized quite easily.
    (B) I don't think I could be hypnotized.
22. I would prefer to do
    (A) ballet dancing
    (B) interpretative, impromptu dancing
23. Regarding memory, I am better at
    (A) recalling names and dates
    (B) recalling where things were in a room or picture
24. When it comes to getting instructions, I prefer
    (A) verbal instructions
    (B) demonstration
25. When getting verbal instructions, I generally feel
    (A) restless
    (B) attentive

Scoring:

In the following answer key, circle the answer A or B that you gave for each of the 25 items. Then total your circled responses in Col. I and in Col. II.

Item	*Col. I*	*Col. II*	Item	*Col. I*	*Col. II*
1.	B	A	14.	A	B
2.	A	B	15.	A	B
3.	A	B	16.	B	A
4.	B	A	17.	A	B
5.	A	B	18.	A	B
6.	B	A	19.	B	A
7.	B	A	20.	B	A
8.	B	A	21.	A	B
9.	A	B	22.	B	A
10.	B	A	23.	B	A
11.	A	B	24.	B	A
12.	B	A	25.	A	B
13.	A	B			
			TOTAL =	____	____

Source: Adapted from Steven Altman, Enzo Valenzi, and Richard M. Hodgetts, Organizational Behavior: Theory and Practice. © 1985 by Harcourt Brace & Company, reprinted by permission of Steve Altman.

See Interpretations at the end of the chapter.

GO ONLINE to the Griffin/Van Fleet Assessment Library for online versions of these and other assessments.

LEARNING ABOUT TECHNICAL SKILLS

LEARN

Technology, Product and Service, Industry, and Business Knowledge

Accounting and Financial Management Techniques

- *Budgets*
- *Financial Statements*
- *Ratio Analysis*

Forecasting Techniques

- *Sales and Revenue Forecasting*
- *Technological Forecasting*
- *Other Types of Forecasting*
- *Forecasting Techniques*
  - *Time-Series Analysis*
  - *Causal Modeling*
  - *Qualitative Forecasting Techniques*

Other Planning Techniques

- *Linear Programming*
- *Breakeven Analysis*
- *Simulations*
- *PERT*

Decision-Making Tools

- *Payoff Matrices*
- *Decision Trees*
- *Other Techniques*
  - *Inventory Models*
  - *Queuing Models*
  - *Distribution Models*
  - *Game Theory*
  - *Artificial Intelligence*

Summary and a Look Ahead

technical skills the skills necessary to perform or understand relatively concrete tasks that require specialized knowledge

technology consists of the conversion processes used to transform inputs (such as materials or information) into outputs (such as products or services)

manufacturing a form of business that combines and transforms resources into tangible outcomes that are then sold to others

Not all managers are trained in business schools—some come from engineering, science, liberal arts, agricultural, or other backgrounds. But regardless of their backgrounds, managers need to understand the basic technologies their organizations use. Moreover, all managers need to know about certain technically based procedures used for accounting and finance, as well as other tools and techniques that are often used to make decisions and solve problems. **Technical skills** are the skills necessary to perform or understand relatively concrete tasks that require specialized knowledge.

TECHNOLOGY, PRODUCT AND SERVICE, INDUSTRY, AND BUSINESS KNOWLEDGE

Technology consists of the conversion processes used to transform inputs (such as materials or information) into outputs (such as products or services). Most organizations use multiple technologies, but an organization's *core technology* is its most important. Although most people visualize assembly lines and machinery when they think of technology, the term also can be applied to service organizations. For example, an investment firm like Fidelity uses technology to transform investment dollars into income in much the same way that Union Carbide uses natural resources to manufacture chemical products.

Because manufacturing once dominated US industry, the entire area of management used to be called "production management." **Manufacturing** is a form of business that combines and transforms resources into tangible outcomes that are then sold to others. The Goodyear Tire & Rubber Company is a manufacturer because it combines rubber and chemical compounds and uses blending equipment and molding machines to create tires. Broyhill is a manufacturer because it buys wood and metal components, pads, and fabric and then combines them into furniture.

A **service organization** is one that transforms resources into an intangible output and creates time or place utility for its customers. For example, Merrill Lynch makes stock transactions for customers, Avis leases cars to customers, and local hairdressers cut clients' hair. In 1947 the service sector was responsible for less than half of the US gross national product (GNP). By 1975, however, this figure reached 65 percent, and by 2012 it was more than 80 percent. Managers have come to see that many of the tools, techniques, and methods that are used in a factory are also useful to a service firm. For example, managers of automobile plants and hair salons both have to decide how to design their facilities, identify the best locations for them, determine optimal capacities, make decisions about inventory storage, set procedures for purchasing raw materials, and set standards for productivity and quality.

Managers must also understand the basic products and services created and supplied by the organization. A human resource manager has no need to understand the inner workings of a computer her firm manufacturers. But she should have a basic knowledge of the kinds of computers the firm makes, the customers it serves, and so forth. Likewise, managers need to know the basic dynamics that exist within their industries. For instance, all managers should understand their relative market share, major competitors, and so forth. Further, managers must know the fundamental business model their firm uses. Some computer companies, for example, make their own computer parts and then assemble them into finished units. Others buy pre-assembled components and then use them to build customized computers. It is also generally important for managers to understand basic accounting and financial management.

> *"Technology is a huge issue because we are functionally a technology company with wings."*
>
> JEFF SMISEK
> United CEO[1]
>
> FORTUNE, MAY 2, 2011, P. 53.

ACCOUNTING AND FINANCIAL MANAGEMENT TECHNIQUES

While most organizations have accounting and financial managers to deal with financial resources, all managers should have at least a rudimentary understanding of the accounting and financial management systems and procedures their organizations use. Indeed, all managers play at least a minor role in financial control. **Financial control** is the control of financial resources as they flow into the organization (revenues, shareholder investments), are held by the organization (working capital, retained earnings), and flow out of the organization (pay, expenses). Businesses must manage their finances so that revenues are sufficient to cover costs and still return profits to the firms' owners. Not-for-profit organizations such as universities have the same concerns: Their revenues (from tax dollars or tuition) must cover operating expenses and overhead. US automakers Ford and GM have come to realize that they have to reduce the costs of paying employees they do not need but whom they are obligated to keep due to longstanding labor agreements. Ford offered to cover the full costs of a college education for certain of its employees if they would resign; GM offered lump-sum payments of varying amounts to some of its workers in return for their resignations.[2] A complete discussion of financial management is beyond the scope of this book, but we will examine the control provided by budgets and other financial control tools.

Budgets

A **budget** is a plan expressed in numerical terms.[3] Organizations establish budgets for work groups, departments, divisions, and the whole organization. The usual time period for a budget is one year, although breakdowns of budgets by the quarter or month are also common. Budgets generally are expressed in financial terms, but they may occasionally be expressed in units of output, time, or other quantifiable factors. When Disney launches the production of a new animated cartoon feature, it creates a budget for how much the movie should cost. Several years ago, when movies like *Aladdin* and *The Lion King* were raking in hundreds of millions of dollars, Disney executives were fairly flexible about budget overruns. But, on the heels of several animated flops, such as *Atlantis: The Lost Empire* and *Treasure Planet*, the company had to take a much harder line on budget overruns.[4]

Because of their quantitative nature, budgets provide yardsticks for measuring performance and facilitate comparisons across departments, between levels in the organization, and from one time period to another. Budgets serve four primary purposes. They help managers coordinate resources and projects (because they use a common denominator, usually dollars). They help define the established standards for control. They provide guidelines about the organization's resources and expectations. Finally, budgets enable the organization to evaluate the performance of managers and organizational units.

Most organizations develop and make use of three different kinds of budgets—financial, operating, and nonmonetary. *Table 9.1* summarizes the characteristics of each of these. A *financial budget* indicates where the organization expects to get its cash for the coming time period and how it plans to use it. Because financial

service organization one that transforms resources into an intangible output and creates time or place utility for its customers

financial control the control of financial resources as they flow into the organization (revenues, shareholder investments), are held by the organization (working capital, retained earnings), and flow out of the organization (pay, expenses)

budget a plan expressed in numerical terms

LEARN

TABLE 9.1 TYPES OF BUDGETS

Organizations use various types of budgets to help manage their control functions. The three major categories of budgets are financial, operating, and nonmonetary. There are several different types of budgets in each category. To be most effective, each budget must be matched carefully with the specific function being controlled.

Type of Budget	What Budget Shows
Financial Budget	*Sources and Uses of Cash*
Cash flow or cash budget	All sources of cash income and cash expenditures in monthly, weekly, or daily periods
Capital expenditures budget	Costs of major assets such as a new plant, machinery, or land
Balance sheet budget	Forecast of the organization's assets and liabilities in the event all other budgets are met
Operating Budget	*Planned Operations in Financial Terms*
Sales or revenue budget	Income the organization expects to receive from normal operations
Expense budget	Anticipated expenses for the organization during the coming time period
Profit budget	Anticipated differences between sales or revenues and expenses
Nonmonetary Budget	*Planned Operations in Nonfinancial Terms*
Labor budget	Hours of direct labor available for use
Space budget	Square feet or meters of space available for various functions
Production budget	Number of units to be produced during the coming time period

© CENGAGE LEARNING 2014

LEARN

resources are critically important, the organization needs to know where those resources will be coming from and how they are to be used. The financial budget provides answers to both these questions. Usual sources of cash include sales revenue, short- and long-term loans, the sale of assets, and the issuance of new stock.

For years Exxon was very conservative in its capital budgeting. As a result, the firm amassed a huge financial reserve but was being overtaken in sales by Royal Dutch/Shell. Executives at Exxon were then able to use their reserves to help finance the firm's merger with Mobil, creating ExxonMobil, and to regain the number-one sales position. Since that time, the firm has become more aggressive in capital budgeting to stay ahead of its European rival.

An *operating budget* is concerned with planned operations within the organization. It outlines what quantities of products or services the organization intends to create and what resources will be used to create them. For example, Dell creates an operating budget that specifies how many of each model of its personal computer will be produced each quarter.

A *nonmonetary budget* is simply a budget expressed in nonfinancial terms, such as units of output, hours of direct labor, machine hours, or square-foot allocations. Managers at the lower levels of an organization most commonly use nonmonetary budgets. For example, a plant manager can schedule work more effectively knowing that he or she has 8,000 labor hours to allocate in a week, rather than trying to determine how to best spend $86,451 in wages in a week.

Traditionally, top management and the controller developed budgets and then imposed them on lower-level managers. Although some organizations still follow this pattern, many contemporary organizations now allow all managers to participate in the budget process. As a starting point, top management generally issues a call for budget requests, accompanied by an indication of overall patterns the budgets may take. For example, if sales are expected to drop in the next year, managers may be told up front to prepare for cuts in operating budgets.

As *Figure 9.1* shows, the heads of each operating unit typically submit budget requests to the head of their divisions. An operating unit head might be a department manager in a manufacturing or wholesaling firm or a program director in a social service agency. The division heads might include plant managers, regional sales managers, or college deans. The division head integrates and consolidates the budget requests from operating unit heads into one overall division budget request. A great deal of interaction among managers usually takes place at this stage, as the division head coordinates the budgetary needs of the various departments.

Division budget requests are then forwarded to a budget committee. The budget committee is usually composed of top managers. The committee reviews budget requests from several divisions, and once again,

FIGURE 9.1 DEVELOPING BUDGETS IN ORGANIZATIONS

Most organizations use the same basic process to develop budgets. Operating units are requested to submit their budget requests to divisions. These divisions, in turn, compile unit budgets and submit their own budgets to the organization. An organizational budget is then compiled for approval by the budget committee, controller, and CEO.

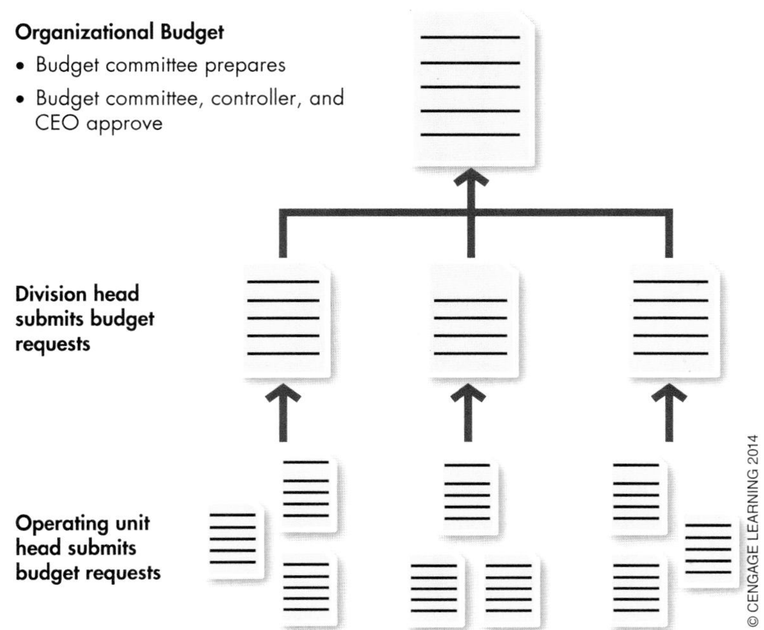

LEARN

corrects duplications and inconsistencies. Finally, the budget committee, the controller, and the CEO review and agree on the overall budget for the organization, as well as specific budgets for each operating unit. These decisions are then communicated back to each manager.

Budgets offer a number of advantages, but they also have weaknesses. On the plus side, budgets facilitate effective control. Placing dollar values on operations enables managers to monitor operations better and pinpoint problem areas. Budgets also facilitate coordination and communication between departments because they express diverse activities in a common denominator (dollars). Budgets help maintain records of organizational performance and are a logical complement to planning. In other words, as managers develop plans, they should simultaneously consider control measures to accompany them. Organizations can use budgets to link plans and control by first developing budgets as part of the plan and then using those budgets as part of control.

> *"I need to understand. I'm the one who signs the letters of representation with the auditors."*
>
> MICHAEL WOODFORD
> former executive at Olympus, discussing a recent financial scandal at the Japanese firm[5]

BLOOMBERG BUSINESSWEEK, FEBRUARY 20-FEBRUARY 26, 2012, P. 72.

On the other hand, some managers apply budgets too rigidly. Budgets are intended to serve as frameworks, but managers sometimes fail to recognize that changing circumstances may warrant budget adjustments. The process of developing budgets also can be very time consuming. Finally, budgets may limit innovation and change. When all available funds are allocated to specific operating budgets, it may be impossible to procure additional funds to take advantage of an unexpected opportunity. Indeed, for these very reasons, some organizations are working to scale back their budgeting systems. Although most organizations are likely to continue to use budgets, the goal is to make them less confining and rigid. Indeed, strong technical skills will help managers to decide when and how to most effectively use budgets.

Moreover, while budgets are the most common means of financial control, other useful tools are financial statements, ratio analysis, and financial audits.

LEARN

Financial Statements

© INGVAR BJORK/SHUTTERSTOCK.COM

A **financial statement** is a profile of some aspect of an organization's financial circumstances. There are commonly accepted and required ways that financial statements must be prepared and presented.[6] The two most basic financial statements prepared and used by virtually all organizations are a balance sheet and an income statement.

The **balance sheet** lists the assets and liabilities of the organization at a specific point in time, usually the last day of an organization's fiscal year. For example, the balance sheet may summarize the financial condition of an organization on December 31, 2013. Most balance sheets are divided into current assets (assets that are relatively liquid, or easily convertible into cash), fixed assets (assets that are longer term in nature and less liquid), current liabilities (debts and other obligations that must be paid in the near future), long-term liabilities (payable over an extended period of time), and stockholders' equity (the owners' claim against the assets).

Whereas the balance sheet reflects a snapshot profile of an organization's financial position at a single point in time, the **income statement** summarizes financial performance over a period of time, usually one year. For example, the income statement might be for the period January 1, 2013, through December 31, 2013. The income statement summarizes the firm's revenues less its expenses to report net income (profit or loss) for the period. Information from the balance sheet and income statement is used in computing important financial ratios.

financial statement a profile of some aspect of an organization's financial situation

balance sheet lists the assets and liabilities of the organization at a specific point in time, usually the last day of an organization's fiscal year

income statement summarizes financial performance over a period of time, usually one year

ratio analysis the calculation of one or more financial ratios to assess some aspect of the financial health of an organization

Ratio Analysis

Financial ratios compare different elements of a balance sheet or income statement to one another. **Ratio analysis** is the calculation of one or more financial ratios to assess some aspect of the financial health of an organization. Organizations use a variety of different financial ratios as part of financial control. For example, *liquidity ratios* indicate how liquid (easily converted into cash) an organization's assets are. *Debt ratios* reflect ability to meet long-term financial obligations. *Return ratios* show managers and investors how much return the organization is generating relative to its assets. *Coverage ratios* help estimate the organization's ability to cover interest expenses on borrowed capital. *Operating ratios* indicate the effectiveness of specific functional areas rather than of the total organization. Walt Disney is an example of a company that relies heavily on financial ratios to keep its financial operations on track.[7]

FORECASTING TECHNIQUES

The various accounting and financial management skills discussed above relate primarily to the control function. Technical skills are also important in planning.[8] To plan, managers must make assumptions about future events. But unlike Harry Potter and his friends, planners cannot simply look into a crystal ball or wave a wand. Instead, they must develop forecasts of probable future circumstances. Forecasting is the process of developing assumptions or premises about the future that managers can use in planning or decision making.

Sales and Revenue Forecasting

As the term implies, sales forecasting is concerned with predicting future sales. Because monetary resources (derived mainly from sales) are necessary to finance both current and future operations, knowledge of future sales is of vital importance. Sales forecasting is something that every business, from ExxonMobil to a neighborhood pizza parlor, must do. Consider, for example, the following questions that a manager might need to answer:

1. How much of each of our products should we produce next week? Next month? Next year?
2. How much money will we have available to spend on research and development and on new-product test marketing?
3. When and to what degree will we need to expand our existing production facilities?

4. How should we respond to union demands for a 5 percent pay increase?
5. If we borrow money for expansion, when can we pay it back?

None of these questions can be answered adequately without some notion of what future revenues are likely to be. Thus, sales forecasting is generally one of the first steps in planning.

Unfortunately, the term *sales forecasting* suggests that this form of forecasting is appropriate only for organizations that have something to sell. But other kinds of organizations also depend on financial resources, and so they also must forecast. The University of South Carolina, for example, must forecast future state aid before planning course offerings, staff size, and so on. Hospitals must forecast their future income from patient fees, insurance payments, and other sources to assess their ability to expand. Although we will continue to use the conventional term *sales forecasting*, keep in mind that what is really at issue is *revenue forecasting*.

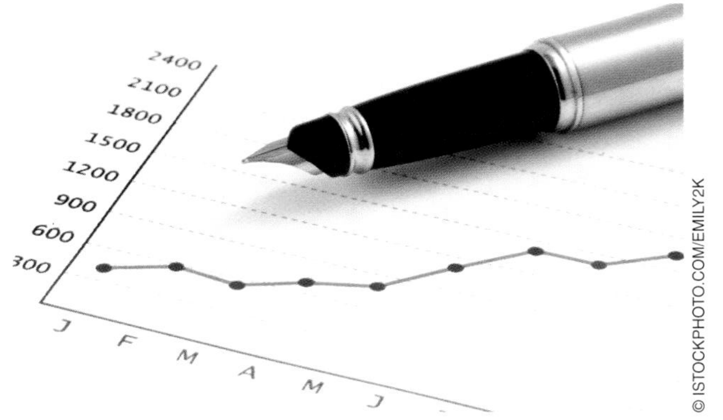

© ISTOCKPHOTO.COM/EMILY2K

Managers use several sources of information to develop a sales forecast. Previous sales figures and any obvious trends, such as the company's growth or stability, usually serve as the base. General economic indicators, technological improvements, new marketing strategies, and the competition's behavior all may be added together to ensure an accurate forecast. Once projected, the sales (or revenue) forecast becomes a guiding framework for various other activities. Raw-material expenditures, advertising budgets, sales-commission structures, and similar operating costs are all based on projected sales figures.

Managers often forecast sales across several time horizons. The longer-run forecasts may then be updated and refined as various shorter-run cycles are completed. For obvious reasons, a forecast should be as accurate as possible, and the accuracy of sales forecasting tends to increase as organizations learn from their previous forecasting experiences. But the more uncertain and complex future conditions will be, the more difficult it is to develop accurate forecasts. To offset these problems partially, forecasts are more useful to managers if they are expressed as a range rather than as an absolute index or number. If projected sales increases are expected to be in the range of 10 to 12 percent, a manager can consider all the implications for the entire range. A 10 percent increase could dictate one set of activities; a 12 percent increase could call for a different set.

Technological Forecasting

Technological forecasting is another type of forecasting used by many organizations. It focuses on predicting what future technologies are likely to emerge and when they are likely to be economically feasible. In an era when technological breakthrough and innovation have become the rule rather than the exception, managers must be able to anticipate new developments. If a manager invests heavily in existing technology (such as production processes, equipment, and computer systems) and the technology becomes obsolete in the near future, then the company has wasted its resources.

The most striking technological innovations in recent years have been in electronics, especially semiconductors. Personal computers, electronic games, and sophisticated communications equipment such as smartphones are all evidence of the electronics explosion. Given the increasing importance of technology and the rapid pace of technological innovation, it follows that managers will grow increasingly concerned with technological forecasting in the years to come.

Other Types of Forecasting

Managers also may use other types of forecasting. Resource forecasting projects the organization's future needs for and the availability of human resources, raw materials, and other necessary equipment and supplies. General economic conditions are the subject of economic forecasts. For example, some organizations forecast the size of the population or market. Some also attempt to forecast future government fiscal policy and various government regulations that might be put into practice. Indeed, almost any component in an organization's environment may be an appropriate area for forecasting.

Forecasting Techniques

To carry out the various kinds of forecasting we have identified, managers use several different techniques. Time-series analysis and causal modeling are two common quantitative techniques.

LEARN

FIGURE 9.2 TIMES-SERIES ANALYSIS EXAMPLE

Because time-series analysis assumes that the past is a good predictor of the future, it is most useful when historical data are available, trends are stable, and patterns are apparent. For example, few time-series analyses yield such clear results because there is almost always considerably more fluctuation in data from year to year.

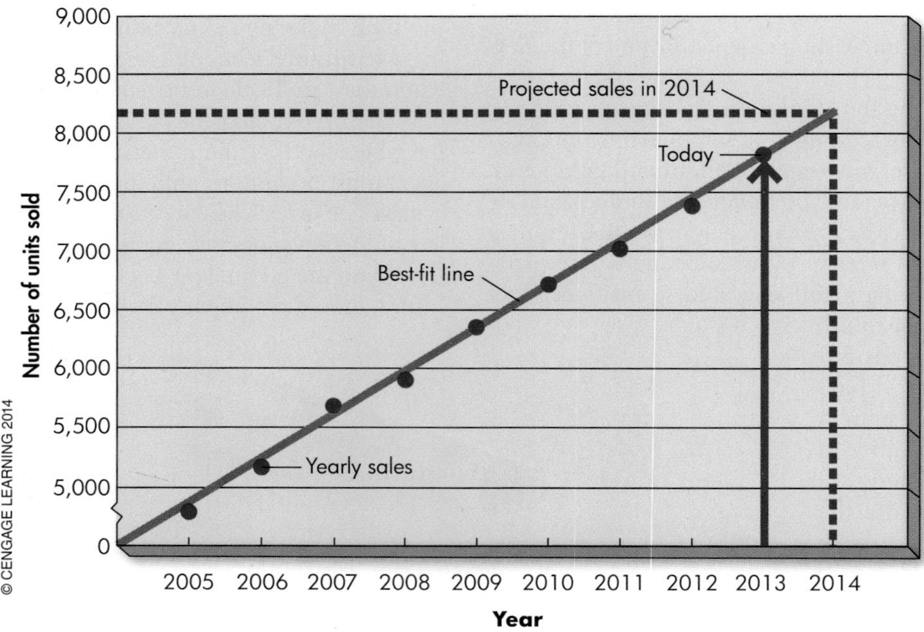

© CENGAGE LEARNING 2014

Time-Series Analysis The underlying assumption of time-series analysis is that the past is a good predictor of the future. This technique is most useful when the manager has a lot of historical data available and when stable trends and patterns are apparent. In a time-series analysis, the variable under consideration (such as sales or enrollment) is plotted across time, and a "best-fit" line is identified. *Figure* 9.2 shows how a time-series analysis might look. The points represent the number of units sold for each year from 2005 through 2013. The best-fit line has also been drawn in. It is the line around which the dots cluster with the least variability. A manager who wants to know what sales to expect in 2014 simply extends the line. In this case, the projection would be around 8,200 units.

Real time-series analysis involves much more than simply plotting sales data and then using a ruler and a pencil to draw and extend the line. Sophisticated mathematical procedures, among other things, are necessary to account for seasonal and cyclical fluctuations and to identify the true best-fit line. In real situations, data seldom follow the neat pattern found in *Figure* 9.2. Indeed, the data points may be so widely dispersed that they mask meaningful trends from all but painstaking, computer-assisted inspection.

Causal Modeling Another useful forecasting technique is causal modeling. Actually, the term causal modeling represents a group of several techniques. *Table* 9.2 summarizes three of the most useful approaches. Regression models are equations created to predict a variable (such as sales volume) that depends on several other variables (such as price and advertising). The variable being predicted is called the *dependent variable*; the variables used to make the prediction are called *independent variables*. A typical regression equation used by a small business might take this form:

$$y = ax_1 + bx_2 + cx_3 + d$$

where

y = the dependent variable (sales, in this case)

x_1, x_2, and x_3 = independent variables (advertising budget, price, and commissions)

a, b, and c = weights for the independent variables calculated during development of the regression model

d = a constant

To use the model, a manager can insert various alternatives for advertising budget, price, and commissions into the equation and then compute y. The calculated value of y represents the forecasted level of sales, given various levels of advertising, price, and commissions.

Econometric models employ regression techniques at a much more complex level. Econometric models attempt to predict major economic shifts and the

TABLE 9.2 CAUSAL MODELING FORECASTING TECHNIQUES

Managers use several different types of causal models in planning and decision making. Three popular models are regression models, econometric models, and economic indicators.

Regression models	Used to predict one variable (called the dependent variable) on the basis of known or assumed other variables (called independent variables). For example, we might predict future sales based on the values of price, advertising, and economic levels.
Econometric models	Make use of several multiple-regression equations to consider the impact of major economic shifts. For example, we might want to predict what impact migration toward the Sun Belt might have on our organization.
Economic models	Various population statistics, indexes, or parameters that predict organizationally relevant variables, such as discretionary income. Examples include cost-of-living index, inflation rate, and level of unemployment.

© CENGAGE LEARNING 2014

LEARN

potential impact of those shifts on the organization. They might be used to predict various age, ethnic, and economic groups that will characterize different regions of the United States in the year 2025 and also to predict the kinds of products and services these groups may want. A complete econometric model may consist of hundreds or even thousands of equations. Computers are almost always necessary to apply them. Given the complexities involved in developing econometric models, many firms that use them rely on outside consultants who specialize in this approach.

Economic indicators, another form of causal model, are population statistics or indexes that reflect the economic well-being of a population. Examples of widely used economic indicators include the current rates of national productivity, inflation, and unemployment. In using such indicators, the manager draws on past experiences that have revealed a relationship between a certain indicator and some facet of the company's operations. Pitney Bowes Data Documents Division, for example, can predict future sales of its business forms largely based on current GNP estimates and other economic growth indexes.

GARY GLADSTONE

Food products companies often use customer-evaluation techniques when introducing new products. This woman, for example, is sampling different flavor options for a new product.

Qualitative Forecasting Techniques Organizations also use several qualitative techniques to develop their forecasts. A qualitative forecasting technique relies more on individual or group judgment or opinion rather than on sophisticated mathematical analyses. The *jury-of-expert opinion* approach involves using the collective judgment of members of top management. That is, top management serves as a collection of experts asked to make a prediction about something—competitive behavior, trends in product demand, and so forth. Their collective judgment then forms the basis of the forecast.

The *sales-force-composition* method of sales forecasting is a pooling of the predictions and opinions of experienced salespeople. Because of their experience, these individuals are often able to forecast accurately what various customers will do. Management combines these forecasts and interprets the data to create plans. Textbook publishers use this procedure to project how many copies of a new title they might sell.

The *customer-evaluation* technique goes beyond an organization's sales force and collects data from customers of the organization. The customers provide estimates of their own future needs for the goods and services that the organization supplies. Managers must combine, interpret, and act on this information. This approach, however, has two major limitations. Customers may be less interested in taking time to develop accurate predictions than members of the organization itself, and the method makes no provision for including any new customers that the organization may acquire. Walmart helps its suppliers use this approach by providing them with detailed projections regarding what it intends to buy several months in advance.

Selecting an appropriate forecasting technique can be as important as applying it correctly. Some techniques are appropriate only for specific circumstances. For example, the sales-force-composition technique is good only for sales forecasting. Other techniques are useful in a variety of situations. Some techniques, such as econometric models, require extensive use of computers, whereas others, such as customer-evaluation models, can be used with little mathematical expertise. For the most part, selection of a particular technique depends on the nature of the problem, the experience and preferences of the manager, and available resources.

LEARN

OTHER PLANNING TECHNIQUES

Of course, planning involves more than just forecasting. Other tools and techniques that are useful for planning purposes include linear programming, breakeven analysis, and simulations.

Linear Programming

Linear programming, a very popular quantitative tool for planning, is a procedure for calculating the optimal combination of resources and activities. It is appropriate when there is some objective to be met (such as a sales quota or a certain production level) within a set of constraints (such as a limited advertising budget or limited production capabilities).

To illustrate how linear programming can be used, assume that a small electronics company produces two basic products—a high-quality cable television tuner and a high-quality receiver for picking up television audio and playing it through a stereo amplifier. Both products go through the same two departments, first production and then inspection and testing. Each product has a known profit margin and a high level of demand. The production manager's job is to produce the optimal combination of tuners (T) and receivers (R) that maximizes profits and uses the time in production (PR) and in inspection and testing (IT) most efficiently. *Table* 9.3 gives the information needed for the use of linear programming to solve this problem.

> *"If you don't have enough or the right kind [of parts], your plant will shut down. Factories are willing to pay a huge convenience premium to ... make sure their supply is safe."*
>
> BASILI ALUKOS
> financial analyst[9]

BLOOMBERG BUSINESSWEEK, FEBRUARY 27-MARCH 4, 2012, P. 48.

The *objective function* is an equation that represents what we want to achieve. In technical terms, it is a mathematical representation of the desirability of the consequences of a particular decision. In our example, the objective function can be represented as follows:

$$\text{Maximize profit} = \$30X_T + \$20X_R$$

Where

R = the number of receivers to be produced

T = the number of tuners to be produced

The \$30 and \$20 figures are the respective profit margins of the tuner and receiver, as noted in *Table* 9.3. The objective, then, is to maximize profits.

However, this objective must be accomplished within a specific set of constraints. In our example, the constraints are the time required to produce each product in each department and the total amount of time available. These data are also found in *Table* 9.3 and can be used to construct the relevant constraint equations:

$$10T + 6R \leq 150$$

$$4T + 4R \leq 80$$

TABLE 9.3 PRODUCTION DATA FOR TUNERS AND RECEIVERS

Linear programming can be used to determine the optimal number of tuners and receivers a home entertainment business might make. Essential information needed to perform this analysis includes the number of hours each product spends in each department, the production capacity for each department, and the profit margin for each product.

	Number of Hours Required per Unit		Production Capacity per Day (in hours)
Department	Tuners (T)	Receivers (R)	
Production (PR)	10	6	150
Inspection and Testing (IT)	4	4	80
Profit Margin	\$30	\$20	

© CENGAGE LEARNING 2014

That is, we cannot use more capacity than is available. And, of course:

$T \geq 0$

$R \geq 0$

The set of equations consisting of the objective function and constraints can be solved graphically. To start, we assume that production of each product is maximized when production of the other is at zero. The resultant solutions are then plotted on a coordinate axis. In the PR department, if $T = 0$ then:

$10T + 6R \leq 150$

$10(0) + 6R \leq 150$

$R \leq 25$

In the same department, if $R = 0$ then:

$10T + 6R \leq 150$

$10T + 6(0) \leq 150$

$T \leq 15$

Similarly, in the IT department, if no tuners are produced,

$4T + 4R \leq 80$

$4(0) + 4R \leq 80$

$R \leq 20$

And, if no receivers are produced,

$4T + 4R \leq 80$

$4T + 4(0) \leq 80$

$T \leq 20$

The four resulting inequalities are graphed in *Figure* 9.3. The shaded region represents the feasibility space, or production combinations that do not exceed the capacity of either department. The optimal number of products will be defined at one of the four corners of the shaded area—that is, the firm should produce 20 receivers only (point C), 15 tuners only (point B), 13 receivers and 7 tuners (point E), or no products at all. With the constraint that production of both tuners and receivers must be greater than zero, it follows that point E is the optimal solution. That combination requires 148 hours in PR and 80 hours in IT and yields $470 in profit. (Note that if only receivers were produced, the profit would be $400; producing only tuners would mean $450 in profit.)

Unfortunately, the graphical method can only handle two alternatives, and our example was extremely simple. When there are other alternatives, a complex algebraic method must be employed. Real-world problems may require several hundred equations and variables. Clearly, computers are necessary to execute such sophisticated analyses. Linear programming is a

LEARN

FIGURE 9.3 THE GRAPHICAL SOLUTION OF A LINEAR PROGRAMMING PROBLEM

Finding the graphical solution to a linear programming problem is useful when considering only two alternatives. When problems are more complex, computers that can execute hundreds of equations and variables are necessary. Virtually all large firms, such as General Motors, Chevron, and Sears, use linear programing.

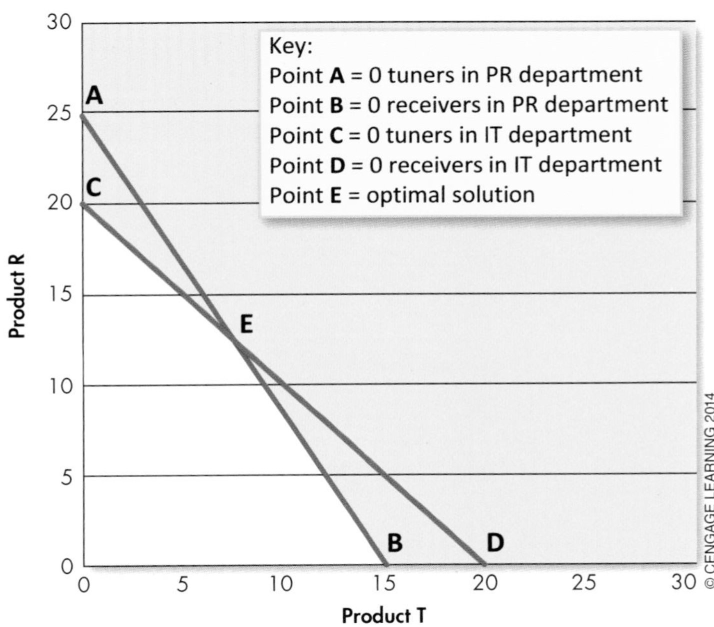

powerful technique, playing a key role in both planning and decision making. It can be used to schedule production, select an optimal portfolio of investments, allocate sales representatives to territories, or produce an item at some minimum cost.

Breakeven Analysis

Linear programming is called a *normative procedure* because it prescribes the optimal solution to a problem. Breakeven analysis is a *descriptive procedure* because it simply describes relationships among variables; then it is up to the manager to make decisions. (This is an example, then, of a manager needing to employ technical skills and then decision-making skills.) We can define breakeven analysis as a procedure for identifying the point at which revenues start covering their associated costs. It might be used to analyze the effects on profits of different price and output combinations or various levels of output.

Figure 9.4 represents the key cost variables in breakeven analysis. Creating most products or services includes three types of costs: fixed costs, variable costs, and total costs. *Fixed costs* are costs that are incurred regardless of what volume of output is being generated. They include rent or mortgage payments on the building, managerial salaries, and depreciation of plant and equipment. *Variable costs* vary with the number of units produced, such as the cost of raw materials and direct labor used to make each unit. *Total costs* are fixed costs plus variable costs. Note that because of fixed costs, the line for total costs never begins at zero.

FIGURE 9.4 COST FACTORS USED IN BREAKEVEN ANALYSIS

To determine the breakeven point for profit on sales for a product or service, the manager must first determine both fixed and variable costs. These costs are then combined to show total costs.

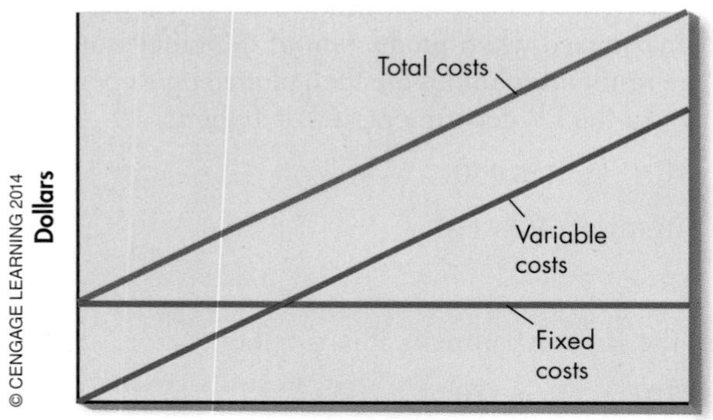

Other important factors in breakeven analysis are revenue and profit. Revenue, the total dollar amount of sales, is computed by multiplying the number of units sold by the sales price of each unit. *Profit* is then determined by subtracting total costs from total revenues. When revenues and total costs are plotted on the same axes, the breakeven graph shown in *Figure 9.5* emerges. The point at which the lines representing total costs and total revenues cross is the breakeven point. If the company represented in *Figure 9.5* sells more units than are

FIGURE 9.5 BREAKEVEN ANALYSIS

After total costs are determined and graphed, the manager then graphs the total revenues that will be earned on different levels of sales. The regions defined by the intersection of the two graphs show loss and profit areas. The intersection itself shows the breakeven point—the level of sales at which all costs are covered but no profits are earned.

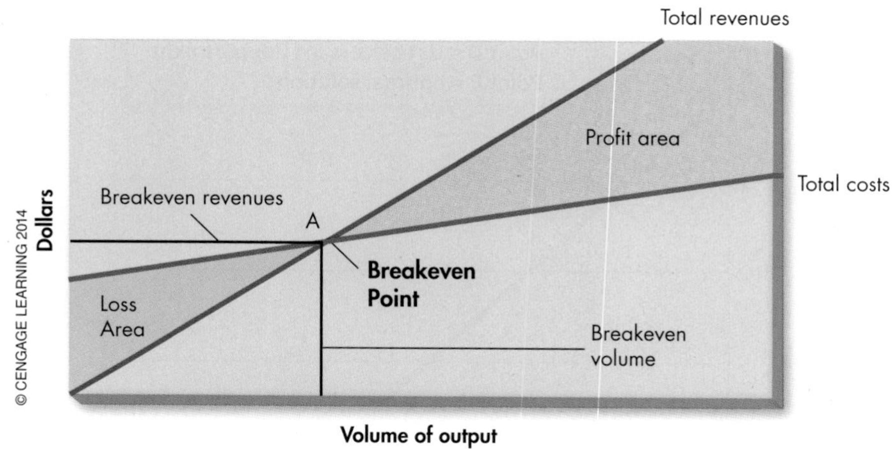

represented by point A, it will realize a profit; selling below that level will result in a loss.

Mathematically, the breakeven point (expressed as units of production or volume) is shown by the formula

$$BP = \frac{TFC}{P - VC}$$

Where

BP = breakeven point

TFC = total fixed costs

P = price per unit

VC = variable costs per unit

Assume that you are considering the production of a new garden hoe with an ergonomically curved handle. You have determined that an acceptable selling price will be \$20. You have also determined that the variable costs per hoe will be \$15, and you have total fixed costs of \$400,000 per year. The question is, how many hoes must you sell each year to break even? Using the breakeven model,

$$BP = \frac{TFC}{P - VC}$$

$$BP = \frac{400{,}000}{20 - 15}$$

$$BP = 80{,}000 \text{ units}$$

Thus, you must sell 80,000 hoes to break even. Further analysis would also show that if you could raise your price to \$25 per hoe, you would need to sell only 40,000 to break even, and so on.

The state of New York used a breakeven analysis to evaluate seven variations of prior approvals for its Medicaid service. Comparisons were conducted of the costs involved in each variation against savings gained from efficiency and improved quality of service. The state found that only three of the variations were cost effective.

Breakeven analysis is a popular and important planning technique, but it also has noteworthy weaknesses. It considers revenues only up to the breakeven point, and it makes no allowance for the time value of money. For example, because the funds used to cover fixed and variable costs could be used for other purposes (such as investment), the organization is losing interest income by tying up its money prior to reaching the breakeven point. Thus, managers often only use breakeven analysis as the first step in planning. After the preliminary analysis has been completed, more sophisticated techniques (such as rate-of-return analysis or discounted-present-value analysis) are used. Those techniques can help the manager decide whether to proceed or to divert resources into other areas.

Simulations

Another useful planning device is simulation. The word *simulate* means to copy or to represent. An organizational simulation is a model of a real-world situation that can be manipulated to discover how it functions. Simulation is a descriptive, rather than a prescriptive, technique. Concepts NREC is an engineering consulting firm that helps clients plan new factories. By using a sophisticated factory simulation model, the firm helped a client cut several machines and operations from a new plant and save more than \$750,000.

LEARN

To consider another example, suppose the city of Houston was going to build a new airport. Issues to be addressed might include the number of runways, the direction of those runways, the number of terminals and gates, the allocation of various carriers among the terminals and gates, and the technology and human resources needed to achieve a target frequency of take-offs and landings. (Of course, actually planning such an airport would involve many more variables than these.) A model could be constructed to simulate these factors, as well as their interrelationships. The planner could then insert several different values for each factor and observe the probable results.

Simulation problems are in some ways similar to those addressed by linear programming, but simulation is more useful in very complex situations characterized

© CLYNT GARNHAM/ALAMY

New airport construction often relies on the use of simulations to determine the optimal arrangements for runways, terminals, gates, and other facilities. The design of this new passenger terminal under construction in Dusseldorf International Airport was based on results from several simulations.

by diverse constraints and opportunities. The development of sophisticated simulation models may require the expertise of outside specialists or consultants, and the complexity of simulation almost always necessitates the use of a computer. For these reasons, simulation is most likely to be used as a technique for planning in large organizations that have the required resources.

LEARN

PERT

A final planning tool that we will discuss is PERT. PERT, an acronym for Program Evaluation and Review Technique, was developed by the United States Navy to help coordinate the activities of 3,000 contractors during the development of the Polaris nuclear submarine, and it was credited with saving two years of work on the project. Most large companies use PERT in different ways. The purpose of PERT is to develop a network of activities and their interrelationships and thus highlight critical time intervals that affect the overall project. PERT follows six basic steps:

1. Identify the activities to be performed and the events that will mark their completion.
2. Develop a network showing the relationships among the activities and events.
3. Calculate the time needed for each event and the time necessary to get from each event to the next.
4. Identify within the network the longest path that leads to completion of the project. This path is called the *critical path*.
5. Refine the network.
6. Use the network to control the project.

Suppose that a marketing manager wants to use PERT to plan the test marketing and nationwide introduction of a new product. *Table* 9.4 identifies the basic steps involved in carrying out this project. The activities are then arranged in a network like the one shown in *Figure* 9.6. In the figure, a number in a circle represents each completed event. Letters on the lines connecting the events indicate the activities. Notice that some activities are performed independently of one another and others must be performed in sequence. For example, test production (activity a) and test site location (activity c) can be done at the same time, but test site location has to be done before actual testing (activities f and g) can be done.

The time needed to get from one activity to another is then determined. The normal way to calculate the time between each activity is to average the most optimistic, most pessimistic, and most likely times, with the most likely time weighted by 4. Time is usually calculated with the following formula:

$$\text{Expected time} = \frac{a + 4b + c}{6}$$

TABLE 9.4 ACTIVITIES AND EVENTS FOR INTRODUCING A NEW PRODUCT

PERT is used to plan schedules for projects, and it is particularly useful when many activities with critical time intervals must be coordinated. Besides launching a new product, PERT is useful for projects such as constructing a new factory or building, remodeling an office, or opening a new store.

Activities	Events
	1. Origin of project
a. Produce limited quantity for test marketing	2. Completion of production for test marketing
b. Design preliminary package	3. Completion of design for preliminary package
c. Locate test market	4. Test market located
d. Obtain local merchant cooperation	5. Local merchant cooperation obtained
e. Ship product to selected retail outlets	6. Product for test marketing shipped to retail outlets
f. Monitor sales and customer reactions	7. Sales and customer reactions monitored
g. Survey customers in test-market area	8. Customers in test-market area surveyed
h. Make needed product changes	9. Product changes made
i. Make needed package changes	10. Package changes made
j. Mass-produce the product	11. Product mass-produced
k. Begin national advertising	12. National advertising carried out
l. Begin national distribution	13. National distribution completed

© CENGAGE LEARNING 2014

FIGURE 9.6 A PERT NETWORK FOR INTRODUCING A NEW PRODUCT

PERT is used to plan schedules for projects. It is particularly useful when many activities with critical time intervals must be coordinated. Besides launching a new product, PERT is useful for projects such as constructing a new factory or building, remodeling an office, or opening a new store.

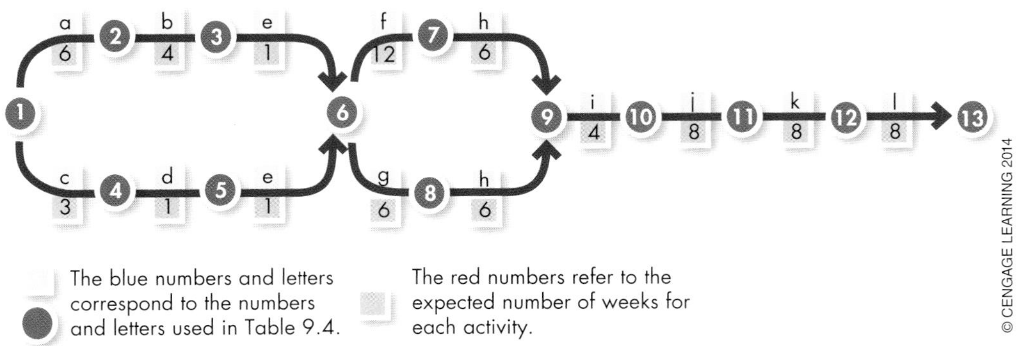

Where

a = optimistic time

b = most likely time

c = pessimistic time

The expected number of weeks for each activity in our example is shown in red along each path in *Figure* 9.6. The critical path—or the longest path through the PERT network—is then identified. This path is considered critical because it shows the shortest time in which the project can be completed. In our example, the critical path is 1-2-3-6-7-9-10-11-12-13, totaling 57 weeks. PERT thus tells the manager that the project will take 57 weeks to complete.

The first network may be refined. If 57 weeks to completion is too long, the manager might decide to begin preliminary package design before the test products are finished. Or the manager might decide that 10 weeks rather than 12 is enough time to monitor sales. The idea is that if the critical path can be shortened, so too can the overall duration of the project. The PERT network serves as an ongoing framework for both planning and control throughout the project. For example, the manager can use it to monitor where the project is relative to where it needs to be. Thus, if an activity on the critical path takes longer than planned, the manager needs to make up the time elsewhere or live with the fact that the entire project will be late.

DECISION-MAKING TOOLS

Managers can also use a number of tools that relate more specifically to decision making than to planning. Again, the application and interpretation of these tools requires the manager to have strong technical skills. Two commonly used decision-making tools are payoff matrices and decision trees.

Payoff Matrices

A payoff matrix specifies the probable value of different alternatives, depending on different possible outcomes associated with each. The use of a payoff matrix requires that several alternatives be available, that several different events could occur, and that the consequences depend on which alternative is selected and on which event or set of events occurs. An important concept in understanding the payoff matrix, then, is probability. A probability is the likelihood, expressed as a percentage, that a particular event will or will not occur. If we believe that a particular event will occur 75 times out of 100, we can say that the probability of its occurring is 75 percent, or 0.75. Probabilities range in value from 0 (no chance of occurrence) to 1.00 (certain occurrence—also referred to as 100 percent). In the business world, there are few probabilities of either 0 or 1.00. Most probabilities that managers use are based on subjective judgment, intuition, and historical data.

The expected value of an alternative course of action is the sum of all possible values of outcomes from that action multiplied by their respective probabilities. Suppose, for example, that a venture capitalist is considering investing in a new company. If he believes there is a 0.40 probability of making \$100,000, a 0.30 probability of making \$30,000, and a 0.30 probability of losing \$20,000, the expected value (EV) of this alternative is

$$EV = 0.40(100{,}000) + 0.30(30{,}000) + 0.30(-20{,}000)$$

$$EV = 40{,}000 + 9{,}000 - 6{,}000$$

$$EV = \$43{,}000$$

FIGURE 9.7 EXAMPLE OF A PAYOFF MATRIX

A payoff matrix helps the manager determine the expected value of different alternatives. A payoff matrix is effective only if the manager ensures that probability estimates are as accurate as possible.

		High inflation (probability of 0.30)	Low inflation (probability of 0.70)
Investment alternative 1	Leisure products company	–$10,000	+$50,000
Investment alternative 2	Energy enhancement company	+$90,000	–$15,000
Investment alternative 3	Food-processing company	+$30,000	+$25,000

© CENGAGE LEARNING 2014

The investor can then weigh the expected value of this investment against the expected values of other available alternatives. The highest *EV* signals the investment that should most likely be selected.

For example, suppose another venture capitalist wants to invest $20,000 in a new business. She has identified three possible alternatives: a leisure products company, an energy enhancement company, and a food-processing company. Because the expected value of each alternative depends on short-run changes in the economy, especially inflation, she decides to develop a payoff matrix. She estimates that the probability of high inflation is 0.30 and the probability of low inflation is 0.70. She then estimates the probable returns for each investment in the event of both high and low inflation. *Figure* 9.7 shows what the payoff matrix might look like (a minus sign indicates a loss). The expected value of investing in the leisure products company is

$$EV = 0.30\,(-10{,}000) + 0.70\,(50{,}000)$$

$$EV = -3{,}000 + 35{,}000$$

$$EV = \$32{,}000$$

Similarly, the expected value of investing in the energy enhancement company is

$$EV = 0.30\,(90{,}000) + 0.70\,(-15{,}000)$$

$$EV = 27{,}000 - 10{,}500$$

$$EV = \$16{,}500$$

And, finally, the expected value of investing in the food-processing company is

$$EV = 0.30\,(30{,}000) + 0.70\,(25{,}000)$$

$$EV = 9{,}000 + 17{,}500$$

$$EV = \$26{,}500$$

Investing in the leisure products company, then, has the highest expected value.

Other potential uses for payoff matrices include determining optimal order quantities, deciding whether to repair or replace broken machinery, and deciding which of several new products to introduce. Of course, the real key to using payoff matrices effectively is making accurate estimates of the relevant probabilities.

Decision Trees

Decision trees are like payoff matrices because they enhance a manager's ability to evaluate alternatives by making use of expected values. However, they are most appropriate when there are several decisions to be made in sequence.

Figure 9.8 illustrates a hypothetical decision tree. The small firm represented wants to begin exporting its products to a foreign market, but limited capacity restricts it to only one market at first. Managers feel that either France or China would be the best place to start. Whichever alternative the firm selects, sales for the product in that country may turn out to be high or low. In France, there is a 0.80 chance of high sales and a 0.20 chance of low sales. The anticipated payoffs in these situations are predicted to be $20 million and $3 million, respectively. In China, the probabilities of high versus low sales are 0.60 and 0.40, respectively, and the associated payoffs are presumed to be $25 million and $6 million. As shown in *Figure* 9.8, the expected value of shipping to France is $16,600,000, whereas the expected value of shipping to China is $17,400,000.

The astute reader will note that this part of the decision could have been set up as a payoff matrix. However, the value of decision trees is that we can extend the model to include subsequent decisions. Assume, for example, that the company begins shipping to China. If high sales do in fact materialize, the company will soon reach another decision situation. It might use the extra revenues to (1) increase shipments to China, (2) build

FIGURE 9.8 EXAMPLE OF A DECISION TREE

A decision tree extends the basic concepts of a payoff matrix through multiple decisions. This tree shows the possible outcomes of two levels of decisions. The first decision is whether to expand to China or to France. The second decision, assuming that the company expands to China, is whether to increase shipments to China, build a plant close to China, or initiate shipping to France.

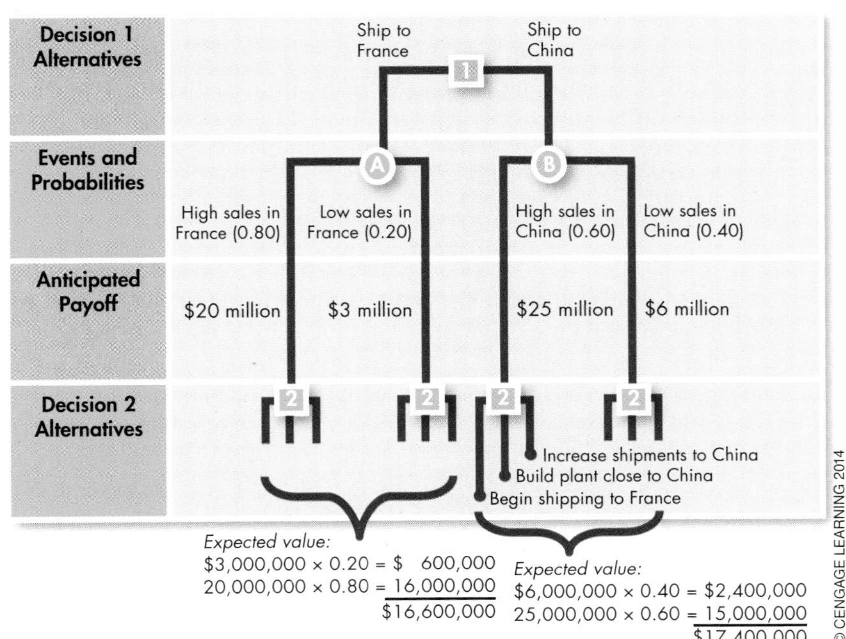

© CENGAGE LEARNING 2014

a plant close to China and thus cut shipping costs, or (3) begin shipping to France. Various outcomes are possible for each decision, and each outcome also will have both a probability and an anticipated payoff. It is therefore possible to compute expected values back through several tiers of decisions all the way to the initial one. As is the case with payoff matrices, determining probabilities accurately is the crucial element in the process. Properly used, decision trees can provide managers with a useful road map through complex decision situations.

Other Techniques

In addition to payoff matrices and decision trees, several other quantitative methods are available to facilitate decision making.

Inventory Models Inventory models are techniques that help the manager decide how much inventory to maintain. Target Corporation uses inventory models to help determine how much merchandise to order, when to order it, and so forth. Inventory consists of both raw materials (inputs) and finished goods (outputs). Colgate Palmolive, for example, maintains a supply of the chemicals it uses to make shaving cream, the cans it uses to pack shaving cream in, and cartons of canned shaving cream ready to be shipped. For finished goods, both extremes are bad: excess inventory ties up capital, whereas a small inventory may result in shortages and customer dissatisfaction. The same holds for raw materials: too much inventory ties up capital, but if a company runs out of resources, work stoppages may occur. Finally, because the process of placing an order for raw materials and supplies has associated costs (such as clerical time, shipping expenses, and higher unit costs for small quantities), it is important to minimize the frequency of ordering. Inventory models help the manager make decisions that optimize the size of inventory. New innovations in inventory management such as just-in-time, or JIT, rely heavily on decision-making models. A JIT system involves scheduling materials to arrive in small batches as they are needed, thereby eliminating the need for a big reserve inventory, warehouse space, and so forth.

Queuing Models Queuing models are included to help organizations manage waiting lines. We are all familiar with such situations: shoppers waiting to pay for groceries at Kroger, drivers waiting to buy gas at an Exxon station, travelers calling American Airlines

LEARN

for reservations, and customers waiting for a teller at Citibank. Take the Kroger example. If a store manager has only one checkout stand in operation, the store's cost for check-out personnel is very low; however, many customers are upset by the long line that frequently develops. To solve the problem, the store manager could decide to keep 20 checkout stands open at all times. Customer would like the short waiting period, but personnel costs would be very high. A queuing model would be appropriate in this case to help the manager determine the optimal number of checkout stands: the number that would balance personnel costs and customer waiting time. Target uses queuing models to determine how many checkout lanes to put in its retail stores.

Distribution Models A decision facing many marketing managers relates to the distribution of the organization's products. Specifically, the manager must decide where the products should go and how to transport them. Railroads, trucking, and airfreight have associated shipping costs, and each mode of transportation follows different schedules and routes. The problem is to identify the combination of routes that optimize distribution effectiveness and distribution costs. Distribution models help managers determine this optimal pattern of distribution.

Game Theory Game theory was originally developed to predict the effect of one company's decisions on competitors. Models developed from game theory are intended to predict how a competitor will react to various activities that an organization might undertake, such as price changes, promotional changes, and the introduction of new products. If Wells Fargo Bank were considering raising its prime lending rate by 1 percent, it might use a game theory model to predict whether Citicorp would follow suit. If the model revealed that Citicorp would do so, Wells Fargo would probably proceed; otherwise, it would probably maintain its current interest rates. Unfortunately, game theory is not yet as useful as its developers expected it to be. The complexities of the real world combined with the limitations of the technique itself restrict its applicability. Game theory, however, does provide a useful conceptual framework for analyzing competitive behavior, and it may prove to be more useful in the future.

© PENKA TODOROVA VITKOVA/SHUTTERSTOCK.COM

Artificial Intelligence Another significant addition to the manager's quantitative tool kit is artificial intelligence (AI). The most useful form of AI is the expert system.[7] An expert system is essentially a computer program that attempts to duplicate the thought processes of experienced decision makers. For example, Hewlett-Packard has developed an expert system that checks sales orders for new computer systems and then designs preliminary layouts for those new systems. HP can now ship the computer to a customer in components for final assembly on site. This approach has enabled the company to cut back on its own final-assembly facilities.

SUMMARY AND A LOOK AHEAD

After reading and studying this chapter, you should have a better understanding of technical skills. Specifically, you should have a clear understanding of the importance of technology, product and service, industry, and business knowledge. You should also see the value of accounting and financial management techniques. In addition, your technical skill set should include familiarity of various forecasting techniques, other planning techniques, and decision-making tools.

The remainder of this chapter provides opportunities for you to continue to develop and refine your own technical skills. For instance, you will be directed to resources where you can visualize both effective and less-effective technical skills. Subsequent sections provide several different opportunities for you to practice and explore technical skills from different perspectives. The chapter concludes with some additional assessment and interpretation data.

VISUALIZING TECHNICAL SKILLS

TECHNICAL SKILLS IN ACTION—1

Your Assignment

Consider the two BizFlix film clips for this chapter.

Casino (1995) is a Martin Scorsese film that presents a long, complex, and beautifully photographed study of Las Vegas gambling casinos and their organized crime connections during the 1970s. It completes Scorsese's trilogy that also includes *Mean Streets* (1973) and *Goodfellas* (1990). Ambition, greed, drugs, and sex destroy the mob's gambling empire. The film includes strong performances by Robert De Niro as Sam "Ace" Rothstein, Joe Pesci as Nicky Santoro, and Sharon Stone as Ginger McKenna.

Doomsday (2008) is a science-fiction thriller in which the Reaper Virus strikes Glasgow, Scotland, on April 3, 2008. It spreads and devastates the population throughout Scotland. Authorities seal off the borders, not allowing anyone to enter or leave the country. No aircraft flyovers are permitted. Social decay spreads, and cannibalistic behavior develops among the few remaining survivors. Eventually, no one is left alive in the quarantined area. The Reaper Virus reemerges in 2032, this time in London, England. Classified satellite images show life in Glasgow and Edinburgh. Prime Minister John Hatcher (Alexander Siddig) and his assistant Michael Canaris (David O'Hara) assign the task of finding the cure to Security Chief Bill Nelson (Bob Hoskins).

Note how technical skills are shown in these two clips.

1. The first clip is part of "The Truth about Las Vegas" sequence that appears early in the film. It follows the scenes of the casino deceiving the Japanese gambler. The scene starts with a close-up of Sam "Ace" Rothstein (Robert De Niro) standing between his two casino executives (Richard Amalfitano and Richard F. Strafella). In a voiceover narration he says, "In Vegas, everybody's gotta watch everybody else." The scene ends after Rothstein describes the former cheaters who monitor the gambling floor with binoculars. What technical skills might be needed for the many levels of monitoring in the casino?
2. The second clip starts at the beginning of the scene entitled "No Rules, No Backup" with a shot of the Department of Domestic Security emblem. The film cuts to Major Eden Sinclair (Rhona Mitra) standing in the rain smoking a cigarette while waiting for Chief Nelson. The sequence ends after Michael Canaris leaves the helicopter while saying to Sinclair, "Then you needn't bother coming back." He closes the helicopter's door. Major Sinclair blows her hair from her face while pondering his last statement. What technical skills will Sinclair need in order for her to perform her task?

VISUALIZE

TECHNICAL SKILLS IN ACTION—2

This exercise gives you an opportunity to think about technical skills that may be involved in management positions you may have in the future.

Your Assignment

1. Think about technical skills and try to identify a scene that illustrates a positive or effective use of such skills in a movie, a TV show, or perhaps a video on YouTube.

2. Now do the same for a scene that illustrates a negative or ineffective use of those same skills.

Share your results with the class and discuss how the positive and negative use of technical skills is shown in each clip. You should also see if you can suggest how the negative situation could have been changed for the better.

PRACTICING YOUR TECHNICAL SKILLS

PRACTICE

APPLYING TECHNICAL SKILLS TO BUDGETING

This exercise gives you practice in applying technical skills related to building a budget and evaluating the effectiveness of a budget.

Although corporate budgets are much more complicated than personal budgets, the steps in creating them are much the same. Both begin with estimates of inflow and outflow. Then both compare actual results with estimated results. And both end with the development of a plan for corrective action.

Your Assignment

1. Prepare your *estimated* personal expenditures and income for one month. Your estimated personal expenditures should represent the amount you spend in a typical month, not what you actually spent. Include food, tuition, rent, car payments, child-care expenses, food, utilities, etc. Then estimate your income from all sources, such as wages, allowance, and loans, and, while technically not income, you should include funds borrowed on credit cards. Calculate the totals.
2. Write down all of your *actual* expenses over the last month. Then write down all of your actual income. If you do not have exact figures, estimate as closely as you can. Calculate the totals.
3. Compare your estimates to your actual expenses and actual income. Are there any discrepancies? What caused the discrepancies?
4. Which did you expect to have for the month—a surplus or a deficit? Which did you actually have? What are your plans for making up any deficit or managing any surplus?
5. Do you regularly use a personal budget? Is a personal budget likely to be helpful to you? Why or why not?

USING YOUR TECHNICAL SKILLS ON THE INTERNET

This exercise will enable you to practice technical skills in using the Internet to obtain information for making a decision.

Assume that you are a business owner seeking a location for a new factory. Your company makes products that are relatively "clean"—that is, they do not pollute the environment and your factory will not produce any dangerous waste products. Thus, most communities would welcome your plant.

You are seeking a place that has a stable and well-educated workforce as well as ample affordable housing, access to quality health care, and a good educational system. You have narrowed your choice to the following towns:

- Santa Cruz, California
- Manhattan, Kansas
- Amherst, Massachusetts
- Madison, Wisconsin
- College Station, Texas
- Athens, Georgia

Your Assignment

1. Use the Internet to research each of these six cities.
2. Rank-order the cities on the basis of the criteria noted.
3. Select the best city for your new factory.

GETTING ORGANIZED

This exercise will help you understand the relative importance of technical skills in coordinating activities in an organization.

Typically, people who start and manage small businesses have the technical skills necessary to perform the operations of the business. But as the business grows, coordinating multiple activities, including some for which the original founder may not be well prepared, becomes a major concern. How to arrange activities to achieve an efficient and effective organization is the question.

Your Assignment

Your organization has grown so that you have four major product offerings. You have to produce the products, market them, finance them, and ship them. You have personnel to deal with each of those activities. The four products are clearly separable and distinct, even though they are not entirely distinct in terms of technology or customer base. Below are some possible ways of organizing your business.

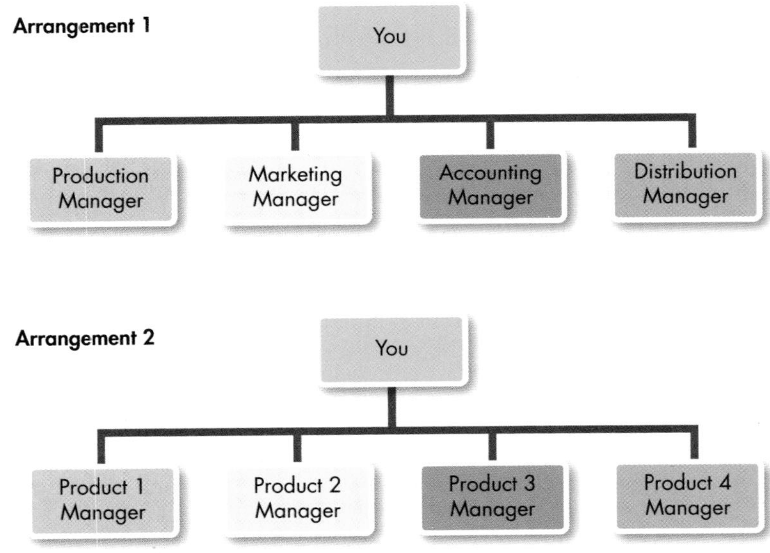

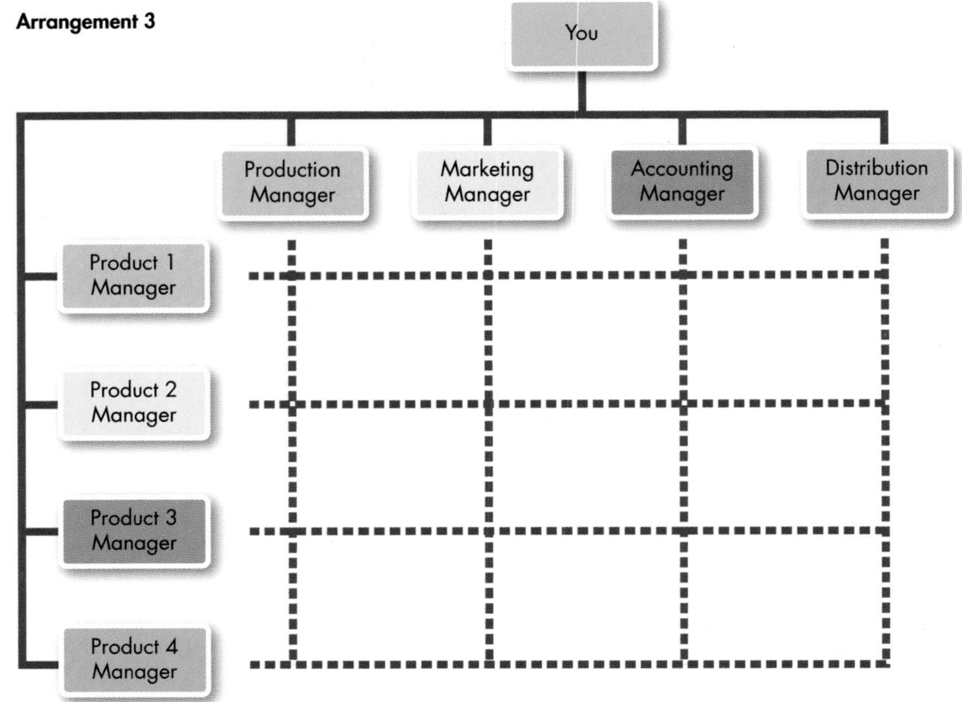

1. What specific technical skills might be required for each of these different organizational arrangements?
2. What seem to be the advantages and disadvantages of each of these?
3. Which arrangement would you use? Why?

USING THE INTERNET TO OBTAIN DATA

This exercise will help you develop and apply technical skills involving the Internet and its potential for providing raw data that can be turned into information that is relevant to important decisions.

Assume that you are a manager for a large national retailer. You are responsible for identifying potential locations for the construction of a warehouse and distribution center. The idea behind such a center is that the firm can use its enormous purchasing power to buy many products in bulk quantities at relatively low prices. Individual stores can then order the specific quantities they need from the warehouse.

The location must include a great deal of land. The warehouse itself, for example, will occupy more than four square acres. In addition, it must be close to railroads and major highways because shipments will be arriving by both rail and truck, although outbound shipments will be exclusively by truck. Other important considerations are that land prices and the cost of living should be relatively low, and weather conditions should be mild to minimize disruptions to shipments.

The firm's general experience is that small to mid-size communities work best. Moreover, warehouses are already in place in the western and eastern parts of the United States, so this new one will most likely be in the central or south central area. Your boss has asked you to identify three or four possible sites.

Your Assignment

1. With the above considerations, use the Internet to identify as many as 10 possible locations.
2. Using additional information from the Internet, narrow down the set of possible locations to three or four.
3. Again using the Internet, find out as much as possible about these potential locations.
4. Prioritize the three or four locations, giving a reason for the first and last positions.

IDENTIFYING TECHNICAL SKILLS RELATED TO QUALITY AND PRODUCTIVITY

This exercise helps you see how technical skills relate to quality, productivity, and operations management.

Assume that you have decided to go into business to make a product like one that you use on a regular basis, for example, computers, CDs, books, or apparel. Do some research to learn as much as you can about how the product is designed, produced, and distributed to consumers, and then complete the assignment below.

Your Assignment

1. Create two columns on a sheet of paper for: (A) all the relevant activities that you already know how to do for this new business (e.g., install software on a computer, sew two pieces of fabric together); and (B) all the activities that you do not know how to do.
2. Rank-order the importance of all the skills regarding this product.
3. Specify where people might learn the skills necessary to perform all the activities for the product you intend to make.
4. Determine how many people you will likely need to employ to have a full skill set available for making and marketing the product.

SPAN OF MANAGEMENT

This exercise will help you understand how technical issues are related to the span of management—the number of employees supervised by a manager.

In general, a less-than-optimal span is likely to be inefficient. For example, if both the manager and his subordinates are all highly competent, it follows logically that the manager can assume responsibility for a greater number of subordinates than would be the case if the competence of the manager or the subordinates were somewhat lower. If the span is too narrow, the manager may have too little work to do; but if the span is too wide, the manager's other work may get neglected.

Various situational factors affect the appropriate span of management that is optimal for a particular situation, including the following:

- The competence of the manager
- The competence of the subordinates
- The physical dispersion of the workstations of subordinates
- The amount of nonsupervisory responsibilities in the manager's job

- The degree of required interaction between the manager and subordinates
- The extent of standardized procedures built into the jobs of subordinates
- The similarity of the tasks being supervised
- The frequency with which new job-related questions and problems arise
- The preferences of the manager and subordinates

Your Assignment

1. Determine the effects of each situational factor noted above on the span of management.
2. Assume that you are a manager. Assess the relative importance that you would place on each situational factor to define your own span of management.
3. Describe how a span that is matched inappropriately with each factor will result in inefficiencies for both managers and subordinates.
4. If situational factors and the existing span of management are matched inappropriately, it may be possible to change one or the other to achieve a better fit. Examine each factor and decide whether it would be easier to change the factor or change the span of management to improve the fit.

For additional information, see Van Fleet, D. D., Span of Management: research and issues. *Academy of Management Journal*, Vol. 26, No. 3 (September 1983; research note): 546–552 and Van Fleet, D. D., & Bedeian, A. G., A history of the span of management. *Academy of Management Review*, Vol. 2, No. 3 (July 1977): 356–372.

PRACTICE

USING SWOT TO EVALUATE WORK-LIFE STRENGTHS AND WEAKNESSES

A technique known as the Strengths, Weaknesses, Opportunities, Threats (SWOT) analysis helps organizations identify their internal capabilities and limitations as well as significant events and trends from the external environment. The SWOT technique also can be useful in understanding your own personal strengths and weaknesses. The following assessment provides an opportunity to better understand the SWOT analysis process and to identify areas for improvement in your readiness for a current or future career.

Your Assignment

Create two lists: one of your *strengths* and one of your *weaknesses*. Judge items as strengths and weaknesses by thinking of them in relation to your current or anticipated future career. For example, creativity may be more valued in a career in marketing while empathy might be more valued in human resources management. If you are having trouble thinking of items or deciding how to classify them, speak to a friend, a fellow student, or someone who knows you well. Their insights can be useful.

1. List the following as *strengths*:
   (A) Work experience in a similar or related field.
   (B) Formal and informal education. This should include degrees earned or expected as well as non-credit courses and other types of training.
   (C) Technical skills or knowledge related to your career. This could include, for example, an IT worker's command of programming languages or an accountant's knowledge of audit procedures.
   (D) Generalized skills. Skills that are valued in just about any job would include leadership, teamwork, communication, and others.

(E) Personal characteristics. Again, most careers call for positive personal characteristics such as initiative, creativity, confidence, optimism, self-discipline, energy, ability to handle stress, and so on.

(F) Job-seeking skills. The ability to present a professional appearance, to network, to mentor others or to be mentored, among others, are job-seeking skills that could be an asset in your career.

2. List the following as *weaknesses*:
   (A) Lack of any of the above; for example, no work experience or no degree
   (B) Areas that are weak or undesirable relative to other job-seekers, such as a low GPA or an unrelated major, weak skills, little technical knowledge, or negative characteristics (i.e., poor self-control or inability to handle criticism)

Now develop two more lists: one of *opportunities* that you may have and another for *threats* to your success. Again, judge items as opportunities and threats by thinking of them in relation to your current or anticipated future career. For example, having good grades may open up opportunities while family issues may be a threat to your career plans. If you are having trouble thinking of items or deciding how to classify them, speak to an advisor, a fellow student, or someone in the field that you think you might pursue. Their insights can be useful.

3. List the following as *opportunities*:
   (A) Furthering your education
   (B) Developing a new skill, e.g., learning a foreign language or a computer program
   (C) Traveling to unique destinations, domestic or foreign
   (D) Taking on a new, challenging assignment
   (E) Volunteering for a social or non-profit organization
4. List the following as *threats*:
   (A) Unforeseen family obligations.
   (B) Changing technology in your field.

Once you have the four lists, carefully assess the importance of each list relative to others and consider how this information may help you further develop your career plans.

IDENTIFYING TECHNICAL SKILLS NEEDED IN DIFFERENT ORGANIZATIONS

This exercise will help you understand the relative importance of technical skills in different kinds of organizations.

Some entrepreneurs have the technical skills that they need to open and run their business successfully. For example, a hair stylist who opens a hair salon, an architect who starts a residential design firm, and a chef who launches a new restaurant all have the technical skills needed (hair styling, blueprint rendering, cooking) to do the work of the organization. In other cases, the entrepreneur who starts the organization may have general management skills but essentially may "buy" required technical skills in the labor market. For example, an entrepreneur with no cooking experience could start a new restaurant by hiring a professional chef to run the kitchen.

Your Assignment

Listed below are examples of ten small businesses that an individual entrepreneur might launch. To help you in answering the questions that follow, think of existing local businesses that fit the general descriptions.

- Retail clothing store
- Computer-clone assembly business
- Tavern
- Sports card retail store
- Aluminum recycling operation
- Used CD retail store
- Drop-in health care clinic
- Gourmet coffee-bean shop
- Business services operation
- Appliance repair shop

1. What specific technical skills are required for each business?
2. For each business, is it imperative that the entrepreneur actually possess the required technical skills, or is it feasible instead to hire others who possess the skills?
3. What are some major factors that determine the viability of buying technical skills in the labor market?

PRACTICE

IMPACT OF ORGANIZATIONAL STRATEGY ON STRUCTURE

This exercise asks you to develop technical skills related to understanding the impact of an organization's strategy on its structure.

Assume that you are a manager of a firm that has developed a new innovative line of athletic performance clothing, such as the Under Armour®. If you are not familiar with Under Armour, visit the website at <www.uabiz.com> and learn about the product.

Your Assignment

Using the information about strategy given in each question below and your knowledge of the Under Armour product, (A) choose the appropriate form of organization structure under each of the five conditions, and (B) tell how each strategy influenced your choice of organization design.

1. What would be the most appropriate organization for Under Armour if its corporate-level strategy were to continue producing a limited line of very similar products for sale in the United States?
2. If its corporate-level strategy were to continue to produce only its original product but to sell it in Asia and Europe as well as in North America, what would be the most appropriate organization for Under Armour?
3. What would be the most appropriate organization for Under Armour if its corporate-level strategy were to move into related areas, using the innovations developed in the design of its heat-handling fabrics to help design other products such as heat-blocking curtains or safety suits for firefighters?
4. If its corporate-level strategy were to use its expertise in fabric innovations to move into other areas such as clothing design, what would be the most appropriate organization for Under Armour?
5. What would be the most appropriate organization for Under Armour if its corporate-level strategy were to use the funds generated by its clothing sales to finance moves into several unrelated industries?

YOUR PROBLEMS

This exercise will help sharpen your technical skills by focusing on real, specific problems.

Your Assignment

1. *Individual class members.* Think about problems associated with the job you hold or have held in the recent past. Would discussing one of those problems with your classmates be (or might have been) of potential value to you? If so, for which problem would such discussion be most beneficial?
   (A) Write your problem on a piece of paper. Concentrate your thinking on that one problem. It may be the most urgent or the most interesting or the only one you can talk about without disclosure problems.
   (B) The best problems to discuss may not be the hardest or the easiest, the most complicated or the simplest. Rather, the best ones to discuss are those for which something can be done. Is the problem you selected really solvable, or is it "always a problem no matter what?"
   (C) What kind of problem is it?

   CHECK ONE: __money? __people? __technical?
   CHECK ONE: __personal? __organizational?

   (D) Your instructor will ask for a show of hands for each of the six possible problem combinations:

	Personal	Organizational
Money		
People		
Technical		

2. *Small groups.* Using the six classifications above, form small groups that have an interest in discussing the same types of problems. Try to keep the groups approximately the same size.
   (A) Group members should introduce themselves to one another and then share their written problems with the whole group. The group should then select one problem to discuss.
   (B) The group should carefully state or restate the problem, generate a few alternative ways to deal with the problem, and then select one solution. A member of the group should be prepared to share this with the class.
3. *The whole class.* The class will reconvene to allow each small group to present the results of its discussion. After all groups have presented, the class selects one problem to discuss more fully.

USE

USING YOUR TECHNICAL SKILLS

PERRIER KEEPS FLOWING

The Perrier story has numerous twists and turns. At first, an attempt was made to develop a spa at the naturally carbonated spring in Vergeze, France. Despite its general popularity, it was not a commercial success. Efforts to bottle the water as a healthy beverage were not successful either. Then along came the Englishman, A. W. St. John Harmsworth. He bought the spring from Louis Perrier in the early 1900s (hence the official name, Source Perrier). By the 1930s, the company was selling almost 20 million bottles per year. By 1992, Perrier was second only to BSN as a global producer of bottled water under such brands as Arrowhead, Calistoga, Contrex, Great Bear, Poland Spring, Vichy, Volvic, and, of course, Perrier.

Adapting to changing consumer tastes and other environmental factors is a source of pride at Perrier, and has proven essential many times. For instance, in 1990 benzene was discovered in the Perrier brand of bottled water. The company quickly pulled all brand Perrier bottled water from the shelves (not just that which was known to be contaminated), found and fixed the problem (a dirty filter), and got the product back in stores in less than three months. While it seems like a short period of time for such a large endeavor, it is a long time in marketing, and competitors raced to take over the shelf space and, hopefully, the market share. Many of Perrier's customers simply switched to other Perrier brands and others moved on to competitors. Motivated to protect its image for distributing only pure spring water, Perrier consolidated brands and spent enormous sums in advertising to reintroduce brand Perrier. It was motivated to protect its image for distributing only pure spring water and felt that the public would continue to be motivated to purchase the famous green-bottled beverage.

Some feel that Perrier overreacted by pulling all of its brand Perrier from shelves and that it might never recover from the absence of product for that length of time. Perrier countered that its motive was to demonstrate its dedication to its customers in providing nothing but the purest product. Both views may be correct, of course, but Perrier was damaged and, as a result, was acquired by Nestlé. In 2004 a crisis erupted when the Nestlé group announced a restructuring plan for Perrier. Then in 2005 a court ordered Perrier to halt restructuring because of a failure to consult adequately with staff. Nevertheless, recovery has occurred. In 2010 Nestlé Waters reported strong growth with its S. Pellegrino, Perrier and Contrex brands.

USE

Case Questions

Go Online

1. How is an awareness of technical skills useful in understanding conditions at Perrier?
2. Which particular technical skills seem to be employed at Perrier?
3. If you were interested in a position in the Perrier organization (or Nestlé Waters), what preparations would you make to have the requisite technical skills for success?
4. Do you think that your skills would be compatible with working at Perrier? Why or why not? If not compatible but you would like them to be, how would you go about changing your skills?

Case References

"Strong first-quarter sales, full-year outlook confirmed," Nestle Press Release, April 22, 2010 www.nestle.com/MediaCenter/PressReleases/AllPressReleases/Q1results2010.htm; Richard Tomlinson, "Troubled Waters at Perrier," *Fortune*, November 29, 2004; "Review/Preview: A Quickened Tempo in 1992 Dealmaking," *Mergers & Acquisitions*, May 1, 1992, p. 7; Gary Hoover, Alta Campbell, Alan Chai, and Patrick J. Spain (eds.) *Hoover's Handbook of World Business 1992* (Austin, TX: The Reference press, 1992), p. 288; Patricia Sellers, "Perrier Plots Its Comeback," *Fortune*, April 23, 1990, pp. 277–278; Daniel Seligman, "Keeping Up," *Fortune*, March 12, 1990, p. 139; Daniel Butler, "Perrier's Painful Period," *Management Today*, August 1990, pp. 72–73.

RESTAURANT OPERATIONS

Red Lobster and Olive Garden are two of the more successful restaurant chains in the United States. The former specializes in seafood and has been around since 1968. It was acquired by General Mills in 1970, and General Mills launched Olive Garden in 1982.

Successful restaurant operations start with raw materials. Red Lobster buys millions of tons of seafood a year from all over the world. Some of it, such as shrimp, is shipped to a St. Petersburg, Florida, plant where it is processed, quick frozen, and packed. Other products, like swordfish, are shipped fresh directly to warehouses around the country. These warehouses then ship both fresh and frozen products to Red Lobster restaurants around the country. This system insures consistent quality while also saving more than 25 cents a pound over the average costs that other seafood restaurants pay. Olive Garden restaurants take an even simpler approach by making pasta on-site. By using prepackaged materials but blending the pasta daily in each restaurant, its costs are around 40 cents a pound as compared with 55 cents a pound for pre-prepared pasta.

Every night the restaurant managers predict their next day of sales using figures from that same day the previous week and the previous year. Ingredients necessary to serve that number of people are then pulled from the freezers and refrigerators and work orders are prepared to get appropriate meals ready to begin the next day. By predicting customer flows using accurate historical data, both Red Lobster and Olive Garden are also able to schedule workers more efficiently. Like most restaurants, they rely heavily on part-time workers and thus have considerable flexibility regarding staffing levels on a day-to-day basis.

Cooking and presentation are also highly standardized in each Red Lobster and Olive Garden restaurant. A one-pound lobster, for example, must be steamed exactly ten minutes. These standards, developed in home-office test kitchens, ensure that food is always prepared the same way. Diagrams show exactly how food is to be arranged on each plate, right down to the location of the parsley. These food placement diagrams are designed to make portions look larger and also to maintain consistency. Managers carry pocket thermometers to spot check food temperature. For example, coffee is never to be served at less than 150 degrees while salads are always to be below 40 degrees. Deviations signal that the kitchen may be behind, a server may be too slow, or there may be a problem with the ovens.

General Mills spun off its restaurant business in 1995 as part of Darden Restaurants. In 2008, despite poor economic conditions, Darden saw its revenues climb. Financial analysts view Darden as one of the restaurant industry's best-operated companies. That was born out when the disastrous oil spill in the Gulf of Mexico threatened fishing, and officials at Darden indicated that they maintain more than one source of supply to counter such emergencies.

Case Questions

1. What technical skills are manifest in the operations of these restaurants?
2. "While technical knowledge is specific to the restaurant business, technical skills can be transferred from any area." Comment.

Go Online

3. Have you ever worked or eaten at a Red Lobster or Olive Garden? Are there are elements of operations management you can recall from your own experiences?
4. If you were interested in a position in one of the Darden restaurants, would your skills be compatible? What must you do to gain the requisite technical skills for success?

Case References

Melissa Nelson, "Oil spill shuts down 19 percent of Gulf fishing," *BusinessWeek*, May 18, 2010 http://www.businessweek.com/ap/financialnews/D9FPHIK84.htm; Yuval Rosenberg, "A stock to stomach tough times," *Fortune*, January 9, 2009 http://money.cnn.com/2009/01/09/magazines/fortune/investing/investor_daily.fortune/index.htm; "Dinnerhouse Technology," *Forbes*, July 8, 1991, pp. 98-99; "Burritos, Anyone?" *Forbes*, March 18, 1991, pp. 52–56; "Cafe Au Lait, a Croissant—and Trix," *BusinessWeek*, August 24, 1992, pp. 50–51.

EXTENDING YOUR TECHNICAL SKILLS

Your instructor may use one or more of these **Group Extensions** to provide you with more opportunities to develop your time-management skills. On the other hand, you may continue your development on your own by doing one or more of the **Individual Extensions**.

These **Group Extensions** are repeated exactly for each of the seven specific skills. Doing the exact **Extension** for different skills will help you to sharpen both the skills and the subtle differences between the several skills.

GROUP EXTENSIONS

- Form small groups of students. Have each group select an organization and a management position. Then have them identify the technical skills needed by a person in that position.
- Form small groups of students. Have each group identify a problem or opportunity facing a business or other organization. Then have them identify the technical skills needed by managers in dealing with that problem or opportunity.
- Form small groups of students. Assign each group one or more corporations to analyze. Have them identify the members who serve on its board of directors and research their backgrounds. Then have the students describe the technical skills of those directors.
- Form small groups of students. Have each group select a job they see regularly (e.g., retail clerk, fast-food worker). Ask them to describe the technical skills needed on that job.
- Form small groups of students. Have students sketch the technical skills they would need if they were going to start a specific type of new business.
- Form small groups of students. Have each group identify examples they have recently faced that illustrate a situation that called for them to use technical skills.

EXTEND

INDIVIDUAL EXTENSIONS

- Go to the library and research a company. Characterize its level of effectiveness and identify the technical skills of its top executives. Share your results with the class.
- Select a highly visible manager and analyze his or her technical skills.
- Interview a manager from a local organization. Learn about the technical skills he or she needs to perform effectively.
- Think of someone you know who is a manager. Describe that person's management position in terms of the type of organization, level in the organization, and the area of management in which he or she practices. What technical skills does that person need to be effective?
- Plan a hypothetical change in your school focusing on the use of technical skills.
- Search the Internet for examples of technical skills in management and compare what you find with the information presented here.

- Albert Einstein, the Nobel Prize-winning physicist, is purported to have said: "Concern for man and his fate must always form the chief interest of all technical endeavors. Never forget this in the midst of your diagrams and equations." What is the managerial lesson conveyed by this quotation?

YOUR TECHNICAL SKILLS NOW

TECHNICAL SKILLS ASSESSMENT

Now that you have completed Chapter 9, it is time again to assess your technical skills. To do so, complete the following instrument. Think about your current situation, job, or organization in which you are a member. You should respond in terms of your current situation and not by how you think you should respond or a manager should respond. If a statement doesn't pertain to your current situation, respond in terms of what you think would be accurate for you in that situation.

Use this scale in your responses.

1	2	3	4	5
Not true at all	Somewhat untrue	Sometimes true Sometimes not	Somewhat true	Completely true

Total your scores and record them in the table at the end of instrument.

Given that many experts suggest the use of 360° feedback in performance appraisal, you may find it useful to obtain the views of others about your managerial skills. You may get a form from your instructor that is designed for others to complete, and then record their scores in the table as well. Areas where there is a large discrepancy between your views and those of others should draw your attention, and you should spend more time developing those skills.

TECHNICAL SKILLS

[Note: The numbers correspond to those on the baseline assessment in Appendix A.]

____ 1. I accomplish a lot.
____ 2. I actively engage in self development.
____ 3. I am able to coordinate tasks.
____ 4. I am able to efficiently utilize available resources (people, materials, equipment, etc.).
____ 5. I am approached by others with technical problems and questions.
____ 6. I am dependable.
____ 7. I am determined to succeed.
____ 8. I am generally an energetic person.
____ 9. I am good with numbers.
____ 10. I am interested in succeeding in my career.
____ 11. I am knowledgeable about my associates and what needs to be done.

____ 12. I am not satisfied with average performance.
____ 13. I am prepared to be flexible to get the job done.
____ 14. I am prepared to do whatever it takes to succeed.
____ 15. I am prepared to keep at a problem until it is solved.
____ 16. I am strongly motivated to "get the job done."
____ 17. I analyze financial information quickly.
____ 18. I can adjust my goals/activities without becoming frustrated.
____ 19. I can identify the important parts of budgets and financial statements.
____ 20. I can read and understand financial or other quantitative information.
____ 21. I can use statistical and quantitative information when necessary.
____ 22. I closely watch expenses.
____ 23. I develop complete, well-detailed plans.
____ 24. I enjoy activities that require me to learn new things.
____ 25. I enjoy improving things.
____ 26. I establish effective and efficient procedures for getting things done.
____ 27. I establish performance standards for those in my organization.
____ 28. I handle details quite well.
____ 29. I have a lot of self-control.
____ 30. I have very high standards for myself and others.
____ 31. I keep up-to-date on technical developments related to my interests.
____ 32. I let others know what and how well I am doing.
____ 33. I make plans that are clear and realistic.
____ 34. I prefer gradual change to sudden change.
____ 35. I read material about my current and future tasks.
____ 36. I readily adapt to new initiatives.
____ 37. I seek feedback about how I am doing.
____ 38. I seldom leave a job unfinished.
____ 39. I set specific learning goals for myself.
____ 40. I strive for excellence in all that I do.
____ 41. I strive for high quality in my work.
____ 42. I tend to keep up with information about my tasks.
____ 43. I tend to stick with problems until they are resolved.
____ 44. I tend to use tried and tested methods.
____ 45. I try not to waste resources.
____ 46. I try to always be prepared.
____ 47. I try to improve my knowledge and skills.
____ 48. I try to keep at a task even when I encounter unexpected difficulties.
____ 49. I try to keep busy all the time.
____ 50. I understand what needs to be done.

Summary of Your Scores

Skill (max. possible score)	**Your Score Now**	**Scores from Others**	**Your Score From Chapter 1**
Technical (250)			

Interpretation of Your Scores

Compare your score with the one you reported at the beginning of Chapter 1. If there is no or only a modest improvement in your score, you should examine the same set of items from the **Managerial Skills Assessment** from Chapter 1 and compare each of them with these to see where change has and has not occurred. You should then spend more time on developing the particular skills where change either decreased or stayed the same.

INTERPRETATIONS

PBS (POWER BASES SCORE) QUESTIONNAIRE

There is no further interpretation. The column totals indicate the extent to which each power base is used. A higher score means the power base is used more. You can compare your scores to those from a national sample of managers, but remember that those do not necessarily represent best scores.

DEFINING QUALITY AND PRODUCTIVITY

The odd-numbered items refer to eight dimensions of quality and are true. Those dimensions are performance, features, reliability, conformance, durability, serviceability, aesthetics, and perceived quality. The even-numbered items are all false.

You should have positive responses for the odd-numbered items and negative responses for the even-numbered ones. If you strongly agree with the odd ones and strongly disagree with the even ones, your total score would be zero.

Which items did you answer incorrectly? Concentrate on learning why the answers are what they are. The American Society for Quality Control defines quality as the total set of features and characteristics of a product or service that bear on its ability to satisfy stated or implied needs of customers.

UNDERSTANDING CONTROL

The odd-numbered items are false and the even-numbered ones, true. You should have positive responses for the even-numbered items and negative responses for the odd-numbered ones. If you agreed strongly with all of the even-numbered ones and disagreed strongly with all of the odd-numbered ones, your total score would be zero.

Which items did you answer incorrectly? Concentrate on learning why the answers are what they are.

ARE YOU TECHNICALLY ORIENTED?

Studies suggest that some people are more technically oriented than others. That is, they solve problems systematically, work best with sequential ideas, and like to solve problems logically. This is in contrast to people who are intuitive problem solvers.

Column I measures your perceived preference for using intuitive functions. Column II measures your perceived preference for using technical functions. A high score in Column II suggests that you are technically oriented. For example, you may be more effective in the planning and operations activities of management than in the intuitive, creative, or human relations aspect of management.

ENDNOTES

[1] *Fortune*, May 2, 2011, p. 53.

[2] "To Shed Idled Workers, Ford Offers to Foot Bill for College," *The Wall Street Journal*, January 18, 2006, pp. B1, B3; "GM's Employees Buyout Offer," *Fast Company*, May 2006, p. 58.

[3] Belverd E. Needles, Jr., Marian Powers, and Susan Crosson, *Principles of Accounting*, 11th ed. (Cincinnati: Cengage Learning, 2012).

[4] "At Disney, String of Weak Cartoons Leads to Cost Cuts," *The Wall Street Journal*, June 18, 2002, pp. A1, A6.

[5] *Bloomberg BusinessWeek*, February 20–February 26, 2012, p. 72.

[6] Needles, Powers, and Crosson, *Principles of Accounting*.

[7] "Mickey Mouse, CPA," *Forbes*, March 10, 1997, pp. 42–43.

[8] There are numerous texts available that discuss and summarize technical procedures for planning and decision. One especially good reference is David Anderson, Dennis Sweeney, Thomas Williams, Jeffrey Camm, James Cochran, Michael Fry, and Jeffrey Ohlmann, *Quantitative Methods for Business*, 12th ed. (Cincinnati: Cengage Learning, 2013).

[9] *Bloomberg BusinessWeek*, February 27–March 4, 2012, p. 48.

CHAPTER 10

ASSESSING LEADERSHIP SKILLS

How Charismatic Are You?

Managerial Leader Behavior Questionnaire

LEARNING ABOUT LEADERSHIP SKILLS

Differences Between Managing and Leading

Understanding the Basics of Leadership

Power and Leadership

Legitimate Power

Reward Power

Coercive Power

Referent Power

Expert Power

Using Power

Leadership Traits

Leadership Behaviors

Michigan Studies

Ohio State Studies

Leadership Grid

Understanding Situational Approaches to Leadership

LPC Theory

Favorableness of the Situation

Favorableness and Leader Style

Flexibility of Leader Style

Path–Goal Theory

Leader Behavior

Situational Factors

The Leader–Member Exchange Approach

Understanding Related Perspectives on Leadership

Substitutes for Leadership

Charismatic Leadership

Transformational Leadership

Cross-Cultural Leadership

Ethical Leadership

Summary and a Look Ahead

VISUALIZING LEADERSHIP SKILLS

Leadership Skills in Action—1

Leadership Skills in Action—2

PRACTICING LEADERSHIP SKILLS

Draw Leadership

Analyze Leadership Style

Managers and Leaders

Who Are the Leaders?

USING LEADERSHIP SKILLS

The Struggles of Leadership

Paper or Not—Xerox Has It Covered

EXTENDING YOUR LEADERSHIP SKILLS

Group Extensions

Individual Extensions

INTERPRETATIONS

How Charismatic Are You?

Managerial Leader Behavior Questionnaire

Transitioning from Managing to Leading

© ISTOCKPHOTO.COM/KALI9

Throughout this book we have emphasized management skills. Now it is time to indicate how you can use those skills to move beyond management and be a leader. This chapter focuses on helping you understand leadership and develop your own leadership skills. We start by examining the differences between managing and leading, and then provide detailed text material to help you learn more about leading and leadership. Following the text section are several cases and exercises to help you further develop and master your leadership skills.

ASSESS

ASSESSING LEADERSHIP SKILLS

HOW CHARISMATIC ARE YOU?

Charismatic leaders seem able to influence others with ease. They articulate a vision, show concern for others, have high expectations, and create high-performing groups and/or organizations. This self-assessment provides a measure of your charismatic potential.

Instructions:
The following statements refer to characteristics you may have. Read each statement carefully and decide the extent to which it applies to you. Then enter that number in the space provided.

Rating Scale
5 – To a Very Great Extent
4 – To a Considerable Extent
3 – To a Moderate Extent
2 – To a Slight Extent
1 – To Little or No Extent

_____ 1. My friends say I should be an actor.
_____ 2. I am confident in my job and social situations.
_____ 3. I love the stage.
_____ 4. When I hear music, I start to keep time with the beat.
_____ 5. I am often the center of attention at social functions.
_____ 6. I generally try to dress to make an impact or create a favorable impression.
_____ 7. When talking to close friends, I may hug or touch them.
_____ 8. I am open and curious, interested in many things.
_____ 9. My friends tell me their problems and ask for my advice.
_____ 10. I am generally assertive.
_____ 11. I tend to be socially free and authentic.
_____ 12. My friends expect me to take the lead in most situations.
_____ 13. I try to understand others' points of view and behavior rather than criticizing them.
_____ 14. I try not to speak in a way that hurts others.
_____ 15. I can easily interact with people of all ages and sexes.
_____ 16. I have a good sense of humor.
_____ 17. I am noted for quick humorous responses.
_____ 18. I smile easily and a lot.

Scoring:

EE	*Total items 4–6*	_____	*SE*	*Total items 16–18*	_____
ES	*Total items 7–9*	_____	*SS*	*Total items 13–15*	_____
EC	*Total items 1–3*	_____	*SC*	*Total items 10–12*	_____
Overall	*Total all items*	_____			

ASSESS

Source: Adapted from Ronald E. Riggio. February 15, 2010. Charisma: What is it? Do you have it? Cutting-Edge Leadership online at www.psychologytoday.com/blog/cutting-edge-leadership/201002/charisma-what-is-it-do-you-have-it (accessed January 18, 2012); Gary Yukl. 2013. *Leadership in Organizations*. 8th ed.; Upper Saddle River, NJ: Pearson Education, Inc.; Howard S. Friedman. 2010. How Charismatic Are You? *O, The Oprah Magazine*, online at www.oprah.com/spirit/How-Charismatic-Are-You (accessed January 17, 2012); and Henrik Edberg. 2009. How to Be Charismatic: 7 Powerful Tips from the Mentalist. Online at www.positivityblog.com/index.php/2009/03/20/how-to-be-charismatic-7-powerful-tips-from-the-mentalist/ (accessed January 17, 2012).

See Interpretations at the end of the chapter.

MANAGERIAL LEADER BEHAVIOR QUESTIONNAIRE

Leadership is now recognized as consisting of a set of characteristics that are important for everyone in an organization to develop. The following assessment surveys the practices or beliefs that you would apply in a management role—that is, your managerial leadership.

Instructions:
The following statements refer to different ways in which you might behave in a managerial leadership role. For each statement, indicate how you do behave or how you think you would behave. Describing yourself may be difficult in some cases, but you should force yourself to make a selection. Record your answers next to each statement according to the following scale:

Rating Scale
5 – Very descriptive of me
4 – Fairly descriptive of me
3 – Somewhat descriptive of me
2 – Not very descriptive of me
1 – Not descriptive of me at all

_____ 1. I emphasize the importance of performance and encourage everyone to make a maximum effort.

_____ 2. I am friendly, supportive, and considerate toward others.

_____ 3. I offer helpful advice to others on how to advance their careers and encourage them to develop their skills.

_____ 4. I stimulate enthusiasm for the work of the group and say things to build the group's confidence.

_____ 5. I provide appropriate praise and recognition for effective performance and show appreciation for special efforts and contributions.

_____ 6. I reward effective performance with tangible benefits.

_____ 7. I inform people about their duties and responsibilities, clarify rules and policies, and let people know what is expected of them.

_____ 8. Either alone or jointly with others, I set specific and challenging but realistic performance goals.

_____ 9. I provide any necessary training and coaching or arrange for others to do it.

_____ 10. I keep everyone informed about decisions, events, and developments that affect their work.

_____ 11. I consult with others before making work-related decisions.

_____ 12. I delegate responsibility and authority to others and allow them discretion in determining how to do their work.

_____ 13. I plan in advance how to efficiently organize and schedule the work.

_____ 14. I look for new opportunities for the group to exploit, propose new undertakings, and offer innovative ideas.

_____ 15. I take prompt and decisive action to deal with serious work-related problems and disturbances.

_____ 16. I provide subordinates with the supplies, equipment, support services, and other resources necessary to work effectively.

_____ 17. I keep informed about the activities of the group and check on its performance.

_____ 18. I keep informed about outside events that have important implications for the group.

_____ 19. I promote and defend the interests of the group and take appropriate action to obtain necessary resources for the group.

_____ 20. I emphasize teamwork and try to promote cooperation, cohesiveness, and identification with the group.

_____ 21. I discourage unnecessary fighting and bickering within the group and help settle conflicts and disagreements in a constructive manner.

_____ 22. I criticize specific acts that are unacceptable, find positive things to say, and provide an opportunity for people to offer explanations.

_____ 23. I take appropriate disciplinary action to deal with anyone who violates a rule, disobeys an order, or has consistently poor performance.

Source: Reprinted from David D. Van Fleet and Gary A. Yukl, *Military Leadership: An Organizational Behavior Perspective*, pp. 38–39. ©1986, with permission from Elsevier Science.

See Interpretations at the end of the chapter.

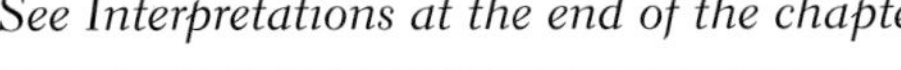

GO ONLINE to the Griffin/Van Fleet Assessment Library for online versions of these and other assessments.

LEARNING ABOUT LEADERSHIP SKILLS

Differences Between Managing and Leading
Understanding the Basics of Leadership
Power and Leadership
Legitimate Power
Reward Power
Coercive Power
Referent Power
Expert Power
Using Power
Leadership Traits
Leadership Behaviors
Michigan Studies
Ohio State Studies
Leadership Grid
Understanding Situational Approaches to Leadership
LPC Theory
Favorableness of the Situation
Favorableness and Leader Style
Flexibility of Leader Style
Path–Goal Theory
Leader Behavior
Situational Factors
The Leader–Member Exchange Approach
Understanding Related Perspectives on Leadership
Substitutes for Leadership
Charismatic Leadership
Transformational Leadership
Cross-Cultural Leadership
Ethical Leadership
Summary and a Look Ahead

Our primary focus in this book has been on management and the skills managers need to be more effective. Many managers also want to go beyond these skills, however, and develop their capabilities as leaders. This chapter provides an introduction to leadership and can serve as an effective transition to thinking about moving from management to leadership. **Leadership** is both a process and a property. As a process—focusing on what leaders actually do—leadership is the use of noncoercive influence to shape the group or organization's goals, motivate behavior toward the achievement of those goals, and help define group or organizational culture.[1] As a property, leadership is the set of characteristics attributed to individuals who are perceived to be leaders. Thus, **leaders** are people who can influence the behaviors of others without having to rely on force or people whom others accept as leaders.

LEARN

DIFFERENCES BETWEEN MANAGING AND LEADING

From these definitions, it should be clear that leadership and management are related, but they are not the same. A person can be a manager, a leader, both, or neither.[2] *Table 10.1* summarizes some of the basic distinctions between management and leadership. At the left side of the table are four elements that differentiate leadership from management. The two columns show how each element differs when considered from a management and from a leadership point of view. For example, when executing plans, managers focus on monitoring results, comparing them with goals, and correcting deviations. In contrast, the leader focuses on energizing people to overcome bureaucratic hurdles to reach goals.

Organizations need both management and leadership if they are to be effective. Leadership is necessary to create change, and management is necessary to achieve orderly results. Management in conjunction with leadership can produce orderly change, and leadership in conjunction with management can keep the organization properly aligned with its environment. Perhaps part of the reason why executive compensation has soared in recent years is the belief that management and leadership skills reflect a critical but rare combination that can lead to organizational success.

leadership the use of noncoercive influence to shape the group or organization's goals, motivate behavior toward the achievement of those goals, and help define group or organizational culture

leadership the set of characteristics attributed to individuals who are perceived to be leaders

leaders people who can influence the behaviors of others without having to rely on force or people whom others accept as leaders

LEARN

TABLE 10.1 DISTINCTIONS BETWEEN MANAGEMENT AND LEADERSHIP

Activity	Management	Leadership
Creating an agenda	*Planning and Budgeting* Establishing detailed steps and timetables for achieving needed results; allocating the resources necessary to make those results happen	*Establishing Direction* Developing a vision of the future, often the distant future, and strategies for producing the changes needed to achieve that vision
Developing a human network for achieving the agenda	*Organizing and Staffing* Establishing some structure for accomplishing plan requirements, staffing that structure with individuals, delegating responsibility and authority for carrying out the plan, providing policies and procedures to help guide people, and creating methods or systems to monitor implementation	*Aligning People* Communicating the direction by words and deeds to everyone whose cooperation may be needed to influence the creation of teams and coalitions that understand the visions and strategies and accept their validity
Executing plans	*Controlling and Problem Solving* Monitoring results versus planning in some detail, identifying deviations, and then planning and organizing to solve these problems	*Motivating and Inspiring* Energizing people to overcome major political, bureaucratic, and resource barriers by satisfying very basic, but often unfulfilled, human needs
Outcomes	Produces a degree of predictability and order and has the potential to produce consistently major results expected by various stakeholders (for example, for customers, always being on time; for stockholders, being on budget)	Produces change, often to a dramatic degree, and has the potential to produce extremely useful change (for example, new products that customers want, new approaches to labor relations that help make a firm more competitive)

Source: Reprinted with permission of The Free Press, a division of Simon & Schuster Adult Publishing Group, from *A Force for Change: How Leadership Differs from Management* by John P. Kotter. Copyright © 1990 by John P. Kotter, Inc.

UNDERSTANDING THE BASICS OF LEADERSHIP

To understand leadership fully, it is necessary to start with the concept of power. It is also instructive to review some of the early approaches to leadership.

Power and Leadership

Power is the ability to affect the behavior of others. A person can have power without actually using it. For example, a football coach has the power to bench a player who is not performing up to par. The coach seldom has to use this power because players recognize that the power exists and work hard to keep their starting positions. In organizational settings, there are usually five kinds of power: legitimate, reward, coercive, referent, and expert power.[3]

power the ability to affect the behavior of others

legitimate power the power defined by the organization to be accorded to people occupying a particular position

reward power the power to give or withhold rewards

Legitimate Power Legitimate power is power granted through the organizational hierarchy; it is the power defined by the organization to be accorded to people occupying a particular position. A manager can assign tasks to a subordinate, and a subordinate who refuses to do them can be reprimanded or even fired. Such outcomes stem from the manager's legitimate power as defined and vested in her or him by the organization. Legitimate power, then, is authority. All managers have legitimate power over their subordinates. The mere possession of legitimate power, however, does not make someone a leader. For example, some subordinates only follow orders that are strictly within the letter of organizational rules and policies. If asked to do something not in their job descriptions, they refuse or do a poor job. The manager of such employees is exercising authority but not leadership.

Reward Power Reward power is the power to give or withhold rewards. Rewards that a manager may control include salary increases, bonuses, promotion recommendations, praise, recognition, and interesting job assignments. In general, the greater the number of rewards a manager controls and the more important the rewards are to subordinates, the greater is the manager's reward power. If the subordinate sees as valuable only the formal organizational rewards provided by the manager, then he or she is not a leader. If the subordinate also wants and appreciates the manager's informal rewards, such as praise, gratitude, and recognition, however, then the manager is also exercising leadership.

(Note that the effective use of reward power also requires the use of diagnostic skills, as discussed in Chapter 6.)

Coercive Power Coercive power is the power to force compliance by means of psychological, emotional, or physical threat. In the past, physical coercion in organizations was relatively common. In most organizations today, however, coercion is limited to verbal reprimands, written reprimands, disciplinary layoffs, fines, demotion, and termination. Some managers may occasionally use verbal abuse, humiliation, and psychological coercion in an attempt to manipulate subordinates. (Most people would agree that these are not appropriate managerial behaviors.) James Dutt, a legendary former CEO of Beatrice Company, once told a subordinate that if his wife and family got in the way of his working a 24-hour day seven days a week, he should get rid of them.[4] The more punitive the elements under a manager's control and the more important they are to subordinates, the more coercive power the manager possesses. On the other hand, the more a manager uses coercive power, the more likely he is to provoke resentment and hostility, and the less likely he is to be seen as a leader.[5]

JUPITERIMAGES

Referent Power Compared with legitimate, reward, and coercive power, which are relatively concrete and grounded in objective facets of organizational life, referent power is abstract. It is based on identification, imitation, loyalty, or charisma. Followers may react favorably because they identify in some way with a leader, who may be like them in personality, background, or attitudes. In other situations, followers might choose to imitate a leader with referent power by wearing the same kind of clothes, working the same hours, or espousing the same management philosophy. Referent power also may take the form of charisma, an intangible attribute of the leader that inspires loyalty and enthusiasm. Thus, a manager might have referent power, but it is more likely to be associated with leadership.

Expert Power Expert power is derived from information or expertise. A manager who knows how to interact with an eccentric but important customer, a scientist who is capable of achieving an important technical breakthrough that no other company has dreamed of, and an administrative assistant who knows how to unravel bureaucratic red tape all have expert power over anyone who needs that information. The more important the information, and the fewer the people who have access to it, the greater is the degree of expert power possessed by any one individual. In general, people who are both leaders and managers tend to have a lot of expert power.

> "It is wise to persuade people to do things and make them think it was their own idea."
>
> NELSON MANDELA
> former president of South Africa[6]

TIME, JULY 21, 2008, P. 46.

Using Power How does a manager or leader use power? Several approaches are possible.[7] The simplest approach is the *legitimate request*, which is based on legitimate power. The manager requests that the subordinate comply because the subordinate recognizes that the organization has given the manager the right to make the request. Most day-to-day interactions between manager and subordinate are of this type. Another use of power is *instrumental compliance*, which is based on the reinforcement theory of motivation. In this form of exchange, a subordinate complies to get the reward the manager controls. Suppose that a manager asks a subordinate to do something outside the range of the subordinate's normal duties, such as working extra hours on the weekend, terminating a relationship with a longstanding buyer, or delivering bad news. The subordinate complies and, as a direct result, reaps praise and a bonus from the manager. The next time the subordinate is asked to perform a similar activity, that subordinate will recognize that compliance will be instrumental in her getting more rewards. Hence the basis of instrumental compliance is clarifying important performance–reward contingencies.

A manager is using *coercion* when she suggests or implies that the subordinate will be punished, fired, or reprimanded if he does not do something. *Rational*

coercive power the power to force compliance by means of psychological, emotional, or physical threat

referent power based on identification, imitation, loyalty, or charisma

expert power derived from information or expertise

LEARN

LEARN

persuasion occurs when the manager can convince the subordinate that compliance is in the subordinate's best interests. For example, a manager might argue that the subordinate should accept a transfer because it would be good for the subordinate's career. In some ways, rational persuasion is like reward power, except that the manager does not really control the reward.

Another way a manager can use power is through *personal identification*. A manager who recognizes that she has referent power over a subordinate can shape the behavior of that subordinate by engaging in desired behaviors: The manager consciously becomes a model for the subordinate and exploits personal identification. Sometimes a manager can induce a subordinate to do something consistent with a set of higher ideals or values through *inspirational appeal*. For example, a plea for loyalty represents an inspirational appeal. Referent power plays a role in determining the extent to which an inspirational appeal is successful because its effectiveness depends at least in part on the persuasive abilities of the leader.

A dubious method of using power is through *information distortion*. The manager withholds or distorts information to influence subordinates' behavior. For example, if a manager agrees to allow everyone to participate in choosing a new group member but subsequently finds one individual whom she really prefers, she might withhold some of the credentials of other qualified applicants so that the desired member is selected. This use of power is dangerous. It may be unethical, and if subordinates find out that the manager has deliberately misled them, they will lose confidence and trust in that manager's leadership.[8]

Leadership Traits

The first organized approach to studying leadership analyzed the personal, psychological, and physical traits of strong leaders. The trait approach assumed that some basic trait or set of traits existed that differentiated leaders from nonleaders. If those traits could be defined, potential leaders could be identified. Researchers thought that leadership traits might include intelligence, assertiveness, above-average height, good vocabulary, attractiveness, self-confidence, and similar attributes.[9]

During the first half of the twentieth century, hundreds of studies were conducted in an attempt to identify important leadership traits. For the most part, the results of the studies were disappointing. For every set of leaders who possessed a common trait, a long list of exceptions also was found, and the list of suggested traits soon grew so long that it had little practical value. Alternative explanations usually existed even for relationships between traits and leadership that initially appeared valid. For example, researchers observed that many leaders have good communication skills and are assertive. Rather than those traits being the cause of leadership, however, successful leaders may begin to display those traits after they have achieved a leadership position.

Although most researchers gave up trying to identify traits as predictors of leadership ability, many people still explicitly or implicitly adopt a trait orientation.[10] For example, politicians are often elected on the basis of personal appearance, speaking ability, or an aura of self-confidence. In addition, traits like honesty and integrity may very well be fundamental leadership traits that serve an important purpose. Intelligence also seems to play a meaningful role in leadership.[11]

job-centered leader behavior paying close attention to subordinates' work, explaining work procedures, and having a keen interest in performance

employee-centered leader behavior having interest in developing a cohesive work group and ensuring that employees are satisfied with their jobs

Leadership Behaviors

Motivated by their lack of success in identifying useful leadership traits, researchers soon began to investigate other variables, especially the behaviors or actions of leaders. The new hypothesis was that effective leaders somehow behaved differently than less effective leaders. Thus, the goal was to develop a fuller understanding of leadership behaviors.

Michigan Studies Researchers at the University of Michigan, led by Rensis Likert, began studying leadership in the late 1940s.[12] Based on extensive interviews with both leaders (managers) and followers (subordinates), this research identified two basic forms of leader behavior: job-centered and employee-centered. Managers using job-centered leader behavior pay close attention to subordinates' work, explain work procedures, and are keenly interested in performance. Managers using employee-centered leader behavior are interested in developing a cohesive work group and ensuring that employees are satisfied with their jobs. Their primary concern is the welfare of subordinates. The two styles of leader behavior were presumed to be at the ends of a single continuum. Although this suggests that leaders may be extremely job centered, extremely employee centered, or somewhere in between, Likert studied only the two end styles for contrast. He argued that employee-centered leader behavior generally tends to be more effective.

Ohio State Studies About the same time that Likert was beginning his leadership studies at the University of Michigan, a group of researchers at Ohio State University also began studying leadership.[13] The extensive questionnaire surveys conducted during the Ohio State studies also suggested that there are two basic leader behaviors or styles: initiating-structure behavior and consideration

LEARN

FIGURE 10.1 THE LEADERSHIP GRID

The Leadership Grid is a method of evaluating leadership styles. The overall objective of an organization using the Grid is to train its managers using organization development techniques so they are simultaneously more concerned for both people and production (9.9 style on the Grid).

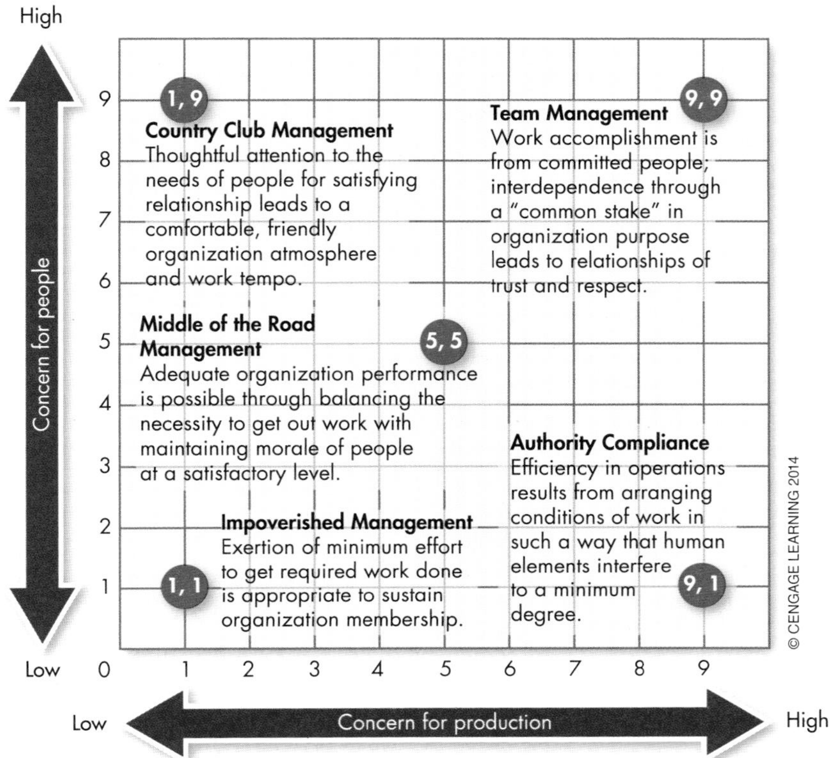

behavior. When using initiating-structure behavior, the leader clearly defines the leader–subordinate role so that everyone knows what is expected, establishes formal lines of communication, and determines how tasks will be performed. Leaders using consideration behavior show concern for subordinates and attempt to establish a warm, friendly, and supportive climate. The behaviors identified at Ohio State are similar to those described at Michigan, but there are important differences. One major difference is that the Ohio State researchers did not interpret leader behavior as being one-dimensional; each behavior was assumed to be independent of the other. Presumably, then, a leader could exhibit varying levels of initiating structure and at the same time varying levels of consideration.

At first, the Ohio State researchers thought that leaders who exhibit high levels of both behaviors would tend to be more effective than other leaders. A study at International Harvester (now Navistar International), however, suggested a more complicated pattern.[14] The researchers found that employees of supervisors who ranked high on initiating structure were high performers but expressed low levels of satisfaction and had a higher absence rate. Conversely, employees of supervisors who ranked high on consideration had low performance ratings but high levels of satisfaction and few absences from work. Later research isolated other variables that make consistent prediction difficult and determined that situational influences also occurred. (This body of research is discussed in the section on situational approaches to leadership.[15])

Leadership Grid Yet another behavioral approach to leadership is the Leadership Grid.[16] The Leadership Grid (originally known as the Managerial Grid) provides a means for evaluating leadership styles and then training managers to move toward an ideal style of behavior. The Leadership Grid is shown in *Figure 10.1*.

initiating-structure behavior clearly defining the leader–subordinate role so that everyone knows what is expected, establishes formal lines of communication, and determines how tasks will be performed

consideration behavior show concern for subordinates and attempt to establish a warm, friendly, and supportive climate

The horizontal axis represents concern for production (similar to job-centered and initiating-structure behaviors), and the vertical axis represents concern for people (similar to employee-centered and consideration behaviors). Note the five extremes of managerial behavior: the 1,1 manager (impoverished management), who exhibits minimal concern for both production and people; the 9,1 manager (authority-compliance), who is highly concerned about production but exhibits little concern for people; the 1,9 manager (country club management), who has exactly opposite concerns from the 9,1 manager; the 5,5 manager (middle-of-the-road management), who maintains adequate concern for both people and production; and the 9,9 manager (team management), who exhibits maximum concern for both people and production.

According to this approach, the ideal style of managerial behavior is 9,9. There is a six-phase program to assist managers in achieving this style of behavior. A.G. Edwards, Westinghouse, the FAA, Equicor, and other companies have used the Leadership Grid with reasonable success. However, there is little published scientific evidence regarding its true effectiveness.

The leader-behavior theories have played an important role in the development of contemporary thinking about leadership. In particular, they urge us not to be preoccupied with what leaders are (the trait approach) but to concentrate on what leaders do (their behaviors). Unfortunately, these theories also make universal generic prescriptions about what constitutes effective leadership. When we are dealing with complex social systems composed of complex individuals, however, few, if any, relationships are consistently predictable, and no formulas for success are infallible. Yet behavior theorists tried to identify consistent relationships between leader behaviors and employee responses in the hope of finding a dependable prescription for effective leadership. As we might expect, they often failed. Other approaches to understanding leadership were, therefore, needed. The catalyst for these new approaches was the realization that although interpersonal and task-oriented dimensions might be useful for describing the behavior of leaders, they were not useful for predicting or prescribing it. The next step in the evolution of leadership theory was the creation of situational models.

UNDERSTANDING SITUATIONAL APPROACHES TO LEADERSHIP

Situational models assume that appropriate leader behavior varies from one situation to another. The goal of a situational theory, then, is to identify key situational factors and to specify how they interact to determine appropriate leader behavior.

LPC Theory

The LPC theory, developed by Fred Fiedler, was the first truly situational theory of leadership.[17] As we will discuss later, LPC stands for least-preferred coworker. Beginning with a combined trait and behavioral approach, Fiedler identified two styles of leadership: task oriented (analogous to job-centered and initiating-structure behavior) and relationship oriented (similar to employee-centered and consideration behavior). He went beyond the earlier behavioral approaches by arguing that the style of behavior is a reflection of the leader's personality and that most personalities fall into one of his two categories—task oriented or relationship oriented by nature. Fiedler measures leadership style by means of a controversial questionnaire called the least-preferred coworker (LPC) measure. To use the measure, a manager or leader is asked to describe the specific person with whom he or she is able to work least well—the LPC—by filling in a set of 16 scales anchored at each end by a positive or negative adjective. For example, 3 of the 16 scales are:

Helpful	8	7	6	5	4	3	2	1	Frustrating
Tense	1	2	3	4	5	6	7	8	Relaxed
Boring	1	2	3	4	5	6	7	8	Interesting

The leader's LPC score is then calculated by adding up the numbers below the line checked on each scale. Note in these three examples that the higher numbers are associated with positive qualities (helpful, relaxed, and interesting), whereas the negative qualities (frustrating, tense, and boring) have low point values. A high total score is assumed to reflect a relationship orientation and a low score, a task orientation on the part of the leader. The LPC measure is controversial because researchers disagree about its validity. Some question exactly what an LPC measure reflects and whether the score is an index of behavior, personality, or some other factor.[18]

concern for production similar to job-centered and initiating-structure behaviors

concern for people similar to employee-centered and consideration behaviors

LPC theory the first truly situational theory of leadership; suggests style of leader behavior is a reflection of the leader's personality and that most personalities fall into one of his two categories—task oriented or relationship oriented by nature

least-preferred coworker (LPC) measure instrument used to measure leader behavior tendencies

© ISTOCKPHOTO.COM/HULTONARCHIVE

Favorableness of the Situation The underlying assumption of situational models of leadership is that appropriate leader behavior varies from one situation to another. According to Fiedler, the key situational factor is the favorableness of the situation from the leader's point of view. This factor is determined by leader–member relations, task structure, and position power. *Leader–member relations* refer to the nature of the relationship between the leader and the work group. If the leader and the group have a high degree of mutual trust, respect, and confidence, and if they like one another, relations are assumed to be good. If there is little trust, respect, or confidence, and if they do not like one another, relations are poor. Naturally, good relations are more favorable.

Task structure is the degree to which the group's task is well defined. A structured task is routine, easily understood, and unambiguous, and the group has standard procedures and precedents to rely on when performing it. An unstructured task is nonroutine, ambiguous, and complex, with no standard procedures or precedents. You can see that a high degree of structure is more favorable for the leader, whereas a low degree is less favorable. For example, if the task is unstructured, the group will not know what to do, and the leader will have to play a major role in guiding and directing its activities. If the task is structured, the leader will not have to get so involved and can devote time to nonsupervisory activities.

Position power is the power vested in the leader's position. If the leader has the power to assign work and to reward and punish employees, position power is assumed to be strong. But if the leader must get job assignments approved by someone else and does not administer rewards and punishment, position power is weak, and it is more difficult to accomplish goals. From the leader's point of view, strong position power is clearly preferable to weak position power. However, position power is not as important as task structure and leader–member relations.

Favorableness and Leader Style Fiedler and his associates conducted numerous studies linking the favorableness of various situations to leader style and group effectiveness.[19] The results of these studies—and the overall framework of the theory—are shown in *Figure 10.2*. To interpret the model, first look at the

FIGURE 10.2 THE LPC THEORY OF LEADERSHIP

Fiedler's LPC (least-preferred coworker) theory of leadership suggests that appropriate leader behavior varies as a function of the favorableness of the situation. Favorableness, in turn, is defined by task structure, leader–member relations, and the leader's position power. According to the LPC theory, the most and least favorable situations call for task-oriented leadership, whereas moderately favorable situations suggest the need for relationship-oriented leadership.

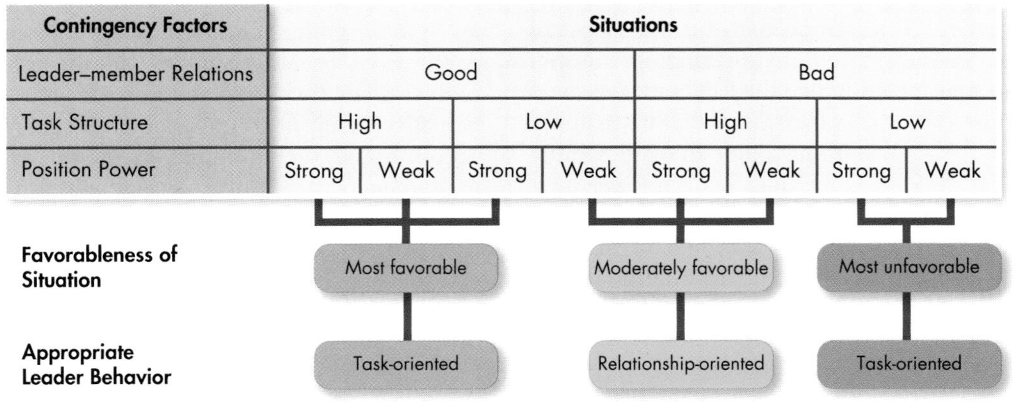

© CENGAGE LEARNING 2014

LEARN

situational factors at the top of the figure. Good or bad leader–member relations, high or low task structure, and strong or weak leader position power can be combined to yield six unique situations. For example, good leader–member relations, high task structure, and strong leader position power (at the far left) are presumed to define the most favorable situation; bad leader–member relations, low task structure, and weak leader power (at the far right) are the least favorable. The other combinations reflect intermediate levels of favorableness.

> *"I listen, but I've got the final say. Then it's up to me to make it work so I don't lose my credibility."*
>
> RICHARD BRANSON
> founder and CEO, Virgin[21]

BLOOMBERG BUSINESSWEEK, NOVEMBER 22–NOVEMBER 28, 2010, P. 122

The degree of favorableness and the form of leader behavior found to be most strongly associated with effective group performance for those situations are shown below each set of situations. When the situation is most and least favorable, Fiedler found that a task-oriented leader is most effective. When the situation is only moderately favorable, however, a relationship-oriented leader is predicted to be most effective.

Flexibility of Leader Style Fiedler argued that, for any given individual, leader style is essentially fixed and cannot be changed; leaders cannot change their behavior to fit a particular situation because it is linked to their particular personality traits. Thus, when a leader's style and the situation do not match, Fiedler argued that the situation should be changed to fit the leader's style. When leader–member relations are good, task structure low, and position power weak, the leader style that is most likely to be effective is relationship oriented. If the leader is task oriented, a mismatch exists. According to Fiedler, the leader can make the elements of the situation more congruent by structuring the task (by developing guidelines and procedures, for instance) and increasing power (by requesting additional authority or by other means).

Fiedler's contingency theory has been attacked on various grounds. Critics argue that the theory is not always supported by research, that his findings are subject to other interpretations, that the LPC measure lacks validity, and that his assumptions about the inflexibility of leader behavior are unrealistic.[20] However, Fiedler's theory was one of the first to adopt a situational perspective on leadership. It has helped many managers recognize the important situational factors they must contend with, and it has fostered additional thinking about the situational nature of leadership. Moreover, Fiedler has attempted to address some of the concerns about his theory by revising it and adding such additional elements as cognitive resources.

path–goal theory of leadership suggests that the primary functions of a leader are to make valued or desired rewards available in the workplace and to clarify for the subordinate the kinds of behavior that will lead to goal accomplishment and valued rewards

Path–Goal Theory

The path–goal theory of leadership was developed by Martin Evans and Robert House.[22] The path–goal theory of leadership suggests that the primary functions of a leader are to make valued or desired rewards available in the workplace and to clarify for the subordinate the kinds of behavior that will lead to goal accomplishment and valued rewards. In other words, the leader should clarify the paths to goal attainment.

Leader Behavior The most fully developed version of path–goal theory identifies four kinds of leader behavior. *Directive leader behavior* lets subordinates know what is expected of them, gives guidance and direction, and schedules work. *Supportive leader behavior* is being friendly and approachable, showing concern for subordinates' welfare, and treating members as equals. *Participative leader behavior* includes consulting with subordinates, soliciting suggestions, and allowing participation in decision making. *Achievement-oriented leader* behavior means setting challenging goals, expecting subordinates to perform at high levels, encouraging subordinates, and showing confidence in subordinates' abilities.

In contrast to Fiedler's theory, path–goal theory assumes that leaders can change their style or behavior to meet the demands of a particular situation. For example, when encountering a new group of subordinates and a new project, the leader may be directive in establishing work procedures and in outlining what needs to be done. Next, the leader may adopt supportive behavior to foster group cohesiveness and a positive climate. As the group becomes familiar with the task and as new problems are encountered, the leader may exhibit participative behavior to enhance group members' motivation. Finally, achievement-oriented behavior may be used to encourage continued high performance.

Situational Factors Like other situational theories of leadership, path–goal theory suggests that appropriate leader style depends on situational factors. Path–goal theory focuses on the situational factors of the personal characteristics of subordinates and environmental characteristics of the workplace.

FIGURE 10.3 THE PATH–GOAL LEADERSHIP FRAMEWORK

The path–goal theory of leadership suggests that managers can use four types of leader behavior to clarify subordinates' paths to goal attainment. Both personal characteristics of the subordinate and environmental characteristics within the organization must be taken into account when determining which style of leadership will work best for a particular situation.

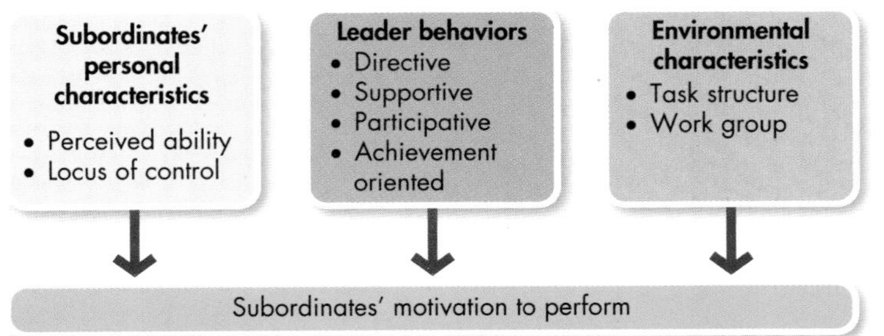

Important personal characteristics include the subordinates' perception of their own abilities and their locus of control. If people perceive that they are lacking in abilities, they may prefer directive leadership to help them understand path–goal relationships better. If they perceive themselves as having many abilities, however, employees may resent directive leadership. Locus of control is a personality trait. People who have an internal locus of control believe that what happens to them is a function of their own efforts and behavior. Those who have an external locus of control assume that fate, luck, or "the system" determine what happens to them. A person with an internal locus of control may prefer participative leadership, whereas a person with an external locus of control may prefer directive leadership. Managers can do little or nothing to influence the personal characteristics of subordinates, but they can shape the environment to take advantage of these personal characteristics by, for example, providing rewards and structuring tasks.

Environmental characteristics include factors outside the subordinates' control. Task structure is one such factor. When structure is high, directive leadership is less effective than when structure is low. Subordinates do not usually need their bosses to tell them repeatedly how to do a routine job. The formal authority system is another important environmental characteristic. Again, the higher the degree of formality, the less subordinates will accept directive leader behavior. The nature of the work group also affects appropriate leader behavior. When the work group provides the employee with social support and satisfaction, supportive leader behavior is less critical. When the group does not derive social support and satisfaction from the group, the worker may look to the leader for this support.

Greater leadership support also may be an important factor in times of change or under unusually stressful conditions. The basic path–goal framework as illustrated in *Figure 10.3* shows that different leader behaviors affect subordinates' motivation to perform. Personal and environmental characteristics are seen as defining which behaviors lead to which outcomes. The path–goal theory of leadership is a dynamic and incomplete model. The original intent was to state the theory in general terms so that future research could explore a variety of interrelationships and modify the theory. Research suggests that the path–goal theory is a reasonably good description of the leadership process. Future investigations along these lines should enable us to discover more about the link between leadership and motivation.[23]

The Leader–Member Exchange Approach

Because leadership is such an important area, managers and researchers continue to study it and develop new ideas, theories, and perspectives. The **leader–member exchange (LMX) model** of leadership, conceived by George Graen and Fred Dansereau, stresses the importance of variable relationships between supervisors and each of their subordinates.[24] Each superior–subordinate pair is referred to as a "vertical dyad." The model differs from earlier approaches in that it focuses on the differential relationships leaders often establish with different subordinates. *Figure 10.4* shows the basic concepts of the leader–member exchange theory.

The model suggests that supervisors establish a special relationship with a small number of trusted subordinates, referred to as "the in-group." The in-group usually receives special duties requiring

leader–member exchange (LMX) model of leadership stresses the importance of variable relationships between supervisors and each of their subordinates

LEARN

FIGURE 10.4 THE LEADER–MEMBER EXCHANGE (LMX) MODEL

The LMX model suggests that leaders form unique independent relationships with each of their subordinates. As illustrated here, a key factor in the nature of this relationship is whether the individual is in the leader's out-group or in-group.

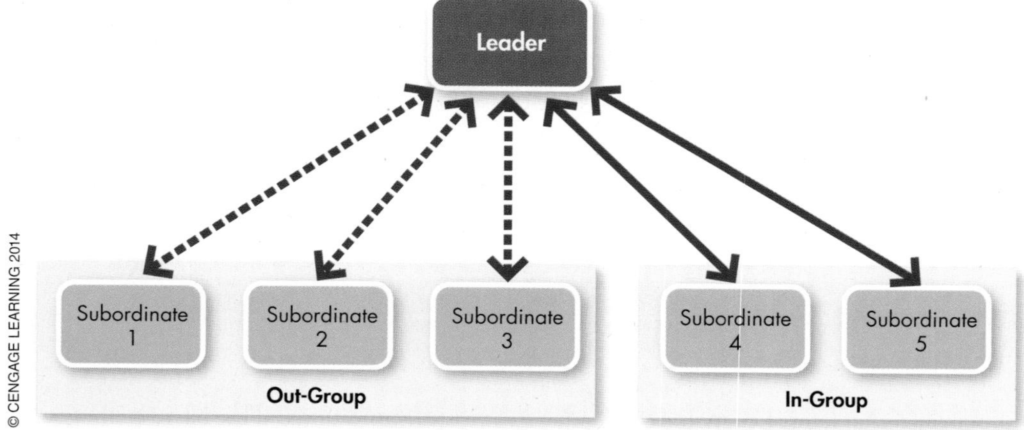

Leader–member exchange theory suggests that leaders form different kinds of relationships with different followers. This leader, for example, appears to be more engaged with the person beside him than with either of the other two individuals present.

responsibility and autonomy; they also may receive special privileges. Subordinates who are not a part of this group are called "the out-group," and they receive less of the supervisor's time and attention. Note in the figure that the leader has a dyadic, or one-to-one, relationship with each of the five subordinates.

Early in his or her interaction with a given subordinate, the supervisor initiates either an in-group or an out-group relationship. It is not clear how a leader selects members of the in-group, but the decision may be based on personal compatibility and the subordinates' competence. Research has confirmed the existence of in-groups and out-groups. In addition, studies generally have found that in-group members have a higher level of performance and satisfaction than do out-group members.[25]

substitutes for leadership identifies situations in which leader behaviors are neutralized or replaced by characteristics of the subordinate, the task, and the organization

UNDERSTANDING RELATED PERSPECTIVES ON LEADERSHIP

Because of its importance to organizational effectiveness, leadership continues to be the focus of a great deal of research and theory building. New approaches that have attracted attention are the concepts of substitutes for leadership, charismatic leadership, transformational leadership, cross-cultural leadership, and ethical leadership.[26]

Substitutes for Leadership

The concept of **substitutes for leadership** was developed because existing leadership models and theories do not account for situations in which leadership is not needed.[27] The existing models simply try to specify what kind of leader behavior is appropriate. The substitutes concept, however, identifies situations in which leader behaviors are neutralized or replaced by characteristics of the subordinate, the task, and the organization. For

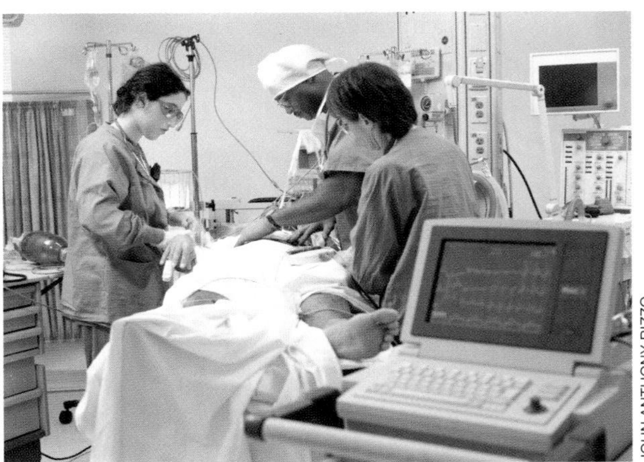
JOHN ANTHONY RIZZO

In some settings a number of different elements can serve as substitutes for leadership. This emergency room team, for example, did not need to wait for instructions to help the patient but instead knew to begin treatment immediately.

example, when a patient is delivered to a hospital emergency room, the professionals on duty do not wait for a leader to tell them what to do. Nurses, doctors, and attendants all go into action without waiting for directive or supportive leader behavior from the emergency room supervisor.

Characteristics of the subordinate that may serve to neutralize leader behavior include ability, experience, need for independence, professional orientation, and indifference toward organizational rewards. For example, employees with a high level of ability and experience may not need to be told what to do. Similarly, a subordinate's strong need for independence may render leader behavior ineffective. Task characteristics that may substitute for leadership include routineness, the availability of feedback, and intrinsic satisfaction. When the job is routine and simple, the subordinate may not need direction. When the task is challenging and intrinsically satisfying, the subordinate may not need or want social support from a leader.

Organizational characteristics that may substitute for leadership include formalization, group cohesion, inflexibility, and a rigid reward structure. Leadership may not be necessary when policies and practices are formal and inflexible, for example. Similarly, a rigid reward system may rob the leader of reward power and thereby decrease the importance of the role. Preliminary research has provided support for the concept of substitutes for leadership.[28]

Charismatic Leadership

The concept of **charismatic leadership**, like trait theories, assumes that charisma is an individual characteristic of the leader. **Charisma** is a form of interpersonal attraction that inspires support and acceptance. All else being equal, then, someone who has charisma is more likely able to influence others than is someone who does not have it. For example, a highly charismatic supervisor will be more successful in influencing subordinate behavior than a supervisor who lacks charisma. Thus, influence is, again, a fundamental element of this perspective.

Robert House first proposed a theory of charismatic leadership, based on research findings from a variety of social science disciplines.[29] His theory suggests that charismatic leaders are likely to have a lot of self-confidence, a firm conviction in their beliefs and ideals, and a strong need to influence people. They also tend to communicate high expectations for follower performance and express confidence in followers. Donald Trump is an excellent example of a charismatic leader. Even though he has made his share of mistakes and generally is perceived as only an "average" manager, many people view him as larger than life.

Most experts acknowledge three elements of charismatic leadership in organizations.[30] First, the leader needs to be able to envision the future, set high expectations, and model behaviors consistent with meeting those expectations. Next, the charismatic leader must be able to energize others through a demonstration of personal excitement, personal confidence, and patterns of success. Finally, the charismatic leader enables others by supporting them, empathizing with them, and expressing confidence in them.[31]

© ANTHONY CORREIA/SHUTTERSTOCK.COM

Charismatic leadership ideas are quite popular among managers today and are the subject of numerous books and articles. Unfortunately, few studies have attempted to test specifically the meaning and impact of charismatic leadership. There also are lingering ethical issues about charismatic leadership that trouble some people. For instance, President Bill Clinton was a charismatic leader. But some of his critics argued that this very charisma caused his supporters to overlook his flaws and to minimize some of his indiscretions. In contrast, President George W. Bush did not possess a high level of charisma, and this may have enabled some critics to magnify his shortcomings.

charismatic leadership assumes that charisma is an individual characteristic of the leader

charisma a form of interpersonal attraction that inspires support and acceptance

LEARN

Transformational Leadership

Another related perspective on leadership has a number of labels: inspirational leadership, symbolic leadership, and transformational leadership. We use the term **transformational leadership** and define it as leadership that goes beyond ordinary expectations by transmitting a sense of mission, stimulating learning experiences, and inspiring new ways of thinking.[32] Because of rapid change and turbulent environments, transformational leaders are considered vital to the success of business.[33]

> "As soon as I arrived, I said that within 90 days we'll make some decisions about the direction of the organization."
>
> SANJAY JHA
> CEO of Motorola Mobility Holdings[34]

FORTUNE, JULY 4, 2011, P. 63.

A widely circulated popular press article once identified seven keys to successful leadership: trusting one's subordinates, developing a vision, keeping cool, encouraging risk, being an expert, inviting dissent, and simplifying things. Although this list was the result of a simplistic survey of the leadership literature, it is nevertheless consistent with the premises underlying transformational leadership. So, too, are recent examples cited as effective leadership. Take the case of 3M. The firm's new CEO is working to make the firm more efficient and profitable while keeping its leadership role in new product innovation. He has also changed the reward system, overhauled procedures, and restructured the entire firm. So far analysts have applauded these changes.

Cross-Cultural Leadership

Another new approach to leadership is based on cross-cultural issues. In this context, culture is used as a broad concept to encompass both international differences and diversity-based differences within one culture. For instance, when a Japanese firm sends an executive to head the firm's operations in the United States, that person will need to become acclimated to the cultural differences that exist between the two countries and to change his or her leadership style accordingly. Japan culture generally is characterized by collectivism, whereas American culture is based more on individualism. The Japanese executive, then, will find it necessary to recognize the importance of individual contributions and rewards, as well as the differences in individual and group roles, that exist in Japanese and US businesses.

Similarly, cross-cultural factors play a growing role in organizations as their workforces become more and more diverse. Most leadership research, for instance, has been conducted on samples or case studies involving white male leaders, because, until recently, most business leaders were white males. As more females, African Americans, and Latinos achieve leadership positions, it may be necessary to reassess how applicable current theories and models of leadership are when applied to an increasingly diverse pool of leaders.

transformational leadership leadership that goes beyond ordinary expectations by transmitting a sense of mission, stimulating learning experiences, and inspiring new ways of thinking

Ethical Leadership

Most people have long assumed that top managers are ethical people. But in the wake of recent corporate scandals, faith in top managers has been shaken. Perhaps now more than ever, high standards of ethical conduct are considered prerequisite for effective leadership. More specifically, top managers are being called on to maintain high ethical standards for their own conduct, to exhibit ethical behavior unfailingly, and to hold others in their organization to the same standards.

Society is scrutinizing the behaviors of top leaders more than ever, and those responsible for hiring new leaders for a business are looking more closely at the background of prospective leaders. The emerging

© ISTOCKPHOTO.COM/KALI9

Cross-cultural leadership is becoming increasingly common in today's global business world. Leaders from one culture who are responsible for leading people from other cultures must work to better understand how their cultural differences might affect their working relationship.

pressures for stronger corporate governance models are likely to further increase commitment to selecting individuals with high ethical standards and to hold them more accountable than in the past for both their actions and the consequences of those actions.[35]

SUMMARY AND A LOOK AHEAD

After reading and studying this chapter, you should have a better understanding of leadership skills. Specifically, you should recognize and be able to articulate the fundamental differences between management and leadership. You also should be able to discuss the basics of leadership, such as power and leadership, early trait perspectives on leadership, and leadership behaviors. In addition, you should be able to describe major situational approaches to leadership such as LPC theory, path–goal theory, and the leader–member exchange perspective. Finally, you should be able to describe such related perspectives on leadership as substitutes for leadership, charismatic leadership, transformational leadership, cross-cultural leadership, and ethical leadership.

The remainder of this chapter provides opportunities for you to continue to develop and refine your own leadership skills. For instance, you will be directed to resources where you can visualize both effective and less effective leadership skills. Subsequent sections provide several opportunities for you to practice and explore leadership skills from different perspectives. The chapter concludes with some additional assessment and interpretation data.

VISUALIZING LEADERSHIP SKILLS

LEADERSHIP SKILLS IN ACTION—1

Your Assignment

Consider the two BizFlix film clips for this chapter.

In *Good Company* (2004) the complexities of corporate America unfold. A corporate takeover brings to star advertising executive Dan Foreman (Dennis Quaid) a new boss who is half his age. Carter Duryea (Topher Grace), Dan's new boss, wants to prove his worth as the new marketing chief at *Sports America*, Waterman Publishing's flagship magazine. Carter applies his unique approaches while dating Dan's daughter, Alex (Scarlett Johansson).

Friday Night Lights (2004) is based on H.G. Bissinger's book about Odessa, Texas, and its passion for Friday night high school football and the Permian High Panthers. Coach Gary Gaines (Billy Bob Thornton) leads the team to the 1988 semifinals where it must compete against a team of much larger players. Fast-moving pace in the football sequences and a slower pace in the serious, introspective sequences give this film many fine moments.

Note how leadership skills are shown in these two clips.

1. The first clip starts with Carter Duryea entering Dan Foreman's office while saying, "Oh, my God, Dan. Oh, my God." Mark Steckle (Clark Gregg) soon follows. Mark is almost violently upset and threatens to fire Dan. Following an extremely tense interaction, the sequence ends with Carter asking, "Any ideas?" Dan Forman says, "One." What leadership skills do the behaviors of Mark and Carter suggest?
2. The second clip begins with a shot of Coach Gaines and the team gathered around him during the half-time break. He starts his speech to the team by saying, "Well, it's real simple. You got two more quarters and that's it." It ends after Gaines says, "Boys, my heart is full. My heart's full." What leadership skills are evident in Gaines handling of this situation?

LEADERSHIP SKILLS IN ACTION—2

This exercise gives you an opportunity to think about leadership skills that may be involved in management positions in your future.

Your Assignment

1. Think about leadership skills and try to identify a scene that illustrates a positive or effective use of such skills in a movie, a TV show, or a video on YouTube.
2. Now do the same for a scene that illustrates a negative or ineffective use of those same skills.

Share your results with the class and discuss how the positive and negative use of leadership skills is shown in each clip. Also, suggest how the negative situation could have been changed for the better.

PRACTICING LEADERSHIP SKILLS

PRACTICE

DRAW LEADERSHIP

This exercise will give you an opportunity to see how your conception of a leader or leadership compares with that of others in your class.

Your Assignment

1. Think about leadership and what that term conveys to you.
2. Now, draw "leadership." On a piece of paper, draw an illustration of what leadership means to you. You are not expected to be an artist, so use stick figures or symbols to convey your impressions.
3. Your instructor will review your drawings and note any patterns or similarities. The class will discuss these patterns and what they suggest about your conception of leadership.

ANALYZE LEADERSHIP STYLE

This exercise will help you develop a conceptual framework for leadership and management. Although leadership and management are the same in some ways, they are more often different.

Most management behaviors and leadership behaviors are a product of individual work experience, so each leader/manager tends to have a unique style. Analyzing leadership/management styles, comparing such styles, and relating them to different organizational contexts often provide rewarding experiences in learning.

Your Assignment

1. Develop a list of questions related to issues you have studied that you want to ask a practicing manager/leader during a face-to-face interview. For purposes of this assignment, a manager or leader is a person whose job priority involves supervising the

work of other people. The leader/manager may work in a business or in a public or private agency.

2. Prior to the actual interview, submit your list of questions to your instructor for approval.
3. Interview the manager/leader, using the questions developed earlier. Do not take more than one hour of the leader/manager's time. Take good notes on his or her comments and on your own observations.
4. Prepare an oral report and then a written report, using your information and responses to the following questions:
   (A) How did you choose and contact the leader/manager you interviewed?
   (B) Without disclosing names, describe the level and responsibilities of your leader/manager.
   (C) Briefly describe the interview setting. How long did the interview last?
   (D) In what way does your leader/manager use decision-making skills?
   (E) In what way does your leader/manager use time-management skills?
   (F) What interpersonal skills did your leader/manager indicate have been most important to him?
   (G) How did your leader/manager feel about being interviewed? How do you know that?

PRACTICE

MANAGERS AND LEADERS

This exercise offers you an opportunity to compare your views about managers and leaders with those of others in your class.

Your Assignment

1. Make a list of ten characteristics of managers and a list of ten characteristics of leaders.
2. Share your lists with other students in small groups and discuss the following:
   (A) Which manager characteristics, if any, appear on different students' lists?
   (B) Which leader characteristics, if any, appear on different students' lists?
   (C) Which characteristics, if any, do students put on both their manager list and their leader list?
3. Have your group compile one list of ten characteristics of managers and one list of ten characteristics of leaders.
4. Share all group lists with the entire class, and see if the class can agree on a final list for managers and a final list for leaders. What, if anything, do the final two lists have in common? Do any characteristics appear on both the manager list and the leader list?

WHO ARE THE LEADERS?

This exercise offers you an opportunity to compare your concepts with those of others in your class about who leaders are.

Your Assignment

1. Make a list of ten leaders—individuals whom most everyone would recognize as leaders.

2. In small groups share and discuss your lists.
   (A) Were the same leaders on more than one student's list?
   (B) What, if anything, do these individuals have in common—education, industry, type of jobs held, family history, etc.?
3. Have each group agree on a list of ten leaders and share those group lists with the entire class. What, if anything, do the leaders on the various group lists have in common? If any leader appears to be radically different from the others, discuss what sets that person apart from other leaders and yet makes them one of the best-known leaders.
4. Try repeating the exercise with the possibilities narrowed, e.g., females, Native Americans, minorities, managers/executives, politicians, religious leaders, international, or from a particular industry.

USING LEADERSHIP SKILLS

USE

THE STRUGGLES OF LEADERSHIP

John King was chairman of Babcock International, a large engineering firm, when he was chosen to become chairman of troubled British Airways (BA) and move it from a government organization to a private business. He slashed employment, sold surplus aircraft as well as some real estate holdings, switched insurance agencies, transformed the board of directors, changed advertising agencies, and hired a new chief executive. The new chief executive was chosen specifically because he understood service organizations and management but had no previous experience in the airline industry and so would be open to new ways of operating. That person was Colin Marshall.

Colin Marshall left home as a teenager to go to sea with the Orient Steam Navigation Company. He spent seven years sailing from Britain to Australia before going to Chicago as a management trainee with Hertz. He left Hertz for Avis where he worked in the European division and then in its New York headquarters. Later he moved to its parent company, Norton Simon, Inc., as an executive. Marshall learned a great deal about tough competitive battles by having worked for both Hertz and Avis. In 1981 he moved to apply his experience in retailing, where he rose to deputy chief executive of Sears PLC Holdings (parent company of the Selfridges retail empire and not related to Sears Roebuck). In 1983, he moved from there to the chief executive position at BA.

King and Marshall worked well together. The merger of British Airways and British Caledonia, which took place the same year as the privatization of BA, was so difficult and protracted that many employees were depressed by the time it ended. To ease the tension and enable the new organization to become effective quickly, King and Marshall had a consulting firm throw a party for all employees. The party for 40,000 people was held in an unused hanger and was highly effective in reducing tensions and bringing everyone together.

As Marshall assumed control of BA, he applied his experience with Hertz and Avis to make BA highly competitive and profitable. He emphasized customer service as the way to win competitive battles and won high praise for improvements in service in all areas of BA. In 1990, BA and Aeroflot formed Air Russia to establish routes from Moscow to Europe, the United States, and the Far East. In 1991, thanks to an excellent information system and continued tight cost controls under Marshall's leadership, BA was the world's most profitable carrier. Then in 1992, BA agreed to buy 44 percent of USAir in a move to become the world's first truly global airline.

King stepped down as chairman in 1993 and was replaced by Marshall, while Robert Ayling took over as CEO. Ayling focused on cutting costs, but it wasn't enough. In 1999, despite being named one of the most admired airlines, British Airways reported a tremendous drop in profits. As a result, in 2000, Ayling was removed from his position and Rod Eddington was named as his successor. Eddington set about cutting the workforce further, in response to the slump caused by the September 11 attacks in 2001. Then in 2005, yet another change occurred as William M. Walsh, former Aer Lingus boss, took charge of the company.

In January 2008, British Airways unveiled a new subsidiary, OpenSkies, to take advantage of the liberalization of transatlantic traffic rights. At that time it was the largest airline of the UK and the seventh largest in the world, but it dropped from that position soon after. On July 30, 2008, British Airways and Iberia Airlines announced a merger plan that would result in the two airlines joining forces in an all-stock transaction. The two airlines would retain their separate brands, similar to KLM and Air France, in their merger agreement.

On March 31, 2009, the airline celebrated its 35th anniversary. Then, in a consolidation move designed to help the company return to profitability, British Airways moved to merge with the Spanish flag carrier, Iberia. The merger between the two carriers would create the world's third-largest airline in terms of annual revenue. In early 2010, the merger moved forward, with its planned completion by the end of the year. The combined company would be known as International Airlines Group, although both the Iberia and BA brands will continue to co-exist.

Case Questions

Go Online

USE

1. What skills can you recognize among the various managerial leaders of British Airways?
2. How would you describe King's leadership? Marshall's leadership?
3. How do your skills match up with those of King and Marshall? Are you prepared to be a manager and/or leader?
4. What skills do you feel would be particularly important for helping a struggling company like British Airways?
5. In what other types of companies might a person develop most of the skills needed by leaders of British Airways?

Case References

Slobodan Lekic, "Airlines struggle to return to profitability," *BusinessWeek*, May 27, 2010; Steve Rothwell, "British Airways counts on crew cuts after record loss," *BusinessWeek*, May 21, 2010; Kenneth Labich, "Europe's Sky Wars," *Fortune*, November 2, 1992, pp. 88–91; Richard D. Hylton, "United to BA: Take Off," *Fortune*, September 7, 1992, p. 9; "Getting Extra Mileage From British Air," *BusinessWeek*, August 24, 1992, p. 86; Paula Dwyer, Andrea Rothman, Seth Payne, and Stewart Toy, "Air Raid: British Air's Bold Global Push," *BusinessWeek*, August 24, 1992, pp. 54–61; Nathaniel Gilbert, "British Airways' Fail-Safe I/S Takes Off," *Chief Information Officer Journal*, Spring 1990, pp. 41–44.

PAPER OR NOT—XEROX HAS IT COVERED

The Haloid Photographic Company was founded in 1906. For the first several decades of its existence, Haloid worked to develop and refine xerography, the process of transferring electrostatic images onto plain paper. In 1958 it became Haloid Xerox. In 1959 the company introduced the first simplified office copier, the Xerox 914. Sales and profits skyrocketed immediately as the Xerox 914 became an office staple around the world. Sales soared from \$37 million in 1960 to \$268 million in 1965. The company changed its name to Xerox in 1961.

Success led Xerox to two distinct results—one a blessing, the other a curse. On the positive side, Xerox copiers dominated the market and continued to generate huge revenues and profits for years. On the negative side, Xerox, failing to diagnose changes in the market, grew complacent in the copier market and did a poor job of developing innovations in other key markets. For example, Xerox scientists were among the first to dabble in personal computers and its research labs actually pioneered laser printers. But failure to diagnose the potential for these innovations caused the firm to miss the boat in both industries.

In the 1980s, the company's neglect of its copier business also began to create problems. Indeed, by the time Xerox recognized the threat from Canon and Ricoh, those two firms had drastically cut into market share. Canon actually took over the top position in the color copier market. Observers blamed the fall of Xerox on its bureaucratic organization design and its lethargic approach to new product development.

In 1990, Paul Allaire became CEO with a mandate to get the firm back on track. At the time, Allaire was a 26-year Xerox veteran and was widely regarded for his forward-looking and aggressive approach to management. He quickly arranged for the executive team to undergo an extensive organization development program to make sure they agreed on what they were going to do and how they were going to do it. This activity involved a diagnostic battery of personality tests followed by several days at a Connecticut monastery to process the results and address their differences.

After the executive committee had established a common frame of reference and agreed upon a plan of attack, Allaire began changing the organization. In particular, he and the other executives decided to create the culture and atmosphere of several smaller companies within the umbrella of the Xerox Corporation. They felt that this would promote better market understanding that would lead to innovation while also enhancing peoples' commitment to and involvement with the organization and its goals.

USE

To accomplish these objectives, the entire organization design of the firm was changed. Previously the firm had been organized as a tall hierarchy and was based on functional departmentalization. It became more of a matrix defining relatively autonomous units. While some managers balked at the changes and a few even chose to leave, most of the key people at Xerox felt that the firm was in a much better position to regain its standing in the industry.

Paul Allaire was followed by Anne Mulcahy as CEO in 2001. Mulcahy moved to sustain the progress made by Allaire, only to have horrible economic conditions hold the company back. But she strengthened the firm by continuing to carefully diagnose consumer tastes, monitor market and product developments, and keep Xerox efficient.

Today Xerox has four product divisions: Global Business and Services Group, Global Customer Operations, Global Services, and ACS (Affiliated Computer Services). ACS, an outsourcing firm, was acquired in 2009 at the behest of Ursula Burns, the president. That same year saw the introduction of ColorCube printers that promised to capture much of the color printing market. The commitment of Xerox to the ACS acquisition is reflected in Burns having succeeded Mulcahy as CEO in 2010. This was also notable in that it was the first female-to-female handoff in a major corporation, and Burns was the first black female CEO of a Fortune 500 company.

Case Questions

Go Online

1. What kinds of changes did the different leaders at Xerox face?
2. What skills would be most useful in responding to those changes?
3. Why did Xerox fail to diagnose important environmental changes during the mid-1900s?
4. What leadership skills would seem to be the most important at Xerox? Why?
5. How would you go about developing your leadership skills to prepare for a managerial position at Xerox?

Case References

Geoff Colvin, "Ursula Burns launches Xerox into the future," *Fortune*, April 22, 2010 http://money.cnn.com/2010/04/22/news/companies/xerox_ursula_burns.fortune/index.htm; Patricia Sellers, "Xerox chief charts her new path," *Fortune*, March 10, 2010 http://postcards.blogs.fortune.cnn.com/2010/03/10/xerox-chief-charts-her-new-path/; Anna Kattan, "Xerox bets on pricey printers," *Fortune*, June 1, 2009 http://money.cnn.com/2009/06/01/technology/xerox_pricey_printers.fortune/index.htm; "The New, New Thinking at Xerox," *BusinessWeek*, June 22, 1992, pp. 120–121; Robert Howard, "The CEO as Organizational Architect: An Interview with Xerox's Paul Allaire," *Harvard Business Review*, September–October 1992, pp. 107–121.

EXTENDING YOUR LEADERSHIP SKILLS

Your instructor may use one or more of these **Group Extensions** to provide you with another opportunity to develop your time-management skills. On the other hand, you may continue your development on your own by doing one or more of the **Individual Extensions**.

These **Group Extensions** are repeated exactly for each of the seven specific skills. Doing the exact **Extension** for different skills will help you to sharpen both the skills and the subtle differences between the several skills.

GROUP EXTENSIONS

- Form small groups of students. Have each group select an organization and a management position. Then have them identify the leadership skills needed by a person in that position.
- Form small groups of students. Have each group identify a problem or opportunity facing a business or other organization. Then have them identify the leadership skills needed by managers in dealing with that problem or opportunity.
- Form small groups of students. Assign each group one or more corporations to analyze. Have them identify the members who serve on its board of directors and research their backgrounds. Then have the students describe the leadership skills those directors need to have.
- Form small groups of students. Have each group select a job they see regularly (e.g., retail clerk, fast-food worker). Ask them to describe the leadership skills those workers need to have on that job.
- Form small groups of students. Have students sketch the leadership skills they would need if they were going to start a specific type of new business.
- Form small groups of students. Have each group identify situations they have recently faced that illustrate a situation that called for them to use leadership skills.
- Form small groups of students. Have each group brainstorm a list of skills that they think of when they hear the word *leadership*. Have a representative from each group write its list on the board. Note similarities and differences across the different lists.
- Form small groups of students. Have each group explore the use of power by managers and leaders. What skills do leaders use in their exercise of power?
- Form small groups of students. Have each group identify several different kinds of organizations, and then discuss whether the top executives in those organizations are more managers or more leaders.

EXTEND

INDIVIDUAL EXTENSIONS

- Go to the library and research a company. Characterize its level of effectiveness and identify the diagnostic skills of its top executives. Share your results with the class.
- Select a highly visible manager and analyze his or her diagnostic skills.
- Interview a manager from a local organization. Learn about the diagnostic skills he or she needs to perform effectively.
- Think of someone you know who is a manager. Describe that person's management position in terms of the type of organization, level in the organization, and the area of management in which he or she practices. What diagnostic skills does that person need to be effective?
- Plan a hypothetical change in your school focusing on the use of diagnostic skills.
- Search the Internet for examples of leadership in management and compare what you find with the information presented here.
- Do your skills match better with those of a manager or those of a leader? How will you change to better match the one you prefer?
- Read a biography or autobiography of an effective leader. What are that person's strongest skills?
- Identify two leaders—one who is charismatic and one who is equally effective but not charismatic. What skill differences can you identify?

INTERPRETATIONS

HOW CHARISMATIC ARE YOU?

Riggio suggests that charisma involves six elements. While an overly simplistic measure, your scores indicate the extent to which you seem to have each of those elements. The higher your total score, the more charismatic you are likely to be. Here is a brief description of each of them.

EE (emotional expressiveness). Expressing feelings spontaneously and in a genuine way that affects others.

ES (emotional sensitivity). The ability to read others' emotions and make connections to them.

EC (emotional control). The ability to control emotions and turn them on and off.

SE (social expressiveness). The use of verbal communication skill to engage others in social interaction and speak in public.

SS (social sensitivity). Skill in social situations that enable a person to be tactful and sensitive to surroundings.

SC (social control). Social role-playing that allows a person to fit in with all sorts of people.

For more information see Ronald E. Riggio. 1988. *The Charisma Quotient: What It Is, How to Get It, How to Use It*. NY: Dodd Mead.

MANAGERIAL LEADER BEHAVIOR QUESTIONNAIRE

These statements represent 23 categories of behavior that research has identified as descriptive of managerial leadership. Not all are important in any given situation. Typically, fewer than half of these behaviors are associated with performance in particular situations; thus there is no "right" or "wrong" set of responses on this questionnaire. The behavior categories are:

1. Emphasizing performance
2. Showing consideration
3. Providing career counseling
4. Inspiring subordinates
5. Providing praise and recognition
6. Structuring reward contingencies
7. Clarifying work roles
8. Setting goals
9. Training-coaching
10. Disseminating information
11. Encouraging participation in decisions
12. Delegating
13. Planning
14. Innovating
15. Problem solving
16. Facilitating the work
17. Monitoring operations
18. Monitoring the environment
19. Representing the unit
20. Facilitating cooperation and teamwork
21. Managing conflict
22. Providing criticism
23. Administering discipline

In military organizations at war, inspiring subordinates, emphasizing performance, clarifying work roles, problem solving, and planning seem most important. On the other hand, during peacetime, inspiring subordinates, emphasizing performance, clarifying work roles, showing consideration, providing criticism, and administering discipline seem most important. In business organizations, emphasizing performance, monitoring the environment, clarifying work roles, setting goals, and sometimes innovating seem to be most important. In each of these instances, however, the level of organization, type of technology, environmental conditions, and objectives being sought all help to determine the precise mix of behaviors that will lead to effectiveness. You should analyze your particular situation to determine which subset of these behaviors is most likely to be important and then strive to develop that subset.

ENDNOTES

[1] Gary A. Yukl, *Leadership in Organizations*, 3rd ed. (Englewood Cliffs, N.J.: Prentice-Hall, 1994), p. 5. See also Gregory G. Dess and Joseph C. Pickens, "Changing Roles: Leadership in the 21st Century," *Organizational Dynamics*, Winter 2000, pp. 18–28 and Julian Barling, Amy Christie, and Colette Hoption, "Leadership," in Sheldon Zedeck, (Ed.), *Handbook of Industrial and Organizational Psychology* (American Psychological Association: Washington, D.C., 2010). Michael Watkins, "How Managers Become Leaders," *Harvard Business Review*, June 2012, p. 64–72.

[2] John P. Kotter, "What Leaders Really Do," *Harvard Business Review*, May–June 1990, pp. 103–111 (reprinted in *Harvard Business Review*, December 2001, pp. 85–93). See also Daniel Goleman, "Leadership That Gets Results," *Harvard Business Review*, March–April 2000, pp. 78–88; Keith Grints, *The Arts of Leadership* (Oxford, U.K.: Oxford University Press, 2000).

[3] John R. P. French and Bertram Raven, "The Bases of Social Power," in Dorwin Cartwright (ed.), *Studies in Social Power* (Ann Arbor, MI: University of Michigan Press, 1959), pp. 150–167.

[4] Hugh D. Menzies, "The Ten Toughest Bosses," *Fortune*, April 21, 1980, pp. 62–73.

[5] Bennett J. Tepper, "Consequences of Abusive Supervision," *Academy of Management Journal*, 2000, Vol. 43, No. 2, pp. 178–190; see also Bennett J. Tepper, "Abusive Supervision in Work Organizations: Review, Synthesis, and Research Agenda," *Journal of Management*, 2007, Vol. 33, No. 3, pp. 261–289.

[6] *Time*, July 21, 2008, p. 46.

[7] Thomas A. Stewart, "Get with the New Power Game," *Fortune*, January 13, 1997, pp. 58–62.

[8] Philip M. Podsakoff and Chester A. Schriesheim, "Field Studies of French and Raven's Bases of Power: Critique, Reanalysis, and Suggestions for Future Research," *Psychological Bulletin*, 1985, Vol. 97, pp. 387–411; Robert C. Benfari, Harry E. Wilkinson, and Charles D. Orth, "The Effective Use of Power," *Business Horizons*, May–June 1986, pp. 12–16; and Yukl, *Leadership in Organizations*.

[9] Bernard M. Bass, *Bass & Stogdill's Handbook of Leadership*, 3rd ed. (Riverside, NJ: Free Press, 1990).

[10] Shelley A. Kirkpatrick and Edwin A. Locke, "Leadership: Do Traits Matter?" *Academy of Management Executive*, May 1991, pp. 48–60. See also Robert J. Sternberg, "Managerial Intelligence: Why IQ Isn't Enough," *Journal of Management*, 1997, Vol. 23, No. 3, pp. 475–493.

[11] Timothy Judge, Amy Colbert, and Remus Ilies, "Intelligence and Leadership: A Quantitative Review and Test of Theoretical Propositions," *Journal of Applied Psychology*, 2004, Vol. 89, No. 3, pp. 542–552.

[12] Rensis Likert, *New Patterns of Management* (New York: McGraw-Hill, 1961); Rensis Likert, *The Human Organization* (New York: McGraw-Hill, 1967).

[13] The Ohio State studies stimulated many articles, monographs, and books. A good overall reference is Ralph M. Stogdill and A. E. Coons (eds.), *Leader Behavior: Its Description and Measurement* (Columbus, OH: Bureau of Business Research, Ohio State University, 1957).

[14] Edwin A. Fleishman, E. F. Harris, and H. E. Burt, *Leadership and Supervision in Industry* (Columbus, OH: Bureau of Business Research, Ohio State University, 1955).

[15] Timothy Judge, Ronald Piccolo, and Remus Ilies, "The Forgotten One? The Validity of Consideration and Initiating Structure in Leadership Research," *Journal of Applied Psychology*, 2004, Vol. 89, No. 1, pp. 36–51.

[16] Robert R. Blake and Jane S. Mouton, *The Managerial Grid* (Houston: Gulf Publishing, 1964); Robert R. Blake and Jane S. Mouton, *The Versatile Manager: A Grid Profile* (Homewood, IL: Dow Jones-Irwin, 1981).

[17] Fred E. Fiedler, *A Theory of Leadership Effectiveness* (New York: McGraw-Hill, 1967).

[18] Chester A. Schriesheim, Bennett J. Tepper, and Linda A. Tetrault, "Least Preferred Co-Worker Score, Situational Control, and Leadership Effectiveness: A Meta-Analysis of Contingency Model Performance Predictions," *Journal of Applied Psychology*, 1994, Vol. 79, No. 4, pp. 561–573.

[19] Fiedler, *A Theory of Leadership Effectiveness*; Fred E. Fiedler and M. M. Chemers, *Leadership and Effective Management* (Glenview, IL: Scott, Foresman, 1974).

[20] Lawrence H. Peters, Darrell D. Hartke, and John T. Pohlmann, "Fiedler's Contingency Theory of Leadership: An Application of the Meta-Analysis Procedures of Schmidt and Hunter," *Psychological Bulletin* Vol. 97, pp. 274–285; and Fred E. Fiedler, "When to Lead, When to Stand Back," *Psychology Today*, September 1987, pp. 26–27.

[21] *Bloomberg BusinessWeek*, November 22–November 28, 2010, p. 122

[22] Martin G. Evans, "The Effects of Supervisory Behavior on the Path-Goal Relationship," *Organizational Behavior and Human Performance*, May 1970, pp. 277–298; Robert J. House and Terence R. Mitchell, "Path-Goal Theory of Leadership," *Journal of Contemporary Business*, Autumn 1974, pp. 81–98. See also Yukl, *Leadership in Organizations*.

[23] J. C. Wofford and Laurie Z. Liska, "Path-Goal Theories of Leadership: A Meta-Analysis," *Journal of Management*, 1993, vol. 19, no. 4, pp. 857–876.

[24] George Graen and J. F. Cashman, "A Role-Making Model of Leadership in Formal Organizations: A Developmental Approach," in J. G. Hunt and L. L. Larson (eds.), *Leadership Frontiers* (Kent, OH: Kent State University Press, 1975), pp. 143–165; Fred Dansereau, George Graen, and W. J. Haga, "A Vertical Dyad Linkage Approach to Leadership Within Formal Organizations: A Longitudinal Investigation of the Role-Making Process," *Organizational Behavior and Human Performance*, 1975, Vol. 15, pp. 46–78.

[25] Kathryn Sherony and Stephen Green, "Coworker Exchange: Relationships Between Coworkers, Leader-Member Exchange, and Work Attitudes," *Journal of Applied Psychology*, 2002, Vol. 87, No. 3, pp. 542–548.

[26] Bruce J. Avolio, Fred O. Walumbwa, and Todd J. Weber, "Leadership: Current Theories, Research, and Future Directions," in Susan T. Fiske, Daniel L. Schacter, and Robert Sternberg (eds.), *Annual Review of Psychology 2009* (Palo Alto, CA: Annual Reviews, 2009), pp. 421–450.

[27] Steven Kerr and John M. Jermier, "Substitutes for Leadership: Their Meaning and Measurement," *Organizational Behavior and Human Performance*, December 1978, pp. 375–403.

[28] Charles C. Manz and Henry P. Sims, Jr., "Leading Workers to Lead Themselves: The External Leadership of Self-Managing Work Teams," *Administrative Science Quarterly*, March 1987, pp. 106–129. See also "Living Without a Leader," *Fortune*, March 20, 2000, pp. 218–219.

[29] Robert J. House, "A 1976 Theory of Charismatic Leadership," in J. G. Hunt and L. L. Larson (eds.), *Leadership: The Cutting Edge* (Carbondale, IL: Southern Illinois University Press, 1977), pp. 189–207. See also Jay A. Conger and Rabindra N. Kanungo, "Toward a Behavioral Theory of Charismatic Leadership in Organizational Settings," *Academy of Management Review*, October 1987, pp. 637–647.

[30] David A. Nadler and Michael L. Tushman, "Beyond the Charismatic Leader: Leadership and Organizational Change," *California Management Review*, Winter 1990, pp. 77–97.

[31] Jane Howell and Boas Shamir, "The Role of Followers in the Charismatic Leadership Process: Relationships and Their Consequences," *Academy of Management Review*, 2005, Vol. 30, No. 1, pp. 96–112.

[32] James MacGregor Burns, *Leadership* (New York: Harper & Row, 1978). See also Rajnandini Pillai, Chester A. Schriesheim, and Eric J. Williams, "Fairness Perceptions and Trust as Mediators for Transformational and Transactional Leadership: A Two-Sample Study," *Journal of Management*, 1999, Vol. 25, No. 6, pp. 897–933.

[33] Robert Rubin, David Munz, and William Bommer, "Leading from Within: The Effects of Emotion Recognition and Personality on Transformational Leadership Behaviors," *Academy of Management Journal*, 2005, Vol. 48, No. 5, pp. 845–858.

[34] *Fortune*, July 4, 2011, p. 63.

[35] Kurt Dirks and Donald Ferrin, "Trust in Leadership," *Journal of Applied Psychology*, 2002, Vol. 87, No. 4, pp. 611–628; See also Russell A. Eisenstat, Michael Beer, Nathanial Foote, Tobias Fredberg, and Flemming Norrgren, "The Uncompromising Leader," *Harvard Business Review*, July–August 2008, pp. 51–59.

APPENDIX A

MANAGERIAL SKILLS ASSESSMENT

To assess your managerial skills, complete the following instrument, which covers each of the major skills discussed in the book. Think about your current situation, job, or organization in which you are a member. Respond in terms of your current situation and not by how you think you or a manager should respond. If a statement does not currently pertain to your situation, respond in terms of what you think would currently be accurate for you in that situation.

Use this scale in your responses.

1	2	3	4	5
Not true at all	Somewhat untrue	Sometimes true Sometimes not	Somewhat true	Completely true

Total your scores and record them in the table at the end of instrument.

Given that many experts suggest the use of 360° feedback in performance appraisal, you may find it useful to obtain the views of others about your managerial skills. Your instructor may give you a form designed for others to complete, and you can then record their scores in the table as well. Pay attention to areas in which there is a discrepancy between your views and those of others and spend more time developing those skills.

TECHNICAL SKILLS

____ 1. I accomplish a lot.

____ 2. I actively engage in self development.

____ 3. I am able to coordinate tasks.

____ 4. I am able to efficiently utilize available resources (people, materials, equipment, etc.).

____ 5. I am approached by others with technical problems and questions.

____ 6. I am dependable.

____ 7. I am determined to succeed.

____ 8. I am generally an energetic person.

____ 9. I am good with numbers.
____ 10. I am interested in succeeding in my career.
____ 11. I am knowledgeable about my associates and what needs to be done.
____ 12. I am not satisfied with average performance.
____ 13. I am prepared to be flexible to get the job done.
____ 14. I am prepared to do whatever it takes to succeed.
____ 15. I am prepared to keep at a problem until it is solved.
____ 16. I am strongly motivated to "get the job done."
____ 17. I analyze financial information quickly.
____ 18. I can adjust my goals/activities without becoming frustrated.
____ 19. I can identify the important parts of budgets and financial statements.
____ 20. I can read and understand financial or other quantitative information.
____ 21. I can use statistical and quantitative information when necessary.
____ 22. I closely watch expenses.
____ 23. I develop complete, well-detailed plans.
____ 24. I enjoy activities that require me to learn new things.
____ 25. I enjoy improving things.
____ 26. I establish effective and efficient procedures for getting things done.
____ 27. I establish performance standards for those in my organization.
____ 28. I handle details quite well.
____ 29. I have a lot of self-control.
____ 30. I have very high standards for myself and others.
____ 31. I keep up-to-date on technical developments related to my interests.
____ 32. I let others know what and how well I am doing.
____ 33. I make plans that are clear and realistic.
____ 34. I prefer gradual change to sudden change.
____ 35. I read material about my current and future tasks.
____ 36. I readily adapt to new initiatives.
____ 37. I seek feedback about how I am doing.
____ 38. I seldom leave a job unfinished.
____ 39. I set specific learning goals for myself.
____ 40. I strive for excellence in all that I do.
____ 41. I strive for high quality in my work.
____ 42. I tend to keep up with information about my tasks.
____ 43. I tend to stick with problems until they are resolved.
____ 44. I tend to use tried and tested methods.
____ 45. I try not to waste resources.
____ 46. I try to always be prepared.
____ 47. I try to improve my knowledge and skills.
____ 48. I try to keep at a task even when I encounter unexpected difficulties.
____ 49. I try to keep busy all the time.
____ 50. I understand what needs to be done.

INTERPERSONAL SKILLS

____ 51. I admit and accept responsibility for my own mistakes.
____ 52. I always do my share in group activities.
____ 53. I am ambitious and competitive.
____ 54. I am assertive or forceful when the need arises.
____ 55. I am aware of potential conflicts in dealing with others.
____ 56. I am comfortable in leadership positions.
____ 57. I am generally an outgoing person.
____ 58. I am generally lively and enthusiastic.
____ 59. I am genuinely interested in what others are doing in terms of their careers.
____ 60. I am patient with others.
____ 61. I am pretty good at getting others to adopt my ideas.
____ 62. I am sensitive to other people's needs and feelings.
____ 63. I am very tough mentally and physically.
____ 64. I am willing to take an unpopular position if I feel it is right.
____ 65. I am willing to work long hours when necessary.
____ 66. I assure that those to whom I delegate have the authority and resources to do the work.
____ 67. I avoid compromising too quickly.
____ 68. I can act as a spokesperson for a group.
____ 69. I can be assertive when necessary.
____ 70. I can handle stress and pressure effectively.
____ 71. I care about my relationships with others.
____ 72. I consider the opinions and feelings of others when they are presenting their ideas.
____ 73. I cooperate with others.
____ 74. I delegate when appropriate.
____ 75. I develop and maintain good, cooperative working relationships with others.
____ 76. I feel that people are mostly trustworthy and ethical.
____ 77. I find that people generally live up to my expectations.
____ 78. I generally am aware of the strengths and weaknesses of those in my group.
____ 79. I generally display enthusiasm about meeting objectives and deadlines.
____ 80. I generally earn the attention and respect of others in a group.
____ 81. I genuinely care about the feelings of others.
____ 82. I get along well with coworkers/peers.
____ 83. I get along well with superiors.
____ 84. I give people the opportunity to show what they are capable of.
____ 85. I go out of my way to help people develop.
____ 86. I handle setbacks effectively.
____ 87. I have a wide range of contacts and friends.
____ 88. I have confidence in others.
____ 89. I help others learn when they are doing new tasks.

____ 90. I help resolve conflicting demands among group members.
____ 91. I inspire confidence.
____ 92. I keep others informed as to how things are going.
____ 93. I let others know when they are doing good work.
____ 94. I let others know when they are doing things wrong.
____ 95. I let people know if their performance is not up to what is desired.
____ 96. I listen to the views of others.
____ 97. I prefer to lead rather than follow.
____ 98. I provide advice to others when appropriate.
____ 99. I provide information to others on what they need to do to do well.
____ 100. I recognize and deal with problems between individuals and groups.
____ 101. I recognize and reward others for helping me.
____ 102. I rely on persuasion and expertise to motivate people.
____ 103. I seek additional responsibility to improve myself.
____ 104. I share credit for group work.
____ 105. I take time to get to know people.
____ 106. I tend to be a strong team player.
____ 107. I trust people to do the right thing.
____ 108. I try to always be courteous.
____ 109. I try to avoid being upset when I am criticized.
____ 110. I try to avoid getting irritable or moody when I am under stress.
____ 111. I try to avoid taking sides in arguments.
____ 112. I try to be a good role model.
____ 113. I try to be confident even in ambiguous and stressful situations.
____ 114. I try to be involved in group activities.
____ 115. I try to coach others to help them with their tasks.
____ 116. I try to convey my feelings so that others will know how I feel.
____ 117. I try to create an environment in which people will perform at their best.
____ 118. I try to deal with conflict by focusing on the real reasons underlying the conflict.
____ 119. I try to develop rapport with others.
____ 120. I try to empower people to help them perform better.
____ 121. I try to get everyone involved in group activities.
____ 122. I try to get people to work well together.
____ 123. I try to help others learn from their mistakes.
____ 124. I try to motivate others to do well.
____ 125. I try to provide support for others.
____ 126. I try to see to it that tasks are evenly distributed among group members.
____ 127. I try to set an example through my performance to encourage excellence by others.
____ 128. I try to set high standards of performance for group members.
____ 129. I try to suggest that everyone's work is important.
____ 130. I try to treat everyone fairly.

CONCEPTUAL SKILLS

____ 131. I am capable of thinking "outside the box."
____ 132. I am creative.
____ 133. I am emotionally mature.
____ 134. I am good at abstract thinking.
____ 135. I am good at analyzing problems.
____ 136. I am good at gathering information.
____ 137. I am good at identifying important information.
____ 138. I am good at identifying problems.
____ 139. I am good at solving problems.
____ 140. I am up to new challenges.
____ 141. I am willing to take risks.
____ 142. I can identify resources necessary to accomplish my tasks.
____ 143. I challenge rules and procedures.
____ 144. I deal constructively with my own failures and mistakes.
____ 145. I develop ways to evaluate how I'm doing.
____ 146. I enjoy learning new ways of doing things.
____ 147. I enjoy risks.
____ 148. I focus on performance.
____ 149. I frequently come up with fresh and imaginative approaches to a problem.
____ 150. I frequently originate change.
____ 151. I frequently take the first step to get things done.
____ 152. I generally can solve problems on my own.
____ 153. I handle change with an open mind.
____ 154. I have a good understanding of my strengths and weaknesses.
____ 155. I have high standards for myself.
____ 156. I imagine alternative solutions in solving problems.
____ 157. I initiate new ideas.
____ 158. I keep long-term and short-term goals and activities in perspective.
____ 159. I know my personal learning style and fit situations to that.
____ 160. I make forecasts to prepare for future events.
____ 161. I promote change.
____ 162. I readily take chances.
____ 163. I recognize that there is more to life than work and a job.
____ 164. I seek opportunities to test myself.
____ 165. I sell ideas.
____ 166. I set goals.
____ 167. I strive to do my best.
____ 168. I think a lot about how to get more for less.
____ 169. I try to deal with problems quickly.
____ 170. I try to learn from my mistakes.

DIAGNOSTIC SKILLS

____ 171. I act independently when it is necessary.
____ 172. I adapt quickly to new situations.
____ 173. I am able to visualize the major aspects of problems.
____ 174. I am prepared to bend the rules if necessary.
____ 175. I am systematic and methodical.
____ 176. I am willing to compromise to get agreement.
____ 177. I analyze facts before making decisions.
____ 178. I approach problems by first trying to determine the root cause(s).
____ 179. I ask questions about difficult problems before trying to solve them.
____ 180. I assure that those in my group have the resources needed to succeed.
____ 181. I break problems down into their component parts to better solve them.
____ 182. I define the problem before trying to solve it.
____ 183. I develop potential solutions to problems.
____ 184. I diagnose causes of poor performance before acting to correct it.
____ 185. I focus on questions and problems important to the organization.
____ 186. I frequently have ideas about how to improve group activities.
____ 187. I generally can quickly identify key issues.
____ 188. I identify easy tasks and get them out of the way before tackling more difficult ones.
____ 189. I identify limits to solutions to help overcome them.
____ 190. I like a challenging climate to work in.
____ 191. I like to get the details right.
____ 192. I pitch in and lead by example
____ 193. I seek to understand the symptoms of a problem in order to develop solutions.
____ 194. I try to focus group discussions on the problem at hand.
____ 195. I try to get divergent views on a problem and its solution.
____ 196. I try to get others to develop potential solutions to problems.
____ 197. I try to help others understand and solve problems.
____ 198. I try to take advantage of opportunities as they arise.
____ 199. I use information from my communication networks in analyzing problems.
____ 200. I usually "look before I leap."

COMMUNICATION SKILLS

____ 201. I accurately perceive nonverbal messages.
____ 202. I actively seek advice from others.
____ 203. I am an easy person to work with.
____ 204. I am an excellent communicator.
____ 205. I am aware of my emotional reactions to what is being said in a conversation.
____ 206. I am aware of emotional reactions of others to what is being said in a conversation.
____ 207. I am capable of editing written documents.
____ 208. I am clear and understandable in oral communications.

_____ 209. I am good at expressing my ideas.
_____ 210. I am good at negotiating.
_____ 211. I am good at persuasion.
_____ 212. I am good at reporting information.
_____ 213. I am good at teaching.
_____ 214. I ask for additional explanation if I don't understand something someone says.
_____ 215. I can accurately describe my feelings.
_____ 216. I can be forceful and persuasive in oral communications.
_____ 217. I can facilitate group discussions.
_____ 218. I can interview others fairly well.
_____ 219. I can prepare written reports easily and quickly.
_____ 220. I can provide appropriate feedback.
_____ 221. I can relate well to different types of people.
_____ 222. I can speak effectively in front of a group.
_____ 223. I can work alone or with others.
_____ 224. I coach others to help them.
_____ 225. I contribute to understanding by asking questions.
_____ 226. I counsel others to assist them.
_____ 227. I deal calmly with difficult situations.
_____ 228. I do not become defensive when I am being criticized.
_____ 229. I encourage those around me to feel free to air their feelings, even strong ones.
_____ 230. I enjoy being part of a group.
_____ 231. I enjoy being with others.
_____ 232. I find it easy to express my feelings.
_____ 233. I find it easy to see things from another's point of view.
_____ 234. I generally find what others have to say interesting.
_____ 235. I generally get my point across when talking.
_____ 236. I generally listen without interrupting.
_____ 237. I keep others up-to-date about information and change.
_____ 238. I let others know if they will be affected by something I am doing.
_____ 239. I listen attentively.
_____ 240. I listen more than talk when I'm with others.
_____ 241. I listen to disagreements among others.
_____ 242. I listen to the concerns of others.
_____ 243. I listen to the views and ideas of others.
_____ 244. I listen to what the team wants to do.
_____ 245. I listen well in group situations.
_____ 246. I make a good impression when I give a presentation.
_____ 247. I make my views known without being pushy.
_____ 248. I make sure that people experience no "surprises" from me.
_____ 249. I provide clear, specific feedback.
_____ 250. I provide feedback linked to particular performance or behavior.
_____ 251. I seldom get into arguments.
_____ 252. I set an example for how hard people in my organization should work.

_____ 253. I speak effectively.
_____ 254. I state my views clearly and concisely when speaking with others.
_____ 255. I strive to be in communication networks so that I am aware of important information.
_____ 256. I teach others how to do tasks.
_____ 257. I tend to be good with words.
_____ 258. I tend to provide a lot of information to others.
_____ 259. I try to give others a chance to say what they think.
_____ 260. I try never to be too busy to listen to the problems and concerns of others.
_____ 261. I try to clearly explain the desired results when assigning tasks.
_____ 262. I try to find out what others think before reaching conclusions.
_____ 263. I try to give feedback that will help people solve their own problems.
_____ 264. I try to identify the "real" message in communications from others.
_____ 265. I try to provide feedback on problems rather than personal characteristics.
_____ 266. I try to put myself in the other person's shoes when I talk to them.
_____ 267. I try to respond to people in a helpful way.
_____ 268. I use correct grammar.
_____ 269. I welcome the views of others.
_____ 270. I write clearly and concisely.

DECISION-MAKING SKILLS

_____ 271. I accept responsibility for my actions.
_____ 272. I always plan how deadlines are going to be met.
_____ 273. I am able to deal with ambiguous and uncertain assignments.
_____ 274. I am prepared to let others take the lead.
_____ 275. I avoid making rash decisions.
_____ 276. I can act decisively when necessary.
_____ 277. I can handle conflict.
_____ 278. I can handle tasks that involve large amounts of information.
_____ 279. I can manage groups.
_____ 280. I consider alternatives before making decisions.
_____ 281. I delegate to get things done.
_____ 282. I do not avoid making difficult decisions.
_____ 283. I do what I say.
_____ 284. I don't get involved in the details.
_____ 285. I generally feel that I have made right decisions.
_____ 286. I generally make decisions that are logical and rational.
_____ 287. I have an ability to cut through red tape.
_____ 288. I involve others in making decisions.
_____ 289. I involve others in planning.
_____ 290. I make decisions with others.
_____ 291. I make things happen.

____ 292. I make timely decisions.
____ 293. I rarely hesitate when making decisions.
____ 294. I readily delegate tasks.
____ 295. I seek good input before making decisions.
____ 296. I set difficult goals for myself.
____ 297. I take full responsibility for my decisions.
____ 298. I try to make clear to others why I make the decisions that I do.
____ 299. I usually make sound decisions even under pressure.
____ 300. I weigh my options carefully when making decisions.

TIME-MANAGEMENT SKILLS

____ 301. I almost always complete my tasks on time.
____ 302. I am able to "unwind" after a trying day at work.
____ 303. I am not stressed about deadlines and commitments.
____ 304. I analyze new tasks or assignments to establish their priorities.
____ 305. I deal with higher priority problems and tasks first.
____ 306. I deal with issues one at a time.
____ 307. I don't over-schedule; I leave time for "the unexpected" and relaxation.
____ 308. I exercise to relieve tension.
____ 309. I generally am punctual.
____ 310. I generally can prioritize tasks without too much trouble.
____ 311. I generally manage my time well.
____ 312. I get others to help when necessary.
____ 313. I handle interruptions quickly so that they don't delay my work.
____ 314. I handle paperwork quickly and effectively.
____ 315. I have "confidants" with whom I can release frustrations.
____ 316. I keep a "to do" list.
____ 317. I keep a well-organized and orderly workspace.
____ 318. I keep information and documents in an orderly manner.
____ 319. I know how much time I spend on the various tasks I do.
____ 320. I make good use of time.
____ 321. I meet goals.
____ 322. I minimize distractions that could keep me from working on critical tasks.
____ 323. I organize and schedule my tasks.
____ 324. I organize my activities.
____ 325. I organize my time effectively.
____ 326. I pay attention to details.
____ 327. I practice relaxation techniques (e.g., reciting a mantra, slowing breathing).
____ 328. I prioritize my activities.
____ 329. I respond promptly to written requests.
____ 330. I return phone calls quickly.
____ 331. I seldom have to ask for extensions.

_____ 332. I set and meet deadlines.
_____ 333. I set aside time for planning and scheduling.
_____ 334. I set daily goals and prepare daily "to do" lists.
_____ 335. I set specific deadlines on projects.
_____ 336. I take time to meet with others.
_____ 337. I try to never leave things to the last minute.
_____ 338. I use goal setting to establish priorities for my tasks and activities.
_____ 339. I use plans to manage my tasks.
_____ 340. I work in a tidy and organized way.

Summary of Your Scores

Skill (maximum possible score)	Your Scores	Scores from Others
Technical (250)		
Interpersonal (400)		
Conceptual (200)		
Diagnostic (150)		
Communication (350)		
Decision Making (150)		
Time Management (200)		

Interpretation of Your Scores

	Your Skill Level				
Skill	**Mastery**	**Reasonably proficient**	**Acceptable**	**Needs further development**	**Needs considerable development**
Technical	225 or higher	200 – 224	175 – 199	150 – 174	149 or below
Interpersonal	360 or higher	320 – 359	280 – 319	240 – 279	239 or below
Conceptual	180 or higher	160 – 179	140 – 159	120 – 139	119 or below
Diagnostic	135 or higher	120 – 134	105 – 119	90 – 104	89 or below
Communication	315 or higher	280 – 314	245 – 279	210 – 244	209 or below
Decision Making	135 or higher	120 – 134	105 – 119	90 – 104	89 or below
Time Management	180 or higher	160 – 179	140 – 159	120 – 139	119 or below

APPENDIX B

SKILLS FOR FINDING A JOB

LEARNING ABOUT JOB-FINDING SKILLS

Careers
- *Career Choice*
- *Choosing a Career*
- *Life Stages and Career Stages*
  - *Exploration*
  - *Establishment*
  - *Maintenance*
  - *Decline*
- *Career Development*
  - *Career Planning*
  - *Career Management*
- *Special Career Issues*
  - *Women and Minorities*
  - *Dual Incomes and Dual Careers*

Job Hunting
- *Self-Assessment*
- *Preparing Your Résumé and Applying for a Job*
- *Interviewing*

Good Luck!

VISUALIZING JOB-FINDING SKILLS

Job-Hunting Skills in Action—1

Job-Hunting Skills in Action—2

PRACTICING JOB-FINDING SKILLS

Selecting a Job

Which Job?

Throughout this book we have tried to enable you to learn and develop your management skills. But in order to demonstrate those newly acquired skills, you must put them into practice as a manager. This appendix is designed to help you achieve that goal through learning and developing one final skill—skill at finding a job.

LEARNING ABOUT JOB-FINDING SKILLS

Careers
Career Choice
Choosing a Career
Life Stages and Career Stages
Exploration
Establishment
Maintenance
Decline
Career Development
Career Planning
Career Management
Special Career Issues
Women and Minorities
Dual Incomes and Dual Careers
Job Hunting
Self-Assessment
Preparing Your Résumé and Applying for a Job
Interviewing
Good Luck!

Before focusing on finding a job, you would do well to learn more about careers in general and the many jobs that are available within those careers. No single career works for everyone. Some people engage in only a single career during their lives while others may switch one or more times. While most people always work for others, some people operate their own businesses, and others do some of each. You have to discover which alternative best suits you.

CAREERS

If you tend to think more about a job than a career, you are not unusual. Yet, you almost certainly will have a career. The term *career* simply refers to attitudes and behaviors related to work experience during your life.[1] Thus, it can be applied to every walk of life, and everyone can have a career. A secretary considering how to improve his or her current position and what that might lead to in a few years has a career in mind. A cook learning new recipes and trying to improve performance has a career. Whenever you are thinking about your current job and a future job and how to get from one to the other, you are thinking about your career. And think you should, because only by thinking about your career will you be able to control its various stages and accomplish what you want.

"Give me a fish, and I will eat for today; teach me to fish, and I will eat for the rest of my life."[2] Having a career goal is like learning to fish: It helps you make decisions that shape your life. Having a career goal enables you to adapt to changing conditions at work. It enables you to tolerate some of the boring, frustrating, and even unsafe parts of your job because you view those as necessary steps in moving from one stage of your career to the next. It can also help you to see that your current job is not contributing to your career so that you can better plan when and how to change jobs.

Career Choice

Your initial choice of a career is important, but careers can and do change. No choice is forever. The career you decide to prepare for and follow when you are 16 may be different from the one you select when you are 26. That one, in turn, may be different from the one that you choose at 36, 46, 56, 66, or even 76. But each time you change careers, there are certain factors you will want to consider. Job security is one factor. For example, you would probably not want to start a career in a dying industry such as the manufacture of manual typewriters or horse carriages.

One aspect of career choice is which sector of the economy in which to work. Every sector of our economy needs qualified people. Employment in agriculture has fallen, but agribusiness has grown. Other sectors have grown or fluctuated. The service sector, wholesale and retail trade, and state and local government have seen substantial increases in employment during the past 40 years. Employment in mining and the federal government has stayed relatively stable over that same period. You can also choose the military for part or all of your career. Military employment is substantial even in times of peace. Not-for-profit organizations, which have goals other than making a profit, need people, too. Religious, social service, and charitable organizations and foundations need people. You need to consider all sectors of the economy and all of these different organizations when making your career choice.

Choosing a Career

Making a career choice involves three steps. The first is understanding yourself including your skills.[3] The second is understanding possible careers and jobs. Finally, you must understand the fit between you and your career. Simple as this seems, it can be difficult to do, but you should try to go through this process periodically during your life.

Ask yourself what you really want out of life. Just exactly what are your overall goals and aspirations? Do you want to lead a calm, peaceful life? Do you want to invent something? Do you want to be rich? What would it take to achieve what you want? Do you have the necessary skills and abilities? Ask yourself what you find interesting and exciting—what do you like to do?

Now ask these same questions about many possible careers. What do the careers you choose require in terms of skills and abilities? What do they provide people in terms of emotional involvement and excitement? What are the goals associated with various careers? A career as a professional forester may lead to very different accomplishments than a career as a politician.

Finally, look for the fit between you and your career. Look for a match between your goals and those of different careers, as well as for matches in terms of interests. If you find one or more careers that match your goals and interests fairly well, examine the required skills and abilities. If you do not have those skills and abilities, can you get them by going to school or by reading about them? Counselors and books are available to help you work through these steps.[4]

Life Stages and Career Stages

Our lives take place in a series of stages—childhood, adolescence, young adulthood, adulthood, and senescence or old age. Each of these stages is associated with an age range, although the years are only approximate. For instance, childhood lasts until about age 13, adolescence until around age 25, and old age until we die. Movement from one stage to another can be turbulent, but things generally settle down again after each transition. Your wants and needs likely differ considerably from one stage to another.

Closely related to life stages are career stages. Career stages are even less exact than life stages in terms of the age at which they occur, and, of course, there is no career stage that corresponds to childhood. There are four career stages: exploration, establishment, maintenance, and decline.

Exploration During the exploration stage, you develop a better understanding of yourself and various occupations. People at this early stage are eager to succeed, ready to upgrade their skills through training of some kind, and generally young, although they won't be if a second career cycle is ready to occur. This stage continues through your first or entry-level job in this career cycle, which could include beginning your own business.

Establishment The establishment stage begins with a trial period—a continuation of the exploration stage. During this period you might hold several jobs as you learn more about the occupational choices available. After the trial period, accomplishment and advancement occur. Now you begin to settle down in a career, learning it, and performing well in it. You become less dependent on others and more independent. You start to form an occupational identity and establish relationships with others in the organization.

Job-hopping becomes common throughout this stage, and you may find that you can move up faster and earn more money by changing jobs. A former top executive at Walmart, Jack Shewmaker, held eight jobs in 11 years before joining Walmart. Afterwards, he stayed with Walmart, and rose from district manager in 1970, when he joined the firm, to president, a position he held from 1978 until 1984.[5] Job-hopping also is partly a function of companies going outside for top leaders. For example, Gould, Inc. recruited James F. McDonald from IBM to be its new CEO. In 1984, Digital Equipment Corporation brought in its new finance vice president from Ford Motor Company. A major consulting firm, the Hay Group, Inc., found that companies using outsiders in key jobs exceeded rate-of-return goals more often than those that relied on insiders.[6]

Maintenance The maintenance stage can follow one or more patterns—continued growth, leveling off, stagnation, or early decline. Career changes may result from the latter patterns, and you will start over again. People at this stage of their careers frequently begin to act as mentors for younger members of the organization, showing them the ropes and helping them along. They usually begin to re-examine their goals in life and to rethink their long-term career plans.

Decline The decline stage usually means the end of full-time employment and facing retirement and other end-of-career options. The overriding question is "What do I do now?" You may begin a new career or you may level off in your current career. Individuals at this stage generally begin to recognize that they are growing old and adjust in a variety of ways—some positive, such as helping others, and some not so positive, such as becoming indifferent or even giving up.

Career Development

Your career is important to you, and the careers of members of organizations are important to the success of those organizations. Career development is the careful, systematic approach to ensuring that sound career choices are made. It involves an individual element—career planning, and an organizational element—career management.

Career Planning Much like career choice, career planning is more detailed and involves carefully specifying how to move within a career once the choice has been made. How do you achieve success in your career? What is the route to follow? Does the area in which you begin matter? Are there certain positions in which you must be sure to gain experience? Some companies provide formal assistance in career planning.

First, develop a written plan. Think in terms of where you want to be at the end of some long-term period, say, 20 years. Now, in order to be at that point in 20 years, where do you need to be in ten years? Work backward to develop an answer; then work backward again to see where you need to be in five years and in one year. Knowing where you need to be in one year to achieve your 20-year goal should be vital information for shaping your decision today.

As you plan your career, you may become aware of deficiencies in your skills, experience, or abilities. You may discover, for instance, that to accomplish your ten-year objectives, you need to learn a foreign language. You can start learning now. Recognizing what your deficiencies are provides you with the opportunity to rectify them through training or by moving to a new job to gain additional experience.

You should review your career plan from time to time, perhaps every three or four years, but no less frequently than every five years. This will enable you to see whether you are accomplishing your objectives, whether you need to work harder, whether you need more training, development, and experience, or whether you need to rethink your objectives. This periodic review also serves to keep your long-term objectives in your mind so that they are not driven out by short-term crises.

If you are pursuing your career within an organization, you must develop your plan in conjunction with others in the organization. Talk with those with whom you work to get their advice. If your company has a formal career management system, check with those who administer it to see whether your plan makes sense within the organization.

Career Management Many organizations, including firms like AT&T, Bank of America, General Electric, General Foods, General Motors, and Sears, offer career management help.[7] Career management is distinct from training and development programs, which most companies provide either in-house (that is, they do the training themselves) or by sending employees to programs conducted by trade groups, universities, or consulting firms. Career management includes career counseling, career pathing, career resources planning, and career information systems.

Career counseling can be informal or formal. Informal advice from a superior to a subordinate is one form; another is from interviews and performance evaluation sessions. A more formal method is to have special career counseling, provided by a personnel department that is available to all personnel or only to those who are being moved down, up, or out of the organization.

Career pathing refers to the identification of coherent progressions of jobs—tracks, routes, or career paths—that are of particular interest to the organization. As with counseling, these may be either formal or informal. The organization may specify a path that follows a particular sequence; an example is a university that states that the positions of assistant professor and associate professor are the normal progression toward becoming a full professor. Or the path may be informal, in which case "everyone knows" that you must first hold jobs A and B to get to job C.

Although they are useful for planning purposes, career paths should not be taken as absolutes. The organization that changes *normally* to *must* is unable to recognize unique situations and exceptional talent when they occur. In the past, for instance, most executives got to the top by working in only a single firm, whereas today many executives have been with several companies on their way to the top. The increasing number of women in executive positions is also bringing changes in traditional career paths. A system that is not flexible enough to permit this will prevent some extremely talented people from reaching the top.

Career resources planning refers to the use of careful planning techniques in career management. The organization makes plans and forecasts of personnel needs, develops charts that show the planned progressions of employees, prepares inventories of human resource needs based on assessments of existing personnel, and monitors the implementation of these plans.

Career information systems are more than just internal job markets (which means that openings within the organization are announced on bulletin boards or in newsletters and memoranda, and members of the organization have a first shot at getting these jobs). Career information systems combine internal job markets with formal career counseling and the maintenance of a career information center for employees. Thus, a career information system can motivate as well as develop the organization's employees.

Companies that have formal career development programs generally are more effective in utilizing using their human resources than those that do not have such programs. Additionally, these programs enable organizations to cope with the numerous government regulations concerning human resources and to recognize and respond to a wide variety of career issues.

Special Career Issues

Women and Minorities All too frequently, women and minorities have felt that some careers were closed to them, most often because discrimination prevented people from those groups from entering those careers in sufficient numbers to set an example for others. When the potential pool of talent is artificially or arbitrarily reduced in some way, the economy suffers, because organizational effectiveness is not what it might be. Therefore, it is important to recognize that members of any group can and do succeed in all careers.

More and more women enter the workforce every year. More than half of the females over 16 years old are now employed, and nearly half of the working population now consists of women. Both of these statistics represent huge increases from conditions at the start of this century. For that matter, there has been significant growth in recent years. Many of these women own their own businesses. In fact, women-owned businesses were one of the fastest-growing parts of the American economy during the 1970s and 1980s. Despite the rapid growth and that nearly three million businesses are owned by women, relatively little is known about the career pattern of successful businesswomen.[8] And women certainly are not confined to small businesses; women have excelled even in some of the largest corporations in the United States.[9]

Executive search firms suggest that there are career differences between male and female corporate officers.[10] The men tend to be older and have been with their companies longer. One study found that both groups worked 55-hour weeks, although the men earned substantially more than the women. Further, most of the women felt that they had made great personal sacrifices to get where they were. Twenty percent had never married, as opposed to less than 1 percent of the men; 20 percent were separated or divorced, as opposed to about 4 percent of the men; 95 percent of the men had children, but more than half of the women were childless. Nevertheless, the number of female officers has risen dramatically over the past decade or so, and women have joined the boards of companies such as Black & Decker and Smith Kline Beckman Corporation.[11] Because there are different issues in the careers of men and women and because of gender discrimination, women need to be particularly attentive to planning their careers.[12]

Members of minority groups also succeed in a wide variety of careers. Government assistance exists in a variety of forms to help members of minority groups who are interested in starting and running their own businesses. The Minority Business Development Agency began in the Department of Commerce in 1969. The United States Department of the Interior, through the Bureau of Indian Affairs, began the Indian Business Development Fund in 1970 to help Native Americans secure funds for starting businesses. The Economic Development Administration began a Minority Contractors Assistance Program in 1971 to help minorities in the construction industry. Professional and technical assistance such as accounting and engineering help is provided under Section 406 of the Equal Opportunity Act. Some private groups, like the Cuban American Foundation, also are available to assist minorities in owning their own businesses.[13]

In summary, women and minorities can and do have successful careers. Perhaps they do face additional obstacles in their careers, but difficulties exist for men and whites as well. In recent years, research has suggested that the most important action for everyone to achieve career success is to be seen, to be visible, to be noticed, and to be appreciated by others in your organization.[14]

Dual Incomes and Dual Careers More than half of all adult females now work. Because many of these women are married, this means that large numbers of households now have two sources of income. The economic advantages of this are obvious. Indeed, in the absence of children, there are few, if any, financial disadvantages. Problems do occur when there are children, but many companies are taking steps to alleviate some of them by providing flexible hours, more generous personal leaves, daycare centers, and the like.

Most of the problems of dual-income families can be worked out. If a problem arises—for example, a child comes down with a long-term illness—one partner can drop out of the workforce and stay at home to nurse the child back to health. If both partners are pursuing careers, however, the situation changes radically. Interrupting a career is far more devastating than interrupting a series of jobs. Which career should suffer? Whose career is less important? The adjustment for the dual-career family is not easy or obvious, and sometimes one or both partners must make a serious sacrifice of long-term goals. Even such things as scheduling vacations can become problematic because both parties must take time off at the same time.[15]

The long-term illness of a child is not a problem most dual-career couples face, of course. Promotions and reassignments that involve transfers to new locations are far more common and can be extremely disruptive. One partner's career may best be served by taking the new assignment, but the other partner's career may best be served by remaining. Which career is more important? What if both people work for the same company and one is a far better performer? One is moving up rapidly, while the other moves slowly or not at all (or, even worse, gets fired). This kind of friction can tear a marriage apart.

Resolving these conflicts is not easy. It is particularly difficult now because not many people are experienced enough to offer advice, although some tentative advice is becoming available.[16] Obviously, a key element in dual-career families is to adopt a "family" or "we/us" view rather than an "I/me" view. This might mean deciding to relocate to help partner A now with the understanding that the next major career decision will help partner B. (Of course, when partner B's turn comes, partner A may get cold feet.)

JOB HUNTING

With all of this in mind, then, you are ready to begin your quest for a job. Job hunting can be a long drawn-out task, so it's best to approach it with the idea that you will eventually be successful. And you should not be discouraged if it takes longer than you initially anticipate. You need to understand yourself—your skills, your strengths and your weaknesses—in order to prepare an effective résumé and cover letters as well as to interview effectively. And, of course, you need to obtain information about industries and organizations to target your search for a job. The rest of this appendix sketches ideas to assist you with your job searching.

Self-Assessment

The key to useful self-assessment is honesty. Yet, despite our most honest efforts, we may not see ourselves as others see us. For this reason, it is useful to obtain the views of others, particularly others in the work environment, about our strengths and weaknesses. Try to combine both your views and those of others as you conduct your self-assessment.

What skills do you have that would appeal to a potential employer? How current are those skills? What knowledge do you have that would enable you to add value to an organization? How current is that knowledge? Make a list of these and highlight key words among those lists. Be sure that you consider knowledge and skills in technical, interpersonal, conceptual, diagnostic, communication, decision-making, and time-management.

Consider your priorities. You are seeking a job, but what would you give up to obtain that job? Are you willing to relocate? Is your family? Will you take a reduction in compensation? If so, how much? As you consider your priorities, think about issues such as your time; the job location; travel involved; potential for new challenges; potential for advancement; who your coworkers will be; to whom you will report; what the fringe benefits are including vacation, retirement, insurance, and the like; and how secure or stable the new job might be.

Consider your career goals. Where do you want to be in ten years? Five years? One year? Will this new job help you achieve those goals? Will it help you acquire knowledge and skills you need to achieve those goals? Will it open new opportunities and/or contacts for you that will assist you in achieving your goals?

Finally, consider the types of jobs and organizations with which you are most comfortable and those with which you are least comfortable. Do you prefer small organizations or larger ones? Do you prefer highly predictable hours and working conditions or a degree of uncertainty and flexibility? Do you prefer working with people, computers, equipment, "things," or "paper"? You can no doubt identify other job and/or organizational elements that you either prefer to have or prefer to avoid in a new situation. Make a list of those and keep it ready to refer to as opportunities arise.

Preparing Your Résumé and Applying for a Job

A résumé is a summary of your qualifications and experience for a job. There is no one correct way to prepare a résumé. Its very name clearly suggests that it is not a detailed accounting of everything that describes you and your credentials; it is a summary. Yet, there is not a fixed length for one. You strive for completeness and brevity in the same document, and the resulting length may be from one to perhaps four or even five pages. Old "rules" about only one page (or two) no longer apply in most fields, but you should be aware of the norm in your field and follow that norm.

In today's job market, you need two versions of your résumé. A nice, clean paper version to deliver to potential employers when asked and an electronic version to use for seeking a job online through the Internet. An electronic version of a résumé is known as an e-résumé and can be very useful for many job searches. You should recognize, of course, that many successful job searches have been and will continue to be conducted without the use of electronic searches.

These two versions differ not only in the media used but also in the nature of the content. A paper résumé emphasize verbs—action words—to call the reader's attention to what you have done. An e-résumé emphasizes nouns—name words—to enable people to find you easier with computerized search programs or engines. Your paper résumé might say that you taught workshops or that you came up with a new advertising slogan on you current job, while your e-résumé would say that you were a workshop instructor or that you are currently a copywriter in an advertising department. You also should be careful to avoid keyword (verbs or nouns) that provide information about political or religious affiliations or that suggest your views on controversial issues. You also should not include personal information about your appearance, marital status, or the like.

As you prepare your résumé, you will find that there actually are five versions of résumés in use today. Two paper versions and three electronic ones. The traditional paper résumé is formatted so that it is pleasant to look at—not cramped with text from top to bottom and side to side, nor with huge margins and lots of white space. Increasingly, though, organizations are asking for paper résumés that can be readily scanned into an electronic database. Scannable résumés have no boldfacing, underlining, italics, or fancy fonts. They should also not have columns or bullets because some scanners cannot handle those formatting devices.

An e-résumé is much like a scannable paper résumé. It should have little font variation and no graphics. Indeed e-résumés are best done in plain text or ASCII (pronounced *ask-ee*). A formatted e-résumé is also much like a formatted paper résumé. It contains fonts and graphics that indicate something about your personality. Finally, some e-résumés are done as Web pages. These typically are even fancier, but you should be aware that some organizations won't look at Web pages. You should also be aware that some sites for uploading or posting your résumé online have specific instructions that you must follow. If you don't re-do your résumé to fit their specifications, they will simply trash it and you will lose any opportunities that posting there would have provided. Follow any and all instructions provided by an organization. Don't assume that the organization will permit you to use whatever format or approach that you are most comfortable with.

The language you use in your résumé needs to be current. It tells prospective employers that you have kept your skills and knowledge up-to-date. Carefully consider what terms or phrases would catch a prospective employer's eye and then use these keywords on your résumé. Be sure to use the keywords in context, however, not merely in some sort of list. Also, be careful to avoid the repetitive use of keywords; they lose their impact if they are used repeatedly. Again, remember that keywords on paper résumés are verbs while those on e-résumés are nouns.

In terms of format, identify and follow the current practice in your field. E-résumés should have line lengths of no more than 65 characters (remember that spaces are characters). Easy fonts to scan, fax, and so on are Times New Roman and Courier. Use 10- or 12-point type size, and remember that a scannable paper résumé and a plain-text e-résumé will have only one font and type size in the whole résumé.

Current practice in your field is important for determining whether or not to have a career objective and/or an introductory paragraph. Some fields use one or the other, some use neither. Always put your most recent information first (reverse chronological order—your current job, then the one before that, etc.). An e-résumé may well be longer than a paper one because most will require a separate line for each piece of new information, whereas in some cases, it would be easy to put several items on the same line on a paper résumé.

The order of information may vary across fields, too. A common arrangement, however, is name, address, career objective or introductory paragraph (if common in your field), your work experience (most recent first), education (majors, minors, concentrations and institutions), hobbies and/or interests (this is optional and a lot of people don't use it; we recommend that you not include it unless it is very common in your field), references (at least indicate that you can and will furnish them if asked, and, of course, obtain permission before using anyone as a reference).

Once you have assembled the information and prepared a first draft, proofread, proofread, proofread! Résumés that have spelling errors, typographical errors, or grammar errors won't get you very far. If you prepare your résumé on a computer, use its spell-check program, but do not substitute that for proofreading. Before submitting your résumé, it is also a good idea to show it to friends or colleagues to get their reactions. They may notice something that you have overlooked.

Once you have completed your résumé, you are ready to apply for jobs. In some cases mailing or faxing your résumé along with a cover letter will constitute your application. (If mailing, be sure that the paper for your resume, cover letter, and envelope match.) In other cases, the organization will require you to complete an application form. Indeed, some organizations will require you to use only their application form and will not accept your résumé. Upon receiving your application, most organizations will send you an EEO/AA form to complete and send in. That information is used solely for providing reports to government agencies and is not used in the hiring process, so you need not have any concerns about filling it out. At this stage, some organizations may telephone you to ask specific questions beyond those on application forms.

If all goes well, you will be asked to come in for an interview. That, too, is an important step, so our next section provides some guidance on interviewing.

Interviewing

Always remember that the interview is a two-way process. The organization is getting information it wants and giving you information it wants you to have. You should give the information sought by the organization, but also ask questions to obtain information that you want beyond what the organization furnishes.

Before the interview, do your homework. Find out as much as you can about the organization, the industry in which it operates, and the specific job in which you are interested. Review your résumé and your qualifications for the job, and prepare answers to broad questions about yourself regarding the kind of work interests you most and how you plan your day. You can find potential questions in a variety of sources.[17] Rehearse potential responses, and practice interviewing with a friend or relative, if possible.

Be aware that there are several different types of interviews, and be prepared for each of them. First, there are structured or directed interviews and unstructured or nondirected ones. The structured/directed interviews follow a carefully constructed set of questions, and the interviewer will not deviate from that set. The unstructured/nondirected interviews are more informal and allow for more freedom of expression. Group or board interviews (two or more interviewers at once) are likely to be used when you will work in a collaborative environment (the former at lower organizational levels than the latter). Stress interviews may be used if the position is going to be one in which significant stress is likely to be encountered and the organization is attempting to determine how well you handle stress. Typically such interviews involve rapid-fire questions with little time to consider answers and tricky questions designed to be "turned back" on you. Some employers like to use stress interviews for all positions, and you should carefully consider whether or not you would be comfortable working for such employers. There are also telephone interviews. These may be any one of those above with the difference being that they are conducted by telephone instead of in person. Essentially all of the recommendations presented here (with the exception of how to dress) are as applicable to a telephone interview as one conducted face-to-face.

The day of the interview, be sure to leave early to ensure that unforeseen events don't cause you to be late. It is far better to be early than late. Be well groomed and dress appropriately for the type of organization and job. Don't snack while waiting, and don't chew gum or smoke. If you use a breath mint, dispose of it before the interview starts. Make sure that you have multiple copies of your résumé and your list of references in case more than one person is involved in the interview process.

Shake hands as you meet the interviewer(s) and make sure you remember his or her name. During the interview respond promptly but, if a question requires some thought before answering, by all means, take your time to think. Speak clearly, and listen carefully. Be truthful, but don't put yourself down. Show enthusiasm for the organization and the job as well as a willingness to be cooperative. Have your questions in mind—you may even have them on note cards to consult during the interview—and ask them when it seems appropriate. As the interview concludes, thank the interviewer.

After the interview, make careful notes of everything that was said. Points may emerge that are not clear and you need to be prepared to obtain clarification when (if?) your next contact occurs. Send a short letter of thanks within a day or so of the interview, and follow up with a telephone call a week or so after that. Finally, evaluate yourself so that you can do even better on your next interview.

GOOD LUCK!

From here, we wish you luck. Frequently that's what it takes at this stage, because there are so many qualified people seeking the same jobs. Be sure to follow up with prospective employers just in case.

VISUALIZING JOB FINDING SKILLS

JOB-HUNTING SKILLS IN ACTION—1

Your Assignment

Consider the first BizFlix film clip for the Transitioning From Managing to Leading chapter (Chapter 10).

In Good Company (2004) the complexities of corporate America unfold. A corporate takeover brings star advertising executive Dan Foreman (Dennis Quaid) a new boss who is half his age. Carter Duryea (Topher Grace), Dan's new boss, wants to prove his worth as the new marketing chief at *Sports America*, Waterman Publishing's flagship magazine. Carter applies his unique approaches while dating Dan's daughter, Alex (Scarlett Johansson).

Note how career or job-hunting skills are evident in this clip.

1. The clip starts with Carter Duryea entering Dan Foreman's office while saying, "Oh, my God, Dan. Oh, my God." Mark Steckle (Clark Gregg) soon follows. Mark is almost violently upset and threatens to fire Dan. Following an extremely tense interaction, the sequence ends with Carter asking, "Any ideas?" Dan Forman says, "One." Carter just put his job and career on the line. What career or job-hunting skills may he need if things go well? What if things don't go well?

JOB-HUNTING SKILLS IN ACTION—2

This exercise gives you an opportunity to think about job-hunting skills that may be involved as you or your classmates graduate.

Your Assignment

1. Think about career or job-hunting skills and try to identify a scene that illustrates a positive or effective use of such skills in a movie, TV show, or a video on YouTube.
2. Now do the same for a scene that illustrates a negative or ineffective use of such skills.

PRACTICING JOB FINDING SKILLS

SELECTING A JOB

This exercise requires you to use your skills in choosing a job for yourself.

Assume that you will soon graduate from college and have received three job offers, as summarized below.

- Offer No. 1 ($32,000)—an entry level position in a large company in a very attractive location. However, you see promotion prospects as being relatively limited, and you know that you are likely to have to relocate frequently.
- Offer No. 2 ($29,000)—a position with a new start-up company, which means working especially long hours. If the company survives for a year, however, opportunities there are unlimited. You may need to move occasionally, but not for a few years.
- Offer No. 3 ($35,000)—a position in the family business. You will start as a middle manager and you can control your own transfers, but you know that some people in the company may resent you because of your family ties.

Your Assignment

1. List the rewards or opportunities that you believe would result from each job.
2. List the downside or problems that you might anticipate with each job.
3. For the outcomes you noted in items 1 and 2, decide how important each reward or problem is to you. (*Hint:* Rank-order the positives and the negatives.)

4. Considering the positives and the negatives to which you gave the most weight, which job would you select from among these three offers?
5. What other outcomes will be important to you in selecting a job?

WHICH JOB?

This exercise gives you practice in defining problems and opportunities in order to choose a job from among several alternatives.

To make an appropriate job choice, the applicant first needs to understand his or her abilities, preferences, and goals. In this exercise, you get the opportunity to make a decision for someone else so that your risks are minimal. You could use the same approach, however, for your own job decision-making.

Your Assignment

Pat is nearing graduation. After months of sending out resumes and interviewing, Pat thinks that there are five possible job opportunities: BIG company, SMALL company, CITY government, FAMILY business, and starting her/his OWN business. Pat has made estimates of the probability of actually getting an offer for each of these and ranked the immediate desirability of each. In addition, Pat also has estimated the probability of his success in each job. Finally, Pat has given some thought to the long-term impact of the jobs; that is, which of these jobs is most likely to result in long-term career success or development. Because considerable time and other resources will be needed to finally secure the job, Pat needs to decide which job to pursue from this point. The figures Pat derived are shown below.

Job	Immediate Desirability Rank	Probability of Getting an Offer	Probability of Success on the Job	Long-term Career Impact
BIG	3	0.70	0.60	Moderate
SMALL	1	0.50	0.80	High
CITY	2	0.80	0.80	Moderate
FAMILY	5	1.00	0.50	Low
OWN	4	1.00	0.20	Unknown

1. Focusing on job success, use Pat's information to decide which job he/she should pursue.
2. Now do the same thing focusing on most likely final offer.
3. If you were Pat, what would you do? Why?

ENDNOTES

[1] Douglas T. Hall, *Careers in Organizations* (Santa Monica, Calif.: Goodyear, 1976).

[2] R. N. Bolles, *What Color Is Your Parachute? 2012: A Practical Manual for Job-Hunters and Career-Changers* (Berkeley, Calif.: Ten Speed Press, 2011).

[3] Diane Cole, "Assess Your Skills to Reduce Career Doubts," *The Wall Street Journal, The College Edition of the National Business Employment Weekly*, Spring 1990, pp. 7–8.

[4] One excellent book is R. N. Bolles, *What Color Is Your Parachute? 2012: A Practical Manual for Job-Hunters and Career-Changers* (Berkeley, Calif.: Ten Speed Press, 2011).

[5] H. Gilman and K. Blumenthal, "Two Wal-Mart Officials Vie for Top Post," *The Wall Street Journal*, July 23, 1986, p. 6.

[6] J. A. Byrne and A. L. Cowan, "Should Companies Groom New Leaders or Buy Them?" *BusinessWeek*, September 22, 1986, pp. 94–96.

[7] B. A. Duval and R. S. Courtney, "Upward Mobility: The GF Way of Opening Employee Advancement Opportunities," *Personnel*, May–June 1978, pp. 43–53; P. G. Benson and G. C. Thornton III, "A Model Career Planning Program," *Personnel*, March–April, 1978, pp. 30–39.

[8] D. D. Bowen and R. D. Hisrich, "The Female Entrepreneur: A Career Development Perspective," *Academy of Management Review*, vol. 11, no. 2 (1986), pp. 393–407.

[9] Anne M. Russell, "High-Tech Corporate Careers: Where Career Ladders Are Like Roller Coasters," *Working Woman*, May 1, 1989, pp. 55–86.

[10] "Male vs. Female: What a Difference It Makes in Business Careers," *The Wall Street Journal*, December 9, 1986, p. 1.

[11] "Women Directors Now Bring Strong Management Credentials to Boards," *The Wall Street Journal*, August 19, 1986, p. 1.

[12] Kathy Cannings and Claude Montmarquette, "Managerial Momentum: A Simultaneous Model of the Career Progress of Male and Female Managers," *Industrial and Labor Relations Review*, January 1, 1991, pp. 212–228; Gary N. Powell and Lisa A. Maniniero, "Cross Currents in the River of Time: Conceptualizing the Complexities of Women's Careers," *Journal of Management*, June 1, 1992, pp. 215–237.

[13] "Winning Friends and Influencing People," *Hispanic Business*, July 1, 1989, pp. 20–25.

[14] Walter Kiechel III, "The Importance of Being Visible," *Fortune*, June 24, 1985, pp. 141–143.

[15] Constanza Montana, "Career Couples Find Vacations Hard to Plan," *The Wall Street Journal*, August 4, 1986, p. A15.

[16] Ronya Kozmetsky and George Kozmetsky, *Making It Together: A Survival Manual for the Executive Family* (New York: Free Press, 1981).

[17] See, for example, M. Yate, *Hiring the Best* (Avon, MA: Adams Media, 2006).

GLOSSARY

A

absenteeism the rate at which employees do not show up for work

administrative model (*of decision making*) describes how decisions often actually are made; argues that managers (1) use incomplete and imperfect information, (2) are constrained by bounded rationality, and (3) tend to "satisfice" when making decisions

agreeableness a person's ability to get along with others

areas of management marketing, financial, operations, human resource, administrative, and other areas

authoritarianism the extent to which a person believes that power and status differences are appropriate within hierarchical social systems such as organizations

avoidance a negative consequence that employees avoid by engaging in a desired behavior

B

balance sheet lists the assets and liabilities of the organization at a specific point in time, usually the last day of an organization's fiscal year

behavior modification (OB Mod) an integrated procedure for using reinforcement theory

"big five" personality traits five fundamental personality traits that are especially relevant to organizations: agreeableness, conscientiousness, neuroticism, extraversion, and openness

bounded rationality decision makers are limited by their values and unconscious reflexes, skills, and habits

budget a plan expressed in numerical terms

burnout a feeling of exhaustion that may develop when someone experiences too much stress for an extended period of time

business-level strategy the set of strategic alternatives from which an organization chooses as it conducts business in a particular industry or market

C

centralization the process of systematically retaining power and authority in the hands of higher-level managers

charisma a form of interpersonal attraction that inspires support and acceptance

charismatic leadership assumes that charisma is an individual characteristic of the leader

coalition an informal alliance of individuals or groups formed to achieve a common goal

coercive power the power to force compliance by means of psychological, emotional, or physical threat

common strength an organizational capability possessed by a large number of competing firms

communication the process of transmitting information from one person to another

communication network the pattern through which the members of a group or team communicate

communication skills the manager's abilities both to effectively convey ideas and information to others and to effectively receive ideas and information from others

competitive disadvantage an organization is not implementing valuable strategies that are being implemented by competing organizations; organizations with a competitive disadvantage can expect to attain below-average levels of performance

compressed work schedule working a full 40-hour week in fewer than the traditional five days

conceptual skills the manager's ability to think in the abstract

concern for people similar to employee-centered and consideration behaviors

concern for production similar to job-centered and initiating-structure behaviors

conflict the result of a disagreement among two or more individuals, groups, or organizations

conscientiousness the number of goals on which a person focuses, including effective time management and meeting work obligations

consideration behavior show concern for subordinates and attempt to establish a warm, friendly, and supportive climate

content perspectives (*on motivation*) theories and concepts that address the question of what factors in the workplace motivate people

contingency planning the process of making decisions in advance regarding alternative courses of action to be taken if an intended course of action is unexpectedly disrupted or rendered inappropriate

contributions (*psychological contract*) what an individual offers to the organization—effort, skills, ability, time, loyalty, and so forth

control the regulation of organizational activities so that some targeted element of performance remains within acceptable limits

controller manager who is responsible for helping line managers with their control activities, for coordinating the organization's overall control system, and for gathering and assimilating relevant information

controlling monitoring the organization's progress toward its goals

control standard a target against which subsequent performance will be compared

corporate-level strategy the set of strategic alternatives from which an organization chooses as it manages its operations simultaneously across several industries and several markets

creativity the ability of an individual to generate new ideas or to conceive of new perspectives on existing ideas

crisis management the set of procedures the organization uses in the event of a disaster or other unexpected calamity

D

decentralization the process of systematically delegating power and authority throughout the organization to middle and lower-level managers

decisional roles entrepreneur, disturbance handler, resource allocator, and negotiator roles

decision making selecting a course of action from a set of alternatives

decision making the act of choosing one alternative from among a set of alternatives

decision-making process recognizing and defining the nature of a decision situation, identifying alternatives, choosing the "best" alternative, and putting it into practice

decision-making skills the manager's ability to accurately recognize and define problems and opportunities and to then select an appropriate course of action to solve problems and capitalize on opportunities

decision-making skills the manager's ability to correctly recognize and define problems and opportunities and to then select an appropriate course of action to solve problems and capitalize on opportunities

delegation the process by which managers assign a portion of their total workload to others

deliberate strategy a plan chosen and implemented to support specific goals

Delphi group used to form a decision from a consensus of expert opinion

diagnostic skills skills that enable a manager to visualize the most appropriate response to a situation

diagnostic skills the manager's ability to visualize the most appropriate response to a situation

distinctive competence something the organization does exceptionally well.

diversity exists in a community of people when its members differ from one another along one or more important dimensions

dysfunctional behaviors behaviors detract from, rather than contribute to, organizational performance

E

education early childhood, high school, college, graduate study, and/or continuing education that contribute to managerial effectiveness

effective making the right decisions and successfully implementing them

effective communication the process of sending a message in such a way that the message received is as close in meaning as possible to the message intended

effective strategies those that promote a superior alignment between the organization and its environment and the achievement of strategic goals

efficient using resources wisely and in a cost-effective way. For example, a firm such as Honda, which produces high-quality products at relatively low costs, is efficient

effort-to-performance expectancy the individual's perception of the probability that effort will lead to high performance

emergent strategy pattern of action that develops over time in an organization in the absence of mission and goals or despite mission and goals

emotional intelligence (EQ) the extent to which people are self-aware, can manage their emotions, can motivate themselves, can express empathy for others, and possess social skills

employee-centered leader behavior having interest in developing a cohesive work group and ensuring that employees are satisfied with their jobs

empowerment the process of enabling workers to set their own work goals, make decisions, and solve problems within their sphere of responsibility and authority

equity theory process theory that contends that people are motivated to seek social equity in the rewards they receive for performance

escalation of commitment adhering to a decision beyond a point after it has become clear that it is wrong

ethnicity refers to the ethnic composition of a group or organization

expectancy theory process perspective that suggests that motivation depends on two things—how much we want something and how likely we think we are to get it

experiences summer jobs while in school, internships, entry-level professional jobs, jobs from an earlier (different) career, and jobs to which a person is promoted and that contribute to managerial effectiveness

expert power derived from information or expertise

extinction occurs when a behavior is repeated because it is rewarded but then stops when the reward is removed

extraversion a person's comfort level with relationships

F

financial control concerned with the organization's financial resources

financial control the control of financial resources as they flow into the organization (revenues, shareholder investments), are held by the organization (working capital, retained earnings), and flow out of the organization (pay, expenses)

financial statement a profile of some aspect of an organization's financial situation

fixed-interval schedule provides reinforcement at fixed intervals of time, regardless of behavior

fixed-ratio schedule gives reinforcement after a fixed number of behaviors, regardless of the time that elapses between behaviors

flexible work schedules gives employees more personal control over the times they work

G

gainsharing programs designed to share the cost savings from productivity improvements with employees

general adaptation syndrome Three-stage process of alarm, resistance, and exhaustion

glass ceiling describes a barrier that keeps women from advancing to top management positions in many organizations

goal-setting theory process theory of motivation that assumes that behavior is a result of conscious goals and intentions

grapevine an informal communication network that can permeate an entire organization

groupthink occurs when the desire for consensus and cohesiveness overwhelms the goal of reaching the best possible decision

H

horizontal communication involves colleagues and peers at the same level of the organization

I

incentive pay plans individual incentive plans reward individual performance on a real-time basis

income statement summarizes financial performance over a period of time, usually one year

individual differences personal attributes that vary from one person to another

inducements (*psychological contract*) what an organization provides to the individual—pay, career opportunities, job security, status, and so forth

informational roles monitor, disseminator, and spokesperson roles

initiating-structure behavior clearly defining the leader–subordinate role so that everyone knows what is expected, establishes formal lines of communication, and determines how tasks will be performed

innovation the managed effort of an organization to develop new products or services or new uses for existing products or services

interacting groups and teams (*for decision making*) the most common form of decision-making group; an existing or a newly designated group or team is asked to make a decision

interpersonal roles figurehead, leader, and liaison roles

interpersonal skills the manager's ability to communicate with, understand, and relate to both individuals and groups

interpersonal skills the manager's abilities to understand and relate to both individuals and groups, as well as to motivate others to perform at their highest levels

intuition an innate belief about something, without conscious consideration

J

job-centered leader behavior paying close attention to subordinates' work, explaining work procedures, and having a keen interested in performance

job sharing two part-time employees share one full-time job

L

leader–member exchange (LMX) model of leadership stresses the importance of variable relationships between supervisors and each of their subordinates

leaders people who can influence the behaviors of others without having to rely on force or people whom others accept as leaders

leadership (*as a process*) the use of noncoercive influence to shape the group or organization's goals, motivate behavior toward the achievement of those goals, and help define group or organizational culture

leadership (*as a property*) the set of characteristics attributed to individuals who are perceived to be leaders

leading the set of processes used to get members of the organization to work together to further the interests of the organization

least-preferred coworker (LPC) measure Instrument used to measure leader behavior tendencies

legitimate power the power defined by the organization to be accorded to people occupying a particular position

levels of management top, middle, and first-line managers

locus of control the extent to which people believe that their behavior has a real effect on what happens to them

LPC theory the first truly situational theory of leadership; suggests style of leader behavior is a reflection of the leader's personality and that most personalities fall into one of his two categories—task oriented or relationship oriented by nature

M

Machiavellianism behavior directed at gaining power and controlling the behavior of others

management a set of activities (including planning and decision making, organizing, leading, and controlling) directed at an organization's resources (human, financial, physical, and information) with the aim of achieving organizational goals in an efficient and effective manner

management by wandering around practice of keeping in touch with what is going on by wandering around and talking with people

management teams consist of managers from various areas and coordinate work teams

managerial innovations changes in the management process by which products and services are conceived, built, and delivered to customers

manufacturing a form of business that combines and transforms resources into tangible outcomes that are then sold to others

Maslow's hierarchy of needs content perspective that suggests there are five levels of needs arranged in a hierarchy of importance

merit pay pay awarded to employees on the basis of the relative value of their contributions to the organization

motivation the set of forces that cause people to behave in certain ways

N

neuroticism the extent to which a person commonly experiences unpleasant emotions such as anger, anxiety, depression, and feelings of vulnerability versus poise, calmness, resilience, and security

nominal group used most often to generate creative and innovative alternatives or ideas

nonprogrammed decisions decisions that are relatively unstructured and occur much less often

nonverbal communication a communication exchange that does not use words or uses words to carry more meaning than the strict definition of the words themselves

O

openness a person's rigidity of beliefs and range of interests

operations control concerned with the processes the organization uses to transform resources into products or services

operations control focuses on the processes the organization uses to transform resources into products or services

oral communication takes place in conversations, group discussions, telephone calls, and other situations in which the spoken word is used to express meaning

organizational citizenship the behavior of individuals who make a positive overall contribution to the organization

organizational opportunities areas that may generate higher performance

organizational strengths skills and capabilities that enable an organization to conceive of and implement its strategies

organizational threats areas that increase the difficulty of an organization's performing at a high level

organizational weaknesses skills and capabilities that do not enable an organization to choose and implement strategies that support its mission

organization change any substantive modification to some part of the organization

organizing determining how to group and coordinate activities and resources

outcomes in expectancy theory, the perceived consequences of motivated behavior

P

participation occurs when employees have a voice in decisions about their own work

participation the process of giving employees a voice in making decisions about their own work

path–goal theory of leadership suggests that the primary functions of a leader are to make valued or desired rewards available in the workplace and to clarify for the subordinate the kinds of behavior that will lead to goal accomplishment and valued rewards

performance behaviors the total set of work-related behaviors that the organization expects the individual to display

performance-to-outcome expectancy the individual's perception that performance will lead to a specific outcome

personality the relatively stable set of psychological attributes that distinguish one person from another

personal skills centered around and drawn from self-awareness, emotional intelligence, values, ethics, priorities, motivation, and self-control

person-job fit the extent to which the contributions made by the individual match the inducements offered by the organization

piece-rate incentive plan the organization pays an employee a certain amount of money for every unit she or he produces

planned change change that is designed and implemented in an orderly and timely fashion in anticipation of future events

planning setting an organization's goals and deciding how best to achieve them

positive reinforcement a method of strengthening behavior by providing a reward or a positive outcome after a desired behavior is performed

postaction control focuses on the outputs of the organization after the transformation process is complete

power the ability to affect the behavior of others

preliminary control concentrates on the resources—financial, material, human, and information—the organization brings in from the environment

prioritization the ability to understand the relative importance of different goals and activities

problem-solving teams temporary teams established to attack specific problems in the workplace

process perspectives (*on motivation*) theories and concepts that focus on why people choose certain behavioral options to satisfy their needs and how they evaluate their satisfaction after they have attained these goals

product development teams combinations of work teams and problem-solving teams that create new designs for products or services that will satisfy customer needs

programmed decisions decisions that are relatively structured or recur with some frequency (or both)

psychological contract the overall set of expectations held by an individual with respect to what he or she will contribute to the organization and what the organization will provide in return

punishment a negative consequence following undesired behavior

R

ratio analysis the calculation of one or more financial ratios to assess some aspect of the financial health of an organization

rational model of decision making a prescriptive approach that tells managers how they should make decisions; it rests on the assumptions that managers are logical and rational and that they make decisions that are in the best interests of the organization

reactive change piecemeal response to circumstances as they develop

referent power based on identification, imitation, loyalty, or charisma

reinforcement theory suggests that behavior that results in rewarding consequences is likely to be repeated, whereas behavior that results in punishing consequences is less likely to be repeated

resource deployment (*as part of strategy*) specifies how the organization will distribute its resources across the areas in which it competes

reward power the power to give or withhold rewards

reward system the formal and informal mechanisms by which employee performance is defined, evaluated, and rewarded

risk uncertainty about future events

risk management the process of protecting the firm and its assets by reducing the potential consequences of risky future events

risk propensity the extent to which a decision maker is willing to gamble when making a decision

risk propensity the degree to which a person is willing to take chances and make risky decisions

risk propensity the degree to which an individual is willing to take chances and make risky decisions

S

satisficing decision makers tend to search only until they identify an alternative that meets some minimum standard of sufficiency rather than conducting an exhaustive search for the best possible alternative

scope (*as part of strategy*) specifies the range of markets in which an organization will compete

screening control focuses on meeting standards for product or service quality or quantity during the actual transformation process itself

self-awareness the extent to which we are aware of how we are seen by others

self-efficacy a person's belief about his or her capabilities to perform a task self-esteem the extent to which a person believes that he or she is a worthwhile and deserving individual

service organization one that transforms resources into an intangible output and creates time or place utility for its customers

state of certainty (*in decision making*) situation in which the decision maker knows with reasonable certainty what the alternatives are and what conditions are associated with each alternative

state of risk (*in decision making*) situation in which the availability of each alternative and its potential payoffs and costs are all associated with probability estimates

state of uncertainty (*in decision making*) situation in which the decision maker does not know all the alternatives, the risks associated with each, or the likely consequences of each alternative

strategic control focuses on how effectively the organization's corporate, business, and functional strategies are succeeding in helping the organization meet its goals

strategic imitation the practice of duplicating another firm's distinctive competence and thereby implementing a valuable strategy

strategic leadership the capability to understand the complexities of both the organization and its environment and to lead change in the organization in order to achieve and maintain a superior alignment between the organization and its environment

strategic management a way of approaching business opportunities and challenges—a comprehensive and ongoing management process aimed at formulating and implementing effective strategies

strategy a comprehensive plan for accomplishing an organization's goals

strategy formulation the set of processes involved in creating or determining the strategies of the organization

strategy implementation the methods by which strategies are operationalized or executed within the organization

stress an individual's response to a strong stimulus

structural control concerned with how the elements of the organization's structure are serving their intended purpose

substitutes for leadership identifies situations in which leader behaviors are neutralized or replaced by characteristics of the subordinate, the task, and the organization

sustained competitive advantage a competitive advantage that exists after all attempts at strategic imitation have ceased

SWOT an acronym for strengths, weaknesses, opportunities, and threats

T

team a small number of people with complementary skills who are committed to a common purpose, performance goals, and approach for which they hold themselves mutually accountable

technical innovations changes in the physical appearance or performance of a product or service, or of the physical processes through which a product or service is manufactured

technical skills the manager's abilities to perform or understand relatively concrete tasks that require specialized knowledge

technical skills the skills necessary to perform or understand relatively concrete tasks that require specialized knowledge

technology consists of the conversion processes used to transform inputs (such as materials or information) into outputs (such as products or services)

telecommuting allowing employees to spend part of their time working offsite, usually at home

time-management skills the manager's ability to prioritize work, to work efficiently, and to delegate appropriately

transformational leadership leadership that goes beyond ordinary expectations by transmitting a sense of mission, stimulating learning experiences, and inspiring new ways of thinking

turnover the rate at which people quit their jobs

two-factor theory of motivation content perspective based on two different dimensions, one ranging from satisfaction to no satisfaction and the other ranging from dissatisfaction to no dissatisfaction

Type A individuals who are extremely competitive, very devoted to work, and have a strong sense of time urgency

Type B individuals who are less competitive, less devoted to work, and have a weaker sense of time urgency

V

valence in expectancy theory, an index of how much an individual values a particular outcome

variable-interval schedule uses time as the basis for reinforcement, but the time interval varies from one reinforcement to the next

variable-ratio schedule varies the number of behaviors needed for each reinforcement

variable work schedules deviation from the traditional work schedule that starts at 8:00 or 9:00 in the morning and ends at 5:00 in the evening, five days a week

vertical communication communication that flows up and down the organization, usually along formal reporting lines

virtual teams teams that may never actually meet together in the same room—their activities take place digitally via teleconferencing and other electronic information systems

Vroom's decision tree approach uses decision trees to determine the degree to which subordinates should be encouraged to participate in decision making based on characteristics of the situation

W

work teams tend to be permanent and are the teams that do the daily work of an organization

written communication relies on written media such as letters, memos, reports, emails, and web posting

INDEX

A

AACSB (American Assembly of Collegiate Schools of Business), 6
Abercrombie & Fitch, 155, 206, 292
Absenteeism, 124–125
Accountability
 delegation process and, 59 (figure)
 too much, as resistance to control, 207
Accounting and financial management, 329–331
Accuracy, effective control and, 205–206
Achievement-oriented leader, 374
Activities
 controlling, monitoring and evaluating, 16
 organizing resources and, 15–16
Adaptation, as purpose of control, 199
Adidas, 290
Administrative managers, 14
Administrative model, 288–289
Advanced Micro Devices, 155
Aer Lingus, 383
Affinity diagrams, in decision-making (exercise), 306–307
A.G. Edwards, 372
Age, as dimension of diversity, 115
Aging U.S. workforce (figure), 116
Agreeableness, as personality trait, 35–36
Airbus, 202, 203, 204, 283, 285, 286, 287
Aladdin (movie), 329
Allaire, Paul, 384
All channel pattern of communication (figure), 247
Alstead, Troy, 13
Alternative dispute resolution, 123–124
Alternatives, decision making
 evaluating, 285–286
 identifying, 285
 implementing, 287–288
 recognizing and defining, 285
 selecting, 286–287
Alukos, Basili (quote), 338
Amalfitano, Richard, 345
Amazon.com, 10
American Airlines, 166
American Assembly of Collegiate Schools of Business, 6
American Express, 207
American Messenger, 89–90
Americans with Disabilities Act of 1990, 117
America Pop Inc., 21
AmeriHost, 21
Amnesty International, 44–45
Amoco, 211
Analytical decision-making style, 316
Anderson, Abram, 135–136
Apple Computer, 162, 165
Application growth, 162
Application launch, 161–162
Areas of management, 14
Arkin, Alan, 216
Arthur Andersen, 284
Artificial intelligence, 344
Art of management, 32–33
Assessment. *See* Self-assessment
Associated Press, 14
Atkinson, J.W., 140–141
Atlantis: The Lost Empire (movie), 329
AT&T, 66, 212
Auditory learning style, 48
Authoritarianism, as personality trait, 38
Authority, delegation and, 59 (figure)
Avoidance, reinforcement, 208
Ayling, Robert, 383

B

Babcock International, 382
Baby boom generation, 115, 120
Baby Mama (movie), 255
Baesler, Randy (quote), 286
Balance sheet, 332
Ballmer, Steve (quote), 60
Banyu, 180
Barriers to communication
 individual, 252–253
 organizational, 253–254
 overcoming (table), 254
 table, 253
Battelle, 225
Battle Creek Toasted Corn Flake Company, 178–179
Baymont Inns, 21
Beatrice Company, 369
Because I Said So (movie), 256
Beecham Group, 123
Behavior, leader/leadership
 leader-member exchange (LMX) approach, 375–376
 leadership grid, 371–372
 LPC theory of, 372–374
 Michigan studies, 370
 Ohio State studies, 370–371
 path–goal theory, 374–375
Behavior, managing workplace
 organizational citizenship, 125
 outcome of interpersonal, 105–106
 performance behaviors, 124
Behavior, understanding others' (exercise), 173–174
Behavior Activity Profile, type A measure, 94–95
Behavioral decision-making style, 316
Behavioral process, decision making and
 administrative model, 288–289
 coalitions and decision making, 289
 escalation of commitment, 290
 ethics and decision making, 291
 intuition and, 289–290
 risk propensity and decision making, 291
Behavioral stress, 65
Behavior modification
 defined, 210
 programs, 210
Belongingness needs, 108–109
Bergin, Patrick, 216
Best alternative, decision making and, 281
Best Apparel of Seattle, 134
Best Buy, 12
Big five personality traits
 agreeableness, 35–36
 conscientiousness, 36
 defined, 35
 extraversion, 36–37
 figure, 36
 neuroticism, 36
 openness, 37
Birthrates, declining, 115
Bissinger, H. G., 126, 379
BizFlix films, 126, 171, 216, 255, 298, 345, 379
Black, Lucas, 126
Blankfein, Lloyd (quote), 64
Blumenthal, Neil, 11
BMW, 41
Body language
 communication and, 244
 nonverbal communication and, 252
Body Shop, 44–45
Boeing, 41, 119, 199, 202, 283, 285, 286, 287
Booth, Lewis (quote), 34
Bounded rationality, 288
Branson, Richard (quote), 374
Breakeven analysis, 338–339
 cost factors use in (figure), 338
 figure, 338
Brin, Sergey, 15
British Airways, 383
British Petroleum, 211, 297
Brodsky, Norm, 59–60
Broyhill furniture, 328
Budget(s)
 apply technical skills to (exercise), 346
 defined, 329
 developing in organizations (figure), 331
 financial forecasting, 334–336. *See also* Financial forecasting
 financial statements, 332
 ratio analysis, 332
 types of (figure), 330
Bundy, McGeorge, 130–131
Burch, Tory (quote), 155
Bureau of Labor Statistics, 299–300
Burnout, as consequence of stress, 65–66
Busfield, Timothy, 299
Bush, George W., 221, 377
Business-level strategy, 156

C

Cameron, D., 269–270
Campbell, Joseph, 135–136
Campbell Soup Company, 135–136
Canon camera, 163, 244
Career choices, making (exercise), 299–300
Carter Hawley Hale Stores, 88
Casey, Jim, 89–90
Cash, James (quote), 105
Casino (movie), 345
Catalyst organization, 88–89
Caterpillar, 41, 166–167, 169
Causal modeling, forecasting technique, 334–335

Cause and effect, understanding relationships, 197–198 (figure)
CBS broadcasting, 41
Cellular telephones, 249
Cendant Hotel Group, 21
Centralization/decentralization (diagnostic skills exercise), 217–218
Century 21 real estate, 41
Chain pattern, communication (figure), 247
Challenger space shuttle, 294
Chambers, John (quote), 61
Champion Spark Plug Company, 205, 206
Change
  manage during (exercise), 127
  organization, weighing alternatives (exercise), 222–223
  resistance to, innovation and, 164
  surviving in period of (exercise), 128–129
Change, managing
  comprehensive approach to, 167–168
  external forces, 166
  internal forces, 166
  Lewin change model, 167
  organizational, 165–166
  resistance to, 168–169
  planned *vs.* reactive, 166–167
  steps in the change process (figure), 167
Channels of communication, 244
Charisma
  assessing your (exercise), 364–365, 386
  defined, 377
Charismatic leadership, 377
Charlie Wilson's War (movie), 171
Cheating, conceptual skills and (exercise), 175–176
Chevrolet Gear and Axle, 207
Chevron, 9
Chick-fil-A, 125
Chief executive officer (CEO), 13
Chief information officer, 248–249
Chiron, 155
Chrysler, 119, 206
Citicorp, 41
Citizenship, organizational, 125
Civil Rights Act of 1964, 115
Clark, Richard T., 180
Claude Ryan, 89–90
Clifford, Clark M., 130–131
Clinton, Bill, 377
Cluster chain, of grapevine communication, 250
Coalitions, decision making and, 289
Coca-Cola, 41
Coercive power, 220, 369
Colgate-Palmolive, 120, 165, 343
Colgate Venture Company, 165
Common strength, 157
Common team reward system, 214
Communication
  across time zones (exercise), 262
  decision making and, 302–303
  decision making and, in small business (exercise), 308–309
  defined, 242
  effectiveness, improving, 254–255
  effectiveness, time-management skills (exercise), 75–76
  electronic, 248–249
  gender differences in (self-assessment), 240–241, 269–270
  horizontal, 248
  improving individual skills, 254
  improving organizational, 254–255
  interpersonal, in organizations, 244–246
  listening skills (figure), 255
  managing organizational, 252–255
  meaning of, 242–243
  in networks and teams, 246–247
  nonverbal, 251–252
  organizational barriers to, 253–254
  overcoming barriers to (figure), 254
  overcoming resistance to change and, 169
  process, 243 (figure), 244
  role in management, 242–243
  selecting modes of (exercise), 127–128
  style, self-assessment, 237–239, 268–269
  two-way, 254
  using (exercises), 256–262
  vertical, 247–248
Communication network, 246
Communication skills
  assessing your (exercises), 236–241, 268–270
  as core management skill, 10 (figure)
  defined, 11
  diversity in the workplace, 118
  practice (exercises), 256–262
  using (exercises), 262–264
Comparison, equity theory and, 113
Competitive advantage, 157
Competitive disadvantage, 158
Competitiveness, as conflict in the workplace, 121–122
Competitive parity, 157
Compressed work schedules, 211
Compromise, conflict and, 123
Conant, Douglas R., 136
Conaty, William (quote), 114
Concepts NREC, 339
Conceptual decision-making style, 316
Conceptual skills
  behavior, understanding others' (exercise), 173–174
  to cheat or not (exercise), 175–176
  as core management skill, 10 (figure)
  defined, 11
  extending your (exercises), 181–182
  factors affecting organizational design (exercise), 176
  goal-setting questionnaire (exercise), 146–147
  job values as perceived by students and employers (exercise), 174–175
  learning from other organizations, 175
  making predictions (exercise), 176–177
  management functions, (exercises), 172–178
  quality and financial performance, relationship between (exercise), 177–178
  self-assessment, 182–184
  teams, determine why successful (exercise), 178
  think about (exercise), 172
  using (exercises), 178–181
  visualizing (exercise), 171
Concern
  for people, 372
  for production, 372
Conflict, managing
  causes of, 121–122
  methods for (table), 122
  nature of, 121
  organizational, nature of (figure), 121
Confrontation, conflict and, 123–124
Connor, Marcia, 48
Conoco, 225
Conscientiousness, as personality trait, 36
Consequences, alternatives in decision making, 286
Consideration behavior, 371
Consolidated Edison, 41
Consolidated Freightways, 41
Consumer Digital Imaging Group, 22
Content perspectives on motivation
  defined, 108
  needs hierarchy approach, 108–109
  two-factor theory, 109–110
Continental Airlines, 14, 200, 282
Contingencies and crisis, decision making during, 296–298
Contingency factors, in LPC theory (figure), 373
Contingency planning
  defined, 296
  figure, 297
Contributions, psychological contract and, 106
Control
  characteristics of effective, 205–206
  diagnostic skills and, 199–201
  managing, 206–207
  operations. *See* Operations control
  understanding, technical skills (exercise), 324–325, 359
Controller, 201
Controlling
  defined, 16
  figure, 15
Control standards
  compare performance against, 203
  corrective action, determine need for, 203–204
  defined, 201–202
  measure performance, 203
Control systems
  decision making (exercise), 303–304
  designing, diagnostic skills, 201–203
Convergent thinking, 159
Coppola, Sophia, 126
Core management skills
  communication, 11
  conceptual, 11
  decision-making, 11–12
  diagnostic, 11
  figure, 10
  interpersonal, 10–11
  technical, 12
  time-management, 9–10
Corning Glass, 205, 215
Corporate-level strategy, as strategic alternative, 156
Correll, A. D., 166
Costner, Kevin, 298–299
Cost reduction decisions (exercise), 304
Costs
  fixed, 338
  minimizing, control and, 200
Cottage industry, 249
Co-variation, 198
Coverage ratios, 332
Covey, Stephen, 70
Creative process
  figure, 159
  insight, 160
  preparation, 159–160
  verification, 160
Creativity, conceptual skills (exercise), 147–150
Creativity, managing
  creative individual, 159
  creative process, 159–160
  enhancing creativity in organizations, 160–161
Credibility, lack of, barriers to communication and, 253
Crisis management, 296
Cross-cultural leadership, 378
Culinova, 165
Cultural differences, communication skills (exercise), 262–263
Culture
  cross-cultural leadership and, 378
  nonverbal communication and, 252
  organizational, innovation and, 165
  in the workplace, 117–118
Curie, Irene, 159
Curie, Marie, 159
Curie, Pierre, 159
Customer-evaluation, qualitative forecasting, 335

D

DAFT management, 20
Dansereau, Fred, 375–376
Data, use Internet to obtain (exercise), 348–349
Days Inn, 21
Debt ratios, 332
Decentralization-centralization
  continuum, 60–61
  diagnostic skills exercise, 217–218
Decisional roles, 17–18, 243
Decision-making
  announcing unpopular, communication skills (exercise), 260–261
  behavioral process and, 288–291. *See also* Behavioral process, decision making and
  communicating a (exercise), 258
  conditions (figure), 283
  contingencies and crisis, 296–298

defined, 281
ethics in (diagnostic skills exercise), 219
group and team, 292–294
participation in, decision trees, 294–296
participative and group, 291–294. *See also* Participative and group decision making
rational model of, 284–288. *See also* Rational model of decision making
understanding (exercise), 131
Decision-making context
about, 281–282
conditions for making decisions, 282–284
kinds of decisions, 282
Decision-making process
defined, 281
evaluating alternatives in (figure), 286
following up and evaluating results, 288
Decision-making skills
choosing team members, 300–302
communicating and, in small business, 308–309
communication and, 302–303
as core management skill, 10 (figure)
cost reduction decisions, 304
defined, 11–12, 281
evaluating training, 305
extending (exercises), 312–313
financial forecasting and, 338
individual *vs.* nominal group decision making, 306
journaling and affinity diagrams, 306–307
making career choices, 299–300
organization, designing new, 307–308
organizational control, examining, 303–304
planning and, 15
rational model of, 284–288
risk management, 170
self-assessments, 274–280
using (exercises), 309–311
visualizing (exercises), 298–299
Decision-making styles
exercises, 274, 278–280, 314–315, 316–317
figure, 295
Decision-making tools, financial forecasting, 341–344
artificial intelligence, 344
decision trees, 342–343
distribution models, 344
game theory, 344
inventory models, 343
payoff matrices, 341–342
queuing models, 343–344
Decision situation, recognizing, 285
Decision trees, 294–296, 342–343
Delegation, effective
defined, 58
problems in, 59–60
process of, 58–59
reasons for, 58
Deliberate strategy, 156
Dell, Michael, 41, 155, 252
Dell Computer, 41, 155, 204–205, 252, 330
Delphi group, 292–293
Delta Air Lines, 122, 166
Demands that cause stress (exercise), 73–74
De Niro, Robert, 345
Dense code, UPS, 90
Dependent variables, 334
Descriptive procedure, financial forecasting, 338
Diagnosing problems (exercise), 222
Diagnostic skills
assessing, organization management, 190–191
as core management skill, 10 (figure)
defined, 11, 197
practicing (exercises), 217–223
self-assessments, 227–229
using (exercises), 224–226
visualizing (exercises), 216–217
Differences, individual, 106–108
Digital Equipment Corporation, 119
Directive decision-making style, 316
Directive leader behavior, 374–375
Disabilities, diversity and, 117
Discrimination, racial, in the workplace, 115
Discrimination/generalizability, as personal skill, 39
Disney, 282, 329
Disseminator, as informational role, 17
Distinctive competence, 155, 157–158
Distribution models, financial decision-making tool, 344
Disturbance handler, as managerial role, 18
Divergent thinking, 159
Diversity
aging U.S. workforce (figure), 116
defined, 114–115
dimensions of, 115–117
disabilities and, 117
discrimination, racial, in the workplace, 115
ethnicity and. *See* Ethnicity
immigration and, 117
reasons for increased, 115
religious beliefs and, 117
sexual orientation and, 117
working with, 117–118
Doomsday (movie), 345
Dorrance, John, 135–136
Douglas, Frederick, 159
Dow Chemical Company, 14
Drawing accounts, 213
Draw leadership (exercise), 380
Duke, Mike (quote), 14
Duke Energy, 297
Dunn, Brian, 12
DuPont, 180
Dutt, James, 369
Dysfunctional behaviors, 124–125

E

E. Merck, 179
Eastman Kodak, 22
Eastman Chemical, 22
Econometric modeling, 334–335
Edison, Thomas, 159
Education
overcoming resistance to change and, 169
role of, 33–34
skill development and, 31–32
using your skills, 44–45
Efficient, 9
Effort-to-performance expectancy, 11
Electronic communication, information systems, 248–249
Eli Lily, 14
Email, as form of communication, 245–246, 249
Emancipation Proclamation, 159
Emergent strategy, 156
Emery Air Freight, 210
Emotional intelligence, 38–39
empathy and, 39
managing emotions, 39
motivating oneself, 39
self-awareness, 39
social skill, 39
Empathy
emotional intelligence and, 39
in the workplace, 117–118
Emperor's Club, The (movie), 298–299
Employee-centered leader behavior, 370
Employee participation
decision making, 291–292
overcoming resistance to control, 207
Employees
motivating, 108–114. *See also* Motivating employees
rewarding diagnostic skills and, 208–215. *See also* Rewarding employees
Employee stock ownership plans (ESOPs), 215
Empowerment
defined, 291
motivation and, 210
techniques and issues in, 211
Encode meaning, communication, 244
Enterprise Rent-A-Car, 206–207
Entrepreneur
assessing personality traits of (exercise), 132–133
determine why individuals become (diagnostic skills exercise), 18–19, 218
as managerial role, 18
Environmental characteristics, path–goal theory of leadership, 375
Environmental factors, as barrier to communication, 253
Environmental Protection Agency (EPA), 42
EQ. *See* Emotional intelligence, 38–39
Equal employment opportunity, 117
Equicor, 372
Equity and justice, dealing with, (diagnostic skills exercise), 223
Equity theory of motivation, 112–114
Escalation of commitment, decision making and, 290
Esteem needs, 109
Ethical leadership, 378–379
Ethics
in decision making (diagnostic skills exercise), 219
decision making and, 291
issues in communication (exercise), 259
organizational code of, 40 (figure)
personal values, priorities, at work, 39–41
Ethnicity
as dimension of diversity, 115
minorities in the workplace, 116–117
trends in the U.S. (figure), 117
Evans, Martin, 374–375
Executive MBA programs, 33 (table)
Expectancy theory, of motivation
defined, 110
effort-to performance expectancy, 111
extension, 113 (figure)
figure, 111
outcomes and valences, 112
performance-to-outcome expectancy, 111–112
Expectations, price, quality and (diagnostic skills exercise), 221–222
Experience
role of, 34
skill development and, 31, 32, figure
Expert power, 369
Exploration in Personality (H. A. Murray), 140–141
External forces for change, 166
Extinction, reinforcement, 209
Extraversion
MBTI framework, 133–134
as personality trait, 36–37
ExxonMobile, 41, 330
Eye contact, nonverbal communication and, 252

F

Facebook, 11
Face-time, 89, 249
Facilitation, overcoming resistance to change and, 169
Facsimile machines, 249
Families and Work Institute (The National Study of the Changing Workforce), 88
Family, managing stress and, 66
Feasibility, alternatives in decision making, 285–286
Federal Emergency Management Agency (FEMA), 296–297
Federal Trade Commission (FTC), 42
Feedback, communication and, 254, 258 (exercise)
Feedback skills questionnaire (self-assessment), 239–240, 269
Feedback style, self-assessment, 193–195, 230 (interpretation)
Feeling, MBTI framework, 133–134
Fey, Tina, 255

Fiat S.p.A., 41
Fiedler, Fred (LPC theory), 372–374
Field of Dreams (movie), 298–299
Figurehead, 16
Film, Photofinishing, and Entertainment Group, 22
Financial budget, 329–330
Financial control, 200, 329
Financial forecasting
  activities and events for introducing new product, 340 (figure)
  breakeven analysis, 338–339
  causal modeling, 334–335
  decision-making tools, 341–344. *See also* Decision making tools, financial forecasting
  linear programming, 336–338
  Programing Evaluation and Review Technique (PERT), 340–341
  qualitative techniques for, 335–336
  sales and revenue, 332–333
  simulations, 339–340
  technological, 333
  time-series analysis (figure), 334
Financial managers, 14
Financial resources
  control and, 200
  defined, 9
Financial statements, 332
Five forces model, of competitive environment, 158
Fixed costs, 338
Fixed-interval schedule, reinforcement, 209
Fixed-ratio schedule, reinforcement, 209
Flexibility
  effective control and, 205
  of leader style, in LPC theory, 374
Flexible work schedule, 212
Flextime work, 88–89, 136
Force-field analysis, overcoming resistance to change and, 169
Ford Motor Company, 14, 41, 210, 284, 329
Forecasting techniques, financial. *See* Financial forecasting
Fortune magazine, 135, 180
Foster, Jodie, 171
Franchise agreement, negotiating (diagnostic skills exercise), 218–219
Friday Night Lights (movie), 126, 379
Friends, managing stress and, 66
Fuji Bank, 41
Fuji Photo, 159
Fulbright, Y. K., 269–270
Functional perspective on management
  controlling, monitoring and evaluating activities, 16
  figure, 15
  leading, motivating and managing people, 16
  organizing, coordinating activities and resources, 15–16
  planning and decision-making, 15

G

Gainsharing programs, 214
Game theory, financial decision-making tool, 344
Gardner, Cathey (quote), 109
GAS (General Adaptation Syndrome), 63 (figure)
Gates, Bill, 121, 131, 160
Gault, Stanley, 309–310
Gender
  differences in communication (self-assessment), 240–241, 269–270
  as dimension of diversity, 115
  glass ceiling and, 116
  pay equity and, 116
General Adaptation Syndrome, 63 (figure)
General Electric, 41, 120, 155, 156, 215
General Foods, 165
Generalizability/discrimination, personal skills and, 39
General Mills, 34, 178–179, 204, 354–355
General Motors, 41, 110, 122, 169, 289
Genesis Community Health, 42
Georgia-Pacific, 166, 200
German Corporate Employees Union (DAG), 311
Gilboa, Dave, 11
Gilbreth, Frank, 90
Gilmartin, Raymond, 155, 180
Girl Scouts of America, 42
Glaser, Jon, 256
Glass ceiling, 116
Goal difficulty, 114
Goals
  competing, conflict and, 123
  personal goal sheet (exercise), 77–78
  staircase your (exercise), 74–75
Goal-setting theory, 114, 184
Goal specific goal, 114
Good Company (movie), 379
Goodfellas (movie), 345
Goodyear
  decision making at, 309–310
  as manufacturer, 328
Google, 11, 15
Gossip chain, 250
Government organizations, management of, 42
Graen, George, 375–376
Grapevine, informal organizational communications, 250–251
Graphic Communications Group, 22
Great Society, 130
Gregg, Clark, 379
Gretsch, Joel, 299
Group and team decision making
  advantages and disadvantages, 293 (table), 294
  forms of, 292–293
  managing, 294
Group communication (exercise), 256–257
Group extensions
  communication skills, 265
  conceptual skills, 181–182
  decision-making skills, 312
  diagnostic skills, 226–227
  interpersonal skills, 137
  leadership skills, 385
  learning skills, 47
  managerial skills, 23
  technical skills, 356
  time-management skills, 91
Group reward system, 214
Groupthink, 293–294
GTE company, 88
Gutierrez, Carlos, 179
Gyllenhaal, Jake, 216

H

Habitat for Humanity, 39
Hackman, J. Richard (quote), 112
Haloid Photographic Company, 383–384
Hanks, Tom, 171
Hard Rock, 290
Harmsworth, A. W. St. John, 354
Harris Bank, 88
Health maintenance organizations (HMOs), 42
Health risks, as job stressor, 64
Healthcare, managing, 42
Hepatitis C Trust, 45
Hernandez, Jason, 13
Herring, Joanne, 171
Hershey, 155
Herzberg, Frederick, 109–110
Hewlett-Packard, 17, 164, 165, 212
High self-awareness, 35
Hirsch, Emile, 298
HMOs (health maintenance organizations), 42
Hoechst, 254
Hoffman, Philip Seymour, 171
Hoffmann, Gaby, 299
Holiday Inn, 21
Home Depot, 202
Honda, 9, 205
Horizontal communication, 248
Hoskins, Bob, 345
House, Robert, 374–375, 377
Human resource managers, 14
  communicating information (exercise), 259–260
Human resources
  control and, 200
  defined, 9
Hurricanes, Katrina/Rita, 296–297
Hygiene factors, satisfaction and, 109–110

I

IBM, 88, 212
ICI America, 180
Images, nonverbal communication and, 252
Immelt, Jeffrey, 155
Immigration, diversity and, 117
Important tasks, 70
Inamori, Kazuo, 46–47
Inappropriate focus, as resistance to control, 207
Incentive pay plans, 213
Incentive reward systems, 213–214
Income statement, 332
Incremental innovation, 162
Incubation, creative process and, 160
Independent variables, 334
Individual, creative
  background, experiences, creativity, 159
  cognitive abilities and, 159
  personality traits and, 159
Individual barriers, to communication, 252–253
Individual communication (exercise), 256–257
Individual differences, understanding
  defined, 107
  nature of, 107–108
  person-job fit, 107
  psychological contract, 106–107
Individual extensions
  communication skills, 265–266
  conceptual skills, 182
  decision-making skills, 312–313
  diagnostic skills, 227
  interpersonal skills, 137
  leadership skills, 386
  learning skills, 47
  managerial skills, 23
  technical skills, 356–357
  time management, 91–92
Individual skills, communication, improving, 254
Individual stress, consequences of, 65
Individual *vs.* nominal group decision making (exercise), 306
Inducements, psychological contracts and, 106
Industrial Light & Magic (ILM), 157
Inefficiency, rewards for, as resistance to control, 207
Informal communication in organizations
  figure, 250
  grapevine, 250–251
  management by wandering around, 251
  nonverbal, 251–252
Informational roles, 17–18, 243
Information distortion, power and, 370
Information resources
  control and, 200
  defined, 9
Information systems, 248–249
In-group, leader-member exchange, 375–376
Initiating-structure behavior, 371
Innovate, failure to
  lack of resources, 164
  opportunities, failure to recognize, 164
  resistance to change, 164
Innovation
  application, 161
  decline, 162
  defined, 161
  development, 161
  maturity, 162
Innovation, forms of
  product *vs.* process, 163–164
  radical *vs.* incremental, 162
  technical *vs.* managerial, 162–163
Innovation, managing
  failure to innovate, 164
  forms of innovation, 162–164
  innovation process, 161–162

process, figure, 161
product and process innovation, economic return and (figure), 163
promoting innovation, 164–165. *See also* Organizational innovation, promoting
Innovation process
application growth, 162
application launch, 161–162
development, 161
innovation application, 161
innovation decline, 162
innovation maturity, 162
Innovative attitudes scale (exercise), 150–152
Insight, creative process and, 160
Inspirational appeal, power and, 220, 370
Instrumental compliance, power and, 220, 369
Intel, 67
Interacting groups and teams, 292
Interdependence, conflict and, 123
Intergroup conflict, 122
Internal environment (exercise), 78
Internal-external control sampler (exercise), 274–275, 315
International Airlines Group, 383
International business, communication in (exercise), 260
International Harvester, 371
International Olympic Committee, 42
International operations, 14, 41–42
International training (diagnostic skills exercise), 225–226
Internet
to obtain data, technical skills (exercise), 348–349
as personal technology, 249
technical skills on (exercise), 346–347
at work, 40–41
Interpersonal communication, in organizations
form, choosing right, 245–246
oral communication, 245
written, 245
Interpersonal demands, as stressor, 65
Interpersonal dynamics, of organizations, 105
Interpersonal nature of organizations
about, 104–105
interpersonal dynamics, 105
outcomes of interpersonal behaviors, 105–106
Interpersonal problem solving, 123
Interpersonal roles
communication, 243
defined, 16
Interpersonal skills
change and, 127–128, 129 (exercise)
communication, selecting mode of (exercise), 127–128
conflict and, 121
as core management skill, 10 (figure)
defined, 10–11, 104
extending (exercises), 136–137
perceptual process (exercise), 129–130
personality traits, identify for jobs (exercise), 132
practicing (exercises), 127–128
self-assessment, needs, 100
using your (exercises), 134–136
visualizing, in action (exercises), 126
Intrapreneurship, in organizations, 165
Introduction to Motivation, An (Atkinson), 140–141
Introversion, MBTI framework, 133–134
Intrusions, in meetings, 61–62
Intuition
behavioral process, decision making and, 289–290
MBTI framework, 133–134
Inventor, 165
Inventory models, financial decision-making tools, 343
iPad, 14

J

J. C. Penny, 122, 123, 285, 287
Jago, Arthur, 294
Jha, Sanjay (quote), 378
JIT (just-in-time), 343
Job-centered leader behavior, 370
Job involvement, self-assessment, 100–101
Jobs, Steve, 131, 164
Job sharing, 212
Job skills, management skills, 19 (exercise)
Job values (conceptual skills exercise), 174–175
Johansson, Scarlett, 126, 379
Johari Window, 129, 130
John Hancock, 211
Johns Manville, 66
Johnson, David W., 135–136
Johnson, Lyndon Baines (President), 130
Johnson & Johnson, 180
Jokes, in the workplace, 118
Jones, James Earl, 299
Jones, Vinnie, 216
Journaling, affinity diagrams, in decision making (exercise), 306–307
Judging, MBTI framework, 133–134
Jury-of-expert opinion, qualitative forecasting, 335
Justice and equity, dealing with issues (diagnostic skills exercise), 223
Just-in-time (JIT), 343

K

Kansas City Royals, 286
Katrina (hurricane), 296–297
Keaton, Diane, 256
Keegan, Robert, 310
Kelco and Calgon Vestal Laboratories, 180
Kelleher, Herb, 34
Kellogg, creativity at, using conceptual skills (exercise), 178–179
Kellogg, John Harvey, 178–179
Kellogg, W. K., 178–179
Kelly Services, 41
Kelly-Springfield, 309
KinderCare Learning Centers, 41
Kinesthetic learning style, 48
King, John, 382
Kinnear, Greg, 255
Kinsella, W. P., 298–299
Kline, Kevin, 298
Kozlowski, Dennis, 38
Krispy Kreme, 155
Kroger, 344
K Shoes, 120
Kullman, Ellen, 225
Kyocera Corporation, 46–47

L

Lafley, A.G., 155, 246 (quote)
Lancaster, Burt, 299
Leader-member exchange (LMX) approach to leadership, 375–376 (figure)
Leader-member relations, 373–374
Leader(s)
defined, 367
as manager, 16
strategic, 155
Leadership
charismatic, 377
cross-cultural, 378
defined, 367
ethical, 378–379
management *vs.*, 367–368, 368 (figure)
power and leadership, 368–370. *See also* Power, leadership and
substitutes for, 376–377
traits, 370
transformational, 378
Leadership, situational approaches to
LPC theory, 372–374
path-goal theory, 374–375. *See also* Path-goal theory, of
Leadership behaviors, studies of
leader-member exchange (LMX) approach, 375–376
See also Behaviors, leadership
Leadership grid, behaviors, 371–372, 371 (figure)
Leadership skills (exercises)
analyze, 380–381
assessing, 364–366
draw leadership, 380
extensions, 385–386
managers and leaders, 381
struggles of using, 382–383
visualizing, 379–380
who are leaders?, 381–382
Xerox, 383–385
Leading
defined, 16
figure, 15
motivating and managing people, 16
Learning goals
exercises, 43–44
explore yours and others (exercises), 44
Learning skills (exercises)
assessing yours, 28–29
Body Shop and education, 44–45
extending, group/individual, 47
learning at Kyocera, 46–47
management, 21–22
what is your learning style?, 47–48
Learn More Know (Marcia Conner), 48
Least-preferred coworker (LPC) measure
defined, 372–373
favorableness and leader style, 373–374
favorableness of the situation, 373
figure, 373
flexibility of leader style, 374
Legitimate power, 368
Legitimate request, power and, 220, 369
Level of competitive rivalry, (five forces model), 158
Levels of control, 200–201
Levels of management, 13–14
Levi Strauss, 41
Lewin, Kurt, 167
Lewin change model, 167
Liaison role, of manager, 16
Likert, Rensis, 370
Lincoln, Abraham, 159
Lincoln Electric, 213
Linear programming, financial forecasting, 336–338
graphical solution (figure), 339
production data (table), 338
Lion King, The (movie), 329
Liotta, Ray, 298–299
Liquidity ratios, 332
Listening skills
more and less effective (figure), 255
poor, as barrier to communication, 253
Litchfield, Paul, 309–310
Little League Baseball, 42
Livengood, Scott, 155
LMX model of leadership, 375–376 (figure)
Locus of control, as personality trait, 37–38, 375
L'Oréal, 45
Loss, feelings of, resistance to change and, 168
Lost in Translation (movie), 126
Low self-awareness, 35
LPC theory, least-preferred coworker, 372–374. *See also* Least-preferred coworker (LPC) measure
Lucas, George, 157
Lufthansa, decision making in (exercise), 310–311

M

Machiavelli, Nicolo *(The Prince)*, 38
Machiavellianism, as personality trait, 38
Mackay, David, 179
Mackey, John (quote), 9
Management
areas of, 14
communication role in, 242–243
defined, 8
leadership *vs.*, 367–368 (figure)
risk. *See* Risk management
role perspective on, 16–18
science and art of, 32–33
scope of, 41–42
span of, technical skills (exercise), 349–350
what is?, 8–9

Management by wandering around, 251
Management functions, conceptual skills and
identify generalizations (exercise), 172
new business startup, choosing (exercise), 172–173
Management levels
first-line, 14
middle managers, 13
top managers, 13
Management perspective, functional, 15–18
Management skills
core, 9–12, 10 (figure)
extending, group and individual, 23
job skills, 19 (exercise)
motivation and (exercise), 128
organizational compass, 12–14
rate your basic, 4–6, 24
self-described profile of basic, 6–7, 24
think about, 20–21 (exercise)
using your, 21–22 (exercise)
Management teams, 119
Managerial innovations, 163
Managerial leader behavior questionnaire (exercise), 364–366, 387
Managerial roles, ten basic, 17 (table)
Managerial work, nature of, 19–20 (exercise)
Mintzberg on, 30
research, 24
Manager(s)
delegation process and, 59 (figure)
diversity, working with, 117–118
informational roles of, 17
as leader, 16
liaison role of, 16
roles of decisional, 17–18
types of, 14
Managing
change and (exercises), 127
control and. *See* Control, managing
emotion, emotional intelligence and, 39
group and team decision-making process, 294
innovation, 161–165. *See also* Innovation, managing
leading *vs.*, 367–368
meetings, controlling intrusions and, 61–62
stress, 62–67
teams, 118–120. *See also* Teams, managing
workplace behaviors, 124–125
Managing organizational communication, 252–255
improving effectiveness, 254–255
individual barriers to, 252–253
organizational barriers to, 253–254
Mandela, Nelson (quote), 369
Manufacturing, 328
Marketing managers, 14
Marriot, Bill, 251
Mars candy, 155, 204
Marshall, Colin, 382
Maslow's hierarchy of needs, 108–109
Massachusetts General Hospital, 180
Massey Ferguson, 41
Matsushita Electric Industrial Co., 157
Maxwell, Wayne, 14
MBA programs, 33 (table)
MBTI (Myers-Briggs Type Indicator), 37
McDonald, Bob (quote), 158
McDonald's, 34, 67, 161, 175
Mean Streets (movie), 345
Medicaid, 130
Medical consequences of stress, 65
Medicare, 130
Meetings
guidelines for effective, 62 (table)
scheduling, controlling intrusions and, 61–62
Mental abilities, assessing your, 29
learning and, 48
Merchants Parcel Company, 89–90
Merck & Company, 14, 124, 155, 203, 225
creativity at, 179–181
Merit pay, 212–213
Merit reward systems, 212–213
Metalloy, 199
Metropolitan Life Insurance, 41
Michigan studies, leadership behaviors, 370
Microsoft, 16–17, 121, 160, 212, 215
Middle managers, 13
Mintzberg, H., 16, 18, 19, 24, 30
Mitra, Rhona, 345
Model of skill development, 31–32
Monetary budget, 330
Monitor, as informational role, 17
Monsanto Company, 14, 41, 164
Moore, Mandy, 256
Motivating employees
content perspective on motivation, 108–110
equity theory of, 112–114
expectancy theory of motivation, 110–112. *See also* Expectancy theory of motivation
goal-setting theory, 114
leading and, 16
Motivating oneself, emotional intelligence and, 39
Motivation
defined, 108
empowerment and participation, 210
implications of reinforcement perspectives, 210
process perspective on, 110–114
reinforcement theory, 208
techniques and issues, in empowerment, 211
skills related to (exercise), 128
types of reinforcement, 208–209
Motivation factors, two-factor theory of, 110 (figure)
Motorola, 120, 248, 310
Mozart, 159
Mulcahy, Anne, 155, 282 (quote), 384
Murray, Bill, 126
Murray, H. A., 140–141
Murray's Manifest Needs, 140–141
Myers, Isabel, 133
Myers-Briggs Framework, personalities, 37, 133–134

N

Nabisco, 135–136, 168
Napoleon (quote), 290
Napster, 219
NASA, 14, 16, 294
National Labor Relations Board, 135
National Science Foundation, 42
National Study of the Changing Workforce, The (Families and Work Institute), 88
Nature *vs.* nurture, 35
Navistar International, 371
Needs
belongingness, 108–109
esteem, 109
hierarchy approach, to motivation, 108–109
relating needs to reality (diagnostic skills exercise), 217
security, 108
self-actualization, 109
self-assessment, 100
Negotiator, as managerial role, 18
Nestlé S. A., 41, 354
NetFlix, 212
Networks, communication in work teams and, 246–247
Neuroticism, as personality trait, 36
New York Times, The, 249
New York Times Company, 41
Nike, 290
Nikon, 163
Nintendo, 165
Nishi, Kazuhiko, 121
Nobel Prize, 159, 180, 288, 306
Noise, in communication, 244
NOK auto parts, 199
Nokia, 165
Nominal group
defined, 293
individual decision making *vs.* (exercise), 306
Nonprogrammed decisions, 282
Nonverbal communication, 251–252
Nordstrom, John W., 134–135
Nordstrom stores, 134–135
Normative approach, to financial forecasting, 338
Norton Simon Inc., 382
Not-for-profit companies, managing, 42

O

Obama, Barack (President), 221
Objective facts, 33
Objective function, linear programming, 338
Objectivity, effective control and, 206
OB Mod, 210
Occupational Outlook Handbook (Bureau of Labor Statistics), 128
Occupational Safety and Health Act of 1970, 264
O'Hara, David, 345
Ohio State studies, leadership behaviors, 370–371
Olive Garden, restaurant operations (case), 354–355
Omron Corporation, 159
Open-door policy, 61–62
Openness, as personality trait, 37
Operating budget, 330
Operating ratios, 332
Operational planning, 15
Operations managers, 14
Operations of control
defined, 200, 204
forms of (figure), 204
postaction control, 205
preliminary control, 204
screening control, 204–205
Opportunities, failure to recognize, 164
Oral communication, 245
Organizational barriers, to communication, 253–254
Organizational change
comprehensive approach to, 167–168
defined, 166
forces for, 166
planned *vs.* reactive, 166–167
weighing alternatives (diagnostic skills exercise), 222–223
Organizational characteristics, substitutes for leadership and, 377
Organizational citizenship, 125
Organizational climate, self-assessment, 191–193, 229–230
Organizational communication, 247–248
grapevine chains of communication in (figure), 250
horizontal, 248
management by wandering around, 251
managing, 252–255
nonverbal, 251–252
vertical, 247–248
Organizational compass, 12 (figure)
areas of management, 14
defined, 12
levels of management, 13–14
Organizational complexity, coping with, 200
Organizational design, factors affecting (conceptual skills exercise), 176
Organizational ethics, personal values, priorities and, 39–41
Organizational innovation
culture and, 165
intrapreneurship and, 165
reward system for, 164
Organizational management, self-assessment, 190–191, 229
Organizational opportunities, 158
Organizational skills, improving communication, 254–255
Organizational strategy, technical skills (exercise), 352
Organizational strengths, evaluating, 157–158. *See also* Strengths, organizational
Organizational structure preferences, self-assessment, 195–196, 230–231
Organizational threats, 158
Organizational weaknesses, 158
Organization-based fitness programs, 67

Organization control system, examining, (decision-making exercise), 303–304
Organizations
aging workers and, 115–116
conflict between, 122
decentralization–centralization, 60–61
designing a new, decision making (exercise), 307–308
developing budgets in (figure), 331
diversity and, 114–115
formal communication in (figure), 247
forms of communication in, 244–249
identifying technical skills needed in (exercise), 351–352
informal communications in, 249–252
interpersonal nature of, 104–106
intrapreneurship in, 165
learning from others, conceptual skills, 175
managing conflict in, 122–124
nature of conflict in (figure), 121
providing reinforcement in, 209–210
psychological contracts and, 106–107
stress management and, 66
Organizing
coordinating activities and resources, 15–16
defined, 15
technical skills (exercise), 347–348
Orient Steam Company, 382
OSHA, change and, 166
Outcomes, 112
Outgroups, in LMX model of leader behavior, 376
Overcontrol, as resistance to control, 206–207
Owen, Clive, 171

P

Pacific Gas & Electric, 41
Page, Larry, 15, 163 (quote), 210 (quote)
Pan American World Airways, 290
Parker Brothers, 161
Participation
decision-making trees, 294–296
defined, 291
motivation and, 210
overcoming resistance to change, 168–169
Participative and group decision making, 291–292
Participative leader behavior, 374
Path–goal theory of leadership
defined, 374
framework (figure), 375
leader behavior, 374
situational factors of, 374–375
Pauling, Linus, 306
Pay equity, gender and, 116
Payoff matrices, as decision-making tool, 341–342
Pepperidge Farm, 135–136
PepsiCo, 204
Perceiving, MBTI framework, 133–134
Perception, resistance to change and, 168
Perceptual process, understanding (exercise), 129–130
Performance
behaviors, 124
measure, 203
reward system to motivate, 212–215
Performance-based reward system, 215
Perot, H. Ross, 252
Perrier company, 353–354
Personal characteristics, path–goal theory, of leadership, 375
Personal conflict, in the workplace, 121
Personal electronic technology, communication and, 249
Personal goal sheet (exercise), 77–78
Personal identification, power and, 220, 370
Personality
assessing your (exercise), 133–134
big five personality traits, 35–37. *See also* Big five personality traits
Myers-Briggs framework, 37
personality traits at work, 37–38
types A and B, 63
Personality traits
authoritarianism, 38
creativity and, 159
identify for specific jobs (exercise), 132
locus of control, 37–38
Machiavellianism, 38
risk propensity, 38
self-efficiency, 38
self-esteem, 38
Personal risk taking, assessment, 152–153
Personal skills, development of, 31 (figure), 32
emotional intelligence, 38–39
generalizability/discrimination, 39
personality, understanding your, 35–38
personal values, ethics, and priorities, 39–41
self-awareness, 35
Person–job fit, individual differences and, 107
PERT (Program Evaluation and Review Technique), 340–341
Pesci, Joe, 345
Philip Morris Companies, 14, 211
Photocopying, 249
Physical condition, managing stress and, 66
Physical control, 200
Physical demands, as stressor, 64
Physical resources, 9
Piece-rate incentive plan, 213
Pien, Howard, 155
Pioneer, 225
Pitney Bowes Data Documents Division, 335
Planned change, 166–167
Planning
assessing your skills, 53
contingency (figure), 297
defined, 15
financial. *See* Financial forecasting
integration with control and, 205
self-assessment, 95
Plant managers, 13
Played (movie), 216
Plummer, Christopher, 171
Poehler, Amy, 255
Polaroid, 161
Poole, S., 269–270
Porter, Linda, 244
Porter, Michael, 158
Position power, 373
Positive reinforcement, 208
Postaction control, 205
Power
of buyers (five forces model), 158
of suppliers (five forces model), 158
using different methods of (diagnostic skills exercise), 220
using different types of (diagnostic skills exercise), 220–221
Power, leadership and
coercive, 369
expert, 369
leadership behaviors, 370–372
leadership traits, 370
legitimate power, 368
power, defined, 368
referent, 369
reward power, 368–369
using, 369–370
Power Bases Score questionnaire, 322–323
Predictions, making (conceptual skills exercise), 176–177
Preliminary control, 204
Preparation, creative process and, 159–160
Presentations
communication skills (exercise), 257
slide, communication skills (exercise), 261
President, 13
Price, quality and expectations (diagnostic skills exercise), 221–222
Prince, The (Machiavelli), 38
Prioritization
defined, 57
misjudging, 58
setting priorities, 57–58
of tasks, 70
time-management and (exercise), 80–88
Prizes, reward system, 214
Problem recognition, in decision making, 285
Problems, diagnosing (exercise), 222
Problem-solving
questionnaire (exercise), 275–278, 315–316
teams, 118–119
technical skills and, 353
Process perspective on motivation
defined, 110
expectancy theory, 110–112
Procter & Gamble, 34, 155, 210
Product and process innovation, effects on economic return (figure), 163
Product champion, 165
Product development teams, 119
Production data, linear, financial planning (table), 338
Productivity, quality and, defining, technical skills (exercise), 323–324, 348–349, 359
Profit, breakeven analysis, 338
Profit-seeking companies, scope of management in, 41–42
Profit-sharing approach, to rewards, 214–215
Programing Evaluation and Review Technique (PERT), 340–341
introducing a new product (figure), 340
network for introducing new product (figure), 341
Programmed decisions, 282
Prototypes, 160
Prudential Insurance, 14, 41, 169
Psychological consequences of stress, 65
Psychological contract
contributions, 106
defined, 106
figure, 106
individual differences and, 106–107
inducements and, 106
Public Broadcasting System (PBS), 42
Public relations managers, 14
Public Workers' Union (OTV), 311
Punishment, reinforcement, 208

Q

Qantas Airlines, 204
Quaid, Dennis, 379
Qualitative financial forecasting, techniques, 335–336
Quality
financial performance and (conceptual skills exercise), 177–178
relative to price and expectations (diagnostic skills exercise), 221–222
Quality and productivity
self-assessment, technical skills, 323–324, 359
technical skills (exercise), 348–349
Quality control, 200
Queuing models, financial decision-making tools, 343–344

R

Race, ethnicity and, in workplace, 116–117
Radical innovation, 162
Rand Corporation, 292
Ratio analysis, 332
Rational model of decision making
defined, 284
figure, 285
identifying alternatives, 285. *See also* Alternatives, decision-making
recognizing and defining decision situation, 285

Rational persuasion, 369–370
Reactive change, 166–167
Reality, relating needs to (diagnostic skills exercise), 217
Receivers, barriers to communication and, 253
Recording Industry Association of America, 219
Red Lobster, restaurant operations (exercise), 354–355
Reebok, 122
Referent power, 369
Refreezing, change and, 167
Regan, Julie, 245
Regression, 334
Reinforcement theory, motivation, 208
  elements of (figure), 209
  implications of, 210
  in organizations, 209–210
  types of, 208–209
Relaxation, managing stress and, 66
Reliant Energy, 297
Religion, diversity and, 117
Rendition (movie), 216
Research and development (R&D), 14
Resistance to change, overcoming
  education and communication, 169
  facilitation, 169
  force-field analysis, 169
  participation, 168–169
Resistance to change, understanding
  feeling of loss, 168
  perceptions, different, 168
  threatened self-interests, 168
  uncertainty, 168
Resource allocator, as managerial role, 18
Resource base, expand, conflict and, 123
Resource deployment, 156
Resources
  control and, 200
  lack of, failure to innovate and, 164
  organizing, coordinating activities and, 15–16
  types of, 9
Responsibility, delegation and, 59 (figure)
Restaurant operations (case), 354–355
Return ratios, 332
Revenue and sales forecasting, 332–333
Revenue forecasting, 333
Rewarding employees, using rewards effectively (figure), 208
Reward power, 368–369
Rewards for inefficiency, as resistance to control, 207
Reward system
  common team and group, 214
  defined, 212
  employee stock ownership plans (ESOPs), 215
  inventive, 213–214
  merit, 212–213
  organizational innovation and, 164
  performance-based, 215
  prizes and awards, 214
  profit-sharing, 214–215
  substitutes for leadership and, 377
  using to motivate performance, 212–215
Rhone-Poulenc, 254
Risk, 169
Risk management
  defined, 169
  risk propensity, 169–170
Risk propensity
  decision making and, 291
  defined, risk management and, 169–170
  as personality trait, 38
Rita (hurricane), 296–297
Roberts, Julia, 171
Rockwell International, 14
Roddick, Anita, 44–45
Role demands, as stressor, 64–65
Role perspective on management
  decisional roles, 17–18
  informational roles, 17
  interpersonal roles, 16–17
  ten basic roles, 17 (table)
Roman Catholic Church, 42
Rossi, Mick, 216
Roth, Bruce, 160
Royal Dutch/Shell Group, 41
Rubbermaid, 160
Ruiz, Hector, 155
Rusk, Dean, 130–131

S

Sabbaticals, managing stress and, 67
Sabotage, as dysfunctional workplace behavior, 125
Safeway, 41
Saks Fifth Avenue, 134
Sales and revenue forecasting, 332–333
Sales commission, 213
Sales-force-competition, qualitative forecasting, 335
Sales forecasting, 333
Sandberg Sheryl, 11
Sanera, Alicia (quote), 65
Sarsgaard, Peter, 216
Satisfactoriness, in decision making, 285–286
Satisficing, administrative model and, 289
Scanlon, Joseph, 214
Scanlon-type reward systems, 214
Sceppaguerico, Maria (quote), 203
Scheduling meetings, controlling intrusions and, 61–62
Schering-Plough, 180
Schultz, Howard, 13
Science of management, 32
S. C. Johnson & Son, 165
Scope, 155
Scorsese, Martin, 345
Scott, Lee, 252
Screening control, 204–205
Sears company, 41, 157, 168, 204
Security needs, 108
Seiberling, Charles, 309–310
Seiberling, Frank, 309–310
Self-actualization needs, 109, 184
Self-assessment
  charisma, 364–365, 386
  communication skills, 236–239, 266–269
  conceptual skills, goal-setting, 146–147, 182–184
  control, understanding, 324–325
  creativity, conceptual skills, 147–150, 184
  decision making skills, 313–314
  decision making styles, 274, 278–280, 314–317
  diagnostic skills, 227–229
  feedback skills questionnaire, 239–240, 269
  feedback style, 193–195, 230
  gender differences in communication, 240–241, 269–270
  innovative attitudes scale, 150–152, 184
  internal-external control sampler, decision-making, 274–275, 315
  interpersonal skills, 137–140
  job involvement, 100–101, 141
  learning goals, yours and others, 43–44
  learning style, what's yours?, 28–29
  managerial leader behavior questionnaire, 364–366, 387
  mental abilities, assessing yours, 29, 48
  needs, 100, 140–141
  organizational climate, 191–193, 229–230
  organizational management, 190–191, 229
  organizational structure preferences, 195–196
  personality type, 133–134
  personal risk taking, 152–153, 184–185
  planning skills, 53, 95
  power bases score questionnaire, technical skills, 322–323, 359
  problem-solving questionnaire, 275–278, 315–316
  profile, basic management skills, 6–7, 24
  quality and productivity, defining, 359
  rate as manager, 4–6, 24
  skill development and, 31 (figure), 32
  stress management, 54–55, 95
  team effectiveness, 101–102, 141
  teams, using, 102–103
  technical orientation, 325–327, 359–360
  technical skills, 357–358
  time-management skills, 52–53, 55–56, 92–94, 96
  type A personality profile, 94–95
  using teams, 141
Self-awareness
  develop, 35
  emotional intelligence and, 39
Self-described profile. *See* Self-assessment
Self-efficiency, as personality trait, 38
Self-esteem, as personality trait, 38
Self-interests, threatened, resistance to change and, 168
Sender communication, 254
Senge, Peter (quote), 33
Sensing, MBTI framework, 133–134
September 11, 2001, 297
Service organization, 328
Setting, nonverbal communication and, 252
7-Eleven, 168
Sexual orientation, diversity and, 117
Shell Oil Company, 34, 211
Shift work, as job stressor, 64
Shimizu Corporation, 159
Shoeless Joe (W. P. Kinsella), 298–299
Signals, conflicting/inconsistent, as barriers to communication, 252–253
Simon, Herbert A., 288
Simulations, financial forecasting, 339–340
Sinegal, Jim (quote), 244
Singapore Airlines, 283
Situational factor, path-goal theory, of leadership, 374–375
Six Sigma, 310
Skill development, model of, 31–32
Skype, 249
Small business, choosing, conceptual skills (exercise), 172–173
Smisek, Jeff (quote), 201, 251, 297, 329
Smith, Roger, 289
Social skill, emotional intelligence and, 39
Sony, 161, 165
Southwest Airlines, 14, 34
Spokesperson, as informational role, 17
Sponsor, 165
Sports America, 379
Spuriousness, 198
Staircase goals (exercise), 74–75
Starbucks, 13, 14, 33, 112, 161, 200
Star Trek (movie), 169
State Farm, 41
State of certainty, 283
State of risk, 283
State of uncertainty, 284
Sterling-Winthrop, 22
Stimulus, 62–63
Stone, Sharon, 345
Strafella, Richard F., 345
Strategic control, 200
Strategic imitation, 158
Strategic leaders, 155
Strategic leadership, 155
Strategic management, 155
Strategic planning, 15
Strategic thinking, 154–155
Strategy
  communicate change in (exercise), 258
  components of, 155–156
  defined, 154–155
  formation, 156
  implementation, 156
Strengths, organizational, 157
  common strength, 157
  distinctive competence, 157–158
  strategic imitation, 158
  sustained competitive advantage, 158
Stress
  behavioral, 65
  burnout, 65–66
  causes of, 64–65
  consequences of, 65–66
  defined, 62

demands that cause (exercise), 73–74
general adaptation syndrome, 63 (figure)
individual, 65
jobs, 79 (exercise)
managing, 66–67
medical consequences of, 65
methods and techniques for managing, 67
psychological consequences of, 65
stressors, 64–65. *See also* Stressors
time-management stress cycle, 63 (figure)
withdrawal behaviors, 65
Stress management
assessing your skills, 54–55
self-assessment, 95
Stressor(s)
about, 62–63
identifying, 79 (exercise)
interpersonal demands as, 65
organizational, 64 (figure)
physical demands, 64
role demands as, 64–65
task demands, 64
Stride Rite Corporation, 88
Structural control, 200
Structure, task, 373
Subordinate
delegation process and, 59 (figure), 60
LMX leadership theory, 376
substitute for leadership and, 377
Substitutes for leadership, 376–377
Support group, managing stress and, 66
Supportive leader behavior, 374
Sustained competitive advantage, 158
SWOT analysis, formulating strategy and
evaluate work-life strength/weakness (exercise), 350–351
figure, 157
organizational strengths, evaluating, 157–158
organizational threats and opportunities, 158
organizational weaknesses, evaluating, 158
using to formulate, 157–158

T

Taco Bell, 202
Tactical planning, 15
Tactile learning style, 48
Target, 41
Target Corporation, 343
Task characteristics, substitutes for leadership and, 377
Task demands, as stressor, 64
Task environment, 78 (exercise)
Task structure, 373
Tasks, prioritize, 70, 78 (exercise)
Taxpayer revolts, 42
Team effectiveness inventory, self-assessment, 101–102
Team matrix structure, 119
Team members, choosing, decision making skills (exercise), 300–302
Teams
determine why successful, conceptual skills (exercise), 178
using, self- assessment, 102–103
work, communication in networks and, 246–247
Teams, managing
benefits and costs of, 119–120
management teams, 119
problem-solving, 118–119
product development teams, 119
virtual teams, 119
work teams, 118
Technical innovation, 162–163
Technical skills
applying to budgeting (exercise), 346
assessing your (exercises), 322–327
as core management skill, 10 (figure)
defined, 12, 328
extensions, 356–357
identifying in different organizations (exercise), 351–352
Internet, obtain data from (exercise), 348–349
organizational strategy (exercise), 352
organization (exercise), 347–348
orientation to, 359–360
problem-solving, 353
quality and productivity (exercise), 348–349
self-assessments, 357–358
span of management (exercise), 349–350
SWOT, evaluate work-life strength/weakness, 350–351
use on Internet (exercise), 346–347
using your (exercises), 353–356
Technological forecasting, 333
Technology
defined, 328
personal electronic, communication and, 249
Telecommuting, 212, 249
Teleconferencing, 249
Texas Instruments (TI), 156, 165, 212
Theft, as dysfunctional workplace behavior, 125
Thinking
conceptual skills and (exercise), 172
convergent, 159
divergent, 159
MBTI framework, 133–134
strategic. *See* Strategic thinking; Thinking strategy
SWOT analysis to formulate (figure), 157
types of strategic alternatives, 156
Thinking strategy
components of, 155–156
formation and implementation, 156–157
See also Strategic thinking
Thompson, Jane, 157
Thornton, Billy Bob, 126, 379
Threat of new entrants (five forces model), 158
Threat of substitutes (five forces model), 158
3M Company, 18, 156–157, 160, 164
Time-and-motion study, 90
Time flexibility, time-management exercises, 88–90
Timeliness, effective control and, 206
Time magazine, 14
Time-management skills
assessing your, 92–94
behavior activity profile, assessment, 52–53
communication effectiveness (exercise), 75–76
as core management skill, 10 (figure)
as core skill, 9–10
defined, 9, 57
develop your (exercise), 80
group and individual extensions, 91–92
how is time being spent? (exercise), 76–77
practice (exercises), 69–73
prioritization, understanding, 57–58
prioritize tasks, 78 (exercise)
self-assessment, 55–56, 96
stress and, 66
stressful jobs, 79 (exercise)
tasks, prioritizing (exercise), 80–88
time flexibility (exercises), 88–90
using effectively (exercise), 80
visualizing in action (exercises), 68–69
Time-management stress cycle, 63 (figure)
Time-series analysis (figure), 334
Time-zones, communicating across (exercise), 262
Top-management teams, 119
Top managers, 13
Total costs, 338
Toucan-Do, 245
Toyota, 41
Toys "R" Us, 204
Training
evaluating (decision making exercise), 305
international (diagnostic skills exercise), 225–226
Transformational leadership, 378
Transmitting information, communication, 244
Treasure Planet (movie), 329
Treasury Department, 11
Trump, Donald, 377
Turnover, as dysfunctional workplace behavior, 125
Two-factor theory of motivation, 109–110 (figure)
Two-way communication, 254
Tyco International, 38
Type A personality, 63
self- assessment, 94–95
Type B personality, 63

U

Uncertainty, resistance to change and, 168
Under Armour®, 352
Unfreezing, change and, 167
Ungar, Nicolas, 134
Unilever, 41
Union Carbide, 17, 124
Unions, change and, 166
United Airlines, 14, 41, 166, 200, 251, 282
United Auto Workers, 123, 167, 169
United Parcel Service, 89–90
United Way of America, 42
University of South Carolina, 333
Urgent tasks, 70
U.S. Postal Service, 42

V

Vacation incentives, 213
Vagelos, P. Roy, 180
Valences, 112
Variable costs, 338
Variable-interval schedule, reinforcement, 209
Variable-ratio schedule, reinforcement, 209
Variable work schedules, 211
Verification
creative process and, 160
develop, overcoming resistance to control, 207
Vertical communication, 247–248
Vertical dyad, 375–376
Vice president, 13
Vietnam War, 130
Violence
as dysfunctional workplace behavior, 125
workplace, communication skills (exercise), 263–264
Virtual teams, 119
Visualization, skill development, 31 (figure), 32
Visualizing exercises
communication skills, 255–256
conceptual skills, 171
decision-making skills, 298–299
diagnostic skills, 216–217
interpersonal skills, 126
leadership skills, 379–380
technical skills, 345–346
time-management skills, 68–69
Visual learning style, 47
Vodafone, 165
Voser, Peter, 61
Vroom, Victor, 294
Vroom's decision tree
about, 291
approach, to decision making, 294
development-driven (figure), 296
time-driven (figure), 295

Wagner, Jenny, 14
Wall Street Journal, The, 104, 168
Walmart, 252, 297
Walsh, William M., 383
Walt Disney, 165
Warby Parker, 11
Warner-Lambert, 160
War on Poverty, 130

Warren, DeAnna, 42
Washington, Denzel, 171
WD-40 Company, 213
Weakness, evaluating organizational, 158
Weber, Juergen, 311
Wellness stress program, 66
Wells Fargo, 41
Westinghouse, 168, 372
Weyerhaeuser, 114
Wheel pattern, communication (figure), 247
Whistler Corporation, 199, 201
Whitman, Meg, 131
Whitney, Meredith (quote), 12
Wilson Sporting Goods, 120
Winchell, Mike, 126
Withdrawal behaviors, as consequence of stress, 65
Woodford, Michael (quote), 331
Work flexibility
  alternative forms of work arrangements, 211–212
  exercises, 88–90
Workforce, aging U.S. (figure), 116
Workplace violence, communication skills (exercise), 263–264
Work stress, causes of, 64 (figure)
Work teams, 118
World Bank, 11
World War II, 115, 161
Wozniak, Steve, 164
Written communication, 245
Wyndham Worldwide, 21

X

Xerox, 41, 88, 155
  leadership skills (exercise), 383–385

Yahoo! Inc., 61
Yetton, Philip, 294
Y2K, 296
YMCA, 66–67
Y pattern, communication (figure), 247

Z

Zalaznick, Lauren (quote), 37
Zuckerberg, Mark, 11